D0421768

THE PRENTICE-HALL SERIES IN MARKETING
Philip Kotler, Series Editor

ABELL/HAMMOND	Strategic Market Planning
COREY	Industrial Marketing: Cases and Concepts, 3rd ed.
GREEN/TULL	Research for Marketing Decisions, 4th ed.
KEEGAN	Multinational Marketing Management, 3rd ed.
KLEPPNER/RUSSELL/VERRILL	Otto Kleppner's Advertising Procedure, 8th ed.
KOTLER	Marketing Management, 5th ed.
KOTLER	Marketing for Nonprofit Organizations, 2nd ed.
KOTLER	Principles of Marketing, 2nd ed.
LOVELOCK	Services Marketing: Text, Cases, and Readings
MYERS/MASSY/GREYSER	Marketing Research and Knowledge Development
RAY	Advertising and Communication Management
STERN/EL-ANSARY	Marketing Channels, 2nd ed.
STERN/EOVALDI	Legal Aspects of Marketing Strategy: Antitrust and Consumer Protection Issues
URBAN/HAUSER	Design and Marketing of New Products

PRENTICE-HALL INTERNATIONAL SERIES IN MANAGEMENT

Legal Aspects of Marketing Strategy: Antitrust and Consumer Protection Issues

Louis W. Stern

John D. Gray Professor of Marketing

Northwestern University

Thomas L. Eovaldi

Professor of Law

Northwestern University

Prentice-Hall, Inc., Englewood Cliffs, N.J. 07632

Library of Congress Cataloging in Publication Data

STERN, LOUIS W., (date)
    Legal aspects of marketing strategy.

    Includes index.
    1. Trade regulation—United States.   2. Marketing—Law
and legislation—United States.   3. Antitrust law—United
States.   4. Consumer protection—Law and legislation—
United States.   I. Eovaldi, Thomas L.   II. Title.
KF1609.S74   1984   343.73'08   83-24612
ISBN 0-13-528084-2   347.3038

Editorial/production supervision and
    interior design: Rick Laveglia
Cover design: Wanda Lubelska
Manufacturing buyer: Ed O'Dougherty

© 1984 by Prentice-Hall, Inc., Englewood Cliffs, New Jersey 07632

All rights reserved. No part of this book may be
reproduced, in any form or by any means,
without permission in writing from the publisher.

Printed in the United States of America

10   9   8   7   6   5   4   3   2   1

ISBN 0-13-528084-2

Prentice-Hall International, Inc., *London*
Prentice-Hall of Australia Pty. Limited, *Sydney*
Editora Prentice-Hall do Brasil, Ltda., *Rio de Janeiro*
Prentice-Hall Canada Inc., *Toronto*
Prentice-Hall of India Private Limited, *New Delhi*
Prentice-Hall of Japan, Inc., *Tokyo*
Prentice-Hall of Southeast Asia Pte. Ltd., *Singapore*
Whitehall Books Limited, *Wellington, New Zealand*

Contents

Preface xix

1

**The Scope and Enforcement of Laws
Regulating Marketing Strategy 1**

OVERVIEW OF THE LEGAL SYSTEM 2

    Nature and Hierarchy of Laws 2

        The Constitution 2
        Legislation and Administrative Agency Rules 4
        Judicial Decisions 4

LAW ENFORCEMENT BY MAJOR FEDERAL
   AGENCIES 5

   The Antitrust Division of the Department of
      Justice 5

         Criminal Proceedings 5
         Civil Matters 5
         Advisory Opinions 5

   The Federal Trade Commission 7

         The Complaint and Judicial Process 7
         Consent Orders, Advisory Opinions, and Rules 8
         Injunctions and Consumer Redress 9

   Enforcement Agency Discretion 9

PENALTIES AND REMEDIES FOR VIOLATIONS OF
   THE LAW 10

   The Range of Sanctions for Violation of Law 10

         Criminal Sanctions 11
         Civil Penalties 11
         Punitive Damages 12
         Actual Damages (and Class Actions) 12
         Loss of License 13
         Other Remedies 13

ORGANIZATION OF THE TEXT 15

CONCLUSION 17

2

Legal Issues Related to Internal Development of Products 19

PROTECTION OF TRADE SECRETS AND CONFIDENTIAL
   INFORMATION 20

   When Is Information a Trade Secret? 21
   Protection of Secrets by Employee Agreements
      23

Avoiding Liability for Use of Ideas Submitted by
   Outsiders 24
Scope of the Privilege to Copy an Unpatented
   Product 25

PROTECTION OF INNOVATIONS THROUGH PATENT
   LAWS 26

Definition and Duration of Patents 26
The Domain of Patents 27
Rationale for Patents 28
Antitrust and Patents 29
Criteria for Patentability 29
The Patenting Process 29
Scope of Patent Rights 31
The Antitrust Limits of Licensing 33

   Refusals and Royalties 33
   Controlling Prices 34
   Controlling Distribution 34
   Using Cross-licensing and Patent Pools 36

Challenging Patents and Obtaining Remedies 37

PROTECTION OF LITERARY AND ARTISTIC WORKS
   THROUGH COPYRIGHT LAW 38

Subject Matter Protected 39
Formalities of Obtaining and Protecting a
   Copyright 40
Duration of a Copyright 41
Licensing of Copyrights 41
Rights of the Copyright Owner 42

PROTECTING TRADEMARKS AND TRADE
   IDENTITY 43

Trademarks and Trade Names Distinguished 43
Types of Trademarks 44
General Trademark Law Principles 44
Trademarked Rights Exist Only When the Mark Is
   Put into Actual Use 46
Extension of Mark to Different Products 47
Infringement of Trademarks and the "Likelihood
   of Confusion" Test 48

Relief Available in Infringement Actions 49
Legal Considerations in Choosing a Trademark 50

Avoiding Infringement of Existing Marks 50
Specific Prohibitions on Federal Registration 51
Protection of Trade Names 52

Guides for Choosing Trademarks 52

Strong Marks versus Weak Marks 52
Deceptive Marks 55
State Restrictions on Trade Names 55

Protection against Loss of Trademark Rights 56

Abandonment 56
Infringement 56
Preventing a Mark from Becoming Generic 56
Licensing or Assigning Trademarks 57

Some Permissible Uses of Another's
Trademark 57

Comparative Advertising 57
Repair Services 58
Replacement Parts 58
Reconditioned Products 58
Repackaging and Reprocessing 59

CONCLUSION 59

Case 1: Compco Corporation v. Day-Brite Lighting, Inc. 62

Case 2: Anti-Monopoly, Inc. v. General Mills Fun Group, Inc. 65

3

Legal Issues Related to Product Quality 76

THE LAW OF WARRANTIES 77

Express Warranties under the Uniform
Commerical Code 79
The Implied Warranties of Merchantability and
Fitness for a Particular Purpose 80
Disclaimer of Implied Warranties 83
Limiting Remedies for Warranty Breach 85

The Magnuson–Moss Warranty Act's Labeling and
Disclosure Requirements 86

  Full Warranty Requirements 86
  Disclosure Requirements 87
  Presale Availability Requirements 88
  All Other Sales 88
  Other Important Magnuson–Moss Act Provisions 89

PRODUCT LIABILITY LAW 89

Tort Law and Liability for Product-Related
Injuries 90
Tort Liability Standards for Different Types of
Product Defects 92
Liability Theories for Defective Designs 94

  The Deviation from the Norm Test 94
  The Restatement (Second) of Torts Test 94
  The Unreasonable Seller Test 95.
  The Risk–Utility Test 95
  *A Hybrid Consumer Expectations and Risk–Utility
    Test 96*

Defenses to Product Liability Actions 97
Product Liability Insurance 98

GOVERNMENT REGULATION OF FOODS, DRUGS,
AND CONSUMER PRODUCTS 99

Regulation of Food Products 103

  Food Identity Standards 103

Regulation of Drugs, Devices, and Cosmetics 104
Regulation of Products by the Consumer Product
Safety Commission 106

  *The CPSC's Authority to Ban Unsafe
    Products 107*
  *The CPSC's Authority to Set Safety
    Standards 108*
  Is the Product within the CPSC's Jurisdiction? 109
  *CPSC Information Gathering and
    Dissemination 110*

PACKAGING AND LABELING REGULATIONS 110

The Fair Packaging and Labeling Act 111
State Unit Pricing Laws 111

Other Product Labeling and Disclosure
Requirements 112

CONCLUSION 113

Case 1: *A&M Produce Co.* v. *FMC Corp.* 117

Case 2: *Grimshaw* v. *Ford Motor Co.* 129

4

Antitrust Issues Related to the Addition of Products or Services by Merger, Acquisition, or Joint Venture 151

DEFINITIONS 152

GOVERNMENT RESPONSE TO MERGERS 154

HORIZONTAL MERGERS 159

CONGLOMERATE MERGERS 167

Deep-Pocket Mergers 168
Potential Entrant Mergers 169

DEFENSES AVAILABLE TO DEFENDANTS 172

"Failing Firm" Defense 172
"Toehold" Defense 173
"Efficiencies" Defense 174

GOVERNMENT MERGER GUIDELINES 174

Defining the Relevant Market 175
Market Concentration 176

CONCLUSION 179

U.S. Department of Justice Merger Guidelines (1982) 183
Statement of Federal Trade Commission Concerning Horizontal
Mergers 204

Case 1: *Brown Shoe Co., Inc.* v. *United States* 214

Case 2: *Federal Trade Commission* v. *Procter & Gamble Co.* 229

5

Antitrust Issues and Pricing Strategy 236

PRICE FIXING 238

> Dominant Cases 239
> Frequency of Price Fixing 241
> Scope of the Per Se Rule 242
> Exceptions to the Per Se Rule 243
> Liability in Price Fixing 245

EXCHANGING PRICE INFORMATION 245

> Significant Cases 246
> Rules of Thumb 249

PARALLEL PRICING 250

> Significant Cases 251
> The Content of "Parallelism Plus" 253
> Price Leadership 255
> Delivered Prices 255

PREDATORY PRICING 257

> Classic Cases 258
> Controversy over Predatory Pricing 259
> Sales-Below-Cost Laws 26

DISCRIMINATORY PRICING 263

> Discriminate in Price 265
> Different Purchasers 265
> Commodities of Like Grade and Quality . . . Are
>   Sold 266
> Substantially Lessen Competition 267
>
> > *Primary Level 268*
> > *Secondary Level 269*
> > *Tertiary Level 270*
>
> Cost Justification Defense 271

Good Faith Defense 272

> *The Price Being Met Must Be Lawful 272*
> *The Price Must Be Met and Not Undercut 272*
> *The Competition Being Met Must Be at the Primary*
>   *Level 273*

Sales at "Unreasonably Low Prices" 274
Price Discrimination by Buyers 274

CONCLUSION 276

> **Case 1:** *American Tobacco Co. et al.* **v.** *United States* **280**

> **Case 2:** *Great Atlantic & Pacific Tea Co., Inc.* **v.** *Federal Trade*
>   *Commission* **291**

6

Antitrust Issues and Marketing Channel Strategy 300

EXCLUSIVE DEALING 302

Major Cases 303
Sherman and FTC Act Cases 307

TYING CONTRACTS 307

Major Cases 308
Patents, Copyrights, and Trademarks 310

> *Patents 311*
> *Copyrights 311*
> *Trademarks 312*

Related Policies Subject to Scrutiny 315
The Per Se Issue 317

TERRITORIAL AND CUSTOMER RESTRICTIONS 319

Territorial Restrictions 319
Customer Restrictions 324

RESALE PRICE MAINTENANCE 325

Some Significant Cases 327

RECIPROCITY 330

REFUSALS TO DEAL 331

FUNCTIONAL DISCOUNTS 334

VERTICAL INTEGRATION 337

Vertical Integration by Merger 338
Vertical Integration by Internal Expansion 341
Problems Created by Dual Distribution 343

Price Squeezes 343
Horizontal Combinations or Conspiracies 345

CONCLUSION 346

Case 1: *Continental T.V., Inc. et al.* v. *GTE Sylvania, Inc.* 349

Case 2: *United States Steel Corp. et al.* v. *Fortner Enterprises, Inc.* 362

7

Legal Aspects of Promotion Strategy: Advertising 369

ADVERTISING AND THE FEDERAL TRADE COMMISSION 370

Deceptive Acts or Practices 370

The Meaning of Deception 370
Implied Representations 374
The Defense of Puffing 375

Unfair Acts or Practices 377

Advertising Substantiation 378

Federal Trade Commission Remedies 380

Affirmative Disclosure Orders 381
Corrective Advertising 381
Multiple Product Orders 385
Other FTC Remedial Powers 386

Federal Trade Commission Rule Making 387

REGULATION OF SPECIFIC PROMOTIONAL
PRACTICES 388

Deceptive Demonstrations or Mock-ups 389
Endorsements and Testimonials 390

What Is an Endorsement? 390
Celebrity Endorsements 390
Consumer Endorsements 391
Expert Endorsements 392
Using a Seal of Approval of a Third Party 393
Disclosing Connections 393

Promotions Based on Price 394

Price Surveys 394
Cents-Off Labeling 394
Introductory Offers 395
Economy Size Labeling 395
Price Reductions 396
Bait Advertising and Unavailability of Advertised
Products 396
Validity of Restrictions on Price Advertising 397
Unit Pricing 398
Scanning and Price Marking 399

Promotions of Warranties 399
Credit Advertising 400

COMPETITOR ACTIONS AGAINST DECEPTIVE
ADVERTISING 401

Comparative Advertising and the Lanham Act 403
Comparative Advertising and Consumer
Preference Tests 405
State Law Regarding Comparative Advertising 406

CONCLUSION 409

**Federal Trade Commission: Policy Planning Protocol — Deceptive
and Unsubstantiated Claims 412**

Case 1: *Warner–Lambert Company* **v.** *Federal Trade
Commission* **415**

Case 2: *American Home Products Corp.* **v.** *Johnson & Johnson* **432**

8

Legal Aspects of Sales Promotion and Personal Selling Practices 445

SWEEPSTAKES AND CONTESTS 445

PERSONAL SELLING AND COERCION 447

Selling in the Purchaser's Home 448
Special Restrictions on Personal Selling 449

MAIL-ORDER SELLING 450

Unordered Merchandise 450
Negative Option Mail-Order Plans 451
Prompt Shipping Requirements 451

REFERRAL SALES 452

BROKERAGE AND PROMOTIONAL ALLOWANCES 452

Brokerage Allowances 453
Promotional Allowances 453

CONCLUSION 456

Case 1: *Encyclopedia Britannica, Inc.* v. *Federal Trade Commission* **458**

Case 2: *Federal Trade Commission* v. *Henry Broch & Co.* **469**

9

Antitrust Issues and Achieving Market Dominance 475

THE MEANING OF MONOPOLIZATION 476

MAJOR PRECEDENT-SETTING CASES 477

Standard Oil (1911) 479
United States Steel (1920) 480
Alcoa (1945) 482
United Shoe Machinery (1953) 484
Du Pont (1956) 485
Grinnell (1956) 487

CONTEMPORARY CASES 488

IBM (1975, 1978, 1979, 1982) 488

Telex v. *IBM* 488
U.S. v. *IBM* 489

AT&T (1982) 490
Berkey–Kodak (1979) 491
Kellogg (1982) 492
General Foods (1982) 493
Borden (1976), Xerox (1975), and
Exxon (1981) 494

PROBLEMS WITH MONOPOLIZATION CASES 495

POTENTIAL PROBLEMS: THE EUROPEAN
SITUATION 497

CONCLUSION 498

Case 1: *United States* v. *Alumimum Co. of America* 501

Case 2: *United States* v. *Grinnell Corp. et al.* 516

10

Conjectures about the Future of Antitrust and Consumer Protection Law Enforcement 523

THE GOALS OF ANTITRUST AND CONSUMER PROTECTION 524

Antitrust 524
Consumer Protection 525

CONTEMPORARY VERSUS TRADITIONAL
  PERSPECTIVES 526

    Antitrust 526
    Consumer Protection 530

GENERAL ISSUES IN THE ENFORCEMENT OF
  ANTITRUST AND CONSUMER PROTECTION
  LAWS 532

THE FUTURE OF ANTITRUST AND CONSUMER
  PROTECTION 535

Indexes 537

Preface

The law and our legal system have a pervasive impact on marketing activities. Decisions of marketing executives frequently raise issues which should be carefully evaluated as to their legal consequences before they are implemented. The failure to appreciate these legal implications can lead to seriously damaging, if not disastrous, results for a firm.

Despite the importance of law to strategic marketing decision-making, students and practitioners of marketing receive little or no formal training, either in college or in executive development programs, about our legal system or the multitudinous laws which govern the activities of a firm as it seeks to successfully compete in the marketplace. Our hope and expectation in writing this book is that both audiences will have a readily useable resource for obtaining a relatively detailed working knowledge of risks and opportunities which inhere in our legal system's regulation of marketing activities.

Because of our respective backgrounds, interests, and areas of teaching, we have emphasized legal issues which arise from two major areas of public policy concern, namely, antitrust law and consumer protection law. We have organized the presentation of these legal issues around the four elements of the "marketing mix," i.e., pricing, product, channels of distribution, and promotion. We do not discuss the details of marketing strategy in this book, because we presume that readers will have some familiarity with marketing principles and strategic issues as reflected in texts such as Philip Kotler's *Marketing Management: Analysis, Planning, and Control, 5th ed.* Nor do we comprehensively treat all of the legal topics which lawyers would include as being within the scope of antitrust law or consumer protection law; rather, we have selectively focused on the aspects of those laws which most directly implicate strategic marketing decisions.

Our exposition of the law which relates to marketing activities reflects other beliefs and biases which deserve mention. For example, we focus heavily on law which is made by judges. We frequently discuss the facts, arguments, opinions, and unresolved issues involved in the major court decisions relating to marketing activities. In addition, at the end of each of the eight substantive chapters, we have reprinted the text of important opinions in actual court cases. The heavy emphasis on judge-made law and the inclusion of actual court opinions is based on our strong belief that no textual exposition of the "law" can do justice to the complexity of litigation and the difficulties faced by courts in deciding actual controversies. Because many readers of this book will not have had the occasion to read an actual court opinion, we felt that this minimum of exposure to the decision-making and "law creation" process of courts is essential to the education of all students of marketing. Our textual discussion of a variety of cases hopefully will convey the important messages that (a) "statutory law," as enacted by Congress or by state legislatures, frequently is so general, vague, or imprecise that courts are required to create their own rules for interpreting and applying any given statute; (b) "case law," which consists of past court decisions, plays a major role in future court decisions, as courts try to adhere to their "precedents;" and (c) the "law" which ultimately evolves from the interaction of legislatures and courts is frequently uncertain and always subject to change.

The emphasis which we place on judicial precedent also reflects our view that the major contours of the law relating to marketing practices exhibit remarkable stability. Perhaps this is not all that surprising, since statutes presumably reflect basic policies derived from widely held beliefs about the legitimacy of much business activity: fraud, price-fixing, and other obviously illegitimate restrictions of fair competition have long been considered illegal and undoubtedly will continue to be illegal in the future. Although the legality of some marketing practices is not as clear-cut and can be viewed differently when political forces result in changes of philosophy at various law enforcement agencies, we have focused on precedents because we feel that these relatively more durable strands of law should be given more emphasis than the current views of changeable administrations. For example, while the relaxed antitrust and consumer protection enforcement attitudes of the executive officeholders under President Ronald Reagan's administration may have given marketing executives a little less to be worried about, the likelihood exists that the relief will not be permanent. In any case, marketing executives must be continuously concerned about lawsuits brought by private parties invoking basic legal rules and doctrines which are not changeable by officeholders.

Our treatment of legal issues relating to marketing practices also reflects our belief that, in a text of this nature, greater emphasis should be given to federal law than to state or local law. Our belief is based on legal realities. Focusing heavily on federal law makes sense because (1) federal law is "supreme" and will override any inconsistent state laws; (2) federal law may be the only law where states have not enacted their own laws to govern marketing practices; and (3) for some legal topics, federal law serves as a model for state law which is, for all practical purposes, substantively identical to the federal law. Marketing executives must, however, be aware that the body of state law on antitrust and consumer protection issues is growing rapidly and is playing an increasingly important role in influencing marketing decisions. Strategists must seek advice elsewhere about many of these laws.

Despite our caveat about state law, our emphasis on federal law is not exclusive because, for a large number of legal and marketing issues, no federal law exists. Thus, for example, in the area of product liability law, marketing practices are regulated almost exclusively by state law. Our discussion of the constraints of state product liability on product policy decisions reflects the paramount importance of state statutes and judicial decisions.

We hope that the joint collaboration of a marketing professor and a law professor in writing a book of this nature (the first such occurrence, to our knowledge) has resulted in a unique product. We hope that the combination has led to very positive benefits in the form of insights from both our worlds. We realize that our treatment of many subjects has barely scratched the surface of the law; each chapter could be expanded into a book on its own. But we do believe that we have provided enough information for students and executives to be alerted to most of the legal issues raised by strategic marketing decisions. Indeed, from an executive's perspective, the information contained in this book should provide ample signals as to the need for further legal advice regarding most marketing decisions. Because lawsuits are excessively time consuming and expensive, we hope that more of them can be avoided as a result of increased awareness of the outright illegality of some strategies and of the value of seeking additional detailed legal advice regarding other strategies.

The overall organization of the text is spelled out at the end of Chapter 1; we will not repeat that discussion here. However, the reader is urged to turn to that short section now in order to obtain a notion about the breadth of coverage offered. Also, we have purposely made the Table of Contents comprehensive so that readers can locate subjects relatively quickly.

In writing this text, we have relied extensively on the help and assistance of a great number of people. We cannot thank them all, but some deserve special mention. First and foremost, we want to thank our spouses, Ruth and Marina, for providing the love, support, and space we both needed in order to complete this text. Second, our research assistants, Patrick J. Kaufmann and

Maureen McNamara, provided invaluable help; their suggestions, insights, and information-gathering skills made this book possible. Third, the typing assistance and/or word processing wizardry of Laura Pooler, Marion Davis, Martha Koning, Sarah Mingo, Pat Franklin, and Jacy Brown is gratefully acknowledged. Finally, we would like to thank John Connelly (formerly an editor with Prentice-Hall) for his enthusiasm about and support of this project; we hope his faith in us has been fulfilled. Elizabeth Classon succeeded John, and we are similarly appreciative of her enthusiasm, attention, and support.

We also owe a special debt of gratitude to those who provided a careful and thorough review and criticism of our earlier drafts—Lee E. Preston, Jerome Lamet, John Cady, Patrick Murphy, and Gary M. Ropski. Their excellent suggestions led to significant improvement of our product. They, of course, bear no responsibility for any shortcomings in the final effort; that responsibility is completely ours.

Louis W. Stern
Evanston, Illinois

Thomas L. Eovaldi
Chicago, Illinois

Note on Citations

Throughout the text we have provided a moderate level of footnote referencing to our sources. Many of these references are to legal materials which may be unfamiliar to many readers. Below we list and briefly describe some of these references.

CITATION   *EXPLANATION*

CASES

U.S.
The official report of decisions of the United States Supreme Court, published by the U.S. Government Printing Office, Washington, D.C.

F.2d
Federal Reporter, second series. The official report of decisions of the Circuit Courts of Appeal of the United States, published by West Publishing Co., St. Paul, Minnesota. Numbers which precede "F.2d" indicate the volume number, while numbers which follow "F.2d" indicate the page on which the case begins. Material in parentheses indicates the Circuit Court which decided the case and the date of the decision.

F. Supp.
Federal Supplement. The official report of decisions of the United States District Courts, published by West Publishing Co., St. Paul, Minnesota. Material in parentheses indicates the court which decided the case and the date of the decision.

F.T.C.
Federal Trade Commission Reports. The official report of decisions of the Federal Trade Commission, published by the U.S. Government Printing Office, Washington, D.C.

(state courts)
Decisions of the appellate courts of the states generally are reported in an official state publication and in an unofficial "regional" reporter published by the West Publishing Co., St. Paul, Minnesota. Where feasible, we have cited to both the official and unofficial versions. Thus, a case citation to "____ Ill. 2d. ____, ____ N.E.2d____ (19__)" indicates that the court opinion can be found in the designated volume at the indicated page of both the Illinois Supreme Court Reports (second series) and the Northeastern Reporter (second series).

STATUTES

U.S.C. or U.S.C.A.
United States Code. The official codification of the statutes of the United States, published by the U.S. Governmment Printing Office. An unofficial version of the code is called "United States Code Annotated," or U.S.C.A., and is published by West Publishing Co., St. Paul, Minnesota.

C.F.R.	Code of Federal Regulations. The authorative collection of regulations promulgated by the regulatory agencies of the federal government; published by the U.S. Government Printing Office, Washington, D.C.
Fed. Reg.	Federal Register. The daily record of activities of the federal regulatory agencies, published by the U.S. Government Printing Office, Washington, D.C. Recent activities are reported here before they are compiled in the Code of Federal Regulations.
Cong. Rec.	Congressional Record. The official record of proceedings in the United States Congress (House of Representatives and Senate), published daily by the U.S. Government Printing Office, Washington, D.C.
(state statutes)	Citations to state statutes may be to either the official compilation or to an unofficial collection. An example of a reference to an unofficial source would be "Ill. Ann. Stat., ch.____, §____ (Smith-Hurd 19__)," which refers to a specific chapter and section of the Annotated version of Smith-Hurd's Illinois Statutes published by West Publishing Co., St. Paul, Minnesota.

REPORTING SERVICES

BNA, ATRR	The Antitrust and Trade Regulation Reporter, published weekly by the Bureau of National Affairs, Inc., Washington, D.C.
CCH Trade Reg. Rep.	The Trade Regulation Reporter, published in loose-leaf form, with bi-weekly reports of current events, by Commerce Clearing House, Inc., Chicago, Illinois.

Note on Editing of Cases

At the end of Chapters 2 through 9, we have reprinted two important court decisions involving the subject of the Chapter. These decisions have been heavily edited, usually by omitting excessive citation to legal authority. Frequently we have not indicated these omissions. Where footnotes have been omitted, the remaining footnotes have been renumbered.

1

The Scope and Enforcement of Laws Regulating Marketing Strategy

Decisions relating to the setting or implementation of marketing strategy are both seriously incomplete and highly risky if they are made without a reasonable understanding of the requirements of antitrust and consumer protection laws. This straightforward assertion seems more trite than profound until one begins to take account of the number of public and private lawsuits filed each year under these laws and the absolute cost (e.g., legal fees, executive time, etc.) associated with litigation. Then it becomes immediately obvious that either marketing executives do not have a "reasonable" understanding of these laws, or they have made too many erroneous calculations regarding their ability to avoid prosecution for "borderline" practices in which they knowingly have engaged.

The purpose of this text is not to indicate when risks with the law are appropriate or inappropriate. Indeed, given the costs of lawsuits, such risks are likely to be increasingly inappropriate. Rather, the emphasis throughout is to provide present or prospective marketing executives with enough knowledge about potential legal difficulties so that they will know when to obtain further advice from legal counsel. In other words, this text makes no pretense about

1

being the "last" or "complete" word in this extremely complex and, frequently, tortuous area. The objective is awareness and enlightenment, as opposed to completeness.

The approach to achieving this objective has been to address federal laws and court decisions that relate to the four main areas of marketing study, the so-called "four P's" of marketing: product, price, place (marketing channels), and promotion.[1] The primary focus is on discussions of major Supreme Court and, occasionally, Circuit Court of Appeals decisions interpreting and applying federal antitrust and consumer protection laws. The emphasis given to court decisions reflects the fact that, in many areas of law affecting marketing strategy, court precedents provide the main guidelines for organizations attempting to comply with the laws. For the most part, antitrust and consumer protection laws were written in an extremely vague and general way. Because of their vagueness (e.g., they incorporate such undefined phrases as "unfair or deceptive acts or practices" and "substantially lessen competition"), they may be little more than legislative commands that the judiciary or administrative agencies (such as the Federal Trade Commission) develop, through their decisions, more specific parameters for industry to follow. The end result is, therefore, that court decisions, and particularly those of the Supreme Court, are critical to an understanding of the state of antitrust enforcement and consumer protection regulation in the United States.

Thumbnail sketches of the major antitrust and consumer protection laws covered by this text are presented in Table 1-1. Specific sections of these statutes are detailed in a number of chapters where such detailing is appropriate (e.g., the chapter on mergers and acquisitions discusses Section 7 of the Clayton Act). Attention has also been given to a number of rules, particularly those promulgated by the Federal Trade Commission, related to individual aspects of product and promotional strategies.

The various laws and their related mechanisms are an integral part of the broader legal system of the United States. Some comprehension of that system and the allocation of regulatory authority within it is important to an understanding of the particular laws and court decisions that are discussed in the remainder of the book. Accordingly, a brief overview of the United States' legal system is presented next.

OVERVIEW OF THE LEGAL SYSTEM

Nature and Hierarchy of Laws

The Constitution.

The federal constitution allocates governmental power among the three branches of the federal government (executive, legislative, and judicial), and leaves other governmental power to the states. The Constitution also

---

[1] See Philip Kotler, *Marketing Management: Analysis, Planning, and Control*, 4th ed. (Englewood Cliffs, N.J.: Prentice-Hall, Inc., 1980).

Table 1-1

Major Antitrust and Consumer Protection Laws Covered in this Text

Statute	Main Provisions	Chapter(s) Addressing
Sherman Act, Section 1	Prohibits entering into a contract, combination, or conspiracy in restraint of trade	2, 5, 6
Sherman Act, Section 2	Prohibits monopolizing or attempting to monopolize trade	4, 9
Clayton Act	Where the effect may be substantially to lessen competition or tend to create a monopoly:	
Section 2 (as amended by the Robinson–Patman Act)	Prohibits discrimination among purchasers to an extent that cannot be justified by a difference in cost or as an attempt made, in good faith, to meet the price of a competitor	5, 6, 8
Section 3	Prohibits entering into exclusive dealing and tying contracts	6
Section 7 (as amended by the Celler–Kefauver Act)	Prohibits acquiring the stock or the assets of competing corporations	4, 6
Federal Trade Commission Act Section 5	Prohibits the use of unfair methods of competition	5, 6, 9
As amended by the Wheeler–Lea Act, Section 3	Prohibits employing unfair or deceptive acts or practices	3, 7, 8
Magnuson–Moss Warranty Act	Requires disclosure of warranty terms in easily understood language, and labeling of warranties as "full" or "limited"	3
Trademark Act of 1946 (Lanham Act)	Provides for registration of trademarks and prohibits false representations by competitors	2, 7
Copyright Act of 1976	Provides for rights in literary or artistic works against copying by others	2
Food, Drug, and Cosmetic Act	Regulates the conditions under which foods, drugs, and cosmetics can be marketed	3
Consumer Products	Provides for the banning of dangerous consumer products and sets standards for safety of products	3

establishes the rights of persons (including corporations and other business organizations), protects those rights from improper governmental invasion, and limits the exercise of governmental power in other important ways. One important principle embedded in this scheme of government is that rights guaranteed by the federal constitution cannot be abridged by government. Another important principle is that laws that have been validly enacted at the federal level cannot be subverted by conflicting laws enacted at the state and local level.

While it is not intuitively obvious why these principles have any applicability to a book on the legal aspects of marketing strategy, they do play an important role. For example, the United States Supreme Court recently has held that "commercial speech" (a concept that includes advertising and other communicative promotional activities) is part of "the freedom of speech," which is protected against federal and state governmental abridgement by the first and fourteenth amendments of the United States Constitution.[2] This means that governments cannot enact laws that restrict the ability of firms to advertise, unless those laws are enacted in order to further other important and legitimate governmental objectives and are the least restrictive methods of achieving those objectives (or unless the laws simply prohibit false or deceptive advertising).[3]

The principle upholding federal over state law where the two are in conflict has, for example, been applied to state attempts to impose standards for the weighing, packaging, and labeling of products. Courts have held that some of these state laws are totally preempted by federal law requirements and can be ignored by firms without any risk of incurring a sanction for the violation of the state law.

Legislation and Administrative Agency Rules.

The Constitution authorizes Congress to enact laws in many specific areas, including the regulation of interstate commerce. Laws that have been validly enacted by Congress may directly regulate marketing practices. However, as noted previously, Congress has frequently passed "general" laws in the antitrust and consumer protection areas. Accordingly, the specific content of any law may be ascertained only by further search, either of court decisions interpreting the law or of rules or decisions of administrative agencies. Judicial and administrative interpretations of a statute are as much a part of the "law" as if they had been expressly enacted by Congress.

Judicial Decisions.

Clearly, the courts play a critical role by interpreting the laws that Congress has enacted and by determining whether Congress has acted in violation of the Constitution. In addition, through their decisions, particularly at the state level, courts *create* categories of law, referred to as "the common law."[4] Numerous subcategories of this body of law have a significant impact on marketing practices. For example, state courts have created "tort law,"[5] the con-

---

[2] *Virginia State Bd. of Pharmacy* v. *Virginia Citizens Consumer Council, Inc.,* 425 U.S. 748 (1976); *Bates* v. *State Bar of Arizona,* 433 U.S. 350 (1977).

[3] *Central Hudson Gas* v. *Public Service Comm'n,* 447 U.S. 557 (1980).

[4] See Oliver Wendell Holmes, Jr., *The Common Law* (Boston: Little, Brown & Co., 1945); Lawrence M. Friedman, *A History of American Law* (New York: Simon & Schuster, Inc., 1973).

[5] William L. Prosser, *Handbook of the Law of Torts,* 4th ed. (St. Paul, Minn.: West Publishing Co., 1971).

tent of which does not exist in any readily ascertainable form such as a code or statute; rather, it consists of the holdings of courts in specific controversies in which persons who have been injured by products sold to the public have sought monetary recoveries against firms that designed and marketed them. Whenever an appellate court (a court that sits in review of decisions of state or trial courts) enters a judgment requiring a firm to compensate a plaintiff, a precedent has been established that will control decisions by courts in future disputes. The facts of the case and the language used by the court in explaining its decision must be consulted for guidance as to what must be done in the future to avoid or minimize liability.

LAW ENFORCEMENT BY MAJOR FEDERAL AGENCIES

More than 20 different federal agencies have some kind of jurisdiction over legal infractions with regard to marketing strategies, tactics, and practices. However, two agencies play such a paramount role with regard to antitrust and consumer protection laws that their activities have been isolated and highlighted throughout this book. These agencies are the Antitrust Division of the U.S. Department of Justice and the Federal Trade Commission (FTC).

The Antitrust Division of the Department of Justice[6]

The Antitrust Division enforces the Sherman Act and, along with the Federal Trade Commission, the Clayton Act. It has a staff of over 200 persons, including lawyers and economists, and initiates several hundred investigations each year, which result in approximately 100 criminal and slightly fewer civil cases being filed. As differentiated from the FTC, the Antitrust Division is predominantly an investigative and enforcement (as opposed to a research and adjudicative) agency.

Criminal Proceedings.

The Antitrust Division has sole authority for instituting criminal complaints under the antitrust laws. Criminal cases generally involve serious, clearly proscribed violations of the antitrust laws, such as price-fixing conspiracies.

Criminal cases are frequently disposed of by accepting a defendant firm's plea of *nolo contendere,* by which the firm indicates that, while it does not want to admit guilt, it also does not wish to contest the charges. Instead, the firm is willing to accept any punishment the court might have ordered if the firm had pled guilty or had been found guilty after a trial. One reason that a firm might enter a plea of *nolo contendere* is that, by doing so, it avoids a judicial finding that it violated the antitrust laws. Any such finding can be used

---

[6] See, generally, Lawrence Sullivan, *Handbook of the Law of Antitrust* (St. Paul, Minn.: West Publishing Co., 1977) and Aran D. Neale and D. G. Goyder, *The Antitrust Laws of the United States,* 3d ed. (New York: Cambridge University Press, 1980).

by private parties in civil treble damage actions as *prima facie* evidence of an antitrust violation, thus saving potential plaintiffs the cost of gathering evidence and proving a violation in a trial. However, on the negative side, the *nolo contendere* plea may alert interested parties to the fact that some violation may have occurred and may trigger a serious inquiry into the defendant's actions, resulting in future civil lawsuits.

The Antitrust Division has ample authority to conduct detailed investigations of conduct that it suspects may violate the antitrust laws. If the Division suspects that criminal activity is involved, it may convene a grand jury, which can subpoena witnesses and compel the production of documents. The proceedings of the grand jury are secret, although under special circumstances civil litigants may be allowed to have access to some of the testimony and records.

Civil Matters.

If the Antitrust Division does not expect to be able to establish criminal violations of the antitrust laws, it may conduct investigations pursuant to its authority to enforce the laws in civil actions. In this event, the Division is authorized to use civil investigative demands (CIDs) to obtain information and evidence.

The Division often disposes of civil matters by consent decree. In these cases, the Division enters into settlement negotiations with parties suspected of having violated the antitrust laws. If an agreement can be reached, the agreement will be embodied into a decree and will be filed with a court. The Antitrust Procedures and Penalties Act requires the Division to file the decree for public comment and to prepare a statement disclosing the theory of the proposed case and the effects of the settlement. The court then holds public hearings and must make findings as to whether the decree is in the public interest.

As in the case of *nolo contendere* pleas in criminal cases, a consent decree cannot be used as evidence of a violation of the antitrust laws in civil actions brought by private parties, unless the Division negotiates for and includes a clause in the decree providing for this effect. The use of such clauses is relatively rare, and thus the entry of a consent decree may be seen as preventing litigation by private parties. However, the reality is that, as in *nolo contendere* situations, other parties are likely to believe that "where there's smoke, there's fire," and accordingly will seriously contemplate bringing private civil actions against businesses who enter into consent decrees with the government.

Advisory Opinions.

When businesses are in doubt as to the possible legality under the antitrust laws of any proposed course of conduct, an advisory opinion may be requested from the Division. A written statement consisting of a full and complete disclosure of the facts pertaining to a proposed course of conduct can be submitted to the Division, and the Division can, in its discretion, disclose its present intention as to its enforcement policy. Such opinions are particularly prevalent with respect to proposed mergers and acquisitions. But even when the Division indicates that no enforcement action is contemplated, it can withdraw its opinion at any time and initiate enforcement proceedings. However, the department has never initiated *criminal* enforcement proceedings after withdrawing an advisory opinion in which it indicated an intent not to proceed.

The Federal Trade Commission

Established in 1914, the Federal Trade Commission is an independent federal agency responsible to Congress but consisting of five commissioners who are appointed by the president and confirmed by the Senate. It has a staff of about 1,500 persons divided among three bureaus: Economics, Consumer Protection, and Competition. The FTC does economic, consumer, and financial research; promulgates rules; investigates and prosecutes complaints; and adjudicates cases.

Originally created to deal with difficult anticompetitive problems, the jurisdiction of the FTC now is seen as a dual one; it not only polices anticompetitive conduct, but it also serves to protect consumers more directly through its authority to prevent both deceptive and unfair practices. It has power to enforce antitrust laws (a power that it shares with the Antitrust Division of the Justice Department)[7] and sole authority to enforce the Federal Trade Commission Act's ban against "unfair methods of competition" and its ban on "unfair or deceptive acts or practices."[8] Courts consistently have held that the act cannot be directly enforced by private parties. (However, most states allow injured consumers and competitors to bring actions against practices that would be considered unfair or deceptive under the FTC Act.) The FTC also enforces a number of other consumer protection acts, including the Truth in Lending Act, the Fair Credit Reporting Act, and the Magnuson–Moss Warranty Act.

The Complaint and Judicial Process.

The FTC, after staff investigation, can issue a complaint alleging in detail the unfair or deceptive acts or practices that it believes a respondent has committed. The complaint can be brought before an administrative law judge specifically empowered to hear FTC complaints. The decision of the judge is final unless it is reviewed by the Commissioners, either on the appeal of the FTC staff or of the respondent. The end result of such a proceeding may be the entry of a cease and desist order against the respondent. This order is similar to

---

[7] See *United States* v. *Louisiana Pacific Corp.*, 1982–83 Trade Cases ¶65,114 (D. Ore. Dec. 28, 1982). Sherman Act violations can be attacked by the FTC as unfair trade practices under Section 5 of the FTC Act. Scherer points out that the overlapping of responsibilities of the Antitrust Division and the FTC "poses coordination problems that are not always solved successfully. A positive attribute of the dual enforcement approach is a tendency for one agency's oversights to be corrected by actions of the other agency." See F. M. Scherer, *Industrial Market Structure and Economic Performance,* 2nd ed. (Chicago: Rand McNally College Publishing Co., 1980), p. 495. However, this overlap came under considerable "fire" during the Reagan administration; it was viewed by some officials in that administration as an unnecessary duplication of efforts.

[8] Federal Trade Commission Act, 15 U.S.C. § 45.

an injunction entered by a court in that, if the FTC feels that the order is later violated, it can bring an action in which a court can impose a civil penalty in the amount of $10,000 for each violation of order.

The FTC also is authorized to bring actions in court seeking an award of civil penalties against those who violate its prior "determinations" in cease and desist proceedings. This FTC power means that even parties who were not respondents in proceedings that lead to the entry of a cease and desist order must follow the precedent created by the order if they have knowledge of the order. The FTC sends copies of its "determinations" to members of industries likely to be affected by them, thereby ensuring that firms that violate its precedents will be doing so with "knowledge" and therefore can have civil penalties entered against them.

Consent Orders, Advisory Opinions, and Rules.

Of all the potential violations referred to or discovered by the FTC, few are handled in a formal manner. More likely, if the FTC believes that a violation has occurred, it is likely to enter into some sort of settlement negotiations that can terminate with a "consent order." The consent order has the advantage that no violation of law is admitted. This is much like the *nolo contendere* plea available through the Antitrust Division of the Justice Department. Between 150 and 200 of these consent decrees are issued every year; considerably fewer formal complaints are initiated.

The FTC also will issue advisory opinions as to whether a proposed course of action (but not a currently operative business practice) would be in violation of the FTC Act. While these staff opinions are not binding in the sense of precluding the FTC from challenging the practice, it is not likely that the FTC would take any kind of punitive action regarding conduct that it has previously approved; instead, it would seek to have the practice declared illegal and prohibited in the future.

More detailed guidance as to the legality of a contemplated course of action is available from the FTC in two forms. One form is called an "industry guide." Violations of these rules carry no direct penalty because the guides are not final determinations that, under all circumstances, the prohibited conduct is "unfair or deceptive." Instead, "guides" merely are views of the FTC as to what might constitute unfair or deceptive acts or practices. No sanction for violation of a guide can be entered until the FTC brings an action in which it is determined that the act or practice complained of actually is "unfair" or "deceptive." Many guides have been issued, including guides for the household furniture industry, the feather and down products industry, the watch industry, the dog and cat food industry, and the mail-order insurance industry. Many of these guides are under review, and they appear to be falling into disuse.

A more important form of detailed guidance, Trade Regulation Rules, are directly enforceable as law. These rules are issued by the FTC after extensive hearings. They define with specificity the acts or practices that are deceptive or unfair. Violations of these rules can lead to the imposition of civil penalties of up to $10,000 for each violation and can be the basis of a court order requiring a violator to provide compensation to those injured by the rule violation. Rules exist on numerous practices, and some of them cover entire industries. Examples include rules on the incandescent light bulb industry, the funeral industry, games of chance in the food retailing and gasoline industries, care labeling of wearing apparel, negative option sales plans, door-to-door selling, mail-order merchandising, franchising and business opportunity ventures, advertising of ophthalmic goods and services, and labeling and advertising of home insulation.

Injunctions and Consumer Redress.

The commission also has authority to seek preliminary and permanent injunctions against conduct that violates the Federal Trade Commission Act. The FTC rarely uses this authority; most of its injunction actions involve false advertising of foods, drugs, or medical procedures, where there is some serious risk of harm to the public health from the false advertising. The FTC also can ask courts to require violators of the Act to provide consumer redress to victims harmed by a violation. Consumer redress might take the form of paying damages to customers injured by a deceptive practice, refunding the proceeds of sales induced by deceptive practices, or notifying the public of the deception. The FTC also issues refund orders without going to court, although some doubt exists as to whether Congress has given the FTC this authority.

Enforcement Agency Discretion

In a number of places throughout this text, reference is made to the considerable discretion that the Antitrust Division of the Justice Department and the Federal Trade Commission have in deciding which cases to prosecute. The significance of this discretion is very great relative to determining the current course of antitrust and consumer protection law enforcement. However, this discretionary significance must be kept in perspective. Changes in antitrust and consumer protection enforcement policy frequently occur when administrations change, which means that certain policies have very short life-spans in the case of unsuccessful presidential reelection attempts. In addition, the current officeholders cannot define the scope of operation of the antitrust laws, in particular, because their beliefs are likely to have little impact on private litigation, unless they decide to enter private cases on an *amicus curiae* or "friend of the court" basis. Even then, the courts have the final word in deciding whether the law has been violated and in making awards of treble damages. With regard to the significance of an administration's stance and the capacity of appointed officials to institute changes, one commentator has observed:

They . . . may not be in power very long. Furthermore, it's the federal courts that decide what the law is, and most of the judges were appointed by some prior Administration, which had a different attitude about antitrust matters. Finally, the bulk of litigation is private, and, there, the government's opinion has only an indirect, psychological effect.[9]

For an antitrust or consumer protection policy to have long-lasting effect, it generally must be reflected in a Supreme Court decision. Only a few precedent-setting antitrust or consumer protection cases are decided by the Court each year, and consequently the administration in power has little ability to change the law through its litigation efforts. By and large, this text focuses on those precedent-setting cases and ignores the personal philosophies of individual administrations.

PENALTIES AND REMEDIES FOR VIOLATIONS OF THE LAW

One important aspect of the U.S. legal system is that the same substantive law often can be enforced by different parties. For example, laws frequently declare that the violation of a statute is both a crime and a civil law violation. The government agency responsible for enforcing the criminal laws may bring an action in court seeking the imposition of a criminal sanction such as a monetary fine, a sentence of imprisonment, or both. And a person or firm who was injured by the same conduct might be able to commence an action in court seeking a civil remedy authorized by the statute (or implied by a court). Civil remedies might include awards of damages (to compensate the victim of the law violation, to punish the violator, or both) or the entry of an injunction (which might prohibit similar conduct by the violator in the future and subject the violator of the injunction to other, more powerful sanctions, such as imprisonment). The most common example of such dual enforcement is relative to the antitrust laws, where Congress provided for both criminal and civil sanctions for violations.

The Range of Sanctions for Violation of Law

Knowledge of a law's substance is important for marketing executives, but knowledge of actual consequences that can occur if a law is violated may be even more important. Lawyers refer to this latter aspect of law as the "remedy" (to distinguish it from the law's "substance"). In evaluating the appropriateness of various alternative marketing proposals, it is essential to consider the probability of each proposal's being challenged by a governmental agency or a private party, of its being found to have violated a law, and the seriousness of the sanctions that can be imposed if a violation of law is established. In the following paragraphs we briefly describe the types of sanctions that might be available to a court; of course, whether they are actually available will depend on the statute and the facts relating to the violation.

[9] See Bureau of National Affairs, *Antitrust & Trade Regulation Reporter* 44 (Jan. 27, 1983), p. 208 (hereinafter ATRR).

Criminal Sanctions.

Many laws relating to marketing strategies and tactics permit the government to seek and courts to impose criminal sanctions. These sanctions might include imprisonment for the individuals who violated the law and monetary fines for both the individual and the firm. Thus, executives who conspired to fix prices among competing firms have been sentenced to jail, and their firms have been required to pay large monetary fines to the government. The use of the imprisonment sanction is on the increase; prior to 1970, only four sentences of imprisonment had been imposed on violators of the Sherman Antitrust Act, but between 1971 and 1979, 405 persons were sentenced to and served terms of imprisonment.[10] Price fixing is the offense that accounts for the majority of imprisonments for violation of antitrust laws. Criminal sanctions also are authorized for a variety of consumer protection laws, such as regulations relating to the safety of foods, drugs, and other consumer products. And false advertising frequently is declared to be a crime at both the state and federal levels. Similarly, use of the U.S. mails in a scheme to defraud other persons is a federal crime.

Civil Penalties.

Many statutes authorize the government to bring an action to recover a *civil penalty* against those who violate a law. Although there is little practical difference between a fine and a civil penalty (both require the offending firm to make a payment to the government), there are some practical differences, such as the degree of certainty with which the violation must be proved by the government. In any event, large civil penalties have been entered for violations of laws relating to marketing practices. For example, in 1982, Reader's Digest Corporation was ordered to pay the government $17 million for violating an order of the Federal Trade Commission which prohibited the mailing of solicitations for magazine subscriptions that resembled checks.[11] A 1982 study of FTC civil penalty cases shows that three factors account for most of the variation in the size of the civil penalty awarded: the size of the firm, the firm's ability to pay, and the culpability of the firm. Somewhat surprisingly, the size of consumer injury was not a statistically significant variable.[12]

Multiple Damages.

Statutes frequently authorize private parties to recover a multiple of the actual damages caused by conduct that violated a law regulating marketing practices. For example, the federal antitrust laws provide for the trebling of any award of actual damages caused by a violation.[13] These awards can be significant: defendants in the lumber, folding carton, and electrical equipment industries, among others, have been ordered to pay millions of dollars to

---

[10] Project, *White Collar Crime: Second Annual Survey of Law,* 19 Am. Crim. L. Rev. 173, 266 n. 757 (1981).

[11] *Readers Digest* v. *FTC,* 662 F.2d 955 (3rd Cir. 1981), *cert. denied,* 102 S. Ct. 1253 (1982).

[12] Study of Phyllis Altrogge, as described in 43 ATRR 1226, Dec. 23, 1982.

[13] Clayton Act, § 4, 15 U.S.C. § 15 (1976).

plaintiffs.[14] Many consumer protection laws provide that successful plaintiffs can recover a minimum dollar amount, together with the costs of the action and reasonable attorney's fees. The award of attorney's fees to the winner of a lawsuit can induce victims to bring suit and thus lead to increased private enforcement of a law.

Punitive Damages.

Under the common law of most states, courts can make an award of punitive damages against firms who willfully and deliberately engage in conduct that wrongfully injures another person. The purpose of an award of punitive damage is to punish the firm and to set an example so as to deter others from engaging in the same wrongful conduct. Various verbal formulations exist to define the circumstances under which an award of punitive damages is appropriate, but they all convey the same basic message: the firm's conduct must be highly reprehensible. Thus, courts use terms such as "malicious," "reckless," "abusive," and "gross" to refer to a defendant's conduct. In order to find a defendant sufficiently culpable to support an award of punitive damages, the defendant must have been aware that its conduct was wrongful and must have acted with intent to cause harm to the plaintiff.

Punitive damages awards have been entered with increasing frequency in cases involving marketing practices. These judgments may be much larger than the fines that could have been imposed for violations of criminal laws. For example, the law of products liability furnishes many instances where very large punitive damages have been awarded. In these cases, proof of the requisite element of conscious choice of conduct in violation of the law was not very difficult, especially when the defendant improperly designed the product by consciously choosing one product design over other safer but more costly alternative designs. The Ford Motor Company is involved in numerous personal injury actions in which an award of punitive damages would be consistent with most verbal formulations of the appropriate legal standard; one jury award of punitive damages has been upheld on appeal in the amount of over $2 million.[15] Liability was based on the failure of Ford to design its Pinto gasoline tank in a way that would have made it less resistant to rupture in a rear-end collision.

Actual Damages (and Class Actions).

Unless statutes provide for additional remedies, liability usually is imposed in an amount designed to compensate the injured party for actual damages caused by the violation. Thus, when firms are found to have made false representations about their products, purchasers who relied on the false representations are allowed to recover the difference in value between what the product actually is worth and what it would have been worth if the representations had been true.

---

[14] See 44 ATRR (Feb. 17, 1983), p. 330.

[15] *Grimshaw* v. *Ford Motor Co.*, 174 Cal. Rptr 348 (Cal. App. 1981) (Excerpts from this case are contained at pages 129–150).

Similarly, when false representations are made about another firm's product that cause a loss of business, damages can be awarded for profits that are lost as a result of consumer response to the false representation. But proving the amount of loss is very difficult, because there may be numerous explanations for a firm's loss of business that have nothing to do with a competitor's false representations.

In many situations, lawsuits are unlikely to be filed simply because the amount of actual damage to individual consumers is so small; few individuals would find that the costs and risks of litigation would be worth the possible amount that could be recovered. However, litigation is considerably more likely if the action can be brought as a *class action*. This procedural device allows one injured party to bring suit on behalf of all similarly situated injured parties. The amount in controversy (damages to all persons, rather than just the damage caused to any particular plaintiff) is raised to a much higher level in class actions, thereby inducing attorneys to bring cases where their compensation is based on a percentage of the total amount recovered. In addition, many states have enacted statutes that supplement the common law by authorizing a court to order a losing party to pay the litigation expenses and the antitrust or attorney's fees of parties who successfully establish that antitrust or consumer protection laws have been violated.

Congress has taken an extra step to ensure that violators of the antitrust laws do not escape liability because they have inflicted small injuries. It has authorized the Attorneys General of the states to bring suit on behalf of the citizens of the state who have been injured by antitrust violations. Frequently, this authority (called *parens patriae*) is given in addition to the authority already possessed by these officials to enforce state antitrust laws. The significance of these enforcement actions is illustrated by cases brought by the attorney general of New York in which refunds of $6.7 million to consumers were obtained from 25 milk producers who had entered into a price-fixing agreement.[16]

Loss of License.

Some states have required firms to obtain licenses prior to engaging in specific businesses. The licenses can be revoked or suspended for failure to comply with consumer protection requirements built into the licensing law. For example, New York will revoke licenses of automobile repair shops if it is found that the shops willfully fail to provide "quality repairs." A 1982 case upheld the validity of this law and affirmed a 15-day suspension of a repair shop.[17]

---

[16] See 43 ATRR 1132, Dec. 23, 1982. *Parens patriae* suits are specifically authorized by the Hart–Scott–Rodino Antitrust Improvement Act of 1976, Public Law 94-435 (Sept. 30, 1976). However, the Supreme Court, in 1983, dealt a setback to such suits by denying state attorneys general the right to obtain secret information gathered by federal grand juries in related criminal antitrust cases. See Stephen Wermiel, "Top Court Deals a Blow to States' Antitrust Suits," *Wall Street Journal,* March 30, 1983, p. 4.

[17] *Montgomery Ward & Co.* v. *N.Y. Dep't of Motor Vehicles,* 456 N.Y.S. 2d 274 (App. Div., 1982).

Other Remedies.

While the foregoing monetary and penal sanctions pose a large potential risk for violators of antitrust and consumer protection laws, courts can often use other remedial measures, which could prove to be even more significant than the largest possible criminal or monetary sanction. Some of these remedies include the following:

INJUNCTIONS. An injunction is an order entered by a court that prohibits (or compels) future conduct. While the order itself carries no direct monetary consequence, violations of injunctions are considered to be a flaunting of the authority of the court for which powerful criminal and civil sanctions are available, including imprisonment for as long as the order is not being obeyed. Injunctions are entered in cases involving infringement of trademarks, copyrights, and patents, theft of trade secrets, breach of postemployment noncompetition contracts, potentially anticompetitive mergers, false comparative advertising, and other similar conduct.

Frequently, illegal conduct can be effectively dealt with only by imposing an injunction, especially when compensatory damages cannot be proven with sufficient certainty and precision. For example, in a lawsuit involving false or deceptive advertising, damages theoretically could be recovered by injured competitors; the damage that is caused by false advertising is a loss of sales and profits. However, actual proof of the exact amount of lost profits caused by the false advertising is always difficult and often impossible. Because courts will not make an award of damages unless they are proven with sufficient certainty, the only remedy available as a practical matter is an injunction against future false advertising.

CEASE AND DESIST ORDERS. These orders are entered in proceedings conducted by the Federal Trade Commission involving deceptive advertising, price maintenance, price discrimination, and other unfair competitive matters. They are similar to injunctions, except that the statute provides for the entry of civil, rather than criminal, penalties for violation of a cease and desist order. One restrictive aspect of such orders is that they usually do more than simply prohibit a repetition of conduct found to be unlawful. In other words, courts have accepted the notion that the FTC should be able to "fence in" a lawbreaker, thereby closing "all roads to the prohibited end," not just those involved in any particular case. For example, when Sears, Roebuck and Company was found to have engaged in unsubstantiated advertising for one particular product (Lady Kenmore dishwashers), the FTC also prohibited Sears from engaging in unsubstantiated advertising for all of Sears' multitude of other products.[18] Cease and desist orders can, therefore, result in the subsequent imposition of sanctions that are more severe than otherwise would be the case in the absence of the prior violation.

[18] *Sears Roebuck & Co.* v. *FTC,* 676 F.2d 385 (9th Cir. 1982).

DIVESTITURE. This order is used when corporate mergers or acquisitions are found to be anticompetitive and in violation of the antitrust laws. The effect of such an order is to require the undoing of a corporate merger or acquisition. Although doubt exists as to whether private litigants can seek divestiture or dissolution of anticompetitive combinations, governments clearly can pursue this type of remedy. An example of the divestiture remedy occurred when Ford Motor Company was required to divest itself, through sale, of its acquisiton of the Autolite Sparkplug Company,[19] and when Du Pont was compelled to divest itself completely of its 63 million shares of General Motors Corporation.[20]

LOSS OF RIGHTS IN PATENTS, COPYRIGHTS, AND TRADEMARKS. Courts have the authority to declare that patents, copyrights, and trademarks are not enforceable. Thus, loss of these valuable rights can impose serious consequences for a firm. This remedy has been used when those holding patent rights were found to have abused those rights by, for example, restraining trade through tying the sale of unpatented products to the sale of the patented product.

THE COST OF LITIGATION ITSELF. Although the remedies mentioned in the preceding paragraphs will be levied (absent some sort of negotiated settlement) only if a firm is found to have violated a particular law regulating marketing practices, a successful defense of such an action may itself be a form of punishment. The costs of defending litigation are enormous and include not only the direct costs of attorneys, but include lost time of employees, damage to the firm's reputation, and distraction from other important activities that may be vital to the future of the firm. Nevertheless, in certain situations, the benefits of litigation may overweigh the costs (e.g., the costs of defending a patent might be worth a considerable expenditure of litigation effort); similarly, the establishing of a legal precedent may confer benefits that are important to the strategy of the firm.

ORGANIZATION OF THE TEXT

This text has been written for marketing executives and students of marketing. It is not a law book, although there is considerable emphasis on legal issues, terminology, and theory. Given its primary audience, the text has been structured according to the key and critical elements of the marketing mix so that, as strategy is considered for any one of a number of different marketing variables, the reader may refer directly to the most pertinent part of the text for immediate insights into potential legal problems.

The starting point for effective marketing is the marketplace. Once unmet needs have been assessed and target markets selected, organizations then must

---

[19] *Ford Motor Co.* v. *U.S.*, 405 U.S. 562 (1972).

[20] *United States* v. *E. I. Du Pont de Nemours and Co.*, 366 U.S. 316 (1961).

turn to developing methods, services, or products by which those identified needs will be satisfied. In developing products and services for attacking markets, it is necessary to keep ideas as secret as possible from competitors. Also, once a product or service is developed, questions arise about attaching trademarks to it and thereby giving it a unique public character. If the product represents a major breakthrough, it may even be possible to consider obtaining a patent for it. If the product is an original work of authorship, copyright protection may be available. The antitrust and consumer protection issues surrounding all these elements of new product policy—trade secrets, trademarks, patents, and copyrights—are discussed in Chapter 2.

Once a product is developed, trademarked, patented, and/or copyrighted, and then commercialized, it is sometimes found that, due to inadequate foresight on the part of its developers, the product is unsafe or below proper quality levels. These safety and quality issues have become a nightmare for many marketing executives, and therefore, it is imperative that attention be focused on the legalities surrounding them *prior* to product introduction. Chapter 3 deals with such issues as product liability, warranties, and government safety requirements, all of which are major considerations in the setting of product strategy.

Rather than develop a product from "scratch," numerous organizations have acquired "new" products by merging with other organizations or by forming joint ventures. Merger and acquisition policy can therefore be viewed as an extension of product policy, at least for a great many firms. It involves, in effect, a "make or buy" decision. The whole area of antitrust law dealing with horizontal mergers (i.e., mergers between companies on the same level of distribution) is discussed in Chapter 4.

Pricing is the subject of Chapter 5. Included are discussions of horizontal price fixing, price information exchanges, parallel pricing, predatory pricing, delivered pricing, and discriminatory pricing. No area of antitrust law creates more controversy or generates more hard-nosed enforcement agency reactions than the pricing area. It is one that is laced with land mines. Furthermore, there is no adequate map for finding one's way through the minefield, although the content of Chapter 5 should help considerably.

Chapter 6 focuses on antitrust issues surrounding marketing channel strategies and tactics. It covers such policy areas as exclusive dealing, tying agreements, territorial and customer restrictions, resale price maintenance, and vertical mergers (i.e., mergers between organizations located on different levels of distribution), among others. It deals with the incentives that marketing executives employ to entice more effort and support from marketing channel members and the possible legal problems of using those incentives.

Chapters 7 and 8 deal with the various ways in which marketing executives might choose to communicate with customers relative to the products and services they have available to satisfy their needs. Chapter 7 concerns itself with the host of consumer protection laws surrounding advertising, while Chapter 8 focuses on legal issues circumscribing sales promotion and personal selling.

If marketing executives are truly successful in combining the various marketing mix elements in effective ways, they may enable their firms to achieve positions of dominance in the markets selected for attack. Once achieved, these positions of dominance may be the subject of considerable antitrust scrutiny, regardless of the methods used to win out in the competitive battle. Therefore, even before embarking on a quest for large market shares, marketing executives are well advised to consider what might lie ahead if they actually succeed. This topic is the subject of Chapter 9. The final chapter in the book, Chapter 10, provides a perspective on current topics in antitrust and consumer protection enforcement and gives an indication of what might lie ahead.

It should be noted that the text focuses mainly on federal statutes and court cases promulgated under them. Many details of state law have been ignored. It would be a mistake of major proportions if a marketing executive were to fail to recognize that, in every state in the United States, legal restrictions on competitive strategy exist and numerous consumer protection regulations apply to marketing practices. It is vitally important that the reader be forewarned about the myopic nature of this text, because state law can be as equally constraining as federal law. While we obviously believe that federal law is extremely important, we do not want to minimize, by our exclusion, the significance of state law to the setting of marketing strategies.

It is also worth noting that we have not addressed in this book any of the numerous federal credit-oriented consumer protection laws, such as the Truth in Lending Act, the Fair Credit Reporting Act, the Fair Credit Billing Act, the Equal Credit Opportunity Act, or the Fair Debt Collection Practices Act, as we have preferred to focus on legislation that more directly affects marketing strategy relating to price, product, marketing channels, and promotion. This purposive omission does not mean that credit-oriented laws are unimportant for marketing executives; rather, it simply reflects the emphasis of the text on strategic issues surrounding the four most highly visible elements of the marketing mix.[21]

CONCLUSION

The goals of maintaining a competitive economy and of protecting consumers are reflected in legislation at every governmental level and in the law created by courts. While Congress is usually the principal moving force behind most legislation in this area, the final result—the actual guidelines to which industry must adhere—is often established by court cases. To a large extent, then, antitrust and consumer protection law is largely case law, although statutes, regulations, and rules addressing consumer protection are sometimes slightly

---

[21] Readers interested in specific aspects of credit-oriented legislation might consult David G. Epstein and Steve H. Nickles, *Consumer Law,* 2d ed. (St. Paul, Minn.: West Publishing Co., 1981).

more specific than those found in antitrust. But both sets of laws are vague, to put it mildly. Therefore, marketing strategists face a double task. First, they must understand the laws, and then they must understand the court interpretations of the laws. It is likely that both tasks will present considerable difficulty and consternation.

The Antitrust Division of the Department of Justice and the Federal Trade Commission are the two main enforcement agencies with which this text is concerned, basically because the primary focus of the text is on federal law. For both agencies, efforts are more bent toward settlement than they are toward trial. Their resources are even more limited than most of the corporations they challenge, and, therefore, settlement (either by making available nolo contendere pleas or consent decrees or via other means) is generally preferred, unless the agencies are desirous of establishing a precedent through the court system. In the latter case, they must bring the case to trial. But most of the time, the agencies will use advisory opinions, guides, rules, and other means at their disposal to avoid confrontation while assuring proper business conduct.

The enforcement agencies and the courts have at their disposal a large number of penalties and remedies that can be applied against violators. They range all the way from criminal sanctions (and imprisonment) to large fines, punitive damages (trebled damages, in the case of antitrust violations), short-term injunctions, and cease and desist orders. But perhaps the greatest deterrent to antitrust and consumer protection law violation is the cost of the defense itself. When lawyers' fees and executive time are totaled, even the most trivial matter becomes very expensive. Furthermore, the threat of government action is not the only concern. Rather, private lawsuits account for 95 percent of all the lawsuits filed in the antitrust and consumer protection area. And beyond this fact is the realization that, if one lawsuit is lost to one plaintiff, other plaintiffs are waiting in the "wings" to use what has already been learned in pursuit of the defendant.

Given all these potential consequences, it seems relatively clear why present and future marketing executives might want to avail themselves of the information in this text. At the very least, calculation of risks will be much more realistic, once the appropriate weights for legal indiscretions have been factored into the strategic equation.

2

Legal Issues Related
to Internal Development
of Products

The essence of successful marketing is innovation and creativity. To acquire, maintain, or increase any given share of a market (and once acquired, prevent erosion of the share), a firm constantly must search for new ways of responding to the needs of its customers via new product ideas, new production techniques, new distribution plans, and new promotional strategies. In the process of seeking and using new means for attacking markets, it may become important for the firm to maintain secrecy for these innovations so that they are not appropriated and used by competitors. In maintaining secrecy, the firm may wish to avail itself of opportunities that the legal system offers to acquire and protect its innovations against appropriation or use by others. This chapter describes important features of the legal system for creating and maintaining trade values in such intangibles as trade secrets, patents, copyrights, and trademarks.

Unfortunately, for the firm desiring protection against the use of its ideas, designs, and symbols by others, the law is not overly expansive. Perhaps the closest that the law comes to giving absolute protection is in the form of a patent. But while a genuinely novel discovery can receive protection for years, a cost associated with receiving this benefit is public disclosure of the discovery with the concomitant risk that others will be able to learn enough through the disclosure to make a different, and better, invention and obtain their own 17-year patent monopoly. A trademark can receive protection for a virtually indefinite period as long as the mark continues to serve as shorthand reference by consumers for the identity of the product's source. But a trademark offers absolutely no protection against copying and selling a product that has not been patented, as long as purchasers are not confused as to which firm is producing the product. Nor does copyright offer any protection for attempts to exclusively use new ideas; the copyright laws protect only the right to publish or perform a copy of the original work. The ideas embodied in the work can be freely used by others.

The alternative to obtaining legal protection consists of keeping the innovation a secret for as long as possible while exploiting its market value. The law does offer some assistance in keeping ideas secret, but, for the most part, once the secrecy is lost and the ideas become publicly known, they are available for anyone to use. The law relating to the protection of trade secrets will be discussed in the next section. Succeeding sections of the chapter discuss patents, copyrights, and trademarks, respectively.

PROTECTION OF TRADE SECRETS
AND CONFIDENTIAL INFORMATION

In general, if a genuine "trade secret" exists, agreements between a firm and its employees that prevent the secret from being communicated to competitors or from being used upon termination of employment will be upheld in court. In addition, if a secret is appropriated by competitors through unlawful methods such as theft, unauthorized surveillance, or bribery of employees, courts can impose a monetary sanction on those who unlawfully divulged or obtained the trade secret. On the other hand, public policies that protect trade secrets are in conflict with the ideal of "free and open" competition. They are also in conflict with the ideal of encouraging individuals to deploy "human capital" (knowledge and skills) to its most productive use. And in some respects, enforcement of restraints against the use of *unpatented* trade secrets is in conflict with the underlying policy of the patent laws (i.e., that unpatentable trade secrets can be freely used by anyone).

Thus, this area of the law illustrates the difficult process of judicial reconciliation of competing policies. Decisions in this area can be properly understood only by careful analysis of the factual settings out of which the controversies arise. And, as in a number of areas of the law that affect marketing practices, there is no federal law of trade secrets; accordingly, the generalities presented here must be qualified by noting that results may be different in particular states.

When Is Information a Trade Secret?

For a firm to obtain any legal protection for unpatented ideas, the information must satisfy the law's requirements for being classified as a "trade secret." A trade secret has been defined as follows:

> Information, including a formula, pattern, compilation, program, device, method, technique, or process, that (i) derives independent economic value, actual or potential, from not being generally known to, and not being readily ascertainable by proper means by, other persons who can obtain economic value from its disclosure or use, and (ii) is the subject of efforts that are reasonable under the circumstances to maintain its secrecy.[1]

Courts consider a wide variety of factors in determining whether information is a trade secret. These factors can be phrased as questions, which, if they can be answered affirmatively, will increase the likelihood that the information will be classified as a trade secret:

1. Is the information known only within a firm and not among competing firms?
2. Do only a selected and small number of employees have access to the information?
3. Does the firm employ measures to protect the information from disclosure?
4. Has the firm expended efforts in developing the information?
5. Would acquisition or duplication of the information by others be difficult and costly?
6. Is the information valuable to the firm and to its competitors?[2]

Courts have applied these factors to give protection to blueprints and specifications for industrial fans,[3] designs for a radio cabinet,[4] customer lists and individualized formulas developed for each customer,[5] and the specifications and relationships embodied in a tape recording machine (although the general idea and approach of the process of reducing inertia in the machine was not protectable).[6]

The element of secrecy is critical to any attempt to obtain legal protection for the holder of an idea. If a competitor independently discovers the information or process legitimately by, for example, using its own internal product development processes, the firm may not prevent use of that information. If an

---

[1] National Conference of Commissioners on Uniform State Laws, Uniform Trade Secrets Act, §1(4). The National Conference proposes laws for adoption by the states and attempts to propose statutes that will unify the law and be acceptable in all jurisdictions. As of this date, few states have adopted the Act. The Act is discussed in Klitzke, *The Uniform Trade Secrets Act,* 64 Marquette L. Rev. 277 (1980). A detailed treatment of trade secrets law can be found in James Pooley, *Trade Secrets: How to Protect your Ideas and Assets* (Berkeley, CA: Osborne/McGraw-Hill:, 1982).

[2] Restatement, Torts, Section 757, comment b.

[3] *ILG Industries, Inc.* v. *Scott,* 49 Ill. 2d 88, 273 N.E.2d 393 (1971).

[4] *Piedot* v. *Zenith Radio Corp.,* 308 Ill. App. 197, 31 N.E.2d 385 (1941).

[5] *Heatbath Corp.* v. *Ikfovits,* 117 Ill. App. 2d 158, 254 N.E.2d 139 (1969).

[6] *Winston Research Corp* v. *Minnesota Mining and Mfg. Co.,* 350 F.2d 134 (9th Cir. 1965).

idea is embodied in a product and the idea can be discovered by examination of the product (such as through a process commonly known as "reverse engineering"), then, in the absence of patent protection, anyone is free to use the idea. Several cases illustrate this point: protection has been denied for valve designs evident from the valves themselves and for a manufacturing process for electronic rectifiers (when only one process was feasible and the steps in the process were variable only to an insignificant degree).[7]

Similarly, if the idea is voluntarily disclosed to others without any understanding or agreement as to the need to preserve secrecy, legal protection will be lost. Thus, exhibiting a novel toy at a trade show will result in a loss of secrecy status for any ideas embodied in the toy; even an employee with inside knowledge of the new toy is free to develop a competing product using the discovery.[8] Here the federal patent policy predominates: if the idea is in the public domain and is not patentable, copying is permitted. However, in 1979, the Supreme Court indicated that licensing and royalty agreements that were entered into when a trade secret existed may be enforceable even after the ideas have come into the public domain.[9]

An interesting case that raised difficult issues about the proper scope of legitimate efforts to discover secrets involved the taking of photographs from an airplane of a construction site for a new methanol manufacturing plant owned by Du Pont.[10] Alleging that the photographs would reveal a highly secret but unpatented process for producing methanol, which had been developed at great expense, had been safeguarded against disclosure, and which had given Du Pont a competitive advantage, the Du Pont company sought an injunction against circulation of the photographs, an injunction against further aerial photography, and damages for the disclosure. The photographers defended on the ground that their actions occurred in public airspace, did not violate any confidential relation, and otherwise were not fraudulent or illegal. The court held that Du Pont was justified in bringing suit against this "improper means" of obtaining trade secrets, since Du Pont had been taking reasonable steps to keep the process secret and since a requirement that the construction project be covered by a temporary roof would be unreasonable. While the boundaries of the "improper means" rule are not precise, and probably would not protect against discovery of trade secrets open to plain view, the conduct used by Du Pont's competitor offended the court's sense of business morality.

Courts also have insisted that a trade secret possess some degree of uniqueness or novelty, although it is clear that the originality need not rise to the level of patentability. Furthermore, very general ideas that have not been con-

---

[7] *Futurecraft Corp.* v. *Clary Corp.*, 205 Cal. App. 2d 279, 23 Cal. Rptr. 198 (1962); *Sarkes Tarzian, Inc.* v. *Audio Devices, Inc.*, 166 F. Supp. 250 (S.D. Cal. 1958).

[8] *Aurora Products Canada, Ltd.* v. *Tyco Industries, Inc.*, No. 058377 (Conn. Super., July 26, 1982), 43 ATTR 327 (Aug. 12, 1982).

[9] *Aronson* v. *Quick Point Pencil Co.*, 440 U.S. 257 (1979). See also *Kewanee Oil Co.* v. *Bicron Corp.*, 416 U.S. 470 (1974).

[10] *E. I. Du Pont de Nemours & Co.* v. *Christopher*, 431 F.2d 1012 (5th Cir. 1970).

verted to valuable information in a business, and that the owner does not have the capability of exploiting, are not protectable as trade secrets.[11]

The security measures adopted by the owner of a trade secret are of importance to courts in determining whether a real secret exists. If a firm (1) keeps a production process guarded and limits access to the workplace by requiring passes and permits, (2) requires any visitors to sign agreements against disclosing what is observed, (3) keeps relevant documents under lock and key and out of view, and (4) requires employees to execute agreements that indicate the secret nature of the information and that obligate the employee to keep the information secret, the chances of obtaining trade secret protection are improved. Conversely, if such security measures are not taken, protection is likely to be denied.[12]

Protection of Secrets by Employee Agreements

The law gives protection to a firm with a genuine trade secret by enforcing contracts in which employees agree not to use the trade secret or disclose it to outsiders or competitors. As part of any employment relationship, the law implies a duty of loyalty and fidelity to the interests of the employer; disclosure of trade secrets and confidences to others clearly would violate these duties.[13] But firms should not rely upon such general, legally implied duties; instead, employees should be asked to execute agreements not to divulge or use trade secrets obtained as part of the employment relationship. These agreements should make known to the employee precisely what is considered to be a trade secret and express the employee's obligation not to reveal the confidence.[14] One advantage of using such agreements is that they will suggest to a court, in any subsequent trade secret litigation, that the employer does take steps to preserve secrecy and that the information is in fact a valuable trade secret.

If an employee has obtained access to trade secrets as a result of the employment relationship, and the employment relationship subsequently is terminated, legal issues are raised as to whether the former employee and any new employer can be restrained from using the trade secret. Courts often will be willing to restrain use of a secret by entering an injunction against both the employee and the new employer. The firm claiming the right to continued secrecy should notify the new employer of the areas in which the employee has obtained knowledge of trade secrets, as this may assist in recovering damages

---

[11] *Vendo Co.* v. *Stoner,* 58 Ill. 2d 289, 321 N.E.2d 1 (1974). (Plaintiff's idea for a vending machine held not a trade secret; the defendant developed the idea with considerable effort and plaintiff did not have the know-how to construct the machine.)

[12] *Capsonic Group, Inc.* v. *Plas-Met Corp.,* 46 Ill. App. 3d 436, 361 N.E.2d 41 (1977).

[13] See Annotation, 30 A.L.R. 3d 631.

[14] See Arthur Sidel and Ronald Panitch, *What the General Practitioner Should Know about Trade Secrets and Employment Agreements* (Philadelphia, Pa.: American Law Institute, 1973). This book contains suggested agreements to cover all trade secret and confidential relation situations.

as well as obtaining an injunction in the event the employee violates the obligation not to divulge secrets.[15] Reminding the former employee of the existence of the agreement not to divulge secrets also may help in subsequent legal actions.

In some instances, a firm may be able to prove that the new employer hired the former employee for the very purpose of obtaining access to the trade secrets known to the employee. In that case, the competitor may have violated tort law, which protects against interference with contractual relationships;[16] in addition, there is a possibility, however remote, that such action can be considered a theft of trade secrets and actionable under criminal laws.[17] Theft, espionage, and other such illegal methods of obtaining knowledge of trade secrets clearly can be prohibited and punished by courts, both civilly as well as criminally.[18]

Avoiding Liability for Use of Ideas Submitted by Outsiders

Occasionally, someone outside a firm may approach the firm with an offer to disclose a new idea that would be of benefit to the firm. These situations present risks for firms since subsequent use of ideas disclosed in confidence can lead to an obligation to reasonably compensate the person who submitted the idea. For example, Procter & Gamble received an idea for putting a blue substance in a laundry powder. When P&G subsequently marketed "Blue Cheer," liability was imposed for using the idea submitted by the outsider; although the court could have imposed liability on an express or implied contract theory, or on a misuse of trade secret theory, the court used a theory of unjust enrichment and held that Procter & Gamble was obligated to pay the outsider the value of the idea it had received.[19]

Although subsequent use by a firm of information submitted to it in confidence always is somewhat risky, use of the information is not invariably illegal. Before liability is imposed, courts will insist that the outsider's idea be both novel and concrete; liability will not be imposed for use of vague and general ideas (unless, of course, there is a clear, express contract governing the matter). Since the line between concrete and vague ideas is elusive, many firms have established a special department staffed by a nontechnical person to deal with the problem of unsolicited idea submission. Formal records are kept as to the

---

[15] However, as Edmund Kitch has noted, this strategy may be counterproductive as it may alert the new employer to the existence of a valuable secret and may intensify efforts to discover the information. See Kitch, "Rights in Information: Report on An Inquiry," p. 6 (undated; mimeo).

[16] See Dobbs, *Tortious Interference with Contractual Relationships.* 34 Ark. L. Rev. 335 (1980).

[17] *United States* v. *Bottone,* 365 F.2d 389 (2d Cir. 1966) (upholding conviction under 18 U.S.C. §2314 for theft and interstate transportation of documents and microorganisms in elaborate scheme for pirating trade secrets). See also, Annotation, 84 A.L.R.3d 967.

[18] Prosecutions have been commenced against persons who allegedly stole information about computers. Drinkhall, "Mitsubishi Electric, Four Employees, Indicted on Charge of Conspiring to Steal IBM Data," *Wall Street Journal,* July 20, 1982, p. 6, col. 1.

[19] *Galanis* v. *Procter & Gamble Corp.,* 153 F. Supp. 34 (S.D.N.Y. 1957).

date the idea was received and its specific content. Some firms go even farther and refuse to discuss outsider submissions in the absence of a specific agreement as to the use of and compensation for any ideas to be submitted and an agreement that the idea is not submitted in confidence. If an outsider submits an idea that already has evolved internally, no liability will be imposed to compensate an outsider for the same suggestion. To guard against a possible argument that subsequent use of an internally developed idea actually came from an outsider, firms should keep elaborate notes as to the time and place of, and employees involved in, the discovery of new ideas and trade secrets.

Scope of the Privilege to Copy an Unpatented Product

As explained in the next section, it may be possible to obtain a patent on an invention, and the patent laws will prohibit the use of the invention without the permission of the patent holder. But if a product does not embody any patented invention, the law will do very little against those who decide to develop and market a similar, or even an identical, product. If a product is not sufficiently novel to be patentable, or if a patent has expired, the law's general policy favoring competition allows the production and sale of products by competitors at lower prices. In the *Sears, Roebuck and Company* case, the Supreme Court held that Sears was free to produce and sell copies of a pole lamp made by Stiffel Company, since Stiffel did not have a valid patent on the lamp.[20] The Court held that state laws, which had been used to impose sanctions on Sears for the act of copying the unpatented product, were unconstitutional because the laws violated the supreme federal policy of competition. Under the rule established by this case, a firm is free to copy and sell a product that is not patented.

The freedom to copy and sell an unpatented product is limited only by the law of unfair competition: the privilege to copy does not allow one to both copy another's product *and* to confuse consumers as to who is marketing the product. Thus, in the *Sears* case, while Sears was free to copy and sell lamps designed by Stiffel, if Stiffel could have shown that buyers of Sears lamps thought that they were buying lamps made by Stiffel, an injunction could have been obtained against Sears. However, Sears could not have been totally prohibited from marketing its imitation of Stiffel's lamps; it could only have been required to take whatever steps would have been necessary to prevent consumer confusion as to the manufacturing source of the lamps, such as clearly labeling its lamps to indicate that the lamps were not made by Stiffel. In short, the policy favoring the copying of unpatented products is limited only to the extent necessary to achieve the goal of avoiding consumer confusion as to the true identity of the actual source of a product.

When consumer confusion as to the source of a product results from the copying of the shape or packaging of another's product, the law is less clear,

---

[20] *Sears, Roebuck & Co.* v. *Stiffel Co.,* 376 U.S. 225 (1964).

particularly where the copying produces other consumer benefits. A case raising these issues is *Inwood Laboratories, Inc.* v. *Ives Laboratories, Inc.*[21] There, when a patent expired on a drug, several manufacturers copied the drug, including its shape, size, and color, and marketed the drug, using its generic name. When the original maker discovered that the "look-alike" drugs were being substituted by pharmacists when filling prescriptions that called for the original drug, it brought suit against the "look-alike" drug manufacturers to stop the manufacture and sale of the copies. The generic drug makers countered that they could not be held legally responsible for the undisclosed substitutions by independent pharmacists and that copying the shape and color of the unpatented drug was functional to patients, doctors, and hospitals and should not be restricted. The Supreme Court did not provide a definitive answer as to the legality of this form of product copying. But the law does seem reasonably clear outside of the drug copying area; when the copying of the packaging and trade dress of another firm's product serve no functional purpose, courts will enjoin the use of confusingly similar packaging. Thus, the makers of "Rubik's Cube," an unpatented puzzle, were able to obtain an injunction against the makers of "Wonderful Puzzles" to prohibit the use of confusingly similar packaging.[22]

PROTECTION OF INNOVATIONS THROUGH PATENT LAWS

In the process of seeking new ways of solving old problems, individuals within organizations or acting on their own sometimes make startling and truly unique discoveries. When this occurs, the question of whether to patent the discovery arises.

Definition and Duration of Patents

A patent is an exclusive right conferred on an invention by a government for a limited period. It authorizes the inventor to make, use, transfer, or withhold whatever may be patented. Even more importantly from a legal perspective, it grants the inventor the right to *exclude* others from making, using, or selling the invention or to admit them on his own terms. In the United States, a patent code was adopted by Congress under the broad authority of Article 1, Section 8 of the Constitution, which urges the promotion of "the progress of science and useful arts, by securing for limited times to authors and inventors the exclusive right to their respective writings and discoveries."

In the United States, patents are granted for a 17-year period and are not renewable.[23] The reason for the 17 years is anchored in history. English patent

---

[21] 102 S. Ct. 2182 (1982).

[22] *Ideal Toy Corp.* v. *Plawner Toy Mfg. Co.*, 685 F.2d 78 (3rd Cir. 1982).

[23] Different countries and the European Economic Community (Common Market) have different laws and regulations relating to patents and licensing. Furthermore, the territorial scope of a patent is limited to the jurisdiction of the country that grants it. An American who wishes to protect his or her invention in other countries must take out patents under their laws.

law granted exclusive rights to a relatively simple device for 14 years. It was reasoned that it would take apprentice workmen 7 years to become proficient in the manufacture of the new product and that the employer ought to have an additional 7-year apprentice generation to make a profit from large-scale production. But when it came to much more complicated inventions, the English gave the inventor another 7 years to reap his rewards. Congress did away with the confusing distinction between complicated and simple inventions and compromised on 17 years for all patents.

From a modern marketing perspective, the 17-year life of the patent is an anachronism, growing out of a handicraft economy and bearing no functional relation to the requirements of machine technology. As Wilcox has pointed out, "There is no reason why the duration of protection should be the same in every case. The period permitted might well be related to the time required to recover the sums invested in research and development."[24] Indeed, this suggestion brings us full circle, back to the notion developed by the English. In fact, as mentioned later, some recent legislation considered by Congress and passed by the Senate leads in the direction of varying the patent life of products.

The Domain of Patents

Patent law covers processes of production (art, manufacture), the implements employed in such processes (engine, machine), and the products resulting from them (manufacture, composition of matter, and botanical plants). It encompasses, as composition of matter, not only such chemical products as dyestuffs, plastics, and synthetic fibers, but also foods and medicines, products to which the patent privilege is not generally extended under the laws of other countries. Patents are, however, not available for novel theories or thoughts. For example, in *Gottschalk* v. *Benson,*[25] the Supreme Court held that a mathematical formula for converting decimal numbers into binary numbers for general use as a program in digital computers was not patentable. The court concluded that the patent application was an attempt to secure protection for an idea—a general mathematical formula—and thus should not be protected by the patent laws.

Patents on ornamental design may relate to the design of the article itself or to designs that are incorporated in it or affixed to it. A design patent is granted for 14 years. Designs, by their nature, are ephemeral and their economic value is often short-lived. In fact, designs may be protected more cheaply and for longer periods by obtaining copyrights. Design protection is generally applicable to products that are durable, such as jewelry and furniture. But fashions, in which the element of design is important, are neither patented nor copyrighted, not because the law excludes them, but because they change too rapidly to be protected by the usual legal processes.[26]

---

[24] Clair Wilcox, *Public Policies Toward Business,* 4th ed. (Homewood, Ill.: Richard D. Irwin, Inc., 1971), pp. 181–182.

[25] *Gottschalk* v. *Benson,* 409 U.S. 63 (1972).

[26] William G. Shepherd and Clair Wilcox, *Public Policies Toward Business,* 6th ed. (Homewood, Ill.: Richard D. Irwin, Inc., 1979), p. 501n.

Obviously, a great many inventions occur without patent protection because of (1) time lags in imitation due to secrecy, lack of know-how, and the like; (2) the outright advantages that come from competitive leadership; and (3) nonpatent barriers to competition such as lack of access to appropriate production facilities, managerial experience, and distribution channels.[27] Furthermore, to get a patent, the inventor must disclose the invention as opposed to keeping it secret. For these reasons, among others, the availability of patent protection is unlikely to be as important a stimulant to innovation as the forces of opportunity and competition.[28]

Rationale for Patents

Governments have chosen to grant exclusive patent rights on inventions for three main reasons: (1) to promote invention, (2) to encourage the development and commercial utilization of inventions, and (3) to encourage inventors to disclose their inventions to the public. A patent monopoly is designed to provide something that consumers value and that they could not have at all or have as abundantly were not patent protection afforded.[29] According to Kamien and Schwartz, invention, innovation, new products, and technological advances may have more to do with promoting a viable, healthy, and competitive economy than anything else. Patent protection encourages innovation because it enhances the possibility of a profit payoff.[30]

A patent is a legal device to ensure that there can be a property right in certain ideas. Therefore, the temporary right of a patentee to exclude others is a means of preventing a competitor from taking a "free ride" on the efforts, energy, and creativity expended in formulating the invention. Without a patent system, prevention of "free riding" would be severely limited.[31] The patent laws prevent free riders from denying the inventor a return on his or her investment and ingenuity. The general rule seems to be that a patentee is entitled to extract a monopoly income by reducing utilization of an invention, even if other goods and services are also restricted, provided that in each case the restriction of the invention is confined as narrowly and specifically as technology and the practicalities of administration will permit. The idea of a patent is that the patentee will get a reward directly proportional to the usefulness of the invention.

---

[27] Patents cluster tightly in certain industries, especially in drugs, photocopying, aerospace, and electrical equipment. Over large areas of industry, patents are virtually absent and irrelevant.

[28] For confirmation and documentation, see F. M. Scherer, *Industrial Market Structure and Economic Performance*, 2nd ed. (Chicago: Rand McNally College Publishing Company, 1980), pp. 439–458. See, also, C. A. Taylor and Z. A. Silbertson, *The Economic Impact of the Patent System* (New York: Cambridge University Press, 1973).

[29] Ward S. Bowman, Jr., *Patent and Antitrust Law* (Chicago: University of Chicago Press, 1973), p. 1.

[30] Morton I. Kamien and Nancy L. Schwartz, *Market Structure and Innovation* (New York: Cambridge University Press, forthcoming).

[31] Bowman, op. cit., p. 2.

Antitrust and Patents

The patent system creates a source of tension with the antitrust laws because the holder of a patent is in a position of monopoly with regard to the invention he has patented. In addition, certain kinds of restrictive agreements made by the patent holder (such as an exclusive license to make or sell the patented product in a defined territory) may, in the absence of a patent, be in violation of the antitrust laws. However, it is important to note that the granting of a monopoly right to the use of an invention does not necessarily confer monopoly power. The extent of monopoly power given depends on the availability of substitutes and the elasticity of demand. If numerous substitutes are available and/or if demand is relatively elastic, then the extent of monopoly power is diminished. Also, the nature of the patent[32] and the relationship of the patent to existing, complementary patents[33] are also factors enhancing or limiting the degree of monopoly power involved. Nevertheless, the monopoly right granted by a patent runs counter to the whole body of antitrust law developed in this country since the 1890s to promote and protect the free enterprise system. Therefore, as we shall see later, when there is conflict between the antitrust laws and patent protection, the antitrust laws generally prevail.

Criteria for Patentability

To be patentable, an invention must be (1) novel, (2) nonobvious, (3) useful, and (4) adequately disclosed.[34] However, with regard to the third criterion (an invention must be useful), Bowman has articulated argued that "*usefulness* is a proper precondition for *reward,* but not for *patentability.* The market performs more reliably than patent examiners in determining usefulness. . . .[35]

The most important criteria appear to be the first two: an invention must be novel and nonobvious. The broad rule is that a patent will be issued if the differences between an invention and the prior art are substantial and that the invention would not have been obvious to someone reasonably skilled in the art. But the obviousness of inventions and the substantiality of their differences from the prior art are still matters of judgment.

The Patenting Process

To initiate the patenting process, an inventor files a patent application in the U.S. Patent and Trademark Office. The application must include certain specific portions, including an abstract, a written description of the invention, one or more claims, the required filing fee, and a declaration by the inventor that

[32] For example, an improvement patent may be used to extend the life of the original monopoly.

[33] For example, it is possible to "fence in" a specific technology by securing enough patents within a given field.

[34] Ernest Gellhorn, *Antitrust Law and Economics in a Nutshell* (St. Paul, Minn.: West Publishing Co., 1976), p. 346.

[35] Bowman, op. cit., p. 33.

he believes himself to be the original and sole inventor of the claimed subject matter. Each patent applicant is under a duty to disclose to the patent examiner relevant prior art and other information of which he is aware that may have an impact on the patentability of the invention. Failure to adhere to this "duty of full disclosure" may be grounds for invalidating the issued patent. However, as Wilcox and Shepherd observe,

> The preparation of a patent application is an art in itself. The broader they can be made, without appearing to be limitless, the wider the area of monopoly. The less informative they can be made, without appearing to withhold essential facts, the less likelihood that the technology involved will be disclosed to possible competitors.[36]

During any given year, there are over 100,000 applications filed and over 200,000 patents pending. The number of patents issued per year runs around 80,000. The typical patent, when granted, has been pending more than three years. The Patent Office examines applications ex parte or from one side only. Given the flood of patent applications with which it must cope and the scarcity of its resources, it is not surprising that many of the patents granted by the Patent Office overlap with others. It is rare, though, that patents are taken to court, but when they are, there is a 60 percent chance, based on past experience, that the courts will find that the plaintiff's patent was *not* infringed or that the patent was lacking in validity. This situation can be interpreted two ways. First, because of the large numbers of patents that are not reviewed by a court, it is obvious that the word of the Patent Office passes at face value most of the time. Given the undermanned condition of the Patent Office, which prevents it from subjecting patent applications to thorough scrutiny, this is somewhat appalling. Second, the uncertainty concerning the validity of patents that results from litigation weakens the operation of the patent system and dilutes the value of the patent grant. As one jurist has remarked, "A patent is merely a license to bring a lawsuit."[37] In recognition of the latter weakness, Congress passed a bill in 1980 aimed at strengthening existing patents in infringement suits. The legislation allows the patent holder or a challenger to ask the Patent Office to reexamine the patentability of an invention.

On the other hand, from the point of view of the patent seeker, it is likely that he or she can expect, due to a number of different factors, to receive more than 17 years of protection for an invention. First, a patent is likely to be pending for 3 or more years. Also, the duration of monopoly may be prolonged by dividing complicated inventions into several parts—the steps in the process, the elements in a compound, or the sections of a machine—and applying for separate patents at judicious intervals. Improvement patents are granted. And, during the period of patent protection, a firm may have developed a productive organization, market outlets, control over markets, and a

---

[36] Clair Wilcox and William G. Shepherd, *Public Policies Toward Business*, 5th ed. (Homewood, Ill.: Richard D. Irwin, Inc., 1975), p. 257.

[37] *Guide* v. *Desperak*, 144 F. Supp. 182, 186 (1956).

monopoly of skilled personnel that will make it difficult, if not impossible, for others to enter the field when its patents have expired. In addition to these means of extending the 17-year period, the Senate has passed a bill that would increase a patent's life for as long as 7 years to compensate patent holders for the time it takes to get regulatory clearance by such agencies as the Food and Drug Administration. For example, it has been shown that by the time the FDA has reviewed a patented new drug for safety and effectiveness, less than 10 years remain in the average life of the patent. Besides drugs for humans and animals, products potentially eligible for this patent extension include food additives, pesticides, medical devices, and other substances subject to federal premarketing regulations.

Scope of Patent Rights

Once a patent is granted, the individual patentee has clear and unrestricted rights to exclusive use of the patented process or machinery, or to exclusive production and sale of the patented product, in any volume or at any price the patentee may wish to establish. Indeed, if a patent owner makes a business decision based on reasonable considerations that it is not economically feasible for him to practice the patented invention, such nonuse would be permissible, and the patent should be fully enforceable against others. In *Special Equipment Co.* v. *Coe*,[38] the Supreme Court explicitly stated that, in granting a patent, it made no difference whether the grantee ever intended to make use of the patented invention. Most, perhaps 90 percent, of all patents are unused because they have no commercial value. Another possible reason, among others, for nonuse is that the patent holder may have substantial sums invested in a competing product or in a process that embodies an earlier technology. Thus, the patent may be used to prevent competitors from securing a differential advantage. Such suppression of patents is not illegal; nevertheless, it clearly defeats the fundamental purpose of the patent law.

On the other hand, the fact that violations for nonuse are rare does not mean that they could not be found under specific circumstances. Exploitation of patent rights can run afoul of the antitrust laws (the Sherman Act, Section 3 of the Clayton Act, and Section 5 of the FTC Act) if a patent or a group of patents is used as a tool for creating a more extensive monopoly or a greater restraint of trade than has been bestowed in the "basic monopoly" stemming from the patent or patents in question.[39] If nonuse is based on, say, a collusive agreement to suppress patented inventions in order to "fence in" the technology or to "block in" a competing technology, antitrust violations may exist.[40]

It is also of questionable legality for a single firm to attain control over a great many individual patents, covering most or all of the many processes, machines, or products needed for a firm to operate in an industry. In such a

---

[38] 324 U.S. 370 (1945).

[39] Joe S. Bain, *Industrial Organization*, 2nd ed. (New York: John Wiley & Sons, Inc., 1968), p. 554.

[40] *Hartford-Empire Co.* v. *U.S.*, 323 U.S. 386, 431 (1945).

circumstance, a firm would, via the accumulation of patents, gain the ability to exclude competitors and secure predominant market occupancy of a whole industry. As Scherer observes,

> Examples of massive patent portfolios being accumulated by single firms have been found in the following industries: synthetic fibers, cellophane, plastics, synthetic leather, synthetic rubber, photo supplies, tranquilizers, radio, television, shoe machinery, data-processing equipment, electric lamps, telephone equipment, copying processes, and can-closing machines, to name just a few.[41]

Acquisition of patents by purchase or by exclusive license[42] may be used as evidence of monopolization or attempted monopolization under Section 2 of the Sherman Act if the acquisition has been made by a firm holding a dominant position in a market. The existence of several consent decrees presents strong indications that where a company has amassed a patent portfolio that threatens undue maintenance of industry domination, even though the patents may have been acquired through internal research, antitrust law may require some sort of alteration in the patent situation in the industry.

From a patent holder's strategic management perspective, a primary concern may be to exclude others from practicing his invention, irrespective of whether he, himself, puts it to use. The only way a patentee can prevent infringement under the present patent system is to file a lawsuit in federal court. Sometimes the mere threat of litigation can discourage companies, especially smaller concerns, from marketing products that would compete with those of the patentee.[43] However, a patentee probably could not obtain a preliminary injunction unless he had actually practiced the invention in the open market. In other words, in the absence of an actual market "test" of the alleged infringement, a patentee would have to go through the entire process of trying the case in order to stop the infringement.[44] Even if the patentee were to win the case, the infringer could still appeal. Resolution of the issue might come after the product life of the article or process is exhausted.[45] There is always the possibility that, within the five or six years that it would take to get the litigation resolved, no one would have invented a better product. But if the patent holder calculates that the life cycle will be relatively short and that the likelihood of infringement is high, he may decide to license his patent in order to be certain to generate decent profits rather than take a risk and not recoup an adequate return if the market becomes volatile. In other words, if the patent holder comes to the conclusion that others will probably infringe, he

---

[41] Scherer, op. cit., p. 451.

[42] The true exclusive license permits the licensee to exercise the full range of patent rights, including prohibiting even the patent owner from manufacturing, using, or selling the patented item or process.

[43] See Sanford L. Jacobs, "Patent Lawsuits Can Be Used to Keep the Competition Away," *Wall Street Journal,* October 12, 1981, p. 27. However, the institution of infringement suits in bad faith can constitute evidence of monopolization or attempted monopolization. See *Otter Tail Power Co.* v. *U.S.,* 410 U.S. 366 (1973).

[44] C. Lee Cook, Jr., and John R. Murphy, "Dramatization: Patent–Antitrust Considerations," 49 *Antitrust L. J.,* 441 (1981).

[45] In order to reduce the difficulty and amount of time consumed in obtaining decisions in patent cases, Congress in 1982 created a single appeals court to rule on patent cases appealed from the federal district courts, and this court hears all patent appeals from the Patent and Trademark Office.

might well consider licensing others and collect royalties rather than get nothing. Other options might be (1) to get a head start first and then license the patent or (2) to litigate infringers in the hope that a more lucrative licensing arrangement will be forthcoming as a result of the lawsuit. In any case, licensing is an extremely important strategic consideration. Unfortunately, from the firm's perspective, this area generates a host of legal issues, especially when the patentee, via licensing, tries to restrict competition.

The Antitrust Limits of Licensing

Licensing is usually done for a fee (called a royalty), the amount charged frequently being based on usage. Licensing is often favored by public policy agencies because, from a social welfare point of view, it tends to expand the use of the invention, increase competition in its use, and disperse the technology, thereby encouraging improvements. On the other hand, licensing also has its drawbacks relative to social welfare because it tends to encourage the development of intimate relations among competitors, lessen the likelihood of challenges to invalid patents, and discourage the invention of more efficient alternatives.[46]

In many nations, patent holders can solidify their control over licensees by prescribing prices at which the product can be sold, imposing output quotas, and limiting licensees to particular markets or fields of use. Such restrictions have come under increasing attack in the United States, but they have not yet been ruled illegal when enforced *unilaterally* by the patentee. Indeed, the patentee–licensor may impose restrictions upon the use of the patent that in other circumstances might violate antitrust law.[47] In fact, he may generally impose restraints reasonably necessary to protect the patented object and the patent itself. However, he may not, under the Sherman Act, use a licensing system affecting several competitors that effectively eliminates competition among them or within a market.[48]

Refusals and Royalties.

Patent holders can refuse to license certain parties; they are not obligated to license everybody. If they make unilateral decisions to license A and not B, such arrangements are perfectly permissible, especially if the patent holders are small companies or have rather weak or minimal market positions. (If the patent holders are dominant firms, their freedom to refuse may be severely curtailed.) In addition, a patent empowers the owner to exact royalties as high as can be negotiated using the monopoly leverage granted to the patentee. How-

---

[46] Gellhorn, op. cit., p. 348.

[47] When attempting to sort out the legal constraints on marketing strategy in the patent area, it is important to understand that there are virtually no statutes that define what a corporate or individual patent holder can or cannot do. Rather, actions are governed by precedents established in scores of legal cases. For a comprehensive listing of cases, see Bowman, op. cit., and Rupert, *The Relationship of Patent Law to Antitrust Law,* 49 Antitrust L. J., 763 (1981).

[48] *U.S.* v. *U.S. Gypsum Co.,* 333 U.S. 364 (1948).

ever, patent holders who license competing licensees must be wary of the effect that the royalty base or rate may have. If the royalty base or rate creates *discriminatory* royalty obligations among competing licensees such that competition among the licensees is injured, an unfair method of competition in violation of Section 5 of the FTC Act, and patent misuse, may exist.[49]

Controlling Prices.

Relative to pricing strategy and patents, the Supreme Court has never abandoned a rule first announced in 1902 that a patentee may enforce minimum price clauses in its licensing arrangements.[50] The most notorious decision dealing with this issue, however, came 20 years later in a lawsuit involving General Electric's patent on electric lamps.[51] GE had granted a license to Westinghouse, indicating that electric lamps made using the patent had to be sold at the same price that GE was charging and distributed through the same means. (GE had devised an "agency" or consignment distribution system, divided into retail and industrial user markets aimed at retail price maintenance, which it wanted to continue; hence the price restrictions to Westinghouse.) The Court held that the license did *not* violate the antitrust laws, because, it reasoned, part of the right of a patent is to acquire profit by setting the price at which the product is sold. Therefore, according to the Court, it is permissible for the patent holder to restrict the price at which a licensee may sell a patented product in order to protect the profit that the patentee should receive.

Given its overwhelmingly and consistently negative stand on price fixing of any kind throughout the years,[52] the Supreme Court's decision in the GE case was somewhat bizarre. Although it has never overruled the GE decision, it has distinguished the rule whenever possible. The GE rule of patent licensing containing price control now appears to be limited to cases involving a *single* licensee, that is, when price control is enforced unilaterally.[53] Nevertheless, in deciding whether to license A and not to license B, it is not illegal for a marketing manager to have in his or her *own* mind that A does not cut prices and B does.[54]

Controlling Distribution.

With regard to distribution strategy, the patent law specifically authorizes the granting of an exclusive right to a patented invention in a limited geographic area less than all of the United States. But, as with price control is-

---

[49] Rupert, supra note 47.

[50] 186 U.S. 70 (1902).

[51] *U.S.* v. *General Electric Co.,* 272 U.S. 476 (1926).

[52] See Chapter 5.

[53] Gellhorn, op. cit., p. 357. See *U.S.* v. *Line Material Company,* 333 U.S. 287 (1948) and *U.S.* v. *Huck Mfg. Co.,* 382 U.S. 197 (1965), where attempts to overturn the GE doctrine were thwarted by a 4–4 split among the participating Supreme Court justices.

[54] Cook and Murphy, op. cit., p. 443.

sues, such arrangements must be made *unilaterally;* they cannot involve collusion among the various licensees (all of whom may be competitors) and the patent holder.

While it is possible to establish territorial restrictions, it is not possible to use a patent as a means for managing an entire distribution channel made up, for example, of a manufacturer, wholesalers, and retailers. The manufacturer may be able to limit the territories of wholesalers via licensing, but his ability to restrict the retailers is highly constrained.[55] The terms of a patent license cannot legally include a restriction on the resale of a patented good once sold by the licensee (in this example, a wholesaler) to an initial purchaser (here, a retailer). Nor can they probably include a restriction on the sale price of an unpatented good made with the patented process or machine that is licensed. In the specific case of a method or a process, the patent holder is not permitted to control the manufacture or sale of the product produced by the method. The only way the holder can control what the licensee does with the end product is to obtain a patent on the end product itself, because if the patent is limited to the method of making it, once the licensee has practiced that method, the invention, from the point of view of patent law, is finished.

One famous case that is at odds with the constraints on distribution strategy just outlined is *General Talking Pictures Corp.* v. *Western Electric Co.*[56] GTP had a patent on vacuum tube amplifiers that were appropriate for use in both industrial and consumer goods. It gave a license to manufacture and sell the amplifier to several companies serving each sector separately. In the license agreements, there was a restriction prohibiting the licensee from using the product to make other types of products than those allowed by the license. Western Electric was licensed only for consumer goods, but went ahead and made an industrial good as well, which it then resold to an industrial purchaser. The Court found that the infringement action against Western Electric *and* Western Electric's customer by GTP was valid, thereby upholding the right of the patent holder to control the use of a patented product *after* it had been sold by the original licensee. Although this case has never been overturned by the Supreme Court, it is similar in nature to the *GE* case cited earlier in that it seems clearly out of step with decisions after 1938.[57]

Another distribution strategy influenced by patent cases is the use of tying contracts or agreements. The subject of such contracts is addressed in considerable detail in Chapter 6. However, relative to patents, a patent holder may not, under the Sherman and the Clayton Acts, license the use of a patented process or machine on condition that the licensee purchase or lease unpatented goods from the patent holder. Doing so, it is reasoned, would extend the monopoly from a patented to an unpatented good, where the effect would be sub-

[55] *American Industrial Fastener Corp.* v. *Flushing Enterprises, Inc.*, 362 F. Supp. 32 (N.D. Ohio, 1973). The court here found a per se violation of the antitrust laws. It should be noted that this case was tried and decided prior to the *Sylvania* decision [*Continental TV, Inc.* v. *GTE-Sylvania, Inc.*, 433 U.S. 36 (1977)], which is discussed extensively in Chapter 6.

[56] 305 U.S. 124 (1938).

[57] See, for example, *U.S.* v. *Univis Lens Co.*, 316 U.S. 241 (1942).

stantially to lessen competition or create a monopoly in a line of commerce.[58] The courts have struck down contracts, among others, requiring radio manufacturers licensed under RCA patents to buy their tubes from RCA, requiring lessees of IBM data-processing equipment to buy their tabulating cards from IBM, and requiring the purchase of rivets by lessees of patented riveting machines. In these cases, the contracts were found substantially to lessen competition because the patent holder dominated the market for the process or product to which the unpatented commodity was tied. But tying contracts have also been invalidated in cases where the patent holder was far from having a monopoly. Thus, in the *International Salt* case,[59] the Supreme Court held that a contract requiring the users of a patented salt dispenser to purchase salt from its producer was unreasonable *per se*.

Even in the face of the seemingly rigid approach to tying contracts, there have been some more recent cases that have bent the "rule." In *U.S.* v. *Jerrold Electronics*,[60] the Supreme Court, by affirming a district court decision, approved a tie-in of an engineering service contract to the purchase of highly complex equipment, but only during the early, developmental stages of a business in which the technology was innovative and unproven. However, as the technological knowledge became more widespread and definitive, the Suprem Court indicated that such a restraint would not be justified. And, in an even more recent case,[61] the Supreme Court in a five-to-four decision decided that Rohm & Haas's tying of a certain unpatented chemical compound "propanil" to a patented *method* of selectively controlling weeds and crops was not a misuse of its patent. By operation of law, purchasers of propanil from Rohm & Haas receive an implied license to use the patented method. The only way it has been possible for users to obtain a license to perform the patented process has been to buy propanil from R&H.

Using Cross-Licensing and Patent Pools.

Several firms in the same industry may agree to cross-license or pool their different patents that cover complementary processes, machines, or products. A cross-license is an agreement in which all or part of the consideration for licensing one patent is a license under another. When multiple rights of several owners are involved, an arrangement for the interchange of such rights is called a patent pool. By themselves, cross-licensing agreements or patent pools do not violate antitrust laws and indeed can sometimes convey substantial procompetitive benefits. For example, since 1915, patents have been pooled and licenses granted freely in the automobile industry without restriction and without charge. Patents covering all but the more recent inventions are thus thrown open to the entire industry, and smaller and newer firms may use them without contributing inventions of their own. Since the pool was estab-

---

[58] Bain, op. cit., p. 555.

[59] *International Salt Co.* v. *U.S.*, 332 U.S. 392 (1947). See, also, discussion of this case in Chapter 6.

[60] 187 F.Supp. 545 (E.D. Pa., 1960), *aff'd per curiam*, 365 U.S. 567 (1961).

[61] *Dawson Chemical Co.* v. *Rohm & Haas Co.*, 448 U.S. 176 (1980).

lished, no manufacturers of automobiles have appeared as plaintiff and defendant in an infringement suit.[62]

Cross-licensing arrangements can, however, violate the Sherman Act when (1) they result in the regimentation and elimination of competition in an industry; (2) they limit each party to the pooling arrangement to a particular field of use or to a particular territory; (3) they result in price fixing; (4) they are entered into for the purpose of excluding a competitor from the marketplace; or (5) they include limitations on the resale of unpatented goods.[63] In addition, one danger with patent pooling is that, in effect, a cartel will be established in the industry by the cooperation among firms. These pools often result from disputes between persons holding various patent rights, where the parties get together and pool their patents rather than fight each other. According to Scherer,

> Some of the most egregious price-fixing schemes in American economic history were erected on a foundation of agreements to cross-license complementary and competing patents. Industries cartelized at one time or another in this way include electric lights, glass bottles, parking meters, eyeglasses, magnesium, synthetic rubber, titanium paint pigments, radio broadcasting equipment, motion picture production, gypsum board, hardboard, machine tools, bathtubs, and a host of other electrical and chemical products.[64]

Where a patent pool is used to gain a monopoly for the member firms, the pool will be declared illegal.[65] Also, if the cross-licensing or patent pooling arrangement is used to suppress competition, it also will be declared illegal. For example, Singer was, at one time, the only U.S. manufacturer of a zigzag sewing machine. It had 62 percent of the U.S. market; the Japanese had 22 percent and European imports, 16 percent. Singer had conflicting patent claims with two European companies. The three companies agreed to drop their claims in return for royalty-free cross-licenses. As part of the agreement, one of the European companies assigned its patent to Singer, taking a license back, in return for cash and a promise by Singer to enforce the patent. Singer then sued the Japanese companies importing into the United States for patent infringement. The Court found that Singer was in violation of the antitrust laws because it was attempting to restrain the Japanese competition while concurrently protecting its two European allies.[66]

Challenging Patents and Obtaining Remedies

The path of patents is strewn with litigation. A major countercharge that defendants have been permitted to use in infringement suits is that patents have been employed to violate the antitrust laws. When such charges are successful-

[62] Wilcox and Shepherd, op. cit., pp. 269–270.

[63] Rupert, op. cit., p. 772 and footnote 70, p. 772, for relevant cases.

[64] Scherer, op. cit., p. 452.

[65] *Hartford–Empire Co.* v. *U.S.*, 323 U.S. 386 (1945).

[66] *U.S.* v. *Singer Mfg. Co.*, 374 U.S. 174 (1963).

ly upheld, the courts have refused to enforce the patents. Although not invalidated, patents have been rendered ineffective and their use as instruments of anticompetitive practice destroyed.

Other judicial actions have sought to remove barriers to entry. For example, it has generally been held that compulsory licensing is an appropriate remedy in antitrust actions where patent licensing abuses are proven and the compulsory license is required to obtain effective change in the industry.[67] However, even in cases where the defendant has not engaged in abusive practices in the use of its patents, compulsory licensing may be necessary in order to reduce the defendant's monopoly power, which it has acquired as a result of its other business practices.[68] In addition, scores of consent decrees have been accepted providing for the frequently royalty-free licensing of all applicants. Other decrees have called for the provision of necessary know-how. For example, American Can was directed to provide technical specifications and, if necessary, expert assistance relative to its licensing of can-closing equipment. Similar stipulations have been made of Owens-Corning Fiberglas, Eastman Kodak, IBM, and General Electric.[69]

Irrespective of the possible remedies available in the event of patent abuses, the entire subject of patents and their significance is one that has been the subject of controversy for decades.[70] The mere thought of the government granting a firm or an individual a monopoly regarding the manufacture and sale of any item, with the possible exception of a public utility, is probably enough to send shivers down the back of even lukewarm antitrusters. It is not our purpose to debate here the pros and cons of the patent system. It would, however, be well to close this discussion on patents by repeating Kamien and Schwartz's observation that invention, innovation, new products, and technological advances may have more to do with advancing competition than the antitrust laws, and that as long as patent protection encourages innovation, it is serving a highly important economic function.[71]

PROTECTION OF LITERARY AND ARTISTIC WORKS THROUGH COPYRIGHT LAW

The Constitution authorizes Congress to enact legislation that protects "writings" of "authors" (i.e., literary and artistic works) from unauthorized copying by others.[72] Congress exercised this authority most recently in the Copyright

---

[67] Compulsory licensing is an accepted feature of patent laws abroad. Typically, it can be invoked when a patent recipient fails to utilize an invention in the domestic market within a specific period of time, when licensing is essential to bring a complementary invention into use, or when the patent owner abuses a patent position, e.g., by restricting supply excessively. See Scherer, op. cit., p. 456.

[68] Rupert, op. cit., p. 774. See especially, *U.S.* v. *United Shoe Machinery Corporation,* 110 F. Supp. 295 (D. Mass. 1953), *aff'd per curiam,* 347 U.S. 521 (1954).

[69] Shepherd and Wilcox, op. cit., p. 515.

[70] For excellent analyses, see Scherer, op. cit., pp. 439–458; Bowman, op. cit.; and Taylor and Silbertson, op. cit.

[71] Kamien and Schwartz, op. cit.

[72] United States Constitution, Article I, Section 8.

Act of 1976.[73] The previous law, the Copyright Act of 1909, remains applicable to some aspects of works created under its provisions, but, otherwise, the new Act is applicable to works created after its effective date, January 1, 1978, and to many aspects of works created earlier.[74]

Subject Matter Protected

For a literary or artistic work to be protected, it must meet the constitutional requirements that it be a "writing" and that its creator be an "author." The Supreme Court, in *Goldstein* v. *California,*[75] has indicated that a "writing" consists of any physical rendering of the product of creative intellectual or esthetic labor. Under this definition, virtually any work could be protected, and thus the precise contours of protection have been left to Congressional definition, although the Court has held the intellectual effort used to create a trademark was not worthy of copyright protection. The constitutional requirement that copyright protection can be extended by Congress only to "authors" means that (1) only the person whose labor created the work can obtain protection, and (2) only original works can be protected (authorship connotes some degree of originality and not mere copying of previous works).[76]

The 1976 act gives a general grant of protection to original works of authorship fixed in any tangible medium of expression, and then enumerates seven specific (but not exclusive) categories of works that will be protected:

1. Literary works, including books, periodicals, pamphlets, scripts, catalogs, directories, product labels, computer programs, and data bases.
2. Musical works, including accompanying words.
3. Dramatic works, including accompanying music.
4. Pantomimes and choreographic works, if reduced to some tangible form (probably film or videotape).
5. Pictorial, graphic, and sculptural works, such as cartoons, photographs, prints and art reproductions, maps, globes, charts, diagrams, models, architect's drawings, and fabric designs.
6. Motion pictures and other audiovisual works.
7. Sound recordings.[77]

Copyright protection can be obtained for compilations and for derivative works. Compilations are works "formed by the collection and assembling of preexisting materials or data."[78] Derivative works are those based on preexisting works, and may consist of "a translation, fictionalization, motion picture version, sound recording, art reproduction, abridgement, condensation, or any other form in which the pre-existing work may be recast, transformed or adapted."[79] These derivative works and compilations, in order to be

[73] 17 U.S.C. Section 101 et seq. (1976 & Supp. V, 1981).

[74] Id., at Section 106.

[75] 412 U.S. 546 (1973).

[76] C. McManis, *The Law of Unfair Trade Practices* (St. Paul, Minn.: West Publishing Co., 1982).

[77] Copyright Act of 1976, Section 102.

[78] C. McManis, supra note 76, at 235.

[79] Id.

copyrightable, must, of course, have sufficient originality to merit protection and must not infringe any copyrights held by others.

Several classes of work are not eligible for copyright protection. For example, utilitarian features of an invention cannot be copyrighted; they must receive protection, if at all, under the patent laws. However, if pictorial, graphic, or sculptural matter can be separated from the article, those aspects can be copyrighted. Similarly, ideas, processes, discoveries, concepts, and methods of operation cannot be protected under the copyright laws; their protectability will be determined by patent law or by trade secret law.

While the policy of the law is to protect original expressions but to avoid giving any protection to facts and ideas, the process of drawing lines between these two domains is not easy. For example, courts have held that the author of literary fiction has protection not only for the literal words chosen, but also for the structural patterns in the work. Similarly, the author of a factual work has protection for any originality in the selection or arrangement of the facts, although it obviously is not possible to copyright the facts themselves. Thus, if two authors use the same facts to independently produce nearly identical works (such as a map or an alphabetized directory), each may be able to copyright the work but may be unable to claim that the other's work is an infringement (as long as direct copying cannot be established).[80]

Courts also have made clear that trademarks are not copyrightable. Trademark law, as discussed in the next section of this chapter, seeks to protect consumers against being confused as to the source of goods or services. Since it is possible for the same trade symbol to be used on different types of goods without causing any consumer confusion, there is no need to grant a totally exclusive right to use the symbol, as would be the case if the symbol could be copyrighted. However, labels that incorporate a trademark can be copyrighted, and use of the labels by others can be prevented.[81]

Formalities of Obtaining and Protecting a Copyright

The 1976 Copyright Act provides that a work of authorship is protected under federal copyright law as soon as the work is fixed in any tangible medium of expression. To avoid loss of protection, authors (unless publishing no more than a small number of copies) must place a notice of copyright on copies publicly distributed. The notice consists of three elements: (1) a symbol (an encircled letter ⓒ for visual works, or an encircled letter ⓟ for sound recordings), (2) the year when the work was first published, and (3) the copyright owner's name. To be able to enforce rights in court, it is necessary to register and deposit a copy of the work in the Library of Congress's Copyright Office.[82]

---

[80] C. McManis, supra note 76, at 239.

[81] Id., at 240.

[82] Copyright Act of 1976, Section 411.

Duration of a Copyright

A copyright, once obtained under the new act, lasts for the life of the author plus an additional 50 years in most cases. A different, specific time is specified for anonymous works, pseudonymous works, or works for hire: 75 years from date of publication or 100 years from date of creation, whichever occurs first. Other terms of duration apply for works protected under the prior act and for works that had only common law protection when the new act became effective. (The new Act abolished common law protection; therefore, the nature of such protection is not discussed here.)

Licensing of Copyrights

A copyright may be sold or licensed. To be valid, sales and exclusive licenses must be in writing and signed by the owner or the owner's agent. Nonexclusive licenses need not be in writing; oral agreements and agreements evidenced by conduct have been upheld. Purchasers or exclusive licensees must make sure that the sale or license is recorded in the Copyright Office so that exclusive rights can be enforced against other unauthorized users.

Most arrangements for the sale or license to use copyrighted works are simply matters of contractual agreement between the parties. However, some categories of works are subject to *compulsory licensing,* which means that others are privileged to use a copyrighted work upon payment of fees or charges as set by the Copyright Office, even though the copyright owner has not agreed to the use. The way compulsory licensing works depends upon the use that is to be made of the work. For example, if a person desires to use a nondramatic musical work in a recording, notice must be served on the owner of the copyright, and monthly royalties on sales of recordings must be paid directly to the owner at the rate of $0.0275 per recording, or $0.005 per minute of playing time, whichever is larger.[83] If the work is to be played on a juke box, a flat royalty of $8 per year per juke box is paid to the Copyright Office and later distributed to authors by the Copyright Royalty Tribunal.[84] Similarly, a compulsory license for transmission of copyrighted works over cable television may be obtained by cable operators (unless precluded by prior licensing agreements); royalties, usually a percentage of the gross receipts of the cable system (currently 3.75 percent), are paid to the Copyright Royalty Tribunal and later distributed to copyright owners.

One other peculiarity of copyright law should be noted; both the old and new acts allow the original author (copyright holder) or heirs of the author to terminate any license regardless of whether such termination rights were reserved or waived in the contract of license (unless the work was originally

---

[83] C. McManis, supra note 76, at 245.

[84] Id., at 245–46.

made "for hire"). Specific time periods within which this termination right must be exercised are specified in the act, as well as necessary formalities for exercising the right, such as notice and recording.

Because of the high transaction costs of negotiating individual licensing agreements between copyright owners and potential users, authors frequently assign their rights to organizations who, in turn, authorize use by others for a preset fee. Organizations, such as the American Society for Composers, Artists, and Publishers (ASCAP), hold many copyrights for musical works and recordings; broadcasters and other private commercial users (e.g., restaurants playing recorded music) are required by the terms of the copyright assignment to ASCAP to pay ASCAP a fee, which is later distributed to authors.

Rights of the Copyright Owner

The owner of a copyright has extremely valuable rights to prevent copying of the protected work and distribution of copies of the work by others. In addition to these rights, the owner has the exclusive right to adapt the original work for preparation of derivative works. Thus, the holder of a copyright on a play has the right to adapt the play for use in a motion picture, which also can be copyrighted. But there are important exceptions to these rights. For example, the holder of a sound recording copyright cannot prevent others from publicly playing the recording. And various special interests, such as libraries and educational broadcasters, are allowed certain rights to copy, perform, or display copyrighted works without the permission of the copyright owner. Furthermore, the very notion of compulsory licensing suggests that certain copyright owners cannot prevent copying, performance, or display of their copyrighted works. All copyright holders are subject to a "fair use" exception, which means that copyrighted works can be used for purposes of teaching, research, comment, criticism, and news reporting without violating the rights of the copyright holder. Many factors are to be considered by courts in determining whether any use of copyrighted material is a fair use, but the most important factor is whether the use substantially diminishes the value of the copyrighted work. This factor was stressed by the Court in *Sony Corp* v. *Universal City Studios,*[85] which held that home videotaping of copyrighted movies broadcast by television stations did not impair the potential market for the movies and therefor did not violate the rights of the copyright owners.

The legal remedies available for copyright infringement include an injunction against copying, performance, or distribution; recovery of damages or, alternatively, the infringer's profits; attorney's fees; and statutory damages, in lieu of actual damages, of not less than $250 nor more than $10,000 per infringed work, as determined by the court, with an increase of up to $50,000 for willfull infringement.

[85] 52 U.S.L.W. 4090, 4098–4100 (U.S., Jan.17, 1984), *rev'g*, 659 F.2d 963 (9th Cir. 1981).

PROTECTING TRADEMARKS AND TRADE IDENTITY

Businesses frequently invest considerable resources and effort in establishing an identity for the firm and its products and services. This identity helps to direct the search by potential first-time customers for the firm's output. If customers are satisfied with their initial purchases, this firm or product identity then serves as a shorthand device for associating a particular source of supply with a satisfactory quality–price relationship and allows the building up of goodwill and reputation, which should pay off in future sales.

In these efforts to establish and maintain a firm's corporate image and product identity and to reap the benefits of a good reputation, the law of trademarks plays a crucial role. For example, if a new product is to be marketed, the choice of a name for the product may determine whether the firm is liable for infringing a similar name that is being used by another firm. The choice of a product name also may affect the ability of a firm to obtain registration of the name under the federal trademark laws, and registration plays a crucial role in expanding the territorial reach of a trademark and in preventing competitors from adopting confusingly similar marks. Finally, once a mark has been established (and registered), the firm should be aware of the need to take actions that will minimize the risk that a mark will lose its enforceability and significance. This section will explore each of these issues after describing some of the basic principles relating to trademarks and clarifying some of the confusing terminology that permeates this area of marketing and law.

Trademarks and Trade Names Distinguished

The terms "brand" or "brand names" are frequently used in marketing literature to describe the use of names, words, symbols, and marks to identify goods and services or to associate those goods and services with a particular firm. The law tends to use different terminology. In particular, the federal trademark statute distinguishes between "trademarks" and "trade names" by permitting trademarks to be registered under the law, but prohibiting the registration of trade names. Trademarks are defined by the statute as including any "word, name, symbol or device or any combination thereof adopted and used by a manufacturer or merchant to *identify his goods* and distinguish them from those manufactured by others."[86] Trade names, on the other hand, are defined as the "individual names and surnames, firm names and trade names used by manufacturers, industrialists, merchants, agriculturalists, and others to *identify their businesses, vocations, or occupations. . . .*"[87] While the statute is perhaps more confusing than illuminating, the basic distinction between these terms is that "trademark" refers to *goods* while "trade name" refers to the business enterprise itself. The distinction is as important for federal registration purposes as it is simple: "Acme Clothing Company, Incorporated" would

---

[86] Trademark Act of 1946, §45, 15 U.S.C. §1127 (1976) (emphasis added).

[87] Id.

be considered an unregistrable trade name, but separate use of "ACME," especially if printed in distinctive form and accompanied by the ™ or ℠ symbol prior to registration, or ® symbol after registration would qualify as a trademark.

In theory, Congress has chosen to give protection only to symbols and those names that are graphically memorable and that are then associated by the public with goods and used by purchasers to distinguish one seller's goods from those of another. In practice, there may be little significant difference between marks and names; as demonstrated later, it is possible to obtain federal trademark protection for short but significant components of most trade names,[88] and state law may protect both names and marks from being used by others.

Types of Trademarks

Federal law also recognizes differences between "service marks," "certification marks," and "collective marks," allowing them to be registered and protected.[89] A *service mark* is a mark used in connection with the sale of services. Since services do not involve a tangible object to which a mark can be attached, the law recognizes and protects the identity of a business itself (and may allow protection to what would otherwise be an unregistrable trade name if applied to a product). For example, "Jones Transmission Repair Service, Inc.," may be a registrable service mark.

A *certification mark* is a device to indicate regional origin, nature of material, method of manufacture, quality, or labor source. Thus, the "Good Housekeeping Seal of Approval" would qualify as a certification mark, as would the mark of the International Ladies Garment Workers Union, the mark used to certify that a garment is made of 100 percent wool, and the term "Roquefort" for cheese.

Collective marks are symbols used by members of an association or group to signify that the user of the mark is a bona fide member of the group. The mark is not applied to goods or services sold by the group. Thus, a symbol used on a letterhead to indicate that the business is a member of a trade association would be a collective mark.

For the most part, these differences between types of marks are small, and all four types of marks can be registered and protected. In the remainder of this section the term "trademark" is used to include all the above terms unless differences are legally significant, in which case the differences are noted and the different treatments described.

General Trademark Law Principles

The general purpose of the law of trademarks is to protect consumers from being misled as to the identity of the producer of a product. For the honest and ethical firm, this policy coincides with the firm's interest in establishing

[88] See infra, at p. 52.

[89] Trademark Act of 1946, §45, 15 U.S.C. §1127 (1976).

and protecting its identity, reputation, and goodwill. For such firms, the law protecting trademarks is an ally against unscrupulous competitors who attempt to trade on the firm's previously established goodwill and reputation by engaging in actions that confuse, deceive, or mislead the consumer as to the identity of the producer of goods or services. The law of trademarks is not the only law that protects a firm against such improper methods of competition; properly seen, trademark law is part of a larger body of law known as the law of unfair competition.

The law of unfair competition is part of our common law, which means that, for the most part, the law is judge-made and is uniform within, but not necessarily between, states. These laws, and not federal law, basically determine when a firm has acquired legally protectable rights in a mark. However, an important federal law, the Lanham Act, extends significant protection and procedural advantages to firms that have acquired rights to marks and have registered such marks under that act.

The advantage of registering a mark under federal law is that registration provides constructive notice to any subsequent user of the same or similar mark that the holder of the registration claims the exclusive right to its use. While registration of a mark cannot prohibit the continued use of an identical or confusingly similar but unregistered mark by a prior user, registration can be effective to prevent future expansion by that user into markets not served by the prior user at the time of registration. And when use of a similar mark by another person does not begin until after federal registration, the registrant can enjoin the infringing use when actual consumer confusion results. In the *Dawn Donuts* case, for example, the defendant, a local food retailer, had been using the mark "Dawn" for a number of years in the Rochester, New York, market in connection with its bakery goods without knowledge that plaintiff had federally registered the same mark before defendant's use began. Plaintiff had not entered the Rochester market but had used the mark in other markets in connection with its dough mixes and its licensed retail bakeries. The court held that because plaintiff's "Dawn Donuts" mark had been federally registered before defendant began using the same mark, the defendant could be prohibited from using the mark if plaintiff ever actually expanded into the Rochester market.[90]

While simple registration of a trademark under federal law does not confer on the registrant any rights that the registrant did not have under state law before registration, registration does confer several procedural advantages. Registration indicates the registrant's *prima facie* ownership and exclusive rights to use the registered mark. Initially, this *prima facie* status does not preclude others from raising all legal or equitable defenses that could have been asserted even if the mark had not been registered. But when the mark becomes "incontestable" (by continuous use for five consecutive years subsequent to registration), the registration does become "conclusive evidence of the registrant's exclusive right to use the registered mark in commerce on or in connec-

[90] *Dawn Donut Co.* v. *Hart's Food Stores, Inc.*, 267 F.2d 358 (2d Cir. 1959).

tion with the goods or services specified. . . ." Although this "conclusive evidence" is subject to a number of statutory defenses (such as fraudulent acquisition, abandonment, loss of distinctiveness, prior use of the mark by the defendant before the owner's registration, and use to violate antitrust laws),[91] the advantage of acquiring the status of incontestability is significant.

The status of incontestability can be used to defeat a defense often raised to an infringement suit (i.e., that the registered mark was merely descriptive of the goods at the time of registration). If the mark has become incontestable, this defense simply cannot be raised in an infringement action. Thus, the leading case of *Union Carbide Corp.* v. *Ever-Ready, Inc.,*[92] held that even if the mark "Ever-Ready" was descriptive and had not acquired a secondary meaning at the time it was registered (and therefore could have been attacked during the first five years after registration), once the mark had become incontestable, the defense of "descriptiveness" could not be asserted.

Trademark Rights Exist Only When the Mark Is Put Into Actual Use

One common misconception applies to trademarks: that one merely has to think up a clever design for a mark and then register the design with the government in order to obtain the exclusive right to use the mark. Unfortunately, for the firm that has conceived a clever design or trademark, this misconception can prove dangerous. Under American legal principles, the right to use a trademark is acquired only by actual use of the trademark on goods or services and by the association of the trademark by the consuming public with those particular goods or services. Only after such actual use and association can the trademark be protected by state law or registered under the Lanham Act.

Firms should be aware that the United States is unique in its requirement of actual use of a mark before registration is allowed and protection is obtained; in most other countries, registration is allowed before goods using the mark are sold. In fact, many countries require that before a mark for imported goods can be registered, a registered mark must be in existence in the country where the product is made. For firms that have not sold goods in the United States using the mark, the registration requirement presents a dilemma, since the mark cannot be registered in the United States. To resolve the dilemma, Congress provided for a "Supplemental Register" upon which

---

[91] These defenses are:
1. The registration was obtained fraudulently;
2. The mark has been abandoned;
3. The mark is being used with the owner's acquiescence to misrepresent the source of goods or services;
4. The mark alleged to be an infringement is merely an individual's name not used as a mark or is used in good faith as a description of goods or their geographic origin;
5. The mark was adopted and used before the owner's registration (this defense is good only in the geographic area of prior use);
6. The alleged infringing mark was actually registered and used prior to the second registration;
7. The mark is or has been used to violate the antitrust laws. 15 U.S.C. §1115.

[92] 531 F.2d 366 (7th Cir. 1976).

United States companies could register their marks without first using them; this registration can then be used in order to obtain registration under the laws of foreign countries.[93]

The requirement that a mark actually be used before it can be registered means that there is considerable risk to the firm that has conceived a good idea for a mark and is preparing to develop and market goods or services using the mark. Considerable expense may be incurred in getting ready for production and in designing and printing labels, packages, and promotional material. Yet, it is entirely possible that a competitor is further along in this process and will be the first to reach the market with goods using the same or a confusingly similar mark. The law will give protection to the first person who actually uses the mark in connection with products or services that are actually sold. United States law thereby fosters a "race to the marketplace" by those who are seeking to use a potentially valuable trademark and protects the rights of those who win the race. Thus, the Burger King enterprise was not able to prevent use of the "Burger King" name by a local restaurant that had begun its operations prior to plaintiff's federal registration of the "Burger King" trademark.[94]

Extension of Mark to Different Products

Because the basic underlying principle of trademark ownership rests upon prior actual use of a mark in connection with the sale of goods or services, difficulties arise when a firm wishes to extend its previously used mark to a new product line. Many cases have reached somewhat surprising results by holding that a mark well known in connection with one product line can be appropriated by different marketers of dissimilar products. For example, the owner of the Johnnie Walker trademark as applied to Scotch whiskey was not able to enjoin the use of the Johnny Walker name by a different company engaged in the marketing of shoes. The court reasoned that because purchasers of shoes would not conclude that the whiskey marketer had become engaged in the marketing of shoes, there was little likelihood of consumer confusion and therefore no need for an injunction. But where the "V-8" trademark (applied to a vegetable juice cocktail) was appropriated by a marketer of vitamins, the court was able to conclude that consumers mistakenly might infer that the vegetable juice supplier had extended its mark to a new line of products including vitamins. Thus, on this finding of a likelihood of consumer confusion, the use of the V-8 mark for vitamins was prohibited. Some states have enacted

---

[93] Pattishall, *The Use Rationale and the Trademark Registration Treaty*, 61 American Bar Ass'n Journal 83 (1975). The differing registrability requirements of nations present interesting and difficult legal issues. For example, the United States has entered into conventions and treaties with other nations that provide for protection of trademarks before they are actually used. Section 44(d) of the Lanham Act allows marks that have been registered in a country that is a party to these treaties and conventions to be registered in the United States, even though they have not been used here. This registration was held to give priority to a Canadian company even though the Canadian company and a United States company began using the mark at the same time. *SCM Corp. v. Langis Foods, Ltd.,* 539 F.2d 196 (D.C. Cir. 1976).

[94] *Burger King of Florida, Inc. v. Hoots,* 403 F.2d 904 (7th Cir. 1968).

laws that restrict the practice of taking a free ride on another's well-established name; these laws might help firms avoid the "dilution" of the value of a trademark.

Infringement of Trademarks and the "Likelihood of Confusion" Test

The ultimate value of acquiring a legally protectable interest in a trademark lies in the ability to take legal action against other firms that might use the same or a deceptively similar mark. Use of a protected mark by another firm can cause great injury in several ways. First, and most important, a direct loss of revenue and income will occur as sales are diverted. Second, if purchasers never become aware that they have mistakenly purchased goods that were not produced by the owner of the trademark, and if those goods do not meet the expectations of the purchaser as to quality, the owner of the trademark has suffered a loss of reputation and might lose revenue and profits in the future. Finally, even if the purchaser becomes aware of the mistaken purchase, there is always the danger that the purchaser will decide that any price premium demanded by the owner of the mark simply is not justified.

The ability to protect rights in a trademark is relatively straightforward if a firm has registered the mark and if an alleged infringer is copying, or "counterfeiting," the mark. In that situation, the main difficulties in obtaining an injunction against unauthorized use of a mark lie in identifying the offenders and the channels of supply of the counterfeit goods.[95] But if a competing firm has adopted a trademark that is not a direct copy and is using the mark in a good faith effort to identify the firm's own goods, the ability to stop the competitor's use of the mark will turn on the question of whether consumers of the general class of goods are likely to be confused as to the source of the goods or services. No hard and fast rules can be laid down in this area; courts frequently base their decisions on the totality of all circumstances involved in each case, and it is rare that two cases are completely similar.

The approach of courts to the question of likelihood of confusion is typified by the case of *Exxon Corporation* v. *Texas Motor Exchange of Houston, Inc.*[96] The ultimate holding of the court was that the "Exxon" trademark was infringed by the mark "Texxon," but not by the mark "Tex-On." Standard Oil Company changed its name to Exxon Corporation in late 1972 and adopted "Exxon" as its national trademark, incurring great expense to advertise and

---

[95] The problem of outright pirating of a trademark apparently is widespread. In the case of the Rolling Stones musical group, their recent nationwide tour was accompanied by widespread sale of T-shirts, buttons, pins, trinkets, and other merchandise bearing the trademark of the Stones. Designers, sports teams, soft drink companies, and the National Football League all have had to resort to court actions in order to obtain injunctions against the sale of items bearing unauthorized trademarks. In some cases, courts have been persuaded to issue ex parte seizure orders where other legal relief (such as damages) would not be available because of the itinerant nature of the sellers of the counterfeit merchandise. See Bassett, "*Trademark Attorneys Get Tough*," National Law Journal, Dec. 21, 1981, p. 1, col. 13.

[96] 628 F.2d 500 (5th Cir. 1980).

promote the mark throughout the United States. A few months later, Texxon was selected as a new name for Texxon Motor Centers, Incorporated, a company that provided automobile repair services in the Houston, Texas, area. Standard Oil then filed an infringement action. In determining whether there was a likelihood of confusion, the court examined several factors: (1) the Exxon mark was found to be a strong mark, rarely used by others and not a common word; (2) the design of the marks was not similar, even though both marks used block letters and similar colors; (3) the goods and services provided under each mark were similar—auto repairs; (4) the market for the goods is identical—members of the car-driving public; (5) the retail outlets were dissimilar, Exxon using retail service stations, Texxon using warehouse-type buildings; (6) the advertising media used by the parties was substantially identical—both used radio, television, newspaper, and yellow page advertising; (7) survey evidence indicated a high degree of confusion between the Texxon and Exxon marks, but no significant confusion existed when the Exxon and Tex-On marks were compared.

Inasmuch as the ultimate legality of the use of any particular mark is whether the mark creates a likelihood of confusion in the minds of prospective purchasers as to the source of goods or services, the most important evidence often is a survey of consumers in the relevant market. Such survey evidence is now widely accepted into evidence and seemingly is relied upon more and more by courts in the decision process. As this type of evidence becomes determinative of infringement disputes, criticism has been voiced as to the appropriateness of the research design and as to the validity of many research findings. Although most surveys simply measure whether the mark used by an alleged infringer causes survey respondents to associate the mark with the plaintiff's business, in the future it can be anticipated that such simple research designs will be questioned and that more sophisticated designs will be employed to determine whether and to what extent confusion exists and causes consumers to purchase under mistaken beliefs as to the source of a product.[97]

Relief Available in Infringement Actions

Whenever a trademark has been infringed, the injured party is entitled to relief through the courts. Generally, this relief can be in the form of either injunctive relief against future infringement or damages (including lost profits) caused by past infringement. Recovery of damages is difficult. Courts require proof that any loss of business was caused by the infringement. Proving this causation is difficult. Evidence that the plaintiff's sales declined after the infringement occurred is not sufficient, standing alone, to prove that the infringer's actions were the cause of the sales decline; the possibility always exists that losses were caused by other factors, such as general economic declines or

[97] Sidney J. Levy and Dennis W. Rook, "Brands, Trademarks and the Law," in Ben M. Enis and Kenneth J. Roering, eds., *Review of Marketing 1981* (Chicago, Ill.: American Marketing Association, 1981), pp. 185, 189–90.

genuine consumer preference for products other than the plaintiff's products. However, injunctive relief is available if the plaintiff's evidence shows "a reasonable basis for the belief that the plaintiff is likely to be damaged . . . ."[98] While courts are reluctant to grant monetary compensation to a plaintiff in the absence of fairly definitive proof of actual injury caused by the defendant, injunctive relief is more readily allowed, as an injunction "poses no likelihood of a windfall for the plaintiff . . . [and] the complaining competitor gains no more than that to which it is already entitled—a market free of false advertising."[99]

Legal Considerations in Choosing a Trademark

After a firm has developed a new product for introduction into the market, the firm must decide whether it would be useful to create a new trademark for use in connection with the product. Obviously, this decision must be made before the packaging, labeling, and promotional material is prepared and before the product itself is produced, since the trademark should be affixed to and prominently displayed on the product and its packaging and promotion. Less obviously, the decision as to the form and content of the trademark must be made in light of legal principles so that risks will be avoided and the benefits of the use of a trademark will be maximized. The risks to be avoided include the risk that a trademark will infringe someone else's trademark. The benefits of proper choice of a trademark include the ability to prevent competitors from adopting and using a confusingly similar mark and the ability to invoke the protections of the federal trademark law. In the next sections, we explore the legal aspects of the choice of a trademark.

Avoiding Infringement of Existing Marks.

Once a mark has been selected as a candidate for use on a new product, the firm must determine whether the mark belongs to someone else. Unless reasonable assurance can be obtained that the mark can be used and later registered, there is little utility in preparing to market a product under a mark that cannot be protected or that will result in infringement of an existing mark.

Under the common law, and under the Lanham Act, liability attaches to the use of a trademark that is the same as, or confusingly similar to, a trademark that has been adopted and used by another firm. Since trademarks are not required to be registered in public offices, no certain way exists of completely eliminating the risk that a trademark which is thought to be new and original actually is confusingly similar to a trademark used by another firm. But even though the risk of accidental infringement cannot be eliminated, steps can be taken to minimize this risk. Searching all available information sources for prior use of the trademark and avoiding adoption and use of the

---

[98] *Johnson & Johnson* v. *Carter-Wallace, Inc.,* 631 F.2d 186, 190 (2d Cir. 1980).

[99] Id., at 192.

same or confusingly similar marks is the only way to minimize the risk of accidental infringement, and the more thorough the search, the less the risk. Fortunately, professional searching services exist that can perform fairly thorough investigations of state and federal trademark registers, telephone and trade directories, fictitious name registers, and numerous other sources that would reflect prior trademark or trade name use.

The dangers of failing to discover a prior use of a trademark are illustrated by the case involving Goodyear's use of a trademark "Big Foot" for an automobile tire design that it developed.[100] Goodyear had invested considerable sums in preparation for its new product introduction but had failed to learn that a small retailer of tires was using the "Big Foot" name on a line of tires it was distributing locally. Goodyear was held liable to the small retailer for infringing the retailer's trademark; in addition, the retailer was allowed to recover from Goodyear for injury to the retailer's reputation, which resulted from consumer perception that the small retailer was infringing Goodyear's trade name and attempting to confuse the public. This latter theory of recovery, relatively new at the time of its introduction, has subsequently received widespread support by legal commentators.

Specific Prohibitions on Federal Registration.

Federal trademark law constrains the choice of a trademark through specific prohibitions against registration. Three specific classes of marks cannot be registered:

1. Marks that consist of "immoral" or "scandalous" matter or which are contemptuous or disparaging of individuals (living or dead), institutions, beliefs or national symbols;[101]
2. Marks that consist of or include flags, coats of arms, or other insignia of cities, states, or the federal government or foreign nations;[102]
3. Marks that consist of the name, image, or signature of a living individual (unless the individual gives written consent).[103]

Apart from these specific restrictions, there are two general limits on registrability: (1) registration should not be permitted for marks that are "likely . . . to cause confusion, or to cause mistake, or to deceive" others because of prior use of a similar or identical trademark or trade name;[104] and (2) registration is not permitted for a mark that is merely descriptive (either functionally or geographically) or that is primarily a surname unless the mark has become "distinctive" (i.e., the mark has acquired "secondary meaning").[105]

---

[100] *Big O Tire Dealers, Inc.* v. *Goodyear Tire & Rubber Co.*, 408 F. Supp. 1219 (D. Col., 1976), *aff'd and modified on other grounds*, 561 F.2d 1365 (10th Cir. 1977), *cert. dismissed*, 434 U.S. 1052 (1978).

[101] 15 U.S.C. §1052(a).

[102] 15 U.S.C. §1052(b).

[103] 15 U.S.C. §1052(c).

[104] 15 U.S.C. §1052(d).

[105] 15 U.S.C. §1052(f).

The Patent and Trademark Office maintains a list that classifies goods and services; a mark can be registered only for specific classifications for which the mark is actually being used. This limitation implements the notion that rights to use trademarks are not actually acquired by registration but are acquired only by actual use of the mark in connection with actual sales of goods or services.

These rules (likelihood of confusion and classifications of goods) can lead to peculiar results. For example, the trademark "Johnnie Walker" has been held to be infringed by use on cigarettes[106] but not, as mentioned earlier, by use on men's shoes.[107] The "Beefeater" mark for gin was infringed by "Beef/Eater" for a restaurant,[108] but "Holiday Inns" was not infringed by "Holiday Out in America" for a trailer park.[109]

Protection of Trade Names.

Although registration under the federal act extends only to marks (trademarks, service marks, certification marks, or collective marks) and does not extend to trade names, this limitation should not serve as a deterrent to obtaining federal protection for the major component of a company name. While the Patent and Trademark Office probably will refuse to register as a trademark the full corporate name of a business, such as "American Ever-Ready Company," registration would be allowed of "Ever-Ready" as a mark applied to flashlights if some part of the name were emphasized by distinctive type style.

Guides for Choosing Trademarks

Strong Marks versus Weak Marks.

The choice of a trademark for a product should be guided in part by a desire to obtain the maximum legal protection for the mark and thereby prevent others from using a confusingly similar mark. The choice process should be undertaken in recognition of the law's varied protection, which depends, in part, on the characterization of the trademark as either "weak" or "strong." A weak mark might be thought of as a word that praises or describes (e.g., "premium" or "best"), while a strong mark can be thought of as coined or fanciful (e.g., "Exxon" or "Xerox").

If a court or the trademark office categorizes a trademark as "weak," then protection will not be given to the mark unless the first user of a mark can demonstrate that the mark has acquired what is called "secondary meaning." This secondary meaning refers to an association on the part of the consumer

---

[106] 110 U.S.P.Q. 249 (Com. Pat. 1956); *John Walker & Sons, Ltd.* v. *Tampa Cigar Co.*, 222 F.2d 460 (5th Cir. 1955) (cigars).

[107] *John Walker & Sons, Ltd.* v. *Modern Shoe Co.*, 213 F.2d 322 (C.C.P.A. 1954).

[108] *Beef/Eater Restaurants, Inc.* v. *James Burrough, Ltd.*, 398 F.2d 637 (5th Cir. 1968).

[109] *Holiday Inns, Inc.* v. *Holiday Out in America*, 481 F.2d 445 (5th Cir. 1973).

between the goods or services to which the mark relates and a particular source (or certifier of quality) of the goods or services. In other words, it is not necessary that a mark be associated with a particular manufacturer in the minds of consumers; it is only necessary that consumers associate the product and its mark with some particular or exclusive source. This association allows consumers to make inferences about the quality of the goods or the reputation of the entity that manufactures them. It is this association or identity between the mark and the manufacturer that must be established in order to merit legal protection.

In addition to marks that are merely descriptive of a product or one of its uses, functions, or attributes (e.g., "bright" and "shiny"), a second category of "weak" marks are geographic names. For example, "Swiss" for cheeses or watches, "Boston" for beans, or "Colombia" for coffee would be unprotectable in the absence of demonstrable secondary meaning. Since these marks or names merely indicate the geographic source of a product, the law has not allowed a particular marketer to appropriate such a general geographic name for exclusive use. Particularly since geographic locations may indicate a particular level of manufacturing skill, others should be free to use that geographic designation. Of course, even such a geographic name can acquire secondary meaning in the sense that a particular manufacturer or marketer becomes associated with goods bearing that geographic designation (e.g., "Old Milwaukee" beer). In that case, the mark will be protected against use by other direct competitors, but proof of secondary meaning is often problematical and always risky.

The third category of weak marks are family names. Particularly if the family name is a common one (Johnson, Smith) is it probable that someone else has already adopted and used such a name. Although an individual generally has a privilege to adopt and use one's own name as a trademark, there are two major disadvantages in taking this approach. First, although all users of the same name originally carried the same risk, it is possible that secondary meaning has attached to one particular use of the name. Subsequent use by others having the same genuine name would be prohibited and would constitute an infringement if a likelihood of confusion existed. Thus, although the makers of "Johnson's Wax" ran a considerable risk when first introducing their product, at some point the Johnson's name became associated with a particular manufacturing source. After that point, all other Johnsons would run a risk of infringing that mark by selling wax products in the same geographic area where "Johnson's Wax" was known to refer to a particular source. To view the matter from the position of the Johnson's Wax Company, there was a considerable risk that others could adopt and use the name in the early stages of the development and marketing of the product under the Johnson's name. This risk should be minimized, if possible, by choice of a stronger name.

The fourth category of weak marks would include so-called laudatory descriptions of quality. For example, "premium," or "the world's finest" would not be given much protection in the absence of a demonstrated secondary meaning. Although there are numerous examples of such marks that have acquired secondary meaning such as Pabst Blue Ribbon beer or Gold Medal flour, there is considerable risk that others could use the same laudatory descriptions and, correspondingly, a reduced probability that the description will ever acquire secondary meaning.

The other general category of marks, "strong" marks, can also be thought as of consisting of several subcategories. For example, courts often extend protection without proof of secondary meaning to the use of marks that are considered "coined" or "fanciful." Such marks are advantageous in that courts are not likely to uphold defenses to infringement actions based on the concept of "innocent infringement." This defense, if successful, could protect a firm against monetary liability for using a mark already used by another firm, although it will not prevent a court from entering an injunction barring use of the infringing mark in the future. The innocent infringement defense, to be successful, requires that the court believe the infringer's assertion that the infringing mark was adopted without knowledge of the prior use of the mark by the plaintiff and without any intent to take business away from the plaintiff as a result of consumer confusion. If plaintiff used a strong mark, the defendant's assertion is not very credible. Thus, Johnson's Wax Company might be able to enjoin a Fred Johnson from marketing a "Johnson's Wax" product, but is not likely to win a money judgment against Fred if Fred claims to have chosen the mark innocently. On the other hand, the second user of a fanciful mark such as "Exxon," "GAF," or "RCA" probably would be liable for damages as well as an injunction because courts would find it difficult to believe that adoption of the term Exxon, GAF, or RCA was anything other than a deliberate and intentional copying of a mark, for which substantial damages could be awarded.

Strong marks are also recognized when a mark is chosen that is not descriptive but that does suggest some benefit of using the product. Such marks might include "Sure" for deodorant or "Black Flag" for insect spray. These marks will receive protection in the absence of proof of secondary meaning simply because they are distinctive. Although they are somewhat suggestive, they are not merely descriptive of the product.

Occasionally, a firm will choose a foreign word for a trademark. Some risks are associated with this practice. First, if the words chosen are descriptive of the product in the foreign language, United States law will also find that the marks are descriptive and will not allow registration or protection in the absence of proof of secondary meaning. The assumption here seems to be that many consumers might well know the foreign language. Second, if there is any possibility of future export sales of products using a foreign word, firms should ensure that subtle meanings of the foreign word are not derogatory or humorous in the minds of the foreign consumers. For example, the mark "Enco" for gasoline worked well in this country but was found to mean "Stalled Car" in Japanese; this restricted the marketability of the product under that mark in Japan.[110] Furthermore, foreign countries also recognize and give protection to trademarks based on the first to register under the foreign law. Accordingly, if exporting is a possibility, checking for prior registrations in possible countries of export should be done before a mark is adopted for use in the United States.

Deceptive Marks.

The choice of trade name can lead to problems with the Federal Trade Commission if the name chosen is deceptive. For example, Dollar-A-Day car rental company was required to change its name to Dollar car rental company because the name falsely suggested that automobiles could be rented for one dollar per day.[111]

State Restrictions on Trade Names.

Firms that sell a form of professional service (medical, dental, optical, legal, engineering, architectural, etc.) may be restricted in their choice of a firm name (and a related trademark) by state and local laws that prohibit professional practice under an assumed or fictitious name. The asserted state policy for such laws is that consumers of professional services are entitled to know the identities of the individuals providing services, and the use of a trade name tends to obscure the identities of individual practitioners and allow disreputable practitioners to hide their past low reputation. Opponents of such laws contend that they are enacted by lobbying groups that seek to prevent the "commercialization" of these fields of practice.

The validity of these laws was challenged on the ground that they conflict with the principle that truthful commercial speech is protected under the first amendment to the United States Constitution. In a 1979 decision, *Friedman* v. *Rogers*,[112] the Supreme Court held that states could enact these laws without violating first amendment rights, since the regulation was designed to prevent a form of deception, and deceptive commercial speech is not protected by the first amendment. While the reasoning of the Court completely overlooks the informative value of the trademarks and the marketplace pressures to maintain a firm's reputation, and while the decision arguably is inconsistent with later first amendment cases, the *Friedman* decision remains a viable precedent and compels a cautious approach to state and local restrictions on the use of trade names. However, a recent case struck down as violative of first amendment rights a local law that prohibited a restaurant chain from using its trademark "Sambos." The city had prohibited use of the trademark on the ground that it was racially offensive, but the Court of Appeals decided that this interest was not sufficiently important to justify infringement of the firm's right to choose its trade name.[113]

[110] Levy & Rook, supra note 97, at 185.

[111] *Resort Car Rental System, Inc.* v. *Federal Trade Comm'n,* 518 F.2d 962 (9th Cir. 1975).

[112] 440 U.S. 1 (1979).

[113] *Sambo's Restaurants, Inc.* v. *City of Ann Arbor,* 663 F.2d 686 (6th Cir. 1981).

Protection against Loss of Trademark Rights

Once rights in a trademark have been established, the firm should take steps to avoid loss or dilution of those rights. Registration of the mark under federal law, as explained earlier, will go a long way toward assuring continued protection against infringement, and the registration should be renewed at the end of the first 5-year period and at the end of each subsequent 20-year period in which it is desired to continue using the mark. But, in addition, four other major pitfalls need to be avoided:

Abandonment.

If a firm ceases using a mark for any extended period, there is a risk that abandonment can be found. The federal registration statute creates a presumption of abandonment if nonuse continues for a 2-year period. Extenuating circumstances can demonstrate that nonuse is not intended to be an abandonment; one case held that an 18-month delay between the first sale under the mark and the beginning of full production was a normal delay in preparation for full-scale manufacture of the goods. During that delay, the mark was not abandoned and therefore could not be adopted by a competitor.

Infringement.

Once the right to use a mark has been established, it is important to take action against competitors who infringe the mark. Government publications of applications for new marks should be scrutinized on a regular basis, and sales representatives should be alerted to competitors using confusingly similar marks. Directories and catalogs of competitors should be examined for infringements. Action should be taken to stop infringers or to oppose registrations of confusingly similar marks. Failure to take action could lead to a loss of distinctiveness of a mark and its subsequent cancellation. Inaction should also be a bar to later infringement actions; courts regularly deny relief to persons who fail to assert rights in a timely fashion.

Preventing a Mark from Becoming Generic.

Another reason for policing the actual ways in which a mark is used is that some marks can actually become shorthand words for the product itself. When that happens, the mark actually does no more than describe generically a class of similar goods and is no longer associated by consumers with any particular source. Such marks then are subject to cancellation and can be used by all competitors to describe their own products.[114] Marks such as aspirin, cellophane, and shredded wheat (and more recently, a game called "Monopoly") originally indicated to consumers that the product came from a particular source, but over time the marks came to be associated with all similar products regardless of who made them. Uniquely named products should be on

---

[114] See Osborne, *How To Prevent Trademarks From Becoming Generic,* 27 Practical Lawyer 81 (1981).

guard to protect their marks. A common method of avoiding "genericide" is to use the word "brand" in connection with any mention of the goods themselves (which should be referred to by another preexisting name). For example, the phrase "buy Xerox *brand* copiers" might forestall the apparent tendency to use the word "xerox" for all copiers.

Licensing or Assigning Trademarks.

Although trademarks have many characteristics that resemble property rights, there is some risk in treating them as though they were fully transferrable and assignable. The risk arises from the fact that trademarks are protected from use by others precisely because they indicate to consumers that the goods originate from a common source. An assignment or sale of the right to use a mark thus can actually misdescribe the source of goods if the mark obscures the fact that the original source no longer has any connection with the goods. However, licensing or assignment or sale of a mark is possible as long as the goodwill of the original owner is transferred with the mark, or as long as the original owner continues to exercise control over use of the mark by, for example, establishing standards for production of goods by licensees and making sure that the standards are adhered to by licensees.[115]

Some Permissible Uses of Another's Trademark

Although the owner of a trademark generally has the exclusive right to use the mark, the law has allowed other businesses to use the owner's mark. Use of another's mark is permitted, to varying degrees, under the following circumstances:

Comparative Advertising.

The law generally favors the use of advertisements that compare features or prices of competing products. Unless direct reference can be made to the trademark or trade name of the compared product, there will be little incentive for competitors to disclose differences in products through advertising. Accordingly, the law permits direct use of another's mark in comparative advertising. An example of a permitted comparison involved one firm's representation that its perfume was the equivalent of "Chanel No. 5" at a much lower price. The court allowed the use of the trade name "Chanel No. 5" as long as the equivalence claim was truthful.

However, if the use of a competitor's trademark creates confusion or misunderstanding, the use of the mark will be restricted by courts. In one case, Robot-Coupe International Corporation ran an ad which announced that it was importing and selling food processors that formerly had been imported by

---

[115] The exercise of control over a trademark licensee presents difficult problems of antitrust, as some franchisors have been held to have illegally tied the use of the trademark to purchases of other products. See, *Siegel* v. *Chicken Delight, Inc.,* 448 F.2d 43 (1971); but compare *Krehl* v. *Baskin-Robbins Ice Cream Co.,* 50 United States Law Week 2421 (9th Cir. 1982).

Cuisinarts, Incorporated. The ad stated: "Robot-Coupe. It's Pronounced Robo Coop." Underneath, in smaller type, the ad stated: "(It Used To Be Pronounced Cuisinart)." Cuisinart presented evidence that newspaper food critics interpreted the ad to mean that Cuisinart had either changed its name or gone out of business, and the court enjoined use of the phrase "It Used To Be Called Cuisinart."[116]

Repair Services.

Some products, if properly maintained and repaired, have a sufficiently long useful life that businesses specialize in the repair of the product. Courts generally have permitted a repair service to use the trademark associated with the product as long as the public is not confused as to whether the service provider is affiliated with the product seller. In a series of cases involving repair shops that specialized in the repair of Volkswagen vehicles, courts permitted repair shops to use the Volkswagen name and mark as long as the name and mark were not given prominence in advertising or in signs. Thus, in *Volkswagen* v. *Church*,[117] a repair service was allowed to use the Volkswagen trade name if it used the word "Independent" in connection with the name and did not use Volkswagen's distinctive color scheme, circled emblem, or lettering style. But other cases involving Volkswagen prohibited use of the phrases "Volkswagen Sales," "Volkswagen Service," "Volkswagen Repair," "VW Sales," "VW Service," and "VW Parts."[118]

Replacement Parts.

Products that can be used as replacement parts in products made or sold under a competitor's trademark or trade name can refer to or use that mark or name in any truthful indication of compatibility. Thus, in *American-Marietta Co.* v. *Krigsman*,[119] the defendant was permitted to describe sponge mop refills for its own brand and for that of a competitor by advertising: "This refill fits the O-Cedar 76 and Crown 400." Since no evidence was presented that consumers were misled to believe that the refill manufacturer was affiliated with the manufacturer of O-Cedar mops, the court permitted the advertising and packaging representations to continue.

Reconditioned Products.

More difficult issues are presented when secondhand goods are reconditioned and resold under the brand name of the original manufacturer. The danger to be avoided here is the possibility that the purchaser of the reconditioned goods might attribute defective reconditioning to the owner of the underlying trademark. Despite this danger, the Supreme Court, in *Champion Spark Plug Co.* v. *Sanders*,[120] allowed the defendant to sell reconditioned spark

[116] *Cuisinarts, Inc.* v. *Robot-Coupe Int'l Corp.*, 509 F.Supp. 1036 (S.D. N.Y. 1981).

[117] 411 F.2d 350 (9th Cir. 1969).

[118] *Volkswagenwerk Aktiengesellschaft* v. *Karadizian*, 170 U.S.P.Q. 565 (C.D. Cal. 1971).

[119] 275 F.2d 287 (2d Cir. 1960).

[120] 331 U.S. 125 (1947).

plugs bearing the Champion trademark. The Court gave primary emphasis to the interest of the defendant in truthfully selling the reconditioned product. As long as the reconditioned products are clearly and distinctly sold as repaired or reconditioned rather than new, and as long as the manufacturer is not identified with the inferior qualities of the product resulting from wear and tear or the reconditioning process, use of the manufacturer's trademark is legal.

Repackaging and Reprocessing.

Very difficult legal questions are raised when one firm's product is purchased by another firm and is repackaged, altered, or incorporated into another product and then resold using the manufacturing firm's trademark or trade name. In a decision that has been heavily criticized but never overruled, the Supreme Court refused to prohibit the defendant from purchasing and repackaging plaintiff's perfume and face powder and reselling the products by describing them as having been made by the plaintiff. The Court did require the defendant to use plaintiff's trademark in only a collateral or subordinate way (i.e., so that it would not stand out from the rest of the label) and to clearly indicate that the defendant was the repackager of the product. If these precautions result in the elimination of any consumer confusion, one firm's mark can be used by another. And if, as other courts have suggested, the product should be accompanied with proper labels and instructions for use, the user must repackage so as to pass along the owner's instructions and label warnings.[121]

CONCLUSION

This chapter has outlined the various ways in which the legal system affects marketing decisions relating to the development and attempted exploitation of new product ideas. Attention has focused on the protection of trade secrets and on the use of patents, copyrights, and trademarks.

During the process of developing a new product, the law allows a firm to take steps to protect itself against the possibility that its secret new product ideas and information will become public knowledge or will fall into the hands of a competitor. To take advantage of the law's protection of trade secrets, the firm must take sufficient security precautions against disclosure of the information to unauthorized persons. In addition, contractual arrangements must be devised to make clear to employees that they are not authorized to reveal trade secrets to anyone, even on leaving employment with the firm. Finally, contractual arrangements and clearance procedures must be established for the receipt of ideas submitted by outsiders; in the absence of a clear understanding, there is significant risk that the submitter of an idea that later is turned to profit will be entitled to substantial compensation for the idea.

During the course of research for product development, some truly novel inventions can occur. In that event, the firm must decide whether the invention would qualify for protection under the patent laws and, if so, whether other considerations might outweigh the possible benefits of obtaining a pa-

---

[121] *Clairol, Inc.* v. *Boston Discount Center of Berkeley, Inc.*, 608 F.2d 1114 (6th Cir. 1979).

tent. Those benefits include the possibility of having a monopoly over the use of the product for up to 17 years. In many circumstances, this potential monopoly will not be of sufficient commercial value to warrant the attempt to obtain a patent, but in some circumstances the effort undoubtedly should be undertaken. Three types of patents are available: utility patents, design patent, and plant patents. Several classes of subject matter exist for utility patents: process, machine, manufactured article, and composition of matter. In addition, improvement patents are also available. If discoveries meet the tests of having utility, being truly novel, and not being obvious from prior inventions, a patent can be obtained. However, to obtain the patent, detailed procedures must be followed and complete and full disclosure of the invention must be made to the public.

While the obtaining of a patent can result in the acquisition of a valuable, legally protected monopoly, the attempt to exploit that monopoly, particularly through the process of licensing others to use the patent, presents certain risks of violating the antitrust laws. Licensing can injure competition in ways not authorized by patent policy and can result in antitrust liability. While some unilateral decisions about licensing are held to be legal, some pricing and distribution strategies present risks of illegal discrimination or resale price maintenance and impermissible territorial market allocation, particularly if there is any evidence from which a court might infer that decisions were made collusively. Also illegal are attempts to extend the patent beyond the patented product by, for example, requiring purchasers of the patented product to also purchase other goods from the patent owner. In addition to liability for antitrust violations, misuse of the patent can lead a court to completely invalidate the patent.

Ideas that are reduced to some tangible form, such as literary and artistic works of authors, can receive a limited form of protection under the copyright laws; the law protects the author against unauthorized copying and distribution of the work by others. Books, periodicals, plays, movies, recordings, compositions, and other published works can qualify for this form of protection. However, the protection offered by the law is limited to the form of the expression; the ideas and facts embodied in the work, once published, are in the public domain and their use by others cannot be restricted. Special formalities must be followed in order to be able to enforce copyrights in court. The usual life of a copyright is measured by the life of the author plus 50 years.

The law also allows firms to obtain valuable rights in trademarks used to identify the firm and its products. Because the law offers a variety of levels of protection for different types of trademarks and trade names, the choice of a trademark may be critical to its ultimate value to the firm. In addition, the initial choice of a trademark must be preceded by careful investigation to discover any prior use of the same mark or one that is confusingly similar. Failure to discover a prior use not only can lead to liability for infringement, it can result in the inability to obtain nationwide protection for the mark under federal law. Since the purpose of the law of trademarks is to assist customers in identifying and assuring the source of supply of a product associated with a particular mark, trademark owners must take steps to avoid public use of the trademark as a shorthand reference for the product; if a trademark comes to be used as a generic term for the product itself, exclusive rights to use the trademark can be lost.

Apart from these rather limited and narrow protections for expressions, trademarks, trade secrets, and novel inventions, the overall policy of the law is to encourage competition. Thus, if a product is not protected under one of these legal doctrines, competitors are perfectly free to copy the product in its entirety and sell it to consumers at a lower price. The only restrictions on copying products that are not patented or copyrighted, and whose features can be discovered without violating trade secret law, are restrictions designed to prevent consumers from being deceived as to the identity of the firm producing the product. This limitation is not a serious one and can be overcome easily by making sure that the producing firm's identity is prominently displayed so as to negate any inference that it is made by another firm. If this is done, the law extends protection to any firm that decides to copy, produce, and market an unpatented, uncopyrighted product developed by another firm. The underlying desire is, supposedly, to foster competition and confer benefits on consumers through the production of lower-priced products. Even patents and copyrights, while conferring monopoly power, are also supposedly procompetitive because they encourage inventors and authors to exercise their creative talents. These incentives are expected to benefit consumers by bringing forth a greater supply of novel discoveries and valuable writings than would be the case in their absence, thus contributing to increased consumer welfare.

Case 1
Compco Corporation *v.* Day-Brite Lighting, Inc.

Supreme Court
376 U.S. 234 (1964)

Mr. JUSTICE BLACK delivered the opinion of the Court.

As in *Sears, Roebuck & Co.* v. *Stiffel Co.,* the question here is whether the use of a state unfair competition law to give relief against the copying of an unpatented industrial design conflicts with the federal patent laws. Both Compco and Day-Brite are manufacturers of fluorescent lighting fixtures of a kind widely used in offices and stores. Day-Brite in 1955 secured from the Patent Office a design patent on a reflector having cross-ribs claimed to give both strength and attractiveness to the fixture. Day-Brite also sought, but was refused, a mechanical patent on the same device. After Day-Brite had begun selling its fixture, Compco began making and selling fixtures very similar to Day-Brite's. This action was then brought by Day-Brite. One count alleged that Compco had infringed Day-Brite's design patent; a second count charged that the public and the trade had come to associate this particular design with Day-Brite, that Compco had copied Day-Brite's distinctive design so as to confuse and deceive purchasers into thinking Compco's fixtures were actually Day-Brite's, and that by doing this Compco had unfairly competed with Day-Brite. The complaint prayed for both an accounting and an injunction.

The District Court held the design patent invalid; but as to the second count, while the court did not find that Compco had engaged in any deceptive or fraudulent practices, it did hold that Compco had been guilty of unfair competition under Illinois law. The court found that the overall appearance of Compco's fixture was "the same, to the eye of the ordinary observer, as the overall appearance" of Day-Brite's reflector, which embodied the design of the invalidated patent; that the appearance of Day-Brite's design had "the capacity to identify [Day-Brite] in the trade and does in fact so identify [it] to the trade"; that the concurrent sale of the two products was "likely to cause confusion in the trade"; and that "[a]ctual confusion has occurred." On these findings the court adjudged Compco guilty of unfair competition in the sale of its fixtures, ordered Compco to account to Day-Brite for damages, and enjoined Compco "from unfairly competing with plaintiff by the sale or attempted sale of reflectors identical to, or confusingly similar to" those made by Day-Brite. The Court of Appeals held there was substantial evidence in the record to support the District Court's finding of likely confusion and that this finding was sufficient to support a holding of unfair competition under Illinois law.[1] Although the District Court had not made such a finding, the appellate court observed that "several choices of ribbing were apparently available to meet the functional needs of the product," yet Compco "chose precisely the same design used by the plaintiff and followed it so closely as to make confusion likely." A design which identifies its maker to the trade, the Court of Appeals held, is a "protectable" right under Illinois law, even though the design is unpatentable. We granted certiorari.

To support its findings of likelihood of confusion and actual confusion, the trial court was able to refer to only one circumstance in the record. A plant manager who had installed some of Compco's fixtures later asked Day-Brite to service the fixtures, thinking they had been made by Day-Brite. There was no testimony given by a purchaser or by anyone else that any customer had ever been misled, deceived, or "confused," that is, that anyone had ever bought a Compco fixture thinking it was a Day-Brite fixture. All the record shows, as to the one instance cited by the trial court, is that both Compco and Day-Brite fixtures had been installed in the same plant, that three years later some repairs were needed, and that the manager viewing the Compco fixtures—hung at least 15 feet above the floor and arranged end to end in a continuous line so that identifying marks were hidden—thought they were Day-Brite fixtures and asked Day-Brite to service them. Not only is this incident suggestive only of confusion *after* a purchase had been made, but also there is considerable evidence of the care taken by Compco to prevent customer confusion, including clearly labeling both the fixtures and the containers in which they were shipped and not selling through manufacturers' representatives who handled competing lines.

Notwithstanding the thinness of the evidence to support findings of likely and actual confusion among purchasers, we do not find it necessary in this case to determine whether there is "clear error" in these findings. They, like those in *Sears, Roebuck & Co.* v. *Stiffel Co.,* were based wholly on the fact that selling an article which is an exact copy of another unpatented article is likely to produce and did in this case produce confusion as to the source of the article. Even accepting the findings, we hold that the order for an accounting for damages and the injunction are in conflict with the federal patent laws. Today we have held in *Sears, Roebuck & Co.* v. *Stiffel Co.,* that when an article is unprotected by a patent or a copyright, state law may not forbid others to copy that article. To forbid copying would interfere with the federal policy, found in Art. I, §8, cl. 8, of the Constitution and in the implementing federal statutes, of allowing free access to copy whatever the federal patent and copyright laws leave in the public domain. Here Day-Brite's fixture has been held not to be entitled to a design or mechanical patent. Under the federal patent

---

[1] The Court of Appeals also affirmed the holding that the design patent was invalid. No review of this ruling is sought here.

laws it is, therefore, in the public domain and can be copied in every detail by whoever pleases. It is true that the trial court found that the configuration of Day-Brite's fixture identified Day-Brite to the trade because the arrangement of the ribbing had, like a trademark, acquired a "secondary meaning" by which that particular design was associated with Day-Brite. But if the design is not entitled to a design patent or other federal statutory protection, then it can be copied at will.

As we have said in *Sears,* while the federal patent laws prevent a State from prohibiting the copying and selling of unpatented articles, they do not stand in the way of state law, statutory or decisional, which requires those who make and sell copies to take precautions to identify their products as their own. A State of course has power to impose liability upon those who, knowing that the public is relying upon an original manufacturer's reputation for quality and integrity, deceive the public by palming off their copies as the original. That an article copied from an unpatented article could be made in some other way, that the design is "nonfunctional" and not essential to the use of either article, that the configuration of the article copied may have a "secondary meaning" which identifies the maker to the trade, or that there may be "confusion" among purchasers as to which article is which or as to who is the maker, may be relevant evidence in applying a State's law requiring such precautions as labeling; however, and regardless of the copier's motives, neither these facts nor any others can furnish a basis for imposing liability for or prohibiting the actual acts of copying and selling. Cf. *Kellogg Co.* v. *National Biscuit Co.,* 305 U. S. 111, 120 (1938). And of course a State cannot hold a copier accountable in damages for failure to label or otherwise to identify his goods unless his failure is in violation of valid state statutory or decisional law requiring the copier to label or take other precautions to prevent confusion of customers as to the source of the goods.[2]

Since the judgment below forbids the sale of a copy of an unpatented article and orders an accounting for damages for such copying, it cannot stand.

Reversed.

---

[2] As we pointed out in *Sears, Roebuck & Co.* v. *Stiffel Co.,* there is no showing that Illinois has any such law.

Case 2
Anti-Monopoly, Inc., *v.* General Mills Fun Group, Inc.,

United States Court of Appeals, Ninth Circuit.
Decided Aug. 26, 1982.

684 F.2d 1316

DUNIWAY, Circuit Judge:

This is the second appeal in this case. Our first opinion is reported in *Anti-Monopoly, Inc.* v. *General Mills Fun Group*, 9 Cir., 1979, 611 F.2d 296 (*Anti-Monopoly I*). On remand the district court again found that the "Monopoly" trademark was valid and had been infringed by Anti-Monopoly, Inc. *Anti-Monopoly, Inc.* v. *General Mills Fun Group, Inc.*, N.D.Cal., 1981, 515 F.Supp. 448 (*Anti-Monopoly II*). We reverse and remand for further proceedings.

I. PRIOR PROCEEDINGS

General Mills is the successor to Parker Brothers, Inc., which had produced and sold a game it called Monopoly since 1935. Parker Brothers registered "Monopoly" as a trademark in that year. In 1973 Anti-Monopoly, Inc. was established to produce and sell a game it called Anti-Monopoly. General Mills claimed that this infringed its trademark. This action was then brought by Anti-Monopoly, seeking a declaratory judgment that the registered trademark "Monopoly" was invalid, and cancelling its registration. In a counterclaim, General Mills sought declaratory and injunctive relief upholding its trademark, and the dismissal of the action. The case was tried without a jury in 1976. The court entered a judgment for General Mills. We reversed and remanded for further consideration of (i) the validity of the trademark, (ii) infringement of the trademark, if it is valid, by Anti-Monopoly, and (iii) state law claims concerning unfair competition and dilution. We also chose to defer consideration of (iv) Anti-Monopoly's defense that General Mills had unclean hands. On remand, after hearing further evidence, the district court again entered a judgment for General Mills.

IV. GENERIC TERMS—THE LAW.

Our opinion in *Anti-Monopoly I* binds both this court and district court. There, we set out the law about generic terms and explained how it was to be applied to the particular facts of this case. *Anti-Monopoly I* 611 F.2d at 300–306. In this opinion, we assume that the reader will be familiar with that opinion. Here, we emphasize what we consider to be its essence. A word used as a trademark is not generic if "the primary significance of the term in the minds of the consuming public is not the product but the producer. . . . [W]hen a trademark primarily denotes a product, not the product's producer, the trademark is lost." A registered mark is to be cancelled if it has become "the common descriptive name of an article," and no incontestable right can be acquired in such a mark. We said "Even if only one producer—Parker Brothers—has ever made the MONOPOLY game, so that the public necessarily associates the product with that particular producer, the trademark is invalid unless source indication is its primary significance." *Anti-Monopoly I,* 611 F.2d at 302. "It is the source-denoting function which trademark laws protect, and nothing more." *Id.* at 301. "[O]ne competitor will not be permitted to impoverish the language of commerce by preventing his fellows from fairly describing their own goods." *Id.,* quoting *Bada Co.* v. *Montgomery Ward & Co.,* 9 Cir., 1970, 426 F.2d 8, 11. "[W]hen members of the consuming public use a game name to denote the game itself, and not its producer, the trademark is generic and, therefore, invalid."

V. WAS THE TERM "MONOPOLY" GENERIC AT THE TIME OF REGISTRATION?

Anti-Monopoly, Inc. claims that the term "Monopoly" was generic at the time when Parker Brothers registered it. On this question, the trial judge made the following findings:

> Plaintiff [Anti-Monopoly] attempted to show at trial that at the time of Parker Brothers' trademark registration, MONOPOLY was already a widely played game known by that name. The evidence introduced to support this contention consists chiefly of isolated and sporadic examples of individuals playing old oilcloth games referred to in some instances as "Monopoly," the "Landlord's Game," or some other variation thereof.
>
> *   *   *   *   *
>
> In order to be "generic," the name MONOPOLY, in the minds of the consuming public, must primarily denote product rather than source. It remains unclear how widely played the precursors to modern MONOPOLY were in the 1920s and early '30s. Plaintiff has simply made no showing as to what the public conception of the term was at that juncture or indeed how widely played it actually was. As Clarence [sic] Darrow, and later his successor, Parker Brothers, popularized a specific game they called MONOPOLY, this court cannot find that the trademark when registered denoted "a game" rather than the "game's producer." Because Anti-Monopoly has the burden of showing genericness by convincing evidence, this finding must be for defendant.

515 F.Supp. at 451–452. The district court found also that Darrow was the inventor of the game (*Id.,* at 451) and that the game was "created" by Darrow. *Id.* at 452 n.1. (The quotation marks are in the original.)

We have already held that the district court placed too heavy a burden on Anti-Monopoly, Inc. Moreover, the court's reference to Darrow as the inventor or creator of the game is clearly erroneous. The record shows, as we stated in *Anti-Monopoly I*, that "The game of 'Monopoly' was first played from 1920 to 1932 on various college campuses by a small group of individuals, many of whom were related by blood or marriage. In late 1932 or early 1933 one of these players introduced Charles Darrow to the game, and gave him a handmade game board, rules, and associated equipment. Immediately thereafter Darrow commenced commercially producing and selling 'Monopoly' game equipment." 611 F.2d at 299.

We have re-examined the entire record on appeal. Here is what it shows. At some time between 1904 and 1934, the game of monopoly developed. Early equipment was handmade and copied from earlier handmade equipment. All the witnesses presented by Anti-Monopoly insisted that the game was known as "Monopoly" by all who played it, although in most cases the name did not appear on the board itself. The game was played in Reading, Pennsylvania, sometime between 1911 and 1917, but this date may be a little early. In the early 1920's the game was played at Princeton University, Massachusetts Institute of Technology, Smith College, the University of Pennsylvania, and Haverford College. On occasion the rules were privately printed. The game was offered to, but rejected by, Milton-Bradley, a leading competitor of Parker Brothers. It was played in and around Reading, Pennsylvania from the early 1920's to the early 1930's. It may have been brought there from the University of Pennsylvania. Players in Reading made up and sold some half dozen sets of equipment at Williams College and the University of Michigan. The game next appeared in Indianapolis, where some players marketed it under the name "Finance." (Players in Reading sold some of those games too.) The game of monopoly was brought to Atlantic City, New Jersey in 1931 or thereabouts. The street names used in the game were then changed to Atlantic City street names. The game was taught to Darrow. He sold it to Parker Brothers in 1935, claiming that it was his own invention. Parker Brothers also bought the Finance game from its owners.

It is true that Darrow, in his correspondence with Parker Brothers, claimed to have invented the game and offered to sign an affidavit stating his story. However, Robert B. M. Barton, the former President of Parker Brothers, who negotiated with Darrow in 1935, testified that he did not believe Darrow's claim. A precursor of monopoly, the Landlord's Game, was patented by Mrs. Maggie Elizabeth Phillips of Washington, D.C. in 1904 and again in 1924. Parker Brothers purchased this game from her in 1934 or thereabouts.

In 1957, Barton, the President of Parker Brothers, in a letter to an inquirer, wrote: "So far as we know The Landlord's Game, invented by Mrs. Elizabeth Maggie Phillips of Washington, D.C., was the basic game for both FINANCE and MONOPOLY. Mrs. Phillips patented her game and we purchased her patent. Mr. Charles Darrow later made many improvements in The Landlord's Game and called his game MONOPOLY. He, too, secured a patent which he assigned to us. Because of the fact that we purchased all three games, it does not make very much difference to us who invented either one of the games. . . ."

The evidence clearly shows that the game of monopoly was played by a small number of people before Darrow learned of it, and that these people called the game "monopoly." It is unclear just how many people played. General Mills offered testimony that it was not widespread throughout the United States. The burden of proof was on Anti-Monopoly to show that the term was generic. We cannot presume that the evidence offered by Anti-Monopoly is the tip of the iceberg. Thus, we are faced with the following legal question: if a game is known about by a small number of people and they all call it by a particular term, may one member of the group appropriate that name by registering it as a trademark?

Ordinarily, because the trial judge imposed too heavy a burden on Anti-Monopoly, we would be required to remand for new findings made under the proper burden. However, because we have concluded that the evidence, construed most favorably to Anti-Monopoly, does not show that "Monopoly" had become generic before Parker Brothers registered it as its trademark, and because our holding in Part VI, *post,* is dispositive of the case, such a remand is unnecessary here.

When a small number of people use a particular thing and call it by a particular name, one which is not a common descriptive term for the thing, a person may appropriate the name and register it as a trademark. The purpose of the doctrine that generic terms cannot be made trademarks is to prevent the appropriation of a term that is already in wide use among those who are potential purchasers of the thing that the term describes. If those who might purchase the thing know it by a particular name, then to forbid the use of that name by potential producers will erect unwarranted barriers to competition. As we said in *Anti-Monopoly I,* "Trademarks . . . are not properly used as patent substitutes to further or perpetuate product monopolies," 611 F.2d at 300. On the other hand, where, as here, the potential market is nationwide, and where the name is used only by a small number of scattered consumers, appropriation of the name as the trademark of one who produces for that potential market does not restrain competition to a significant degree.

We agree with the trial judge's conclusion that "Monopoly" had not become generic before Parker Brothers registered it as a trademark.

VI. HAS "MONOPOLY" BECOME GENERIC SINCE IT WAS REGISTERED?

This question is discussed, and the trial court's findings of fact appear in *Monopoly II,* 515 F.Supp. at 452–455. Under the heading "FINDINGS OF FACT," the following appears:

1. The court again finds as fact each fact found in this Opinion as set forth in the foregoing.

2. As a game trademark, MONOPOLY primarily denotes its producer, Parker Brothers, and primarily denoted its producer when registered.

Id. at 455. We consider finding 2 to be one of ultimate fact, and "clearly erroneous."

The district court also said "'Primary significance' logically implies a hierarchical priority over a competing alternative." Dictionary definitions are in accord. Funk & Wagnalls' New Standard Dictionary gives "primary 1. First in . . . thought or intention. 2. First in degree, rank or importance, most fundamental, chief. . . ." Webster's New International Dictionary (2d Ed.) gives "1. First in . . . intention; 2. First in . . . importance; chief, principal. . . ." We are not sure what the district court meant by a "competing alternative." To us, this carries some suggestion of "either, or." Yet it is nearly always the case, as the district court recognized, that a trademark will identify both the product and its producer. Indeed, its value lies in its identification of the product with its producer.

In its opinion, the district court supports its finding 2 as follows:

> The difficulty in this regard arises due to the public's dual usage of the tradename, denoting both product and source. For example, the mark "Ford" to the average consumer denotes *both* car and motor company. However, to demonstrate "primary significance" it is necessary to show more than a high percentage of the consuming public who recognize MONOPOLY as a brand name (as defendant has done: 63% of those polled recognized MONOPOLY as a "brand name"). It is necessary to show more than a public awareness that Parker Brothers is the sole manufacturer of MONOPOLY (55% correctly identified Parker Brothers in defendant's survey). "Primary significance" logically implies a hierarchical priority over a competing alternative.
>
> Yet the cumulative weight of the evidence does satisfy this court that the primary significance of MONOPOLY in the public's eye is to denote a "Parker Brothers' Game" (*i.e.,* source) in contradistinction to that "popular game of MONOPOLY" (product). Parker Brothers has expended substantial time, energy, and money in promoting and policing their trademark, expending over $4 million in advertising expenditures. One result of these diligent efforts has been the extraordinary success Parker Brothers has achieved in creating public source awareness. Over 55% of the American public correctly identified Parker Brothers as the producer of the game. *Cf. Selchow & Righter Co.* v. *Western Printing & Lithographing Co.,* D.C., 47 F.Supp. 322, 326 (court finding it "very evident that any ordinary customer, going into a store, and asking for the game "PARCHEESI" had no information as to who might have manufactured and produced the game.") An even more impressive display of the amount of goodwill which Parker Brothers has imbued through its various games—especially MONOPOLY—is *the finding of plaintiff's survey that one out of three MONOPOLY purchasers do so primarily because "they like Parker Brothers' products."* Hence, source attribution is a dominant perceived effect of the MONOPOLY trademark. This court cannot say from the facts before it that it is not the "primary significance" of the mark.

Id. at 454–455 (emphasis in the original).

In considering whether these findings, and finding 2, are clearly erroneous, we have in mind an obvious proposition. The word "Monopoly," while not in its ordinary meaning descriptive of the game "Monopoly," is an ordinary English word, and it does describe the objective of the game. This was recognized in the rules of the game published by Parker Brothers in 1935. They begin with:

> BRIEF IDEA OF THE GAME
> THE IDEA OF THE GAME is to BUY and RENT or SELL properties so profitably that one becomes the wealthiest player and eventual MONOPOLIST.

A Monopolist has a monopoly. By choosing the word as a trademark, Parker Brothers subjected itself to a considerable risk that the word would become so identified with the game as to be "generic."

In *Anti-Monopoly II*, the district court also said this: "Unless the Ninth Circuit standard is meant to foreclose the possibility of trademark protection for any producer of a unique game whose corporate name does not appear in the title of the game (*e.g.,* 'SCRABBLE,' 'TOWER OF BABBLE'), then its test cannot be used here to thwart MONOPOLY's trademark rights." 515 F.Supp. at 455. Nothing in our opinion in *Anti-Monopoly I* even hints at the relevance of whether or not the corporate name of the producer of a game appears in the title of the game, and our opinion does not foreclose the possibility of trademark protection of the name of the game that does not embody the corporate name of its producer. But our opinion does squarely hold as follows: "Even if only one producer—Parker Brothers—has ever made the MONOPOLY game, so that the public necessarily associates the product with that particular producer, the trademark is invalid unless source identification is its primary significance." 611 F.2d at 302.

The district court obviously felt that our opinion in *Anti-Monopoly I* gave Anti-Monopoly an easier task in trying to show that "Monopoly" has become generic than the district court would give. Nevertheless, both we and the district court are bound by our decision in *Anti-Monopoly I.*

We now consider whether finding 2 of the district court is clearly erroneous. We conclude that it is.

As we have seen, the district court relied in part upon the fact that General Mills and its predecessor have spent time, energy, and money in promoting and policing use of the term "Monopoly." That fact, however, is not of itself sufficient to create legally protectable rights. It is not, of itself, enough that over 55% of the public has come to associate the product, and as a consequence the name by which the product is generally known, with Parker Brothers. Even if one third of the members of the public who purchased the game did so because they liked Parker Brothers' products, that fact does not show that "Monopoly" is primarily source indicating. The very survey on which the district court placed emphasis by italicizing its result shows that two thirds of the members of the public who purchased the game wanted "Monopoly" and did not care who made it.

The real question is what did Parker Brothers and General Mills get for their money and efforts? To us, the evidence overwhelmingly shows that they very successfully promoted the game of Monopoly, but that in doing it they so successfully promoted "Monopoly" as "the name of the game," that it became generic in the sense in which we use that term in trademark law. We recognize that "there is evidence to support" the trial court's findings, [but] "on the entire trial evidence [we are] left with the definite and firm conviction that a mistake has been committed."

The principal evidence in the case was in the form of consumer surveys, and to these we now turn.

A. The Brand-name Survey.

General Mills conducted a survey based upon a survey approved by a district court in the "Teflon" case, *E. I. Du Pont de Nemours & Co.* v. *Yoshida International, Inc.,* E.D.N.Y., 1975, 393 F.Supp. 502. In the survey conducted by General Mills, people were asked whether "Monopoly" is a "brand-name," and were told: "By *brand* name, I mean a name like *Chevrolet,* which is made by *one* company; by common name, I mean 'automobile,' which is made by a number of different companies." (Emphasis in the original.) The results of this survey had no relevance to the question in this case. Under the survey definition, "Monopoly" would have to be a "brand name" because it is made by only one company. This tells us nothing at all about the *primary* meaning of "Monopoly" in the minds of consumers.

It is true that the witness through whom the survey was introduced testified on direct examination that as a result of it his opinion was that "Monopoly" primarily denotes source or producer. However, on cross-examination and redirect examination it became clear that this witness had done no more than reduplicate the "Teflon" survey (with appropriate substitutions and slight additions) and had no opinion on the relevance of this survey to any issue in the present case. The brand-name survey is not even some evidence to support finding 2; it is no evidence to support it.

B. The "Thermos" Survey.

Anti-Monopoly's first survey was based upon that used in the "Thermos" case, *King-Seeley Thermos Co.* v. *Aladdin Industries, Inc.,* D.Conn., 1962, 207 F.Supp. 9, 20–21, *aff'd,* 2 Cir., 1963, 321 F.2d 577. In Anti-Monopoly's survey people were asked the question: "Are you familiar with business board games of the kind in which players buy, sell, mortgage and trade city streets, utilities and railroads, build houses, collect rents and win by bankrupting all other players, or not?" About 53% said they were. Those people were then asked: "If you were going to buy this kind of game, what would you ask for, that is, what would you tell the sales clerk you wanted?" About 80% said: "Monopoly."

The witness through whom this survey was introduced testified that Anti-Monopoly gave his firm the questions used in the "Thermos" survey and asked it to conduct a similar one. Anti-Monopoly provided the wording of the questions in the present survey as well. The research firm was responsible for deciding how to reach a sample that would adequately represent the population of the United States. The witness gave no testimony as to the relevance of the results of the survey to the issues in the case.

In one of its briefs, General Mills points out that the survey used in the "Thermos" case was described as "generally corroborative of the court's conclusions drawn from other evidence," and that the district court which decided the "Teflon" case found a "Thermos"-like survey defective because "the design of the questions more often than not [focused] on supplying the inquirer a 'name,' without regard to whether the principal significance of the name supplied was 'its indication of the nature or class of an article, rather than an indication of its origin,' *King-Seeley Thermos Co., supra,* 321 F.2d at 580." *E. I. Du Pont de Nemours & Co., supra,* 393 F.Supp. at 527. Be that as it may, we think that the results of this survey are compelling evidence of a proposition that is also dictated by common sense: an overwhelming proportion of those who are familiar with the game would ask for it by the name "Monopoly."

C. The Motivation Survey.

After the remand to the district court, Anti-Monopoly commissioned a further survey. This survey was based upon the following language from our opinion in *Anti-Monopoly I*:

> It may be that when a customer enters a game store and asks for MONOPOLY, he means: "I would like Parker Brothers' version of a real estate trading game, because I like Parker Brothers' products. Thus, I am not interested in board games made by Anti-Monopoly, or anyone other than Parker Brothers." On the other hand, the consumer may mean: "I want a 'Monopoly' game. Don't bother showing me Anti-Monopoly, or EASY MONEY, or backgammon. I am interested in playing the game of Monopoly. I don't much care who makes it."
>
> In the first example, the consumer differentiates between MONOPOLY and other games according to source-particular criteria. In the second example, source is not a consideration. The relevant genus, or product category, varies accordingly. At the urging of Parker Brothers, the district court erred by first defining the genus, and then asking the "primary significance" question about the wrong genus-species dichotomy. The proper mode of analysis is to decide but one question: whether the primary significance of a term is to denote product, or source. In making this determination, the correct genus-species distinction, that is, the correct genericness finding, follows automatically.

611 F.2d at 305–306. The wording of the questions was provided by Dr. Anspach, Anti-Monopoly's president, and by the expert who testified at trial. The expert had studied our first opinion. The survey was designed to ascertain the use of the term "Monopoly" by those who had purchased the game in the past or intended to do so in the near future. It was conducted by telephone. The results were as follows: 92% were aware of "Monopoly," the business board game produced by Parker Brothers. Of that 92%, 62% either had "purchased 'Monopoly' within the last couple of years" or intended to purchase it in the near future. Those people were asked why they had bought or would buy monopoly. The answers exhibited the following pattern: 82% mentioned

some aspect of the playing of the game (e.g., that they played it as a kid, it was a family game, it was enjoyable, it was fun to play, it was interesting), 14% mentioned some educational aspect of the game, 7% mentioned the equipment (e.g., saying it was durable) or said they were replacing a set, 1% spoke of price, 34% gave other reasons neutral to the issues in this case (e.g., it was for a gift, the game was a classic, people like the game). The percentages total more than 100 because respondents often gave more than one reason.

The people who said that they had purchased the game within the last couple of years or would purchase it in the near future were then given a choice of two statements and were asked which best expressed their reasons. Sixty-five percent chose: "I want a 'Monopoly' game primarily because I am interested in playing 'Monopoly,' I don't much care who makes it." Thirty-two percent chose: "I would like Parker Brothers' 'Monopoly' game primarily because I like Parker Brothers' products."

A very similar "intercept survey" was conducted by face to face interviews. The results were very close to those of the telephone survey, but the expert did not claim that the intercept study was validly projectable.

The district court indicated its reasons for rejecting this survey. Insofar as these are findings of fact they must be accorded the deference required by Rule 52(a), and giving them that deference, we hold them to be clearly erroneous. The district court's major objection to the survey was that it sought an explanation of an actual purchaser's motivation in purchasing the game rather than the primary significance of the word. This objection cannot stand. In our earlier opinion we made it clear that what was relevant was the sense in which a purchaser used the word "Monopoly" when asking for the game by that name. The survey was a reasonable effort to find that out and was modelled closely on what we said in our opinion.

The district court thought that the survey was invalidated by the fact that in the first question people were asked if they were "aware of 'Monopoly,' the business board game *produced by Parker Brothers*" (emphasis supplied). It supposed that the presence of the emphasized words somehow inhibited those who might otherwise have responded to later questions that they bought the game because it was produced by Parker Brothers. No evidence or expert opinion was given to support this view and it has no inherent plausibility.

In a footnote the district court said of this survey that "other methodological deficiencies abound." One suggested deficiency is that Professor Anspach suggested the language that was used. This is taken to be evidence of "inherent bias." General Mills argues to us that little weight should be given to this survey because it was devised by Dr. Anspach and the survey firm without the mediation of a trademark attorney. We find no merit in these objections.

The district court found that the study was "overwhelmingly prone to errors of subjective grading." No doubt it was referring to the process by which responses were categorized as, for example, education, enjoyable, "played it as a kid," or equipment. This process of categorization was not purely mechanical, and did involve some use of human judgment. However, we are not prepared to dismiss every process that includes the operation of human judgment as "overwhelmingly prone to errors of subjective grading." Nor do we find any special reasons to suspect the exercise of judgment in the case of this survey. The categories that were listed strike us as reasonable ones.

Neither the district court nor General Mills claims that there were *in fact* errors of judgment, but only that there might have been. The raw responses to the survey were at one point offered in evidence by Anti-Monopoly, but the offer was withdrawn after General Mills objected, citing F.R. Evidence 705, 1005 and 1006, and the district judge said: "if [counsel for General Mills had] asked for them, he could have received them. If he received them, he could have turned them over to his expert to check them out and see if they give a reliable or non-reliable basis for the opinion. But since he didn't ask for them, I don't think they should go into evidence." Under these circumstances, General Mills cannot now argue that the raw responses were not in fact correctly categorized.

Finally, in the same footnote, the district court suggested that the result that 82% of monopoly purchasers buy for "product related" reasons *cannot be reconciled* with the other result that 32% of actual or potential buyers chose the statement "I would buy Parker Brothers' 'monopoly' game primarily because I like Parker Brothers' products." This is a misconception of the survey results. The comparable figure to the 32% is the 65% who chose the statement "I want a 'monopoly' game primarily because I am interested in playing 'monopoly,' I don't much care who makes it." The 82% who gave "product related" answers no doubt had both product related and source related reasons for buying, and, with some, enough to reduce 82% to 65%, the source related reason was stronger when the person had to choose. But it is still true that 65% chose product, rather than source.

We conclude that the findings regarding the survey are clearly erroneous, and that it does support the conclusion that the primary significance of "Monopoly" is product rather than source.

D. The Tide Survey.

General Mills introduced a survey that was intended as a *reductio ad absurdum* of the motivation survey. It showed that when asked to supply a reason for buying Tide about 60% of those who might buy it now or in the future said that they would buy Tide because it does a good job. However, when asked "Would you buy Tide primarily because you like Procter and Gamble's products, or primarily because you like Tide detergent?" about 68% indicated the latter reason. There were various respects in which this survey was different from the motivation survey used by Anti-Monopoly, but we shall not suddenly attach great importance to technical considerations. We suspect that these results tend to show that the general public regards "Tide" as the name of a particular detergent, having particular qualities, rather than as one producer's brand name for the same detergent which is available from a variety of sources. We do not know whether the general public thinks this, or if it does, is correct in thinking this, or whether Procter and Gamble intend them to think it. If the general public does think this, and if the test formulated in *Anti-Monopoly I* could be mechanically extended to the very different subject of detergents, then Procter and Gamble might have cause for alarm. The issue is not before us today. The motivation survey conducted by Anti-Monopoly, Inc. was in accordance with the views we expressed in *Anti-Monopoly I*. The results in the *Tide* Survey are of no relevance to this case.

E. Conclusion.

We hold that Finding 2 is clearly erroneous because, although there is some evidence to support it, our examination of the evidence leaves us with the definite and firm conviction that a mistake has been committed. We hold that, as applied to a board game, the word "Monopoly" has become "generic," and the registration of it as a trademark is no longer valid.

VII. OTHER ISSUES.

The district court must determine whether Anti-Monopoly is taking reasonable care to inform the public of the source of its product, and if it finds that this is not so may enjoin the sale of anti-monopoly save upon appropriate conditions. *Anti-Monopoly I,* 611 F.2d at 307.

We remand the case. The district court shall enter judgment for Anti-Monopoly, Inc. on the question of trademark validity and take whatever actions are necessary and consistent with this opinion.

3

Legal Issues Related
to Product Quality

In theory, marketing executives should be free to determine just how much quality they wish to build into their products. If complete information about all competing products were available, buyers could be fully knowledgeable about differing quality levels, could bargain with sellers using this knowledge, and could arrive at purchase prices that would take into account realistic expectations of performance. However, complete information is never available, and even it it were, buyers would likely be overwhelmed in trying to assimilate and comprehend all of it. Indeed, the difficulties faced by buyers in their efforts to sort through product offerings have been compounded over time by the increasing complexity of products, the proliferation of product offerings, the development of highly impersonal markets, the widening physical separation of buyers and sellers, and the scarcity of search time available to buyers.

Beginning in the early part of the twentieth century, the law began to respond to the dilemma faced by buyers. The result has been a steady expansion of legislative and judicial activity that constrains the ability of firms to choose the level of quality that they will offer to the market, especially if the product is capable of causing bodily injury. For example, in the early 1900s, concerns about the safety of food and drug products led to the enactment of federal legislation designed to keep dangerous drugs and unhealthy foods off the market. More recently, concerns about injuries resulting from the marketing of unsafe products led to the enactment of legislation regulating specific products such as automobiles, flammable fabrics, and children's toys. And, in 1972, the increasing concern about injuries caused by all types of consumer products led to the creation of the federal Consumer Product Safety Commission. These federal enactments have empowered regulators to set minimum safety standards for a whole range of products and, in certain cases, to ban the manufacture and sale of certain highly dangerous products.

The general concern for safety is also reflected in the evolution of the common law. In the 1960s and 1970s the law of torts evolved to impose "strict liability" on sellers of goods that are found to be "defective" and "unreasonably dangerous" and that cause personal injury to purchasers and users of the goods. This liability is imposed even though a firm has exercised "due care" in designing and manufacturing a product. In addition to tort law, contract law imposes constraints (as well as opportunities) on the product quality decision (both safety and non-safety aspects) through the creation and enforcement of warranties relating to a product's level of performance. Warranties impose obligations on the firm, but they also present the firm with an opportunity to differentiate itself from competitors by offering higher levels of protection to customers in the event a product fails to comply with representations as to quality.

In this chapter, we first examine the law of warranties and explain the significant difference between "express" and "implied" warranties. Attention is also focused on the provisions of the Magnuson–Moss Warranty Act. Then we look at the increasingly important issue of product liability as it has developed through the law of torts. And finally we examine government efforts to make products safer by directly regulating product quality and by providing more information to consumers about product quality and about safe methods of using dangerous products. Agencies such as the U.S. Department of Agriculture, the Food and Drug Administration, the Consumer Product Safety Commission, and the Federal Trade Commission, all play major roles in regulating product quality, and their actions, taken together, have an important impact on the latitude available to marketing executives as they bring their firms' products to market.

THE LAW OF WARRANTIES

A warranty is commonly thought of as the written document that accompanies the sale of a product and that sets forth the obligations of a seller if the product proves to be defective. This conception of a warranty is correct as far as it goes, but the law actually imposes obligations on sellers in addition to those that the seller *expressly* agrees to make. These further obligations are known as *implied warranties.* Both "express" and "implied" warranties are governed by state laws. Considerable uniformity among the states has resulted from the adoption of the Uniform Commercial Code (UCC) by all states except Louisiana.[1]

The two types of warranties are very different. The source of an *express* warranty obligation is the *agreement* between the seller and the purchaser, whereas the source of an *implied* warranty is *the law*. In other words, the UCC will impose a warranty obligation on a seller of *goods* even if the seller has not expressly agreed to warrant the product. Although the UCC does provide some freedom for a seller to *disclaim* these legally imposed implied warranties or to specify the limits of relief that a buyer can obtain if an implied warranty is *breached*, there are definite limits on the marketer's ability to disclaim warranties or limit remedies for breach. (These limitations will be explained in subsequent sections.)

Despite the basic difference between express and implied warranties, they do share one feature in common, namely, the circumstances under which courts impose liability for breach of a warranty. For a firm to be held liable, the injured party must establish that: (1) the product was a "good" sold by a "merchant"; (2) the seller made a warranty, either express or implied or both, and the injured party is entitled to enforce the warranty;[2] (3) the product did not comply with the warranty at the time of the sale (i.e., the warranty was "breached"); (4) reasonably quantifiable and specific damages were caused by the breach of warranty. Even if the plaintiff is able to establish all these elements, the seller still may escape liability by showing that the injured party failed to give notice within a reasonable time of the breach of warranty,[3] failed to bring suit within the time specified in the applicable statute of limitations,[4]

---

[1] The Uniform Commercial Code is a proposal of the National Conference of Commissioners on Uniform State Laws. Although 49 states have enacted the basic Code, total uniformity has not been achieved, since some states have enacted variations on the proposed statutory language, and since, for some warranty sections of the Code, uniformity was never contemplated as states were given various alternatives that they might adopt while enacting the entire Code.

[2] At common law, a warranty given by a seller extended only to those persons who directly dealt with the seller. This requirement, known as the *privity* requirement, insulated manufacturers from liability to consumers when the manufacturer distributed the goods through independent retailers. (This privity rule is known as *vertical* privity.) Furthermore, retail sellers were not liable if loss caused by the defective goods was sustained by someone other than the purchaser. Thus, if a husband purchased defective goods but the defect injured someone other than the husband, such as the husband's spouse, child, or guest, the retail seller was not liable for the loss. (This rule is referred to as *horizontal* privity.)

The UCC takes no position on the issue of vertical privity, leaving that issue to "developing case law on whether the seller's warranties, given to his buyer who resells, extend to other persons in the distributive chain." UCC §2-318, comment 3. Judicial decisions have, for all practical purposes, eliminated the vertical privity requirement in consumer warranty actions. Thus, under case law and under the Magnuson–Moss Warranty Act, all sellers are liable to the ultimate consumers of their products, at least for personal injury caused by a breach.

With respect to horizontal privity, the UCC proposed three alternatives for adoption by the states. Alternative A extends the warranty to natural persons who are family members or guests in the home if personal injury results and was reasonably foreseeable. Twenty-nine states have adopted this alternative. Alternative B extends the warranty to all persons who foreseeably could be personally injured by a breach of the warranty. Eight states have adopted this alternative. And alternative C follows alternative B with respect to persons covered by the warranty but expands coverage to include economic loss as well as personal injury (unless a seller excludes or limits liability for economic loss). Five states have adopted alternative C. 1A *Uniform Laws Annotated* (St. Paul, Minn.: West Publishing Co., 1976), pp. 52–53.

[3] UCC §2-607(3)(a).

[4] The UCC sets a 4-year period as the time within which litigation must be commenced after a breach has occurred. The parties to the contract may agree to reduce the period to not less than 1 year. UCC §2-715. Other litigation periods may be applicable if an injured buyer brings suit under a tort theory. (See the discussion in the Product Liability section.)

assumed the risk of a defect, or otherwise misused the product. (Product misuse and assumption of risk negate a causal connection between the breach of warranty and the plaintiff's damage; these *defenses* to liability are discussed in greater detail later in the product liability section.)

Damages recoverable for a warranty breach include *loss of bargain* (measured by the difference between the value of the product if it had complied with the warranty and the value of the defective product actually delivered)[5] plus *incidental* and *consequential* damages.[6] The incidental damages category includes the cost of storing the defective goods and the expenses incurred in acquiring a substitute product. The consequential damages category includes injury to the person or to property. Thus, if a defective tire has a blowout and causes a driver to lose control of the automobile and to collide with another automobile with resulting injury to both occupants, the seller could be held liable for damage to both cars and for injury to both occupants. Because liability for damage caused by a breach of warranty can be extensive, and because the seller's culpability or fault in selling a product that does not conform to its warranties is irrelevant to the liability question, sellers may desire to minimize their exposure by disclaiming warranties or limiting the remedies available for breaching the warranty. The extent to which this can be done will be explained in subsequent sections.

Express Warranties under the Uniform Commercial Code

The Uniform Commercial Code governs the creation of express warranties by sellers of products. The UCC provides that warranties are created in three ways: (1) "any affirmation of fact or promise" that "relates to the goods and becomes part of the basis of the bargain" creates an express warranty that the goods will conform to the affirmation or promise; (2) any "description of goods which is made part of the basis of the bargain" creates an express warranty that the goods conform to this description; and (3) use of a "sample or model" also creates a warranty that the goods will conform to the sample or model.[7]

The code makes clear that a warranty can be created even though the seller does not use the terms "warrant" or "guarantee."[8] Nor is the seller's desire or intent to avoid the making of a warranty relevant; a seller who makes factual representations or promises, describes the goods, or uses a sample or model has made a warranty regardless of the seller's actual intent.[9] Since advertising, labeling, and promotional communications often contain factual representations, and since statements made by salespersons are attributable to the firm, sellers must carefully scrutinize and monitor these communications to make sure that they match actual product performance.

[5] UCC §2-714(2).

[6] UCC §2-715.

[7] UCC §2-715.

[8] Id.

[9] Id.

The UCC does make clear that "puffing" about the value of a product does not create a warranty: "An affirmation merely of the value of the goods or a statement purporting to be merely the seller's opinion or commendation of the goods does not create a warranty."[10] However, for a seller, the risk is large that courts will find an express warranty rather than a "puff" or an "opinion," especially when a purchaser has suffered bodily injury as a result of using a defective product. As we discuss more fully in Chapter 7, courts increasingly are willing to find warranties from loose sales talk and advertising. Thus, firms may find that they have created warranties even when they have not intended to do so.

Although the UCC requires that a plaintiff establish that the warranty was "part of the basis of the bargain,"[11] courts are split on whether a plaintiff is required by this language to introduce some evidence of actual *reliance* upon the seller's representations. The current uncertainty on the reliance issue is exemplified by two cases. In *Interco, Inc.* v. *Randustrial Corp.*,[12] express warranties were held to have been created solely through representations in the seller's promotional material; reliance on these representations was not required to be shown. However, in *Hagenbuch* v. *Snap-On Tools Corp.*,[13] statements that were made in a seller's catalog concerning a hammer were held to have created no express warranty since the buyer did not show any reliance upon these statements. The court in *Interco* did qualify its approval of the rule that representations in promotional material can create actionable express warranties without proof of reliance by noting that "the catalog, advertisement or brochure must at least have been read" in order for the language in such promotional material to be "part of the basis of the bargain." Realistically, neither the *Interco* qualification nor the *Hagenbuch* rule offer much hope for firms seeking to avoid express warranty liability; most purchasers will be able to make out a credible claim of actual reliance on any express representations.

The Implied Warranties of Merchantability and Fitness for a Particular Purpose

The Uniform Commercial Code creates implied warranties of "merchantability" and "fitness" for a "particular purpose" in any contract for the sale of goods by a "merchant."[14] Merchantability means that the goods are "fit for

---

[10] Id.

[11] UCC §2-313.

[12] 533 S.W.2d 257 (Mo. App. 1976).

[13] 339 F.Supp. 676 (D.N.H. 1972).

[14] UCC §2-314. The Code also imposes an implied warranty of fitness for a particular purpose: "[w]here the seller at the time of contracting has reason to know any particular purpose for which the goods are required and that the buyer is relying on the seller's skill or judgment to select or furnish suitable goods, there is unless excluded or modified under the next section an implied warranty that the goods shall be fit for such purpose." UCC §2-315. In most consumer contexts, this warranty will not differ from the implied warranty of merchantability, which is discussed in the text.

the ordinary purposes for which such goods are used" and that the goods conform to representations made on labels and packages.[15] "Fitness for a particular purpose" means that goods are suitable for uses other than their ordinary uses; the warranty is made whenever the seller has reason to know that the buyer is relying on the seller's skill and judgment to select and furnish goods which are suitable for the buyer's special needs. We do not discuss the implied warranty of fitness in any great detail. Sellers should be aware that, when dealing with a sophisticated buyer, the precise nature of the obligation to furnish a suitable product should be the subject of negotiation and should be clearly spelled out in a written agreement. When dealing with unsophisticated buyers, there is some risk that an unintended fitness warranty will arise when sales personnel are alerted to the special needs of the buyer and are aware that the buyer is relying on the sales agent to choose and furnish a somewhat special product; however, any added risk is minimized because of the fact that most buyers will have rather ordinary needs which sellers are obligated to satisfy under the implied warranty of merchantability. In any event, sellers may be able to disclaim this warranty or limit liability for its breach. (See the following two sections.)

The statutory definition of merchantability offers little guidance on what quality level is being demanded of a seller. Although many cases have been litigated on the question of whether a product was merchantable, few usable generalities about the standard have evolved. Court decisions often turn upon (1) the nature of the loss (i.e., whether the product caused personal injury or only economic loss); (2) evidence of comparable product offerings in the marketplace; (3) normal consumer expectations about similar products; and (4) labeling of the product. It is clear that perfection is not required; fish chowder that contained bones[16] and shelled nuts with some shell fragments[17] have been held merchantable. But chicken bones in a pot pie and worms in canned vegetables have been held to breach the warranty of merchantability.[18] Similarly, defects are tolerated in used goods that would breach a merchantability standard for new goods.[19] Products that produce allergic reactions in an appreciable segment of buyers may be unmerchantable unless the allergy risk is mentioned on the label.[20] Proof that a firm's product complied with industry or government standards may be a necessary, although not always a sufficient, condition to establish that the product was merchantable.[21]

---

[15] UCC §§2-314 (2)(c) & (f).

[16] *Webster* v. *Blue Chip Tea Room, Inc.*, 198 N.E.2d 309 (Mass. 1964).

[17] *Coffer* v. *Standard Brands, Inc.*, 226 S.E.2d 534 (N. Car. App. 1976).

[18] *DeGraff* v. *Myers Foods, Inc.*, 1 U.C.C. Rep. 110 (Pa. Com. Pleas 1958); *Maze* v. *Bush Bros. & Co.*, 9 U.C.C. Rep. 1201 (Tenn. App. 1971).

[19] *Overland Bond & Investment Corp.* v. *Howard*, 292 N.E.2d 168 (Ill. App. 1972).

[20] *Zirpola* v. *Adam Hat Stores, Inc.*, 4 A.2d 73 (N.J.L. 1939); *Harris* v. *Belton*, 65 Cal. Rptr. 808 (Cal. App. 1968).

[21] *Handrigan* v. *Apex Warwick, Inc.*, 275 A.2d 262 (R.I. 1971).

Since the UCC applies only to "sales" of "goods" by "merchants,"[22] the question of whether a particular product is covered by the UCC has presented difficult questions. The case law is split on the question of whether a "sale" includes a lease of personal property. One recent New Jersey case held that the implied warranty of merchantability extends to a truck leasing service.[23] The rendition of services may not be covered. The New York courts have held that the UCC's implied warranty of merchantability was not given by a firm that undertook the installation of a burglary or fire alarm system; the court viewed such an arrangement as basically a service, to which the Uniform Commercial Code does not apply.[24] Whether the implied warranty of merchantability extends to blood transfusions or the actions of beauty parlor operators is still unresolved. The UCC is explicit about one difficult issue: it provides that "the serving for value of food or drink" is a sale of goods.[25]

Even if the UCC's implied warranty of merchantability is inapplicable because the transaction is not a sale of goods, courts frequently have imposed a warranty of quality as a matter of common law. For example, one court imposed a warranty that a repair service would be performed with "skillful" workmanship.[26] While courts in many states now hold service providers to a slightly lower standard (negligence or ordinary care), the common law is in a state of evolution and there is a fairly clear trend to impose higher quality standards on service providers, whether they be thought of as professionals (e.g., doctors, lawyers) or ordinary service providers. Courts may be expected to respond affirmatively to policy arguments on behalf of consumers of substandard services that such purchasers are in the same position as product purchasers with respect to their ability to protect themselves against unknown defects. And since service providers, like product sellers, are in a better position to minimize defects and to spread the costs of injury to all users of the service, judicial imposition of a higher standard of quality on service providers seems appropriate.

Until recently, sellers of housing units have not been saddled with an implied warranty; but several courts have imposed a "warranty of habitability" in sales of new homes, and the trend seems to be growing.[27] Some courts have extended this warranty to second purchasers who acquired the home within one year of its construction.[28]

---

[22] "Merchant" is defined as "a person who deals in goods of the kind [sold] or otherwise by his occupation holds himself out as having knowledge or skill peculiar to the practices or goods involved in the transaction. . . ." UCC §2-104(1).

[23] *Cintrone v. Hertz Truck Leasing & Rental Service,* 45 N.J. 434, 212 A.2d 769 (1965).

[24] *Craig v. The American District Telegraph Co.,* 91 Misc. 2d 1063, 399 N.Y.Supp. 2d 164 (1977).

[25] UCC, §2-314(1).

[26] *Jeffreys v. Hickman,* 132 Ill. App. 2d 272, 269 N.E.2d 110 (1971).

[27] See, e.g., *Petersen v. Hubschman Const. Co.,* 76 Ill. 2d 31, 389 N.E.2d 1154 (1979).

[28] *Redarowicz v. Ohlendorf,* 92 Ill. 2d 171, 441 N.E.2d 324 (1982).

Disclaimer of Implied Warranties

Although sellers can avoid the making of express warranties by making no representations in promotional material that could be construed as warranties, the implied warranties are imposed as a matter of law regardless of any affirmative representations of the marketer. Nevertheless, the drafters of the UCC recognized a need to allow the parties to a sales transaction to override these legally imposed terms by bargaining for and agreeing to the sale of a product without any warranties, express or implied. Accordingly, the UCC allows the implied warranties of merchantability and fitness to be *disclaimed* under appropriate conditions.

The concept of a *disclaimer* of the warranty should be distinguished from a *limitation on the remedy for breach* of a warranty. Disclaiming a warranty means that no warranty is given and therefore nothing can be breached for which remedies would be available. A limitation of remedy, on the other hand, acknowledges that some warranty has been given but purports to specify the consequences, financial or otherwise, of the seller's breach of that warranty. Limitations of remedy are discussed later.

The warranty of merchantability may be disclaimed if the disclaimer uses the word "merchantability," if the disclaimer is "conspicuous," and if it is calculated to be brought to the attention of the consumer.[29] The code also allows all implied warranties to be excluded by using expressions such as "as is," "with all faults," or other language that "in common understanding calls the buyer's attention to the exclusion of the warranties and makes plain that there is no implied warranty."[30] The question of whether any particular disclaimer will be enforced ultimately will depend upon a judicial determination of whether a disclaimer was sufficiently "conspicuous." A firm's chances of prevailing on that question are increased when the communication effectiveness of a disclaimer is beyond doubt; firms should print disclaimers in boldface capital letters, use contrasting colors, and locate the disclaimer near the top and on the front of any written agreement with the buyer. Nevertheless, courts will construe disclaimers narrowly in cases involving consumers; and there is always the possibility that a court will view the disclaimer as "unconscionable"[31] and simply refuse to enforce it. In transactions between businesses, warranty disclaimers almost always will be upheld.

One additional legal doctrine may prevent disclaimers from becoming effective. The law creates an implied warranty of merchantability at the time a

[29] UCC §2-316(2). The Code provides that disclaimers of the implied warranty of fitness for a particular purpose (see note 14 supra) must be in writing and be conspicuous.

[30] UCC §2-316(3).

[31] The UCC contains a general provision in §2-302 that allows a court to deny enforcement of any contract or term that the court finds "unconscionable" at the time the contract was made. While scholars have engaged in a raging debate over whether this provision allows a court to override warranty disclaimers and remedy limitations authorized elsewhere by the Code, it is clear that most courts presume that they have authority to police against and deny enforcement of unconscionable contracts, including warranty disclaimers and remedy limitations.

binding contract is entered into by the parties. If the disclaimer is not in that contract, but instead is contained in a document inside a sealed package that the buyer first sees when opening the package after the product has been purchased, the disclaimer will be viewed as an ineffective attempt at modifying an already existing contract, which included the implied warranty. Compliance with the presale availability requirements of the federal Magnuson–Moss Warranty Act (discussed later) may protect firms from the operation of this rule.

Several states have enacted special legislation that prevents sellers from disclaiming the implied warranty of merchantability or limiting its duration when goods are sold to consumers.[32] The theory behind such legislation is that consumers are unable to protect themselves from sellers who want to assume no responsibility for goods that they sell. In these states, sellers cannot escape responsibility for some minimum quality level, no matter how low the price for which the product is sold and no matter how clearly both the seller and the buyer want the sale to occur without warranties. Under the banner of consumer protection, freedom to contract has been limited.[33]

Another legal constraint on the ability of sellers to disclaim the implied warranties is the Magnuson–Moss Warranty Act (MMWA).[34] The Act provides that if a supplier[35] makes any written warranty[36] to, or enters into a service contract[37] with, a consumer, implied warranties may not be disclaimed or modified.[38] Thus, a firm's decision to offer any sort of written warranty or service contract is a decision not to disclaim implied warranties. But the MMWA does allow a firm to limit the *duration* of the implied warranty to the period of the written warranty, if the limitation is "reasonable," "conscionable," and

[32] See Millspaugh and Coffinberger, *Sellers' Disclaimer of Implied Warranties: The Legislatures Strike Back*, 13 U.C.C. L.J. (1980), p. 160.

[33] The UCC makes clear that if a buyer examines goods or refuses the seller's request for examination, "there is no implied warranty with regard to defects which an examination ought in the circumstances to have revealed." UCC §2-316(3)(b).

[34] 15 U.S.C. §2301 et seq. A detailed guide to the intricacies of this law can be found in Curtis R. Reitz, *Consumer Protection under the Magnuson–Moss Warranty Act* (Philadelphia: American Law Institute, 1978).

[35] "Supplier" includes "any person engaged in the business of making a consumer product directly or indirectly available to consumers." 15 U.S.C. §2301(4).

[36] A written warranty under the Magnuson–Moss Warranty Act is somewhat less encompassing than an express warranty under the UCC. The MMWA applies only to "written warranties," which are defined as (a) written affirmations of fact or written promises that relate to the nature of the material or workmanship and affirm or promise that such material or workmanship is defect free or will meet a specified level of performance over a specified period of time, or (b) written undertakings to repair, refund, replace, or take other remedial action if the product fails to meet the specifications set forth in the undertaking. 15 U.S.C. §2301(6). Recently, a court has held that this definition relates only to those warranties that are contained in a document marked "warranties;" the Act therefore does not apply to representations made in advertising, manuals, brochures, or other forms of communication. Thus, when General Motors' written warranty document made no mention of the quality level of its transmissions, it could not be charged with violating the MMWA by substituting allegedly inferior transmissions. *Skelton* v. *General Motors Corp.*, 660 F.2d 311 (7th Cir. 1981), *cert. den.* 102 Sup. Ct. 2238 (1982). In order for an express warranty under the UCC to be a warranty to which the Magnuson–Moss Act applies, the Federal Trade Commission has indicated that a time period must be mentioned. Thus, affirmations of fact, such as information disclosures, while being express warranties under the UCC, will not be written warranties within the MMWA. FTC, Interpretations of Magnuson–Moss Warranty Act, 16 C.F.R. §700.3(a) (1982).

[37] "The term 'service contract' means a contract in writing to perform, over a fixed period of time or for a specified duration, services relating to the maintenance or repair (or both) of a consumer product." 15 U.S.C. § 2301(7).

[38] 15 U.S.C. §2308(a).

is "set forth in clear and unmistakable language and prominently displayed on the face of the warranty."[39] However, the FTC has advised that if a service contract is used instead of a warranty, the firm may not limit the duration of implied warranties pursuant to this section of MMWA.[40] And if a firm decides to offer a "full" warranty, even this limitation on the duration of the implied warranty is not permitted.[41]

Another constraint on disclaiming warranties flows from the law's concern for the personal safety of users of consumer products. Liability for personal injury caused by "defective and unreasonably dangerous" products cannot be avoided. Although the UCC permits the implied warranty of merchantability to be disclaimed (and most states have not restricted this ability to disclaim), tort law, under either negligence or strict liability principles, probably will not give effect to any contractual attempts of firms to limit liability for personal injury caused by defective and unreasonably dangerous products.[42]

Limiting Remedies for Warranty Breach

As the preceding sections have made clear, a firm may not be able to disclaim the implied warranty of merchantability (either because of noncompliance with the UCC or because of the restrictions in the MMWA). However, it may be possible to limit the nature and extent of the buyer's *remedy* for a breach of the warranty. In other words, although the warranty itself cannot be disclaimed or negated, the nature and extent of the seller's liability under the warranty can be specified in the contract. Sellers may want to limit remedies in order to escape liability that the UCC would otherwise impose for a warranty breach. Under the UCC, breaching sellers are liable not only for the loss of the value of the goods; they also are liable for incidental and consequential damages. Thus, a truck seller may be liable for costs of alternate transportation when the truck malfunctions and may be liable for personal injuries or property damages that result from a collision caused by the defect. One seller was held liable for damages to a house that burned as a result of defective wiring in an automobile parked in an attached garage.[43]

The UCC indicates that the buyer's remedies can be limited to "return of the goods and repayment of the price" or to "repair and replacement of nonconforming goods or parts."[44] Apparently, the MMWA does not preclude such a limitation on the remedies for a breach of warranty of merchantability since, even under a "full" warranty, the act permits the exclusion or limitation of liability for consequential damages if the "exclusion or limitation conspicuously appears on the face of the warranty."[45]

---

[39] 15 U.S.C. §2308(b).

[40] FTC Advisory Opinion, Nov. 17, 1978, 43 Fed. Reg. 57244 (Dec. 7, 1978).

[41] 15 U.S.C. §2304(a)(2).

[42] *Vandermark* v. *Ford Motor Co.,* 391 P.2d 168 (Cal. 1964).

[43] *Riley* v. *Ford Motor Co.,* 442 F.2d 670 (5th Cir. 1971).

[44] UCC §2-719(1)(a).

[45] 15 U.S.C. §2304(a)(3).

Whether a firm's attempts to limit liability for incidental and consequential damages for a warranty breach will be successful is always problematical. Courts can narrowly construe the language of the limitation against the seller and can also invoke countervailing policies in the UCC to override such limitations. For example, courts have found that a remedy limitation "fail[ed] of its essential purpose" and therefore was not enforceable where the exclusive remedy under the warranty was for the repair and replacement of defective parts and where numerous repair attempts had not produced an operable automobile.[46] Furthermore, courts are authorized by the UCC to deny enforcement of a limitation or exclusion of consequential damages if the clause is "unconscionable."[47] (Such a limitation is *prima facie* unconscionable to the extent that it limits consequential damages "for injury to the person in the case of consumer goods."[48]) With courts declaring both warranty disclaimers and remedy limitations unconscionable, the chances of seller success in remedy limitation cases are considerably reduced.

The Magnuson–Moss Warranty Act's Labeling and Disclosure Requirements

The Magnuson–Moss Warranty Act was enacted to give consumers more information about warranties that accompanied consumer products. The act's premise was that consumers could use the information to selectively shop for those products that offered the best warranty protection, thereby stimulating competition among sellers. The act imposes three major requirements on firms that choose to give a written warranty. Firms must (1) designate the warranty as either a "full (statement of duration) warranty" or a "limited warranty," depending on whether or not the warranty meets the standards for a full warranty as set forth in the act; (2) "fully and conspicuously disclose in simple and readily understood language the terms and conditions" of the warranty; and (3) make the terms of the warranty available to the consumer prior to the sale of the product.[49] These requirements are discussed in this section.

Full Warranty Requirements.

The Magnuson–Moss Warranty Act requires that each written warranty be conspicuously labeled as either a "FULL" warranty or a "LIMITED" warranty. Congress wanted to protect consumers by allowing them to quickly determine whether a product was being sold with or without comprehensive warranty protections. Accordingly, it divided all warranties into two classes and established rigorous standards for calling a warranty a full warranty. Be-

---

[46] *Riley* v. *Ford Motor Co.*, supra note 43; *Goddard* v. *General Motors Corp.*, 60 Ohio 2d 41, 396 N.E.2d 761 (1979).

[47] UCC §2-719(3).

[48] *Id.* See Samuels, *The Unconscionability of Excluding Consequential Damages Under the Uniform Commercial Code When No Other Meaningful Remedy Is Available*, 43 U.Pitt.L.Rev. 197 (1981).

[49] 15 U.S.C. §§2302 & 2303. Requirements (1) and (2) apply only to consumer products costing more than $5.00; requirement (3) applies only to products costing more than $10.00. The FTC has changed the dollar limits for requirements (1) and (2) to $15.00. 16 C.F.R. §§701.3(a) and 702.3 (1982).

cause of these rigorous standards for a full warranty, and because a firm is required to choose between only two categories of warranty, the choice of whether to offer a full or a limited warranty is not an easy one, particularly if consumers have strong preferences for a full warranty and if a firm's competitors are offering a full warranty.

To qualify as a full warranty, a warrantor must (1) remedy promptly and without charge any defect, malfunction, or failure to conform to the terms of the warranty; (2) permit the consumer to obtain either a replacement or a refund if the malfunction cannot be repaired after a reasonable number of attempts; (3) not exclude or limit consequential damages for breach of the written or implied warranties (unless the limitation "conspicuously appears on the face of the warranty"); and (4) place no limit on the duration of implied warranties.[50]

If a firm designates a warranty as a full warranty, the act does not allow the firm to impose any duties on the consumer, such as requiring the consumer to return the product to the place of original purchase, unless the warrantor can demonstrate that the duty is reasonable. One court found such a requirement reasonable; the product was a recreational vehicle, and the court relied on testimony showing that the buyer was fully informed at the time of purchase that warranty service required that the goods be returned to the dealer for repairs and regular maintenance.[51] The FTC has found unreasonable any duty imposed on consumers to return a warranty registration card.[52]

If a firm gives a full warranty, the firm's duties under the warranty (e.g., to repair, replace, or refund) cannot be limited to the first purchaser of the product unless that restriction is made clear in the labeling portion of the warranty. Thus, the label "FULL warranty for as long as you own this product" would restrict warranty rights to the first purchaser, but a designation of "Full 3-year warranty" would mean that the firm's obligations under the warranty extend to each person who becomes the owner of the product during the 3-year period.[53]

Disclosure Requirements.

To improve the informative function of warranties, the Magnuson–Moss Act authorized the Federal Trade Commission to require written warranties to contain specified items of information. In line with the dictates of the Act, the FTC has enacted rules that require disclosure (in a single document using "simple and readily understood language") of the following items of information for warranted products costing more than $15:[54]

---

[50] 15 U.S.C. §2304.

[51] *Pratt* v. *Winnebago Ind.*, 463 F. Supp. 709 (W.D.Pa. 1979).

[52] FTC Interpretation of MMWA, 16 C.F.R. §700.7 (1982). However, the firm can suggest that return of a registration card would serve as proof of the date of purchase; but if this suggestion is made, the consumer must be notified that failure to return the card will not affect rights under the warranty. Ibid.

[53] Ibid., §700.6(b).

[54] 15 U.S.C. §§2302. The Federal Trade Commission has promulgated rules implementing this section. See 16 C.F.R. §701.1 (1981).

1. The identity of the persons to whom the warranty extends (if the warranty does not extend to every owner during the warranty term).
2. A description of the products, parts, characteristics, components, or properties covered.
3. A statement of what the warrantor will do in the event of a defect and the items or services that the warrantor will pay for or provide.
4. The time period or other measurement of warranty duration.
5. The step-by-step explanation of the procedure that the consumer should follow to obtain the benefits of the warranty, including the name and address of the warrantor.
6. Information about the availability of dispute settlement procedures.
7. Limitations on the duration of implied warranties and any exclusions of or limitations on recovery of incidental or consequential damages, together with statements indicating that state law may not allow these limitations or exclusions.

Presale Availability Requirements.

Congress gave the Federal Trade Commission authority to specify the manner in which warrantors could comply with the act's requirement that the terms of warranties be made available to consumers before the product was purchased. The FTC has promulgated two special rules and one general rule for making the terms of warranties available to consumers before a product is purchased. The rules apply to consumer products costing more than \$15.[55]

Special Rules

CATALOG AND MAIL-ORDER SALES. If the product is offered through a catalog or mail-order promotion, the seller must include either the full text of any written warranty or a statement that the full text can be obtained free of charge by writing to a stated address. The text or statement must be provided on the page describing the product or on the facing page, or in an information section of the catalog or solicitation that is clearly referenced by page number.[56]

DOOR-TO-DOOR SALES. If the product is offered for sale in a door-to-door sales transaction, both an oral disclosure and written statement must be given to the buyer prior to the consummation of the sale that the sales representative has a copy of the warranty, which may be inspected at any time during the sales presentation.[57]

All Other Sales

In all other sales, the seller of a consumer product must make the text of a written warranty available to the buyer prior to the sale. Four alternative ways for doing this are authorized: (1) displaying the text of the warranty in close proximity to the displayed product; (2) providing "ready access" to an indexed binder prominently entitled "Warranties" and containing copies of warranties for all products sold in the department (these binders must be prominently displayed, or signs must be prominently displayed that inform the consumer of the availability of the binder); (3) displaying the package on

---

[55] 16 C.F.R. §702 (1981).

[56] 16 C.F.R. §702.3(c) (1982).

[57] 16 C.F.R. §702(d)(2) (1982).

which the text of the warranty is clearly visible; or (4) posting near the product a notice that contains the text of the warranty.

The FTC attempted to enforce the presale availability rule against a large retailer, Montgomery Ward & Co., which had opted to use the binder method. The FTC interpreted its rule as requiring that at least one set of binders be available on each selling floor and that signs be posted in each department as to the existence and location of the binders. The Court of Appeals upheld the "one binder per floor" requirement, but refused to go along with the FTC's interpretation of the rule as requiring a sign in each department, since the rule only required that signs be placed in "prominent locations in the store or department."[58]

The FTC also has approved the use of ultrafiche and microfiche viewing systems as a method of satisfying the presale availability requirements. These systems will meet the FTC's presale availability requirements only if (1) the reading machines are labeled with operating instructions, (2) employees are available to assist consumers in using the readers, (3) the reading material on the cards consists only of warranty texts (i.e., other promotional material cannot appear on the cards), (4) the warranty texts must be grouped by product class on the same row or column of the card, and (5) each card must contain a clear product index.

Other Important Magnuson–Moss Act Provisions.

Several features of the act affect litigation regarding warranties. One feature allows firms to establish informal dispute resolution mechanisms, which (if the mechanism complies with rules of the Federal Trade Commission) buyers must use before bringing any action in court for breach of warranty.[59] Another feature of the act allows a court to award attorneys' fees to any consumer who prevails in an action to enforce any warranty.[60] This change in the total amount that a consumer can recover makes suits much more likely against warrantors who do not live up to their warranties.

PRODUCT LIABILITY LAW

The law of warranties places constraints on a firm's choice of product quality but does not completely foreclose all choices; it is possible, from a strictly legal point of view, for a firm to avoid warranty liability by making no express warranties, providing no service agreements, and conspicuously disclaiming all implied warranties. But other branches of the law are not so tolerant of a decision to market a product that might cause injury to the purchaser. Many products cannot be marketed unless they meet minimum safety requirements. These requirements flow from two principal sources.

[58] *Montgomery Ward & Co.* v. *FTC,* 691 F.2d 1322 (9th Cir. 1982).

[59] 15 U.S.C. §2310(a). The Federal Trade Commission has implemented standards for informal dispute resolution mechanisms that satisfy this section. See 16 C.F.R. §703 (1981). These requirements are exceptionally rigorous and few warrantors have adopted them.

[60] 15 U.S.C. §§2310(d)(2).

One major constraint on product quality is the common law, principally "tort" law. In this field of law, courts impose monetary liability on firms whose products have caused personal injury. As explained later, liability originally depended upon a showing that the firm had acted negligently (i.e., the firm failed to exercise that degree of due care and caution as would be exercised by reasonable marketers in similar circumstances). Today, in most states, liability is "strict," in the sense that the fault or negligence of the manufacturer is irrelevant; liability is imposed if the product is dangerously defective and the defect is unexpected by consumers and causes injury.[61]

A second source of legal constraint on product quality is regulatory in nature. Governments have acted, usually through regulatory agencies, to ban some unsafe products and to establish minimum safety standards for others. Beginning with the regulation of foods and drugs at the turn of the twentieth century, federal legislation has become increasingly comprehensive, first covering specific product categories (automobiles, flammable fabrics, children's toys), then extending to any "hazardous substance," and finally covering all "consumer products." The following discussion explores the legal climate covered by tort law. Then we examine legislation dealing with unsafe products.

Tort Law and Liability for Product-Related Injuries

Tort law consists of principles developed by judges as part of the common law. This field of the law is concerned with compensating one person for harm caused by the wrongful conduct of another. The legal principles developed by courts seek to define the standards of conduct of our society, the violation of which (if harm results) will lead to the imposition of an order requiring the violator of the standard to compensate the person harmed. At one time, the "negligence" rule was the principal doctrine under which sellers of products might be held liable if a product proved defective and caused injury. The negligence rule establishes a standard of ordinary care, or reasonableness: only by failing to exercise the degree of care that reasonably prudent sellers would exercise in similar circumstances does a seller incur liability for injuries caused by a defective product. Although this standard may seem somewhat vague, the results in decided cases are not difficult to understand. Producers of goods have been held liable for failing to establish reasonable inspection procedures for detecting defects in the manufacturing process; and sellers who know of dangerous aspects of their products are liable for failing to take reasonable measures to eliminate the dangers or to warn users about them. Although at one time the duty of care extended only from a seller to the seller's immediate purchaser, today the duty to carefully manufacture products has gradually been extended until it clearly reaches any purchaser of the product, members of the purchaser's family, guests, and even bystanders having no relation to

---

[61] Liability for the sale of a product that fails to comply with warranties also is "strict" in this same sense: if a warranty is breached, liability may follow regardless of the marketer's fault. The standard of liability is set by the marketer's express and implied representations. Such standard can exceed the standard that would be set by tort law.

the purchaser. In short, the seller's duty extends to any person who might foreseeably be injured if a product is negligently made.

By the 1960s, the requirement that a plaintiff who has suffered injury from a defective product establish that the marketer of the product was negligent came to be seen as somewhat unjust. Since an injured party often is not in a position to demonstrate that a defective product was a result of a defendant's negligence, courts and juries are free to find that the defect is simply a case of accident and not preventable by the exercise of ordinary care. The doctrine of *res ipsa loquitur* (literally, "the thing speaks for itself") does help some injured plaintiffs and presents risks to sellers. Under this doctrine, if the defect is one that would not ordinarily have occurred in the absence of negligence, the plaintiff is relieved of the burden of introducing evidence of the seller's negligence, and the seller is required to establish that it exercised due care in manufacturing the product. A seller could wax eloquent about the cleanliness of his plant and the thoroughness of his inspection procedures, yet a mouse in a soda bottle suggests, and juries are entitled to find, some degree of negligence.

Despite the existence of the *res ipsa* rule, dissatisfaction prevailed with the negligence principle. Courts searched for new liability rules and ultimately borrowed the liability-without-fault principle from other areas of tort law and from contract law dealing with breach of warranties. However, while the concept of liability without fault is inherent in the warranty theory of liability, that theory of recovery has some major limitations, which can be determinative in some cases and can bar recovery even where recovery seems entirely appropriate. Warranty liability requires the giving of timely notice that the warranty has been breached. Also, some courts require the plaintiff to be a direct purchaser from the seller (i.e., to be in contractual privity with the defendant). And finally, warranties, being contractual in nature, can be completely disclaimed or never expressly made.

These shortcomings of the warranty action, coupled with dissatisfaction as to the requirement of proving fault in a negligence action, caused courts to recognize a new basis of recovery for bodily injuries caused by defective products. This doctrine, called *strict liability in tort*, has been accepted by the courts of nearly all the states. As a result, firms can be held liable for injuries caused by a product if the product was in a "defective" condition and "unreasonably dangerous" when it left the control of the marketer.[62] All members of the channel of distribution, from manufacturers through retailers, are saddled with joint liability, although it is possible for the courts to reallocate liability to the party who actually was responsible for the existence of the defect. Lia-

---

[62] This formulation of the liability standard is found in the Restatement (Second) of Torts, §402A:

(1) One who sells any product in a defective condition unreasonably dangerous to the user or consumer or to his property is subject to liability for physical harm thereby caused to the ultimate user or consumer, or to his property, if (a) the seller is engaged in the business of selling such a product, and (b) it is expected to and does reach the user or consumer without substantial change in the condition in which it is sold. (2) The rule stated in Subsection (1) applies although (a) the seller has exercised all possible care in the preparation and sale of his product, and (b) the user or consumer has not bought the product from or entered into any contractual relation with the seller.

Increasingly, courts of most states are adopting this standard of liability.

bility is imposed even though a firm has exercised all due care in the manufacture, design, and packaging of a product.

The strict liability in tort doctrine has been adopted because of a policy that favors compensation of persons injured by defective products regardless of the ability of the injured party to demonstrate the "fault" of the seller. Courts have come to believe that many product injuries simply are not avoidable and that it is unjust to deny recovery to a person who has been injured by a defective product even if it has been carefully made. The strict liability doctrine also is thought to advance the goal of encouraging the development of safer products. Since the cost of product-related injuries will be treated as a cost of doing business, courts expect sellers to minimize these costs by striving to reduce the level of product defects. For those injuries that are not avoided, their cost should be borne initially by the producer of the product and spread among all purchasers through the pricing mechanism or through insurance. Although economists are increasingly vocal in their efficiency-based criticism of strict liability rules,[63] courts seemingly are firmly wedded to this new liability standard. Firms must learn to cope with the liability-without-fault rule.

Thus, liability for injuries caused by defective products can be imposed under two basic legal theories, each having two subcategories. Under contractual theories, a seller can be liable for breach of express warranty or breach of implied warranty. Under tort theories, liability can be imposed under negligence rules or under the strict liability in tort theory. We have discussed the warranty liability of marketers in the previous section; we now turn to the potential liability of businesses under tort theories.

Tort Liability Standards for Different Types of Product Defects

When a firm is charged with having marketed a "defective" product (under either negligence or strict liability rules), three different categories of product defect can be identified. In the first category, which can be thought of as *manufacturing process defects,* the product allegedly is not in compliance with either the manufacturer's own designs and specifications or with the standards commonly used in the industry. Although a manufacturer's compliance with such specifications and standards will not be conclusive on the issues of whether the manufacturer was negligent or the product was defective, such standards usually can be admitted into evidence and considered by the court (or jury).[64] When a product does not comply with a firm's own standards or

---

[63] See, e.g., Priest, *The Best Evidence of the Effect of Product Liability Law on the Accident Rate,* 91 Yale L.J. 1386 (1982).

[64] Firms should be aware of and attempt, at a minimum, to comply with product safety standards promulgated by various private organizations, such as the American National Standards Institute (ANSI), since evidence of compliance with such standards usually can be admitted into evidence. See *Nordstron* v. *White Metal Rolling & Stamping Corp.,* 453 P.2d 619 (Wash. 1969) (safety standard for portable metal ladders). ANSI promulgates standards for both industrial and consumer products. Recent examples include electrostatic air cleaners, outdoor gas grills, and shredder-baggers. See *BNA Product Safety & Liability Reporter,* Jan. 1, 1982, p. 7.

industry guides, injured plaintiffs will usually be able to recover on either negligence or strict liability principles. Through this branch of tort law, firms are encouraged to closely monitor their production processes to make sure that they are turning out goods that meet the firm's, or the industry's, standards of quality and freedom from defects.

A second category of defect involves *inadequate warnings or instructions.* Here, sellers are liable for failing to provide buyers with information about risks that will be encountered if the product is used improperly. Sellers must provide information to purchasers on how dangers may be avoided and on emergency procedures for dealing with an improper use, such as ingestion of a poison. (Some of these warnings are mandated by government safety regulations; these regulations are discussed later in this chapter.) Warnings must be provided even if the seller supplies accessories to prevent injuries. Thus, in *Garza* v. *Spudnik Equipment Company,*[65] the equipment manufacturer was held liable for failing to warn of the danger that its potato piler might overturn if the stabilizing outriggers (which the manufacturer had supplied) were not installed and used. Because the stabilizers could be removed, failure to warn of the danger of removal was held to be negligent.

The adequacy of a warning may depend upon its prominence, its specific wording, and its general communicative effectiveness. In addition, a warning that otherwise might be adequate can be negated by other communications. For example, in *Incollingo* v. *Ewing,*[66] a court held that the activities of drug salesmen in "overpromoting" a drug and in discouraging physicians from reading the detailed product literature could result in liability for failure to give an adequate warning of the risks of using the drug.

One group of cases suggests that no matter how adequate the warnings and instructions concerning a dangerous product, the seller nevertheless may be liable for injuries caused by the product. In essence, the seller can be found negligent for placing the product on the market. These cases are exemplified by *Drayton* v. *Jiffe Chemical Corp.,*[67] in which liability was imposed for injuries caused by a liquid drain cleaner with an excessively high concentration of a caustic chemical, and by *Ruggeri* v. *Minnesota Mining & Manufacturing Co.,*[68] in which a seller was held liable because an adhesive was excessively flammable for its intended use even though the warnings about the flammability were otherwise adequate. These cases can be seen as a species of "design defect" cases (discussed later). Where a slight change in design or composition of the product would have avoided a potentially fatal injury while not impairing the utility of the product, adequate warnings are no substitute for failure to make the design change, and liability will be imposed.[69] In essence, such a judicial

[65] *Garza* v. *Spudnik Equipment Co.,* No. 80-3110 (9th Cir., Nov. 27, 1981), *cert. denied,* 50 U.S. Law Week, 3948 (U.S., June 1, 1982).

[66] 282 A.2d 206 (Pa. 1971).

[67] 395 F. Supp. 1081 (N.D. Ohio 1975).

[68] 63 Ill. App. 3d 525, 380 N.E.2d 445 (1978).

[69] See *Uloth* v. *City Tank Corp.,* 384 N.E.2d 1188 (Mass. 1978).

determination is analogous to a determination by the Consumer Product Safety Commission (CPSC) that, if a product is excessively hazardous in its current formulation, it must be banned. About the only type of product for which adequate warnings will be a substitute for a dangerous condition are those products where no alternative design is possible, yet the product has considerable utility—the "unavoidably unsafe" product such as useful medications that also have serious side effects.[70]

In the third category, *design defects,* the challenge is to the product designs and specifications themselves, and the seller is charged with failing to adopt a safer alternative design. Thus, in *Micallef* v. *Miehle Co.,*[71] a printing press manufacturer was held liable for failing to install a guard on its printing press which would have protected the plaintiff–operator from suffering an injury to his hand. This category of defect presents a most serious risk for firms as the "defect," if it is found to exist, applies to all products sold that incorporate the challenged design. Exposure to liability is thus greater than in the manufacturing defect case, where the defect usually is a relatively limited error or random variation in the production or assembly process.

Liability Theories for Defective Designs

The precise nature of a firm's exposure to liability for defective product designs is uncertain at this point in the evolution of tort law. An examination of recent tort litigation reveals at least five different formulations applied by courts to determine whether a product has been defectively designed.

The Deviation from the Norm Test.

Under this test, a product is defective if it is below the quality level of most similar products, and injury results from this deviation. The most famous case using this test is *Greenman* v. *Yuba Power Products, Inc.,*[72] where a lathe manufacturer was found liable for injuries caused by its failure to use a proper fastening device that had been incorporated into the lathes of most competitors.

The Restatement (Second) of Torts Test.

Under this test, a jury can impose liability on a seller by simply concluding that the product was sold in a "defective" condition "unreasonably dangerous" to the buyer. The court gives the jury no additional guidance on these concepts, and the jury is left with considerable discretion to impose liability out of sympathy for the injured plaintiff. The comments to the restatement

---

[70] See *Gaston* v. *Hunter,* 588 P.2d 326 (Ariz. App. 1978), in which warnings to physicians about the serious side effects of the experimental drug chymopapain relieved the marketer of liability for injury to a patient that resulted from use of the drug.

[71] 39 N.Y.2d 376, 348 N.E.2d 571 (1976).

[72] 59 Cal.2d 57, 377 P.2d 897, 27 Cal. Rptr. 697 (1963).

add only minimal clarification to the apparent open-endedness of this standard. They suggest that the issues of "defect" and "unreasonably dangerous" should be determined in light of the contemplation of the "ordinary" consumer, possessing the "ordinary" knowledge common to the community as to the characteristics of the product.

The Unreasonable Seller Test.

Under this test (which frequently is coupled with the Restatement test), a product can be found defective in design if a "prudent manufacturer aware of the risk involved" would not have placed the product in the channels of commerce.[73] This test requires juries to assess the probable actions of "prudent" manufacturers and obviously leaves much room for variable determinations of liability based on product designs.

The Risk–Utility Test.

Under this test, which is receiving more widespread acceptance from courts and commentators, the judge or jury is asked to determine whether the risk of harm resulting from a particular design choice is outweighed by the utility of the design. Evidence is presented to the judge and jury on numerous aspects of the design choice process. These aspects include (1) the availability of safer alternative designs; (2) the cost of modifying the design and the impact on the product's utility; and (3) the consumer's ability to avoid harm by exercising care in view of obvious dangers or clear warnings and instructions for safe use. Courts also consider the frequency and seriousness of injuries that might result from the alleged design defect. Thus, a hood latch was found to be not defective in its design when only seven cases of inadvertent opening occurred in seven years.[74]

In some states, the risk–utility test is applied by the judge in deciding whether to send a case to the jury for the ultimate determination of liability. In these states, only if the judge decides that the utility of the chosen design did not outweigh its risks will the jury be permitted to decide liability. In those states, the jury may be asked to apply one of the other tests described here, but usually will not be entrusted to apply a full risk–utility test.

Although the risk–utility test appears to introduce a somewhat greater degree of certainty in liability determinations regarding product designs, there still is a great deal of uncertainty in weighing the factors that are relevant to the decision. Furthermore, judges and juries may balk at applying a purely economic analysis when loss of life or serious injury has occurred. And there is no assurance that courts will accept a seller's calculations of the economic

[73] See *Turner v. General Motors Corp.*, 584 S.W.2d 844, 850 (Tex. 1979) (jury properly allowed to determine defectiveness of crashworthiness design of automobile roof).

[74] *Roach v. Kononen*, 269 Or. 457, 525 P.2d 125 (1974).

value of life or limb, or concur in the firm's judgment that alternative designs would have diminished the utility of the product to an unacceptable level. Thus, even this test leaves sellers with very little by way of concrete guidance as to appropriate product design decisions.

A Hybrid Consumer Expectations and Risk–Utility Test.

Under this test, recently adopted by the California Supreme Court in *Barker* v. *Lull Engineering Co.,* a product can be found defective in design

> (1) if the plaintiff demonstrates that the product failed to perform as safely as an ordinary consumer would expect when used in an intended or reasonably foreseeable manner, or (2) if the plaintiff proves that the product's design proximately caused his injury and the defendant fails to prove, in light of the relevant factors . . . that on balance the benefits of the challenged design outweigh the risk of danger inherent in such design.[75]

This approach shifts the burden to the seller of demonstrating that, on balance, its safety design decision was correct in light of all risks and benefits of alternative designs. This test places a heavy burden and considerable risk on firms regarding safety designs.

The obligation to design a product safely extends to all uses of the product that are foreseeable. At one time, automobile manufacturers were successful in arguing that they had no duty to design cars that would be safe for occupants in a crash, on the theory that it was not reasonably foreseeable that cars would be involved in crashes or accidents.[76] That holding was abandoned in 1977 in the case of *Huff* v. *White Motor Co.*[77] Now manufacturers are expected to design their products to be as safe as "an ordinary consumer would expect."[78] Since it is not possible to predict how judges and juries will decide what the ordinary consumer would expect, it behooves those in the distribution channel to be aware of all possible uses of their products and to design them so that they are not unreasonably dangerous to all users under all conditions. Such precautions may be necessary to avoid the imposition of substantial liability in the event that personal injury results. For example, automobile manufacturers have been held liable for injuries caused when occupants of automobiles were burned by gasoline that escaped from the gasoline tank when the tank was ruptured in an accident.[79] It is estimated that gas tank design defect cases have already cost manufacturers over $50 million in judgments and legal fees, and many more cases are pending and will certainly arise.[80]

---

[75] 573 P.2d 443, 457-58, 143 Cal. Rptr. 225, 239-40 (Cal. 1978).

[76] See *Evans* v. *General Motors Corp.,* 359 F.2d 822 (7th Cir. 1966).

[77] 565 F.2d 104 (7th Cir. 1977).

[78] *Barker* v. *Lull,* supra note 75, at 457, 143 Cal. Rptr. at 239.

[79] *Grimshaw* v. *Ford Motor Co.,* 119 Cal. App. 3d 757, 174 Cal. Rptr. 348 (1981) (damages of $2.8 million compensatory and $3.5 million punitive in accident involving the Ford Pinto automobile).

[80] See Lauter, "Car Fires Ignite High Awards," *Nat'l L.J.,* Dec. 21, 1981, p. 1, col. 1.

Defenses to Product Liability Actions

Whether a firm ultimately will be held liable for injuries caused by a product may depend upon the legal theory invoked by the injured party and the defenses available under state law. For example, one typical defense to product liability actions is based on the timeliness of the commencement of the litigation. Most states have established time periods ("statutes of limitation") within which an injured person must commence litigation. These periods may vary depending on whether the theory of the litigation is based on contract (i.e., warranty) or tort (i.e., negligence or strict liability) principles. If the statute imposes a 3-year limit on tort actions and a 4-year limit on warranty actions, a plaintiff will not be able to commence litigation under the doctrine of strict tort liability if 3 years have elapsed since the injury occurred. But a plaintiff might be able to base an action on a breach of warranty theory (either express or implied), and since a warranty action is considered to be governed by contract principles, such an action might not be barred until 4 years have elapsed after a product-related injury occurred.

Other defenses to product liability actions relate to the behavior of the injured plaintiff in using the product. Various forms of improper behavior by users of a product can lead to the avoidance of liability. Considerable doctrinal uncertainty exists as to the circumstances under which firms can avoid liability for injuries caused by their products. Tort law principles are evolving rapidly, and many states have not yet reached a degree of certainty as to the types of plaintiff misconduct that should prevent an injured plaintiff from recovering all or a part of damage caused by a product. For example, the failure of an injured person to buckle an automobile seatbelt was held to be "contributory negligence" and a bar to an action based on a negligence theory; however, the contributory negligence was not a bar to an action based on the theory of strict liability.[81] Even where the plaintiff's theory is based on negligence, recovery may be allowed. Many states have relaxed the older rule (which absolutely barred recovery on a negligence theory if the plaintiff was also negligent) in favor of a "comparative negligence" rule, under which a plaintiff can recover a portion of the injuries caused by the defendant's negligence.

On the other hand, even where strict liability cannot be avoided by showing that the plaintiff was negligent, courts do recognize that some forms of behavior by plaintiffs should prevent recovery against the manufacturer of the product. For example, many courts will deny recovery under strict liability theories if it can be shown that the plaintiff discovered the product defect and was aware of the dangers of using it, but nevertheless unreasonably used the product and suffered injury. Similarly, recovery might be denied by many

---

[81] See *Vizzini* v. *Ford Motor Co.*, 569 F.2d 754 (3d Cir. 1977) (failure of deceased to buckle seat belts was contributory negligence and therefore a complete defense to a negligence action, but was not a defense to a strict liability action).

courts if the plaintiff used the product in a way not reasonably forseen by the manufacturer.

We cannot explore these difficult doctrinal uncertainties here nor predict with any degree of confidence how these policy questions will be resolved. Realistically, the avoidance of liability is problematical at best and will depend on not only the state of evolving tort law but on jury determinations of highly unpredictable questions such as whether a plaintiff's actions were reasonable under the circumstances and whether a plaintiff was aware of a defect and assumed the risk that the defect might cause injury.

In any action seeking to recover for injuries related to a product defect, the injured party is required to demonstrate that the injuries were *caused* by a product actually manufactured by the defendant. This *causation* element normally is rather straightforward, and there is little doubt as to the identity of the manufacturer. But in some situations the identity of the producer of a defective product cannot be precisely identified. These situations involve products whose harmful characteristics are not known or do not become manifest for many years after the product was manufactured. Asbestos products and some drugs are examples of this type of product. A case involving the drug DES, which has a long latency period before its cancer-causing propensities become manifest in daughters of mothers who took the drug during pregnancy, was decided by the California Supreme Court. In *Sindell* v. *Abbott Laboratories, Inc.,*[82] the plaintiff was unable to identify which firm had manufactured the drug and sued several manufacturers on the theory that each manufacturer should be held liable for that portion of the plaintiff's injuries represented by each manufacturer's share of the total sales of the drug. The Court upheld this theory, although it allowed individual firms to escape liability if the firm could establish that its drug could not have been consumed by the plaintiff's mother.

This market-share liability theory has implications for manufacturers of generic products, since all manufacturers of the same generic product are potentially liable for their market share of injuries caused by defects inherent in the product. Some commentators have suggested that generic drug manufacturers should design their products and packaging in distinctive ways (and thereby become nongeneric) so that purchasers would certainly remember whether they consumed such a distinctive product. Others have suggested that careful long-term record keeping as to the distribution of the product would allow the manufacturer to offer conclusive proof that its product could not have been consumed by the plaintiff.

Product Liability Insurance

Strict liability for defective products presents considerable risk for firms. With liability being based on the existence of a defect rather than on the negligence of the seller, there is little that can be done to escape liability for personal injuries caused by a product that is found to be defective. While extra care and

[82] 26 Cal. 3d 588, 163 Cal. Rptr. 132 (1980).

caution can go a long way toward minimizing liability by discovering defects before the product reaches the market, ultimately a firm faces liability simply because courts have insisted that product-related injuries are to be treated as a cost of doing business. In that event, any particular firm might want to avoid the risk of a devastatingly large liability by obtaining insurance against this risk.

Obtaining insurance against the risks of liability for defective products has become a subject of considerable controversy in the past few years. Apparently, some businesses simply are not able to obtain insurance coverage at *any* premium level; other businesses have been faced with drastic increases in premiums. Some state legislatures have attempted to place limits on exposure for products sold many years ago by enacting "statutes of repose," which prohibit actions based on product defects where the product was sold or placed in service more than a certain period before an injured plaintiff files a lawsuit.[83] And, more recently, Congress has enacted legislation that will allow firms to organize their own collective insurance companies without fear that such collusive action might violate the antitrust laws.[84] Whether these organizations will be able to provide insurance protection at reasonable rates remains to be seen.

GOVERNMENT REGULATION OF FOODS, DRUGS, AND CONSUMER PRODUCTS

In addition to the requirements imposed on firms by warranty and tort law, many products are subject to extensive oversight by various government agencies. For example, foods, drugs, devices, and cosmetics are subject to regulation by the Food and Drug Administration, as are products that emit radiation, such as microwave ovens; meat, poultry, and egg products are regulated by the United States Department of Agriculture; alcohol, tobacco, and firearm products are regulated by the United States Treasury Department; and automobiles are regulated by a division of the United States Department of Commerce.

Much of this regulation is comprehensive. For example, under the Food, Drug, Device and Cosmetic Act, products must be safe, properly and nondeceptively labeled, and not adulterated or misbranded. Labels must contain specified information (e.g., drug labels must include appropriate directions for use and must indicate specific risks of consuming the product). Products that do not meet these quality or labeling requirements can be seized and condemned, and criminal sanctions and injunctions can be used against violators of the requirements.

An extensive, but by no means complete, list of products and the federal agencies that regulate the manufacture or sale of each product is contained in Table 3-1.

---

[83] See McGovern, *The Variety, Policy and Constitutionality of Product Liability Statutes of Repose*, 30 Am. U. Law Rev. 579 (1981).

[84] See Product Liability Risk Retention Act, 15 U.S.C. §3901 et. seq. (Supp V, 1981).

Table 3-1

Federal Agency and Products Regulated	Nature of Regulation[a]					
	Packaging Requirements	Labeling or Disclosure Requirements	Minimum Quality or Performance Standards	Mandatory Warranties	Grading Standards or Testing Protocols	Licenses or Permits
Department of Agriculture	X	X	X		X	X
Meat and meat products						
Poultry and poultry products						
Eggs and egg products						
Fruits						
Vegetables						
Seeds						
Department of Commerce	X	X				
Seafood						
Fire detection devices						
Fire extinguishing devices						
Consumer products						
Fruits						
Vegetables						
Testing laboratories						
Consumer Product Safety Commission	X	X	X		X	
Consumer products						
Flammable fabrics						
Poisons						
Hazardous substances						
Bicycles						
Toys						
Refrigerators						
Department of Energy						
Energy-consuming consumer products, including:						

Dishwashers
Refrigerators and freezers
Clothes washers and dryers
Water heaters
Air conditioners
Home heating equipment
Televisions
Furnaces
Kitchen ranges and ovens
Humidifiers and dehumidifiers

Environmental Protection Agency

Motor vehicles
Engines
Fuels and fuel additives
Noise emitting and reducing products
Insecticides, pesticides, and rodenticides
Poisons
Insect and rodent traps and repellents

Federal Trade Commission

Light bulbs
Binoculars
Transistor radios
Sewing machines
High-fidelity amplifiers
Energy-consuming appliances
Consumer commodities and products
Foods
Drugs
Cosmetics
Medical devices
Wool, fur, and textile products
Cigarettes

Table 3-1 (Cont'd)

Federal Agency and Products Regulated	Nature of Regulation[a]					
	Packaging Requirements	Labeling or Disclosure Requirements	Minimum Quality or Performance Standards	Mandatory Warranties	Grading Standards or Testing Protocols	Licenses or Permits
Food and Drug Administration						
Foods						
Drugs						
Cosmetics						
Medical devices						
Biological products	X	X				
Hearing aids			X		X	X
Radiation-emitting products (Microwave ovens)						
Clinical laboratories						
Department of Housing and Urban Development						
Land						
Mobile homes		X	X			
Department of Transportation						
Motor vehicles						
Tires		X	X		X	
Boats						
Department of the Treasury						
Imported goods						
Alcoholic beverages	X	X				
Tobacco products						X

[a] The possible forms of regulation that might be exercised by each agency are indicated by an X in the appropriate column; however, the agency may not be authorized to exercise all forms of regulation with respect to all the products within its jurisdiction.

Two product categories are examined in some detail next: foods and drugs (together with devices and cosmetics). In addition, we have also focused on the activities of the Consumer Product Safety Commission, since it has authority to regulate the widest variety of consumer products. However, a comprehensive discussion of the governmental regulation of *each* type of product offered in the marketplace is not presented in this text. As a general caveat, we believe that marketing executives should be cautioned that they will need considerable particularized expert advice to determine whether their products are subject to governmental packaging, labeling, and safety standards and requirements. In addition, state and local governments may regulate products that are also regulated at the federal level; accordingly, it is necessary for executives to be aware of these regulations as well.

Regulation of Food Products

The marketing of food and food products is subject to regulation by two federal agencies, the U.S. Department of Agriculture and the Food and Drug Administration (located in the U.S. Department of Health and Human Services). The USDA has authority over agricultural products such as meat, poultry, eggs, fruits, and vegetables, and the FDA has authority over most other food products. Both agencies are authorized to inspect the manufacturing and processing facilities through which these products pass or in which they are made. In addition to the inspection of plants, the USDA is required to inspect the products themselves if the products consist of meat or poultry. Both agencies can take action against the manufacture, sale, distribution, or receipt of products that are deemed "adulterated" or "misbranded" (see Appendix). Both agencies have authority to establish standards of identity and appropriate names for products within their respective jurisdictions. In addition, the USDA has established quality grading systems for most products under its jurisdiction, although use of its grading systems is not required.

Food Identity Standards.

Congress authorized the USDA and FDA to enact standards of identity in 1938 in order to allow the government to act against "economic adulteration." This particular form of consumer fraud consisted of practices such as adding water to milk, chicory to coffee, cereal to sausage, and additional sugar to jam (thereby diluting the content of the principal ingredient), without disclosing the extent of the dilution or adulteration to the consumer and thereby passing off the diluted product as an unadulterated equivalent. While commentators have suggested that requirements for disclosing ingredients in labeling would maximize consumer welfare, the government agencies continue to promulgate precise recipes for specific foods and meat products.[85]

---

[85] Merrill and Collier, *Like Mother Used to Make: An Analysis of FDA Food Standards of Identity,* 74 Colum. L. Rev. 561 (1974).

Courts have generally deferred to agency discretion in the promulgating of standards of identity and have even gone so far as to allow the agencies to prescribe preparation processes for the sole purpose of ensuring that a food product tastes as the consumer expects it to taste. For example, in *Atlas Powder Co.* v. *Ewing,*[86] the court upheld the FDA's prohibition of the use of a softening agent in bread products. Even though consumers could not tell the difference between fresh bread and artificially softened older bread, and although there was no evidence of any nutritional differences in products, the FDA's prohibition was upheld in order to prevent consumer deception as to bread freshness. However, some standards of identity that specified a preparation process rather than a list of acceptable ingredients and that were designed to preserve consumer expectations as to taste of the product have been struck down by courts. For example, the court in *Tennessee Valley Ham Co., Inc.* v. *Bergland*[87] found that a regulation setting standards for "country" and "country-style" hams and pork shoulders could not be supported on a rational basis. The Department of Agriculture had not investigated consumer preferences and expectations as to the taste of "country" or "country-style" hams. The court also found that the minimum cure and aging periods were not based on relevant evidence.

Regulation of Drugs, Devices, and Cosmetics

Drugs,[88] devices,[89] and cosmetics[90] are subject to even more extensive regulation than foods. For example, a "new drug"[91] cannot be marketed until it has been approved by the FDA; the FDA will not approve a new drug application unless it believes that the drug is generally recognized by experts as being safe and effective. This premarket approval process is lengthy and costly and has been blamed for a supposed lag in the marketing of new drugs. Drugs that are generally recognized as safe and effective can be marketed without having to go through this process.

The question of whether a drug is "new" and must go through the complete new drug approval process has arisen in connection with the marketing of "generic" drugs. These drugs, also known as "copycat" or "me-too" drugs,

[86] 201 F.2d 347 (3d Cir. 1952).

[87] 493 F. Supp. 1007 (W.D. Tenn. 1980).

[88] "Drug" is defined by the FFDCA as an article that is "(A) recognized in the Official U.S. Pharmacopeia . . . (B) . . . intended for use in the diagnosis, cure, mitigation, treatment, or prevention of disease in man or other animals; and (C) . . . intended to affect the structure or any function of the body of man or other animals . . ." 21 U.S.C. §321(g)(1).

A "device" is defined as "an instrument, apparatus, implement, machine, contrivance, implant, [or] in vitro reagent . . . which is . . . intended for use in the diagnosis . . . cure, mitigation, treatment, or prevention of disease . . . or . . . intended to affect the structure or any function of the body . . ." and which does not work through chemical action or metabolization. 21 U.S.C. §321(h) (1976).

[89] FFDCA, §201(h), 21 U.S.C. §321(h) (1976).

[90] FFDCA, §201(i), 21 U.S.C. §321(i) (1976). C23.10.

[91] A "new drug" is a drug that was not regulated under prior law and is not generally recognized by experts as safe and effective, or is so recognized but has not been used for a sufficiently long period of time or administered to a sufficiently large number of users. FFDCA, §201(p), 21 U.S.C. §321(p) (1976).

contain the same active ingredients as drugs that the FDA had previously approved but whose patent protection has expired, thus allowing competitors to manufacture and sell the drug at competitive prices. If the generic drug contains the same active ingredients but different inactive ingredients than the previously approved drug, the FDA requires the generic drug to go through the entire new drug application process if there is any reasonable possibility that the presence of different inactive ingredients will make the generic drug less safe and effective than the pioneer drug. The Supreme Court, in *United States* v. *Generix Drug Corp.,*[92] upheld the FDA's requirements. A generic drug manufacturer had objected to the FDA requirements on the ground that compliance with the full new drug application requirements would deprive consumers of the opportunity to purchase prescription drugs at lower prices. But the District Court had found that differences in inactive ingredients could result in different bioavailabilities of the active ingredients (comparing the generic drug and the pioneer drug) and that these differences might make the generic drug less safe and effective. Faced with these findings, the Supreme Court upheld the FDA interpretation of the statute. The District Court did require the FDA to show a "reasonable possibility" that a generic drug is not bioequivalent to an approved drug in order to enjoin distribution of the generic drug. The effect of the Supreme Court's decision is that generic drug marketers must either make sure that the generic drug is an exact copy of the pioneer drug or that any differences in the drugs are virtually certain to produce no different impact on users.

Because of the differing requirements for premarketing clearance of foods and drugs, disputes frequently arise as to whether a particular product is a drug or a food. For example, the FDA contended that a product known as a "starch blocker" was a drug and not a food, even though it was derived from a food and was supposed to be consumed as part of a diet. Because no safety and effectiveness testing had been evaluated by the FDA, the agency said the product could not lawfully be sold. A court supported the FDA and ordered that the product be removed from the market.[93]

The FDA publishes a list of those drugs that it considers as meeting the "generally recognized as safe and effective" standard.[94] The agency is in the process of evaluating the safety and effectiveness of therapeutic classes of over-the-counter drugs; to date, the review process has been completed for only one class, antacids.[95] Drugs that are not found to be generally recognized as safe and effective after this review process will be removed from the market unless they can successfully meet the FDA's standards of approval for new drugs.

Like foods, the Food, Drug, and Cosmetic Act defines the conditions under

---

[92] 51 U.S.L.W. 4282 (U.S., Mar. 22, 1983).

[93] *Nutrilab, Inc.* v. *Schweiker,* 547 F. Supp. 880 (N.D. Ill. 1982), *Aff'd,* 713 F.2d 335 (7th Cir. 1983).

[94] Drugs that the FDA considers to be generally recognized as safe and effective are listed at 21 C.F.R. 182 (1982).

[95] OTC Review of Antacids 21 C.F.R. 331 (1982).

which drugs and devices will be considered "adulterated" or "misbranded" and therefore not marketable (see Appendix).

In addition to its authority to deal with adulterated and misbranded articles, the FDA also has other important powers. For example, it can ban devices that present an unreasonable and substantial risk of illness or injury or of substantial deception. It can order the manufacturer of such a device to repair, replace, or refund the purchase price of such a device if it was not manufactured properly, given the state of the art at the time of manufacture, and if a notice to users will not eliminate the unreasonable risk of harm. The FDA can publicly disseminate information about imminent dangers to health or gross deceptions of consumers; the FDA has done this frequently when food is suspected to contain poison such as botulism. Although the FDA cannot compel a product recall, it can obtain a seizure and condemnation order from a court.

Most prescription drugs are not required to carry warning labels, since the physician involvement in the treatment and prescribing process is presumed to result in the consumer's being adequately informed as to risks of harm. Several product liability cases have reinforced this notion by indicating that users of prescription drugs cannot recover from drug manufacturers for failure to provide warnings to the consumer as to contraindications for use.[96] However, the FDA has authority to require pharmacists to include "patient package inserts" when dispensing certain drugs. The most notable example of this requirement involves warnings as to risks associated with oral contraceptives. Proposals have been made to abolish this program on the ground that patients are being frightened into avoiding the use of needed medications, although studies suggest that few consumers actually have these reactions to the inserts.[97]

Regulation of Products by the Consumer Product Safety Commission

Apart from regulation of specific products by highly specialized agencies such as the FDA, the regulatory agency with jurisdiction over most other products is the Consumer Product Safety Commission. The CPSC was established by Congress in 1972 in response to public concern over the safety of all consumer products. The CPSC was established for several purposes: (1) to protect the public against unreasonable risks of injury associated with consumer products; (2) to develop uniform safety standards for products that would preempt conflicting state and local regulations; (3) to promote research into the causes of and methods of preventing product-related deaths, illnesses, and injuries; and (4) to assist consumers in evaluating the comparative safety of consumer products.[98] In addition to administering the Consumer Product Safety Act, the CPSC administers several acts that predated the Commission, including the

[96] *Seley* v. *G. D. Searle, Inc.*, 67 Ohio St. 2d 192, 423 N.E.2d 831 (1981).

[97] *Consumer Reports*, July 1982, p. 346.

[98] Consumer Product Safety Act, 15 U.S.C. §2051 (1976).

Flammable Fabrics Act, the Federal Hazardous Substances Act, and the Poison Prevention Packaging Act of 1970. Before the CPSC can act under the general provisions of the Consumer Product Safety Act, it is compelled to determine whether regulation under one of these earlier acts would be adequate.[99]

The CPSC's Authority to Ban Unsafe Products

Acting under the Federal Hazardous Substances Act, the CPSC may act to declare a product a "hazardous substance" or a "banned hazardous substance." A hazardous substance is defined as any substance that is toxic, corrosive, an irritant, a strong sensitizer, flammable or combustible, or that generates pressure through decomposition, heat, or other means, if substantial personal injury or illness may foreseeably result from usual handling or use or from ingestion by children.[100] In addition, any toy that presents an electrical, mechanical, or thermal hazard is a hazardous substance.[101] All hazardous substances intended for use by children can be banned, as can any other hazardous substance (if intended or packaged for household use) if, notwithstanding cautionary labeling, the degree or nature of the hazard is such that "public health and safety can adequately be served" only by a ban.[102] Although the CPSC usually acts through full rule-making procedures, it has authority to declare a hazardous substance a "banned hazardous substance" when it presents an "imminent hazard to the public health."[103]

Acting pursuant to the Federal Hazardous Substances Act, the CPSC has banned some fireworks devices.[104] It also has acted, pursuant to the Child Protection Act of 1966 and the Child Protection and Toy Safety Act of 1969, to ban the sale of toys that present thermal, electrical, or mechanical hazards (by virtue of wires, attachments, protrusions, etc. that might cause lacerations, puncture wounds, aspiration, or other injury).[105] Under this rule, toy rattles, dolls, stuffed animals, pacifiers, cribs, and bicycles are banned if they present such hazards or fail to comply with detailed regulations.[106]

In the period since it came into existence, the CPSC, acting under the Consumer Product Safety Act, has banned unstable refuse bins, flammable contact adhesives, lead-based paints, and certain asbestos-containing products. A recent controversy at the CPSC involves urea formaldehyde insulation for homes. The CPSC believes that the product, after it is installed in a home (by being pumped into walls of existing homes), gives off fumes that penetrate the

[99] Ibid., §2079(d).

[100] Federal Hazardous Substances Act, 15 U.S.C. §1261(f) (1976). All these terms are further defined in the same statute.

[101] Ibid.

[102] Ibid., §1261(q)(1).

[103] Ibid., §1262(e)(2).

[104] 16 C.F.R. §1630 (1982).

[105] 16 C.F.R. §1500.18 (1982).

[106] Ibid.

living environment and may cause cancer. The CPSC concluded that the product could not be made safe in use and therefore it completely banned the product. However, the ban was overturned because of insufficient evidence to support the finding that the cancer risk was "unreasonable."[107]

The shipping or receipt of misbranded[108] or banned hazardous substances is prohibited and punishable by fine or imprisonment unless done in good faith,[109] and such products can be seized and destroyed. All marketers in the distribution chain can be compelled to repurchase banned hazardous substances from those to whom the article was sold, paying the purchase price plus transportation charges to return the article.[110]

The CPSC's Authority to Set Safety Standards

Under the Consumer Product Safety Act, the CPSC's major authority is to set product safety standards that are "reasonably necessary to prevent or reduce an unreasonable risk of injury"[111] associated with a particular product; in fact, product bans are appropriate only if the CPSC finds that no standard would adequately protect the public from the unreasonable risk of injury.[112]

Product manufacturers (and private labelers) are required to certify that any applicable product standards have been met. The manufacture, distribution, importation, or sale of a banned hazardous product or a product that does not meet safety standards, is prohibited.[113] If a firm discovers that its product does not meet any applicable product safety standard, it must notify the commission.[114] The CPSC can bring suit to seize any product that is "imminently hazardous";[115] the firm can be required to recall the product by giving notice to purchasers and to repair, replace or refund the price of the product.[116]

The CPSC has promulgated detailed safety standards for the following products: architectural glazing materials, matchbooks, walk-behind power mowers, swimming pool slides, bicycles, cellulose insulation, CB base station and TV antennas, and gas-fired space heaters. When the CPSC establishes a standard, it also frequently will specify the testing protocols for determining whether a product fails to meet the standard. For example, test protocols have been established for determining toxicity, skin and eye irritability, flammabili-

---

[107] *Gulf South Insulation* v. *Consumer Product Safety Comm'n,* 701 F.2d 1137 (5th Cir. 1983).

[108] A "misbranded hazardous substance" is a hazardous household substance that does not have proper packaging or labeling under the Poison Prevention Packaging Act or fails to have a label containing conspicuous warnings, identification of hazards, precautionary measures, first-aid instructions, and other required information 15 U.S.C. §1261(p).

[109] 15 U.S.C. §1264.

[110] 15 U.S.C. §1274.

[111] Consumer Product Safety Act, 15 U.S.C. §2056 (1976 & Supp V, 1981).

[112] Ibid., §§2057, 2058.

[113] Ibid., §2068.

[114] Ibid., §2064(1).

[115] Ibid., §2061.

[116] Ibid., §§2064(c) & (d), 50 U.S. Law Week, April 13, 1982. p. 2600.

ty, sound loudness, sharpness of points and edges, and so on. The CPSC also establishes exemptions from bans or labeling requirements under appropriate circumstances.

Two of the CPSC's safety standards promulgated under this section have been successfully challenged in court on the ground that the CPSC did not have sufficient evidence to justify the promulgation of a safety standard. In *Aqua Slide 'N' Dive Corp.* v. *CPSC,* [117] the CPSC's requirement of warning signs on swimming pool slides was not supported by substantial evidence that signs were reasonably necessary to eliminate or reduce an unreasonable risk. And in *Southland Mower Co.* v. *CPSC,* [118] the CPSC's foot-probe test for determining the safety of lawn mower discharge chutes was rejected because no reliable evidence indicated the number of injuries that would be prevented by use of the foot-probe test.

These judicial reviews of CPSC safety standards require that the CPSC accurately assess the frequency and severity of injury before embarking on the process of promulgating a safety standard; they also require the CPSC to accurately balance the costs of complying with the standard against the benefits to be gained from implementing the standard. Thus, although swimming pool slide injuries do produce serious injuries, they are very few in number. The CPSC warning requirement was condemned because there was no evidence that a warning would have prevented any substantial proportion of the relatively few injuries.

Is the Product within the CPSC's Jurisdiction?

The question of what products are covered by the Consumer Product Safety Act is not an easy one. For example, the CPSC asserted that an aerial tramway at an amusement park was a consumer product since it was produced or distributed "for personal use, consumption or enjoyment of a consumer . . . in recreation." The assertion of jurisdiction was upheld by the courts,[119] but Congress responded to these decisions by removing such permanently affixed rides from the category of "consumer products."[120] Although Congress has clearly excluded some products from coverage under the Act (tobacco products, motor vehicles, pesticides), coverage questions remain ambiguous in many cases. The CPSC's assertion of coverage has been upheld with respect to lawn mowers,[121] wired glass (as covered by the CPSC's architectural glazing materials rule),[122] and refuse bins located in an apartment complex and in violation of a

[117] 569 F.2d 831 (5th Cir. 1978).

[118] 619 F.2d 499 (5th Cir. 1980).

[119] *Robert K. Bell Enterprises, Inc.* v. *Consumer Product Safety Comm'n,* 484 F. Supp. 1221 (D. Okla. 1980); *State Fair of Texas* v. *Consumer Product Safety Comm'n,* 481 F. Supp. 1070 (D.Tex. 1979).

[120] Omnibus Budget Reconciliation Act of 1981, Pub. L. No. 97-35, §1213, 95 Stat. 724 (1981), amending 15 U.S.C. §2052(a)(1). Other amusement rides that are not permanently fixed to a site are consumer products under CPSC jurisdiction.

[121] *Southland Mower Co.* v. *Consumer Product Safety Comm'n,* 619 F.2d 499 (5th Cir. 1980).

[122] *ASG Industries* v. *Consumer Product Safety Comm'n,* 593 F.2d 1323 (D.C. Cir. 1979).

CPSC standard;[123] but jurisdiction over aluminum branch-circuit residential wiring has been denied.[124]

CPSC Information Gathering and Dissemination

One function that was given to the CPSC was to gather information about product accidents and to provide information to the public about the relative dangerousness of products. In attempting to carry out this mandate, the CPSC frequently requires firms to compile and furnish information about injuries related to the firm's products.

Disclosure of information can be unjustly harmful to a seller. On one occasion, the CPSC gathered information on injuries caused by television sets and then proposed to disseminate the information. The CPSC was enjoined from doing so because the CPSC had not taken the required steps to assure the accuracy and fairness of the information contained in the reports.[125] The Court found that not all manufacturers had been asked to respond to the request for data, that some questions about accident data were ambiguous, and that the data which the CPSC proposed to release did not form a reliable basis upon which consumers might make safety comparisons; accordingly, the CPSC was enjoined from releasing the data.

In any event, firms must receive advance notice before information is released that might identify them, either directly or indirectly. At that time, the firm can institute suit to restrain the disclosure because of any inaccuracy or unfairness in the publicity or because of the confidential or trade secret nature of the data. Congress recently provided that firms could submit comments in opposition to the proposed disclosure; at the request of the firm, such comment must be included with any CPSC disclosure of information.[126]

PACKAGING AND LABELING REGULATIONS

In many situations, the question of whether a product is defective and unreasonably dangerous or is unsafe will depend on the warnings and directions for use that are affixed to the product itself or to its packaging. We have not explored these labeling requirements in detail because, at least in the case of heavily regulated products, the labeling requirements are extremely detailed, complex, and specific to a particular product. We cannot include here the myriad of labeling requirements that consume thousands of pages of printed regulations. Instead, we focus on one law that has extremely widespread appli-

---

[123] *United States* v. *One Hazardous Product,* 487 F. Supp. 581 (D.N.J. 1980).

[124] See decision of U.S. District Court Judge Thomas A. Flannery, in CPSC suit against 26 manufacturers of wiring, as reported in *Consumer Reports,* 1982, p. 131. But see *Kaiser Aluminum & Chemical Corp.* v. *Consumer Product Safety Commission,* 574 F.2d 178 (D.C. Cir. 1979).

[125] *GTE Sylvania Inc.* v. *Consumer Product Safety Comm'n,* 598 F.2d 790 (3d Cir. 1979), *aff'd,* 447 U.S. 102 (1980).

[126] 15 U.S.C. §2055(b)(1).

cation, the Fair Packaging and Labeling Act, and then briefly describe laws that require disclosure of pricing and other information designed to assist consumers in making more informed purchasing decisions.

The Fair Packaging and Labeling Act

The most important general labeling law is the federal Fair Packaging and Labeling Act (FPLA),[127] which is implemented by regulations of the Federal Trade Commission[128] and of the Food and Drug Administration. The Act applies to all "consumer commodities." The purpose of the act was to allow consumers to obtain "accurate information as to the quantity of the contents" of a packaged commodity and thus to "facilitate value comparisons." The FTC was given authority to exempt products from coverage under the Act if the ability of consumers to make value comparisons would not be aided by the labeling requirements of the Act. A few FTC interpretations seem surprising: sponges, waxes, and solvents for home use are consumer commodities, but rubber gloves and clothes pins are not.[129]

The FPLA requires that each packaged consumer commodity bear a label specifying the identity of the commodity, the name and place of business of the manufacturer, packer, or distributor, the net quantity of the contents, and, if applicable, a statement of the net quantity used in estimating the number of servings, uses, or applications contained within the package. The net quantity should be expressed in units making value comparisons easier for consumers. Standards of measurement and preferred methods of expressing units of measurement are specified in the regulations. Locations, type sizes, and other features of labeling also are specified by the regulations. The extent of variability in net contents is prescribed, but only in general terms.

The FTC has enacted special rules for particular products, such as film, candles, sponges, Christmas tree ornaments, chamois, and vacuum cleaner replacement bags. And detailed regulations exist to prevent deceptive use of "cents-off," "introductory offer," and "economy size" representations on labels.[130]

State Unit Pricing Laws

The FPLA and its accompanying regulations have been criticized on the ground that value comparisons have not been significantly enhanced. The FPLA does not require firms to adopt standard package sizes or to disclose either the price of the package or a price for each unit of the product contained in the package. The law thus does little by way of accomplishing its stated purpose of facilitating value comparisons. To fill some of this void, several

[127] Fair Packaging and Labeling Act, 15 U.S.C. §1451 (1976 of Supp V, 1981).

[128] The FTC regulations are codified at 16 C.F.R. Part 500 (1982).

[129] 16 C.F.R. Part 503 (1982).

[130] 16 C.F.R. Part 502 (1982).

states and municipalities have enacted *unit pricing laws* that require retailers to provide consumers with standardized price-per-unit-of-quantity information for many products.

Other Product Labeling and Disclosure Requirements

During the decades of the 1960s and 1970s, consumer lobbying groups petitioned for and obtained enactment of numerous federal laws that require sellers to disclose information about quality and the cost of operating or maintaining the product. Many of these disclosure laws require that specific information appear on a label attached to the product. Some of the products covered by these disclosure requirements and the information that must be disclosed are listed in Table 3-2.

Space limitations preclude discussion of the details of all these packaging and labeling laws; nor can all the numerous types of laws even be mentioned. Although each series of enactments has been a response to an expression of consumer desire for more information or protection, serious questions are being raised as to the cost-effectiveness of the regulations and the need for government intervention in this area.

Table 3-2

Product	Information
Automobile tires	Tires must be tested and graded, and the grades for expected treadwear, traction, and resistance to heat damage must appear on a label attached to the tire.
Residential thermal insulation	Insulation must be tested according to a protocol, and its relative insulating ability must be indicated by an R-value.
Household appliances	The amount of energy consumed by the appliance during a year must be disclosed on a label that also shows the range of energy costs for all appliances in the product class.
Gasoline	The octane rating of the gasoline, measured according to a procedure established by the FTC, must be disclosed on the pump.
Clothing	The FTC requires that clothing be labeled with instructions as to the proper care and method of cleaning the garment.
Automobiles	The estimated number of miles that the automobile will travel on a gallon of gasoline in both city and highway driving, as measured by the Environmental Protection Agency, must be indicated on a label attached to the automobile.
Light bulbs	The average life of the light bulb and the amount of light produced by the bulb must be disclosed on the package.
Credit costs	The cost of credit (the "finance charge") and the cost expressed as an "annual percentage rate" must be disclosed to consumers under the Truth in Lending Act.

CONCLUSION

This chapter has described the myriad of laws that affect a firm's decisions about the quality level of its product offering. These laws seek to advance three major interests. First, they require a firm to abide by and honor its voluntarily assumed contracts and representations about the quality of its offering. Second, they seek to compensate persons who suffer injury as a result of a defect in a product. By making sellers liable for these injuries, the law encourages manufacturers to design and build safer products. Third, the laws seek to provide consumers with more information about products so that consumers can allocate resources in a way that more closely approximates their preferences.

Marketing decisions about the level of quality of a firm's product may be affected by laws which require that products be labeled with informative disclosures. If these required disclosures reveal to consumers that a firm's product is overpriced in relation to the price–quality combination of competitors, then the firm must improve the quality of its product or reduce its price. The law's requirements for disclosing information about the tar and nicotine content of cigarettes and about the gasoline mileage of automobiles undoubtedly have produced considerable concern for managers whose products ranked low on those dimensions of product quality.

The other objectives pursued by the law also have an impact on marketing decisions. By imposing liability on firms for damages caused by defective products, the law encourages firms to offer products that are safer and less likely to cause injury. The imposition of liability for failure to exercise due care in the manufacturing process requires firms to expend additional resources to make sure that production processes are turning out goods that comply with the firm's own quality standards as well as the standards of industry and of government. The imposition of liability for products that are defective because of design choices that result in an unacceptably high risk of injury to consumers forces firms to become aware of alternative product configurations and to carefully balance the costs of safer designs against the benefits of safer products. Although some judicial decisions involving allegedly defective product designs seemingly require firms to compensate injured consumers regardless of the cost or realistic possibilities of producing and selling a safer product, several state courts are showing sensitivity to the reality that a totally safe product would be so costly to produce that it could not be profitably marketed.

The law's imposition of liability for a firm's failure to adequately warn users about the dangers associated with a product requires firms to exercise care in evaluating the communicative effectiveness of its warnings. Firms must be aware not only of all possible uses and users of its products and the risks inherent in each use, but they also must be alert to common *misuses* of their products. They must find ways to communicate to users the nature of the safety risks and the ways of minimizing or avoiding those risks.

The duty implicit in the failure-to-warn-rule complements the duty imposed by the law on firms to honor their expressly assumed quality obligations. Both duties have the effect of enhancing the accuracy of information upon which consumers base their purchasing decisions. By requiring firms to warn users of risks associated with use of a product, consumers are informed of the true nature of the product. And by imposing liability on firms that fail to live up to the representations they make about the quality of their products, the law increases the accuracy of information used by consumers in their purchasing decisions.

Because firms are liable for representations about the safety and quality of their products, marketing managers must be alert to representations made in advertising, labeling, packaging, and other promotional efforts and must make sure that such representations are accurate and do not suggest or encourage conduct by purchasers that might lead to personal injury. Similarly, managers must take care to monitor the communications that are made by sales representatives. These communications may impose liability on firms under express warranty and implied fitness warranty rules. In addition, overly aggressive promotion of products can effectively negate printed warnings that otherwise would satisfy the law's requirements for adequate warnings.

One aspect of product quality, the nature and extent of warranties offered to purchasers, is heavily regulated by both federal and state law. State law generally leaves firms with considerable discretion as to whether a warranty will be offered to purchasers. If a firm chooses to do so, it can offer a product without any warranties, express or implied. A conspicuous disclaimer of the warranty of merchantability, coupled with the failure to make any representations or express warranties regarding product quality and the failure to offer any service contract, will suffice to avoid warranty liability (although it probably will not avoid liability for personal injury caused by a defective product). Again, competitive pressures may force a firm to offer some sort of warranty, and in that case federal law may severely constrain the ability of firms to limit liability under implied warranty theories.

Regulatory agencies play a large role in determining the quality level of a firm's product offering. Foods, drugs, cosmetics, hazardous substances, children's toys, and a host of products that present risks of causing personal injury are subject to numerous requirements, ranging from premarket demonstrations of safety and effectiveness of the product to required packaging and labeling. Firms offering products in these regulated areas must carefully comply with the requirements of the applicable administrative agency; failure to do so could result in seizure and destruction of nonconforming products or embarrassing and expensive product recalls.

Appendix

Under Section 402 of the Federal Food, Drug, and Cosmetic Act, 21 U.S.C. § 342, a *food* is deemed "adulterated" if it

(a) contains any poisonous or deleterious substance injurious to health;
(b) contains unsafe levels of food or color additives, new animal drugs or pesticides or other poisonous or deleterious added substance;*
(c) consists of any filthy, putrid, or decomposed substance or is otherwise unfit for food;
(d) was prepared, packed, or stored under unsanitary conditions;
(e) is contained in any package which makes the food injurious to health;
(f) has been impermissibly radiated;
(g) has been altered, added to, mixed or otherwise reduced in quality or strength or made to appear better or of greater value than it actually is.

Under Section 403 of the Food, Drug, and Cosmetic Act, 21 U.S.C. §343, a *food* is deemed "misbranded" if

(a) its labeling is "false or misleading in any particular";
(b) it is improperly named;
(c) it is an imitation of another food and its label does not prominently use the word "imitation";
(d) its label fails to indicate the name and place of business of the manufacturer, packer, or distributor;
(e) its label does not accurately state the quantity of the contents in terms of weight, measure, or count;
(f) any required label information is not prominently displayed with sufficient conspicuousness that ordinary consumers are likely to read and understand the information under normal conditions of purchase and use;
(g) it fails to comply with any standards of identity and fails to contain the standard name of the food, or if no standard of identity exists, it fails to use the common or usual name of the food and fails to list each ingredient used in its fabrication (except spices, flavorings, and colorings do not have to be specifically itemized);
(h) it is a special dietary food, unless its label bears other information about vitamins, minerals, and other dietary properties as the FDA requires;
(i) its labeling fails to disclose the presence of artificial flavoring or coloring, or any chemical preservative;
(j) if it contains saccharin and its label does not contain a warning that saccharin may be hazardous to health and has been determined to cause cancer in laboratory animals.

*Pursuant to the "Delaney Amendment," food additives are deemed unsafe unless they are affirmatively established to be safe by scientific evidence. Further, the FDA is prohibited from finding that a food additive is safe if it is known to induce cancer when ingested by man or animal.

Under Section 501 of the Food, Drug, and Cosmetic Act, 21 U.S.C. §351, a *drug* or *device* is considered "adulterated" if

(a) it contains any filthy, putrid, or decomposed substance;
(b) it has been prepared, packed or held under unsanitary conditions;
(c) it is not made in accordance with "good manufacturing practices" to assure that it has the safety, identity, strength, quality and purity characteristics which it is represented to possess;
(d) its container is poisonous or deleterious and may make the drug injurious to health;
(e) it contains an unsafe color additive;
(f) its strength, quality or purity falls below the standards set forth in any official drug compendium unless the differences are clearly set forth on the label, or, if the drug is undefined, its strength, quality or purity falls below the levels represented by the seller;
(g) its strength or quality has been reduced by substitution of another substance;
(h) it is a device and it
  1. does not comply with applicable performance standards;
  2. has not been given any required premarket approval by the FDA;
  3. has been banned; or
  4. has not been manufactured, stored, packed, or installed in accordance with applicable regulations.

Under Section 502 of the Food, Drug, and Cosmetic Act, 21 U.S.C. §352, a *drug* or *device* is considered "misbranded" if

(a) its label is false or misleading in any particular;
(b) its package is not labeled with the name and address of the manufacturer, packer or distributor and does not contain an accurate statement of the quantity of the contents in terms of weight, measure, or numerical count;
(c) any required label information is not prominently displayed with such conspicuousness as to make it likely to be read and understood by ordinary consumers under customary conditions of purchase and use;
(d) it is habit-forming and does not contain an appropriate warning;
(e) its label does not bear the established name of the drug or device and the name and quantity of each active ingredient;
(f) its label does not bear adequate directions for use and adequate warnings where use may be dangerous to health;
(g) it is not packaged and labeled as prescribed in an official compendium;
(h) it is subject to deterioration and is not appropriately packaged and labeled with precautions;
(i) its container is misleadingly formed, filled or made;
(j) it is dangerous to health when used as suggested on the label;
(k) it is insulin or an antibiotic and is from a batch for which a certificate of release has not been issued;
(l) it is a prescription drug or a restricted device and its advertisements fail to contain specific information as to its established name, its formula, and other information as to side effects, contraindications and effectiveness;
(m) it was manufactured in an unregistered establishment;
(n) its packaging or labeling does not comply with regulations under the Poison Prevention Packaging Act of 1970;
(o) it is a device and its labeling does not conform to performance regulations.

Case 1
A & M Produce Co. *v.* FMC Corp.,

135 Cal. App. 3d 473 (1982)

WIENER, Associate Justice.

Defendant FMC Corporation (FMC) appeals from the judgment entered in favor of plaintiff A & M Produce Co. (A & M) in the net sum of $255,000 plus $45,000 attorney's fees. Although this case has a rather humble origin arising from the simple business transaction in 1974 when FMC sold A & M an agricultural weight-sizing machine for $32,000, the issues now require our traversing the labyrinthine complexities of the Uniform Commercial Code, only partially illuminated by California precedent. Because of the nature of this case, we believe it helpful to state the facts before describing the issues and the manner in which they are resolved.

I.

A & M, a farming company in the Imperial Valley, is solely owned by C. Alex Abatti who has been farming all of his life. In late 1973, after talking with two of his employees, Mario Vanoni and Bill Billingsley, he decided to grow tomatoes. Although they had grown produce before, they had never grown tomatoes or any other crop requiring a weight-sizer and were not familiar with weight-sizing equipment. At the suggestion of Billingsley, they first spoke with a salesman from Decco Equipment Company regarding the purchase of the necessary equipment. The salesman explained A & M would need a hydrocooler in addition to a weight-sizer and submitted a bid of $60,000 to $68,000 for the equipment. Abatti thought the Decco bid was high, and Billingsley suggested Abatti contact FMC for a competitive bid.

In January 1974, A & M called FMC whose representative, John Walker, met with them at A & M's office. Walker admitted he was not an expert on the capacity or specifics of weight-sizing equipment. Later he brought Edgar Isch of FMC into the negotiations to assist in making the determination on the proper type of equipment. Isch did not say a hydrocooler was required. According to Abatti, Isch recommended FMC equipment because it operated so fast that a hydrocooler was unnecessary thereby saving A & M about $25,000.

117

The parties discussed the capacity of the sizing equipment recommended by Isch. Walker and Isch proposed a preliminary bid of $15,299.55 for the weight-sizer. They obtained Abatti's signature to a "field order" for the equipment to "secure Abatti's consent" to order the equipment. The field order did not state the final price nor list all the necessary material and equipment. The order was on a standard form, printed on both sides, the terms of which were identical to the written contract which Abatti later received. Along with the order, Abatti delivered his $5,000 check as a deposit. Walker and Isch left a copy of the capacity chart for FMC weight-sizers which had been referred to in the negotiations.

The field order was sent to FMC where the proposed lay-out of the packing shed was analyzed by the engineering department, and a final list of essential materials was compiled. Abatti then received a copy of the form contract in the mail. It contained a list of all the equipment and materials being purchased, either typed in blanks on the front of the contract, or handwritten on an attached order sheet. The total bill was for $32,041.80.

For our purposes the provisions of the agreement which are important are: paragraph 3, "Seller's Remedies" outlining the buyer's obligation to pay seller's reasonable attorney's fees in connection with any defaults by the seller; paragraph 4, "Warranty" containing a disclaimer of warranties, in bold print; and paragraph 5, "Disclaimer of Consequential Damages" stating in somewhat smaller print that "Seller in no event shall be liable for consequential damages arising out of or in connection with this agreement. . . ."

Abatti signed the agreement and returned it to FMC with his check for an additional $5,680.60 as a down payment. He never paid the $21,361.20 due "on delivery of equipment." In April 1974 FMC delivered and installed the machinery. A 20-foot extension to A & M's packing house was required to house the equipment. A & M's problems with the FMC equipment began during the third week of May, when it started to pick the tomatoes. Tomatoes piled up in front of the singulator belt which separated the tomatoes for weight-sizing. Overflow tomatoes had to be sent through the machinery again, causing damage to the crop. The damage was aggravated because the tomatoes were not cooled by a hydrocooler, allowing a fungus to spread more quickly within the damaged fruit. Walker was called out and managed to control the overflow by starting and stopping the machine. This effort was counterproductive, however, because it significantly reduced the processing speed. Unlike the Decco machinery, the FMC equipment did not have a speed control.

Abatti unsuccessfully attempted to get additional equipment from FMC and/or Decco. There was insufficient time to set up a new packing shed to hand-pick the tomatoes. Moreover, a search for other packing operators to handle A & M's tomatoes was unavailing. On June 17, A & M closed its shed because the return on the fruit—some of which had been damaged—was inadequate to cover costs. Some tomatoes were sold to a canning plant; most were rejected because they were not cannery tomatoes.

Shortly thereafter, A & M offered to return the weight-sizer to FMC provided FMC would refund A & M's down payment and pay the freight charges. FMC rejected this offer and demanded full payment of the balance due.

A & M then filed this action for damages against FMC for breach of express warranties, breach of implied warranty for a particular use and misrepresentation. A & M dismissed the misrepresentation cause of action at trial. By stipulation the trial was bifurcated to permit the judge to decide FMC's cross-complaint for the balance due on the purchase price and the issue of attorney's fees after the jury returned its verdict on the complaint.

This appeal is the result of a third trial. In the earlier two cases special verdict forms were used. The first case resulted in a hung jury; a new trial was ordered in the second.

After hearing evidence presented to the jury, and additional evidence in the absence of the jury on the nature of the contract's formation and the bargaining position of the respective parties, the court ruled:

> "[I]t would be unconscionable to enforce [the waivers of warranties and waiver of consequential damage] provisions of the agreement, and further that they are not set out in a conspicuous fashion.
> "The Court's ruling is based on all of the circumstances in this case in connection with how the negotiations were conducted, the fact that initially a down payment of—a substantial down payment of $5,000 was made and later on the contract was signed."

Accordingly, the jury viewed only the front of the contract, not the reverse side with its lengthy provisions.

The jury returned a general verdict for $281,326 which the parties agreed to reduce by $12,090.70, the amount already paid to FMC for the machinery. The court found for FMC on its cross-complaint, but awarded plaintiff $45,000 in attorney's fees and prejudgment interest from September 18, 1976.

II.

The major issues in this case involve the validity of FMC's purported disclaimer of warranties and limitation on the buyer's ability to recover consequential damages resulting from a breach of warranty.[1] Resolution of both these issues turns largely on the proper application of the doctrine of unconscionability, which the trial court utilized in precluding enforcement of the

---

[1] There exists some considerable confusion between the concept of disclaiming warranties and the concept of limiting or excluding remedies for breach of warranty. (See discussion in White and Summers. Uniform Commercial Code (2d ed. 1980) §12-11, pp. 471–472.) The former subject deals with the seller's attempt to limit the situations for which he can be held liable for breach. The latter subject assumes a breach has been established but attempts to limit the remedies available to the complaining party. In the instant contract, for example, we find much language located in the "Warranty" section which actually amounts to limitations on remedies available to the buyer. When the terms are properly sorted out, the only warranty appearing in the written document is that the material and workmanship of new equipment will be free from defects for various specified periods of time. Other language in the section purports to limit the remedy for breach of this single warranty to repair or replacement of defective parts, provided that the buyer pays for shipping the equipment to the seller and back at the seller's request.

warranty disclaimer and the consequential damage limitation. Although FMC concedes that California Uniform Commercial Code section 2719[2] allows a court under proper circumstances to declare a consequential damage limitation unconscionable, it argues that unconscionability is inapplicable to disclaimers of warranty, being supplanted by the more specific policing provisions of section 2316. We conclude otherwise, however, and turn our attention to the nature of this often-amorphous legal doctrine, outlining the analytic framework to be used in determining whether a particular contractual provision is unconscionable. That framework is then utilized in finding that the facts of this case, involving a preprinted form sales contract, support the trial court's conclusion that both the disclaimer of warranties and the limitation on consequential damages were unconscionable. We also reject FMC's argument that the consequential damages alleged by A & M were too speculative to be the basis for any damage award.

III.

FMC's initial attack on the judgment alleges prejudicial error by the trial court in not allowing the jury to see the reverse side of the written agreement which contained both a disclaimer of all warranties as well as a provision stating that in the event a warranty was made, the buyer was precluded from recovering consequential damages resulting from a breach of the warranty. The trial court's decision to exclude evidence of the contents of the agreement's reverse side was based on its determination that the warranty disclaimer and the consequential damage exclusions were unconscionable and therefore unenforceable.[3] If this determination was correct—that is, if the trial court properly applied the unconscionability doctrine to the facts of this case—then the reverse side of the contract was appropriately withheld from the jury.[4]

---

[2] All statutory references are to the Commercial Code unless otherwise indicated.

[3] The court's ruling was also based on the inconspicuousness of the disclaimer and exclusion provisions. As to the disclaimer of warranty, we agree with FMC that a disclaimer printed in boldface type twice as large as the other terms of the agreement is conspicuous. Section 1201, subdivision (10), specifically provides:

"A term or clause is conspicuous when it is so written that a reasonable person against whom it is to operate ought to have noticed it. A printed heading in capitals (as: NONNEGOTIABLE BILL OF LADING) is conspicuous. *Language in the body of a form is 'conspicuous' if it is in larger or other contrasting type or color.*" (Italics added.) This definition by its terms precludes the trial court's ruling on this issue. (See *FMC Finance Corp.* v. *Murphree* (1980) 632 F.2d 413, 419.)

In contrast to the provisions of section 2316, subdivision (2), which require that a warranty disclaimer be conspicuous, the code imposes no similar requirement as to consequential damage limitations. This is not to say the conspicuousness of such a term is irrelevant; rather, it it one of several factors bearing on the procedural unconscionability of the limitation. Is will therefore be considered in that context rather than as an independent basis for denying enforcement to the consequential damage exclusion.

[4] FMC has also argued that even if the disclaimer of warranty was unconscionable, evidence of the disclaimer clause's presence in the contract was admissible to suggest that no warranty was ever created by action of the parties. But assuming the unconscionability of the disclaimer, its value toward proving the factual proposition that no warranty was created is slight, and substantially outweighed by the disclaimer's tendency to unfairly prejudice and mislead the jury. (Evid.Code, §352.)

A

Acknowledging that a limitation on consequential damages may be unconscionable (§2719, subd. (3)),[5] FMC asserts the trial court erred in applying that doctrine to the disclaimer of warranties. It contends unconscionability is irrelevant to warranty disclaimer provisions, having been eliminated by the specific statutory requirements of section 2316.[6] Alternatively, FMC suggests the California Legislature's failure to adopt the general Uniform Commercial Code section on unconscionability (§2-302) as part of California's Commercial Code precludes the trial court's reliance on the doctrine in this instance.[7]

While FMC's argument is not without force, we conclude that an unconscionable disclaimer of warranty may be denied enforcement despite technical compliance with the requirements of section 2316. Unconscionability is a flexible doctrine designed to allow courts to directly consider numerous factors which may adulterate the contractual process. Uniform Commercial Code section 2-302 specifies that "any clause of the contract" may be unconscionable. The policing provisions of section 2316 are limited to problems involving the visibility of disclaimers and conflicts with express warranties. But oppression and unfair surprise, the principal targets of the unconscionability doctrine, may result from other types of questionable commercial practices. Moreover, the subtle distinction between an "implied" warranty and an "express" warranty may do precious little to mitigate the exploitation of a party with inferior bargaining power. Yet as long as the warranty remains "implied," section 2316's policing provisions are ineffective.

FMC's contention regarding the status of the unconscionability doctrine in California is similarly unpersuasive. Unconscionability has long been recognized as a common law doctrine which has been consistently applied by California courts in the absence of specific statutory authorization. And although the Legislature did not adopt section 2-302 as part of California's version of

[5] Subdivision (3) of section 2719 provides:
"Consequential damages may be limited or excluded unless the limitation or exclusion is unconscionable. Limitation of consequential damages for injury to the person in the case of consumer goods is invalid unless it is proved that the limitation is not unconscionable. Limitation of consequential damages where the loss is commercial is valid unless it is proved that the limitation is unconscionable."

[6] Section 2316 provides in relevant part:
"(1) Words or conduct relevant to the creation of an express warranty and words or conduct tending to negate or limit warranty shall be construed wherever reasonable as consistent with each other: but subject to the provisions of this division on parol or extrinsic evidence (Section 2202) negation or limitation is inoperative to the extent that such construction is unreasonable.
"(2) Subject to subdivision (3), to exclude or modify the implied warranty of merchantability or any part of it the language must mention merchantability and in case of a writing must be conspicuous. . . . Language to exclude all implied warranties of fitness is sufficient if it states, for example, that 'There are no warranties which extend beyond the description on the face hereof.' "

[7] Section 2-302 provides:
"(1) If the court as a matter of law finds the contract or any clause of the contract to have been unconscionable at the time it was made the court may refuse to enforce the contract, or it may enforce the remainder of the contract without the unconscionable clause, or it may so limit the application of any unconscionable clause as to avoid any unconscionable result.
"(2) When it is claimed or appears to the court that the contract or any clause thereof may be unconscionable the parties shall be afforded a reasonable opportunity to present evidence as to its commercial setting, purpose and effect to aid the court in making the determination."

the Uniform Commercial Code, the identical language, complete with accompanying commentary, was recently enacted as section 1670.5 of the Civil Code. The only significant difference is that section 1670.5, placed under the "Unlawful Contracts" heading of division 3, part 2, title 4 of the Civil Code, applies to all contracts rather than being limited to those sales transactions governed by the Commercial Code. We think the trial court properly entertained A & M's arguments directed at the unconscionability of both the consequential damage exclusion and the warranty disclaimer.[8]

B

We now turn to the principal question involved in this appeal: Whether the trial court erred in concluding that FMC's attempted disclaimer of warranties and exclusion of consequential damages was unconscionable and therefore unenforceable. Before we can answer that question however, we must first concern ourselves with the nature of the unconscionability doctrine.

The Uniform Commercial Code does not attempt to precisely define what is or is not "unconscionable." Nevertheless, "[u]nconscionability has generally been recognized to include an absence of meaningful choice on the part of one of the parties together with contract terms which are unreasonably favorable to the other party." Phrased another way, unconscionability has both a "procedural" and a "substantive" element.

The procedural element focuses on two factors: "oppression" and "surprise."

"Oppression" arises from an inequality of bargaining power which results in no real negotiation and "an absence of meaningful choice." "Surprise" involves the extent to which the supposedly agreed-upon terms of the bargain are hidden in a prolix printed form drafted by the party seeking to enforce the disputed terms. Characteristically, the form contract is drafted by the party with the superior bargaining position.

---

[8] Even were we to accept FMC's position that a warranty disclaimer may not be declared unconscionable, we believe the trial court's decision was harmless error under the circumstances of this case. Subdivision (1) of section 2316 (see *ante,* fn. 6), which FMC admits is applicable, specifically provides that an express warranty takes precedence over an attempted disclaimer where the two are not reasonably reconcilable and where evidence of the express warranty is not precluded by the Parol Evidence Rule. (see §2202.) At trial, A & M attempted to prove that FMC breached both the implied warranty of fitness for a particular purpose (see §2315) which may be negated by a conspicuous disclaimer (§2316, subd. (2)), and various express warranties made by FMC personnel which may not be disclaimed. But after our "examination of the entire cause, including the evidence" (Cal.Const., art. VI. §13), we do not think it reasonably probable the jury could have found breach of an implied warranty without also finding breach of an express one. (See *People* v. *Watson* (1956) 46 Cal.2d 818, 836, 299 P.2d 243; *Alarid* v. *Vanier* (1958) 50 Cal.2d 617, 625, 327 P.2d 897.) Under such circumstances, even had evidence of the disclaimer been before the jury, section 2316 would require them to disregard it where it conflicted with the express warranty.

Our conclusion that any error was harmless is supported by a record which contains more than ample evidence that FMC expressly warranted its weight-sizing machine would pack 1200–1250 cartons per hour. The major dispute in the testimony concerned what size cartons the warranty applied to. Thus, the questions was not so much whether an express warranty had been made, but rather whether the warranty had been breached. In addition, there was no impediment to proof of the express warranty in view of the trial court's implied finding that the parties did not intend the preprinted form contract drafted by FMC to be the "final expression of their agreement with respect to such terms as are included therein. . . ." (§2202.)

Of course the mere fact that a contract term is not read or understood by the non-drafting party or that the drafting party occupies a superior bargaining position will not authorize a court to refuse to enforce the contract. Although an argument can be made that contract terms not actively negotiated between the parties fall outside the "circle of assent"[9] which constitutes the actual agreement, commercial practicalities dictate that unbargained-for terms only be denied enforcement where they are also *substantively* unreasonable. No precise definition of substantive unconscionability can be proffered. Cases have talked in terms of "overly-harsh" or "one-sided" results. One commentator has pointed out, however, that ". . . unconscionability turns not only on a 'one-sided' result, but also on an absence of 'justification' for it," which is only to say that substantive unconscionability must be evaluated as of the time the contract was made. The most detailed and specific commentaries observe that a contract is largely an allocation of risks between the parties, and therefore that a contractual term is substantively suspect if it reallocates the risks of the bargain in a objectively unreasonable or unexpected manner. But not all unreasonable risk reallocations are unconscionable; rather, enforceability of the clause is tied to the procedural aspects of unconscionability such that the greater the unfair surprise or inequality of bargaining power, the less unreasonable the risk reallocation which will be tolerated.

Although there is little California precedent directly on point, the importance of both the procedural and substantive elements of unconscionability finds support by analogy in the recent decision by the Supreme Court in *Graham* v. *Scissor-Tail, Inc., supra,* 28 Cal.3d 807, 171 Cal.Rptr. 604, 623 P.2d 165.[10] Graham, a music promoter, booked concerts for a group of musicians incorporated under the name of "Scissor-Tail." A standard form contract drafted by the musicians' union provided that the arbitrator for all contract disputes was to be selected by the union. Graham challenged enforcement of the clause, arguing that an arbitrator so selected was presumptively biased in favor of the musicians.

The court first determined that the contract was one of adhesion, noting that although Graham was a prominent and successful rock music promoter, the union—which represented nearly all significant musicians—mandated that promotion agreements be "negotiated" pursuant to standard union-prepared contracts. In language closely approximating the "unequal bargaining power"

---

[9] In the words of Professor Murray:

"One of the fundamental concepts of contract law is the concept of *assent.* The basic idea that parties exercise their volition by committing themselves to future action and that the law provides their *circle of assent* with the status of a private law is fundamental to any discussion of contracts. The two basic questions raised are: (1) Did the parties agree to any future action or inaction? (2) If they did agree, what are the terms of their agreement (or, what is their circle of assent)?"

(Murray on Contracts (2d ed. 1974) §352, p. 743; first italics in original, second italics added.)

[10] Although the contract in *Graham* was not governed by the Uniform Commercial Code, and although much of the court's discussion is phrased in non-code terminology, the similarity of factors considered leads to the conclusion that unconscionability is a doctrine fundamental to the operation of contract law, irrespective of the particular application. In apparent recognition of this fact, the Legislature's belated decision to adopt Uniform Commercial Code section 2-302 codifies the unconscionability doctrine in Civil Code section 1670.5, applicable to all types of contracts, rather than as part of the Uniform Commercial Code.

prong of the procedural unconscionability factor, the court concluded that Graham ". . . was required by the realities of his business as a concert promoter to sign [union] form contracts with *any* concert artist with whom he wished to do business. . . ."

Moving next to a discussion paralleling the "unfair surprise" prong of procedural unconscionability, the court determined that Graham was not surprised by the inclusion of the arbitration clause. It relied on the course of dealing between the parties as well as Graham's vast experience in the music industry in concluding that neither the inclusion of the arbitration clause nor its effect were outside of Graham's "reasonable expectations."

Finally, in a discourse resembling substantive unconscionability analysis, the court indicated that " 'contractual machinery [must] operate within some minimal levels of integrity.' " The contract in *Graham* did not attain this "minimal level" because the arbitration clause left the "adhering" party without any real and fair opportunity to prevail in the event of a contractual dispute. In the language of substantive unconscionability, all the risks were allocated to Graham who was forced to accept the contract without negotiation. Not surprisingly, the court's conclusion denying enforcement to the arbitration clause on unconscionability grounds ties procedural and substantive elements together:

> "[W]e are of the view that the 'minimum levels of integrity' which are requisite to a contractual arrangement for the nonjudicial resolution of disputes are not achieved by an arrangement which designates the union of one of the parties as the arbitrator of disputes arising out of employment—especially when, as here, the arrangement is the product of circumstances indicative of adhesion."

With these considerations in mind, we must now determine whether the trial court in this case was correct in concluding that the clauses in the FMC form contract disclaiming all warranties and excluding consequential damages were unconscionable. In doing so, we keep in mind that while unconscionability is ultimately a question of law, numerous factual inquiries bear upon that question. The business conditions under which the contract was formed directly affect the parties' relative bargaining power, reasonable expectations, and the commercial reasonableness of the risk allocation as provided in the written agreement. To the extent there are conflicts in the evidence or in the factual inferences which may be drawn therefrom, we must assume a set of facts consistent with the court's finding of unconscionability if such an assumption is supported by substantial evidence.

Turning first to the procedural aspects of unconscionability, we note at the outset that this contract arises in a commercial context between an enormous diversified corporation (FMC) and a relatively small but experienced farming company (A & M). Generally, ". . . courts have not been solicitous of businessmen in the name of unconscionability." This is probably because courts view businessmen as possessed of a greater degree of commercial understanding and substantially more economic muscle than the ordinary consumer.

Hence, a businessman usually has a more difficult time establishing procedural unconscionability in the sense of either "unfair surprise" or "unequal bargaining power."

Nevertheless, generalizations are always subject to exceptions and categorization is rarely an adequate substitute for analysis. With increasing frequency, courts have begun to recognize that experienced but legally unsophisticated businessmen may be unfairly surprised by unconscionable contract terms, and that even large business entities may have *relatively* little bargaining power, depending on the identity of the other contracting party and the commercial circumstances surrounding the agreement. This recognition rests on the conviction that the social benefits associated with freedom of contract are severely skewed where it appears that had the party actually been aware of the term to which he "agreed" or had he any real choice in the matter, he would never have assented to inclusion of the term.

Both aspects of procedural unconscionability appear to be present on the facts of this case. Although the printing used on the warranty disclaimer was conspicuous (see *ante,* fn. 4), the terms of the consequential damage exclusion are not particularly apparent, being only slightly larger than most of the other contract text. Both provisions appear in the middle of the back page of a long preprinted form contract which was only casually shown to Abatti. It was never suggested to him, either verbally or in writing, that he read the back of the form. Abatti testified he never read the reverse side terms. There was thus sufficient evidence before the trial court to conclude that Abatti was in fact surprised by the warranty disclaimer and the consequential damage exclusion. How "unfair" his surprise was is subject to some dispute. He certainly had the opportunity to read the back of the contract or to seek the advice of a lawyer. Yet as a factual matter, given the complexity of the terms and FMC's failure to direct his attention to them, Abatti's omission may not be totally unreasonable. In this regard, the comments of the Indiana Supreme Court in *Weaver* v. *American Oil Company,* 276 N.E.2d at pp. 147–148 are apposite:

> "The burden should be on the party submitting [a standard contract] in printed form to show that the other party had knowledge of any unusual or unconscionable terms contained therein. The principle should be the same as that applicable to implied warranties, namely that a package of goods sold to a purchaser is fit for the purposes intended and contains no harmful materials other than that represented."

Here, FMC made no attempt to provide A & M with the requisite knowledge of the disclaimer or the exclusion. In fact, one suspects that the length, complexity and obtuseness of most form contracts may be due at least in part to the seller's preference that the buyer will be dissuaded from reading that to which he is supposedly agreeing. This process almost inevitably results in a one-sided "contract."

Even if we ignore any suggestion of unfair surprise, there is ample evidence of unequal bargaining power here and a lack of any real negotiation over the terms of the contract. Although it was conceded that A & M was a large-scale farming enterprise by Imperial Valley standards, employing five persons on a regular basis and up to fifty seasonal employees at harvest time, and that Abatti was farming some 8,000 acres in 1974, FMC Corporation is in an entirely different category. The 1974 gross sales of the Agriculture Machinery Division alone amounted to $40 million. More importantly, the terms of the FMC form contract were standard. FMC salesmen were not authorized to negotiate any of the terms appearing on the reverse side of the preprinted contract.[11] Although FMC contends that in some special instances, individual contracts are negotiated, A & M was never made aware of that option. The sum total of these circumstances leads to the conclusion that this contract was a "bargain" only in the most general sense of the word.

Although the procedural aspects of unconscionability are present in this case, we suspect the substantive unconscionability of the disclaimer and exclusion provisions contributed equally to the trial court's ultimate conclusion. As to the disclaimer of warranties, the facts of this case support the trial court's conclusion that such disclaimer was commercially unreasonable. The warranty allegedly breached by FMC went to the basic performance characteristics of the product. In attempting to disclaim this and all other warranties, FMC was in essence guarantying nothing about what the product would do. Since a product's performance forms the fundamental basis for a sales contract, it is patently unreasonable to assume that a buyer would purchase a standardized mass-produced product from an industry seller without any enforceable performance standards. From a social perspective, risk of loss is most appropriately borne by the party best able to prevent its occurrence. Rarely would the buyer be in a better position than the manufacturer–seller to evaluate the performance characteristics of a machine.

In this case, moreover, the evidence establishes that A & M had no previous experience with weight-sizing machines and was forced to rely on the expertise of FMC in recommending the necessary equipment. FMC was abundantly aware of this fact. The jury here necessarily found that FMC either expressly or impliedly guaranteed a performance level which the machine was unable to meet. Especially where an inexperienced buyer is concerned, the seller's performance representations are absolutely necessary to allow the buyer to make an intelligent choice among the competitive options available. A seller's attempt, through the use of a disclaimer, to prevent the buyer from reasonably relying on such representations calls into question the commercial reasonableness of the agreement and may well be substantively unconscionable. The trial court's conclusion to that effect is amply supported by the record before us.

---

[11] The transcript of FMC salesman John Walker's testimony reads as follows:

"Q All right. Now do you negotiate the terms of those contracts, or are they preprinted and that's the way you use them?

"A They are sent by our legal department, with the exception of payment terms are negotiable, but not the "Whereases" and "Wherefores."

"Q So you don't separately negotiate the terms on the back and the other terms, other than payment terms?

"A I'm not empowered to do that, sir."

As to the exclusion of consequential damages, several factors combine to suggest that the exclusion was unreasonable on the facts of this case. Consequential damages are a commercially recognized type of damage actually suffered by A & M due to FMC's breach.[12] A party ". . . should be able to rely on their existence in the absence of being informed to the contrary . . . ." This factor is particularly important given the commercial realities under which the contract was executed. If the seller's warranty was breached, consequential damages were not merely "reasonably foreseeable"; they were explicitly obvious. All parties were aware that once the tomatoes began to ripen, they all had to be harvested and packed within a relatively short period of time.

Another factor supporting the trial court's determination involves the avoidability of the damages and relates directly to the allocation of risks which lies at the foundation of the contractual bargain. It has been suggested that "[r]isk shifting is socially expensive and should not be undertaken in the absence of a good reason. An even better reason is required when to so shift is contrary to a contract freely negotiated." But as we noted previously, FMC was the only party reasonably able to prevent this loss by not selling A & M a machine inadequate to meet its expressed needs.[13] "If there is a type of risk allocation that should be subjected to special scrutiny, it is probably the shifting to one party of a risk that *only* the other party can avoid."

In summary, our review of the totality of circumstances in this case, including the business environment within which the contract was executed, supports the trial court's determination that the disclaimer of warranties and the exclusion of consequential damages in FMC's form contract were unconscionable and therefore unenforceable. When non-negotiable terms on preprinted form agreements combine with disparate bargaining power, resulting in the allocation of commercial risks in a socially or economically unreasonable manner, the concept of unconscionability as codified in Uniform Commercial Code sections 2-302 and 2-719, subdivision (3), furnishes legal justification for refusing enforcement of the offensive result.

IV.

FMC claims that even if the disclaimer of consequential damages is invalid, the damage award should be set aside because it is speculative. Civil Code section 3301 provides that "[n]o damages can be recovered for a breach of contract which are not clearly ascertainable in both their nature and origin." The general rule under this statute is that ". . . where the operation of an

---

[12] In the absence of an exclusion, the code provides that consequential damages are generally recoverable. (§ §2714, subd. (3) and 2715, subd. (2).) The general rule regarding limitations on available remedies was stated by the court in *Chemetron Corporation* v. *McLouth Steel Corporation* (N.D.Ill.1974) 381 F.Supp. 245, 250:

"While parties may agree to limit the remedies for breach of their contract, the policy of the Uniform Commercial Code disfavors limitations and specifically provides for their deletion if they would act to deprive a contracting party of reasonable protection against breach." (Fn. omitted.)

[13] We recognize that a buyer may be able to restrict the *amount* of consequential damages, but the Code already imposes a duty to mitigate damages. (See §2-715, subd. (2)(a).) In any event there is no contention here that any actions by A & M artificially inflated the consequential loss suffered.

unestablished business is prevented or interrupted, damages for prospective profits that might otherwise have been made from its operation are not recoverable for the reason that their occurrence is uncertain, contingent and speculative." However, *Grupe,* which FMC cites, also stands for the exception to the rule: "[A]nticipated profits dependent upon future events are allowed where their nature and occurrence can be shown by evidence of reasonable reliability."

FMC does not argue on appeal that the evidence the trial court heard on the issue was itself speculative. That evidence included size of the crop and market price of the type of tomato A & M grew. Although A & M had never grown tomatoes before, Abatti was an experienced farmer. Moreover, the crop itself was in good condition at harvest time. There was no evidence of crop damage from harvesting to those tomatoes actually picked, nor was there any evidence that transportation of the crop would have posed a problem. These circumstances make the exception to the rule applicable and provide ample support for the trial court's decision to allow the award of consequential damages.

Case 2
Grimshaw *v.* Ford Motor Co.,

174 Cal. Rptr. 348 (Cal. App. 1981).

TAMURA, Acting Presiding Justice.

A 1972 Ford Pinto hatchback automobile unexpectedly stalled on a freeway, erupting into flames when it was rear ended by a car proceeding in the same direction. Mrs. Lilly Gray, the driver of the Pinto, suffered fatal burns and 13-year-old Richard Grimshaw, a passenger in the Pinto, suffered severe and permanently disfiguring burns on his face and entire body. Grimshaw and the heirs of Mrs. Gray (Grays) sued Ford Motor Company and others. Following a six-month jury trial, verdicts were returned in favor of plaintiffs against Ford Motor Company. Grimshaw was awarded $2,516,000 compensatory damages and $125 million punitive damages; the Grays were awarded $559,680 in compensatory damages.[1] On Ford's motion for a new trial, Grimshaw was required to remit all but $3½ million of the punitive award as a condition of denial of the motion.

Ford appeals from the judgment and from an order denying its motion for a judgment notwithstanding the verdict as to punitive damages. Grimshaw appeals from the order granting the conditional new trial and from the amended judgment entered pursuant to the order.

Ford assails the judgment as a whole, assigning a multitude of errors and irregularities, including misconduct of counsel, but the primary thrust of its appeal is directed against the punitive damage award. Ford contends that the punitive award was statutorily unauthorized and constitutionally invalid. In addition, it maintains that the evidence was insufficient to support a finding of malice or corporate responsibility for malice. Grimshaw's cross-appeal challenges the validity of the new trial order and the conditional reduction of the punitive damage award.

FACTS

Since sufficiency of the evidence is in issue only regarding the punitive damage award, we make no attempt to review the evidence bearing on all of the litigated issues. Subject to amplification when we deal with specific issues, we shall set out the basic facts pertinent to these appeals in accordance with es-

---

[1] The jury actually awarded Grimshaw $2,841,000 compensatory damages and $125 million punitive damages and the Grays $659,680 compensatory damages. Pursuant to stipulation that sums previously received by plaintiffs from others should be deducted from the amounts awarded by the jury, the judgment was modified to reflect compensatory damages in favor of Grimshaw for $2,516,000 and in favor of the Grays for $559,680.

tablished principles of appellate review: We will view the evidence in the light most favorable to the parties prevailing below, resolving all conflicts in their favor, and indulging all reasonable inferences favorable to them.

The Accident:

In November 1971, the Grays purchased a new 1972 Pinto hatchback manufactured by Ford in October 1971. The Grays had trouble with the car from the outset. During the first few months of ownership, they had to return the car to the dealer for repairs a number of times. Their car problems included excessive gas and oil consumption, down shifting of the automatic transmission, lack of power, and occasional stalling. It was later learned that the stalling and excessive fuel consumption were caused by a heavy carburetor float.

On May 28, 1972, Mrs. Gray, accompanied by 13-year-old Richard Grimshaw, set out in the Pinto from Anaheim for Barstow to meet Mr. Gray. The Pinto was then six months old and had been driven approximately 3,000 miles. Mrs. Gray stopped in San Bernardino for gasoline, got back onto the freeway (Interstate 15) and proceeded toward her destination at 60–65 miles per hour. As she approached the Route 30 off-ramp where traffic was congested, she moved from the outer fast lane to the middle lane of the freeway. Shortly after this lane change, the Pinto suddenly stalled and coasted to a halt in the middle lane. It was later established that the carburetor float had become so saturated with gasoline that it suddenly sank, opening the float chamber and causing the engine to flood and stall. A car traveling immediately behind the Pinto was able to swerve and pass it but the driver of a 1962 Ford Galaxie was unable to avoid colliding with the Pinto. The Galaxie had been traveling from 50 to 55 miles per hour but before the impact had been braked to a speed of from 28 to 37 miles per hour.

At the moment of impact, the Pinto caught fire and its interior was engulfed in flames. According to plaintiffs' expert, the impact of the Galaxie had driven the Pinto's gas tank forward and caused it to be punctured by the flange or one of the bolts on the differential housing so that fuel sprayed from the punctured tank and entered the passenger compartment through gaps resulting from the separation of the rear wheel well sections from the floor pan. By the time the Pinto came to rest after the collision, both occupants had sustained serious burns. When they emerged from the vehicle, their clothing was almost completely burned off. Mrs. Gray died a few days later of congestive heart failure as a result of the burns. Grimshaw managed to survive but only through heroic medical measures. He has undergone numerous and extensive surgeries and skin grafts and must undergo additional surgeries over the next 10 years. He lost portions of several fingers on his left hand and portions of his left ear, while his face required many skin grafts from various portions of his body. Because Ford does not contest the amount of compensatory damages awarded to Grimshaw and the Grays, no purpose would be served by further description of the injuries suffered by Grimshaw or the damages sustained by the Grays.

Design of the Pinto Fuel System:

In 1968, Ford began designing a new subcompact automobile which ultimately became the Pinto. Mr. Iacocco, then a Ford Vice President, conceived the project and was its moving force. Ford's objective was to build a car at or below 2,000 pounds to sell for no more than $2,000.

Ordinarily marketing surveys and preliminary engineering studies precede the styling of a new automobile line. Pinto, however, was a rush project, so that styling preceded engineering and dictated engineering design to a greater degree than usual. Among the engineering decisions dictated by styling was the placement of the fuel tank. It was then preferred practice in Europe and Japan to locate the gas tank over the rear axle in subcompacts because a small vehicle has less "crush space" between the rear axle and the bumper than larger cars. The Pinto's styling, however, required the tank to be placed behind the rear axle leaving only 9 or 10 inches of "crush space"—far less than in any other American automobile or Ford overseas subcompact. In addition, the Pinto was designed so that its bumper was little more than a chrome strip, less substantial than the bumper of any other American car produced then or later. The Pinto's rear structure also lacked reinforcing members known as "hat sections" (2 longitudinal side members) and horizontal cross-members running between them such as were found in cars of larger unitized construction and in all automobiles produced by Ford's overseas operations. The absence of the reinforcing members rendered the Pinto less crush resistant than other vehicles. Finally, the differential housing selected for the Pinto had an exposed flange and a line of exposed bolt heads. These protrusions were sufficient to puncture a gas tank driven forward against the differential upon rear impact.

Crash Tests:

During the development of the Pinto, prototypes were built and tested. Some were "mechanical prototypes" which duplicated mechanical features of the design but not its appearance while others, referred to as "engineering prototypes," were true duplicates of the design car. These prototypes as well as two production Pintos were crash tested by Ford to determine, among other things, the integrity of the fuel system in rear-end accidents. Ford also conducted the tests to see if the Pinto as designed would meet a proposed federal regulation requiring all automobiles manufactured in 1972 to be able to withstand a 20-mile-per-hour fixed barrier impact without significant fuel spillage and all automobiles manufactured after January 1, 1973, to withstand a 30-mile-per-hour fixed barrier impact without significant fuel spillage.

The crash tests revealed that the Pinto's fuel system as designed could not meet the 20-mile-per-hour proposed standard. Mechanical prototypes struck from the rear with a moving barrier at 21-miles-per-hour caused the fuel tank to be driven forward and to be punctured, causing fuel leakage in excess of the standard prescribed by the proposed regulation. A production Pinto crash tested at 21-miles-per-hour into a fixed barrier caused the fuel neck to be torn from the gas tank and the tank to be punctured by a bolt head on the differential housing. In at least one test, spilled fuel entered the driver's compartment through gaps resulting from the separation of the seams joining the real wheel wells to the floor pan. The seam separation was occasioned by the lack of reinforcement in the rear structure and insufficient welds of the wheel wells to the floor pan.

Tests conducted by Ford on other vehicles, including modified or reinforced mechanical Pinto prototypes, proved safe at speeds at which the Pinto failed. Where rubber bladders had been installed in the tank, crash tests into fixed barriers at 21-miles-per-hour withstood leakage from punctures in the gas tank. Vehicles with fuel tanks installed above rather than behind the rear axle passed the fuel system integrity test at 31-miles-per-hour fixed barrier. A Pinto with two longitudinal hat sections added to firm up the rear structure passed a 20-mile-per-hour rear impact fixed barrier test with no fuel leakage.

The Cost to Remedy Design Deficiencies:

When a prototype failed the fuel system integrity test, the standard of care for engineers in the industry was to redesign and retest it. The vulnerability of the production Pinto's fuel tank at speeds of 20 and 30-miles-per-hour fixed barrier tests could have been remedied by inexpensive "fixes," but Ford produced and sold the Pinto to the public without doing anything to remedy the defects. Design changes that would have enhanced the integrity of the fuel tank system at relatively little cost per car included the following: Longitudinal side members and cross members at $2.40 and $1.80, respectively; a single shock absorbent "flak suit" to protect the tank at $4; a tank within a tank and placement of the tank over the axle at $5.08 to $5.79; a nylon bladder within the tank at $5.25 to $8; placement of the tank over the axle surrounded with a protective barrier at the cost of $9.95 per car; substitution of a rear axle with a smooth differential housing at a cost of $2.10; imposition of a protective shield between the differential housing and the tank at $2.35; improvement and reenforcement of the bumper at $2.60; addition of eight inches of crush space a cost of $6.40. Equipping the car with a reinforced rear structure, smooth axle, improved bumper and additional crush space at a total cost of $15.30 would have made the fuel tank safe in a 34 to 38-mile-per-hour rear end collision by a vehicle the size of the Ford Galaxie. If, in addition to the foregoing, a bladder or tank within a tank were used or if the tank were protected with a shield, it would have been safe in a 40 to 45-mile-per-hour rear impact. If the tank had been located over the rear axle, it would have been safe in a rear impact at 50 miles per hour or more.

Management's Decision to Go Forward
with Knowledge of Defects:

The idea for the Pinto, as has been noted, was conceived by Mr. Iacocco, then Executive Vice President of Ford. The feasibility study was conducted under the supervision of Mr. Robert Alexander, Vice President of Car Engineering. Ford's Product Planning Committee, whose members included Mr. Iacocca, Mr. Robert Alexander, and Mr. Harold MacDonald, Ford's Group Vice President of Car Engineering, approved the Pinto's concept and made the decision to go forward with the project. During the course of the project, regular product review meetings were held which were chaired by Mr. MacDonald and attended by Mr. Alexander. As the project approached actual production, the engineers responsible for the components of the project "signed off" to their immediate supervisors who in turn "signed off" to their superiors and so on up the chain of command until the entire project was approved for public release by Vice Presidents Alexander and MacDonald and ultimately by Mr. Iacocca. The Pinto crash tests results had been forwarded up the chain of command to the ultimate decision-makers and were known to the Ford officials who decided to go forward with production.

Harley Copp, a former Ford engineer and executive in charge of the crash testing program, testified that the highest level of Ford's management made the decision to go forward with the production of the Pinto, knowing that the gas tank was vulnerable to puncture and rupture at low rear impact speeds creating a significant risk of death or injury from fire and knowing that "fixes" were feasible at nominal cost. He testified that management's decision was based on the cost savings which would inure from omitting or delaying the "fixes."

Mr. Copp's testimony concerning management's awareness of the crash tests results and the vulnerability of the Pinto fuel system was corroborated by other evidence. At an April 1971 product review meeting chaired by Mr. Mac-Donald, those present received and discussed a report (Exhibit 125) prepared by Ford engineers pertaining to the financial impact of a proposed federal standard on fuel system integrity and the cost savings which would accrue from deferring even minimal "fixes."[2] The report refers to crash tests of the in-

---

[2] The "FUEL SYSTEM INTEGRITY PROGRAM FINANCIAL REVIEW" report included the following:

"PRODUCT ASSUMPTIONS

"To meet 20 mph movable barrier requirements in 1973, fuel filler neck modifications to provide breakaway capability and minor upgrading of structure are required.

"To meet 30 mph movable barrier requirements, original fuel system integrity program assumptions provided for relocation of the fuel tanks to over the axle on all car lines beginning in 1974. Major tearup of rear and center floor pans, added rear end structure, and new fuel tanks were believed necessary for all car lines. These engineering assumptions were developed from limited vehicle crash test data and design and development work.

"Since these original assumptions, seven vehicle crash tests have been run which now indicate fuel tank relocation is probably not required. Although still based heavily on judgment, Chassis Engineering currently estimates that the 30 mph movable barrier requirement is achievable with a reduced level of rear end tearup.

"In addition to added rear-end structure, Chassis Engineering believes that either rubber 'flak' suits (similar to a tire carcass), or alternatively, a bladder lining within the fuel tank may be required on all cars with flat fuel tanks located under the luggage compartment floor (all cars, except Ford/Mercury/Lincoln and Torino/Montego station wagons). Although further crash tests may show that added structure alone is adequate to meet the 30 mph movable barrier requirement, provisions for flak suits or bladders must be provided. The design cost of a single flak suit, located between the fuel tank and the axle, is currently estimated at $(4) per vehicle. If two flak suits (second located at the rear of the fuel tank), or a bladder are required, the design cost is estimated at $(8) per vehicle. Based on these estimates, it is recommended that the addition of the flak suit/bladder be delayed on all affected cars until 1976. However, package provision for both the flak suits and the bladder should be included when other changes are made to incorporate 30 mph movable barrier capability. A design cost savings $10.9 million (1974–1975) can be realized by this delay. Although a design cost provision of $(8) per affected vehicle has been made in 1976 program levels to cover contingencies, it is hoped that cost

tegrity of the fuel system of Ford vehicles and design changes needed to meet anticipated federal standards. Also in evidence was a September 23, 1970, report (Exhibit 124) by Ford's "Chassis Design Office" concerning a program "to establish a corporate [Ford] position and reply to the government" on the proposed federal fuel system integrity standard which included zero fuel spillage at 20 miles per hour fixed barrier crash by January 1, 1972, and 30 miles per hour by January 1, 1973. The report states in part: "The 20 and 30 mph rear fixed barrier crashes will probably require repackaging the fuel tanks in a protected area such as above the rear axle. This is based on moving barrier crash tests of a Chevelle and a Ford at 30 mph and other Ford products at 20 mph. Currently there are no plans for forward models to repackage the fuel tanks. Tests must be conducted to prove that repackaged tanks will live without significantly strengthening rear structure for added protection." The report also notes that the Pinto was the "[s]mallest car line with most difficulty in achieving compliance." It is reasonable to infer that the report was prepared for and known to Ford officials in policy-making positions.

The fact that two of the crash tests were run at the request of the Ford Chassis and Vehicle Engineering Department for the specific purpose of demonstrating the advisability of moving the fuel tank over the axle as a possible "fix" further corroborated Mr. Copp's testimony that management knew the results of the crash tests. Mr. Kennedy, who succeeded Mr. Copp as the engineer in charge of Ford's crash testing program, admitted that the test results had been forwarded up the chain of command to his superiors.

Finally, Mr. Copp testified to conversations in late 1968 or early 1969 with the chief assistant research engineer in charge of cost-weight evaluation of the Pinto, and to a later conversation with the chief chassis engineer who was then in charge of crash testing the early prototype. In these conversations, both men expressed concern about the integrity of the Pinto's fuel system and complained about management's unwillingness to deviate from the design if the change would cost money.

The Action:

Grimshaw (by his guardian ad litem) and the Grays sued Ford and others. Grimshaw was permitted to amend his complaint to seek punitive damages but the Grays' motion to amend their complaint for a like purpose was denied. The cases were thereafter consolidated for trial.[3] Grimshaw's case was submitted to the jury on theories of negligence and strict liability; the Grays' case went to the jury only on the strict liability theory.

---

reductions can be achieved, or the need for any flak suit or bladder eliminated after further engineering development.

"Current assumptions indicate that fuel system integrity modifications and 1973 bumper improvement requirements are nearly independent. However, bumper requirements for 1974 and beyond may require additional rear end structure which could benefit fuel system integrity programs."

[3] Plaintiffs settled with the other defendants before and during trial; the case went to verdict only against Ford Motor Company.

FORD'S APPEAL

Ford seeks reversal of the judgment as a whole on the following grounds: (1) Erroneous rulings relating to Mr. Copp's testimony; (2) other erroneous evidentiary rulings; (3) prejudicial misconduct by plaintiffs' counsel; (4) instructional errors; and (5) jury misconduct. On the issue of punitive damages, Ford contends that its motion for judgment notwithstanding the verdict should nave been granted because the punitive award was statutorily unauthorized and constitutionally invalid and on the further ground that the evidence was insufficient to support a finding of malice or corporate responsibility for malice. Ford also seeks reversal of the punitive award for claimed instructional errors on malice and proof of malice as well as on the numerous grounds addressed to the judgment as a whole. Finally, Ford maintains that even if punitive damages were appropriate in this case, the amount of the award was so excessive as to require a new trial or further remittitur of the award.

In the ensuing analysis (ad nauseam) of Ford's wideranging assault on the judgment, we have concluded that Ford has failed to demonstrate that any errors or irregularities occurred during the trial which resulted in a miscarriage of justice requiring reversal.

II. OTHER EVIDENTIARY RULINGS

Ford contends that the court erroneously admitted irrelevant documentary evidence highly prejudicial to Ford. We find the contention to be without merit.

(1) Exhibit No. 125:

Exhibit No. 125 was a report presented at a Ford production review meeting in April 1971, recommending action to be taken in anticipation of the promulgation of federal standards on fuel system integrity. The report recommended, *inter alia,* deferral from 1974 to 1976 of the adoption of "flak suits" or "bladders" in all Ford cars, including the Pinto, in order to realize a savings of $20.9 million. The report stated that the cost of the flak suit or bladder would be $4 to $8 per car. The meeting at which the report was presented was chaired by Vice President Harold MacDonald and attended by Vice President Robert Alexander and occurred sometime before the 1972 Pinto was placed on the market. A reasonable inference may be drawn from the evidence that despite management's knowledge that the Pinto's fuel system could be made safe at a cost of but $4 to $8 per car, it decided to defer corrective measures to save money and enhance profits. The evidence was thus highly relevant and properly received.

(2) Exhibits Nos. 95 and 122:

Ford urges that a report (Exhibit No. 95) and a motion picture depicting Ford's crash test No. 1616 (Exhibit No. 122) should have been excluded because they were irrelevant and highly prejudicial to Ford in that they showed that in a 21.5-mile-per-hour crash of a 1971 Pinto prototype into a fixed barrier the filler neck of the fuel tank separated allowing fluid to spill from the tank, whereas no such filler neck separation occurred in the Gray vehicle. Under the test for ascertaining relevancy of evidence to which we have previously alluded, we find no abuse of discretion in the court's ruling. Not only did the filler neck separation show the vulnerability of the Pinto fuel system in a 21.5-mile-per-hour fixed barrier test, but crash test No. 1616, as Ford conceded, resulted in a puncture of the fuel tank from the exposed bolt heads on the differential housing. Thus, the exhibits showed the defect in the Pinto's gas tank location and design, the hazard created by the protrusions on the differential housing, and, in addition, they served as evidence of Ford's awareness of those defects. Exhibits Nos. 95 and 122 were properly received in evidence.

(3) Exhibit No. 82:

Ford contends admission into evidence over its objection of a report known as the "Chiara memorandum" (Plaintiffs' Exhibit No. 82) was error. The report, dated February 1971, was a Ford engineering study of the costs of a proposal for a fuel tank over the axle and a tank within a tank for a Ford-Mercury automobile. Ford argues that the study was irrelevant because it pertained to an entirely different car to be built four years later. Mr. Copp testified, however, that the information in the study could be applied equally to the Pinto. The study showed that the cost of placing the gas tank over the axle with protective shield was about $10 and that a tank within a tank with polyurethane foam between tanks would have cost about $5. Whether the probative value of the evidence was outweighed by the danger of undue prejudice was a matter for the trial judge.

IV. INSTRUCTIONS

Ford complains of instructional errors on design defect and superseding cause.

(1) Design Defects:

Some two weeks before this case went to the jury, the Supreme Court in *Barker* v. *Lull Engineering Co.,* 20 Cal.3d 413, 143 Cal.Rptr. 225, 573 P.2d 443, formulated the following "two-pronged" definition of design defect, embodying the "consumer expectation" standard and "risk–benefit" test: "First, a product may be found defective in design if the plaintiff establishes that the product failed to perform as safely as an ordinary consumer would expect when used in an intended or reasonably foreseeable manner. Second, a product may alternatively be found defective in design if the plaintiff demonstrates that the product's design proximately caused his injury and the defendant fails to establish, in light of the relevant factors, that, on balance, the benefits of the challenged design outweigh the risk of danger inherent in such design." The "relevant factors" which a jury may consider in applying the *Barker* "risk–

benefit" standard include "the gravity of the danger posed by the challenged design, the likelihood that such danger would occur, the mechanical feasibility of a safer alternative design, the financial cost of an improved design, and the adverse consequences to the product and to the consumer that would result from an alternative design." Under the risk–benefit test, once the plaintiff makes a prima facie showing that the injury was proximately caused by the product's design, the burden shifts "to the defendant to prove, in light of the relevant factors, that the product is not defective."

Ford requested two instructions purporting to set out the *Barker* tests for design defect,[4] but the court gave only the following instruction: "A product is defective in design if the product has failed to perform as safely as an ordinary consumer would expect when used in an intended or reasonably foreseeable manner." Ford complains that the failure to give the balance of the other requested instruction constituted prejudicial error. For the reasons set out below, we conclude that the contention lacks merit.

Initially, *Barker* does not mandate a jury instruction on both prongs of the tests in a design defect case. The *Barker* court referred to the two standards for evaluating design defect as "alternative tests" and in its suggested instruction phrased the tests in the disjunctive.[5] The court stated that the alternative risk–benefit prong of the *Barker* test was designed to aid the injured party in establishing design defects because " '[i]n many situations . . . the consumer would not know what to expect, because he would have no idea how safe the product could be made.' " The court referred to the fact that numerous California decisions have recognized this fact by making it clear "[t]hat a product may be found defective in design even if it satisfies ordinary consumer expectations, if through hindsight the jury determines that the product's design embodies 'excessive preventable danger,' or, in other words, if the jury finds that the risk of danger inherent in the challenged design outweighs the benefits of such design." Thus, the risk–benefit test was formulated primarily to aid injured persons. The instant case was submitted solely on the consumer expectation standard because the trial had been virtually completed before the *Barker* decision was rendered in which our high court for the first time articulated the risk–benefit standard of design defect.

---

[4] The two requested instructions on design defect read:

"A product is defective in design if the product has failed to perform as safely as an ordinary consumer would expect when used in an intended or reasonably foreseeable manner."

"In determining whether or not the Pinto automobile was defectively designed, you may consider, among other relevant factors, the gravity of the danger posed by the challenged design, the likelihood that such danger would occur, the mechanical feasibility of a safer alternative design, the financial cost of an improved design, the adverse consequences to the product and to the consumer that would result from an alternative design, the extent to which its design and manufacture matched the average quality of other automobiles and the extent to which its design and manufacture deviated from the norm for automobiles designed and manufactured at the same point in time."

[5] The *Barker* court held "that a trial judge may properly instruct the jury that a product is defective in design (1) if the plaintiff demonstrates that the product failed to perform as safely as an ordinary consumer would expect when used in an intended or reasonably foreseeable manner, *or* (2) if the plaintiff proves that the product's design proximately caused his injury and the defendant fails to prove, in light of the relevant factors discussed above, that on balance the benefits of the challenged design outweigh the risk of danger inherent in such design.

Ford therefore cannot complain of the failure to instruct on the risk–benefit test. Indeed, had the risk–benefit prong of the design defect instruction as formulated in *Barker* been given, Ford would have been entitled to complain of prejudice. The instruction provides that a product is defective in design if "plaintiff proves that the product's design proximately caused his injury *and the defendant fails to prove*, . . . that on balance the benefits of the challenged design outweigh the risk of danger inherent in such design." (*Id.*, at p. 435, 143 Cal.Rptr. 225, 573 P.2d 443, emphasis supplied.) Had the jury been so instructed, Ford could have justifiably claimed prejudice because the case had not been tried on the assumption that under a risk–benefit analysis Ford had the burden of proving that the product was not defective.

Finally, even had it been proper to instruct on the risk–benefit test, Ford's requested version of the standard was defective in two important respects. First it omitted the crucial element of the manufacturer's burden of proof in the risk–benefit posture. Nor did Ford offer a separate instruction covering the subject of the burden of proof. Second, the proposed instruction erroneously included among the "relevant factors," "the extent to which its [Pinto's] design and manufacture matched the average quality of other automobiles and the extent to which its design and manufacture deviated from the norm for automobiles designed and manufactured at the same point in time." In a strict products liability case, industry custom or usage is irrelevant to the issue of defect. The *Barker* court's enumeration of factors which may be considered under the risk–benefit test not only fails to mention custom or usage in the industry, the court otherwise makes clear by implication that they are inappropriate considerations. *Barker* contrasts the risk–benefit strict liability test with a negligent design action, stating that "the jury's focus is properly directed to the condition of the product itself, and not to the reasonableness of the manufacturer's conduct. Thus, [the court explains] the fact that the manufacturer took reasonable precautions in an attempt to design a safe product or otherwise acted as a reasonably prudent manufacturer would have under the circumstances, while perhaps absolving the manufacturer of liability under a negligence theory, will not preclude the imposition of liability under strict liability principles if, upon hindsight, the trier of fact concludes that the product's design is unsafe to consumers, users, or bystanders." In *Foglio*, we held that an instruction permitting the jury in a strict products liability case to consider industry custom or practice in determining whether a design defect existed constituted error.

For the reasons stated above, the other instructions Ford requested which would have permitted the jury to consider custom or usage in the trade in determining whether a design defect existed were also properly refused.[6]

---

[6] Ford offered the following instructions on custom or usage in the trade:

"In determining whether the automobile involved in this case was defective, you may consider (the extent to which) (whether) its design and manufacture conformed to the state of the art or the custom of the trade at the time of its design and manufacture."

"The term, 'state of the art,' as used in the previous instruction, means the practice usually and customarily engaged in by automobile manufacture[r]s in the United States at the time of the design and manufacture of the automobile in this case."

(2) Superseding Causes:

Ford requested the following instruction on superseding cause: "If you find that the gasoline tank in the 1972 Pinto automobile was improperly located or protected but that the fire would have occurred even if the tank had been properly located or protected, its location or protection was not a substantial factor in bringing about the fire and was, therefore, not a contributing cause thereof." Instead, the court gave the following instruction: "If you find that the defects alleged to exist in the 1972 Pinto did in fact exist but that the fire and resulting injuries would have occurred even if the defects did not exist, the defects were not a substantial factor in bringing about the fire and therefore were not contributing factors to the resulting injuries." Ford assigns the refusal of its instruction and the giving of the other instruction as error.

Ford contends that one of its defenses to the claims based on the design of the fuel tank and its location and protection was that the impact speed was so great that the fuel tank rupture and fire would have occurred without regard to the location and protection of the fuel tank. It concedes that defense would have been of no avail as to compensatory damages had the jury found that the Pinto stalled on the freeway because of a carburetor defect but that it could have been a defense to punitive damages because that claim rested entirely on Ford's conduct with respect to the fuel tank's design position and protection. Ford argues that its proffered instruction was "accurate and complete" and tailored to fit its defense based on the fuel tank location and protection and that the instruction given by the court, using the word "defects" instead of the precise claimed defects pertaining to the fuel tank, effectively eliminated Ford's superseding cause defense as to the fuel tank. It argues that under the instruction as given if the jury found only that the carburetor was defective and was a substantial cause of the fire, then it could conclude that all of the claimed defects were substantial causes of the fire and that no superseding cause had intervened. We find no merit in the contentions.

Initially, we note that Ford's proffered instruction was not "accurate and complete." One of the major defects which plaintiffs claimed caused the fire in the interior of the vehicle was the susceptibility of the rear wheel wells to separate from the floor pan. There was substantial evidence to support a finding that such defect existed. Ford's instruction failed completely to take this major defect into account. Second, Ford's argument that use of the word "defect" in the instruction given by the court permitted the jury to conclude that if it found that a defective carburetor was a substantial factor in causing the fire, the other alleged defects relating to location of the fuel tank and the rear structure of the car were then also substantial causes of the fire is such a strained and obscure interpretation that it could not have been indulged by any reasonable juror. None of the attorneys attempted to interpret the instruc-

"In determining whether the automobile involved in this case was defective, you may consider (the extent to which) (whether) its design and manufacture matched the average quality of other and (the extent to which) (whether) its design and manufacture deviated from the norm for automobiles designed and manufactured at the same point in time."

tion in the manner now suggested by Ford. Indeed, argument of counsel on both sides made it clear that the only "defects" referred to in the instruction on superseding cause were those involving the gasoline tank and rear structure of the vehicle, not the carburetor.

Ford's reliance on *Self* v. *General Motors Corp.*, 42 Cal.App.3d 1, 116 Cal.Rptr. 575, for its contention that the court's instruction was inadequate is misplaced. In *Self*, the trial court failed to give any instruction on superseding cause and the reviewing court held that the failure to give the superseding cause instruction proffered by the defendant was error. Here the court refused Ford's version of a superseding cause instruction but gave its own which adequately covered the subject. A party has the right to have the jury instructed on his theory of the case but does not have the right to require his phraseology; the court may modify an instruction or give an instruction of its own in lieu of the one offered provided it correctly instructs the jury on the issue.

VI. PUNITIVE DAMAGES

Ford contends that it was entitled to a judgment notwithstanding the verdict on the issue of punitive damages on two grounds: First, punitive damages are statutorily and constitutionally impermissible in a design defect case; second, there was no evidentiary support for a finding of malice or of corporate responsibility for malice. In any event, Ford maintains that the punitive damage award must be reversed because of erroneous instructions and excessiveness of the award.

(1) "Malice" Under Civil Code Section 3294:

The concept of punitive damages is rooted in the English common law and is a settled principle of the common law of this country. The doctrine was a part of the common law of this state long before the Civil Code was adopted. When our laws were codified in 1872, the doctrine was incorporated in Civil Code section 3294, which at the time of trial read: "In an action for the breach of an obligation not arising from contract, where the defendant has been guilty of oppression, fraud, or malice, express or implied, the plaintiff, in addition to the actual damages, may recover damages for the sake of example and by way of punishing the defendant."[7]

---

[7] Section 3294 was amended in 1980 (Stats. 1980, ch. 1242, §1, p.—, eff. Jan. 1, 1981) to read:

"(a) In an action for the breach of an obligation not arising from contract, where the defendant has been guilty of oppression, fraud, or malice, the plaintiff, in addition to the actual damages, may recover damages for the sake of example and by way of punishing the defendant.

"(b) An employer shall not be liable for damages pursuant to subdivision (a), based upon acts of an employee of the employer, unless the employer had advance knowledge of the unfitness of the employee and employed him or her with a conscious disregard of the rights or safety of others or authorized or ratified the wrongful conduct for which the damages are awarded or was personally guilty of oppression, fraud, or malice. With respect to a corporate employer, the advance knowledge, ratification, or act of oppression, fraud, or malice must be on the part of an officer, director, or managing agent of the corporation.

"(c) As used in this section, the following definitions shall apply:

"(1) 'Malice' means conduct which is intended by the defendant to cause injury to the plaintiff or conduct which is carried on by the defendant with a conscious disregard of the rights or safety of others.

Ford argues that "malice" as used in section 3294 and as interpreted by our Supreme Court in *Davis* v. *Hearst,* 160 Cal. 143, 116 P. 530, requires *animus malus* or evil motive—an intention to injure the person harmed—and that the term is therefore conceptually incompatible with an unintentional tort such as the manufacture and marketing of a defectively designed product. This contention runs counter to our decisional law. As this court recently noted, numerous California cases after *Davis* v. *Hearst, supra,* have interpreted the term "malice" as used in section 3294 to include, not only a malicious intention to injure the specific person harmed, but conduct evincing "a conscious disregard of the probability that the actor's conduct will result in injury to others."

In *Taylor* v. *Superior Court, supra,* 24 Cal.3d 890, 157 Cal.Rptr. 693, 598 P.2d 854, our high court's most recent pronouncement on the subject of punitive damages, the court observed that the availability of punitive damages has not been limited to cases in which there is an actual intent to harm plaintiff or others. The court concurred with the *Searle* court's suggestion that conscious disregard of the safety of others is an appropriate description of the *animus malus* required by Civil Code section 3294, adding: "In order to justify an award of punitive damages on this basis, the plaintiff must establish that the defendant was aware of the probable dangerous consequences of his conduct, and that he wilfully and deliberately failed to avoid those consequences."

Ford attempts to minimize the precedential force of the foregoing decisions on the ground they failed to address the position now advanced by Ford that intent to harm a particular person or persons is required because that was what the lawmakers had in mind in 1872 when they adopted Civil Code section 3294. Ford argues that the Legislature was thinking in terms of traditional intentional torts, such as, libel, slander, assault and battery, malicious prosecution, trespass, etc., and could not have intended the statute to be applied to a products liability case arising out of a design defect in a mass produced automobile because neither strict products liability nor mass produced automobiles were known in 1872.

A like argument was rejected in *Li* v. *Yellow Cab Co.,* 13 Cal.3d 804, 119 Cal.Rptr. 858, 532 P.2d 1226, where the court held that in enacting section 1714 as part of the 1872 Civil Code, the Legislature did not intend to prevent judicial development of the common law concepts of negligence and contributory negligence. As the court noted, the code itself provides that insofar as its provisions are substantially the same as the common law, they should be construed as continuations thereof and not as new enactments (Civ.Code, §§4, 5), and thus the code has been imbued "with admirable flexibility from the standpoint of adaptation to changing circumstances and conditions." In light of the

"(2) 'Oppression' means subjecting a person to cruel and unjust hardship in conscious disregard of that person's rights.

"(3) 'Fraud' means an intentional misrepresentation, deceit, or concealment of a material fact known to the defendant with the intention on the part of the defendant of thereby depriving a person of property or legal rights or otherwise causing injury."

common law heritage of the principle embodied in Civil Code section 3294,[8] it must be construed as a "continuation" of the common law and liberally applied "with a view to effect its objects and to promote justice." (Civ.Code, §§ 4, 5.) To paraphrase *Li* v. *Yellow Cab Co.,* the applicable rules of construction "permit if not require that section [3294] be interpreted so as to give dynamic expression to the fundamental precepts which it summarizes."

The interpretation of the word "malice" as used in section 3294 to encompass conduct evincing callous and conscious disregard of public safety by those who manufacture and market mass produced articles is consonant with and furthers the objectives of punitive damages. The primary purposes of punitive damages are punishment and deterrence of like conduct by the wrongdoer and others. In the traditional noncommercial intentional tort, compensatory damages alone may serve as an effective deterrent against future wrongful conduct but in commerce related torts, the manufacturer may find it more profitable to treat compensatory damages as a part of the cost of doing business rather than to remedy the defect. Deterrence of such "objectionable corporate policies" serves one of the principal purposes of Civil Code section 3294. Governmental safety standards and the criminal law have failed to provide adequate consumer protection against the manufacture and distribution of defective products. Punitive damages thus remain as the most effective remedy for consumer protection against defectively designed mass produced articles. They provide a motive for private individuals to enforce rules of law and enable them to recoup the expenses of doing so which can be considerable and not otherwise recoverable.

We find no statutory impediments to the application of Civil Code section 3294 to a strict products liability case based on design defect.

(2) Constitutional Attacks on Civil Code Section 3294:

Ford's contention that the statute is unconstitutional has been repeatedly rejected. Ford's argument that its due process rights were violated because it did not have "fair warning" that its conduct would render it liable for punitive damages under Civil Code section 3294 ignores the long line of decisions in this state beginning with *Donnelly* v. *Southern Pacific Co.* (1941) *supra,* 18 Cal.2d 863, 869–870, 118 P.2d 465, holding that punitive damages are recoverable in a nondeliberate or unintentional tort where the defendant's conduct constitutes a conscious disregard of the probability of injury to others. The related contention that application of Civil Code section 3294 to the instant case would violate the ex post facto prohibition of the federal Constitution because at the time it designed the 1972 Pinto Ford had no warning that its conduct could be punished under Civil Code section 3294 is equally without merit.

---

[8] The doctrine was expressed in *Dorsey* v. *Manlove,* supra, 14 Cal. 553, as follows: "But where the trespass is committed from wanton or malicious motives, or a reckless disregard of the rights of others, or under circumstances of great hardship or oppression, the rule of compensation is not adhered to, and the measure and amount of damages are matters for the jury alone. In these cases the jury are not confined to the loss or injury sustained, but may go further and award punitive or exemplary damages, as a punishment for the act, or as a warning to others." (*Id.,* at p. 556.)

This constitutional prohibition extends to criminal statutes and penalties, not to civil statutes. Moreover, at the very least since *Toole* v. *Richardson-Merrell Inc.,* it should have been clear that a manufacturer of a dangerous, defective product might be liable for punitive damages if it knowingly exposed others to the hazard.

Equally without merit is the argument that the statute permits an unlawful delegation of legislative power because it fails to provide sufficient guidance to the judge and jury. As we have explained, the doctrine of punitive damages and its application are governed by common law principles. Judicial development of common law legal principles does not constitute an unlawful usurpation of legislative power; it is a proper exercise of a power traditionally exercised by the judiciary. The precise contention now advanced has been previously rejected.

The argument that application of Civil Code section 3294 violates the constitutional prohibition against double jeopardy is equally fallacious. This prohibition like the ex post facto concept is applicable only to criminal proceedings.

The related contention that the potential liability for punitive damages in other cases for the same design defect renders the imposition of such damages violative of Ford's due process rights also lacks merit. Followed to its logical conclusion, it would mean that punitive damages could never be assessed against a manufacturer of a mass produced article. No authorities are cited for such a proposition; indeed, as we have seen, the cases are to the contrary. We recognize the fact that multiplicity of awards may present a problem, but the mere possibility of a future award in a different case is not a ground for setting aside the award in this case, particularly as reduced by the trial judge. If Ford should be confronted with the possibility of an award in another case for the same conduct, it may raise the issue in that case. We add, moreover, that there is no necessary unfairness should the plaintiff in this case be rewarded to a greater extent than later plaintiffs. As Professor Owen has said in response to such a charge of unfairness: "This conception ignores the enormous diligence, imagination, and financial outlay required of initial plaintiffs to uncover and to prove the flagrant misconduct of a product manufacturer. In fact, subsequent plaintiffs will often ride to favorable verdicts and settlements on the coattails of the firstcomers." That observation fits the instant case.

(3) Sufficiency of the Evidence to Support the Finding of Malice and Corporate Responsibility:

Ford contends that its motion for judgment notwithstanding the verdict should have been granted because the evidence was insufficient to support a finding of malice or corporate responsibility for such malice. The record fails to support the contention.

"The rules circumscribing the power of a trial judge to grant a motion for judgment notwithstanding the verdict are well established. The power to grant such a motion is identical to the power to grant a directed verdict; the judge cannot weigh the evidence or assess the credibility of witnesses; if the evidence is conflicting or if several reasonable inferences may be drawn, the motion should be denied; the motion may be granted ' " 'only if it appears from the evidence, viewed in the light most favorable to the party securing the verdict, that there is no substantial evidence to support the verdict.' " '

There was ample evidence to support a finding of malice and Ford's responsibility for malice.

Through the results of the crash tests Ford knew that the Pinto's fuel tank and rear structure would expose consumers to serious injury or death in a 20 to 30 mile-per-hour collision. There was evidence that Ford could have corrected the hazardous design defects at minimal cost but decided to defer correction of the shortcomings by engaging in a cost–benefit analysis balancing human lives and limbs against corporate profits. Ford's institutional mentality was shown to be one of callous indifference to public safety. There was substantial evidence that Ford's conduct constituted "conscious disregard" of the probability of injury to members of the consuming public.

Ford's argument that there can be no liability for punitive damages because there was no evidence of corporate ratification of malicious misconduct is equally without merit. California follows the Restatement rule that punitive damages can be awarded against a principal because of an action of an agent if, but only if, "(a) the principal authorized the doing and the manner of the act, or (b) the agent was unfit and the principal was reckless in employing him, or (c) the agent was employed in a managerial capacity and was acting in the scope of employment, or (d) the principal or a managerial agent of the principal ratified or approved the act." The present case comes within one or both of the categories described in subdivisions (c) and (d).

There is substantial evidence that management was aware of the crash tests showing the vulnerability of the Pinto's fuel tank to rupture at low speed rear impacts with consequent significant risk of injury or death of the occupants by fire. There was testimony from several sources that the test results were forwarded up the chain of command. Vice President Robert Alexander admitted to Mr. Copp that he was aware of the test results; Vice President Harold MacDonald, who chaired the product review meetings, was present at one of those meetings at which a report on the crash tests was considered and a decision was made to defer corrective action; and it may be inferred that Mr. Alexander, a regular attender of the product review meetings, was also present at that meeting. MacDonald and Alexander were manifestly managerial employees possessing the discretion to make "decisions that will ultimately determine corporate policy" (*Egan* v. *Mutual of Omaha Ins. Co., supra*). There was also evidence that Harold Johnson, an Assistant Chief Engineer of Research, and Mr. Max Jurosek, Chief Chassis Engineer, were aware of the results of the crash tests and the defects in the Pinto's fuel tank system. Ford contends those two individuals did not occupy managerial positions because Mr. Copp testified that they admitted awareness of the defects but told him they were powerless to change the rear-end design of the Pinto. It may be inferred from the testimony, however, that the two engineers had approached management about redesigning the Pinto or that, being aware of management's attitude, they decided to do nothing. In either case the decision not to take corrective action was made by persons exercising managerial authority. Whether an employee acts in a "managerial capacity" does not necessarily depend on his "level" in the corporate hierarchy. As the *Egan* court said: " 'Defendant should not be allowed to insulate itself from liability by giving an employee a nonmanagerial title and relegating to him crucial policy decisions.' " While much of the evidence was necessarily circumstantial, there was substantial evidence from which the jury could reasonably find that Ford's management decided to proceed with the production of the Pinto with knowledge of test results revealing design defects which rendered the fuel tank extremely vulnerable on rear impact at low speeds and endangered the safety and lives of the occupants. Such conduct constitutes corporate malice.

(4) Instructions on Malice:

In its instructions to the jury, the trial court defined malice as follows: " 'Malice' means a motive and willingness to vex, harass, annoy or injure another person. Malice may be inferred from acts and conduct, such as by showing that the defendant's conduct was wilful, intentional, and done in conscious disregard of its possible results." The court also instructed the jury that plaintiff Grimshaw had the burden of proving "[t]hat the defendant acted with malice which may be inferred from defendant's conduct if the conduct was wilful, intentional and done in conscious disregard of its possible result."

On appeal, Ford contends that the phrase "conscious disregard of its possible results" used in the two instructions would permit a plaintiff to impugn almost every design decision as made in conscious disregard of some perceivable risk because safer alternative designs are almost always a possibility. Ford argues that to instruct the jury so that they might find "malice" if any such "possibility" existed was erroneous; it maintains that an instruction on "malice" in products liability must contain the phrase "conscious disregard of [the probability/a high probability] of injury to others," in order to preclude prejudicial error. Ford cites *Dawes* v. *Superior Court, supra,* recently decided by this court, for its authority.

The instruction on malice as given by the court was former BAJI 14.71 with a one-word modification. BAJI 14.71 then read in pertinent part: " 'Malice' means a motive and willingness to vex, harass, annoy or injure another person. Malice . . . may be inferred from acts and conduct such as by showing that the defendants' conduct, was wilful, intentional, and done in reckless disregard of its possible results." The instruction as given merely substituted the word "conscious" for the word "reckless."[9] The phrase "wilful, intentional and

[9] The 1980 revision of BAJI uses the expression "conscious disregard of the plaintiff's rights." The trial court's substitution in the instant case was apparently in response to *G. D. Searle & Co.* v. *Superior Court, supra,* (1975) 49 Cal.App.3d 22, 29–32, 122 Cal.Rptr. 218, which criticized the use of the term "reckless" in defining malice and suggested that "conscious disregard" would be a more accurate expression of the required state of mind.

done in reckless disregard of its possible results" used in former BAJI 14.71 seems to have made its first appearance in *Toole* v. *Richardson-Merrell Inc., supra.* The *Toole* formulation has been repeated since in a number of decisions. In *Schroeder,* the Supreme Court approved the *Toole* expression of the kind of behavior which would support a punitive award, stating: "But 'intent,' in the law of torts, denotes not only those results the actor desires, but also those consequences which he knows are substantially certain to result from his conduct. (Rest.2d Torts, §3a; Prosser, Torts (4th ed. 1971) pp. 31–32.) The jury in the present case could reasonably infer that defendants acted in callous disregard of plaintiffs' rights, knowing that their conduct was substantially certain to vex, annoy, and injure plaintiffs. Such behavior justifies the award of punitive damages. As stated in *Toole* v. *Richardson-Merrell Inc.* (1967) 251 Cal.App.2d 689, 713, 60 Cal.Rptr. 398, 29 A.L.R.3d 988: 'malice in fact, sufficient to support an award of punitive damages . . . may be established by a showing that the defendant's wrongful conduct was wilful, intentional, and done in reckless disregard of its possible results.'

In *Dawes* v. *Superior Court, supra,* this court noted that "since 1974 at the latest, and probably since a much earlier date, the term 'malice' as used in Civil Code section 3294 has been interpreted as including a conscious disregard of the *probability* that the actor's conduct will result in injury to others." (Emphasis supplied.) Our use of the term "probability" was not intended to effect a change in the law as set forth in *Toole, Schroeder,* and the other cases which have echoed the *Toole* formulation. Rather, it was meant to reflect correctly what the cases have been stating, albeit in varying ways, as an essential ingredient of the concept of malice in unintentional torts and to express this essential ingredient in the most precise manner possible. Although the *Toole* formulation of the rule used the expression "possible results," those words were preceded by the pejoratives "wilful," "intentional" and "reckless disregard." Taking the statement as a whole, it is our view that probability that the conduct will result in injury to another is implicit in *Toole.* This was also apparently how the Supreme Court viewed it in *Schroeder.* We agree with Ford, however, that to be as accurate as possible, the rule should be expressed in terms of probability of injury rather than possibility. Viewed in this way, the salient question for this appeal becomes whether the instruction given by the court resulted in a miscarriage of justice because it failed to use "probability." As we explain below, we are convinced that it did not.

A judgment may not be set aside on the ground the jury was misdirected unless reviewing court, after an examination of the entire cause, including the evidence, shall be of the opinion that the error resulted in a miscarriage of justice. Prejudice from an erroneous instruction is never presumed; it must be effectively demonstrated by the appellant. One of the factors to be considered in measuring the effect of an erroneous instruction is whether a party's argument to the jury may have given the instruction a misleading effect. Finally, an instruction should be interpreted in a manner that will support rather than defeat a judgment if it is reasonably susceptible to such an interpretation.

Applying the above precepts to the instant case, Ford has failed to demonstrate prejudice from the claimed defect in the instructions on malice. When the instructions are read as a whole, the jury could not possibly have interpreted the words "conscious disregard of its possible results" to extend to the innocent conduct depicted by Ford. The term "motive and willingness . . . to injure" and the words "wilful," "intentional," and "conscious disregard" signify *animus malus* or evil motive. As the *Searle* court explained, the term "conscious disregard" itself denotes a "highly culpable state of mind." The jury was instructed that Ford was not required under the law to produce either the safest possible vehicle or one which was incapable of producing injury. The instructions on malice manifestly referred to conduct constituting conscious and callous disregard of a substantial likelihood of injury to others and not to innocent conduct by the manufacturer. Further, plaintiffs made no attempt in their arguments to the jury to give the instructions on malice the interpretation to which Ford says they are susceptible. Plaintiffs did not argue possibility of injury; they argued that injury was a virtual certainty and that Ford's management knew it from the results of the crash tests. Thus, the instructions on malice, even assuming them to have been erroneous because the word "possible" was used instead of "probable," did not constitute prejudicial error.

(6) Amount of Punitive Damage Award:

Ford's final contention is that the amount of punitive damages awarded, even as reduced by the trial court, was so excessive that a new trial on that issue must be granted. Ford argues that its conduct was less reprehensible than those for which punitive damages have been awarded in California in the past; that the 3½ million dollar award is many times over the highest award for such damages ever upheld in California; and that the award exceeds maximum civil penalties that may be enforced under federal or state statutes against a manufacturer for marketing a defective automobile. We are unpersuaded.

In determining whether an award of punitive damages is excessive, comparison of the amount awarded with other awards in other cases is not a valid consideration. Nor does "[t]he fact that an award may set a precedent by its size" in and of itself render it suspect; whether the award was excessive must be assessed by examining the circumstances of the particular case. In deciding whether an award is excessive as a matter of law or was so grossly disproportionate as to raise the presumption that it was the product of passion or prejudice, the following factors should be weighed: The degree of reprehensibility of defendant's conduct, the wealth of the defendant, the amount of compensatory damages, and an amount which would serve as a deterrent effect on like conduct by defendant and others who may be so inclined. Applying the foregoing criteria to the instant case, the punitive damage award as reduced by the trial court was well within reason.[10]

In assessing the propriety of a punitive damage award, as in assessing the propriety of any other judicial ruling based upon factual determinations, the evidence must be viewed in the light most favorable to the judgment. Viewing the record thusly in the instant case, the conduct of Ford's management was reprehensible in the extreme. It exhibited a conscious and callous disregard of public safety in order to maximize corporate profits. Ford's self-evaluation of its conduct is based on a review of the evidence most favorable to it instead of on the basis of the evidence most favorable to the judgment. Unlike malicious conduct directed toward a single specific individual, Ford's tortious conduct endangered the lives of thousands of Pinto purchasers. Weighed against the factor of reprehensibility, the punitive damage award as reduced by the trial judge was not excessive.

Nor was the reduced award excessive taking into account defendant's wealth and the size of the compensatory award. Ford's net worth was 7.7 billion dollars and its income after taxes for 1976 was over 983 million dollars. The punitive award was approximately .005% of Ford's net worth and approximately .03% of its 1976 net income. The ratio of the punitive damages to compensatory damages was approximately 1.4 to one. Significantly, Ford does not quarrel with the amount of the compensatory award to Grimshaw.

Nor was the size of the award excessive in light of its deterrent purpose. An award which is so small that it can be simply written off as a part of the cost of doing business would have no deterrent effect. An award which affects the company's pricing of its product and thereby affects its competitive advantage would serve as a deterrent. The award in question was far from excessive as a deterrent against future wrongful conduct by Ford and others.

Ford complains that the punitive award is far greater than the maximum penalty that may be imposed under California or federal law prohibiting the sale of defective automobiles or other products. For example, Ford notes that California statutes provide a maximum fine of only $50 for the first offense and $100 for a second offense for a dealer who sells an automobile that fails to conform to federal safety laws or is not equipped with required lights or brakes (Veh.Code, §§24007, 24250 et seq.; 26300 et seq., 42000; 42001); that a manufacturer who sells brake fluid in this state failing to meet statutory standards is subject to a maximum of only $50 (Bus. & Prof.Code, §13800 et seq.); and that the maximum penalty that may be imposed under federal law

---

[10] A quantitative formula whereby the amount of punitive damages can be determined in a given case with mathematical certainty is manifestly impossible as well as undesirable. (Mallor & Roberts, *supra*, 31 Hastings L.J. 639, 666–667, 670.) The authors advocate abandonment of the rule that a reasonable relationship must exist between punitive damages and actual damages. They suggest that courts balance society's interest against defendant's interest by focusing on the following factors: Severity of threatened harm; degree of reprehensibility of defendant's conduct, profitability of the conduct, wealth of defendant, amount of compensatory damages (whether it was high in relation to injury), cost of litigation, potential criminal sanctions and other civil actions against defendant based on same conduct. (*Id.*, at pp. 667–669.) In the present case, the amount of the award as reduced by the judge was reasonable under the suggested factors, including the factor of any other potential liability, civil or criminal.

for violation of automobile safety standards is $1,000 per vehicle up to a maximum of $800,000 for any related series of offenses (15 U.S.C. §§1397–1398). It is precisely because monetary penalties under government regulations prescribing business standards or the criminal law are so inadequate and ineffective as deterrents against a manufacturer and distributor of mass produced defective products that punitive damages must be of sufficient amount to discourage such practices. Instead of showing that the punitive damage award was excessive, the comparison between the award and the maximum penalties under state and federal statutes and regulations governing automotive safety demonstrates the propriety of the amount of punitive damages awarded.

GRIMSHAW'S APPEAL

Grimshaw has appealed from the order conditionally granting Ford a new trial on the issue of punitive damages and from the amended judgment entered pursuant to that order.

Grimshaw contends that the new trial order is erroneous because (1) the punitive damages awarded by the jury were not excessive as a matter of law, (2) the specification of reasons was inadequate; and (3) the court abused its discretion in cutting the award so drastically. For reasons to be stated, we have concluded that the contentions lack merit.

The court prefaced its specification of reasons with a recitation of the judicially established guidelines[11] for determining whether a punitive award is excessive. The court then observed that there was evidence in the record (referring to Exhibit 125) which might provide a possible rational basis for the 125 million dollar jury verdict which would dispel any presumption of passion or prejudice,[12] adding, however, that the court was not suggesting that the amount was warranted "or that the jury did utilize Exhibit 125, or any other exhibits, and if they did, that they were justified in so doing." The court then noted, based on the fact that Ford's net worth was 7.7 billion and its profits during the last quarter of the year referred to in the financial statement introduced into evidence were more than twice the punitive award, that the award was not disproportionate to Ford's net assets or to its profit generating capacity. The court noted, however, that the amount of the punitive award was 44 times the compensatory award, the court stated that while it did not consider that ratio alone to be controlling because aggravating circumstances may justify a ratio as high as the one represented by the jury verdict, it reasoned that the ratio coupled with the amount by which the punitive exceeded the com-

[11] The court stated that "the principles by which the propriety of the amount of punitive damages awarded will be judged are threefold: (1) Is the sum so large as to raise a presumption that the award was the result of passion and prejudice and therefore excessive as a matter of law; (2) Does the award bear a reasonable relationship to the net assets of the defendant; and (3) Does the award bear a reasonable relationship to the compensatory damages awarded."

[12] Exhibit 125 was the report by Ford engineers showing savings which would be realized by deferring design changes to the fuel system of Ford automobiles to meet the proposed governmental standards on the integrity of the fuel systems.

pensatory damages (over 122 million dollars) rendered the jury's punitive award excessive as a matter of law.

Grimshaw contends that the court erred in determining that the ratio of punitive to compensatory damages rendered the punitive excessive as a matter of law. The trial court, however, did not base its decision solely on the ratio of punitive to compensatory. It took into account the ratio, the "aggravating circumstances" (the degree of reprehensibility), the wealth of the defendant and its profit generating capacity, the magnitude of the punitive award, including the amount by which it exceeded the compensatory. Those were proper considerations for determining whether the award was excessive as a matter of law. When a trial court grants a new trial for excessive damages, either conditionally or outright, a presumption of correctness attaches to the order and it will not be reversed unless it plainly appears that the judge abused his discretion.

Grimshaw also contends that the order granting a new trial was invalid for lack of adequate specification of reasons. We find that contention equally lacking in merit. When a motion for new trial is granted for excessive damages the specification of reasons should indicate the respects in which the evidence dictated a smaller verdict but, as the court observed in *Neal* different considerations bear upon the adequacy of the reasons where the amount of punitive rather than compensatory damages is the primary concern. In such cases the specification is adequate if it reveals how the court applied the decisional guidelines for assessing the propriety of the amount of the punitive damage award to the evidence in the particular case. This the trial court did in the instant case. Its specification of reasons adequately enables a reviewing court to determine whether there is a substantial basis in law and fact for the order granting the conditional new trial.

Finally, Grimshaw contends the court abused its discretion in reducing the award to 3½ million dollars as a condition of its new trial order and urges this court to restore the jury award or at least require a remittitur of substantially less than that required by the trial court.

We cannot say that the judge abused the discretion vested in him by Code of Civil Procedure section 662.5 or that there is "no substantial basis in the record" for the reasons given for the order. Finally, while the trial judge may not have taken into account Ford's potential liability for punitive damages in other cases involving the same tortious conduct in reducing the award, it is a factor we may consider in passing on the request to increase the award. Considering such potential liability, we find the amount as reduced by the trial judge to be reasonable and just. We therefore decline the invitation to modify the judgment by reducing the amount of the remittitur.

DISPOSITION

In *Richard Grimshaw* v. *Ford Motor Company,* the judgment, the conditional new trial order, and the order denying Ford's motion for judgment notwithstanding the verdict on the issue of punitive damages are affirmed.

4

Antitrust Issues Related to the Addition of Products or Services by Merger, Acquisition, or Joint Venture

Rather than expend all the time, energy, and resources attempting to expand an existing line or create a totally new line of products or services via internal development and commercialization, an organization may decide to merge with, acquire, be acquired by, or form a joint venture with another organization. The possibility of engaging in such expansionary activities is available to profit and not-for-profit organizations alike. While mergers, acquisitions, and joint ventures permit virtually instant diversification for the participating organizations, they are far from risk-free from the viewpoint of marketing management. Because they generally involve acquiring established products, they may permit the organizations to avoid the trials and tribulations of commercialization and the difficulties associated with the introductory period of the product life cycle. However, they bring with them the problems of all marriages, especially those basic compatibility issues relating to goals, means, personalities, and values. The task of matching interests and assimilating management styles was no more easy for Du Pont and Conoco or R.J. Reynolds and Heublein or Coca-Cola and Columbia Pictures than it has been for any newlyweds. Furthermore, most mergers, acquisitions, and joint ventures take place between relatively mature companies whose major products may also be in the mature stage of the product life cycle. Adjustments and adaptations are impeded by calcified methods of doing business. Nevertheless, mergers, acquisitions, and joint ventures do permit firms to deepen or extend their product lines, find new routes to the marketplace, or simply diversify their product or service portfolios. And certainly such activities provide instantaneous growth for both organizations, bringing with it all the advantages and disadvantages that come with larger size (e.g., greater access to capital markets versus increased bureaucratization).

Our concern here is not with the rationale for engaging in mergers, acquisitions, or joint ventures. Rather, assuming that the firm is considering such a move, our task is to examine the legal developments in this area. Indeed, one of the most serious and confusing points at issue between business and government is the role mergers and acquisitions should be permitted to assume in corporate strategy. Here we discuss the federal antitrust laws and their application to specific cases of horizontal and conglomerate amalgamations. (While we define what is meant by a "vertical" merger, a discussion of vertical integration via merger is left for Chapter 6. Our focus now is only on product policy, that is, the addition of products to an organization's portfolio through mergers or acquisitions.)

DEFINITIONS

Mergers are generally classified into three separate groups: horizontal, vertical, and conglomerate. The definitions employed by the Federal Trade Commission are as follows:[1]

Horizontal mergers: the companies involved produce one or more of the same, or closely related, products in the same geographic market.

Vertical mergers: the companies involved had a potential buyer–seller relationship prior to the merger.

Conglomerate mergers are classified into three subcategories: product extension, market extension, and other.

Product extension mergers: the companies involved are functionally related in production and/or distribution but sell products that do not compete directly with one another (e.g., a soap manufacturer acquiring a bleach manufacturer).

Market extension mergers: the companies involved manufacture the same products, but sell them in different geographic markets (e.g., a fluid milk processor in Washington acquiring a fluid milk processor in Chicago).

Other (or "pure") conglomerate mergers: the companies involved are essentially unrelated (e.g., a shipbuilding company buying an ice cream manufacturer).

Table 4-1 presents FTC data on the acquisitions of manufacturing and mining firms with assets of $10 million or more, by merger category, for 1979 compared with 1978, 1948–1978, and 1967–1978. The dominant category is conglomerate, even though there was a surge in large horizontal mergers in

[1] Federal Trade Commission, *Statistical Report on Mergers and Acquisitions 1979* (Washington, D.C.: U.S. Government Printing Office, July 1981), pp. 102–103.

Table 4-1

Large Acquisitions in Manufacturing and Mining by Type of Acquisition, 1979 Compared with 1978, 1948–1978, and 1967–1978[a]

Type of Acquisition	Number				Assets[b]			
	1948–1978	1967–1978	1978	1979	1948–1978	1967–1978	1978	1979
Horizontal	16.9%	14.3%	19.8%	5.2%	16.8%[c]	15.7%	28.5%	2.5%
Vertical	10.2	7.6	11.7	5.2	9.2	7.0	15.1	7.3
Conglomerate	72.9	78.1	68.5	89.7	74.0	77.3	56.4	90.4
Production Extension	43.0	42.7	33.3	42.3	33.7	31.8	28.0	35.9
Market Extension	3.9	3.5	0.0	2.1	5.9	5.0	0.0	0.3
Other	25.9	32.3	35.1	45.4	34.4	40.5	28.4	54.2
Total	100.0%	100.0%	100.0%	100.0%	100.0%	100.0%	100.0%	100.0%
Total number	1,926	1,139	110	97	—	—	—	—
Total dollars (in millions)[c]	—	—	—	—	$108,990.7	$80,889.8	$10,724.3	$12,867.1

[a] Not included in the tabulation are companies for which data were not publicly available.

[b] Sums may not always add due to rounding.

[c] Acquired firms with assets of $10 million or more.

Source: Federal Trade Commission, *Statistical Report on Mergers and Acquisitions, 1979* (Washington, D.C.: U.S. Government Printing Office, July 1981), pp. 109 and 110.

1978. Given the government statistics on mergers over time, it seems unmistakable that the U.S. law has had a strong effect on channeling mergers into the conglomerate category. (Merger activity in industrialized nations without antitrust statutes analogous to those in the United States continues to be predominantly horizontal.[2])

Table 4-1 does not really tell the full story, because it reflects only relatively large mergers. There are roughly over 2,000 mergers each year in the United States.[3] Selected large mergers that took place in the late 1970s are listed in Table 4-2 merely as illustrations. For those familiar with some of the mergers enumerated in Table 4-2, it is clear that the categories provided by the Federal Trade Commission are not always mutually exclusive. The dividing line between a product extension merger and a horizontal merger is, for example, not always evident. We will return to this point later, because it has a bearing on antitrust enforcement efforts. It is also important to note that a number of massive mergers and acquisitions have taken place in more recent history, perhaps reflecting a general relaxation of the government's merger policy. Some of the more expensive acquisitions that were consummated in 1982 alone are listed in Table 4-3.

GOVERNMENT RESPONSE TO MERGERS

From the viewpoint of antitrust, growth by internal expansion has, historically, been looked upon more favorably than growth by acquisitions and mergers. The general belief is that growth internally expands investment and production and hence increases competition, while growth by merger and acquisition in some sense removes a competitor or a supplier or a customer from the market. In any event, there is no necessary increase in net investment or of production.[4] In general, agreements between independent companies, especially direct competitors, have been viewed as dangerous to competition, because their likely impact is the restriction of output and consequently increased prices.

The landmark law relating to mergers is the 1950 Celler–Kefauver Act amendment to Section 7 of the Clayton Act. Prior to the passage of the Celler–Kefauver amendment, firms could grow at will through asset acquisitions, because the Sherman Act of 1890 prohibited only a few obvious monopoly consolidations, and the Clayton Act of 1914 applied only to stock acquisitions. In fact, as case precedents evolved, the Sherman Act became increasingly impotent in controlling mergers unless the merging firms were on the verge of attaining substantial monopoly power. For example, in *United States* v. *Colum-*

---

[2] F. M. Scherer, *Industrial Market Structure and Economic Performance*, 2nd ed. (Chicago: Rand McNally College Publishing Co., 1980), p. 559.

[3] There is some indication that in the early 1980s mergers and acquisitions were being consummated at an increasing rate. For example, the number of mergers and acquisitions completed in 1981 rose 58% from 1980, and their dollar volume almost doubled to more than $70 billion. The 2,314 transactions completed in 1981 represented a 27% increase over 1968 volume at the height of that decade's merger boom. See "Mergers, Acquisitions Rose 53% Last Year, Hay Group Study Says," *Wall Street Journal*, Jan. 28, 1982, p. 48.

[4] E. T. Grether, *Marketing and Public Policy* (Englewood Cliffs, N.J.: Prentice-Hall, Inc., 1966), p. 547.

Table 4-2

Selected Mergers, by Type of Acquisition, 1975–1979

Acquiring Company	Acquired Company
Horizontal	
Honeywell	Incoterm Corp.
Consolidated Foods Corp.	Chef Pierre Inc.
Eaton Corp.	Cutler–Hammer Inc.
General Signal	Leeds & Northrup
Harper & Row, Publ.	J. B. Lippincott
LTV Corp.	Lykes Corp.
Vertical	
Interspace Corp.	Allied Thermal
Thyssen AG	The Budd Co.
Coca-Cola Bottling NY	Jeanette Corp. Co.
VSI Corp.	Liquidonics Inds.
Arcata National	Keyes Fibre Co.
Petrolane Inc.	Signal Drilling Co.
Conglomerate	
Product Extension	
Eli Lilly	Cardiac Pacemakers
Continental Telephone	Executone Inc.
Louisiana–Pacific	Fibreboard Corp.
Gould Inc.	Hoffman Electronics
Cadbury Schweppes	Peter Paul Inc.
Philip Morris	Seven-Up Co.
Mattel Inc.	Western Publishing
Avon Products Inc.	Tiffany & Co.
Market Extension	
Herald Co.	Booth Newspapers
Bell Tel Canada	Cook Electric Co.
Olympia Brewing	Lone Star Brewing
St. Gobain–Mousson	Certain-Teed Corp.
Mickelberry Corp.	Neuhoff Bros. Packers
BTR, Ltd.	SW Industries Inc.
Other	
Nestle SA	Alcon Laboratories
B. F. Goodrich	Continental Conveyor
Beatrice Foods	Culligan International
Warner–Lambert	Entenmanns Inc.
Johnson Controls	Globe–Union
Esmark Inc.	STP Corp.
McGraw–Edison Co.	Studebaker–Worthington

Source: Federal Trade Commission, *Statistical Report on Mergers and Acquisitions, 1979* (Washington, D.C.: U.S. Government Printing Office, July 1981), pp. 157–166.

bia Steel Co.,[5] a case brought under the Sherman Act, U.S. Steel, the largest company in an industry not known for price competition was allowed to purchase its largest "steel fabrication" competitor (Consolidated Steel).

The Sherman Act, in its application to combinations, was punitive and corrective. Section 7 of the Clayton Act was designed to be preventive. The test of illegality in the Sherman Act required proof of accomplished monopolization or of intent to monopolize. The test in the Clayton Act was easier to

[5] 334 U.S. 495 (1948).

Table 4-3

Examples of Very Large Acquisitions, in Order of the Value of the Deal, in 1982

Acquiring Company	Business	Acquired Company	Business	Value of the Deal (billions)
U. S. Steel	Steel	Marathon Oil	Oil and gas	$5.96
Occidental Petroleum	Oil and gas	Cities Service	Oil and gas	4.02
Connecticut General	Insurance	INA	Insurance	1.93
Allied	Oil, gas, chemicals	Bendix	Automotive products	1.82
American General	Insurance	NLT	Insurance	1.54
R. J. Reynolds	Tobacco and food	Heublein	Distilling	1.37
Norfolk & Western	Railroad	Southern	Railroad	1.36
Union Pacific	Oil, gas, railroad	Missouri Pacific	Railroad	1.17
Baldwin–United	Financial services	MGIC	Insurance and real estate	1.16
Smith Kline	Pharmaceuticals	Beckman	Medical instruments	1.01
Coca-Cola	Soft drinks	Columbia Pictures	Motion pictures	0.75

Source: Robert Steyer, "Deals of the Year," *Fortune*, Jan. 24, 1983, pp. 49–50.

meet; it required only a reasonable probability that competition would be substantially lessened at some future date. However, Section 7 banned only purchases of *stock*. Thus, all a firm had to do in order to avoid its reach was to acquire the *assets* of the other firm.

The main provision of Section 7 as amended in 1950 reads as follows:

> No corporation engaged in commerce shall acquire, directly or indirectly, the whole or any part of the stock or other share capital and no corporation subject to the jurisdiction of the Federal Trade Commission shall acquire the whole or any part of the assets of another corporation engaged also in commerce, where, in any line of commerce in any section of the country, the effect of such acquisition may be substantially to lessen competition or tend to create a monopoly.

Thus, the revision was calculated to close the stock versus assets loophole. Furthermore, the words "part of the assets" have been held to cover even the purchase of a single trademark by one company from another (e.g., the acquisition by Lever Brothers from Monsanto Chemical Company of the trademark "All" relating to detergents).

Underlying the passage of the Celler–Kefauver Amendment seemed to be several concerns of Congress. The fundamental concern was the rising tide of economic concentration in the economy, which the FTC reported at the time as being due primarily to horizontal mergers. Such concentration was feared because it would facilitate direct and indirect collusion among sellers. In addition, Congress wanted to retain control over industry and to protect small business. Other values that entered into the development of the statute were (1) its relevance for vertical and conglomerate as well as horizontal mergers, (2) its emphasis that mergers could be forbidden when the trend toward lessening competition was still in its incipiency, (3) its focus on competition, not competitors, which meant that mergers could be restrained that merely lessened competition, and (4) its use of the word "may," which lowered the standard of proof so that only *probable* anticompetitive effects need be shown.[6]

Two more recent laws are also important in the merger area. A rider to a 1973 bill gave the Federal Trade Commission authority to seek preliminary injunctions against mergers, a power the Justice Department already had. And the 1976 Antitrust Improvements Act (which inserted a new clause 7a in the Clayton Act) makes advance notification of mergers compulsory if one party to the merger has yearly sales or assets of at least $100 million and the other party at least $10 million, and if the acquiring company, as a result of the merger, reaches a position where it holds either 15 percent or $50 million worth of voting securities or assets in the acquired company. The law imposes a 15- to 30-day waiting period following initial notification before the merger can be consummated so as to allow the FTC or the Justice Department to seek a preliminary injunction to restrain the merger if they believe such restraint is desirable.

Before we turn to look at the specific antitrust actions involving mergers, it

---

[6] Ernest Gellhorn, *Antitrust Law and Economics in a Nutshell* (St. Paul, Minn.: West Publishing Co., 1976), pp. 304–305.

is important to note at the onset that the lines of policy with respect to mergers are basically set by the Supreme Court through precedents from their decisions. The Antitrust Division of the Attorney General's Office in the Department of Justice and the Federal Trade Commission can influence the policy process directly by the kinds of cases that they bring and the theories that they apply. The Supreme Court then may have an opportunity to react to the theories and to interpret Congress' will in the antitrust area, if a case makes it all the way through the court system. But private litigants can and do file numerous merger cases under the federal statutes, especially as a result of "unfriendly" takeover attempts,[7] and unless the enforcement agencies decide to join these private cases, their orientations will only be felt indirectly in them.

It is also important to note that the temper of the times relative to merger policy is changing. First, in recent history, power has been placed in the hands of enforcement agency officials who, by and large, believe that the attitude toward mergers prior to 1980 was too restrictive. This more laissez-faire attitude is reflected in the Justice Department's merger guidelines discussed later. Second, and most important, the analytic style of the Supreme Court's decisions in antitrust cases has shifted since early 1974 and is now, on balance, different in focus and form from what it was in the 1960s and early 1970s.[8] The Warren Court (1954–1968) had the task of establishing the first real merger policy. In applying the merger law, the Warren Court placed heavy reliance on a structural analysis of markets and on developing rules that outline for businessmen in advance which mergers are likely to be challenged, primarily through examining the market shares of the merging firms. The antitrust enforcement agencies won all 12 merger decisions during 1958–1969. With the retirement of Chief Justice Warren in 1969 and the appointment of Chief Justice Burger, followed by the appointment of Justices Blackmun, O'Connor, Powell, Rehnquist, and Stevens to replace Justices Black, Douglas, Fortas, Harlan, and Stewart, a structuralist antitrust generation of Supreme Court justices began to phase out and a "realist" generation, as Bock calls it, began to emerge.[9] The Court under Chief Justice Burger has been less quick to apply presumptions of illegality derived from market share statistics and other data. It has also been more willing to accept district judges' findings of fact.

Doubtless, the changed orientation both on the Court and in the enforcement agencies will have an effect on how mergers should be viewed from a legal perspective, but the actual content of that effect is indeterminant until the Court deals with more merger cases. In the interim, precedents exist, and it is these precedents to which businesspersons, forming a merger policy, must mainly attend as opposed to conjectures on what a more "realistic" Court will do.

---

[7] See, for example, *Marathon Oil Co.* v. *Mobil Corp.*, 530 F. Supp. 315, *affirmed*, 669 F.2d 378 (6th Cir. 1981).

[8] Betty Bock, *Antitrust and the Supreme Court—An Economic Exploration* (New York: The Conference Board, Information Bulletin No. 73, 1980), p. 3.

[9] Ibid.

HORIZONTAL MERGERS

Over the years, the following factors have been found relevant in testing horizontal mergers:

1. The degree of concentration in the relevant market.
2. The rank and shares of the acquiring and acquired company in the relevant market.
2. Changes, and particularly decreases, in the number of companies operating in an expanding market.
4. Changes in barriers to entry.
5. The elimination of a major independent company from a generally oligopolistic market.

These factors were emphasized so strongly by the Warren Court, the Justice Department, and the FTC that the following observation accurately described the state of affairs in the merger arena at the end of the 1960s:

> if there is an overall rule for horizontal mergers . . . , it is that neither actual nor potential competitors can safely merge if the acquiring company is a major company and if the acquired company is a strong competitor in its own right and concentration in the relevant market is high; nor can a viable independent with relatively low market shares be acquired if concentration in the relevant market is high, the number of companies is declining in the face of expanding demand, and the acquiring company is a dominant one in the market affected.[10]

Such a perspective will no doubt be loosened under the Burger Court and by application of the 1982 merger guidelines. As we shall see later, some general loosening has already begun. And yet the theme implied in the past history of antitrust cases is such a significant one that it is unlikely that it will be reversed entirely. Indeed, it should be expected that the variables examined will remain much the same, but that narrow presumptions of illegality or even more flexible standards will be more commonplace than per se rules.

To determine whether a merger, under the Celler–Kefauver Amendment, may substantially lessen competition or tend to create a monopoly "in any line of commerce in any section of the country," a product market ("line of commerce") and a geographic market ("section of the country") must first be defined prior to the calculation of market shares and, concomitantly, an assessment of the degree of economic concentration. Supposedly, a "relevant market," inclusive of both product and geographic considerations, has been properly delineated if, in the face of price increases or output restrictions on the part of firms within the market, other firms with substitute products would not enter the market promptly enough or in sufficient scale to cause a reduction of the price or an increase of the output to their previous levels. As Sullivan observes,

> If sufficient supply would promptly enter from other geographic areas, then the "defined market" is not wide enough in geographic terms; if sufficient supply

---

[10] Betty Bock, *Mergers and Markets*, 6th ed. (New York: The Conference Board, Study in Business Economics No. 100, 1968), p. 7.

would promptly enter in the form of products made by other producers which had not been included in the product market as defined, then the market would not be wide enough in defined product terms. A "relevant market," then, is the narrowest market which is wide enough so that products from adjacent areas or from other producers in the same area cannot compete on substantial parity with those included in the market.[11]

The decision with respect to "relevant market" may be crucial. If markets are narrowly defined, a substantial lessening of competition will be more frequent than if they are broadly defined.

Defining relevant markets is no simple matter.[12] In Clayton Act proceedings (as well as in Sherman Act cases), courts have tended to determine the outer boundaries of a relevant market through a consideration of "the reasonable interchangeability of use or the cross-elasticity of demand between the product itself and substitutes for it."[13] However, this concept, while theoretically appealing, has been difficult to apply in practice because of the absence of defensible data relative to cross-elasticities of demand, which basically measure the change in the quantity demanded of one product as the price of another product is raised or lowered when all other influencing factors are held constant. In fact, the courts have gone beyond the concept of "outer boundaries" and have delineated submarkets that exist within the broader market, making the probability of a substantial lessening of competition higher than would be the case if the outer boundaries tests were used. (For example, a submarket might be defined as the market for reconstituted lemon juice within the more encompassing lemon juice market, which would, of course, include the juice from fresh lemons.) As stated in the now infamous *Brown Shoe* case,

> The boundaries of such a submarket may be determined by examining such practical indicia as industry or public recognition of the submarket as a separate economic entity, the product's peculiar characteristics and uses, unique production facilities, distinct customers, distinct prices, sensitivity to price changes, and specialized vendors.[14]

We will not engage in a debate with the Court over the criteria to be used (and their possible inconsistencies) or over the relevance of the submarket concept. We will, however, insert two cynical observations, one by Richard Posner, formerly a University of Chicago professor of law and now a federal judge, and the other by Max Ways of *Fortune* magazine. Posner has commented that

---

[11] Lawrence A. Sullivan, *Handbook of the Law of Antitrust* (St. Paul, Minn.: West Publishing Co., 1977), p. 41.

[12] For a discussion of this issue, see Thomas W. Dunfee, Louis W. Stern, and Frederick D. Sturdivant, "Bounding Markets in Merger Cases: Identifying Relevant Competitors," *Northwestern L.R.* 78 (Nov. 1983).

[13] *Brown Shoe Co. v. U.S.*, 370 U.S. 294 (1962) at 325. The term "cross-elasticity of demand" has basically been used as an abstraction. Actual cross-elasticities of demand are rarely ever computed for antitrust purposes. As such, the term has become a very clever "buzz word," which really ought to be dropped from the language of the courts unless it is employed with its originally intended precision. If it were applied as originally defined by economists, it would become immediately apparent that cross-elasticities are not very helpful in defining the relevant sphere of competition.

[14] Ibid.

> If the "outer boundaries" of the market include only the product's good sub-stitutes in both consumption and production . . . , then a submarket would be a group of sellers from which sellers of good substitutes in consumption or pro-duction had been excluded, and these exclusions would deprive any market-share statistics of their economic significance.[15]

Ways has noted,

> If you assume that aluminum wire doesn't compete with copper wire (*U.S.* vs. *Aluminum Co. of America*, 377 U.S. 271, 1964), that a commercial bank doesn't compete with another commercial bank twenty miles away (*U.S.* vs. *Philadelphia National Bank*, 374 U.S. 321, 1963), that a retail shoe market could be arbitrari-ly defined as any city of 10,000 with its "immediate surrounding areas" where both the merging companies had stores (*Brown Shoe* vs. *U.S.* 370 U.S. 294, 1962), then, of course, you can prove quite a lot of "concentration" in a particu-lar market.[16]

In the *Alcoa-Rome*[17] case, for example, the Court indicated that copper wire and cable *and* aluminum wire and cable were separate *product* submarkets, even though, as the District Court found, the two types of conductors require similar production processes, have similar uses and characteristics, and are sold to the same type of customers. The District Court also considered the dif-ference in prices between the two types of conductors and held "that this price difference did not foreclose actual competition." The significance of the market identification portion of the case is that if the product submarket included *both* copper and aluminum conductors, an insignificant amount of competition would have been restrained and the merger would have been allowed.[18] In *U.S.* v. *Continental Can Co.*,[19] a case somewhat similar to *Alcoa-Rome*, the Court held that bottles and cans were in the same relevant product market, a finding totally inconsistent with the line of reasoning in *Alcoa-Rome*. Here the ques-tion involved the potential effect on competition of Continental Can's acquisi-tion of Hazel–Atlas. Continental was the second largest producer of metal containers, and Hazel–Atlas was the third largest producer of glass containers. By finding that the types of containers were interchangeable for some uses, the Supreme Court could then view the merger as horizontal. Because of the size of the respective firms in the now combined can–glass container *product* mar-ket, the Court eventually became convinced that the merger cold have led to a substantial lessening of competition if allowed to stand. According to Scherer, the *Alcoa-Rome* and *Continental Can* decisions exhibit the overriding willingness of the courts, at least prior to 1974, to "accept market definitions that resolve inherent doubts on the side of preventing mergers with possible anti-competitive effects."[20]

[15] Richard A. Posner, *Antitrust Law: An Economic Perspective* (Chicago: University of Chicago Press, 1976), p. 129.

[16] Max Ways, "Antitrust in an Era of Radical Change," *Fortune* 73 (March 1966), p. 131.

[17] *U.S.* v. *Aluminum Co. of America*, 377 U.S. 271 (1964).

[18] Joe L. Welch, *Marketing Law* (Tulsa, Okla.: Petroleum Publishing Co., 1980), p. 43.

[19] 378 U.S. 441 (1964).

[20] Scherer, op. cit., p. 552.

The Celler–Kefauver Act also allows considerable scope for defining *geo-graphic* markets. As indicated in *U.S.* v. *Philadelphia National Bank*,[21] the relevant geographic market "is not where the parties to the merger do business or even where they compete, but where, within the area of competitive overlap, the effect of the merger on competition will be direct and immediate." In *U.S.* v. *Pabst Brewing Company*,[22] the opinion of the majority would seem to indicate that it may suffice to show that competition may be substantially lessened somewhere in the United States without necessarily having to delineate the section by "metes and bounds as a surveyor would lay off a plot of ground."[23]

Aside from the relevant market issue, the history of Section 7 horizontal merger cases after the passage of the Celler–Kefauver Amendment is intriguing and somewhat bewildering. The first major government victory under the new Section 7 came in *U.S.* v. *Bethlehem Steel Corp.*[24] in 1958. Bethlehem, the second largest steel producer in the nation with 16.3 percent of total U.S. ingot capacity, sought to acquire Youngstown Sheet & Tube Co., the sixth largest producer with 4.6 percent of ingot capacity. The companies argued that the merger did not substantially lessen competition because Bethlehem sold most of its output in the East, while Youngstown was primarily active in the Midwest, so that only about 10 percent of their combined output was shipped to customers in overlapping geographic territories. This defense was rejected by the District Court, which held that freight cost barriers to interpenetration of regional markets were overcome sufficiently to view the market as nationwide in scope and that a merger combining such capacity exemplified the substantial lessening of competition Congress sought to outlaw under the new Section 7. The respondents chose not to appeal, so there was no Supreme Court test. In fact, with the possible exception of the companies involved, there are very few antitrust observers who would argue vehemently with the outcome of the case or the reasoning applied to it.

The first substantive Supreme Court test of the Celler–Kefauver Amendment came in 1962 when a lower court decision against the Brown Shoe Company's merger with G. R. Kinney Co. was affirmed.[25] The merger had both horizontal and vertical ramifications. We will deal with only the former in this chapter; the latter are left to Chapter 6. Virtually all aspects of the Supreme Court decision in this case are, however, bathed in controversy.

Both Brown and Kinney were manufacturers and retailers of men's, women's, and children's shoes. The District Court's findings that the merger of the *manufacturing* operations did not violate the antitrust laws was not appealed. Brown was the fourth largest manufacturer of shoes with 4% of the market; Kinney was twelfth largest with 0.5%. The horizontal aspect of the case fo-

---

[21] 374 U.S. 321 (1963).

[22] 384 U.S. 546 (1966).

[23] For a comprehensive discussion of the geographic market issue, see Kenneth G. Elzinga and Thomas F. Hogarty, "The Problem of Geographic Market Delineation in Antimerger Suits," *Antitrust Bulletin* 18 (1973), pp. 45–80.

[24] 168 F. Supp. 576, S.D.N.Y. (1958).

[25] *Brown Shoe Co.* v. *U.S.*, 370 U.S. 294 (1962).

cused instead on the *retailing* operations. The relevant geographic market was defined as cities over 10,000 in which both Brown and Kinney operated stores. In this market, the Court found that the combined share of sales was often very large, exceeding 20 percent for women's shoes in 32 cities and for children's shoes in 31 cities, while exceeding even 50 percent in a few cities. Yet most of these cities were relatively small and did not constitute large markets. Therefore, the critical point, according to the Court, was that "in 118 separate cities the combined shares of the market of Brown and Kinney in the sale of one of the relevant lines of commerce exceeded 5 percent." In assessing whether the merger was anticompetitive or likely to become so, the Court considered the following factors:

1. whether the merger was to take place in an industry not yet concentrated;
2. whether that industry had seen a recent trend towards domination by a few market leaders or had remained fairly consistent in its distribution of market shares among participating companies;
3. whether suppliers had easy access to markets and buyers to suppliers or whether substantial business was foreclosed to competition; and
4. whether new entry to the industry was possible without undue difficulty.[26]

The Court argued that

> In an industry as fragmented as shoe retailing, the control of substantial shares of the trade in a city may have important effects on competition. If a merger achieving 5 percent control were now approved, we might be required to approve future merger efforts by Brown's competitors seeking similar market shares.[27]

While the Court's condemnation of a merger controlling 5 percent of the market where the industry is fragmented seems a curious twist on the merger law's concern with concentration, it is not nearly as curious as the Court's concern with the potential effects of retail *chain* operations on competition. The Court made the following statement on this issue in *Brown Shoe*:

> Of course, some of the results of large integrated or chain operations are beneficial to consumers. Their expansion is not rendered unlawful by the mere fact that small independent stores may be adversely affected. It is competition, not competitors, which the Act protects. But we cannot fail to recognize Congress' desire to promote competition through the protection of viable, small, locally owned businesses. Congress appreciated that occasional higher costs and prices might result from the maintenance of fragmented industries and markets. It resolved these competing considerations in favor of decentralization. We must give effect to that decision.[28]

In the words of Scherer,

> It is possible to interpret the rather muddled *Brown Shoe* opinion as saying that the merger was illegal because it would yield economies and hence lead to the competitive attrition of small retailers. To virtually all economists, such a

[26] A. D. Neale and D. G. Goyder, *The Antitrust Laws of the U.S.A.* (New York: Cambridge University Press, 1980), p. 187.

[27] *Brown Shoe Co.* v. *U.S.*, 370 U.S. 294 (1962) at 344.

[28] Ibid.

rule seems unwise public policy, posing among other things a direct conflict with the efficiency goals of antitrust.[29]

The *Brown Shoe* decision appeared at the time to mean that the principal criterion in assessing a merger was to be its "qualitative substantiality," that is, its overall impact on the competitive process in the particular industry, rather than merely its "quantitative substantiality," the size and market share of the companies involved.[30] In the following year, however, the judgment of the Supreme Court in *U.S.* v. *Philadelphia National Bank*[31] seemed to throw doubt on this interpretation. The Court outlined a minimum threshold where mergers were presumptively illegal and hence did not require evaluation of their economic impact:

> we think a merger which produces a firm controlling an undue percentage share of the relevant market, and results in a significant increase in the concentration of firms in that market is so inherently likely to lessen competition substantially that it must be enjoined in the absence of evidence clearly showing that the merger is not likely to have such anticompetitive effects.[32]

In a footnote, the Court stated that "scholarly opinion" had suggested 20 or 25 percent as a suitable figure at which such an inference could begin to be drawn. However, as Gellhorn correctly points out, the *Philadelphia National Bank* case is not necessarily inconsistent with the *Brown Shoe* case, even though the legal tests that were applied are different.[33] *Brown Shoe* took place in the context of a fragmented industry where the Court insisted on an examination of economic factors, whereas *Philadelphia National Bank* set forth an outside limit for horizontal mergers in concentrated markets.

Gellhorn has also pointed out that in *Alcoa-Rome*[34] and *Continental Can*,[35] two cases having conglomerate merger-product extension overtones that the Court treated as involving strictly horizontal merger issues, the Court only slightly extended the *Brown Shoe–PNB* rule.[36] In the former, the Court held that the dominant firm in a concentrated industry (Alcoa) could not purchase a significant competitive factor (Rome) without unlawfully impairing competition. Rome had been a particularly dynamic force in the copper conductor industry. In *Continental Can*, the court relied primarily on the total market share of the two merged firms (Continental Can and Hazel–Atlas) in the combined can and bottle industries and on the increasing concentration in both industries. As Gellhorn observes, when these two cases are viewed together, it appears as though the market share percentages at which mergers are deemed

---

[29] Scherer, op. cit., p. 556.

[30] Neale and Goyder, op. cit., p. 188.

[31] 374 U.S. 321 (1963).

[32] Ibid.

[33] Gellhorn, op. cit., p. 324.

[34] *U.S.* v. *Aluminum Co. of America,* 377 U.S. 271 (1964).

[35] *U.S.* v. *Continental Can Co.,* 378 U.S. 441 (1964).

[36] Gellhorn, op. cit., p. 325.

illegal were lowered by the Court. However, each case also involved a major merger in a concentrated industry.[37]

The Warren Court's "hard line" on concentration was virtually calcified in a landmark case involving a merger between Von's Grocery Co. and Shopping Bag Stores in Los Angeles.[38] On the face of it, the merger did not appear to pose a serious threat to competition. Market concentration in Los Angeles had not reached high levels before the merger, and the two merging companies had combined sales of only about 8 percent of the market. However, the Justice Department successfully argued that concentration in Los Angeles had been increasing for more than a decade (between 1948 and 1958 the share of grocery store sales held by the top 20 chains rose from 43.8 to 56.9 percent). Furthermore, it showed that much of the remainder of the market was held by small retailers experiencing a high attrition rate; the number of single-store grocery retailers fell from 5,365 in 1950 to 3,818 in 1961. The Court in its decision was primarily interested in helping stem the "tide" of the increase in concentration taking place in Los Angeles. It appears that, in economic terms, the Court wanted to preserve a situation of atomistic competition rather than allow an oligopolistic market to develop. Thus, the reasoning here was similar to that found in *Brown Shoe*. It should, however, be noted that, in a dissenting opinion, Justices Stewart and Harlan argued that the decline in the number of single-unit stores was the result of "transcending social and technological changes" and that competition in Los Angeles grocery retailing remained "pugnacious," with successful new entry at modest initial investment levels perceptibly eroding the market shares of leading firms.[39]

The line of decisions starting with *Brown Shoe* and ending with *Von's Grocery* came to an abrupt end in 1974 when the Burger Court refused to find that an acquisition by General Dynamics might lessen competition or tend to create a monopoly.[40] General Dynamics, which already owned one coal company, had acquired United Electric Coal Company. The effect of the merger was to raise the General Dynamics share of the market in the Eastern Interior Coal Province from 7.6 to 12.4 percent and in the Illinois area from 15.4 to 23.2 percent, representing a significant increase of concentration in both those markets. It is likely that the Warren Court would have considered the merger illegal on this basis alone, but the Burger Court reached back to a footnote in the *Brown Shoe* decision for the proposition that while market share percentages are "the primary index of market power . . . only a further examination of the particular market—its structure, history and probable future—can provide the appropriate setting for judging the probable anticompetitive effect of the merger".[41] In a five-to-four decision, the Court found that the acquired

[37] Ibid., p. 326.

[38] *U.S.* v. *Von's Grocery Co.*, 384 U.S. 270 (1966).

[39] Ibid., at 300.

[40] *U.S.* v. *General Dynamics Corp.*, 415 U.S. 486 (1974).

[41] Ibid., at 498 quoting 370 U.S. 294 (1962) at 322, n. 38.

unit's coal reserves were almost entirely committed under long-term contract, and, therefore, because the acquired company had no real market future, its disappearance as an independent firm would not adversely affect competition. As Scherer has observed,

> *General Dynamics'* primary significance may lie in its demonstration that the new Supreme Court was no longer willing to consistently define markets in a way that gave the benefit of the doubt to the antimerger forces.[42]

Subsequent bank merger cases further suggest that the Court will now more closely examine the meaning of market share percentages before drawing inferences of likely competitive effect.[43] However, it should be carefully noted that in these later cases, the Court described its *General Dynamics* decision as holding that market·share statistics establish a rebuttable presumption of illegality. It should be remembered that this was the formulation employed in *Philadelphia National Bank* under the Warren Court.

Some joint ventures are similar to horizontal mergers in situations where the partners and the seperate entity formed by the partners all compete within the same market, e.g., General Motors' joint venture with Toyota to produce a new subcompact car to be sold in the U.S. In weighing the potential anticompetitive effects of such "horizontal" ventures, the antitrust enforcement agencies and the courts are likely to look at many of the same factors that they would consider in a horizontal merger case, such as the level of concentration in the market, the existence of entry barriers, the likelihood of collusion regarding prices or markets served, and the ability of other firms to compete with the joint venture. In addition, consideration would be given to whether the partners could have *individually* incurred the expense and the effort required to achieve what the joint venture was designed to accomplish, the length of time covered by the joint venture, the purpose of the venture, and the attitude of the partners toward licensing any technological breakthroughs achieved by the venture.

An important issue in horizontal merger cases that has yet to be resolved fully concerns the importance of absolute versus relative concentration measures. Historically, the enforcement agencies and the courts have measured the combined market shares of the top 4, 8, and 20 firms in a given market to determine the extent of concentration. However, it has become increasingly clear that many markets are already highly concentrated and oftentimes dominated by one or two firms holding a large portion of the sales of a given product. In such markets, it would seem logical to take account of the fact that a merger between the medium-sized firms might afford the resulting company increased leverage with which to do battle with the dominant firms in the market.

A New York District Court did, in fact, follow this argument to its logical conclusion in weighing the merits and demerits of a horizontal merger between

---

[42] Scherer, op. cit., p. 555.

[43] *U.S.* v. *Marine Bancorporation,* 418 U.S. 602 (1974) and *U.S.* v. *Citizens & Southern National Bank,* 422 U.S. 86 (1975).

Manufacturers Trust Co. and the Hanover Bank.[44] The court concluded that the gap previously existing in the market structure between the second and third largest banks in New York had narrowed and that the "merger thereby improved the competitive structure and intensified competition for the three leaders." However, this line of reasoning has proved to be the exception rather than the rule in horizontal merger cases. For example, this same argument was raised and rejected in *Philadelphia National Bank* and in *Bethlehem Steel.* As is shown later, the Justice Department in its recent merger guidelines has explicitly endorsed the notion of relative as opposed to absolute concentration. It advocates changing the way in which concentration is measured from the use of four-firm concentration ratios to the Herfindahl–Hirschman Index, which considers the relative market shares of each of the major companies in an industry.[45] Mergers of small- or medium-sized firms in a market may increase the market power of these weaker firms and thereby result in better "market balance" and more intense competition among the remaining rivals.

CONGLOMERATE MERGERS

Concern about conglomerate mergers from an antitrust perspective has generally emphasized two issues: the overall concentration of asset ownership (basically, a political issue) and the competitive superiority of conglomerate firms over firms operating in a single product or geographic market. With regard to the latter issue, some economists feel that the conglomerate merger trend can have three effects. First, the acquiring company may be a potential competitor in a certain market. By acquiring a company already there, rather than entering the market on its own, the conglomerate keeps the number of companies competing in that market from increasing. Second, by remaining on the edge of an oligopolistic market rather than entering it via merger, the potential competitor will have a procompetitive effect on the oligopolists. In other words, they may keep their prices low in order to discourage entry. Economists call such a strategy *limit pricing*, because it purposively limits entry into the market. Third, a multiproduct corporation can use resources generated in one market to overwhelm one-product rivals in another market. This thinking has led to the definition of *conglomerate market power* as "the ability of a conglomerate firm at its discretion to shift marketing emphasis and resources among its markets and activities."[46] All this concern seems like a reaction to large size and diversification rather than to conglomeration per se. In fact, as Gellhorn has cogently observed,

---

[44] *U.S.* v. *The Manufacturers Hanover Trust Co.,* 240 F. Supp. 867 S.D.N.Y. (1965).

[45] For a discussion of the Herfindahl index as applied to the merger area, see Richard A. Posner, *Oligopoly and the Antitrust Laws,* Stanford L. R. 21 (1969), p. 1562. The Justice Department considered the relative market share issue along with entry barriers, growth considerations, and technological issues before deciding to challenge G. Heileman Brewing Co.'s proposed acquisition of Jos. Schlitz Brewing Co. in 1981. See Robert E. Taylor, "Heileman's Plan to Buy Schlitz Opposed by U.S.," *Wall Street Journal,* Oct. 22, 1981, p. 4.

[46] John C. Narver, *Conglomerate Mergers and Marketing Competition* (Berkeley, Calif.: University of California Press, 1967), p. 105.

Whatever the type of conglomerate, the transaction involves firms which are in separate markets, and the merger therefore can have no direct effect on competition. There is no reduction or other change in the number of firms in either the acquiring or acquired firm's market. Foreclosure . . . is generally absent except insofar as the merging parties may engage in reciprocal dealing or supply each other's needs. Nor is there any change in market structure, the firms' market shares, or concentration ratios.[47]

To date, three types of conglomerate acquisitions have been held to violate Section 7 of the Clayton Act: (1) "deep-pocket" acquisitions of dominant firms, (2) potential entrant mergers involving product-extension and market-extension mergers and joint ventures, and (3) acquisitions leading to the creation and potential exercise of reciprocal purchasing leverage. The third type of acquisition more directly pertains to vertical mergers, a topic addressed in Chapter 6. Here we discuss the deep-pocket and potential entrant mergers.

Deep-Pocket Mergers

A deep-pocket merger involves an acquisition of a firm dominant within the relevant competitive market by a firm having managerial and financial resources capable of further entrenching the competitive superiority of the acquired firm. Supposedly, according to the theory, the intrusion of a well-financed, technologically sophisticated, marketing-oriented firm into a market previously populated with small independent sellers increases the likelihood of predatory conduct, which in turn could drive small firms out of business or make them more docile because they fear punishment. The Federal Trade Commission successfully attacked Procter & Gamble's acquisition of the Clorox Company by applying this theory.[48] The Supreme Court, following the suggestions of the Federal Trade Commission, isolated the following anticompetitive factors in declaring the merger illegal:

1. The substitution in the liquid bleach market of the powerful Procter in place of the smaller, but already dominant, Clorox would undoubtedly dissuade smaller firms in the market from active price competition with Procter;
2. Entry barriers would be raised because the volume discounts that Procter could obtain for its own advertising would be placed at the disposal of Clorox;[49]
3. If any competitors in the future did attempt to enter the liquid bleach market, Procter could, at least temporarily, use its profits from other markets for a massive increase in sales promotion and advertisements to support Clorox in resisting the attack;
4. Prior to the merger, Procter had been the most likely entrant to the market: the mere possibility of its own entry (now removed) had had a beneficial effect on the competitive attitudes of the firms in that market.[50]

---

[47] Gellhorn, op. cit., p. 334.

[48] *FTC* v. *Procter & Gamble Co.*, 368 U.S. 568 (1967).

[49] The significance of these discounts as an anticompetitive factor has, in a number of studies, been shown to be low. For a review and appropriate citations, see Scherer, op. cit., pp. 111 and 556.

[50] Neale and Goyder, op. cit., p. 201.

The fourth factor is, of course, associated with the potential entrant theory, which is addressed later.

Similar reasoning to that in the *Procter & Gamble* case appeared in *General Foods Corp. v. FTC*,[51] where General Foods was required to divest itself of the SOS Corporation, a maker of steel-wool pads. The FTC asserted that other current and potential producers of household steel wool had been or might be precluded from competing with General Foods, because of General Foods'

1. Dominant market position, financial resources, and economic power.
2. Advertising ability and experience.
3. Merchandising and promotional ability and experience.
4. Comprehensive line of packaged grocery products.
5. Ability to command consumer acceptance of its products and of valuable grocery-store shelf space.
6. Ability to concentrate on one of its products or on one section of the country the full impact of its promotional, advertising, and merchandising experience and ability.[52]

The FTC rejected General Foods' argument that the acquisition was legal because some 40 other household cleaning devices, such as plastic scouring pads, compete with steel-wool pads.

Despite its successful application in the *P&G* and *General Foods* cases, the deep-pocket theory has not obtained strong scholarly support, and, therefore, it received much less emphasis in the conglomerate merger cases of the 1970s.

Potential Entrant Mergers

A potential entrant merger involves

> an acquisition of a firm within a concentrated relevant competitive market by a firm that is the likely entrant into that market via internal growth. The presumption is that the firms already within the market recognized the acquirer as a likely entrant. As a consequence, these firms engaged in procompetitive behavior by reducing their prices and restricting their profits to make their market appear less attractive to the acquirer. When the acquirer leaves the edge of the market and enters by acquisition, no new competitive entities are created, and the competitive force of the entrant on the edge is lost.[53]

This statement provides the basic idea underlying potential competition theory as it has been applied in conglomerate merger cases. However, two subsets of the theory have been distinguished in a variety of cases, one dealing with *actual* potential entry and the other dealing with *perceived* potential entry. Actual potential entry refers to the loss of a more competitive market that occurs when a firm that might have entered on its own in the future enters a market now by acquisition. Perceived potential entry refers to the situation where a firm without any subjective desire to enter a market may nevertheless be re-

---

[51] 386 F.2d 936 (1967).

[52] Narver, op. cit., p. 85.

[53] Myron L. Erickson, Thomas W. Dunfee, and Frank F. Gibson, *Antitrust and Trade Regulation* (Columbus, Ohio: Grid, Inc., 1977), p. 201. See also Thomas W. Dunfee and Louis W. Stern, *Potential Competition Theory as an Antimerger Tool under Section 7 of the Clayton Act: A Decision Model*, Northwestern L. R. 69 (Jan.–Feb. 1975), pp. 821–871.

garded by those already in the market as a potential entrant, and, as such, it may influence to some degree the pricing and other marketing policies of the existing market participants. Therefore, elimination of either an actual or a perceived potential entrant from the edge of a market via merger with a firm already in the market may have a serious effect on marketing behavior, especially in a concentrated market.

In the decision in *U.S.* v. *El Paso Natural Gas Co.*,[54] the Supreme Court used the phrase "potential competition" for the first time. El Paso bought the stock of Pacific Northwest Pipeline Corporation, a company tapping extensive gas reserves in New Mexico and western Canada. El Paso supplied 50 percent of the natural gas to the California market. Prior to the merger, Pacific had tried to obtain a license to serve the California market and had competed with El Paso on some large utility contracts, causing El Paso to lower its prices. The Federal Power Commission rejected Pacific's application, but Pacific still had its large gas reserves in surrounding states and had the management capability to enter the market. The Supreme Court ordered the merger dissolved because it eliminated a substantial competitive factor (an actual potential entrant), noting that "we would have to wear blinders not to see that the mere efforts of Pacific Northwest to get into the California market, though unsuccessful, had a powerful influence on El Paso's business attitudes within the state."[55]

The potential entrant (or potential competition) theory was applied almost concurrently with the *El Paso* decision to a joint venture involving Penn-Salt and Olin Mathieson.[56] Penn-Salt, prior to the joint venture, had 9 percent of the sodium chlorate industry with a plant in the Northwest. Olin did not manufacture sodium chlorate but sold it in the Southeast for Penn-Salt. Two companies located in the Southeast, Hooker Chemical and American Potash, controlled about 90 percent of the sodium chlorate market at the time. Both Penn-Salt and Olin had done independent studies about building a plant in the Southeast; however, they formed a joint venture instead and built a plant jointly. The District Court found that both Penn-Salt and Olin had the resources and the expertise to enter the market on their own, but, relying on the competitive value of an additional market entrant in a situation where there were only two firms in the market, it upheld the joint venture. The District Court reasoned that competition had been enhanced, not lessened, because one actual entrant was worth more than two on the sideline. However, on review, the Supreme Court remanded the case for further findings, arguing that if there is a probability that one firm will enter a market alone while the other firm remains a threat to enter the market, a venture between the two is unlawful.[57] This case, then, represented another application of the actual potential entry theory.

---

[54] 376 U.S. 651 (1964).

[55] Ibid., at 659.

[56] *U.S.* v. *Penn-Olin Chemical Co.*, 378 U.S. 158 (1964).

[57] On remand, the District Court found that neither Penn-Salt nor Olin would have entered the market by itself. Therefore, the joint venture was held to be legal.

Potential competition theory has also been applied to two market-extension conglomerate merger cases. The first of these cases was *U.S.* v. *Falstaff Brewing Corp.*[58] Falstaff bought Naragansett Brewing Co., which had 20 percent of the highly concentrated New England beer market. Falstaff had 6 percent of the national market but did no business in New England, even though it had studied the possibility of entering the New England market via internal growth. The District Court found that, since Falstaff would not have entered the market without a merger, there was no violation. In other words, Falstaff was not viewed by the court as an actual potential entrant. However, the Supreme Court reversed the decision on the grounds that Falstaff might still have been perceived by the firms in the market as a potential entrant and consequently forced them to constrain their pricing practices. The Court remanded the case, raising two questions for the District Court to answer: (1) Was Falstaff perceived by the firms within the market as a potential competitor? and (2) If it was, would its elimination from the edge of the market significantly affect competition or were others similarly situated? The District Court answered both questions in the negative, and the merger was allowed to stand.

The second of these market-extension cases was *U.S.* v. *Marine Bancorporation et al.*[59] in which Marine Bancorporation, a large national bank headquartered in Seattle, bought another large bank located in Spokane. Marine Bancorporation had no branches in Spokane at the time of the merger. Because Washington state law prohibited the Seattle bank from branching into Spokane, the relevant market was defined not as the state of Washington—in which the two banks might have been potential competitors—but the Spokane metropolitan area. In reasoning not atypical from that found in the *General Dynamics* case, where the Court looked at factors beyond market share, the Court found that, because of the state banking regulations that insulated markets within Washington, the acquisition could not substantially lessen competition by eliminating potential entrants, regardless of the statewide share of the two banks or the degree of concentration in commercial banking in Spokane, where the first three commercial banks accounted for 92 percent of the business.

Despite the flexibility shown in the *Marine Bancorporation* case, the Court reiterated its belief, based on previous cases, that it would still be possible to find a merger illegal on the basis of potential competition theory, even though the Court laid down a difficult burden of proof for antitrust enforcers and private plaintiffs to follow. It stated that a conglomerate merger may be unlawful

> if the target market is substantially concentrated, if the acquiring firm has the characteristics, capabilities, and economic incentive to render it a perceived potential de novo entrant, and if the acquiring firm's pre-merger presence on the fringe of the target market in fact tempered oligopolistic behavior on the part of existing participants in that market.[60]

---

[58] 410 U.S. 526 (1973).

[59] 418 U.S. 602 (1974).

[60] Ibid., at 624–625.

Therefore, plaintiffs must prove that the behavior of sellers in the market entered by merger is oligopolistic, viewed from a negative perspective, and that the acquiring firm's position on the edge of the market prior to the merger constrained insiders' pricing discretion.[61] Indeed, the Justice Department's 1982 merger guidelines take a similar stance; conglomerate mergers are likely to be considered an antitrust violation *only* if they pave the way for potential entry into a concentrated market for which the merger partners could independently develop their own brand. If the market is not concentrated or if there are many potential entrants, then conglomerate mergers are unlikely to be pursued as antitrust violations. The need to determine the number of potential entrants has prompted Posner to criticize the utility of potential competition theory. He has argued that

> There is no practical method of ranking, even crudely, the potential competitors in a market for the purpose of identifying a set of most likely or most feared entrants. And even if one could identify such a set through the methods of litigation, one would not know how to evaluate the elimination of one of its members. There is no theory or evidence that tells us that if the number of equally potential competitors in a market falls from ten to nine or four to three or two to one the pricing decisions of the firms in the market will be affected.[62]

Virtually nothing has been said in this entire discussion about the regulation of *other* or *pure* conglomerate mergers. That is because there are no theories that can relate these mergers to antitrust, with the possible exception of reciprocity advantages, which are discussed later in Chapter 6. The concern regarding other or pure conglomerate mergers is really not over their anticompetitive character in individual markets (which is the thrust of antitrust), but over their political and economic power in the economy as a whole. When massive, unrelated firms merge, such as Du Pont and Conoco, the issue has to do with the concentration of assets and thus the concentration of the wealth of the nation. It would be foolish for anyone to ignore the long-term ramifications of such concentration. But from the perspective of this book, there are no statutes in antitrust or consumer law that can be applied to question their growth, except in instances where the markets of the merged firms overlap. Then the relevant guidelines are found in the horizontal merger precedents.

DEFENSES AVAILABLE TO DEFENDANTS

Aside from arguing that the economic effects of a merger are not likely to be anticompetitive, defendants whose mergers are challenged have available to them three defenses: (1) the "failing firm" defense, (2) the "toehold" defense, and (3) the "efficiencies" defense. Only the first of these has been employed with any success over time.

---

[61] Scherer, op. cit., p. 562.

[62] Posner, op. cit., pp. 122–123. See also Dunfee and Stern, op. cit., for a critique of the theory.

"Failing Firm" Defense

This defense is invoked when the acquired or acquiring company is unlikely to survive as a viable competitor in the absence of a merger. According to the Supreme Court in *Citizens Publishing Co.* v. *U.S.,*[63] the failing company doctrine could only be applied when "the resources of one company were so depleted and the prospect of rehabilitation so remote that it faced grave probability of a business failure." In addition, the Court insisted in that case that there be no other merger prospect with a less severe concentration-increasing effect. In *General Dynamics,* the majority revived the failing firm defense, which had been limited in its application by the Court's statements in *Citizens Publishing.* The Court held that the weaknesses of an acquired company, while not sufficient to make it a failing firm, might still be serious enough to justify a decision that it was unable to compete effectively in the relevant market, so its acquisition would be unlikely to have the anticompetitive effects required for a breach of Section 7.

The enforcement agencies have enjoyed considerable discretion in using the failing firm rationale in borderline situations, including the merger between the McDonnell and Douglas aircraft firms in 1967 and the Penn–Central merger in 1968. In 1976, the Antitrust Division of the Justice Department approved the absorption of "failing" White Motor Corp. by White Consolidated Industries, Inc. And, as Shepherd and Wilcox point out,

> In 1975–78 more than ten sizable mergers took place among brokerage firms, directly raising concentration. This reflected the new competition unleashed by the ending of brokerage fee fixing on May 1, 1975. Though many of the firms were not strictly failing, the [Antitrust] Division (of the Justice Department) permitted the mergers as part of the larger shift to competition. Over 100 viable brokerage firms still remained.[64]

Perhaps the most controversial failing firm merger to be allowed was in 1978 when LTV Corporation was permitted to acquire Lykes Steel. LTV owned Jones & Laughlin Steel Corp. and Lykes owned Youngstown Sheet & Tube Co. The merger created the third largest U.S. steel firm, with about 15 to 25 percent shares of various markets. Neither firm was running losses, but both were in difficulties.

"Toehold" Defense

If a merger involves a small firm in a concentrated market, then an argument could be made that the merger could be procompetitive in that it would create a more effective competitor vis-à-vis the leading firms in the market. For example, although the FTC's order condemning the Kennecott Copper Corporation's acquisition of Peabody Coal was upheld by the 10th Circuit Court of Appeals,[65] there was a suggestion that Kennecott's entry into the coal market

---

[63] 394 U.S. 131 (1964).

[64] William G. Shepherd and Clair Wilcox, *Public Policies toward Business,* 6th ed. (Homewood, Ill.: Richard D. Irwin, Inc., 1979), p. 178.

[65] *Kennecott Copper Corp.* v. *FTC,* 78 FTC 744 (1971), *aff'd on other grounds,* 467 F. 2d 67 (10th Cir. 1972).

might have been allowed had it acquired a small company as a toehold acquisition. This suggestion was consistent with an earlier case in which the FTC had ruled that Bendix Corporation's acquisition of Fram (the third largest manufacturer of automotive oil filters) violated Section 7 because Bendix would have been a likely entrant into the concentrated filter market through acquisition and expansion of a toehold firm.[66]

"Efficiencies" Defense

The prospect of cost savings or other economies resulting from a merger might also be considered as a defense. But the courts have expressed a consistent reluctance to attempt a weighting of potential benefits against adverse structural consequences. In addition, the enforcement agencies will usually not be deterred by claims that a merger will achieve economies. Rather, they require hard evidence, which would stand up in court, that there are net economies that can only be achieved by the merger. In actuality, neither the Justice Department nor the FTC recognizes efficiency as an outright defense; rather, they view it as a factor to be considered in exercising "prosecutorial discretion." The futility of using, in any coherent way, an efficiencies defense has been articulated by Posner:

> Not only is the measurement of efficiency (whether based on economies of scale, superior management, or whatever) an intractable subject for litigation; but an estimate of a challenged merger's cost savings could not be utilized in determining the total economic effect of the merger unless an estimate was also made of the monopoly costs of the merger—and we simply do not know enough about the effect of marginal increases in the concentration ratio under different market conditions to predict the price effects, and hence the monopoly costs, of a challenged merger, against which to compare the projected cost savings of the merger.[67]

Nevertheless, from a societal perspective, certain mergers may lead to increased efficiencies, which in turn lead to greater productivity. In an age where the United States is slipping badly with respect to productivity, especially relative to a number of other highly industrialized nations, the question of an efficiencies defense remains a viable topic for debate and research.

GOVERNMENT MERGER GUIDELINES

On June 14, 1982, the Justice Department issued a set of merger guidelines,[68] which represented a substantial revision of its 1968 guidelines.[69] On the same day, the Federal Trade Commission issued a policy statement on horizontal

---

[66] *Bendix Corp.* v. *FTC,* 77 FTC 73 (1970), *vacated and remanded on other grounds,* 450 F.2d. 534 (6th Cir 1971).

[67] Posner, op. cit., p. 112.

[68] U.S. Department of Justice, *Merger Guidelines,* June 14, 1982.

[69] For a summary of the 1968 *Merger Guidelines,* see Shepherd and Wilcox, op. cit., p. 175.

mergers.[70] To a great extent, the FTC's statement concurs with the guidelines developed by the Justice Department. Both the guidelines and the FTC's policy statement have been reproduced at the end of this chapter. The discussion in this section focuses primarily on the guidelines.

In the language used by the Justice Department,

> The unifying theme of the Guidelines is that mergers should not be permitted to create or enhance "market power" or to facilitate its exercise. A sole seller (a "monopolist") of a product with no good substitutes can maintain a selling price that is above the level that would prevail if the market were competitive. Where only a few firms account for most of the sales of a product, those firms can in some circumstances coordinate, explicitly or implicitly, their actions in order to approximate the performance of a monopolist. This ability of one or more firms profitably to maintain prices above competitive levels for a significant period of time is termed "market power." Sellers with market power also may eliminate rivalry on variables other than price. In either case, the result is a transfer of wealth from buyers to sellers and a misallocation of resources. . . .[71]
> Taken as a whole, . . . the standards in the Guidelines are designed to ensure that, whenever the Department challenges a merger, the firms in the affected market could exercise market power if they were able to coordinate their actions.[72]

The guidelines start out by providing a framework for defining relevant product and geographic markets. Then they turn to a description of the methodology and analysis required to determine the market concentration levels considered likely to reduce competition. The approach suggested by the Justice Department is summarized next.

Defining the Relevant Market

The initial step in scrutinizing the legality of a given merger will be the delineation of a provisional *product* market. Then, employing certain hypotheticals, tests will be made of the boundaries of the product market, particularly regarding potential competition. To determine a provisional product market, it is first necessary to isolate those products that the merging firms' customers view as good substitutes at prevailing prices. The question raised at this point in the analysis is, "What would happen under the assumption that buyers could only respond to an increase in price for a tentatively identified product group by shifting to other products?" In the words of the guidelines, "If readily available alternatives were, in the aggregate, sufficiently attractive to enough buyers, an attempt to raise price would not prove profitable, and the market would prove to have been too narrowly defined."[73] Once the provisional market is defined, it is then tested by asking another question: "How many buyers would be likely to shift to other products within one year if the prices of the products in the provisional market were to increase by 5 percent?" The guide-

---

[70] Federal Trade Commission, *Statement of Federal Trade Commission Concerning Horizontal Mergers,* June 14, 1982.

[71] U.S. Department of Justice, op. cit., pp. 2–3.

[72] Ibid., p. 4.

[73] Ibid., p. 5.

lines further inquire into how many firms would be likely to change to the production and sale of the relevant product within six months if the price rises by 5 percent.

According to the guidelines, the purpose of a *geographic* market definition, in contrast to a product market definition, is "to establish a geographic boundary that roughly separates firms that are important factors in the competitive analysis of a merger from those that are not."[74] Following the same analytical framework as the one established for the product market, the guidelines state that

> The Department will expand the provisional market boundaries to include the locations of firms (or plants) that could make significant sales to customers of firms previously included in the provisional market in response to a small but significant and non-transitory increase in price. As a first approximation, the Department will hypothesize a price increase of five percent and ask how many sellers could sell the product to such customers within one year.[75]

In evaluating geographic substitutability, particular attention will be paid to such factors as evidence of actual shifts of patronage relative to past price changes, price movements in different geographic areas, transportation costs, costs of local distribution, and excess capacity by firms outside the provisional market. The Justice Department also indicates that it will consider existing or potential foreign competition, but that it will be "somewhat more cautious, both in expanding market boundaries beyond the United States and in assessing the likely supply response of specific foreign firms."[76]

In comparison with the past, the impression is that, under the revised guidelines, there will be more sensitivity to such competitive realities as substitute products and rivalry from more distant locales. It is also likely that application of the guidelines relative to defining relevant markets will mean less attention to the notion of "submarkets," as established in *Brown Shoe,* with the end result that market definitions will be expanded.

Market Concentration

The 1968 merger guidelines stressed the notion that market share alone was sufficient to demonstrate monopoly pricing power. They classified industries by four-firm concentration ratios, calculated by summing the market shares of the top four firms in an industry, and spelled out precisely when a horizontal merger would be presumed illegal on the basis of concentration ratio cutoff points. The revised guidelines drop the traditional reference to the ratio and instead rely on the Herfindahl–Hirschman Index (HHI). The HHI is calculated by squaring the percentage market share of each firm and then adding those squares. The HHI approaches zero when a market is occupied by a large number of firms of relatively equal size and reaches a maximum of 10,000 when a market is controlled by a single firm. As stated in the guidelines,

---

[74] Ibid., p. 11.

[75] Ibid., p. 13.

[76] Ibid., p. 14.

The Department divides the spectrum of market concentration as measured by the HHI into three regions that can be broadly characterized as unconcentrated (HHI below 1000), moderately concentrated (HHI between 1000 and 1800) and highly concentrated (HHI above 1800). An empirical study by the Department . . . indicates that the critical HHI thresholds at 1000 and 1800 correspond roughly to four-firm concentration ratios of 50 percent and 70 percent, respectively.[77]

The differences between the four-firm concentration ratio and the HHI can be significant. For example, in a market where the top four companies each have a 15 percent market share, the concentration ratio is 60 percent, but the ratio also equals 60 if one company has 57 percent and the other three have 1 percent each. The first situation would yield an HHI of 900, while the latter would produce an HHI of 3,252. Thus, as pointed out in the guidelines,

> Unlike the traditional four-firm concentration ratio, the HHI reflects both the distribution of the market shares of the top four firms and the composition of the market outside the top four firms. It also gives proportionately greater weight to the market shares of the larger firms, which probably accords with their relative importance in any collusive interaction.[78]

In unconcentrated markets (HHI below 1000), the Justice Department would never challenge mergers. Where the postmerger market is moderately concentrated (HHI between 1000 and 1800), a challenge would still be unlikely, provided that the merger increases the index by less than 100 points. In highly concentrated markets (HHI above 1800), a challenge is unlikely where the merger produces an increase of less than 50 points. If the merger produces an increase in the index of between 50 to 100 points, challenge would be more likely than not. And when the increase exceeds 100 points in highly concentrated markets, a challenge is highly likely. For example, in 1981 the Justice Department challenged the proposed acquisition of Schlitz by Heileman. Heileman was the nation's sixth largest brewer with a 7.5 percent share of the beer market; Schlitz was fourth with 8.5 percent. The number one, two, and three brewers had shares of 28 percent, 21 percent, and 9.5 percent, respectively. The HHI was around 1500, but the proposed merger increased the HHI by over 100 points. In contrast, a proposed merger between Stroh Brewery and Schlitz was approved by the Justice Department in 1982 because it would have increased the HHI by only 70 to 78 points. Stroh accounted for 4.5 to 5 percent of U.S. beer sales. Schlitz's share had dropped to 7.8 percent at the time the merger was suggested.[79]

Other factors, beyond the HHI, will also be taken into consideration in judging whether to challenge a merger. These include the following:

> The amount of technological innovation in an industry (a fast rate of change is a sign of competition).

---

[77] Ibid., pp. 17–18.

[78] Ibid., p. 17.

[79] See Robert E. Taylor, "U.S. Conditionally Permits Stroh to Buy Schlitz, Signaling New Merger Guidelines," *Wall Street Journal,* Apr. 19, 1982, p. 4.

The rate of sales growth (a rapid rate indicates a market will attract competitors).

The amount of risk capital required to enter the industry (low capital requirements suggest ease of entry).

The amount of excess capacity in the industry (lots of excess capacity indicates a weak market that could stand more concentration because excess capacity depresses prices).

Product durability (durable goods such as cars have strong secondary markets that increase competition).[80]

Relative to the proposed Heileman–Schlitz merger, none of these factors were deemed to be favorable to the merger. The Justice Department conducted a full investigation of the beer industry and found high barriers to entry, slow sales growth at only about 2 percent a year, and little technological change.[81]

The guidelines evidence considerable concern about the merger activities of a dominant firm within an industry. In fact, the guidelines indicate that the Justice Department is likely to challenge the merger of any firm with a market share of at least 1 percent with the leading firm in the market, if the leading firm has a market share of 35 percent or more and if it is approximately twice as large as the second largest firm in the market.

The discussion of market concentration up to this point has related to horizontal mergers. However, when the guidelines were promulgated, the Justice Department held to the belief that vertical and conglomerate mergers do not generally produce anticompetitive consequences. In fact, the guidelines suggest that the labels "vertical" and "conglomerate" add nothing to the analysis, and therefore, they refer to these mergers as "nonhorizontal." The discussion of vertical mergers reflects the opinion that such mergers present problems only if they have horizontal consequences. The specific guidelines concerning vertical mergers are outlined in Chapter 6, as well as at the end of this chapter.

Regarding conglomerate mergers, the Justice Department will consider the consequences of acquisitions on both perceived and actual potential competition. Relative to *perceived* potential competition, the guidelines state that "By eliminating a significant present competitive threat that constrains the behavior of the firms already in the market, the merger could result in an immediate deterioration in market performance."[82]

And relative to *actual* potential competition, they state that

> By eliminating the possibility of entry by the acquiring firm in a more pro-competitive manner, the merger could result in a lost opportunity for improvement in market performance resulting from the addition of a significant competitor. The more pro-competitive alternatives include both new entry and entry through a "toehold" acquisition of a present small competitor.[83]

---

[80] See Edward Meadows, "Bold Departures in Antitrust," *Fortune*, Oct. 5, 1981, p. 184.

[81] Robert E. Taylor, "Heileman's Plan to Buy Schlitz Opposed by U.S.," *Wall Street Journal*, Oct. 22, 1981, p. 4.

[82] U.S. Department of Justice, op. cit., p. 30.

[83] Ibid.

However, even though these dangers are recognized, a conglomerate merger will not be challenged unless overall concentration of the acquired firm's market is high, entry is difficult, very few additional potential competitors exist, and/or the market share of the acquired firm is above 5 percent.

Finally, with regard to defenses, the guidelines specify that the Justice Department will be reasonably strict in its application of the failing firm defense. This is in contrast to the Federal Trade Commission, which, in a departure from previous policy, commented in its policy statement that it will "take into account evidence of a failing division . . . that falls short of the technical requirements of the failing company defense." In other words, the FTC will consider acquisitions of "faltering" in addition to "failing" companies as being potentially legal. Another difference between the FTC and the Justice Department is over the question of the weight to be placed on efficiency. The FTC has stated that, in exercising its prosecutorial discretion, it will consider increases in efficiency as a justification for a merger, while the Justice Department has argued that "even if the existence of efficiencies were clear, their magnitude would be extremely difficult to determine." Therefore, the Justice Department will usually not consider the efficiency defense, except in extraordinary circumstances. And, in another departure from the Justice Department guidelines, the FTC declined to adopt the *specific* benchmark figures suggested by Justice for classifying industries and for determining relevant markets because "a more refined treatment of that data is in order." There is also little doubt that defendants in merger cases can be counted on to react with considerable fervor for a long time to come over the frameworks and methodologies suggested by the Justice Department, irrespective of whether they make sense or not from an economics perspective. The complexity of the required analysis alone is likely to strike fear into the hearts of marketing executives and their lawyers, despite the more permissive policy it represents.

CONCLUSION

Over 2,000 mergers and acquisitions are consummated yearly. Clearly, then, the use of mergers and acquisitions (as well as joint ventures) to extend or diversify a firm's product line is perceived as a viable alternative to internal development and commercialization on the part of a large number of executives. If such a route to expansion or diversification is contemplated, it would be wise for a marketing executive to keep in mind the following observations.

First, given court precedents, it would be a highly questionable tactic for a company to acquire another company that markets directly competitive products to those already being sold by the acquiring firm in situations where the acquired or acquiring company's market share is large or where the industry is highly concentrated. While horizontal mergers continue to take place, especially among smaller firms in an industry, they are increasingly being successfully challenged when there is significant market power held by the firms considering the amalgamation. In this chapter, we have discussed a number of horizontal mergers that have been disallowed in past history and have pointed to the challenge of the Heileman–Schlitz merger in more recent history as an indication of a consistent trend. Other horizontal mergers and conglomerate mergers with significant horizontal overlaps (e.g., Gulf Oil Corporation's proposed acquisition of Cities Service Co.; Hospital Corp. of America's acquisition of Hospital Affiliates International, Inc., and Health Care Corp.; American Brands Inc.'s acquisition of Ofrex Group Ltd.; Schlumberger Ltd.'s acquisition of Accutest Corp.; and LTV Corp.'s proposed purchase of Grumman Corp., to name only a few) have also faced challenges by the Justice Department and the Federal Trade Commission in relatively recent times.[84] In addition, joint ventures between competitors are subject to careful antitrust scrutiny, as indicated by the extensive investigation of the proposed General Motors–Toyota joint venture by the Federal Trade Commission during 1983.[85]

Second, in addition to actions taken by the antitrust enforcement agencies, an increase in private lawsuits can be expected. Such actions are especially likely to occur when firms are faced with "unfriendly" takeover bids, as when Marshall Field sued Carter Hawley Hale on antitrust grounds over the latter's attempt to purchase Field's stock, or when Marathon sued Mobil in 1981, or when Martin Marietta sued Bendix in 1982.

On the other hand, diversification via conglomerate merger presents a different picture from an antitrust perspective. With respect to pure conglomerate mergers where there is no market in which the products of the merged companies overlap (e.g., Warner–Lambert's purchase of Entenmanns), there is no known precedent for challenging such mergers successfully, unless it is on reciprocity grounds. The latter is a marketing channel issue and is dealt with in Chapter 6. Precedent does exist, however, for challenging product-extension and market-extension mergers. The basic theory used to prosecute such cases involves the impact of potential competition. There is, allegedly, a procompetitive effect of having a firm, particularly a large corporation, poised on the edge of an oligopolistic market but not entering it. If it decides to enter by internal expansion (i.e., developing a product on its own), then, from the viewpoint of antitrust, this is a positive event, because the number of firms competing in the market increases by one. But if it buys its way into the market or if it is bought up by an in-market firm, then its threatening presence on the

[84] The markets in which these firms competed, making the mergers horizontal, were as follows: Gulf Oil–Cities Service Co. (gasoline distribution, kerosene jet fuel production and distribution, and pipeline transportation of petroleum productions); Hospital Corp. of America–Hospital Affiliates and Health Care Corp. (hospital and inpatient psychiatric care in southeastern Tennessee and northern Georgia); American Brands–Ofrex Group (staplers and fasteners); Schlumberger Ltd.–Accutest (computer-chip test equipment); LTV Corp.–Grumman Corp. (carrier-based aircraft).

[85] See "Questions and Answers Concerning FTC Involvement with the Proposed General Motors-Toyota Joint Venture," *FTC New Notes,* Vol. 21–83, February 18, 1983, p. 1; John Koten, "Chrysler Memo Cites Price-Fixing Charges in Opposition to GM-Toyota Joint Venture," *Wall Street Journal,* April 28, 1983, p. 2; and John Koten, "GM-Toyota Venture Stirs Antitrust and Labor Problems," *Wall Street Journal,* June 10, 1983, p. 1. Decisions affecting the joint venture could set precedents in antitrust law, including whether such arrangements should be evaluated on the basis of the domestic or the world market. The GM-Toyota situation is different from most joint ventures in that it is a horizontal arrangement between companies already in the same business. More typically, companies from different backgrounds enter joint ventures to combine areas of knowledge in starting up a new business. Therefore, joint ventures are generally more similar to conglomerate than they are to horizontal mergers.

edge of the market disappears. The number of competitors does not increase, and the members of the oligopoly can, as the theory would have it, increase their prices and/or restrict their output collectively, earning monopoly profits, without fear of an outsider's intervention into their comfortable cartel.

While this may sound very logical from an economic theory point of view, the concept of potential competition can be called into serious question, and, therefore, prosecuting cases using the theory can be extremely difficult. The reason for this questioning is straightforward; it cannot be determined, with any degree of certainty, just how many potential competitors are actually standing on the edge of any given market or what the effect on the marketing behavior of the firms in the market will be if only one firm enters and the rest remain on the edge. This questioning becomes even more important as the intensity of multinational competition heightens and as global corporations with considerable resources maintain a constant surveillance for new diversification opportunities. For example, it might be possible to assume, without too much fear of contradiction, that companies like Procter & Gamble, R. J. Reynolds, or Coca-Cola represent potential entrants into any lucrative packaged goods segment. And Japanese companies seem ready to enter any U.S. market that shows signs of being profitable. Therefore, potential competition theory, while intriguing, may have little realistic applicability in antitrust cases as the outreach of major corporations worldwide continues to grow.

What this means is that conglomerate mergers are likely to be even more permissible over time, unless, of course, there is a way in which it can be shown that anticompetitive horizontal effects are somehow imbedded in the merger. For instance, the acquisition of Ofrex Group Ltd. by American Brands was classified as a conglomerate merger; however, at the time of the acquisition, American Brands, through its Swingline Co. and Ace Fastener Co. subsidiaries, was the dominant U.S. producer of staplers, and Ofrex's subsidiary, Rexel, Inc., was the fourth largest. In such cases of horizontal overlap, the enforcement agencies may insist that one of the companies divest itself of enough stock, assets, or both to restore competition in the specific market that is affected because of the merger. It is reasonable to predict that conglomerate mergers with significant horizontal overtones will be under considerable scrutiny as merger activity increases.

All this speculation seems very much in line with the more recent version of the merger guidelines issued under the Reagan Administration by the Antitrust Division of the Justice Department. The emphasis in those guidelines is, to a very significant extent, on horizontal mergers. In fact, the guidelines discuss conglomerate and vertical mergers under the heading "Horizontal Effect from Non-Horizontal Mergers." In actuality, the guidelines do not represent a significant softening of the government's position with respect to horizontal mergers in comparison to the guidelines issued in 1968 under a supposedly more liberal administration. Although the techniques for analyzing mergers under the 1982 guidelines are different and more complex, they translate into standards for challenging mergers that would generally accept only slightly more concentration than the 1968 guidelines. In fact, in rare circumstances, the 1982 guidelines could be even more stringent than the earlier ones. For example, the Justice Department is likely to challenge mergers in markets where only two companies dominate sales, such as when a merger expands one of the top two companies so that, after the merger, both of the top two companies end up with more than a 40 percent combined market share. On the other hand, the earlier guidelines defined a market as highly concentrated where four companies commanded 75 percent of sales. Under the 1982 version, use of Herfindahl–Hirschman Index will permit consideration of larger numbers of companies and their relative sizes in determining market concentration. The use of the HHI may permit a general loosening of restrictions on horizontal mergers, especially in situations where the top few firms do not control substantial shares of a market.

Clearly, merger policy is promulgated and pursued within an economic and political climate. The tone of an administration along liberal or conservative dimensions will often permit predictions as to just how difficult it will be for companies to use mergers as an element of marketing and corporate strategy. However, before making any bold predictions, a marketing executive should be forewarned that some of the strictest merger policies in the past were instituted under Republican administrations. The best advice for executives to follow would be for them to pay closer attention to the established court precedents in merger cases, as opposed to getting involved in environmental forecasting. It is for this reason that the discussion in this chapter has focused on those precedents, rather than on predictions of change.

U.S. Department of Justice Merger Guidelines

Issued: June 14, 1982

I. PURPOSE AND UNDERLYING POLICY ASSUMPTIONS

These Guidelines state in outline form the present enforcement policy of the U.S. Department of Justice ("Department") concerning acquisitions and mergers ("mergers") subject to section 7 of the Clayton Act[1] or to section 1 of the Sherman Act.[2] They describe the general principles and specific standards normally used by the Department in analyzing mergers.[3] By stating its policy as simply and clearly as possible, the Department hopes to reduce the uncertainty associated with enforcement of the antitrust laws in this area.

Although the Guidelines should improve the predictability of the Department's merger enforcement policy, it is not possible to remove the exercise of judgment from the evaluation of mergers under the antitrust laws. Difficult factual questions arise under the standards stated below, and the Department necessarily will base its decision on the data that are practicably available in each case. Moreover, the standards represent generalizations to which some exceptions are inevitable. In appropriate cases, the Department will challenge mergers that are competitively objectionable under the general principles of the Guidelines regardless of whether they are covered by the specific standards. Finally, the Guidelines are designed primarily to indicate when the Department is likely to challenge mergers, not how it will conduct the litigation of cases that it decides to bring. Although relevant in the latter context, the factors contemplated in the standards do not exhaust the range of evidence that the Department may introduce in court.[4]

The unifying theme of the Guidelines is that mergers should not be permitted to create or enhance "market power" or to facilitate its exercise. A sole seller (a "monopolist") of a product with no good substitutes can maintain a selling price that is above the level that would prevail if the market were com-

---

[1] 15 U.S.C.A. §18 (1981). Mergers subject to section 7 are prohibited if their effect "may be substantially to lessen competition, or to tend to create a monopoly."

[2] 15 U.S.C.A. §1 (1981). Mergers subject to section 1 are prohibited if they constitute a "contract, combination . . . , or conspiracy in restraint of trade."

[3] They replace a set of Guidelines issued by the Department in 1968, and are subject to further revision in light of subsequent judicial decisions or economic studies. Although changes in enforcement policy may precede the issuance of amended Guidelines, the Department will attempt to conform the Guidelines to such changes as soon as possible.

[4] Parties seeking more specific advance guidance concerning the Department's enforcement intentions with respect to any particular merger should consider using the Business Review Procedure. 28 C.F.R. §50.6.

petitive. Where only a few firms account for most of the sales of a product, those firms can in some circumstances coordinate, explicitly or implicitly, their actions in order to approximate the performance of a monopolist. This ability of one or more firms profitably to maintain prices above competitive levels for a significant period of time is termed "market power." Sellers with market power also may eliminate rivalry on variables other than price. In either case, the result is a transfer of wealth from buyers to sellers and a misallocation of resources.[5]

Although they sometimes harm competition, mergers generally play an important role in a free enterprise economy. They can penalize ineffective management and facilitate the efficient flow of investment capital and the redeployment of existing productive assets. While challenging competitively harmful mergers, the Department seeks to avoid unnecessary interference with that larger universe of mergers that are either competitively beneficial or neutral. In attempting to mediate between these dual concerns, however, the Guidelines reflect the congressional intent that merger enforcement should interdict competitive problems in their incipiency.

II. MARKET DEFINITION AND MEASUREMENT

Using the standards stated below, the Department will define and measure the market for each product or service ("product") of each of the merging firms. A market is a group of products and an associated geographic area with certain economic characteristics that will be described in subsequent paragraphs. In theory, all the demand and supply forces relevant to the evaluation of a merger could be incorporated in the definition of a market. Under the Guidelines, however, market definition is not the exclusive analytical technique through which the Department considers those forces. For example, because the potential new entry from the construction of new facilities and from the substantial modification of existing facilities is not easily captured in conventional market statistics, the Department takes such entry into account in interpreting market statistics.[6] Taken as a whole, however, the standards in the Guidelines are designed to ensure that, whenever the Department challenges a merger, the firms in the affected market could exercise market power if they were able to coordinate their actions.

---

[5] "Market power" also encompasses the ability of a single buyer or group of buyers to depress the price paid for a product to a level that is below the competitive price. Market power by buyers has wealth transfer and resource misallocation effects analogous to those associated with market power by sellers.

[6] In contrast to the comprehensive definition suggested in this paragraph of the text, the market definition used by the Department can be stated formally as follows: "a market consists of a group of products and an associated geographic area such that (in the absence of new entry) a hypothetical, unregulated firm that made all the sales of those products in that area could increase its profits through a small but significant and non-transitory increase in price (above prevailing or likely future levels)." The standards for market definition in the text below implement this definition.

A. Product Market Definition

The first task in market definition is to determine what products to include in the market for the product of the merging firm.[7] In general, the Department seeks to identify a group of products such that a hypothetical firm[8] that was the only present and future seller of those products could raise price profitably. That is, assuming that buyers could respond to an increase in price for a tentatively identified product group only by shifting to other products, what would happen? If readily available alternatives were, in the aggregate, sufficiently attractive to enough buyers, an attempt to raise price would not prove profitable, and the "market" would prove to have been too narrowly defined.

Taking the product of the merging firm as a beginning point, the Department will establish a provisional product market. The Department will include in the provisional market those products that the merging firm's customers view as good substitutes at prevailing prices.[9] The potential weakness of such a market based solely on existing patterns of supply and demand is that those patterns might change substantially if the prices of the products included in the provisional market were to increase. For this reason, the Department will test further and, if necessary, expand the provisional market. The Department will add additional products to the market if a significant percentage of the buyers of products already included would be likely to shift to those other products in response to a small but significant and non-transitory increase in price. As a first approximation, the Department will hypothesize a price increase of five percent and ask how many buyers would be likely to shift to the other products within one year.[10] The Department will continue expanding the provisional market until it satisfies the general profitability standard stated above.[11]

In evaluating product substitutability,[12] the Department will consider any relevant evidence, but will give particular weight to the following factors:

1) Evidence of buyers' perceptions that the products are or are not substi-

---

[7] The analysis that follows will be repeated for each product of each merging firm.

[8] In Sections III(A) and III(C), the Guidelines discuss factors affecting the ability of a group of sellers, by coordinating their actions, to approximate the performance of a single firm.

[9] On occasion, the Department may base this analysis on likely future prices, provided that the relevant price relationships can be projected with confidence.

[10] The purpose of hypothesizing a price increase is to interject a dynamic element in the analysis as a conceptual aid in determining the outer limits of the market. Judged by the effect on rate of return on invested capital, a given percentage price increase may be much more significant in some industries than in others.

Direct evidence of the likely effect of a price increase often will not be available, particularly in the context of the Department's prelitigation evaluation of a merger. As a result, the Department often will have to rely on inferences from the types of circumstantial evidence described in the text below. For consistency, the Department will assume that buyers and sellers immediately recognize the price increase and believe that it will be sustained for the foreseeable future.

[11] The Department normally will not expand the market beyond the point at which this standard is satisfied unless it is convinced that independent competitive concerns exist in a larger market.

[12] In constructing and expanding the provisional market, the Department will not exclude any product that is at least as good a substitute as any product included. The Department will refer to the products included in the market collectively as the "relevant product."

tutes, particularly if those buyers have shifted purchases between the products in response to changes in relative price or other competitive variables;

2) Similarities or differences between the products in customary usage, design, physical composition and other technical characteristics;

3) Similarities or differences in the price movements of the products over a period of years; and

4) Evidence of sellers' perceptions that the products are or are not substitutes, particularly if business decisions have been based on those perceptions.

The analysis of product market definition to this point has assumed that price discrimination—charging different buyers different prices for products having the same cost, for example—would not be possible after the merger. Existing buyers sometimes will differ significantly in their assessment of the adequacy of a particular substitute and the ease with which they could substitute it for the product of the merging firm. Even though a general increase in price might cause such significant substitution that it would not be profitable, sellers who can price discriminate could raise price only to groups of buyers who cannot easily substitute away.[13] If such price discrimination is possible, the Department will consider defining additional, narrower relevant product markets oriented to the buyer groups subject to the exercise of market power.[14]

B. Identification of Firms That Produce the Relevant Product

In most cases, the Department's evaluation of a merger will focus primarily on firms that currently produce and sell the relevant product. In addition to those firms, however, the Department may include additional firms in the market in certain circumstances.[15]

1. *Production Substitution.* The same productive and distributive facilities can sometimes be used to produce and sell two or more products that buyers do not regard as good substitutes. Production substitution refers to the shift by a firm in the use of facilities from producing and selling one product to producing and selling another. Depending upon the cost and speed of that shift, production substitution may allow firms that do not currently produce

[13] Price discrimination requires that sellers be able to identify those buyers and that other buyers be unable profitably to purchase and resell to them.

[14] Price discrimination is discussed in the Guidelines because it is sometimes a manifestation of market power created by a merger. In the context described in the text, a price increase to one group of buyers, reducing quantities purchased by that group, will not be accompanied by a price reduction and output increase to the other group. Hence, its effects on consumer welfare are unambiguously negative. It is important to distinguish that situation from the one in which a firm already possesses market power and is likely to exercise it, whether or not it is able to practice price discrimination. In the latter situation, price discrimination often results in an expansion of output, thus reducing the resource misallocation associated with market power.

[15] The situations described in the text below are particularly subject to difficult questions of degree. In such cases, it is often useful to calculate market shares based on alternative reasonable assumptions—for example, with and then without a particular type of facility arguably capable of easy and economical production substitution. In its evaluation of such cases, the Department will take into account the closeness of the issue, whichever way it is resolved for calculation of market statistics.

the relevant product to respond effectively to an increase in the price of that product.[16]

If a firm has existing productive and distributive facilities that could easily and economically be used to produce and sell the relevant product within six months in response to a small but significant and non-transitory increase in price, the Department will include those facilities in the market.[17] As a first approximation, the Department will hypothesize a price increase of five percent and ask how many firms would be likely to change to the production and sale of the relevant product within six months.[18] Firms that must construct significant new productive or distributive facilities in order to produce and sell the relevant product will not be included in the market, although the Department will consider their competitive significance in evaluating entry conditions generally.[19]

2. *Durable Products.* Some long-lived products may continue to exert competitive influence after the time of original sale. If, under the standards stated in Section II(A), recycled or reconditioned products represent good substitutes for new products, the Department will include in the market firms which recycle or recondition those products.

3. *Internal Consumption.* Captive production and consumption of the relevant product by vertically integrated firms are part of the overall market supply and demand. Such firms are free to buy or sell in the market, and they incur an opportunity cost for units they consume rather than sell. The increase in that cost resulting from an increase in the market price may induce a change in behavior. The Department will include in the market the facilities that are used to produce the relevant product.[20]

C. Identification of Firms That Produce the Relevant Product at Relevant Locations (Geographic Market Definition)

For each product market of each merging firm, the Department will determine the geographic market(s) in which that firm sells. The purpose of geographic

[16] Under other analytical approaches, production substitution sometimes has been reflected in the description of the product market. For example, the product market for stamped metal products such as automobile hub caps might be described as "light metal stamping," a production process rather than a product. The Department believes that the approach described in the text provides a more clearly focused method of incorporating this factor in merger analysis. If production substitution among a group of products is nearly universal among the firms selling one or more of those products, however, the Department may use an aggregate description of those markets as a matter of convenience.

[17] The amount of sales or capacity to be included in the market is a separate question discussed in Section II(D), below.

[18] See note 10, above.

[19] See Section III(B), below.

[20] See note 17, above. In evaluating the competitive significance of internally consumed production, the Department will consider whether the vertically integrated firm, either through sales of the relevant product or through sales of the products in which the relevant product is embodied, could frustrate an effort by the sellers of the relevant product to exercise market power.

market definition is to establish a geographic boundary that roughly separates firms that are important factors in the competitive analysis of a merger from those that are not. Depending on the nature of the product, the geographic market may be as small as a part of a city or as large as the entire world. Moreover, a single firm may operate in a number of economically discrete geographic markets.

In general, the Department seeks to identify a geographic area such that a hypothetical firm that was the only present or future producer of the relevant product in that area could profitably raise price. That is, assuming that buyers could respond to a price increase within a tentatively identified area only by shifting to firms located outside the area, what would happen? If firms located elsewhere readily could provide the relevant product to the hypothetical firm's buyers in sufficient quantity at a comparable price, an attempt to raise price would not prove profitable, and the "market" would prove to have been too narrowly defined.

Taking the location of the merging firm (or each plant, for multi-plant firms) as a beginning point, the Department will establish a provisional geographic market based upon the shipment patterns of that firm and its closest competitors.[21] The potential weakness of such a market boundary based on existing patterns of supply and demand is that those patterns might change substantially if the price within the provisional market were to increase. For this reason, the Department will test further and, if necessary, expand the provisional market. The Department will expand the provisional market boundaries to include the locations of firms (or plants) that could make significant sales to customers of firms previously included in the provisional market in response to a small but significant and non-transitory increase in price. As a first approximation, the Department will hypothesize a price increase of five percent and ask how many sellers could sell the product to such customers within one year.[22] The Department will continue expanding the provisional market until it satisfies the general profitability standard stated above.[23]

In evaluating geographic substitutability,[24] the Department will consider any relevant evidence, but will give particular weight to the following factors:

1) Evidence of buyers actually having shifted their purchases among sellers at different geographic locations, especially if the shifts correspond to changes in relative price or other competitive variables;

---

[21] Because the definition of geographic markets in the Guidelines is an area derived from the location of sellers' facilities, the area may not always exhibit characteristics associated with traditional geographic market definitions that are based, in whole or part, on buyer locations. Nevertheless, as a rule of thumb, the merging firm should make a significant percentage of its sales in the provisional market and firms located outside it collectively should account for a small percentage of total sales there. It is possible that a geographic market could include only one firm.

[22] See note 10, above. In some cases, a general expansion of the market boundaries may overstate the likely supply response. If a specific firm has a particular ability to sell in the provisional market that is not shared by other firms in that firm's area, the Department will treat that firm alone as being in the market.

[23] See note 11, above.

[24] In constructing and expanding the provisional market, the Department will not exclude any area if production there is at least as good a substitute as production that is included.

2) Similarities or differences in the price movements of the relative product in different geographic areas over a period of years;

3) Transportation costs;

4) Costs of local distribution; and

5) Excess capacity by firms outside the provisional market.

The analysis of geographic market definition to this point has assumed that geographic price discrimination—charging different prices net of transportation costs for the same product to buyers in different locations, for example— would not be possible after the merger. As in the case of product market definition, however, where price discrimination is possible,[25] the Department will consider defining additional, narrower geographic markets oriented to those buyer groups subject to the exercise of market power.

In general, the standards stated above will govern geographic market definition, whether domestic or international. The Department, however, will be somewhat more cautious, both in expanding market boundaries beyond the United States and in assessing the likely supply response of specific foreign firms. Although firms located outside the United States may exert an important competitive influence on domestic prices, they may be subject to additional constraints not present in the purely domestic context. For example, changes in exchange rates, tariffs, and general political conditions may limit the ability of such firms to respond to domestic price increases.

D. Calculating Market Shares

The Department normally will include in the market the total sales or capacity[26] of all firms (or plants) that are identified as being in the market in Sections II(B) and II(C). In some cases, however, total sales or capacity may overstate the competitive significance of a firm. With respect to firms included in the market under Sections II(B)(1) (production substitution) and II(B)(3) (internal consumption), for example, the Deparatment will include only those sales likely to be made or capacity likely to be used in the geographic market in response to a small but significant and non-transitory increase in price. As a first approximation, the Department will hypothesize a price of five percent and ask what the likely response of the firms would be within one year.[27] Similarly, a firm's capacity may be so committed elsewhere that it would not be

[25] See notes 13–14, above. Geographic price discrimination against a group of buyers is more likely when other buyers cannot easily purchase and resell the relevant product to them. Such arbitrage is particularly difficult where the product is sold on a delivered basis and where transportation costs are a significant percentage of the final cost.

[26] Market shares can be expressed in terms of dollar sales, physical unit sales, physical capacity, or (in natural resource industries) physical reserves. The availability of data often will determine the measurement base. Where a choice is possible, the Department will use the measurement base that is the best indicator of the likely effect of the merger on market power.

[27] See note 10, above. It follows that some firms included in the market might have little or no sales or capacity attributed to them. Conversely, the present sales or capacity of a firm may understate its competitive significance. This effect is most likely in the acquisition of new or as-yet-unexploited patent rights.

available to respond to an increase in price in the market. In such cases, the Department also may include a smaller part of the firm's sales or capacity.

III. HORIZONTAL MERGERS

Where the merging firms are in the same product and associated geographic market, the merger is horizontal. In such cases, the Department will focus first on the post-merger concentration of the market and the market shares of the merging firms. In some cases with low post-merger market concentration and/or market shares, the Department will be able to determine without a detailed examination of other factors that the merger poses no significant threat to competition. In other cases, however, the Department will proceed to examine a variety of other factors relevant to that question.

A. Concentration and Market Share

Market concentration is a function of the number of firms in a market and their respective market shares.[28] Other things being equal, concentration affects the likelihood that one firm, or a small group of firms, could successfully exercise market power. The smaller the percentage of total supply that a firm controls, the more severely it must restrict its own output in order to produce a given price increase, and the less likely it is that an output restriction will be profitable. Where collective action is necessary, an additional constraint applies. As the number of firms necessary to control a given percentage of total supply increases, the difficulties and costs of reaching and enforcing consensus with respect to the control of that supply also increase.

As an aid to the interpretation of market data, the Department will use the Herfindahl–Hirschman Index ("HHI") of market concentration. The HHI is calculated by summing the squares of the individual market shares of all the firms included in the market under the standards in Section II.[29] Unlike the traditional four-firm concentration ratio, the HHI reflects both the distribution of the market shares of the top four firms and the composition of the market outside the top four firms. It also gives proportionately greater weight to the market shares of the larger firms, which probably accords with their relative importance in any collusive interaction.

The Department divides the spectrum of market concentration as measured by the HHI into three regions that can be broadly characterized as uncon-

---

[28] Markets can range from atomistic, where very large numbers of firms that are small relative to the overall size of the market compete with one another, to monopolistic, where one firm controls the entire market. Far more common, and more difficult analytically, is the large middle range of instances where a relatively small number of firms account for most of the sales in the market.

[29] For example, a market consisting of four firms with market shares of 30 percent, 30 percent, 20 percent and 20 percent has an HHI of 2600 ($30^2 + 30^2 + 20^2 + 20^2 = 2600$). The HHI ranges from 10,000 (in the case of a pure monopoly) to a number approaching zero (in the case of an atomistic market). Although it is desirable to include all firms in the calculation, lack of information about small fringe firms is not critical because such firms do not affect the HHI significantly.

centrated (HHI below 1000), moderately concentrated (HHI between 1000 and 1800) and highly concentrated (HHI above 1800). An empirical study by the Department of the size dispersion of firms within markets indicates that the critical HHI thresholds at 1000 and 1800 correspond roughly to four-firm concentration ratios of 50 percent and 70 percent, respectively. Although the resulting regions provide a useful format for merger analysis, the numerical divisions suggest greater precision than is possible with the available economic tools and information. Other things being equal, cases falling just above and just below a threshold present comparable competitive concerns.

1. *General Standards.* In evaluating horizontal mergers, the Department will consider both the post-merger market concentration and the increase in concentration resulting from the merger.[30] The link between concentration and market power is explained above. The increase in concentration is relevant to several key issues. Although mergers among small firms increase concentration, they are less likely to have anticompetitive consequences. Moreover, even in concentrated markets, it is desirable to allow firms some scope for merger activity in order to achieve economies of scale and to permit exit from the market.

The general standards for horizontal mergers are as follows:

a) *Post-Merger HHI Below 1000.* Markets in this region generally would be considered to be unconcentrated, having the equivalent of at least 10 equally sized firms. Because implicit coordination among firms is likely to be difficult and because the prohibitions of section 1 of the Sherman Act are usually an adequate response to any explicit collusion that might occur, the Department is unlikely to challenge mergers falling in this region.

b) *Post-Merger HHI Between 1000 and 1800.* Because this region extends from the point at which the competitive concerns associated with concentration become significant to the point at which they become quite serious, generalization is particularly difficult. The Department, however, is unlikely to challenge mergers producing an increase in the HHI of less than 100 points.[31] The Department is more likely than not to challenge mergers in this region that produce an increase in the HHI of more than 100 points. In making that decision, however, the Department will take into account the post-merger concentration of the market, the size of the resulting increase in concentration, and the presence or absence of the other factors discussed in Sections III(B) and III(C).

---

[30] The increase in concentration as measured by the HHI can be calculated independently of the overall market concentration by doubling the product of the market shares of the merging firms. For example, the merger of firms with shares of 5 percent and 10 percent of the market would increase the HHI by 100 ($5 \times 10 \times 2 = 100$). [The explanation for this technique is as follows: In calculating the HHI before the merger, the market shares of the merging firms are squared individually. Thus: $(a)^2 + (b)^2$. After the merger, the sum of those shares would be squared. Thus: $(a + b)^2$, which equals $a^2 + 2ab + b^2$. The increase in the HHI therefore is represented by $2ab$.]

[31] Mergers producing increases in concentration close to the 100 point threshold include those between firms with market shares of 25 percent and 2 percent, 16 percent and 3 percent, 12 percent and 4 percent, 10 percent and 5 percent, 8 percent and 6 percent, and 7 percent and 7 percent.

c) *Post-Merger HHI Above 1800.* Markets in this region generally are considered to be highly concentrated, having the equivalent of no more than approximately six equally sized firms. Additional concentration resulting from mergers is a matter of significant competitive concern, and the Department will resolve close questions in favor of challenging the merger. The Department is unlikely, however, to challenge mergers producing an increase in the HHI of less than 50 points.[32] For mergers producing an increase in the HHI of from 50 to 100 points, the Department will base its decision whether to challenge the merger on the post-merger concentration of the market, the size of the resulting increase in concentration, and the presence or absence of the factors discussed in Sections III(B) and III(C). The Department is likely to challenge mergers in this region that produce an increase in the HHI of 100 points or more.[33]

2. *Leading Firm Proviso.* In some cases, typically where one of the merging firms is small, mergers that may create or enhance the market power of a single dominant firm could pass scrutiny under the standards stated in Section III(A)(1). Notwithstanding those standards, the Department is likely to challenge the merger of any firm with a market share of at least 1 percent with the leading firm in the market, provided that the leading firm has a market share that is at least 35 percent and is approximately twice as large as that of the second largest firm in the market. Because the ease and profitability of collusion are of little relevance to the ability of a single dominant firm to exercise market power, the Department will not consider the factors discussed in Section III(C) in this context. Under this standard, an ample market for small acquisitions typically will remain, and it is unlikely that any relevant economies will be limited to mergers involving the largest firm in the market.

B. Ease of Entry

If entry into a market is so easy that existing competitors could not succeed in raising price for any significant period of time, the Department is unlikely to challenge mergers in that market. Under the standards in Section II(B)(1), firms that do not presently sell the relevant product, but that could easily and economically sell it using existing facilities, are included in the market and are assigned a market share. This section considers the additional competitive effects of (1) production substitution where the necessary modifications are more substantial, and (2) entry through the construction of new facilities.

In assessing ease of entry to a market, the Department will consider the likelihood and probable magnitude of entry in response to a small but signifi-

---

[32] Mergers producing increases in concentration close to the 50 point threshold include those between firms with market shares of 12 percent and 2 percent, 8 percent and 3 percent, 6 percent and 4 percent, and 5 percent and 5 percent.

[33] There is some economic evidence that, where one or two firms dominate a market, the creation of a strong third firm enhances competition. The Department has considered this evidence but is not presently prepared to balance this possible gain against the certainty of substantially increased concentration in the market.

cant and non-transitory increase in price.[34] As a first approximation, the Department will hypothesize a price increase of five percent and ask how much new entry would be likely to occur within two years.[35] In most cases in which significant entry is unlikely, the Department will not attempt to differentiate further the degrees of difficulty of entry. In cases where entry is unusually difficult, however, the Department is more likely to challenge a merger.

C. Other Factors

A variety of factors other than concentration, market shares, and ease of entry affect the likelihood that a merger will create, enhance or facilitate the exercise of market power. In evaluating mergers, the Department will consider the following factors as they relate to the ease and profitability of collusion. Where relevant, the factors are most likely to be important where the Department's decision whether to challenge a merger is otherwise close.

1. *Nature of the Product and Terms of a Sale*

(a) *Homogeneity–Heterogeneity of the Relevant Product Generally.* In a market with a homogeneous and undifferentiated product, a cartel need establish only a single price—a circumstance that facilitates reaching consensus and detecting deviation. As the products which constitute the relevant product become more numerous, heterogeneous, or differentiated, however, the problems facing a cartel become more complex. Instead of a single price, it may be necessary to establish and enforce a complex schedule of prices corresponding to gradations in actual or perceived quality attributes among the competing products.[36]

Product variation is arguably relevant in all cases, but practical considerations dictate a more limited use of the factor. There is neither an objective index of product variation nor an empirical basis for its use in drawing fine distinctions among cases. As a result, this factor will be taken into account only in relatively extreme cases where both identification and effect are more certain. For example, when the relevant product is completely homogeneous and undifferentiated, the Department is more likely to challenge the merger. Conversely, when the relevant product is very heterogeneous or sold subject to complex configuration options or customized production, the Department is

---

[34] See note 10, above. In general, entry is more likely when the additional assets necessary to produce the relevant product are short-lived or widely used outside the particular market. Conversely, entry is less likely when those assets are long-lived and highly specialized to the particular application. Entry is generally facilitated by the growth of the market and hindered by its stagnation or decline. Entry also is hindered by the need for scarce special skills or resources and the need to achieve a substantial market share in order to realize important economies of scale. See also Section IV(B)(1)(b), below.

[35] Although this type of supply response will take longer to materialize than those previously considered, its prospect may have a greater deterrent effect on the exercise of market power by present sellers. Where new entry involves the dedication of long-lived assets to a market, the resulting capacity and its adverse effects on profitability will be present in the market until those assets are depreciated.

[36] A similar situation may exist where there is rapid technological change or where supply arrangements consist of many complicated terms in addition to price.

less likely to challenge the merger.[37] Over a significant middle range of the spectrum of product variation, this factor is less likely to affect the Department's analysis.

b) *Degree of Difference between the Products and Locations in the Market and the Next-Best-Substitutes.* The market definition standards stated in Section II require drawing relatively bright lines in order to determine the products and sellers to be considered in evaluating a merger. For example, in defining the relevant product, all "good substitutes" in demand are included. The profitability of any collusion that might occur will depend in part, however, on the quality of the next-best substitute. That is, it matters whether the next-best substitute is only slightly or significantly inferior to the last product included in the relevant product. Similarly, it matters whether the next-most-distant seller is only slightly or significantly farther away than the last seller included in the geographic market. The larger the "gap" at the edge of the product and geographic markets, the more likely the Department is to challenge the merger.

c) *Similarities and Differences in the Products and Locations of the Merging Firms.* There also may be relevant comparisons among the products or sellers included in the market. Where products in a relevant market are differentiated or sellers are spatially dispersed, individual sellers usually compete more directly with some rivals than with others. In markets with highly differentiated products, the Department will consider the extent to which consumers perceive the products of the merging firms to be relatively better or worse substitutes for one another than for other products in the market. In markets with spatially dispersed sellers and significant transportation costs, the Department will consider the relative proximity of the merging firms. If the products or plants of the merging firms are particularly good substitutes for one another, the Department is more likely to challenge the merger.

2. *Information about Specific Transactions and Buyer Market Characteristics.* Collusive agreements are more likely to persist if participating firms can quickly detect and retaliate against deviations from the agreed prices or other conditions. Such deviations are easiest to detect, and therefore least likely to occur, in markets where detailed information about specific transactions or individual price or output levels is readily available to competitors. The Department is more likely to challenge a merger if such detailed information is available to competitors, whether the information comes from an exchange among sellers, public disclosure by buyers, reporting by the press or a government agency, or some other source.

Certain buyer market characteristics also may facilitate detection of deviation from collusive agreements. If orders for the relevant product are frequent, regular and small relative to the total output of a typical firm in the market, collusion is more likely to succeed because the benefits of departing from the collusive agreement in any single transaction are likely to be small relative to

---

[37] This conclusion would not apply, however, where the significance of heterogeneity is substantially reduced through detailed specifications that are provided by the buyer and that form the basis for all firms' bids.

the potential costs. In order to increase its sales significantly in such circumstances, a seller would have to depart from the collusive agreement on a large number of orders. Each such sale takes customers away from other parties to the agreement, a fact that is particularly evident when demand is stable or declining. As a result, the chances of detection and effective response by other sellers increase with the number of such sales. The Department is more likely to challenge a merger where such buyer market characteristics exist.

3. *Conduct of Firms in the Market.* The Department is more likely to challenge a merger in the following circumstances:

a) Firms in the market previously have been found to have engaged in horizontal collusion regarding price, territories, or customers, and the characteristics of the market have not changed appreciably since the most recent finding. The additional concentration resulting from the merger could make explicit collusion more difficult to detect or tacit collusion more feasible.

b) One or more of the following types of practices are adopted by substantially all of the firms in the market: i) mandatory delivered pricing; ii) exchange of price or output information in a form that could assist firms in setting or enforcing an agreed price; iii) collective standardization of product variables on which the firms could compete; and iv) price protection clauses. Although not objectionable under all circumstances, these types of practices tend to make collusion easier, and their widespread adoption by the firms in the market raises some concern that collusion may already exist.

c) The firm to be acquired has been an unusually disruptive and competitive influence in the market. Before invoking this factor, the Department will determine whether the market is one in which performance might plausibly deteriorate because of the elimination of one disruptive firm.

4. *Market Performance.* When the market in which the proposed merger would occur is currently performing noncompetitively, the Department is more likely to challenge the merger. Non-competitive performance suggests that the firms in the market already have succeeded in overcoming, at least to some extent, the obstacles to effective collusion. Additional concentration of such a market through merger could further facilitate the collusion that already exists. When the market in which the proposed merger would occur is currently performing competitively, however, the Department will apply its ordinary standards of review. The fact that the market is currently competitive casts little light on the likely effect of the merger.

In evaluating the performance of a market, the Department will consider any relevant evidence, but will give particular weight to the following evidence of possible non-competitive performance when the factors are found in conjunction:

a) Stable relative market shares of the leading firms in recent years;

b) Declining combined market share of the leading firms in recent years;[38] and

---

[38] The exercise of market power often results in a gradual loss of market share. Fringe firms find it possible and profitable to expand their sales, and new entry may occur.

c) Profitability of the leading firms over substantial periods of time that significantly exceeds that of firms in industries comparable in capital intensity and risk.

IV. HORIZONTAL EFFECT FROM NON-HORIZONTAL MERGERS

By definition, non-horizontal mergers involve firms that do not operate in the same market. It necessarily follows that such mergers produce no immediate change in the level of concentration in any relevant market as defined in Section II. Although non-horizontal mergers are less likely than horizontal mergers to create competitive problems, they are not invariably innocuous. This Section describes the principal theories under which the Department is likely to challenge non-horizontal mergers.

A. Elimination of Specific Potential Entrants

1. *The Theory of Potential Competition.* In some circumstances, the non-horizontal merger[39] of a firm already in a market (the "acquired firm") with a potential entrant to that market (the "acquiring firm")[40] may adversely affect competition in the market. If the merger effectively removes the acquiring firm from the edge of the market, it could have either of the following effects:

a) *Harm to "Perceived Potential Competition."* By eliminating a significant present competitive threat that constrains the behavior of the firms already in the market, the merger could result in an immediate deterioration in market performance. The economic theory of limit pricing suggests that monopolists and groups of colluding firms may find it profitable to restrain their pricing in order to deter new entry that is likely to push prices even lower by adding capacity to the market. If the acquiring firm had unique advantages in entering the market, the firms in the market might be able to set a new and higher price after the threat of entry by the acquiring firm was eliminated by the merger.

b) *Harm to "Actual Potential Competition."* By eliminating the possibility of entry by the acquiring firm in a more pro-competitive manner, the merger could result in a lost opportunity for improvement in market performance resulting from the addition of a significant competitor. The more pro-competitive alternatives include both new entry and entry through a "toehold" acquisition of a present small competitor.

2. *Relation between Perceived and Actual Potential Competition.* If it were always profit-maximizing for incumbent firms to set price in such a way that all entry was deterred and if information and coordination were sufficient to im-

---

[39] Under traditional usage, such a merger could be characterized as either "vertical" or conglomerate," but the label adds nothing to the analysis.

[40] The terms "acquired" and "acquiring" refer to the relationship of the firms to the market of interest, not to the way the particular transaction is formally structured.

plement this strategy, harm to perceived potential competition would be the only competitive problem to address. In practice, however, actual potential competition has independent importance. Firms already in the market may not find it optimal to set price low enough to deter all entry; moreover, those firms may misjudge the entry advantages of a particular firm and, therefore, the price necessary to deter its entry.[41]

3. *Enforcement Standards.* Because of the close relationship between perceived potential competition and actual potential competition, the Department will evaluate mergers that raise either type of potential competition concern under a single structural analysis analogous to that applied to horizontal mergers. The Department first will consider a set of objective factors designed to identify cases in which harmful effects are plausible. In such cases, the Department then will conduct a more focused inquiry to determine whether the likelihood and magnitude of the possible harm justify a challenge to the merger. In this context, the Department will consider any specific evidence presented by the merging parties to show that the inferences of competitive harm drawn from the objective factors are unreliable.

The factors that the Department will consider are as follows:

a) *Market Concentration.* Barriers to entry are unlikely to affect market performance if the structure of the market is otherwise not conducive to monopolization or collusion. Adverse competitive effects are likely only if overall concentration, or the largest firm's market share, is high. The Department is unlikely to challenge a potential competition merger unless overall concentration of the acquired firm's market is above 1800 HHI [a somewhat lower concentration will suffice if one or more of the factors discussed in Section III(C) indicate that effective collusion in the market is particularly likely]. Other things being equal, the Department is increasingly likely to challenge a merger as this threshold is exceeded.

b) *Conditions of Entry Generally.* If entry to the market is generally easy, the fact that entry is marginally easier for one or more firms is unlikely to affect the behavior of the firms in the market. The Department is unlikely to challenge a potential competition merger when new entry into the acquired firm's market can be accomplished by firms without any specific entry advantages under the conditions stated in Section III(B). Other things being equal, the Department is increasingly likely to challenge a merger as the difficulty of entry increases above that threshold.

c) *The Acquiring Firm's Entry Advantage.* If more than a few firms have the same or a comparable advantage in entering the acquired firm's market, the elimination of one firm is unlikely to have any adverse competitive effect. The other similarly situated firm(s) would continue to exert a present restraining influence, or, if entry would be profitable, would recognize the opportunity and enter. The Department is unlikely to challenge a potential competition

---

[41] When collusion is only tacit, the problem of arriving at and enforcing the correct limit price is likely to be particularly difficult.

merger if the entry advantage ascribed to the acquiring firm (or another advantage of comparable importance) is also possessed by three or more other firms. Other things being equal, the Department is increasingly likely to challenge a merger as the number of other similarly situated firms decreases below three and as the extent of the entry advantage over non-advantaged firms increases.

If the evidence of likely actual entry by the acquiring firm is particularly strong,[42] however, the Department may challenge a potential competition merger, notwithstanding the presence of three or more firms that are objectively similarly situated. In such cases, the Department will determine the likely scale of entry, using either the firm's own documents or the minimum efficient scale in the industry. The Department will then evaluate the merger much as it would a horizontal merger between a firm the size of the likely scale of entry and the acquired firm.

d) *The Market Share of the Acquired Firm.* Entry through the acquisition of a relatively small firm in the market may have a competitive effect comparable to new entry. Small firms frequently play peripheral roles in collusive interactions, and the particular advantages of the acquiring firm may convert a fringe firm into a significant factor in the market.[43] The Department is unlikely to challenge a potential competition merger when the acquired firm has a market share of five percent or less. Other things being equal, the Department is increasingly likely to challenge a merger as the market share of the acquired firm increases above that threshold. The Department is likely to challenge any merger satisfying the other conditions in which the acquired firm has a market share of 20 percent or more.

B. Competitive Problems from Vertical Mergers

1. *Barriers to Entry from Vertical Mergers.* In certain circumstances, the vertical integration resulting from vertical mergers could create competitively objectionable barriers to entry. Stated generally, three conditions are necessary (but not sufficient) for this problem to exist. First, the degree of vertical integration between the two markets must be so extensive that entrants to one market (the "primary market") also would have to enter the other market (the "secondary market")[44] simultaneously. Second, the requirement of entry at the secondary level must make entry at the primary level significantly more difficult and less likely to occur. Finally, the structure and other characteristics of the primary market must be otherwise so conducive to non-competitive perfor-

---

[42] For example, the firm already may have moved beyond the stage of consideration and have made significant investments demonstrating an actual decision to enter.

[43] Although a similar effect is possible with the acquisition of larger firms, there is an increased danger that the acquiring firm will choose to acquiesce in monopolization or collusion because of the enhanced profits that would result from its own disappearance from the edge of the market.

[44] This competitive problem could result from either upstream or downstream integration, and could affect competition in either the upstream market or the downstream market. In the text, the term "primary market" refers to the market in which the competitive concerns are being considered, and the term "secondary market" refers to the adjacent market.

mance that the increased difficulty of entry is likely to affect its performance. The following standards state the criteria by which the Department will determine whether these conditions are satisfied.

a. *Need for Two-Level Entry.* If there is sufficient unintegrated capacity[45] in the secondary market, new entrants to the primary market would not have to enter both markets simultaneously. The Department is unlikely to challenge a merger on this ground where post-merger sales (purchases) by unintegrated firms in the secondary market would be sufficient to service two minimum-efficient-scale plants in the primary market. When the other conditions are satisfied, the Department is increasingly likely to challenge a merger as the unintegrated capacity declines below this level.

b. *Increased Difficulty of Simultaneous Entry to Both Markets.* The relevant question is whether the need for simultaneous entry to the secondary market gives rise to a substantial incremental difficulty as compared to entry into the primary market alone. If entry at the secondary level is easy in absolute terms, the requirement of simultaneous entry to that market is unlikely adversely to affect entry to the primary market. Whatever the difficulties of entry into the primary market may be, the Department is unlikely to challenge a merger on this ground if new entry into the secondary market can be accomplished under the conditions stated in Section III(B).[46] When entry is not possible under those conditions, the Department is increasingly concerned about vertical mergers as the difficulty of entering the secondary market increases. The Department, however, will invoke this theory only where the need for secondary market entry significantly increases the costs (which may take the form of risks) of primary market entry.

i) *Increased Cost of Capital as a Barrier to Entry.* More capital is necessary to enter two markets than to enter one. Standing alone, however, this additional capital requirement does not constitute a barrier to entry to the primary market. If the necessary funds were available at a cost commensurate with the level of risk in the secondary market, there would be no adverse effect. In some cases, however, lenders may doubt that would-be entrants to the primary market have the necessary skills and knowledge to succeed in the secondary market and, therefore, in the primary market. In order to compensate for this risk of failure, lenders might charge a higher rate for the necessary capital. This problem becomes increasingly significant as a higher percentage of the capital assets in the secondary market are long-lived and specialized to that

---

[45] Ownership integration does not necessarily mandate two-level entry by new entrants to the primary market. Such entry is most likely to be necessary where the primary and secondary markets are completely integrated by ownership *and* each firm in the primary market *uses* all of the capacity of its associated firm in the secondary market. In many cases of ownership integration, however, the functional fit between vertically integrated firms is not perfect, and an outside market exists for the sales (purchases) of the firms in the secondary market. If that market is sufficiently large and diverse, new entrants to the primary market may be able to participate without simultaneous entry to the secondary market. In considering the adequacy of this alternative, the Department will consider the likelihood of predatory price or supply "squeezes" by the integrated firms against their unintegrated rivals.

[46] Entry into the secondary market may be greatly facilitated in that an assured supplier (customer) is provided by the primary market entry.

market and, therefore, difficult to recover in the event of failure. In evaluating the likelihood of increased barriers to entry resulting from increased cost of capital, therefore, the Department will consider both the degree of similarity in the essential skills in the primary and secondary markets and the degree of specialization of the capital assets in the secondary market.

ii) *Economies of Scale as a Barrier to Entry.* Economies of scale in the secondary market may constitute an additional barrier to entry to the primary market in some situations requiring two-level entry. The problem could arise if the capacities of minimum-efficient-scale plants in the primary and secondary markets differ significantly. For example, if the capacity of a minimum-efficient-scale plant in the secondary market were significantly greater than the needs of a minimum-efficient-scale plant in the primary market, entrants would have to choose between inefficient operation at the secondary level (because of operating an efficient plant at an inefficient output or because of operating an inefficiently small plant) or a larger than necessary scale at the primary level. Either of these effects could cause a significant increase in the operating costs of the entering firm.[47]

c. *Structure and Performance of the Primary Market.* Barriers to entry are unlikely to affect performance if the structure of the primary market is otherwise not conducive to monopolization or collusion.[48] The Department is unlikely to challenge a merger on this ground unless overall concentration of the primary market is above 1800 HHI [a somewhat lower concentration will suffice if one or more of the factors discussed in Section III(C) indicate that effective collusion is particularly likely]. Above that threshold, the Department is increasingly likely to challenge a merger that meets the other criteria set forth above as the concentration increases.[49]

2. Facilitating Collusion through Vertical Mergers

a. *Vertical Integration to the Retail Level.* A high level of vertical integration by upstream firms into the associated retail market may facilitate collusion in the upstream market by making it easier to monitor price. Retail prices are generally more visible than prices in upstream markets, and vertical mergers may increase the level of vertical integration to the point at which the monitoring effect becomes significant. Adverse competitive consequences are unlikely unless the upstream market is generally conducive to collusion and a large

---

[47] It is important to note, however, that this problem would not exist if a significant outside market exists at the secondary level. In that case, entrants could enter with the appropriately scaled plants at both levels, and sell or buy in the market as necessary.

[48] For example, a market with 100 firms of equal size would perform competitively despite a significant increase in entry barriers.

[49] Even if all the conditions above are satisfied, the Department may not challenge a particular merger. The likelihood of significant competitive harm is lower than it is for horizontal mergers identified as competitively objectionable under the standards in Section III, and the extensive pattern of use integration, which is a necessary condition to the competitive problem under discussion, may constitute evidence that substantial economies are afforded by vertical integration. When such economies are present, it might be economically perverse and inequitable to the remaining independent firms to deny them the ability to integrate through merger.

percentage of the products produced there are sold through vertically integrated retail outlets.

The Department is unlikely to challenge a merger on this ground unless i) overall concentration of the upstream market is above 1800 HHI [a somewhat lower concentration will suffice if one or more of the factors discussed in Section III(C) above indicate that effective collusion is particularly likely], and ii) a large percentage of the upstream product would be sold through vertically integrated retail outlets after the merger. Where the stated thresholds are met or exceeded, the Department's decision whether to challenge a merger on this ground will depend upon an individual evaluation of its likely competitive effect.[50]

b. *Elimination of a Disruptive Buyer.* The elimination by vertical merger of a particularly disruptive buyer in a downstream market may facilitate collusion in the upstream market. If upstream firms view sales to a particular buyer as sufficiently important, they may deviate from the terms of a collusive agreement in an effort to secure that business, thereby disrupting the operation of the agreement. The merger of such a buyer with an upstream firm may eliminate that rivalry, making it easier for the upstream firms to collude effectively. Adverse competitive consequences are unlikely unless the upstream market is generally conducive to collusion and the disruptive firm is significantly more attractive to sellers than the other firms in its market.

The Department is unlikely to challenge a merger on this ground unless i) overall concentration of the upstream market is 1800 HHI or above [a somewhat lower concentration will suffice if one or more of the factors discussed in III(C) above indicate that effective collusion is particularly likely], and ii) the allegedly disruptive firm differs substantially in volume of purchases or other relevant characteristics from the other firms in its market. Where the stated thresholds are met or exceeded, the Department's decision whether to challenge a merger on this ground will depend upon an individual evaluation of its likely competitive effect.

3. Evasion of Rate Regulation

Non-horizontal mergers may be used by monopoly public utilities subject to rate regulation as a tool for circumventing that regulation. The clearest example is the acquisition by a regulated utility of a supplier of its fixed or variable inputs. After the merger, the utility would be selling to itself and might be able arbitrarily to inflate the prices of internal transactions. Regulators may have great difficulty in policing these practices, particularly if there is no independent market for the product (or service) purchased from the affiliate.[51] As a

---

[50] See note 49, above.

[51] A less severe, but nevertheless serious, problem can arise when a regulated utility acquires a firm that is not vertically related. The use of common facilities and managers may create an insoluble cost allocation problem and provide the opportunity to charge utility customers for non-utility costs, consequently distorting resource allocation in the adjacent as well as the regulated market.

result, inflated prices could be passed along to consumers as "legitimate" costs. In extreme cases, the regulated firm may effectively preempt the adjacent market, perhaps for the purpose of suppressing observable market transactions, and may distort resource allocation in that adjacent market as well as in the regulated market. In such cases, however, the Department recognizes that genuine economies of integration may be involved. The Department will consider challenging mergers that create substantial opportunities for such abuses.[52]

V. DEFENSES

A. Efficiencies

In the overwhelming majority of cases, the Guidelines will allow firms to achieve available efficiencies through mergers without interference from the Department. Except in extraordinary cases, the Department will not consider a claim of specific efficiencies as a mitigating factor for a merger that would otherwise be challenged.[53] Plausible efficiencies are far easier to allege than to prove. Morever, even if the existence of efficiencies were clear, their magnitude would be extremely difficult to determine.

B. Failing Firm

The "failing firm defense" is a long-established, but ambiguous,[54] doctrine under which an anticompetitive merger may be allowed because one of the merging firms is "failing." Because the defense can immunize significantly anticompetitive mergers, the Department will construe its elements strictly.

The Department is unlikely to challenge an anticompetitive merger in which one of the merging firms is allegedly failing when: 1) the allegedly failing firm probably would be unable to meet its financial obligations in the near future, and 2) it probably would not be able to reorganize successfully under Chapter 11 of the Bankruptcy Act,[55] and 3) it has made unsuccessful good

---

[52] Where a regulatory agency has the responsibility for approving such mergers, the Department will express its concerns to that agency in its role as competition advocate.

[53] At a minimum, the Department will require clear and convincing evidence that the merger will produce substantial cost savings resulting from the realization of scale economies, integration of production facilities, or multi-plant operations which are already enjoyed by one or more firms in the industry and that equivalent results could not be achieved within a comparable period of time through internal expansion or through a merger that threatened less competitive harm. In any event, the Department will consider such efficiencies only in resolving otherwise close cases.

[54] Although its original basis is open to question, the defense is sometimes explained as a balancing of competitive and non-competitive concerns. Under that view, when the elements of the defense are satisfied, there is a conclusive presumption that the anticompetitive dangers associated with the merger are outweighed by the income losses to creditors, stockholders, and communities associated with the failure of the firm. As a general matter, the Department views the incorporation of non-competitive concerns into antitrust analysis as inconsistent with the mandate contained in the antitrust laws. To the extent that the financial health of the firm is relevant to the competitive analysis, the Department, of course, will consider it in that context.

[55] 11 U.S.C.A. §§1101 et seq. (1979).

faith efforts to elicit reasonable alternative offers of acquisition of the failing firm[56] that would both keep it in the market and pose a less severe danger to competition than does the proposed merger. Although these standards are more difficult to apply when the allegedly failing firm is an unincorporated part of a larger parent firm, the Department will recognize the defense in appropriate cases of that type.[57]

---

[56] The fact that an offer is less than the proposed transaction does not make it unreasonable.

[57] The Department is unlikely to challenge an otherwise anticompetitive merger in which one of the merging firms is a financially healthy subdivision of an allegedly failing parent firm when: 1) the parent firm satisfies the above conditions, and 2) the competitive harm from the disappearance of the parent firm from its market would substantially outweigh the competitive harm threatened by the merger, 3) the proposed transaction probably would enable the parent firm to avoid bankruptcy or to reorganize successfully, 4) the third condition stated in the text also has been satisfied with respect to the healthy subdivision, and 5) the merging firm is not capable of independent existence as a business entity. Where the merging firm is capable of independent existence, the Division may insist that the parent company attempt to transfer common stock in it to the parent company's debtors.

STATEMENT OF FEDERAL TRADE COMMISSION CONCERNING HORIZONTAL MERGERS

I. BACKGROUND

The Federal Trade Commission ("Commission") and the Antitrust Division of the Department of Justice ("Antitrust Division") have been reexamining the legal and economic basis for horizontal merger policy. In light of enforcement experience and more recent economic research, the two agencies have both concluded that continued reliance on the Department of Justice's Merger Guidelines, promulgated in 1968 ("1968 Guidelines"), is no longer appropriate. In order to revise the 1968 Guidelines and incorporate new factors that are relevant to current horizontal merger analysis, the Commission and the Antitrust Division formed working groups of lawyers and economists to evaluate past experience under the 1968 Guidelines and to recommend specific modifications. The staffs of both agencies have worked closely in this endeavor. In addition to their research and analytical work, they have also solicited and carefully examined the views of the private bar, the academic and business communities, as well as the public at large.

The Commission is issuing this Statement to express its collective judgment of the reasons why it supports changes in the 1968 Guidelines and to highlight the principal considerations that will guide its horizontal merger enforcement. However, the Department of Justice's 1982 revisions to the 1968 Guidelines will be given considerable weight by the Commission and its staff in their evaluation of horizontal mergers and in the development of the Commission's overall approach to horizontal mergers.[1]

II. MARKET SHARE CONSIDERATIONS

Congress enacted Section 7 of the Clayton Act to prevent the corporate accumulation of market power through mergers.[2] The subsequent amendment to the Clayton Act,[3] while primarily focusing on competitive considerations,[4] also

---

[1] While the Commission supports the Department of Justice's decision to revise the 1968 Guidelines, individual Commissioners, however, may not endorse each specific revision that has been proposed.

[2] Clayton Act, Pub. L. No. 63-212, 38 Stat. 730 (1914) [codified at 15 U.S.C. §18 (1976)].

[3] Celler–Kefauver Act, Pub. L. No. 81-899, 64 Stat. 1125 (1950) [codified at 15 U.S.C. §§18, 21 (1976)].

[4] See IV P. Areeda & D. Turner, *Antitrust Law* 8–14 (1980).

reflected Congress' concern about the overall social and political ramifications of economic concentration attributable to merger activity.[5] Legal analysis of horizontal mergers, however, has focused on the extent to which these mergers confer market power on the acquiring firm or enhance the ability of firms to collude, either expressly or tacitly.

In measuring these market power effects, the courts, the Commission and the Antitrust Division have traditionally looked to market share data and derivative concentration ratios as the principal indicators of market power. Their reliance on such evidence was founded on early empirical economic literature indicating a significant positive relationship between concentration levels, industry performance and profits.[6] In addition, market share data provided an easily ascertainable and relatively objective benchmark to evaluate the potential effects of horizontal mergers.

More recent empirical economic research[7] and well over a decade of practical experience in analyzing and evaluating horizontal mergers, however, have led the Commission to conclude that proper consideration of market realities justifies some revision of market share benchmarks and greater consideration of evidence beyond mere market shares when such evidence is available and in a reliable form. Whether utilizing the Herfindahl–Hirschman index or other concentration measures, the Commission believes that an increase in the threshold market shares is clearly justified on at least three bases. First, current economic analysis suggests that the low combined market share thresholds contained in the 1968 Guidelines, e.g., 8 percent and 10 percent, are unlikely to contribute to oligopolistic behavior or market dominance.[8] Second, the threshold levels in the 1968 Guidelines do not capture as fully as possible economies of scale achieved through merger.[9] Third, the relationship between the number and relative size of firms in the relevant market was not taken into account in the 1968 Guidelines. Recent studies also suggest that poor market performance may be partly a function of firm size disparity. Thus, although far from definitive, this research suggests that particular attention should be given to disparity in market shares between the top one or two firms and the remaining firms in an industry.[10]

For these reasons, while the Commission will continue to look to market share data as an important indicium of the likely competitive effects of a merger, a more refined treatment of that data is in order.

[5] For a discussion of Congress' interest in the non-economic aspects of mergers, see Bok, "Section 7 of the Clayton Act and the Merging of Law and Economics," 74 Harv. L. Rev. 226, 233–49, 306–07 (1960). See also Pitofsky, "The Political Content of Antitrust," 127 U. Pa. L. Rev. 1051 (1979).

[6] See IV P. Areeda & D. Turner, supra note 4, at 52–54. For a discussion of the relevant literature, see generally Pautler, "A Review of the Economic Basis for Broad-Based Horizontal Merger Policy," Federal Trade Commission Staff Working Draft, 18–27 (October 1981).

[7] See literature survey contained in Pautler, supra note 6, at 28–30, 61–74.

[8] Id.

[9] See II P. Areeda & D. Turner, supra note 4, at 291–98; R. Posner, Antitrust Law 112–13 (1976); Fisher & Lande, "Efficiency Considerations in Merger Enforcement," 91 Yale L.J. ——, at Section III (1982) (forthcoming). In certain circumstances, an increase in threshold levels will enhance the ability of smaller firms to exit from the market, thereby facilitating entry. See Pillsbury Co., 93 F.T.C. 966, 1041–42 (1979).

[10] For a detailed discussion of this research, see Pautler, supra note 6, at 78–85.

III. NON-MARKET SHARE CONSIDERATIONS

Current statistical information helps to provide a good snapshot of an industry, but consideration of additional market characteristics, entry barriers being the major example, may provide a clearer and more accurate picture of the competitive dynamics of that industry. Such an inquiry may reveal whether any market power conferred by the merger is likely to persist over time and whether market conditions are conducive either to the exercise of individual firm market power or to collusive-type behavior.

The Commission recognizes, of course, that any type of market analysis, including reliance on market shares, inevitably carries with it an element of imprecision. For example, relevant evidence may be difficult to obtain or, where it is available, may be fragmentary and inconsistent. Further, evidence peculiarly within the control of the parties to the proceeding may be subject to bias and be difficult to verify. Nevertheless, the Commission believes that consideration of factors other than market shares, including qualitative factors, can be useful and desirable. If proper allowance is given to the evidentiary limitations, a balance can be struck that achieves the twin objectives of maintaining reasonable predictability in merger policy while enhancing the quality of the analysis and the correctness of the ultimate outcome.

The following discussion of non-market share factors will serve to define the scope of the merger inquiry and to prevent the analysis from becoming a limitless search for any evidence of possible relevance, since an open-ended examination may prevent the Commission and the courts from providing meaningful and timely guidance to business.

A. Market Power/Duration Factors

As we have noted, market share data can serve as an important preliminary surrogate measure of market power. For a variety of reasons, however, that indicator may not always accurately measure the market power of merging firms. The critical task, then, is to isolate and evaluate those additional factors that are also relevant to the assessment of market power effects.

(1) Marketwide Conditions

Ideally, if we could measure all relevant demand and supply elasticities, we could arrive at relatively precise estimates of market power.[11] Such evidence, however, is rarely, if ever, available and is not readily susceptible to direct measurement. Therefore, other criteria must be utilized to determine the probable impact of a merger. The most probative criteria include: entry barriers; concentration trends (including the volatility of market shares); technological change; demand trends; and market definition. These factors are interrelated and primarily address industrywide conditions rather than firm specific characteristics.

---

[11] Landes & Posner, "Market Power in Antitrust Cases," 94 *Harv. L. Rev.* 937, 939–43 (1981).

The issue of entry barriers is perhaps the most important qualitative factor, for if entry barriers are very low it is unlikely that market power, whether individually or collectively exercised, will persist for long.[12] Conversely, if entry barriers are quite high, the effect may be to exacerbate any market power conferred by the merger. Of course, the evidence relating to entry barriers may not always point clearly to the conclusion that a merger should or should not be allowed. On the other hand, evidence of actual entry, especially recent and frequent new entry, is highly probative, as is evidence of failed entry or the absence of entry over long periods of time. Besides mere entry, effective competition might also depend upon a firm's achieving a certain scale of operation. Evidence of substantial expansion by firms already in an industry, especially nondominant firms, may persuasively indicate that barriers to larger scale are not high. Conversely, evidence of frequent entry, but on a small scale, without significant expansion by fringe firms, may also suggest the existence of barriers to larger scale.

Market power also may be harder to exercise or less likely to endure in the face of rapid technological change or significant upward shifts in demand. Moreover, this kind of evidence may shed light on questions of market definition and the market's propensity towards collusive interdependence. New technology, for example, may signal that the market is being transformed and that traditional boundaries do not accurately measure the degree of product substitutability which actually exists. If these trends are strong, they are likely to result in new entry, declining concentration or unstable market shares. These issues are closely intertwined. Market share fluctuations may represent overt manifestations of underlying market forces and, as such, provide a very useful picture of market dynamics. Of course, like other evidence, the value of such data depends upon the magnitude and likely duration of the shifts that are occurring. Small deviations in market shares, even if they recur on a frequent basis, may be of little significance.

Additionally, the issue of market definition is relevant in determining whether market power exists and can be exercised successfully. The more carefully the lines are drawn, the more confidence can be placed in the predictive value of market share data; but market boundaries cannot always be drawn with fine precision. Where the boundaries are highly blurred, it may be appropriate to take that fact into account, especially at the margin where the market shares are not particularly high.[13]

These factors are important in revealing whether the market shares overstate or understate the competitive impact of a merger. The weight to be assigned this evidence is a critical issue since, as noted above, it will often be impossible to make fine distinctions based on the quantity and quality of the nonstatistical information. For instance, the fact that demand is increasing or new products are being introduced does not necessarily mean that the market

[12] See F. Scherer, *Industrial Market Structure and Economic Performance* 5, 11, 236 (2d ed. 1980); G. Stigler, *The Theory of Price* 220–27 (3d ed. 1966); Demsetz, "Barriers to Entry," 72 *Am. Econ. Rev.* 47 (1982).

[13] See Coca-Cola Bottling Co., 93 F.T.C. 110 (1979); SKF Industries, Inc., 94 F.T.C. 6, 86–87 (1979).

share data should automatically be discounted by some factor. Rather, it is important to look at overall trends to see where the market is heading and at what rate.

Where all of the non-market share evidence consistently points in the same direction, its value will be high. Such evidence will be of even greater significance where the market shares are in the low to moderate range. On the other hand, if the anti competitive potential of a merger is large, as predicted by the combined market shares of the merging parties, other non-market share factors may appropriately be given less weight, even if the adverse effects are relatively shortlived. To be sure, merger analysis properly focuses primarily on long-term competitive implications, but short-term effects should not be ignored, particularly if they are substantial.

(2) Firm-Specific Characteristics

So far, we have focused on marketwide conditions that may bear on the competitive effects of a merger. Factors peculiar to the merging parties can also be of relevance, although some caution should be exercised since this kind of evidence is harder to verify.[14] The most important type of evidence is that which relates to the failing company doctrine, about which we will say more later. However, it is frequently argued by parties to a merger that financial weakness should be considered as a defense by the enforcement agencies. While not endorsing this approach in all its dimensions,[15] the Commission does believe that evidence of individual firm performance can be of use in evaluating the probable effects of a merger, primarily if it indicates that a firm's market share overstates its competitive significance. For example, poor financial performance may accompany new entry or technological change, which itself may be evidence of the firm's declining competitive significance and its lack of prospects for future success or it may be indicative of other changes taking place in the market.[16]

Another issue related to individual company performance concerns the acquisition of firms with small market shares whose competitive potential is unique.[17] Like the previous discussion, the issue here is not so much whether the firm is performing well *per se,* but whether its presence in the market is having some discernible impact on competition. For example, is the firm a disruptive force in an industry that is otherwise susceptible to oligopolistic behavior? Does it have a unique technological capability that can be capitalized to advantage? Obviously, these considerations have more force in markets that are highly concentrated and where the acquiring firm is one of the industry

---

[14] *See* United States v. General Dynamics Corp., 415 U.S. 486, 506–8 (1974); Kaiser Aluminum & Chem. Corp. v. F.T.C., 652 F.2d F.2d 1324, 1338–39 (1981); Pillsbury Co., 93 F.T.C. 966, 1038–39 (1979).

[15] The courts and the Commission have held that evidence of poor financial performance alone is insufficient, as a matter of law, to sanction a merger. *See* United States v. General Dynamics Corp., 415 U.S. 486 (1974); Kaiser Aluminum & Chem. Corp. v. FTC, 652 F.2d 1324, 38–39 (7th Cir. 1981); Pillsbury Co., 93 F.T.C. 966, 1036–39 (1979).

[16] *See* Pillsbury Co., 93 F.T.C. 966 (1979).

[17] *See* United States v. Aluminum Co. of America, 377 U.S. 271, 280–81 (1964); Stanley Works v. FTC, 469 F.2d 498 (2d Cir. 1972), *cert. denied,* 412 U.S. 928 (1973).

leaders. Thus, there may be situations where the market shares of acquired firms clearly understate their competitive significance. This kind of inquiry most likely will involve combined market shares above the Guidelines, but it could, on occasion, involve acquisitions where the combined market shares fall slightly below the triggering threshold levels.

B. Factors Facilitating Collusion

In the preceding section, market conditions that may facilitate or hinder the exercise of market power were discussed. This section focuses on market characteristics that may enhance or detract from the ability of firms to collude or to raise prices and restrict output by interdependent behavior. The Oligopolistic markets, or at least markets with few substantial firms, are more conducive to interdependent behavior than a market without such characteristics. However, the number and size of the firms may not reveal the full picture. Other factors may affect the relative ease or difficulty of achieving or maintaining interfirm coordination. Thus, the Commission believes that it is appropriate to take some account of these considerations, particularly at the pre-complaint stage. The most relevant factors appear to be: the homogeneity (or fungibility) of products in the market; the number of buyers (as well as sellers); the similarity of producers' costs; the history of interfirm behavior, including any evidence of previous price fixing by the firms at issue; and the stability of market shares over time.

The Commission recognizes, of course, that knowledge of the dynamics of collusion or price coordination is far from complete. Moreover, in mergers where individual market power concerns predominate, issues of collusion will be of less importance. Nevertheless, some consideration of these issues should, at the very least, help the courts and enforcement agencies to sort out those cases where there appears to be little, if any, likelihood that an acquisition will contribute significantly to oligopolistic interdependence. Conversely, where the evidence of these factors points strongly in the opposite direction, we will want to examine a merger more closely, even if the market shares are relatively low.

IV. EFFICIENCY CONSIDERATIONS

Mergers may enhance the efficiency of the combining firms in such diverse areas as management, distribution and production. The difficult issue is whether such efficiency gains should be considered, at least as a partial offset to the potential anti-competitive effects of a merger, given the inherent difficulty of accurately predicting and measuring certain efficiencies.[18] Unlike the issues discussed previously, the question here is not whether efficiency considerations reduce or enhance the market power effects of a merger, but

---

[18] See IV P. Areeda & D. Turner, supra note 4, at 146–99; Fisher & Lande, supra note 9.

whether efficiencies should be treated as an independent countervailing factor in merger analysis.

There are two ways merger guidelines might take efficiencies into account. One way is by raising the market share thresholds so that economies of scale generally can be realized to the fullest extent possible. The Commission supports an adjustment in the numerical criteria, in part, for this reason. Such an approach, however, may not account for all possible efficiencies. To accomplish the latter objective, an efficiencies defense could be allowed in individual cases. Of necessity, such a defense would require an assessment of both the magnitude of the efficiencies anticipated from the merger and the relative weight to accord this evidence vis-a-vis the potential market power effects of the merger.

To minimize measurement difficulties, it has been suggested that an efficiencies defense could be limited to measurable operating efficiencies, such as production or plant economies of scale.[19] These efficiencies are also more likely to be of the kind that may eventually represent an improved state of the art available to all producers.[20] While such evidence is appropriate for consideration by the agency in the exercise of its prosecutorial discretion at the precomplaint stage,[21] the Commission believes that there are too many analytical ambiguities associated with the issue of efficiencies to treat it as a legally cognizable defense.[22] To the extent that efficiencies are considered by the Commission as a policy matter, the party or parties raising this issue must provide the Commission with substantial evidence that the resulting cost savings could not have been obtained without the merger and clearly outweigh any increase in market power.

V. FAILING COMPANY DEFENSE AND RELATED ARGUMENTS

The failing company defense recognizes a general preference for having assets productively utilized rather than withdrawn from a market. Whether assets will in fact be withdrawn is a difficult question and depends heavily on evidence under the control of the affected firm. For this reason, the failing com-

---

[19] See IV Areeda & Turner, supra note 4, at 175–96. For a discussion of operating efficiencies and methods of proof, see Fisher & Lande, supra note 9, at Sections III(A), V(A); Muris, "The Efficiency Defense Under Section 7 of the Clayton Act," 30 Case W. Res. L. Rev. 381 (1980).

[20] Where efficiencies flow from factors peculiar to the merged firms, such as improved quality of management, their contribution to the economy as a whole is more problematic.

[21] This procedural approach has been suggested by Williamson, "Economies As An Antitrust Defense Revisited," 125 U. Pa. L. Rev. 699, 734–35 (1977) and by the Section 7 Clayton Act Committee Task Force of the American Bar Association Antitrust Section, "Proposed Revision to the Justice Department's Merger Guidelines," 71 (1982).

[22] Chairman Miller disagrees with this conclusion and believes that scale-type efficiencies should be considered as part of the legal analysis, consistent with the statutory scheme underlying Section 7 of the Clayton Act, see Muris, supra note 19.

pany doctrine imposes rigorous requirements on firms seeking to invoke it.[23] In addition, the restrictions contained in the doctrine reflect the fact that the defense is absolute, regardless of any increased market power accruing to the acquiring firm by virtue of its purchase of the failing company's assets.

Because of proof burdens and general competitive considerations, the suggestion has been made that the doctrine should be relaxed to allow greater latitude for a troubled company to sell its assets to the highest bidder. For example, the doctrine could be liberalized to allow for a failing division defense or to permit a sale to the least objectionable purchaser available, where the technical requirements relating to business failure are otherwise not met, but a substantial risk exists that operations will cease if a merger is not consummated.

An increasing number of mergers evaluated by the Commission involve diversified firms seeking to divest a division or subsidiary. To require subsidization of a division or continuation of unprofitable operations carries its own costs to competition, including diminished efficiency and innovation. Such a result encourages firms to make unsound investments and leads to the inefficient use of capital.[24] The Commission's past reluctance to give legal status to a less-than-failing company defense stems from the difficulty of determining whether the costs of continued operation (until another acceptable purchaser, if any, is found) outweigh the market effects of the proposed merger. For example, with respect to the failing division argument, because of the potential facility to shift overhead and losses among divisions, an individual unit can be made to appear in worse fiscal condition by its parent than in fact is the case.[25]

In light of these considerations, the Commission will take into account evidence of a failing division or other similar evidence that falls short of the technical requirements of the failing company defense. However, due to the difficulties of proof, consideration of this evidence will be limited to the Commission's exercise of its prosecutorial discretion.[26] With respect to any such

---

[23] See, e.g., United States v. General Dynamics Corp., 415 U.S. 486 (1974); United States v. Greater Buffalo Press, Inc., 402 U.S. 549, 555–56 (1971); Citizens Publishing Co. v. United States, 394 U.S. 131, 136–39 (1969); Pillsbury Co., 93 F.T.C. 966, 1031–33, 1036–39 (1979); Reichhold Chems., Inc., 91 F.T.C. 246, 288–91 (1978), aff'd, 598 F.2d 616 (4th Cir. 1979).

[24] Refusal to consider evidence of a failing division has been characterized as unfair in that it requires diversified firms "to absorb losses that independent companies can avoid, or to take risks that the independent lenders would deem improvident." IV P. Areeda & D. Turner, supra note 4, at 112.

[25] See Dean Foods Co., 70 F.T.C. 1146, 1285 (1966); Farm Journal, Inc., 53 F.T.C. 26, 47–48 (1956). The lower courts, however, are clearly divided on the issue of the failing division. Compare FTC v. Great Lakes Chem. Corp., 1981–2 Trade Cas. (CCH) ¶ 64,175 at 73, 592 (N.D. Ill., July 23, 1981); United States v. Reed Roller Bit Co., 274 F. Supp. 573, 584 n. 1 (W.D. Okla. 1967); United States v. Lever Bros. Co., 216 F. Supp. 887 (S.D.N.Y. 1963), with United States v. Blue Bell, Inc., 395 F. Supp. 538, 550 (M.D. Tenn. 1975), and United States v. Phillips Petroleum Co., 367 F. Supp. 1226, 1260 (C.D. Cal. 1973), aff'd per curiam, 418 U.S. 906 (1974). For a discussion of the problems associated with accurately assessing failing division evidence, see generally "Conglomerate Mergers—Their Effects on Small Business and Local Communities," Hearings Before the Subcommittee on Antitrust and Restraint of Trade Activities Affecting Small Business, House of Representatives, 96th Cong., 2d Sess. 49–57, 91–130, 367–435 (1980).

[26] Chairman Miller would permit evidence of a failing division to be raised as a legal defense in a merger proceeding.

analysis, the Commission will look closely at the following factors: the extent and history of a firm's financial difficulties; whether established accounting procedures have been followed; whether a good faith effort to find another purchaser for the firm or division has been made; and whether the proposed purchaser is the least anti-competitive purchaser willing to acquire the firm or division.

VI. MARKET DEFINITION

The predictive value of evidence concerning competitive effects is directly affected by the manner in which the relevant product and geographic markets are defined. Thus, issues of market definition are critically important to sound merger analysis.

A. Product Market

The purpose of product market analysis is to ascertain what grouping of products or services should be included in a single relevant market. Where the cross-elasticity of demand for separate products or services is high, they normally will be within the same product market. Similarly, a high cross-elasticity of supply tends to suggest the existence of a common product market. Therefore, the issue of whether related products or services place a significant constraint on the ability of merging firms to raise prices, limit supply or lower quality, is central to evaluating the competitive effects of a horizontal merger.

Cross-elasticity of demand (or supply) is best measured by the change in the quantity of another product induced by a price rise in the merged firm's product, either over time or in different geographic markets. Since direct evidence of cross-elasticities is generally unavailable, the courts and enforcement agencies look to other, less direct market indicia. For example, the existence of separate product markets may be evidenced by: the persistence of sizeable price disparities for equivalent amounts of different products; the presence of sufficiently distinctive characteristics which render a product suitable only for a specialized use; the preference of a number of purchasers who traditionally use only a particular kind of product for a distinct use; or the judgment of purchasers or sellers as to whether products are, in fact, competitive. In addition, where firms routinely study the business decisions of other firms, including their pricing decisions, such evidence may reflect a single product market. These secondary indicia, however, will be closely scrutinized because of the inherently imprecise and sometimes self-serving nature of this type of evidence. Finally, investment, marketing and production plans may also evidence whether a firm may competitively enter the production and sale of another good. Particularly where such information is detailed and provides the basis for a firm's decision, it will be considered in the product market analysis.

B. Geographic Market

This component of market definition focuses on the extent to which different geographic areas should be combined into a single relevant market. The issue is whether producers of the merged firm's product in other geographic areas place a significant constraint on the ability of the merged firm to raise price or restrict output. As a general proposition, an area is a separate geographic market if a change in the price of the product in that area does not, within a relevant period of time, induce substantial changes in the quantity of the product sold in other areas.

The Commission will consider the following factors relevant to this determination: the relationship between price and quantity (or, if evidence of such relationship is shown not to be available, evidence of independent price movement, collusive pricing or price discrimination within a single area); barriers to trade flows, *e.g.*, high transportation costs, time required to make deliveries or municipal, state, or federal regulation; and shipping patterns (absence of shipments, however, does not necessarily indicate separate geographic markets because, in some circumstances, a slight price rise in one area could precipitate shipments from other areas). Evidence of shipments may be particularly probative when it reflects long-held patterns of trade and industry perceptions.

An additional consideration relevant to geographic market definition concerns the extent to which foreign markets should be included in the analysis. There is increasing evidence that national boundaries may not fully reflect trade patterns or competitive realities in certain instances. At the same time, evidence relating to foreign markets may be very difficult to obtain. Nevertheless, while these limitations may preclude the delineation of larger-than-domestic markets, some consideration should be given to this issue in determining the competitive significance of domestic market share data.

Case 1
Brown Shoe Co., Inc., v. United States

Appeal from the United States District Court for the Eastern District of
Missouri.
No. 4. Argued December 6, 1961.—Decided June 25, 1962.

MR. CHIEF JUSTICE WARREN delivered the opinion of the Court.

I.

This suit was initiated in November 1955 when the Government filed a civil action in the United States District Court for the Eastern District of Missouri alleging that a contemplated merger between the G. R. Kinney Company, Inc.
(Kinney), and the Brown Shoe Company, Inc. (Brown), through an exchange of
Kinney for Brown stock, would violate §7 of the Clayton Act, 15 U. S. C. §18.

In the District Court, the Government contended that the effect of the
merger of Brown—the third largest seller of shoes by dollar volume in the
United States, a leading manufacturer of men's, women's, and children's
shoes, and a retailer with over 1,230 owned, operated or controlled retail outlets[1]—and Kinney—the eighth largest company, by dollar volume, among
those primarily engaged in selling shoes, itself a manufacturer of shoes, and a
retailer with over 350 retail outlets—"may be substantially to lessen competition or to tend to create a monopoly" by eliminating actual or potential competition in the production of shoes for the national wholesale shoe market and
in the sale of shoes at retail in the Nation, by foreclosing competition from "a
market represented by Kinney's retail outlets whose annual sales exceed
$42,000,000," and by enhancing Brown's competitive advantage over other
producers, distributors and sellers of shoes. The Government argued that the
"line of commerce" affected by this merger is "footwear," or alternatively,

---

[1] Of these over 1,230 outlets under Brown's control at the time of the filing of the complaint,
Brown owned and operated over 470, while over 570 were independently owned stores operating
under the Brown "Franchise Program" and over 190 were independently owned outlets operating
under the "Wohl Plan." A store operating under the Franchise Program agrees not to carry
competing lines of shoes of other manufacturers in return for certain aid from Brown; a store
under the Wohl Plan similarly agrees to concentrate its purchases on lines which Brown sells
through Wohl in return for credit and merchandising aid. In addition, Brown shoes were sold
through numerous retailers operating entirely independently of Brown.

that the "line[s]" are "men's," "women's," and "children's" shoes, separately considered, and that the "section of the country," within which the anticompetitive effect of the merger is to be judged, is the Nation as a whole, or alternatively, each separate city or city and its immediate surrounding area in which the parties sell shoes at retail.

In the District Court, Brown contended that the merger would be shown not to endanger competition if the "line[s] of commerce" and the "section[s] of the country" were properly determined. Brown urged that not only were the age and sex of the intended customers to be considered in determining the relevant line of commerce, but that differences in grade of material, quality of workmanship, price, and customer use of shoes resulted in establishing different lines of commerce. While agreeing with the Government that, with regard to manufacturing, the relevant geographic market for assessing the effect of the merger upon competition is the country as a whole, Brown contended that with regard to retailing, the market must vary with economic reality from the central business district of a large city to a "standard metropolitan area"[2] for a smaller community. Brown further contended that, both at the manufacturing level and at the retail level, the shoe industry enjoyed healthy competition and that the vigor of this competition would not, in any event, be diminished by the proposed merger because Kinney manufactured less than 0.5% and retailed less than 2% of the Nation's shoes.

The District Court rejected the broadest contentions of both parties. The District Court found that "there is one group of classifications which is understood and recognized by the entire industry and the public—the classification into 'men's,' 'women's' and 'children's' shoes separately and independently." On the other hand, "[t]o classify shoes as a whole could be unfair and unjust; to classify them further would be impractical, unwarranted and unrealistic."

Realizing that "the areas of effective competition for retailing purposes cannot be fixed with mathematical precision," the District Court found that "when determined by economic reality, for retailing, a 'section of the country' is a city of 10,000 or more population and its immediate and contiguous surrounding area, regardless of name designation, and in which a Kinney store and a Brown (operated, franchise, or plan) store are located."

The District Court rejected the Government's contention that the combining of the manufacturing facilities of Brown and Kinney would substantially lessen competition in the production of men's, women's, or children's shoes for the national wholesale market. However, the District Court did find that the likely foreclosure of other manufacturers from the market represented by Kinney's retail outlets may substantially lessen competition in the manufactur-

---

[2] "The general concept adopted in defining a standard metropolitan area [is] that of an integrated economic area with a large volume of daily travel and communication between a central city of 50,000 inhabitants or more and the outlying parts of the area. . . . Each area (except in New England) consists of one or more entire counties. In New England, metropolitan areas have been defined on a town basis rather than a county basis." II U. S. Bureau of the Census, United States Census of Business: 1954, p. 3.

ers' distribution of "men's," "women's," and "children's" shoes, considered separately, throughout the Nation. The District Court also found that the merger may substantially lessen competition in retailing alone in "men's," "women's," and "children's" shoes, considered separately, in every city of 10,000 or more population and its immediate surrounding area in which both a Kinney and a Brown store are located.

Brown's contentions here differ only slightly from those made before the District Court. In order fully to understand and appraise these assertions, it is necessary to set out in some detail the District Court's findings concerning the nature of the shoe industry and the place of Brown and Kinney within that industry.

The Industry.

The District Court found that although domestic shoe production was scattered among a large number of manufacturers, a small number of large companies occupied a commanding position. Thus, while the 24 largest manufacturers produced about 35% of the Nation's shoes, the top 4—International, Endicott-Johnson, Brown (including Kinney) and General Shoe—alone produced approximately 23% of the Nation's shoes or 65% of the production of the top 24.

In 1955, domestic production of nonrubber shoes was 509.2 million pairs, of which about 103.6 million pairs were men's shoes, about 271 million pairs were women's shoes, and about 134.6 million pairs were children's shoes. The District Court found that men's, women's, and children's shoes are normally produced in separate factories.

The public buys these shoes through about 70,000 retail outlets, only 22,000 of which, however, derive 50% or more of their gross receipts from the sale of shoes and are classified as "shoe stores" by the Census Bureau. These 22,000 shoe stores were found generally to sell (1) men's shoes only, (2) women's shoes only, (3) women's and children's shoes, or (4) men's, women's, and children's shoes.

The District Court found a "definite trend" among shoe manufacturers to acquire retail outlets. For example, International Shoe Company had no retail outlets in 1945, but by 1956 had acquired 130; General Shoe Company had only 80 retail outlets in 1945 but had 526 by 1956; Shoe Corporation of America, in the same period, increased its retail holdings from 301 to 842; Melville Shoe Company from 536 to 947; and Endicott-Johnson from 488 to 540. Brown, itself, with no retail outlets of its own prior to 1951, had acquired 845 such outlets by 1956. Moreover, between 1950 and 1956 nine independent shoe store chains, operating 1,114 retail shoe stores, were found to have become subsidiaries of these large firms and to have ceased their independent operations.

And once the manufacturers acquired retail outlets, the District Court found there was a "definite trend" for the parent-manufacturers to supply an ever increasing percentage of the retail outlets' needs, thereby foreclosing other manufacturers from effectively competing for the retail accounts. Manufacturer-dominated stores were found to be "drying up" the available outlets for independent producers.

Another "definite trend" found to exist in the shoe industry was a decrease in the number of plants manufacturing shoes. And there appears to have been a concomitant decrease in the number of firms manufacturing shoes. In 1947, there were 1,077 independent manufacturers of shoes, but by 1954 their number had decreased about 10% to 970.

Brown Shoe.

Brown Shoe was found not only to have been a participant, but also a moving factor, in these industry trends. Although Brown had experimented several times with operating its own retail outlets, by 1945 it had disposed of them all. However, in 1951, Brown again began to seek retail outlets by acquiring the Nation's largest operator of leased shoe departments, Wohl Shoe Company (Wohl), which operated 250 shoe departments in department stores throughout the United States. Between 1952 and 1955 Brown made a number of smaller acquisitions: Wetherby-Kayser Shoe Company (three retail stores), Barnes & Company (two stores), Reilly Shoe Company (two leased shoe departments), Richardson Shoe Store (one store), and Wohl Shoe Company of Dallas (not connected with Wohl) (leased shoe departments in Dallas). In 1954, Brown made another major acquisition: Regal Shoe Corporation which, at the time, operated one manufacturing plant producing men's shoes and 110 retail outlets.

The acquisition of these corporations was found to lead to increased sales by Brown to the acquired companies. Thus although prior to Brown's acquisition of Wohl in 1951, Wohl bought from Brown only 12.8% of its total purchases of shoes, it subsequently increased its purchases to 21.4% in 1952 and to 32.6% in 1955. Wetherby-Kayser's purchases from Brown increased from 10.4% before acquisition to over 50% after. Regal, which had previously sold no shoes to Wohl and shoes worth only $89,000 to Brown, in 1956 sold shoes worth $265,000 to Wohl and $744,000 to Brown.

During the same period of time, Brown also acquired the stock or assets of seven companies engaged solely in shoe manufacturing. As a result, in 1955, Brown was the fourth largest shoe manufacturer in the country, producing about 25.6 million pairs of shoes or about 4% of the Nation's total footwear production.

Kinney.

Kinney is principally engaged in operating the largest family-style shoe store chain in the United States. At the time of trial, Kinney was found to be operating over 400 such stores in more than 270 cities. These stores were found to make about 1.2% of all national retail shoe sales by dollar volume. Moreover, in 1955 the Kinney stores sold approximately 8 million pairs of nonrubber shoes or about 1.6% of the national pairage sales of such shoes. Of these sales, approximately 1.1 million pairs were of men's shoes or about 1% of the national pairage sales of men's shoes; approximately 4.2 million pairs were of women's shoes or about 1.5% of the national pairage sales of women's shoes; and approximately 2.7 million pairs were of children's shoes or about 2% of the national pairage sales of children's shoes.

In addition to this extensive retail activity, Kinney owned and operated four plants which manufactured men's, women's, and children's shoes and whose combined output was 0.5% of the national shoe production in 1955, making Kinney the twelfth largest shoe manufacturer in the United States.

Kinney stores were found to obtain about 20% of their shoes from Kinney's own manufacturing plants. At the time of the merger, Kinney bought no shoes from Brown; however, in line with Brown's conceded reasons for acquiring Kinney, Brown had, by 1957, become the largest outside supplier of Kinney's shoes, supplying 7.9% of all Kinney's needs.

It is in this setting that the merger was considered and held to violate §7 of the Clayton Act. The District Court ordered Brown to divest itself completely of all stock, share capital, assets or other interests it held in Kinney, to operate Kinney to the greatest degree possible as an independent concern pending complete divestiture, to refrain thereafter from acquiring or having any interest in Kinney's business or assets, and to file with the court within 90 days a plan for carrying into effect the divestiture decreed. The District Court also stated it would retain jurisdiction over the cause to enable the parties to apply for such further relief as might be necessary to enforce and apply the judgment. Prior to its submission of a divestiture plan, Brown filed a notice of appeal in the District Court. It then filed a jurisdictional statement in this Court, seeking review of the judgment below as entered.

THE VERTICAL ASPECTS OF THE MERGER

Economic arrangements between companies standing in a supplier-customer relationship are characterized as "vertical." The primary vice of a vertical merger or other arrangement tying a customer to a supplier is that, by foreclosing the competitors of either party from a segment of the market otherwise open to them, the arrangement may act as a "clog on competition," *Standard Oil Co. of California* v. *United States,* 337 U. S. 293, 314, which "deprive[s] . . . rivals of a fair opportunity to compete."[3] H. R. Rep. No. 1191, 81st Cong., 1st Sess. 8. Every extended vertical arrangement by its very nature, for at least a time, denies to competitors of the supplier the opportunity

[3] In addition, a vertical merger may disrupt and injure competition when those independent customers of the supplier who are in competition with the merging customer, are forced either to stop handling the supplier's lines, thereby jeopardizing the goodwill they have developed, or to retain the supplier's lines, thereby forcing them into competition with their own supplier. See *United States* v. *Bethlehem Steel Corp.,* 168 F. Supp. 576, 613 (D. C. S. D. N. Y.). See also GX 13, R. 215, a letter from Sam Sullivan, an independent shoe retailer, to Clark Gamble, President of Brown Shoe Co.

to compete for part or all of the trade of the customer-party to the vertical arrangement. However, the Clayton Act does not render unlawful all such vertical arrangements, but forbids only those whose effect "may be substantially to lessen competition, or to tend to create a monopoly" "in any line of commerce in any section of the country." Thus, as we have previously noted,

> "[d]etermination of the relevant market is a necessary predicate to a finding of a violation of the Clayton Act because the threatened monopoly must be one which will substantially lessen competition 'within the area of effective competition.' Substantiality can be determined only in terms of the market affected."[4]

The "area of effective competition" must be determined by reference to a product market (the "line of commerce") and a geographic market (the "section of the country").

The Product Market.

The outer boundaries of a product market are determined by the reasonable interchangeability of use or the cross-elasticity of demand between the product itself and substitutes for it.[5] However, within this broad market, well-defined submarkets may exist which, in themselves, constitute product markets for antitrust purposes. *United States* v. *E. I. du Pont de Nemours & Co.,* 353 U. S. 586, 593–595. The boundaries of such a submarket may be determined by examining such practical indicia as industry or public recognition of the submarket as a separate economic entity, the product's peculiar characteristics and uses, unique production facilities, distinct customers, distinct prices, sensitivity to price changes, and specialized vendors. Because §7 of the Clayton Act prohibits any merger which may substantially lessen competition "in *any* line of commerce" (emphasis supplied), it is necessary to examine the effects of a merger in each such economically significant submarket to determine if there is a reasonable probability that the merger will substantially lessen competition. If such a probability is found to exist, the merger is proscribed.

Applying these considerations to the present case, we conclude that the record supports the District Court's finding that the relevant lines of commerce are men's, women's, and children's shoes. These product lines are recognized by the public; each line is manufactured in separate plants; each has characteristics peculiar to itself rendering it generally noncompetitive with the others; and each is, of course, directed toward a distinct class of customers.

Appellant, however, contends that the District Court's definitions fail to recognize sufficiently "price/quality" and "age/sex" distinctions in shoes.

---

[4] *United States* v. *E. I. du Pont de Nemours & Co.,* 353 U. S. 586, 593.

[5] The cross-elasticity of production facilities may also be an important factor in defining a product market within which a vertical merger is to be viewed. Cf. *United States* v. *Columbia Steel Co.,* 334 U. S. 495, 510–511; *United States* v. *Bethlehem Steel Corp.,* 168 F. Supp. 576, 592 (D. C. S. D. N. Y.). However, the District Court made but limited findings concerning the feasibility of interchanging equipment in the manufacture of nonrubber footwear. At the same time, the record supports the court's conclusion that individual plants generally produced shoes in only one of the product lines the court found relevant.

Brown argues that the predominantly medium-priced shoes which it manufactures occupy a product market different from the predominantly low-priced
shoes which Kinney sells. But agreement with that argument would be
equivalent to holding that medium-priced shoes do not compete with low-
priced shoes. We think the District Court properly found the facts to be otherwise. It would be unrealistic to accept Brown's contention that, for example,
men's shoes selling below $8.99 are in a different product market from those
selling above $9.00.

This is not to say, however, that "price/quality" differences, where they exist, are unimportant in analyzing a merger; they may be of importance in determining the likely effect of a merger. But the boundaries of the relevant
market must be drawn with sufficient breadth to include the competing products of each of the merging companies and to recognize competition where, in
fact, competition exists. Thus we agree with the District Court that in this
case a further division of product lines based on "price/quality" differences
would be "unrealistic."

Brown's contention that the District Court's product market definitions
should have recognized further "age/sex" distinctions raises a different problem. Brown's sharpest criticism is directed at the District Court's finding that
children's shoes constituted a single line of commerce. Brown argues, for example, that "a little boy does not wear a little girl's black patent leather
pump" and that "[a] male baby cannot wear a growing boy's shoes." Thus
Brown argues that "infants' and babies'" shoes, "misses' and children's" shoes
and "youths' and boys'" shoes should each have been considered a separate
line of commerce. Assuming, *arguendo,* that little boys' shoes, for example, do
have sufficient peculiar characteristics to constitute one of the markets to be
used in analyzing the effects of this merger, we do not think that in this case
the District Court was required to employ finer "age/sex" distinctions than
those recognized by its classifications of "men's," "women's," and "children's" shoes. Further division does not aid us in analyzing the effects of this
merger. Brown manufactures about the same percentage of the Nation's children's shoes (5.8%) as it does of the Nation's youths' and boys' shoes (6.5%),
of the Nation's misses' and children's shoes (6.0%) and of the Nation's infants'
and babies' shoes (4.9%). Similarly, Kinney sells about the same percentage of
the Nation's children's shoes (2%) as it does of the Nation's youths' and boys'
shoes (3.1%), of the Nation's misses' and children's shoes (1.9%), and of the
Nation's infants' and babies' shoes (1.5%). Appellant can point to no advantage it would enjoy were finer divisions than those chosen by the District
Court employed. Brown manufactures significant, comparable quantities of
virtually every type of nonrubber men's, women's, and children's shoes, and
Kinney sells such quantities of virtually every type of men's, women's, and
children's shoes. Thus, whether considered separately or together, the picture
of this merger is the same. We, therefore, agree with the District Court's conclusion that in the setting of this case to subdivide the shoe market further on
the basis of "age/sex" distinctions would be "impractical" and "unwarranted."

The Geographic Market.

We agree with the parties and the District Court that insofar as the vertical aspect of this merger is concerned, the relevant geographic market is the entire Nation. The relationships of product value, bulk, weight and consumer demand enable manufacturers to distribute their shoes on a nationwide basis, as Brown and Kinney, in fact, do. The anticompetitive effects of the merger are to be measured within this range of distribution.

The Probable Effect of the Merger.

Once the area of effective competition affected by a vertical arrangement has been defined, an analysis must be made to determine if the effect of the arrangement "may be substantially to lessen competition, or to tend to create a monopoly" in this market.

Since the diminution of the vigor of competition which may stem from a vertical arrangement results primarily from a foreclosure of a share of the market otherwise open to competitors, an important consideration in determining whether the effect of a vertical arrangement "may be substantially to lessen competition, or to tend to create a monopoly" is the size of the share of the market foreclosed. However, this factor will seldom be determinative. If the share of the market foreclosed is so large that it approaches monopoly proportions, the Clayton Act will, of course, have been violated; but the arrangement will also have run afoul of the Sherman Act. And the legislative history of §7 indicates clearly that the tests for measuring the legality of any particular economic arrangement under the Clayton Act are to be less stringent than those used in applying the Sherman Act. On the other hand, foreclosure of a *de minimis* share of the market will not tend "substantially to lessen competition."

Between these extremes, in cases such as the one before us, in which the foreclosure is neither of monopoly nor *de minimis* proportions, the percentage of the market foreclosed by the vertical arrangement cannot itself be decisive. In such cases, it becomes necessary to undertake an examination of various economic and historical factors in order to determine whether the arrangement under review is of the type Congress sought to proscribe.

A most important such factor to examine is the very nature and purpose of the arrangement. Congress not only indicated that "the tests of illegality [under §7] are intended to be similar to those which the courts have applied in interpreting the same language as used in other sections of the Clayton Act," but also chose for §7 language virtually identical to that of §3 of the Clayton Act, 15 U. S. C. §14, which had been interpreted by this Court to require an examination of the interdependence of the market share foreclosed by, and the economic purpose of, the vertical arrangement. Thus, for example, if a particular vertical arrangement, considered under §3, appears to be a limited term exclusive-dealing contract, the market foreclosure must generally be significantly greater than if the arrangement is a tying contract before the arrangement will be held to have violated the Act. Compare *Tampa Electric Co.* v. *Nashville Coal*

Co., 365 U. S. 320, and *Standard Oil Co. of California* v. *United States, supra,* with *International Salt Co.* v. *United States,* 332 U. S. 392. The reason for this is readily discernible. The usual tying contract forces the customer to take a product or brand he does not necessarily want in order to secure one which he does desire. Because such an arrangement is inherently anticompetitive, we have held that its use by an established company is likely "substantially to lessen competition" although only a relatively small amount of commerce is affected. *International Salt Co.* v. *United States, supra.* Thus, unless the tying device is employed by a small company in an attempt to break into a market, cf. *Harley-Davidson Motor Co.,* 50 F. T. C. 1047, 1066, the use of a tying device can rarely be harmonized with the strictures of the antitrust laws, which are intended primarily to preserve and stimulate competition. See *Standard Oil Co. of California* v. *United States, supra,* at 305–306. On the other hand, requirement contracts are frequently negotiated at the behest of the customer who has chosen the particular supplier and his product upon the basis of competitive merit. See, *e. g., Tampa Electric Co.* v. *Nashville Coal Co., supra.* Of course, the fact that requirement contracts are not inherently anticompetitive will not save a particular agreement if, in fact, it is likely "substantially to lessen competition, or to tend to create a monopoly." *E.g., Standard Oil Co. of California* v. *United States, supra.* Yet a requirement contract may escape censure if only a small share of the market is involved, if the purpose of the agreement is to insure to the customer a sufficient supply of a commodity vital to the customer's trade or to insure to the supplier a market for his output and if there is no trend toward concentration in the industry. *Tampa Electric Co.* v. *Nashville Coal Co., supra.* Similar considerations are pertinent to a judgment under §7 of the Act.

The importance which Congress attached to economic purpose is further demonstrated by the Senate and House Reports on H. R. 2734, which evince an intention to preserve the "failing company" doctrine of *International Shoe Co.* v. *Federal Trade Comm'n,* 280 U. S. 291. Similarly, Congress foresaw that the merger of two large companies or a large and a small company might violate the Clayton Act while the merger of two small companies might not, although the share of the market foreclosed be identical, if the purpose of the small companies is to enable them in combination to compete with larger corporations dominating the market.

The present merger involved neither small companies nor failing companies. In 1955, the date of this merger, Brown was the fourth largest manufacturer in the shoe industry with sales of approximately 25 million pairs of shoes and assets of over $72,000,000 while Kinney had sales of about 8 million pairs of shoes and assets of about $18,000,000. Not only was Brown one of the leading manufacturers of men's, women's, and children's shoes, but Kinney, with over 350 retail outlets, owned and operated the largest independent chain of family shoe stores in the Nation. Thus, in this industry, no merger between a manufacturer and an independent retailer could involve a larger potential market foreclosure. Moreover, it is apparent both from past behavior of Brown and from the testimony of Brown's President, that Brown would use its ownership of Kinney to force Brown shoes into Kinney stores. Thus, in operation this vertical arrangement would be quite analogous to one involving a tying clause.

Another important factor to consider is the trend toward concentration in the industry. It is true, of course, that the statute prohibits a given merger only if the effect of *that* merger may be substantially to lessen competition. But the very wording of §7 requires a prognosis of the probable *future* effect of the merger.

The existence of a trend toward vertical integration, which the District Court found, is well substantiated by the record. Moreover, the court found a tendency of the acquiring manufacturers to become increasingly important sources of supply for their acquired outlets. The necessary corollary of these trends is the foreclosure of independent manufacturers from markets otherwise open to them. And because these trends are not the product of accident but are rather the result of deliberate policies of Brown and other leading shoe manufacturers, account must be taken of these facts in order to predict the probable future consequences of this merger. It is against this background of continuing concentration that the present merger must be viewed.

Brown argues, however, that the shoe industry is at present composed of a large number of manufacturers and retailers, and that the industry is dynamically competitive. But remaining vigor cannot immunize a merger if the trend in that industry is toward oligopoly. See *Pillsbury Mills, Inc.,* 50 F. T. C. 555, 573. It is the probable effect of the merger upon the future as well as the present which the Clayton Act commands the courts and the Commission to examine.

Moreover, as we have remarked above, not only must we consider the probable effects of the merger upon the economics of the particular markets affected but also we must consider its probable effects upon the economic way of life sought to be preserved by Congress. Congress was desirous of preventing the formation of further oligopolies with their attendant adverse effects upon local control of industry and upon small business. Where an industry was composed of numerous independent units, Congress appeared anxious to preserve this structure. The Senate Report, quoting with approval from the Federal Trade Commission's 1948 report on the merger movement, states explicitly that amended §7 is addressed, *inter alia,* to the following problem:

> "Under the Sherman Act, an acquisition is unlawful if it creates a monopoly or constitutes an attempt to monopolize. Imminent monopoly may appear when one large concern acquires another, but it is unlikely to be perceived in a small acquisition by a large enterprise. As a large concern grows through a series of such small acquisitions, its accretions of power are individually so minute as to make it difficult to use the Sherman Act test against them. . . .
>
> "Where several large enterprises are extending their power by successive small acquisitions, the cumulative effect of their purchases may be to convert an industry from one of intense competition among many enterprises to one in which three or four large concerns produce the entire supply." S. Rep. No. 1775, 81st Cong., 2d Sess. 5. And see H. R. Rep. No. 1191, 81st Cong., 1st Sess. 8.

The District Court's findings, and the record facts, many of them set forth in Part I of this opinion, convince us that the shoe industry is being subjected to just such a cumulative series of vertical mergers which, if left unchecked, will be likely "substantially to lessen competition."

We reach this conclusion because the trend toward vertical integration in the shoe industry, when combined with Brown's avowed policy of forcing its own shoes upon its retail subsidiaries, may foreclose competition from a substantial share of the markets for men's, women's, and children's shoes, without producing any countervailing competitive, economic, or social advantages.

THE HORIZONTAL ASPECTS OF THE MERGER

Thus, again, the proper definition of the market is a "necessary predicate" to an examination of the competition that may be affected by the horizontal aspects of the merger. The acquisition of Kinney by Brown resulted in a horizontal combination at both the manufacturing and retailing levels of their businesses. Although the District Court found that the merger of Brown's and Kinney's *manufacturing* facilities was economically too insignificant to come within the prohibitions of the Clayton Act, the Government has not appealed from this portion of the lower court's decision. Therefore, we have no occasion to express our views with respect to that finding. On the other hand, appellant does contest the District Court's finding that the merger of the companies' *retail* outlets may tend substantially to lessen competition.

The Product Market.

Shoes are sold in the United States in retail shoe stores and in shoe departments of general stores. These outlets sell: (1) men's shoes, (2) women's shoes, (3) women's or children's shoes, or (4) men's, women's or children's shoes. Prior to the merger, both Brown and Kinney sold their shoes in competition with one another through the enumerated kinds of outlets characteristic of the industry.

In Part IV of this opinion we hold that the District Court correctly defined men's, women's, and children's shoes as the relevant lines of commerce in which to analyze the vertical aspects of the merger. For the reasons there stated we also hold that the same lines of commerce are appropriate for considering the horizontal aspects of the merger.

The Geographic Market.

The parties do not dispute the findings of the District Court that the Nation as a whole is the relevant geographic market for measuring the anticompetitive effects of the merger viewed vertically or of the horizontal merger of Brown's and Kinney's manufacturing facilities. As to the retail level, however, they disagree.

The District Court found that the effects of this aspect of the merger must be analyzed in every city with a population exceeding 10,000 and its immediate contiguous surrounding territory in which both Brown and Kinney sold shoes at retail through stores they either owned or controlled.[6] By this definition of the geographic market, less than one-half of all the cities in which either Brown and Kinney sold shoes through such outlets are represented. The appellant recognizes that if the District Court's characterization of the relevant market is proper, the number of markets in which both Brown and Kinney have outlets is sufficiently numerous so that the validity of the entire merger is properly judged by testing its effects in those markets. However, it is appellant's contention that the areas of effective competition in shoe retailing were improperly defined by the District Court. It claims that such areas should, in some cases, be defined so as to include only the central business districts of large cities, and in others, so as to encompass the "standard metropolitan areas" within which smaller communities are found. It argues that any test failing to distinguish between these competitive situations is improper.

We believe, however, that the record fully supports the District Court's findings that shoe stores in the outskirts of cities compete effectively with stores in central downtown areas, and that while there is undoubtedly some commercial intercourse between smaller communities within a single "standard metropolitan area," the most intense and important competition in retail sales will be confined to stores within the particular communities in such an area and their immediate environs.

We therefore agree that the District Court properly defined the relevant geographic markets in which to analyze this merger as those cities with a population exceeding 10,000 and their environs in which both Brown and Kinney retailed shoes through their own outlets. Such markets are large enough to include the downtown shops and suburban shopping centers in areas contiguous to the city, which are the important competitive factors, and yet are small enough to exclude stores beyond the immediate environs of the city, which are of little competitive significance.

The Probable Effect of the Merger.

In the case before us, not only was a fair sample used to demonstrate the soundness of the District Court's conclusions, but evidence of record fully

[6] In describing the geographic market in which Brown and Kinney competed, the District Court included cities in which Brown "Franchise Plan" and "Wohl Plan" stores were located. Although such stores were not owned or directly controlled by Brown, did not sell Brown products exclusively and did not finance inventory through Brown, we believe there was adequate evidence before the District Court to support its finding that such stores were "Brown stores." To such stores Brown provided substantial assistance in the form of merchandising and advertising aids, reports on market and management research, loans, group life and fire insurance and centralized purchase of rubber footwear from manufacturers on Brown's credit. For these services, Brown required the retailer to deal almost exclusively in Brown's products in the price scale at which Brown shoes sold. Further, Brown reserved the power to terminate such franchise agreements on 30 days' notice. Since the retailer was required, under this plan, to invest his own resources and develop his good will to a substantial extent in the sale of Brown products, the flow of which Brown could readily terminate, Brown was able to exercise sufficient control over these stores and departments to warrant their characterization as "Brown" outlets for the purpose of measuring the share and effect of Brown's competition at the retail level. Cf. *Standard Oil Co. of California* v. *United States,* 337 U. S. 293.

substantiates those findings as to each relevant market. An analysis of undisputed statistics of sales of shoes in the cities in which both Brown and Kinney sell shoes at retail, separated into the appropriate lines of commerce, provides a persuasive factual foundation upon which the required prognosis of the merger's effects may be built. Although Brown objects to some details in the Government's computations used in drafting these exhibits, appellant cannot deny the correctness of the more general picture they reveal. . . . They show, for example, that during 1955 in 32 separate cities, ranging in size and location from Topeka, Kansas, to Batavia, New York, and Hobbs, New Mexico, the combined share of Brown and Kinney sales of women's shoes (by unit volume) exceeded 20%. In 31 cities—some the same as those used in measuring the effect of the merger in the women's line—the combined share of children's shoes sales exceeded 20%; in 6 cities their share exceeded 40%. In Dodge City, Kansas, their combined share of the market for women's shoes was over 57%; their share of the children's shoe market in that city was 49%. In the 7 cities in which Brown's and Kinney's combined shares of the market for women's shoes were greatest (ranging from 33% to 57%) each of the parties alone, prior to the merger, had captured substantial portions of those markets (ranging from 13% to 34%); the merger intensified this existing concentration. In 118 separate cities the combined shares of the market of Brown and Kinney in the sale of one of the relevant lines of commerce exceeded 5%. In 47 cities, their share exceeded 5% in all three lines.

The market share which companies may control by merging is one of the most important factors to be considered when determining the probable effects of the combination on effective competition in the relevant market. In an industry as fragmented as shoe retailing, the control of substantial shares of the trade in a city may have important effects on competition. If a merger achieving 5% control were now approved, we might be required to approve future merger efforts by Brown's competitors seeking similar market shares. The oligopoly Congress sought to avoid would then be furthered and it would be difficult to dissolve the combinations previously approved. Furthermore, in this fragmented industry, even if the combination controls but a small share of a particular market, the fact that this share is held by a large national chain can adversely affect competition. Testimony in the record from numerous independent retailers, based on their actual experience in the market, demonstrates that a strong, national chain of stores can insulate selected outlets from the vagaries of competition in particular locations and that the large chains can set and alter styles in footwear to an extent that renders the independents unable to maintain competitive inventories. A third significant aspect of this merger is that it creates a large national chain which is integrated with a manufacturing operation. The retail outlets of integrated companies, by eliminating wholesalers and by increasing the volume of purchases from the manufacturing division of the enterprise, can market their own brands at prices below those of competing independent retailers. Of course, some of the results of large integrated or chain operations are beneficial to consumers. Their expansion is not rendered unlawful by the mere fact that small independent stores may be adversely affected. It is competition, not competitors, which the Act protects. But we cannot fail to recognize Congress' desire to promote competition through the protection of viable, small, locally owned businesses. Congress appreciated that occasional higher costs and prices might result from the maintenance of fragmented industries and markets. It resolved these competing considerations in favor of decentralization. We must give effect to that decision.

Other factors to be considered in evaluating the probable effects of a merger in the relevant market lend additional support to the District Court's conclusion that this merger may substantially lessen competition. One such factor is the history of tendency toward concentration in the industry.[7] As we have previously pointed out, the shoe industry has, in recent years, been a prime example of such a trend. Most combinations have been between manufacturers and retailers, as each of the larger producers has sought to capture an increasing number of assured outlets for its wares. Although these mergers have been primarily vertical in their aim and effect, to the extent that they have brought ever greater numbers of retail outlets within fewer and fewer hands, they have had an additional important impact on the horizontal plane. By the merger in this case, the largest single group of retail stores still independent of one of the large manufacturers was absorbed into an already substantial aggregation of more or less controlled retail outlets. As a result of this merger, Brown moved into second place nationally in terms of retail stores directly owned. Including the stores on its franchise plan, the merger placed under Brown's control almost 1,600 shoe outlets, or about 7.2% of the Nation's retail "shoe stores" as defined by the Census Bureau, and 2.3% of the Nation's total retail shoe outlets. We cannot avoid the mandate of Congress that tendencies toward concentration in industry are to be curbed in their incipiency, particularly when those tendencies are being accelerated through giant steps striding across a hundred cities at a time. In the light of the trends in this industry we agree with the Government and the court below that this is an appropriate place at which to call a halt.

At the same time appellant has presented no mitigating factors, such as the business failure or the inadequate resources of one of the parties that may have prevented it from maintaining its competitive position, nor a demonstrated need for combination to enable small companies to enter into a more mean-

---

[7] A company's history of expansion through mergers presents a different economic picture than a history of expansion through unilateral growth. Internal expansion is more likely to be the result of increased demand for the company's products and is more likely to provide increased investment in plants, more jobs and greater output. Conversely, expansion through merger is more likely to reduce available consumer choice while providing no increase in industry capacity, jobs or output. It was for these reasons, among others, Congress expressed its disapproval of successive acquisitions. Section 7 was enacted to prevent even small mergers that added to concentration in an industry. See S. Rep. No. 1775, 81st Cong., 2d Sess. 5. Cf. *United States* v. *Jerrold Electronics Corp.*, 187 F. Supp. 545, 566 (D. C. E. D. Pa.) aff'd, 365 U. S. 567; *United States* v. *Bethlehem Steel Corp.*, 168 F. Supp. 576, 606 (D. C. S. D. N. Y.).

ingful competition with those dominating the relevant markets. On the basis of the record before us, we believe the Government sustained its burden of proof. We hold that the District Court was correct in concluding that this merger may tend to lessen competition substantially in the retail sale of men's, women's, and children's shoes in the overwhelming majority of those cities and their environs in which both Brown and Kinney sell through owned or controlled outlets.

The judgment is

Affirmed.

Case 2
Federal Trade Commission v. Procter & Gamble Co.

Certiorari to the United States Court of Appeals for the Sixth Circuit.
No. 342. Argued February 13, 1967.—Decided April 11, 1967.

MR. JUSTICE DOUGLAS delivered the opinion of the Court.

This is a proceeding initiated by the Federal Trade Commission charging that respondent, Procter & Gamble Co., had acquired the assets of Clorox Chemical Co. in violation of §7 of the Clayton Act, 38 Stat. 731, as amended by the Celler–Kefauver Act, 64 Stat. 1125, 15 U. S. C. §18.[1] The charge was that Procter's acquisition of Clorox might substantially lessen competition or tend to create a monopoly in the production and sale of household liquid bleaches.

Following evidentiary hearings, the hearing examiner rendered his decision in which he concluded that the acquisition was unlawful and ordered divestiture. On appeal, the Commission reversed, holding that the record as then constituted was inadequate, and remanded to the examiner for additional evidentiary hearings. 58 F. T. C. 1203. After the additional hearings, the examiner again held the acquisition unlawful and ordered divestiture. The Commission affirmed the examiner and ordered divestiture. 63 F. T. C.—. The Court of Appeals for the Sixth Circuit reversed and directed that the Commission's complaint be dismissed. 358 F. 2d 74. We find that the Commission's findings were amply supported by the evidence, and that the Court of Appeals erred.

As indicated by the Commission in its painstaking and illuminating report, it does not particularly aid analysis to talk of this merger in conventional terms, namely, horizontal or vertical or conglomerate. This merger may most appropriately be described as a "product-extension merger," as the Commission stated. The facts are not disputed, and a summary will demonstrate the correctness of the Commission's decision.

---

[1] "No corporation engaged in commerce shall acquire, directly or indirectly, the whole or any part of the stock or other share capital and no corporation subject to the jurisdiction of the Federal Trade Commission shall acquire the whole or any part of the assets of another corporation engaged also in commerce, where in any line of commerce in any section of the country, the effect of such acquisition may be substantially to lessen competition, or to tend to create a monopoly."

At the time of the merger, in 1957, Clorox was the leading manufacturer in the heavily concentrated household liquid bleach industry. It is agreed that household liquid bleach is the relevant line of commerce. The product is used in the home as a germicide and disinfectant, and, more importantly, as a whitening agent in washing clothes and fabrics. It is a distinctive product with no close substitutes. Liquid bleach is a low-price, high-turnover consumer product sold mainly through grocery stores and supermarkets. The relevant geographical market is the Nation and a series of regional markets. Because of high shipping costs and low sales price, it is not feasible to ship the product more than 300 miles from its point of manufacture. Most manufacturers are limited to competition within a single region since they have but one plant. Clorox is the only firm selling nationally; it has 13 plants distributed throughout the Nation. Purex, Clorox's closest competitor in size, does not distribute its bleach in the northeast or mid-Atlantic States; in 1957, Purex's bleach was available in less than 50% of the national market.

At the time of the acquisition, Clorox was the leading manufacturer of household liquid bleach, with 48.8% of the national sales—annual sales of slightly less than $40,000,000. Its market share had been steadily increasing for the five years prior to the merger. Its nearest rival was Purex, which manufactures a number of products other than household liquid bleaches, including abrasive cleaners, toilet soap, and detergents. Purex accounted for 15.7% of the household liquid bleach market. The industry is highly concentrated; in 1957, Clorox and Purex accounted for almost 65% of the Nation's household liquid bleach sales, and, together with four other firms, for almost 80%. The remaining 20% was divided among over 200 small producers. Clorox had total assets of $12,000,000; only eight producers had assets in excess of $1,000,000 and very few had assets of more than $75,000.

In light of the territorial limitations on distribution, national figures do not give an accurate picture of Clorox's dominance in the various regions. Thus, Clorox's seven principal competitors did no business in New England, the mid-Atlantic States, or metropolitan New York. Clorox's share of the sales in those areas was 56%, 72%, and 64% respectively. Even in regions where its principal competitors were active, Clorox maintained a dominant position. Except in metropolitan Chicago and the west-central States Clorox accounted for at least 39%, and often a much higher percentage, of liquid bleach sales.

Since all liquid bleach is chemically identical, advertising and sales promotion are vital. In 1957 Clorox spent almost $3,700,000 on advertising, imprinting the value of its bleach in the mind of the consumer. In addition, it spent $1,700,000 for other promotional activities. The Commission found that these heavy expenditures went far to explain why Clorox maintained so high a market share despite the fact that its brand, though chemically indistinguishable from rival brands, retailed for a price equal to or, in many instances, higher than its competitors.

Procter is a large, diversified manufacturer of low-price, high-turnover household products sold through grocery, drug, and department stores. Prior to its acquisition of Clorox, it did not produce household liquid bleach. Its 1957 sales were in excess of $1,100,000,000 from which it realized profits of more than $67,000,000; its assets were over $500,000,000. Procter has been marked by rapid growth and diversification. It has successfully developed and introduced a number of new products. Its primary activity is in the general area of soaps, detergents, and cleansers; in 1957, of total domestic sales, more than one-half (over $500,000,000) were in this field. Procter was the dominant factor in this area. It accounted for 54.4% of all packaged detergent sales. The industry is heavily concentrated—Procter and its nearest competitors, Colgate-Palmolive and Lever Brothers, account for 80% of the market.

In the marketing of soaps, detergents, and cleansers, as in the marketing of household liquid bleach, advertising and sales promotion are vital. In 1957, Procter was the Nation's largest advertiser, spending more than $80,000,000 on advertising and an additional $47,000,000 on sales promotion. Due to its tremendous volume, Procter receives substantial discounts from the media. As a multiproduct producer Procter enjoys substantial advantages in advertising and sales promotion. Thus, it can and does feature several products in its promotions, reducing the printing, mailing, and other costs for each product. It also purchases network programs on behalf of several products, enabling it to give each product network exposure at a fraction of the cost per product that a firm with only one product to advertise would incur.

Prior to the acquisition, Procter was in the course of diversifying into product lines related to its basic detergent-soap-cleanser business. Liquid bleach was a distinct possibility since packaged detergents—Procter's primary product line—and liquid bleach are used complementarily in washing clothes and fabrics, and in general household cleaning. As noted by the Commission:

> "Packaged detergents—Procter's most important product category—and household liquid bleach are used complementarily, not only in the washing of clothes and fabrics, but also in general household cleaning, since liquid bleach is a germicide and disinfectant as well as a whitener. From the consumer's viewpoint, then, packaged detergents and liquid bleach are closely related products. But the area of relatedness between products of Procter and of Clorox is wider. Household cleansing agents in general, like household liquid bleach, are low-cost, high-turnover household consumer goods marketed chiefly through grocery stores and pre-sold to the consumer by the manufacturer through mass advertising and sales promotions. Since products of both parties to the merger are sold to the same customers, at the same stores, and by the same merchandising methods, the possibility arises of significant integration at both the marketing and distribution levels." 63 F. T.C.—,—.

The decision to acquire Clorox was the result of a study conducted by Procter's promotion department designed to determine the advisability of entering the liquid bleach industry. The initial report noted the ascendancy of liquid bleach in the large and expanding household bleach market, and recommended that Procter purchase Clorox rather than enter independently. Since a large investment would be needed to obtain a satisfactory market share, acquisition of the industry's leading firm was attractive. "Taking over the Clorox business . . . could be a way of achieving a dominant position in the liquid bleach market quickly, which would pay out reasonably well." 63 F. T. C., at—. The initial report predicted that Procter's "sales, distribution and manufacturing setup" could increase Clorox's share of the markets in areas where it was low. The final report confirmed the conclusions of the initial report and emphasized that Procter could make more effective use of Clorox's advertising budget and that the merger would facilitate advertising economies. A few months later, Procter acquired the assets of Clorox in the name of a wholly owned subsidiary, the Clorox Company, in exchange for Procter stock.

The Commission found that the acquisition might substantially lessen competition. The findings and reasoning of the Commission need be only briefly summarized. The Commission found that the substitution of Procter with its huge assets and advertising advantages for the already dominant Clorox would dissuade new entrants and discourage active competition from the firms already in the industry due to fear of retaliation by Procter. The Commission thought it relevant that retailers might be induced to give Clorox preferred shelf space since it would be manufactured by Procter, which also produced a number of other products marketed by the retailers. There was also the danger that Procter might underprice Clorox in order to drive out competition, and subsidize the underpricing with revenue from other products. The Commission carefully reviewed the effect of the acquisition on the structure of the industry, noting that "[t]he practical tendency of the . . . merger . . . is to transform the liquid bleach industry into an arena of big business competition only, with the few small firms that have not disappeared through merger eventually falling by the wayside, unable to compete with their giant rivals." 63 F. T. C., at—. Further, the merger would seriously diminish potential competition by eliminating Procter as a potential entrant into the industry. Prior to the merger, the Commission found, Procter was the most likely prospective entrant, and absent the merger would have remained on the periphery, restraining Clorox from exercising its market power. If Procter had actually entered, Clorox's dominant position would have been eroded and the concentration of the industry reduced. The Commission stated that it had not placed reliance on post-acquisition evidence in holding the merger unlawful.

The Court of Appeals said that the Commission's finding of illegality had been based on "treacherous conjecture," mere possibility and suspicion. 358 F. 2d 74, 83. It dismissed the fact that Clorox controlled almost 50% of the industry, that two firms controlled 65%, and that six firms controlled 80% with the observation that "[t]he fact that in addition to the six . . . producers sharing eighty per cent of the market, there were two hundred smaller producers . . . would not seem to indicate anything unhealthy about the market conditions." *Id.*, at 80. It dismissed the finding that Procter, with its huge resources and prowess, would have more leverage than Clorox with the statement that it was Clorox which had the "knowhow" in the industry, and that Clorox's finances were adequate for its purposes. *Ibid.* As for the possibility that Procter would use its tremendous advertising budget and volume discounts to push

Clorox, the court found "it difficult to base a finding of illegality on discounts in advertising." 358 F. 2d, at 81. It rejected the Commission's finding that the merger eliminated the potential competition of Procter because "[t]here was no reasonable probability that Procter would have entered the household liquid bleach market but for the merger." 358 F. 2d, at 83. "There was no evidence tending to prove that Procter ever intended to enter this field on its own." 358 F. 2d, at 82. Finally, "[t]here was no evidence that Procter at any time in the past engaged in predatory practices, or that it intended to do so in the future." *Ibid.*

The Court of Appeals also heavily relied on post-acquisition "evidence . . . to the effect that the other producers subsequent to the merger were selling more bleach for more money than ever before" (358 F. 2d, at 80), and that "[t]here [had] been no significant change in Clorox's market share in the four years subsequent to the merger" (*ibid.*), and concluded that "[t]his evidence certainly does not prove anti-competitive effects of the merger." *Id.*, at 82. The Court of Appeals, in our view, misapprehended the standards for its review and the standards applicable in a §7 proceeding.

Section 7 of the Clayton Act was intended to arrest the anticompetitive effects of market power in their incipiency. The core question is whether a merger may subtantially lessen competition, and necessarily requires a prediction of the merger's impact on competition, present and future. See *Brown Shoe Co.* v. *United States,* 370 U. S. 294; *United States* v. *Philadelphia National Bank,* 374 U. S. 321. The section can deal only with probabilities, not with certainties. *Brown Shoe Co.* v. *United States, supra,* at 323; *United States* v. *Penn-Olin Chemical Co.,* 378 U. S. 158. And there is certainly no requirement that the anticompetitive power manifest itself in anticompetitive action before §7 can be called into play. If the enforcement of §7 turned on the existence of actual anticompetitive practices, the congressional policy of thwarting such practices in their incipiency would be frustrated.

All mergers are within the reach of §7, and all must be tested by the same standard, whether they are classified as horizontal, vertical, conglomerate[2] or other. As noted by the Commission, this merger is neither horizontal, vertical, nor conglomerate. Since the products of the acquired company are complementary to those of the acquiring company and may be produced with similar facilities, marketed through the same channels and in the same manner, and advertised by the same media, the Commission aptly called this acquisition a "product-extension merger":

> "By this acquisition . . . Procter has not diversified its interests in the sense of expanding into a substantially different, unfamiliar market or industry. Rather, it has entered a market which adjoins, as it were, those markets in which it is already established, and which is virtually indistinguishable from them insofar as the problems and techniques of marketing the product to the ultimate consumer are concerned. As a high official of Procter put it, commenting on the acquisi-

---

[2] A pure conglomerate merger is one in which there are no economic relationships between the acquiring and the acquired firm.

tion of Clorox, 'While this is a completely new business for us, taking us for the first time into the marketing of a household bleach and disinfectant, we are thoroughly at home in the field of manufacturing and marketing low priced, rapid turn-over consumer products.' " 63 F. T. C.—,—

The anticompetitive effects with which this product-extension merger is fraught can easily be seen: (1) the substitution of the powerful acquiring firm for the smaller, but already dominant, firm may substantially reduce the competitive structure of the industry by raising entry barriers and by dissuading the smaller firms from aggressively competing; (2) the acquisition eliminates the potential competition of the acquiring firm.

The liquid bleach industry was already oligopolistic before the acquisition, and price competition was certainly not as vigorous as it would have been if the industry were competitive. Clorox enjoyed a dominant position nationally, and its position approached monopoly proportions in certain areas. The existence of some 200 fringe firms certainly does not belie that fact. Nor does the fact, relied upon by the court below, that, after the merger, producers other than Clorox "were selling more bleach for more money than ever before." 358 F. 2d, at 80. In the same period, Clorox increased its share from 48.8% to 52%. The interjection of Procter into the market considerably changed the situation. There is every reason to assume that the smaller firms would become more cautious in competing due to their fear of retaliation by Procter. It is probable that Procter would become the price leader and that oligopoly would become more rigid.

The acquisition may also have the tendency of raising the barriers to new entry. The major competitive weapon in the successful marketing of bleach is advertising. Clorox was limited in this area by its relatively small budget and its inability to obtain substantial discounts. By contrast, Procter's budget was much larger; and, although it would not devote its entire budget to advertising Clorox, it could divert a large portion to meet the short-term threat of a new entrant. Procter would be able to use its volume discount to advantage in advertising Clorox. Thus, a new entrant would be much more reluctant to face the giant Procter than it would have been to face the smaller Clorox.[3]

Possible economies cannot be used as a defense to illegality. Congress was aware that some mergers which lessen competition may also result in econo-

[3] The barriers to entry have been raised both for entry by new firms and for entry into new geographical markets by established firms. The latter aspect is demonstrated by Purex's lesson in Erie, Pennsylvania. In October 1957, Purex selected Erie, Pennsylvania—where it had not sold previously—as an area in which to test the salability, under competitive conditions, of a new bleach. The leading brands in Erie were Clorox, with 52%, and the "101" brand, sold by Gardner Manufacturing Company, with 29% of the market. Purex launched an advertising and promotional campaign to obtain a broad distribution in a short time, and in five months captured 33% of the Erie market. Clorox's share dropped to 35% and 101's to 17%. Clorox responded by offering its bleach at reduced prices, and then added an offer of a $1-value ironing board cover for 50¢ with each purchase of Clorox at the reduced price. It also increased its advertising with television spots. The result was to restore Clorox's lost market share and, indeed, to increase it slightly. Purex's share fell to 7%.

mies but it struck the balance in favor of protecting competition. See *Brown Shoe Co. v. United States, supra,* at 344.

The Commission also found that the acquisition of Clorox by Procter eliminated Procter as a potential competitor. The Court of Appeals declared that this finding was not supported by evidence because there was no evidence that Procter's management had ever intended to enter the industry independently and that Procter had never attempted to enter. The evidence, however, clearly shows that Procter was the most likely entrant. Procter had recently launched a new abrasive cleaner in an industry similar to the liquid bleach industry, and had wrested leadership from a brand that had enjoyed even a larger market share than had Clorox. Procter was engaged in a vigorous program of diversifying into product lines closely related to its basic products. Liquid bleach was a natural avenue of diversification since it is complementary to Procter's products, is sold to the same customers through the same channels, and is advertised and merchandised in the same manner. Procter had substantial advantages in advertising and sales promotion, which, as we have seen, are vital to the success of liquid bleach. No manufacturer had a patent on the product or its manufacture, necessary information relating to manufacturing methods and processes was readily available, there was no shortage of raw material, and the machinery and equipment required for a plant of efficient capacity were available at reasonable cost. Procter's management was experienced in producing and marketing goods similar to liquid bleach. Procter had considered the possibility of independently entering but decided against it because the acquisition of Clorox would enable Procter to capture a more commanding share of the market.

It is clear that the existence of Procter at the edge of the industry exerted considerable influence on the market. First, the market behavior of the liquid bleach industry was influenced by each firm's predictions of the market behavior of its competitors, actual and potential. Second, the barriers to entry by a firm of Procter's size and with its advantages were not significant. There is no indication that the barriers were so high that the price Procter would have to charge would be above the price that would maximize the profits of the existing firms. Third, the number of potential entrants was not so large that the elimination of one would be insignificant. Few firms would have the temerity to challenge a firm as solidly entrenched as Clorox. Fourth, Procter was found by the Commission to be the most likely entrant. These findings of the Commission were amply supported by the evidence.

The judgment of the Court of Appeals is reversed and remanded with instructions to affirm and enforce the Commission's order.

It is so ordered.

5

Antitrust Issues
and Pricing Strategy

Perhaps the dream of every marketing executive is to so successfully differentiate his or her firm's products or services from those of competitors that price
comparisons by customers would be meaningless. From a marketing perspective, price comparisons can lead to price wars, and in price wars, buyers rather
than sellers have greater power in the marketplace. With greater power at
their disposal, buyers will bargain away the rents available to sellers in order
to increase their own returns.

Besides this general abhorrence of price wars, marketing executives are usually hesitant to use price as the major weapon in their strategic arsenals because a large number of them are housed in firms operating in oligopolistic
industries. A price cut by one firm will probably be met swiftly by another,
given the nature of competition in such industries. For this reason, among
others, oliogopolists prefer to downplay price and, instead, to emphasize other
elements of the marketing mix when winning customers. However, irrespective
of the structure of an industry, competitors are uncontrollable and opportunistic. There are almost always a number of fringe firms who are willing to undercut the prices of major firms, even if the major firms prefer to lead "quiet"

lives. In other words, there can be no certainty in any industry that prices will be stable for long periods of time. Given this fact, there is likely to be an unconscious (if not conscious) desire among at least a few major firms within an industry to stabilize prices through some form of industry-wide agreement. And if an agreement is difficult to consummate, then the next best alternative might be consideration of an exchange of price information among industry members. This exchange would permit public announcements of actual price changes, which, in turn, would give competitors the opportunity to react quickly and meet the new prices. The prospect of quick competitive reaction would tend to dampen the incentive to change prices in the first place and, thus, price stability may be induced simply by instituting the exchange.

On the other hand, marketing executives are well aware of research which indicates that market share and return on investment are positively correlated. The motivation to attain the highest possible share and to retain it, once achieved, is very strong. In the process of attaining and maintaining market share, the strategies and tactics of the firm "on the make" are calculated to make life as uncomfortable as possible for competitors. In fact, if a firm has a considerable treasury, there may even be a strong inclination to eliminate a competitor or two via deep, below-cost price cuts. Clearly, such actions may set off a dreaded price war, but the firm "on the make" may be willing to endure the agony of the war with the knowledge that, sooner or later, its competitor(s) will drop by the wayside, and it will emerge the victor.

Quite apart from the desire either to lead a "quiet" or a "dominant" existence is the fact that most marketing executives would generally prefer to set different prices in different segments of a market. It is obvious that some segments are usually typified by an elastic demand, while others are typified by an inelastic demand. Therefore, if the marketing executive can discriminate between the two segments in his pricing strategy, he may be able to maximize profits, depending, of course, on the costs he incurs in serving the segments. Price discrimination makes abundant sense, from a marketing perspective.

All the above-mentioned activities are circumscribed by antitrust law. In other words, there are constraints associated with price fixing among competitors, exchanging price information, parallel pricing, predatory pricing, and discriminatory pricing. In this chapter, we discuss each topic in turn. The first three are primarily limited by Section 1 of the Sherman Act, which deals with combinations and conspiracies in restraint of trade. The fourth (predatory pricing) is, in part, restricted by Section 2 of the Sherman Act, which addresses monopolization and attempts to monopolize. It is also constrained by the Robinson–Patman Act, along with the fifth topic, discriminatory pricing. The topics overlap; attempts to separate them have been made here for the sake of convenience so that critical court cases addressing specific issues could be isolated at appropriate times. We have, however, left for other chapters those pricing topics that seem directly related to other strategic decision areas in marketing. For example, we have left a discussion of vertical price fixing (resale price maintenance) to Chapter 6 and have left discussion of promotional allowances and services to Chapter 7. On the other hand, we have included in this chapter a discussion of discriminatory pricing, even though we realize that the discriminations basically relate to channel decisions. This is because the Robinson–Patman Act, particularly Section 2(a), pervades (and creates sleepless nights for) the lives of all marketing executives considering the pricing of any product.

PRICE FIXING

When independent business rivals get together to determine prices, they are preventing the forces of competition within their industries from setting prices. From an economist's perspective, prices are the major coordinating mechanisms between production and consumption units. They limit the amount that consumers will purchase and that manufacturers will produce. When prices are manipulated by private forces rather than by market forces, there is the danger that the allocation of resources in the society will not be in accordance with the pattern of consumer choice. Private forces are likely to increase their profits by raising their prices and will limit their output to the quantities that the market will take at the prices they have fixed. Consumers who would be willing to purchase larger quantities of their products at lower prices are left, instead, to buy goods and services that are wanted less (i.e., that are inferior). The resources that are excluded from the superior occupations compete with others for employment in inferior ones and their productivity declines. Thus, the primary effects of price manipulation may be reduced output of desired goods, higher prices, and transfer of income from consumers to producers.

While this is a rather stark and overly simplified depiction of the possible effects of "private" price manipulation in the marketplace, the antitrust laws have emerged basically as a legislative acknowledgment that the coordinative mechanisms provided by prices need some protection. In other words, perfectly competitive markets do not exist in reality. The purpose of the antitrust laws as they relate to pricing is, supposedly, to make certain that the gap between the ideal of "free and open" competition and the reality of imperfect systems dominated by private rules does not become dangerously wide. Indeed, transgressions in the pricing area are treated more seriously by the antitrust enforcement agencies and by the courts than transgressions in any other area of marketing, with the possible exception of product liability when personal injuries are involved.

Section 1 of the Sherman Act proscribes "every contract, combination . . . or conspiracy in restraint of trade or commerce among the several States." The Supreme Court has interpreted the language of Section 1 as making illegal per se all agreements among competing firms to fix prices, to restrict or pool output, to share markets on a predetermined basis, or otherwise directly to restrict the force of competition.[1] The per se doctrine labels as illegal any prac-

---

[1] F. M. Scherer, *Industrial Market Structure and Economic Performance,* 2nd ed. (Chicago: Rand McNally Publishing Co., 1980), p. 497.

tice to which it applies, regardless of the reasons for the practice and without extended inquiry as to its effects. Under a per se rule, it is only necessary for the complainant to prove the occurrence of conduct falling within the class of practices that are "so plainly anticompetitive" that they are subject to per se prohibition. This is in contrast to the "rule of reason" doctrine, which calls for a broad inquiry into the nature, purpose, and effect of any challenged arrangement before a decision is made about its legality. When applying the rule of reason, the courts examine the facts peculiar to the contested practices, their history, the reasons why they were implemented, and their competitive significance.

Following a long series of cases, the perspective of the Supreme Court toward price fixing was summarized, clearly and unequivocably, in a 1956 decision involving McKesson & Robbins, a major drug wholesaler. Chief Justice Warren wrote:

> It has been held too often to require elaboration now that price fixing is contrary to the policy of competition underlying the Sherman Act and that its illegality does not depend on a showing of its unreasonableness, since it is conclusively presumed to be unreasonable. It makes no difference whether the motives of the participants are good or evil; whether the price fixing is accomplished by express contract or by some more subtle means; whether the participants possess market control; whether the amount of interstate commerce affected is large or small; or whether the effect of the agreement is to raise or decrease prices.[2]

The attitude of the federal enforcement agencies and the courts on this issue is also shared on the state level where state antitrust activities against local price fixing are commonplace.

Dominant Cases

In the long series of federal price-fixing cases, two stand out as clearly dominant. The first, *U. S. v. Trenton Potteries Co.*[3] involved charges that the defendants (20 individuals and 23 corporations that manufactured 82 percent of the vitreous pottery [bathroom bowls] in the United States) were combining to restrain trade through the formation of a trade association that fixed prices and limited sales to a select list of non-price-cutting wholesalers. The defendants published standardized price lists through a trade association committee, discussed prices at frequent association meetings, and exhorted one another not to sell at off-list prices. The defendants argued that the prices set were reasonable and that "reasonableness" should be a defense to a prosecution under the Sherman Act. The Court rejected the argument, by saying,

> The aim and result of every price-fixing agreement, if effective, is the elimination of one form of competition. The power to fix prices, whether reasonably exercised or not, involves power to control the market and to fix arbitrary and

---

[2] *U.S.* v. *McKesson & Robbins, Inc.,* 351 U.S. 305 at 309–310 (1956).

[3] 273 U.S. 392 (1927).

unreasonable prices. The reasonable price fixed today may through economic and business changes become the unreasonable price of tomorrow.[4]

Despite the clear rejection of the reasonable price defense, the Court's mention of "power to control the market" left open the possibility of arguing that price fixing may be legal if the conspirators have a relatively small share of the market (i.e., if they lack the power to carry out the agreements they have reached). This impression was fully disspelled in *U.S.* v. *Socony-Vacuum Oil Co.*,[5] the second of the two dominant price-fixing cases.

The backdrop for the *Socony-Vacuum* case is important to its understanding. Oil refining was a depressed industry during the depression years of the 1930s. One group of refiners (the "majors") were fully integrated to the retail level; they had ample production, storage, and distribution capacity. Thus, they could respond to changes in demand by increasing or decreasing their inventories, the amount of gas produced, and changing prices. But another group of refiners ("independents") were not integrated, had limited storage capacity, and often had on their hands so-called distressed gasoline, which they were obliged to offer on the current "spot" market for immediate delivery to retailers. Because prices throughout the industry were affected by prices on the spot market, the majors, in order to inhibit rapid price fluctuations, entered into a concerted program of bidding for and buying distressed gas, which they were capable of storing whenever that was necessary to hold spot prices to a level that they regarded as consistent with overall levels of supply and demand. This concerted program was challenged and found by the Court to violate Section 1.

The defendants argued that the prices set were reasonable. Furthermore, they tried to justify their collusive actions on the grounds of thwarting "competitive evils," such as "ruinous" price cutting. And they also argued that they lacked the power to fully control prices in the spot markets. In his analysis of the decision in this case, Sullivan has pointed out three important conclusions of the Court relative to these claims:

> First, the Court reiterated the position taken in *Trenton Potteries* that reasonableness of prices is no defense, even if, as defendants asserted, the resulting prices were no higher than those which a healthy competitive market would yield. Second, the Court went beyond *Trenton Potteries* to hold that an arrangement fixing prices could not be justified on the ground that it was designed to diminish competitive evils. . . . Finally, the *Socony-Vacuum* opinion flatly stated in an elaborate dictum that a price fixing agreement violated Section 1 regardless of whether the conspirators possessed power to affect prices or had any effect on the price prevailing in the market.[6]

With regard to "competitive evils," the Court bluntly stated that

[4] Ibid., at 396.

[5] 310 U.S. 150 (1940).

[6] Lawrence A. Sullivan, *Handbook of the Law of Antitrust* (St. Paul, Minn.: West Publishing Co., 1977), p. 185.

> Any combination which tampers with price structures is engaged in an unlawful activity. . . . Congress . . . has not permitted the age-old cry of ruinous competition and competitive evils to be a defense to price fixing conspiracies.[7]

And, with regard to its general guidelines for industry, it stated that

> Under the Sherman Act a combination formed for the purpose and with the effect of raising, depressing, fixing, pegging, or stabilizing the prize of a commodity in interstate or foreign commerce is illegal *per se*.[8]

Aside from its adamant stand, the decision in this case is also important because it illustrates that collusive activities directed to controlling the output of a commodity and only consequently affecting prices are treated as equivalent to price fixing.

Frequency of Price Fixing

Despite this loud and very clear message against price fixing and related collusive activities, many industries have not followed its dictates; numerous price-fixing cases have been brought since the time of the *Socony-Vacuum* case. Considerable attention was given to *bid rigging* in some of these cases. Bid rigging occurs where sealed bids are required by a potential customer and are fixed by all or some of the bidders. In some bid-rigging agreements, one firm offers a bid that is lower than the bids of the other conspiring firms; in other cases, identical bids are submitted by all competitors.[9] Because the winning bid is often made public, especially in the case of government contracts, a cartel can identify "chislers" and may find ways of punishing noncompliance.

Perhaps the most infamous price-fixing conspiracy case in the last 50 years involved manufacturers of electrical equipment.[10] Twenty companies and 44 of their employees were indicted under the Sherman Act for conspiring to fix prices on such industrial products as condensers, generators, circuit breakers, insulators, switch gear, and transformers. The basic motive for price fixing proved to be the existence of considerable overcapacity in the industry as a result of the entry of a number of new firms, and the fact that the products involved were often made to specification and sold under a bidding system. Since, for all practical purposes, the products were homogeneous, price was the critical factor in the purchase decisions. Because of overcapacity and the homogeneity of the products, price cutting broke out. The conspiracy ended the price cutting.

As a result of convictions obtained in the electrical equipment conspiracy, 20 firms were fined over $11 million, seven executives were sent to prison for

---

[7] *U.S.* v. *Socony-Vacuum Oil Co.,* 310 U.S. 150 at 218 (1940).

[8] Ibid., at 223.

[9] In a study by the Justice Department, identical bidding was found to be less frequent than had been suspected. See Donald V. Harper, *Price Policy and Procedure* (New York: Harcourt, Brace, Jovanovich, Inc., 1966), p. 98.

[10] See Richard A. Smith, "The Incredible Electrical Conspiracy," *Fortune,* Part I (Apr. 1961), Part II (May 1961).

30 days each, and they and 37 other executives were fined a total of $137,500. Twenty-three executives received suspended 30-day prison sentences and were placed on probation for 5 years.

Even more recently, the three largest supermarket operators in Cleveland, Fisher Foods Inc., First National Supermarkets Inc., and Association of Stop-N-Shop Supermarkets (not related to Boston-based Stop & Shop Cos.), settled civil suits arising from an alleged price-fixing conspiracy by agreeing to distribute $21.5 million of free groceries to area consumers.[11] The government claimed that officers of the three supermarkets secretly met in parking lots, hotels, and an apartment to fix meat and grocery prices in two periods between 1976 and 1978.

Despite the clear per se illegality of price-fixing agreements, as reflected in numerous price-fixing cases across a wide variety of industries, the temptation to earn super-competitive returns or simply to achieve price stability seems irresistible to some companies in almost any industry at least one time in their histories. For example, among the industries involved in price-fixing cases have been those that produce salt, drugs, electrical parts used in television sets and computers, copper and brass tube and pipe, temperature control systems, railroad wheels and pipe flanges and steel rings, newsprint paper, bank services, eyeglasses, flour, bleachers, fertilizers, carbon sheet steel, corrugated containers, plywood, and structural steel. Apparently, environmental factors, industry characteristics (cyclicality in demand, high fixed costs, etc.), and a collusion "culture" have combined to make certain industries more susceptible than others, but, clearly, the practice has been somewhat widespread, to say the least.

Scope of the Per Se Rule

Since 1940, the Court's blanket condemnation in the *Socony-Vacuum* case has been followed consistently. The per se prohibition includes not only express price-fixing agreements, but also conspiracies seeking indirectly to limit price competition through agreements to restrict output, to follow standardized pricing formulas or methods, or to split markets by rotating low bids. Also illegal are agreements that establish minimum and maximum prices below which competitors will not go or which fix differentials in prices to be maintained between sellers. In fact, the prohibition against setting maximum prices has, as recently as 1982, been applied by the Supreme Court to an agreement among doctors in Arizona.[12] The per se rule also applies to resale price maintenance, a topic that is addressed in Chapter 6. In addition, agreements to establish standard charges for services (such as check cashing or the granting of credit), to change prices at the same time, and to refrain from advertising prices are covered by the rule.

---

[11] Margaret Yao, "Three Cleveland Food Chains to Provide Groceries to Settle Price-Fixing Lawsuits," *Wall Street Journal,* Nov. 13, 1981, p. 10.

[12] *Arizona* v. *Maricopa County Medical Society,* 1982-2 Trade Cases #. 64, 792 (U.S. June 18, 1982).

The practice of price "signaling" soon may join the category of per se illegal practices. In the late 1970s, the Federal Trade Commission charged that the country's four antiknock-additive makers, Ethyl Corp., Du Pont Co., PPG Industries, Inc., and Nalco Chemical Corp., negotiated prices indirectly through the press and their customers with the goal of keeping prices uniform during a time of frequent increases. In 1983, the Federal Trade Commission ruled that two of the companies, Du Pont and Ethyl, illegally "signaled" price changes, thereby restraining competition through a series of steps that served to set prices for all the antiknock-additive makers listed in the complaint.[13] Specifically, the companies have been prohibited from:

1. Announcing a price change before the time agreed upon between the company and the purchaser. (Generally, a 30-day notice is given. Notices in excess of the contract requirements permitted "jockeying" to test the waters and settle on a uniform price.)
2. Using a "most-favored-nation" clause in sales or delivery contracts. (Such clauses promise customers they will get the lowest price given to any customer. That discouraged selective discounts, because a company would have to lower its pricing level to all customers, thereby perhaps reducing profits generally.)
3. Setting uniform delivered prices for their anti-knock products. (Under the uniform delivered pricing system, customers all over the country paid the same price, including freight, despite different transportation costs.)

While delivered price systems and exchanges of price information have been challenged in the past (as discussed in detail below), the anti-knock additive case is the first to make it clear that independent, parallel activities that make price coordination easy, even with no agreement at all between the companies, can be declared illegal.

Exceptions to the Per Se Rule

Although a per se rule has certain obvious advantages, its use carries a risk that some activities will be condemned as illegal when the practices actually are beneficial. Even activities that would appear to be forms of price fixing can be useful and not competitively harmful. For example, the Chicago Board of Trade prohibited grain purchases after the board closed unless the grain was already in transit to Chicago and was purchased at the closing bid price. The Justice Department charged that this activity was price fixing, but the Court held that this restraint of trade was not unreasonable.[14] The Court stated that the board's regulation helped competition by promoting the development of a central market, had only an incidental effect on competition, and was limited

---

[13] "FTC Expands Interpretation of Antitrust Law," *Wall Street Journal,* Apr. 4, 1983, p. 6. See, also, *In the Matter of Ethyl Corporation, et al.,* Federal Trade Commission Docket No. 9128, Aug. 5, 1981; Margaret G. Warner, "FTC Aide Bars 4 Gasoline-Additive Firms from Advance Publicity of Price Boosts," *Wall Street Journal,* Aug. 13, 1981, p. 4; "FTC Finds Ethyl and Du Pont Restrained Price Competition For Gas "Antiknock" Compounds," *FTC News Notes,* Vol. 31-83, April 29, 1983, p. 2; and "The FTC Redefines Price-Fixing," *Business Week,* April 18, 1983, p. 37.

[14] *Chicago Board of Trade* v. *U.S.,* 246 U.S. 231 (1918).

to a small part of the grain traded on the board and to an even smaller part of the total grain market. Clearly, the results of this case are difficult to reconcile with the results of other cases in the price-fixing area. Insightfully, Scherer has pointed out some of the possible consequences of the *Chicago Board of Trade* decision:

> the Court may have unwittingly set the stage for a presumption that dealers on an organized exchange were somehow different from others engaged in the hurly-burly of trade, meriting special antitrust immunity that has to some extent persisted even to the present. Similar opportunities to set fees collectively without antitrust prosecution were employed for a long time by members of such professions as medicine, dentistry, law, architecture, and civil engineering. Only during the 1960's and 1970's did these immunities come under significant and largely successful attack.[15]

It should be noted, also, that, contrary to the *Chicago Board of Trade* decision, challenges to the practices of New York Stock Exchange brokers led to the phased elimination of fixed commissions beginning in 1972.[16] There are also other examples where price fixing has been permitted and, in some instances, condoned. As explained in Chapter 2, the owner of a valid patent may legitimately include restrictions in the licenses it unilaterally grants to other firms with respect to price, output, and markets. Furthermore, a host of parties have been exempted from the antitrust laws. In most instances, federal regulators perform price-setting (and thereby, price fixing) duties for the exempted parties. In other instances, special legislation has been enacted permitting them to set prices collectively. A few of the exempted parties and their price-fixing commissions or enabling laws are listed in Table 5-1.

Table 5-1

Exempted Party	Commission or Legislation
Labor unions	Clayton Act
Shipping companies	Federal Maritime Commission
Export trade associations	Webb–Pomerene Act of 1918
Surface transportation companies	Interstate Commerce Commission
Farm cooperatives	Capper–Volstead Act of 1982
Handlers of agricultural commodities	Agricultural Marketing Agreement Act of 1937
Telegraph, telephone, television	Federal Communications Commission
Insurance companies (subject to state control)	McCarran Act of 1945

However, it is important to note that deregulation, especially as it relates to price setting, is well underway for shipping companies, trucks, and telecom-

---

[15] Scherer, op. cit., p. 502. A key decision involving professional fee setting was *Goldfarb* v. *Virginia State Bar Association*, 421 U.S. 773 (1975). See, also, *National Society of Professional Engineers* v. *U.S.*, 435 U.S. 679 (1978).

[16] See H. Michael Mann, "The New York Stock Exchange: A Cartel at the End of its Reign," in Almarin Phillips, ed., *Promoting Competition in the Regulated Markets* (Washington, D.C.: Brookings Institution, 1975), pp. 301–327.

munications companies, among others, and has already been accomplished in the airline industry.

Liability in Price Fixing

Despite certain exceptions, price fixing is generally forbidden in the United States. The deterrents to price fixing are reasonably strong. Besides the possibility of criminal convictions (with prison sentences and fines), the financial risks are large. In price-fixing cases, defendants who lose at trial are liable for treble damages not only for their own antitrust violations but for those of *all* companies found to be co-conspirators, even if the latter have settled out of court. This rule enormously inflates the potential cost of being found guilty.[17] For example, in 1981, a federal appeals court in New Orleans upheld a jury verdict against three Pacific Northwest plywood producers, Weyerhaeuser Co., Georgia-Pacific Corp., and Willamette Industries, Inc., found guilty of conspiring to maintain high prices by manipulating freight rates. Damages assessed against the three defendants could have totaled $2 billion after the tripling permitted under the antitrust laws. The three companies were fortunate to have settled the lawsuit in 1982 by agreeing to pay the plaintiffs $165 million.[18]

On the other side, a small consolation to price fixers is the fact that only their *direct* purchasers can sue for damages, because, according to the controversial *Illinois Brick* decision,[19] to allow recovery by indirect purchasers (such as consumers or retailers when the victim of the price fix was a wholesaler) inevitably would lead to a duplication of financial claims. The court believes that the difficulty of measuring, tracing, and apportioning damages would overcomplicate private antitrust suits and overburden the courts, so that the use of treble-damage actions as a deterrent might be reduced.[20]

While nearly every industrialized Western nation has some kind of antitrust law or competition policy, none is as strict as the American per se rule against price fixing conspiracies. Other countries tolerate pricing agreements within more or less narrowly circumscribed boundaries.[21]

EXCHANGING PRICE INFORMATION

Antitrust cases against price fixing sometimes involve difficult borderline questions of fact concerning whether an explicit agreement exists among competi-

---

[17] See Irwin Ross, "A Philadelphia Lawyer's Class-Action Gold Mine," *Fortune,* Sept. 7, 1981, p. 100.

[18] See Kathryn Christensen, "Three Plywood Companies Lose Appeal of Antitrust Verdict on 'Phantom' Rates," *Wall Street Journal,* Sept. 9, 1981, p. 48, and "Plywood Makers Agree to Settle Antitrust Suit," *Wall Street Journal,* Dec. 15, 1982, p. 3. Members of the roadbuilding industry may not be as fortunate. See Steven Flax, "The Crackdown on Colluding Roadbuilders," *Fortune,* October 3, 1983, pp. 79–85.

[19] *Illinois Brick Co.* v. *State of Illinois,* 431 U.S. 720 (1977).

[20] See A. D. Neale and D. G. Goyder, *The Antitrust Laws of the U.S.A.,* 3rd ed. (New York: Cambridge University Press, 1980), p. 427. However, the Supreme Court has already found some exceptions to the *Illinois Brick* rule. See *Blue Shield of Virginia* v. *McCready,* 50 U.S.L.W. 4723 (U.S. June 21, 1982).

[21] See Scherer, op. cit., p. 504.

tors. Proving an offense under Section 1 of the Sherman Act requires proof of the existence of an agreement—a contract, combination, or conspiracy—in restraint of trade. If an agreement exists and it relates to the fixing of prices, then a per se violation is established. However, if the agreement merely covers an exchange of information concerning prices, output, inventories, or any other aspect of business that might affect prices, then the legality of the agreement will be tested according to the rule of reason. But if the evidence suggests that the parties went further and agreed to use the information jointly to affect prices, then a per se violation has been established, as in *Trenton Potteries.*

Many exchanges of price information are facilitated by trade associations. When trade associations are vehicles for competitors to agree on prices, outputs, market shares, and the like, these activities are viewed as per se illegal. It is only when the information exchanges *might* be leading to anticompetitive behavior in the absence of an explicit price-setting agreement among competitors that the rule of reason is applied.

Significant Cases

During the 1920s, four cases came before the Supreme Court involving the price and other statistical reporting activities of trade associations in the hardwood lumber, linseed oil, maple flooring, and cement industries. In all four cases, the associations concerned were engaged in collecting and disseminating data on production, inventories, orders, sales, and shipments, in preparing and circulating reports on prices and terms of sale, and in operating delivered pricing systems. Some of the associations also held meetings where prices and production were discussed. But no explicit evidence of agreement as to price and production policy was introduced in any of these cases.

The earliest of these cases, *American Column and Lumber Company* v. *U.S.,*[22] involved an association of hardwood manufacturers who adopted an "open competition" plan. This plan was explicitly based on the proposition that "knowledge regarding prices actually made is all that is necessary to keep prices at reasonably stable and normal levels." The Court concluded that, even though no specific agreement to restrict output and fix prices was proved, the conduct of the defendants was "clearly that of men united in an agreement, express or implied, to act together and pursue a common purpose under a common guide." A similar result was reached in *U.S.* v. *American Linseed Oil Company.*[23]

Perhaps the most significant of the four 1920s cases, however, involved the Maple Flooring Manufacturers' Association.[24] Here, an association of 22 manufacturers of hardwood flooring worked out, from information supplied by

---

[22] 257 U.S. 377 (1921).

[23] 262 U.S. 371 (1923).

[24] *Maple Flooring Manufacturers' Association* v. *U.S.,* 268 U.S. 563 (1925).

members, the average member's costs for all dimensions and grades of flooring. The association then circulated these figures to its members in booklets that also showed the freight rates from a base point to several thousand possible consuming centers. Summaries of all sales, prices, and inventories were regularly circulated. Meetings were held regularly to exchange views on the industry's problems,[25] but no discussion of current or future prices took place at these meetings. The Court found that members' prices were not uniform and that, on the whole, they were lower rather than higher than those of manufacturers outside the association, all of which negated an agreement to fix prices. The Court also stated that the mere exchange of information is not "an unreasonable restraint, or in any respect unlawful."

It is important to note that in *Maple Flooring* the Court looked for evidence of agreement by taking into account the "reasonableness" of prices and the competitive situation in the industry. Such factors would not have been given any weight whatsoever if an agreement to fix prices had been obvious.

The fourth significant case in the 1920s was similar to *Maple Flooring*. But in this situation, exchanges of price information among members of the Cement Manufacturers' Protective Association were established for the purpose of preventing fraud on the members of the association.[26] There was no agreement to act in a uniform way. The information helped the members avoid situations where contractors would deliberately overstate their needs for cement, inducing excess supply and thereby driving prices down. The Supreme Court granted limited approval to the information exchange. This approval, later identified as the *controlling circumstance* exception to the antitrust laws, has occasionally been used by lower courts to permit exchanges of price information among competitors.[27]

A case decided in 1936 showed how the rule of reason could work in favor of the enforcement agencies rather than against them, as it had in *Maple Flooring* and the *Cement Manufacturing* cases. Fifteen sugar refining companies had formed The Sugar Institute to administer a "code of ethics" for the industry, which was in a demoralized state because of overcapacity, secret rebates, and other discriminatory concessions.[28] The special feature of the code of ethics provided that, once any refiner announced a price, secret concessions would not be allowed. There was, however, no agreement as to the prices that would be announced. The Supreme Court condemned the agreement not to deviate from an announced price. But rather than finding a per se violation, the Court considered the trading conditions before and after the formation of the institute. It condemned the agreement as an unreasonable restraint, because it found that the agreement had led to a reduction in the frequency of price changes and a "marked increase in margin and a substantial increase in

---

[25] See Neale and Goyder, op. cit., p. 46.

[26] *Cement Manufacturers' Protective Association* v. *U.S.,* 268 U.S. 588 (1925).

[27] Terence H. Benbow, Stephen A. Brown, George M. Burditt, and Susan S. Egan, *Contacts with Trade Associations,* Antitrust L. J. 49 issue 2 (1981), p. 834.

[28] *The Sugar Institute* v. *U.S.,* 297 U.S. 553 (1936).

profits, despite a concededly large excess capacity." On the other hand, the Court did not condemn the industry practice of publicly announcing impending price changes, thereby allowing buyers a period of grace for purchasing at the old price. (This practice, called *price filing*, is very similar to the price signaling questioned in the recent case against the antiknock-additive makers mentioned earlier.[29]) The Court also upheld the circulation of detailed statistics of production, sales, and inventories, provided that the figures were made available to buyers and sellers equally.

Two important cases in the price information exchange area have been decided during the past two decades. The first, *U.S. v. Container Corp. of America*,[30] did not involve a systematic centralized price reporting organization. Instead, the producers supplied to one another upon request (as often as a dozen times per month) information on prices currently or last quoted to particular customers. Once a company received this information from a rival, it usually quoted the same price to that customer; and it was common for buyers to divide orders among producers offering identical quotations. Unlike the members of The Sugar Institute and other trade associations that were the subjects of earlier cases, the defendants were not bound to adhere to price schedules; rather, there was an underlying expectation among all the defendants that, if they supplied the information required, they would in turn be able to obtain reciprocal information at a later date from the other defendants. The majority opinion (applying a rule of reason analysis) concentrated on the structure of the container industry—18 manufacturers of corrugated containers produced about 90 percent of the output in the southeastern United States and only 4 of them accounted for 45 percent of the output—when it emphasized the critical importance of price in the industry. It concluded that the effect of the exchange of information had been to stabilize prices and that it had chilled the vigor of price competition in the industry.[31] Sullivan has, however, quarrelled with the economic analysis of the Court. He has argued that

> On available structural evidence the conclusion of the majority is doubtful. Evidence of power, of a structure facilitating cartelization or interdependence, was no more than borderline. Although the 18 defendants had 90 percent and the largest four of them 45 percent of the southeast market (if, indeed, that was a separate geographical market, as all seemed to assume)—itself, a moderate degree of concentration—the cross-elasticity of demand among the products of different producers (which was displayed by the rapid changes in suppliers by customers), the great ease of entry, and the existing over-capacity, all must have severely limited the potential of defendants to hold prices at supra-competitive levels.[32]

Apart from this criticism, the Court has clearly indicated that agreements to share price information can be anticompetitive and in violation of the Sherman Act.

---

[29] See *In the Matter of Ethyl Corporation, et al.*, op. cit.

[30] 393 U.S. 333 (1969).

[31] See Neale and Goyder, op. cit., p. 49.

[32] Sullivan, op. cit., p. 272.

The second case, *U.S.* v. *United States Gypsum Co.*,[33] was decided in 1978 and involved four leading gypsum companies who were charged with price fixing during the period 1960–1973. They used a price "verification" system; each company would call to find out what price the other firm was currently offering. Using the controlling circumstance exception established in the *Cement Manufacturers* case, the defendants argued that the advance notice was needed to protect them from unwittingly violating the Robinson–Patman Act by cutting prices below competition. The Court refused to find a controlling circumstance in the *Gypsum* case. Instead, it found that the purpose of the information exchange was to suppress and limit competition in violation of the Sherman Act. Indeed, some legal scholars believe that the decision in the *Gypsum* case places in doubt the continuing viability of the controlling circumstance exception.[34]

Rules of Thumb

Generalizations about the legality of agreements to exchange price information are dangerous, because courts seemingly have approached this practice on a case-by-case basis. Slight factual variances among specific cases have permitted different rules to be applied. Nevertheless, there appear to be some broad guidelines, as noted by Wilcox. Price information exchange programs are likely to be lawful when they

—limit price reports to past transactions,
—preserve the anonymity of individual traders,
—make data available to buyers as well as sellers, and
—permit departure from the prices that are filed.[35]

They tend to be viewed with disfavor when

—future prices are reported,
—traders are identified,
—information is withheld from buyers, and
—discussions are held, statements issued, and recommendations made on price and production policies.[36]

Sullivan has observed that:

A purpose and effect analysis which emphasizes the particulars of the program has led courts to uphold price reporting arrangements. Where there is no commitment to comply with published prices, where individual transactions are not identified, where information goes to buyers as well as sellers, and where no audit procedure, common analysis, or suspicious exhortation is associated with price reporting, a purpose and effect analysis *focused only on program details* will tend to validate the program.[37]

[33] 438 U.S. 422 (1978).

[34] See Benbow et al., op. cit., p. 834.

[35] Clair Wilcox, *Public Policies toward Business,* 4th Ed. (Homewood, Ill.: Richard D. Irwin, Inc., 1971), p. 125.

[36] Ibid.

[37] Sullivan, op. cit., p. 269 (emphasis supplied.)

However, the *Container Corp.* case indicated that "program details" are only part of the evidence that courts will evaluate in determining whether a price information exchange program is legal. The Court will look at the program details in the context of the *structure* of the industry. Such an expanded focus may be warranted, because, from an antitrust perspective, the exchange of price information is, as Scherer points out, "unambiguously beneficial [to society] only in the context of purely competitive markets. When the market is oligopolistic, it may impair rather than invigorate rivalry."[38] Where the information exchanged has been made publicly available and the evidence of collusion in price decisions has been weak, defendants in price information exchange cases have succeeded. But the trend has been to make exchanges of price information more hazardous.

PARALLEL PRICING

Parallelism or uniformity in pricing is relatively commonplace in oligopolistic industries. According to economic theory, each seller knows that his competitors must take his reactions into account (and vice versa). Because of the small numbers of competitors in such industries, noncompetitive pricing without an agreement is both feasible and tempting. However, joint profit maximization among competitors in an oligopolistic industry will succeed only if all sellers "participate" by selling above their marginal costs.[39] In nonoligopolistic industries where larger numbers of rivals compete, it is difficult to avoid price competition without "organizing" the market. In the latter case, collusion is often present, and, if present, is usually detected, as we saw in our examination of price information exchanges.

Gellhorn has observed that a traditional interpretation of the Sherman Act would seemingly render interdependent pricing by oligopolists immune from antitrust attack under Section 1 of the Sherman Act because no facial agreement exists.[40] And Section 2 of the Sherman Act also seems inapplicable, because one firm does not have monopoly power.[41] However, the courts have long recognized that agreements (contracts, combinations, or conspiracies) can exist even if they cannot be established by direct testimony; they may be proved by circumstantial evidence. And since agreements can be tacit and informal, an illegal contract can be inferred by courts even in the absence of evidence of meetings among competitors. "It is elementary," said the Supreme Court in the *Eastern States Lumber* case in 1914, "that conspiracies are seldom capable of proof by direct testimony, and may be inferred from the things actually done."[42] In other words, while there may be no direct evidence,

---

[38] Scherer, op. cit., p. 521.

[39] Ernest Gellhorn, *Antitrust Law and Economics in a Nutshell* (St. Paul, Minn.: West Publishing Co., 1976), p. 241.

[40] Ibid., p. 240.

[41] Ibid.

[42] *Eastern States Retail Lumber Assn.* v. *U.S.*, 234 U.S. 600 at 612 (1914).

when a conspiracy is proved by circumstantial evidence, it is deemed to have actually taken place. The legal status of collusion without formal agreement is an important issue, given the prevalent nature of oligopolistic market structures in the economy.

Significant Cases

A seminal case in this area was *Interstate Circuit, Inc., et al.* v. *U.S.*,[43] which was decided a half-century ago. In *Interstate Circuit*, a movie theater chain sent identical letters to eight film distributors demanding that each distributor deny first-run films to exhibitors who either refused to meet a schedule of minimum prices set out in the letter or who showed first-run films as parts of double-feature programs. The letters named all eight distributors, so that each distributor was well aware that the others had received the same demand. The evidence offered in the case showed that all distributors had offices in the same city, that all were contacted by an agent of the chain, that each would gain if all accepted the proposal but lose if it alone accepted, and that all finally responded to the proposal with identical and fairly complex counteroffers. In addition, the Supreme Court noted that the defendants had introduced no witnesses to deny the existence of a conspiracy, even though no evidence was presented to show a formal agreement among them. While the Supreme Court indicated in its decision that the district court was justified in finding an agreement among the distributors, the Court went on to say that, "in the circumstances of this case such agreement . . . was not a prerequisite to unlawful conspiracy. It was enough that, knowing that concerted action was contemplated and invited, the distributors gave their adherence to the scheme and participated in it."[44] The Court noted that the availability of direct evidence of conspiracy is the exception rather than the rule and that the circumstantial evidence not only warranted but virtually demanded a finding of conspiracy. It said,

> It taxes credibility . . . that the several distributors would . . . have accepted . . . and put into operation with substantial unanimity such far reaching changes in their business methods without some understanding that all were to join. . . .[45]

Thus, the distributors were found to have violated Section 1 of the Sherman Act without proof of an express agreement and without even initiating the message that brought about their behavioral change. Yet it is important to see that in this case there was an overt act (the receipt of a letter) to which the conspiracy in restraint of trade could be traced. It is also noteworthy that the Court's decision preceded most empirical and theoretical economic analysis of oligopoly markets in which the central theme of mutually recognized interdependence among industry members is stressed.

[43] 306 U.S. 208 (1939).

[44] Ibid., at 226.

[45] Ibid., at 223.

In 1946, the Supreme Court seemed to go a step beyond *Interstate Circuit* when it expressed the view in *American Tobacco Co.* v. *U.S.*[46] that a common course of conduct was sufficient to warrant the finding of "a unity of purpose or common design"[47] and that "no formal agreement is necessary to constitute an unlawful conspiracy."[48] During the depression of the 1930s, low-priced cigarettes, the "ten cent brands," started to make gains on the high-priced (fifteen cent) brands of the "big three" producers. The latter companies, which did not use and had not previously bid for cheap tobacco and seldom bid against each other even for tobacco of the quality they all did use, all began to bid when cheap tobacco was offered at an auction. As a result, the price of cheap tobacco rose sharply. Concurrently, the big three cut prices on their own brands. Later, after the market share of the cheap brands fell, prices on the major brands were again increased. The evidence of concerted activity in the case, although mainly circumstantial (centering on the parallelism in pricing and purchasing behavior), was persuasive because it was so unlikely that such behavior would have been independently arrived at, given the economic conditions of the 1930s when the conspiracy took place.

The line of cases beginning with *Interstate Circuit* and *American Tobacco* and ending with another movie distribution case[49] decided in 1948 established a doctrine of *conscious parallelism* under which evidence that two or more firms have acted in the same way, each aware of the other's doings, will warrant a finding of conspiracy under Section 1.[50] Indeed, the doctrine had progressed so far that some scholars believed that the courts now would permit an inference of illegal conspiracy solely from evidence of detailed similarity in pricing and nothing more. Such an expansive definition of conspiracy called into question much conduct in oligopolistic industries generally.[51] But this concern was dispelled in subsequent cases, the most significant of which were *Theater Enterprises, Inc.* v. *Paramount Film Distributing Corp. et al.*[52] and *C-O Two Fire Equipment Co.* v. *U.S..*[53]

In *Theater Enterprises,* nine film distributors all refused to grant first-run status to a new theater in a suburban Baltimore shopping center, giving preference instead to established downtown theaters, three of which were owned by distributors. There was no evidence of agreement among the distributors. The Supreme Court refused to infer an illegal conspiracy since the distributors' decisions to deny first-run status could have been taken independently and been based on "individual business judgment motivated by the desire for maximum revenue."[54] Furthermore, the business reasons cited by the defendants

[46] 328 U.S. 781 (1946).

[47] Ibid., at 810.

[48] Ibid., at 809.

[49] *U.S.* v. *Paramount Pictures, Inc.*, 334 U.S. 131 (1948).

[50] Sullivan, op. cit., p. 317.

[51] See William H. Nichols, "The Tobacco Case of 1946," *American Economic Review* 39 (May 1949), p. 296.

[52] 346 U.S. 537 (1954).

[53] 197 F.2nd 489 (9th Cir.), *cert. denied* 344 U.S. 892 (1952).

[54] 346 U.S. 537 at 542 (1954).

for withholding first-run status were compelling. The most important state-ment of the Court on these parallel behavior issues to date was made in this case by Mr. Justice Clark. He wrote,

> The crucial question is whether respondents' conduct toward petitioner stemmed from independent decision or from an agreement, tacit or express. . . . this Court has never held that proof of parallel business behavior conclusively establishes agreement or, phrased differently, that such behavior itself constitutes a Sherman Act offense. Circumstantial evidence of consciously parallel behavior may have made heavy inroads into the traditional attitude toward conspiracy; but "conscious parallelism" has not yet read conspiracy out of the Sherman Act entirely.[55]

Neale and Goyder believe that the decision in *Theater Enterprises* marks the failure of the attempt to extend the meaning of "conspiracy" to cover parallel courses of action—an attempt intended to enable antitrust to be brought to bear more easily on oligopoly situations.[56]

This does not mean that, if the *Interstate Circuit* and *American Tobacco* cases were retried, the decisions would be reversed. It simply means that evi-dence of parallel behavior, standing alone, is not sufficient to establish an agreement in restraint of trade cases involving oligopolists. The *C-O Two* case was helpful in delimiting the boundary between legal and illegal behavior in potential "combination" or "conspiracy" situations. In *C-O Two*, as recounted by Sullivan,

> four competing manufacturers of fire extinguishers had regularly communicat-ed with each other, had engaged in a meticulous program of product standard-ization, raised prices at a time of an industry surplus, made identical bids on public contracts, used substantially identical licensing agreements with distribu-tors (agreements which included resale price fixing provisions) and carefully po-liced these arrangements. On this evidence a finding of conspiracy was warranted.[57]

What these behaviors amounted to were "plus" factors, which went beyond mere conscious parallelism. Indeed, it is the presence or absence of these plus factors that will determine legality or illegality in similar cases.

The Content of "Parallelism Plus"

Evidence of identical behavior by a few large firms is not enough, in itself, to prove an illegal conspiracy in restraint of trade. In other words, oligopolistic behavior alone is not illegal. To be illegal, an apparent uniformity of prices must result from collusion, not from conditions in the market. In this context, collusion means a real "meeting of the minds" in a common endeavor to sup-press or limit price competition.[58] The individual firm must also be under some

---

[55] Ibid., at 540–541.

[56] Neale and Goyder, op. cit., p. 84.

[57] Sullivan, op. cit., p. 318.

[58] See Neale and Goyder, op. cit., pp. 50–51.

fairly effective inhibition with regard to "breaking the price line" when the temptation to do so appears strong.

Even where proof of overt agreement is lacking, identity of behavior may be so complex, so pervasive, and so persistent that agreement may be safely inferred. In each case discussed that found a conspiracy in restraint of trade (i.e., *Interstate Circuit, American Tobacco, Paramount,* and *C-O Two*), there was evidence of one or more of the following:

—a proposal for joint action,
—a complex yet identical set of responses,
—direct communication or an opportunity for it,
—a failure to deny agreement,
—a set of circumstances which made each participant aware that it was in its interest to participate if all did, but adverse to its interest to participate if others did not.[59]

These actions as well as specific occurrences such as chain letters and blacklists certainly qualify as plus factors. The necessary plus can also be inferred when firms have advance knowledge of impending rival actions that could hardly have been gained without covert communications, as in the *American Tobacco* case.[60] Other plus factors are:

the mutual adoption of "price protection" plans discouraging price cutting and the publication of books simplifying the computation of uniform bid prices, as General Electric and Westinghouse did following their 1960 conviction for outright collusion in turbogenerator pricing.[61]

Concerted action can be found only if the evidence as a whole warrants the conclusion that the defendants have together chosen to act in a certain way, that they have, in one way or another, communicated, and given mutual assurances. The state of mutual awareness among oligopolists does not fall within the legal meaning of "conspiracy." Even though such a state of affairs may have restrictive effects on competition, it is beyond the reach of the law of conspiracy so long as the additional bond of a common understanding is lacking.[62] In addition, in a criminal proceeding under Section 1, the Supreme Court, speaking through Chief Justice Burger, held in 1978 that the element of unlawful purpose has to be established in evidence and cannot simply be presumed from proof of an effect on prices (as would be enough to show a civil violation).[63] Therefore, the burden of proving a conspiracy in criminal cases has increased, because the Court's tolerance of circumstantial evidence is lower. However, criminal liability can be found where the defendants have acted with knowledge of the probable consequences of their conduct and where anticompetitive effects have occurred.[64]

---

[59] Sullivan, op. cit., p. 317.

[60] Scherer, op. cit., p. 519.

[61] Ibid., p. 519.

[62] Neale and Goyder, op. cit., p. 86.

[63] *U.S.* v. *United States Gypsum Company,* 438 U.S. 422 (1978).

[64] Ibid.

Price Leadership

In an oligopolistic industry, smaller firms are sometimes forced by the realities of competition to follow the prices charged by an industry leader. The idea that sellers in concentrated markets are generally reluctant to charge different prices from one another, irrespective of size, depends on a number of assumptions about the time lag associated with responses to price changes, the elasticity of demand facing the sellers, and the like.[65] Nevertheless, in the absence of coercion or collusion, price leadership has generally been accepted by the courts. In *U.S.* v. *International Harvester Co.,* the Supreme Court stated,

> the fact that competitors may see proper, in exercise of their own judgment, to follow the prices of another manufacturer, does not establish any suppression of competition or show any sinister domination.[66]

In a more recent case, the Supreme Court upheld the trial court's finding that price changes by smaller companies that closely followed those of the industry leader did not themselves imply the existence of a price-fixing agreement.[67] On the other hand, as Neale and Goyder point out,

> solid evidence of an understanding among firms to abide by the price decisions of an appointed leader would be enough to establish an illegal conspiracy under Section 1. And there have been cases in which the courts have been persuaded to find consciously parallel conduct unlawful by evidence that competitors in an oligopolistic industry have had advance notice of a leading firm's price plans and have then followed similar courses of action.[68]

Delivered Prices

Legal restrictions have also been placed on the use of delivered pricing systems via extension of the conscious parallelism doctrine. Delivered prices have been used to promote price uniformity and stability within an industry. They involve the quotation of selling prices from standard or *base-point* locations in such a way that all customers within a certain area pay the same price for a product regardless of differences in shipping costs from the seller's place of business to the customer's location. For many years, such base-point pricing systems were popular in a variety of industries (e.g., steel, cement, plywood). Almost all of them relied on the cooperation of all, or at least a large majority, of the firms in an industry. Each firm typically agreed to use specified transportation rates in computing the delivered price of its products to its customers. Consequently, the delivered prices quoted by all the firms in an industry would be virtually identical.

A basing point system might come into conflict with the antitrust laws in

[65] Richard A. Posner, *Antitrust Law: An Economic Perspective* (Chicago: University of Chicago Press, 1976), pp. 44–45.

[66] 274 U.S. 693 at 709 (1927).

[67] *U.S.* v. *National Malleable & Steel Castings Co.,* 358 U.S. 38 (1958).

[68] Neale and Goyder, op. cit., p. 51. Neale and Goyder cite *Wall Products Company* v. *National Gypsum Company,* 326 F. Supp. 295 (N.D. Cal. 1971).

several ways.[69] First, it might be found to depend on collusive agreement or conscious parallelism of action and thus reveal a conspiracy in restraint of trade in violation of Section 1 of the Sherman Act. Second, because it avoids competition through adherence to a common course of action, it might be characterized as an unfair method of competition under Section 5 of the Federal Trade Commission Act. Third, the geographic price discrimination resulting from such a system might be found to be injurious to competition and thus be a violation of Section 2(a) of the Clayton Act as amended by the Robinson–Patman Act. It has, however, been argued that the real offense in basing point systems is not the price discrimination that may result from them, but the collusion that is involved in establishing and maintaining them.[70] Therefore, concentration would tend to be on the first and second ways of questioning their legality, rather than the third. In fact, antitrust cases on delivered pricing issues have been concerned essentially with the occurrence of collusive price fixing and not with the merits of base-point pricing as such. Attention has been focused on the collective support given to the formula used as the basis of promoting systematic price stability, rather than on individual use of a price formula.[71]

The most important case on this topic is *Federal Trade Commission* v. *Cement Institute*[72] in which the Supreme Court upheld an FTC order barring cement producers from using base-point pricing. The Institute was shown to have engaged in an active campaign to maintain the pricing system (firing uncooperative employees, selling cement in a price cutter's territory at prices so low that the firm had to capitulate, distributing freight rate books, etc.). The Court ruled that there was substantial evidence in the record to support the FTC's conclusion that cement sellers had in fact agreed with each other to establish this system for fostering monopoly pricing.

A highly significant development in this area of delivered pricing has been the Federal Trade Commission's use of Section 5 of the FTC Act to raise broad questions about oligopoly pricing as it relates to consciously parallel behavior.[73] (And in some cases, firms engaged in delivered pricing have been charged not only with taking part in a tacit conspiracy via conscious parallelism but, as discussed later in this chapter, have also been charged, in the same complaint, with engaging in illegal price discrimination under the Robinson–Patman Act.[74]) The use of Section 5 of the FTC Act is important, because Section 5 does not directly involve the law of conspiracy (like the Sherman Act), but rather primarily focuses on the "unfair methods of competition" employed by *individual* firms. Thus, if an individual firm engages in delivered

---

[69] Wilcox, op. cit., p. 234.

[70] Ibid., p. 241.

[71] Neale and Goyder, op. cit., p. 57.

[72] 333 U.S. 683 (1948).

[73] See *Triangle Conduit and Cable Co. et al.* v. *FTC*, 168 F.2d 175 (7th Cir. 1948).

[74] See, for example, *in re Boise Cascade Corp. et al., decision and final order, Federal Trade Commission docket no. 8958* (Feb. 1978), in addition to the *Glucose* cases discussed later in this chapter.

pricing behavior that is consciously parallel to those of its rivals, the FTC can challenge the pricing scheme, even though no conspiracy might be evident. In fact, there have been interpretations of the FTC Act which indicate that Section 5 permits the FTC to challenge such practices in their "incipiency" (i.e., at the beginning, when they are starting up), if the FTC believes that the practices will eventually lead to anticompetitive consequences.

Neale and Goyder have summarized the present status of delivered pricing systems as follows:

> it seems probable that, given a fairly large trading area with a considerable number of sellers, averaged delivered prices throughout a zone, or prices related to a single basing-point which produced a high degree of price uniformity over a period, would nearly always require and betray an element of collusion. The element of collusion has been found a good deal more elusive, however, in the case of "multiple basing-point" or "freight equalization" schemes, and most of the argument on this topic in the United States has raged about these methods.[75]

PREDATORY PRICING

Section 2 of the Sherman Act states that "Every person who shall monopolize, or attempt to monopolize, or combine or conspire with any person or persons to monopolize any part of the trade or commerce among the several states, or with foreign nations, shall be deemed guilty of a misdemeanour. . . ." While we focus in Chapter 9 on monopoly and monopolization, it is important that, in this chapter, we stop and deal with one of the primary means that might be used to achieve or maintain a monopoly—predatory pricing. Simply put, predatory pricing involves cutting prices to unreasonably low or unprofitable levels in markets where competition is encountered in order to drive others from those markets. The losses that are incurred and/or the profits foregone by the price-cutter are accepted in the expectation that they will be more than made up at a later date by the monopoly profits that can be obtained after the competitive threat from other firms is ended. Thus, the predator's motivation is presumably to secure a monopoly position once rivals have been driven out, enjoying long-run profits higher than they would be if the rivals were permitted to survive.

Firms practicing predatory behavior may be distinguished from other firms along a variety of dimensions. As Sullivan observes, in contrast to the aggressive competitor,

> the predator seeks not to win the field by greater efficiency, better services, or lower prices reflective of cost savings or modest profits. The predatory firm tries to inhibit others in ways independent of the predator's own ability to perform effectively in the market. Its price reduction is calculated to impose losses on other firms, not to garner gains for itself.[76]

---

[75] Neale and Goyder, op. cit., p. 55.

[76] Sullivan, op. cit., p. 111.

There are numerous forms of predatory behavior, such as "predatory investment" in new products, "excessive" promotional spending, "excessive" product variation, and price discrimination.[77] Here we will address only predatory
pricing. In the next section of this chapter, attention is turned to discriminatory pricing. The other forms of predation are included in the general discussion
of monopoly and monopolization in a later chapter.

Classic Cases

The most famous case of alleged predatory pricing was *Standard Oil Company
of New Jersey* v. *U.S.,*[78] which involved the petroleum trust set in motion and
directed by John D. Rockefeller. The Court found that Standard Oil's growth
had occurred primarily from acquisitions of competitors, its pressure on railroads for illegal rebates, its reliance on espionage, and its practice of predatory
pricing, including price warfare waged both overtly and secretly through bo-
gus independent distributors. Standard Oil cut prices sharply in specific local
markets where there was competition while holding prices at much higher levels in markets lacking competition with the goal of softening up its rivals until
they were receptive to merger offers. In the Supreme Court's decision, Chief
Justice White stressed that Standard Oil's power had not been built up "as a
result of normal methods of industrial development, but by new means of
combination which were resorted to in order that greater power might be added. . . ." The whole record demonstrated "the purpose of excluding others
from the trade, and thus centralizing in the combination a perpetual control of
the movements of petroleum and its products in the channels of interstate
commerce." By engaging in a wide variety of sharp practices, the Standard Oil
Trust between 1870 and 1899 attained and maintained a 90 percent share of
the U.S. petroleum refining industry.

In the *Standard Oil* case, the Court articulated its position that the crime of
monopolization involves two elements: (1) the acquisition of a monopoly position and (2) the *intent* to acquire that position and exclude rivals from the industry. It also stated that the essential element of intent could be inferred if
the acts in question unduly restrained competition by going beyond normal
business practice. In *Standard Oil* and in the first *American Tobacco* case,[79]
which immediately followed, the Court examined the defendants' business

---

[77] See Phillip Areeda and Donald F. Turner, *Predatory Pricing and Related Practices under Section 2 of the
Sherman Act,* Harvard L. R. 88 (1975), pp. 720–732. Sullivan, op. cit., p. 113, indicates that the following practices have also been held to be predatory: (1) the action of a newspaper publisher in forcing advertisers to boycott a radio station before it would sell advertising space to them; (2) the repeated expenditure of excessive sums
for advertising upon the introduction of a series of new bread products; (3) the selective payment of excessive
prices for supplies; (4) the obtaining of a controlling interest in a potential competitor in order to vote the stock
to exclude the competitor from monopolized market; and (5) sales by a vertically integrated firm at an excessively high price, so that buyers who compete with its own operations at the next vertical level will not be able to
do so efficiently.

[78] 221 U.S. 1 (1911).

[79] *U.S.* v. *American Tobacco Co.,* 221 U.S. 106 (1911). The 1946 *American Tobacco* case was referenced when
discussing parallel pricing.

methods for gaining power "solely as an aid for discovering (their) intent and purpose." The difference between lawful and unlawful activity by a business with monopoly power was the presence of a "positive drive" for monopolization. Among other activities, American Tobacco had frequently established "fighting brands" that were sold in rivals' local markets at less than cost and on at least one occasion at an effective after-tax price of zero, forcing competitors to sell out. In many cases, the acquired plants were promptly closed down. Such practices were, to the Court, clear evidence of illegal monopolistic intent.

Standard Oil and *American Tobacco* are clearly the dominant cases involving predatory pricing, even though they were decided over 70 years ago. The issue of predatory pricing has been raised in numerous cases since that time. Perhaps the most notorious modern cases have been those brought against IBM by a number of its smaller rivals.[80] In each of these cases, the courts found that IBM was entitled to adopt normal business practices to defend its market share against competitors. For example, in the *Telex* case, which is representative of the others, the plaintiff was a supplier of peripheral equipment to owners or lessees of central processing units produced by IBM and, up to 1970, had been able to offer it at a price below that charged by IBM. IBM reacted to the competition from Telex by making substantial cuts in its own selling prices on various peripheral items and by offering discounts to customers who leased equipment from them for a fixed term of one or two years. It was found that IBM's price cuts still resulted in prices that yielded IBM reasonable profits (i.e., a 20 percent return on sales) and were not therefore "predatory." Each of its products supported itself without cross-subsidization. Thus, IBM's response to competition was held to be "conduct well within the boundaries of permitted competition."

Controversy over Predatory Pricing

There is tremendous controversy among scholars in law and economics with regard to the appropriate way to judge the legality of alleged predatory pricing.[81] Several points at issue underlie the controversy. First, there is the difficult task of distinguishing monopoly intent from the permissible business

---

[80] *Telex Corporation* v. *International Business Machines Corporation,* 510 F.2d 894 (10th Cir. 1975); *ILC Peripherals Leasing Corporation* v. *International Business Machines Corporation,* 458 F. Supp. 423 (N.D. Cal. 1978); *California Computer Products* v. *International Business Machines Corporation,* ATRR A-1 (9th Cir. 1979). However, IBM settled a case instigated by Control Data Corporation giving up, as part of the settlement, its service bureau division. In this situation, it is possible that IBM would have lost the case as a result of the predatory practices alleged of it by Control Data.

[81] Perhaps the most well known of the articles on this subject are the following: John S. McGee, *Predatory Price Cutting: The Standard Oil (N.J.) Case.* J. of L. and E. 1 (Oct. 1958), pp. 137–169; Areeda and Turner, op. cit., pp. 697–733; F. M. Scherer, *Predatory Pricing and the Sherman Act: A Comment,* Harvard L. R. 89 (1976), pp. 869–890; Phillip Areeda and Donald F. Turner, *Scherer on Predatory Pricing: A Reply,* Harvard L. R. 89 (1976), pp. 891–900; F. M. Scherer, "Some Last Words on Predatory Pricing," *Harvard Law Review* 89 (1976), pp. 901–903; Oliver E. Williamson, "Predatory Pricing: A Strategic and Welfare Analysis," *Yale Law Journal* 87 (1977), pp. 284–340.

activity of a firm with massive market power. For example, as Gellhorn indicates,

> a firm could seek to retain monopoly power by predatory pricing, i.e., pricing below its own (and probably its competitors') marginal costs and forcing competitors out of business. What may appear to be predatory pricing to its rivals, however, may in fact be only a competitive pricing response by the monopolist when its costs are significantly lower.[82]

The problem is that with no constraint at all, or a relatively "loose" constraint against predatory pricing, there is the risk that some instances of undesirable predation will go unprosecuted. (This would be called an error of omission or type II error in statistical terminology.) This situation results in the persistence of monopolies and the kind of deadweight loss from resource misallocation usually associated with monopoly pricing.[83] The risks of this kind of error can be reduced by making the constraint against predation tighter (e.g., by prohibiting any price reduction by a monopolist). However, an overly strict constraint will run the risk that genuinely desirable behavior will be prosecuted or deterred. (The error of mistakenly stopping desirable behavior is called an error of commission or type I error.) An optimal rule would reflect the impact of these conflicting forces as well as other elements, such as pure administrative costs, associated with any particular choice of constraint.[84]

Second, an extensive literature seeks to show that predatory pricing is not an effective method of monopolizing.[85] Scholars have questioned whether it is rational for a dominant firm to practice predatory pricing. Given the dominant firm's larger volume of production, it would lose more money during the period of predation than would an equally efficient victim. At the very least, this condition would require that the dominant firm have a substantial amount of resources (a "deep pocket") in order to ride out the period of substantial losses. Even in that situation, the victim, realizing that the predator was losing substantial sums of money, would only need to locate a wealthy "parent" to help it ride out the storm. And even if the predation did succeed in eliminating the victim, it would not be profitable unless the dominant firm could then recoup its temporary losses by charging a monopoly price for some period of time. As Hay has observed,

> this situation requires that there be barriers to entry, and if one firm could enter, there is a strong likelihood that others would be poised to do so as well once the prices were raised back to super-competitive levels. Moreover, since the victim's assets are physically intact, they would presumably be available to be put

---

[82] Gellhorn, op. cit., p. 136. See *Telex Corporation* v. *International Business Machines Corporation*, op. cit., for an illustration of this pricing dilemma.

[83] For a discussion of the economist's concept of deadweight loss, see Scherer, *Industrial Market Structure and Economic Performance*, op. cit., pp. 17–18 and Posner, op. cit., pp. 6–14.

[84] George A. Hay, "A Confused Lawyer's Guide to the Predatory Pricing Literature," in Steven C. Salop (ed.), *Strategy, Predation, and Antitrust Analysis* (Washington, D.C.: Federal Trade Commission, Sept. 1981), p. 167.

[85] Most of this literature is cited in B. S. Yamey, "Predatory Price Cutting: Notes and Comments," *Journal of Law and Economics* 15 (1972), 129–147.

back into action at the first opportunity, either by the victim or by a firm to whom the assets had been sold.[86]

Third, under real-world business conditions, motives may be mixed and practices ambiguous. A price below average or marginal cost may be set for promotional purposes or because it is the best price that can be obtained. It may be difficult to differentiate the transaction that has a significant predatory thrust from that which represents the honest industrial effort of a competitor to deal with the market forces confronting it. Direct evidence of predatory intent will usually be difficult to uncover.

Nevertheless, theoretical economic analysis indicates that pricing below one's own cost to drive out rivals can under some conditions maximize long-run profits. For example, additional analysis has suggested that Standard Oil pursued a sophisticated region-by-region pricing strategy designed to ward off entry by potential competitors.[87] It may pay a firm to absorb losses in one of its markets even beyond what it could ever recoup in order to establish a credible threat that it will pursue the same policy in any market in which an entrant appears. As Hay points out,

> To make this model work requires only good information (i.e., the story of the predation in the first market has to be communicated to the future would-be entrants) and some nontrivial costs of entry and exit (so that unsuccessful entry attempts are not costless).[88]

Even though it may be rare, it is likely that some firms do, on occasion, attempt to drive out or keep out other firms from their markets by predatory, unremunerative (at least in the short-run) behavior.[89] There is a need to police such behavior, but, in doing so, courts in predatory pricing cases have, as Areeda and Turner observe, "generally turned to such empty formulae as 'below cost' pricing, ruinous competition, or predatory intent in adjudicating liability. These standards provide little, if any, basis for analyzing the predatory pricing offense."[90] Therefore, a number of standards have been proposed by a variety of legal scholars, and, in some cases, these standards have applied in actual court cases. Among the proposed standards are the following:[91]

1. No prohibition on pricing at all.
2. Cost-based rules (e.g., Areeda and Turner define as predatory pricing those policies that yield returns below average variable or marginal cost, whichever is lower).[92]

---

[86] Hay, op. cit., pp. 159–160.

[87] Scherer, *Industrial Market Structure . . .* , op. cit., pp. 338 and 528.

[88] Hay, op. cit., pp. 160–161.

[89] A clear-cut example is found in the Supreme Court's decision in *Moore* v. *Mead's Fine Bread Co.,* 348 U.S. 115 (1954), where the seller cut the price of bread in half and this was found to have led to the destruction of a competitor's business.

[90] Areeda and Turner, "Predatory Prices . . . ," op. cit., p. 699.

[91] This list is based on the summary found in Hay, op. cit. pp. 200–201. For more details about and insights into these rules, see Joseph F. Brodley and George A. Hay, *Predatory Pricing: Competing Economic Theories and the Evaluation of Legal Standards,* Cornell L. R. 66 (Apr. 1981), pp. 738–803.

[92] Areeda and Turner, "Predatory Prices . . . ," op. cit.

3. Cost-based rules with provision for exception under certain well-defined circumstances[e.g., in the *Memorex* case, the court rejected IBM's argument that prices may be predatory *only* when they are below marginal or average variable cost (i.e., the Areeda–Turner test). It stated that it would not rule out the possibility of predation where prices were below *total* costs if the evidence pointed to the defendant's *intent* to drive out competitors.][93]
4. Non-cost-based rules (e.g., Williamson's output rule, which would prohibit the dominant firm from increasing output beyond the pre-entry level in response to entry).[94]
5. Ad hoc rules based on inquiry into the long-run welfare implications of pricing behavior in a specific situation (e.g., Scherer believes that such an inquiry might utilize internal evidence of the dominant firm's intent).[95]

In a relatively large number of predatory pricing cases brought during the late 1970s and early 1980s by private parties, several federal appellate judges have adopted the Areeda–Turner test (no. 2 above), making it part of the law for all the district courts in their circuits.[96] For example, in 1977, the Court of Appeals for the 10th Circuit, based in Denver, dismissed a complaint against Kerr–McGee, a diversified chemical company.[97] The complaint had been filed by Pacific Engineering & Production Co., a small firm whose only product was a chemical used in solid-fuel rockets. As a result of severe overcapacity for the chemical, a price-cutting war had broken out, with Kerr–McGee bidding well below its total costs and undercutting Pacific, even though a Kerr–McGee study predicted that Pacific would not survive at the low price levels. Evidence also indicated that Kerr–McGee had taken periodic aerial photographs of Pacific's plant, that an executive of Kerr–McGee had offered a nonexistent "surplus" of the chemical to a Pacific customer at an even lower price, and that Kerr–McGee's future price schedules indicated an intent to raise prices after Pacific's expected demise. Ruling on Pacific's complaint, the court wrote that it found the Areeda–Turner test "extremely valuable" in determining predatory pricing. It then noted that Kerr–McGee's prices had been above variable costs and ruled that the antitrust laws had not been violated.

If the Areeda–Turner test holds, it will mean that marketing executives can breathe relatively easy, because, if they are only required to cover their firms' average variable costs (e.g., short-run expenditures for labor and materials), they can enact very deep price cuts (especially if their firms have high fixed costs) and still stay within the realm of "reasonable" (in contrast to "predatory") pricing. However, the *Memorex* decision (no. 3 above) gave indications that intent might be brought into the picture by some courts, permitting a

---

[93] *ILC Peripherals Leasing Corporation* v. *International Business Machines Corporation*, op. cit.

[94] Williamson, op. cit.

[95] Scherer, "Predatory Pricing . . . ," op. cit.

[96] See William M. Carley, "Laws Against 'Predatory Pricing' by Firms Are Being Relaxed by Many Court Rulings," *Wall Street Journal*, July 14, 1982, p. 46. For discussion and relevant citations, see James D. Hurwitz et al., "Current Legal Standards of Predation," in Steven C. Salop (ed.), op. cit., pp. 101–53 and especially 146–48.

[97] *Pacific Engineering and Production Company of Nevada* v. *Kerr–McGee Corp.*, 551 F.2d 790 (10th Cir.), *cert. denied*, 434 U.S. 977 (1977).

broader definition of predatory behavior. In fact, there really is no consensus on this issue, and the controversy rages on.[98]

Sales-below-Cost Laws

Although emphasis in this text is on federal legislation as interpreted by the courts and enforced by the federal antitrust agencies, it is germane to mention here that about 26 states have sales-below-cost laws (sometimes called unfair sales acts or unfair trade practices acts) that seek to protect firms in all industries from competitors who might sell products or services at less than cost. In addition, over 30 states have sales-below-cost laws applying to *specific* goods, such as cigarettes, milk, and other dairy products. Cost is usually defined in such a way as to cover invoice or replacement cost, whichever is lower, plus a markup to cover the costs of operation including overhead. These laws are intended to prevent predatory pricing. For example, Maine's Unfair Sales Act, which is fairly typical of the general statutes, requires firms, particularly retailers, to charge a margin of at least 5.75 percent above invoice cost for all goods except damaged or deteriorated items. Lower prices may be charged, however, on clear proof that the cost of doing business is less than 5.75 percent.

The state minimum markup laws do not make sales-below-cost illegal per se. They declare it unlawful to advertise, offer to sell, or sell goods below cost only where the intent, or the effect, is to injure competitors and destroy competition. The specific wording of a state law is, however, crucial as to what constitutes statutory presumptions, prima facie evidence, and necessary evidence or proof.[99] And most of the state laws permit selling below cost if done in good faith to meet the price of a competitor.

DISCRIMINATORY PRICING

Basically, discriminatory pricing is selling or purchasing different units of the same commodity at price differentials not directly related to differences in the cost of supply.[100] Such pricing is circumscribed by the Robinson–Patman Act of 1936, which amended Section 2 of the Clayton Act of 1914. Pressure for enactment of a strong price-discrimination law came from relatively small wholesalers and retailers during the Great Depression, who complained that larger rivals were obtaining preferential treatment from suppliers. The argument was made that, if a large firm can purchase supplies at more favorable terms than its smaller rivals, it holds a competitive advantage. The favored

---

[98] For example, see Paul L. Joskow and Alvin K. Klevorick, "A Framework for Analyzing Predatory Pricing Policy," *Yale Law Journal* 89 (1979), pp. 213–270. See, also, William M. Carley, "Ruling in AT&T–MCI Case Indicates Courts' Confusion on Predatory Pricing," *Wall Street Journal*, Jan. 21, 1983, p. 7, and *MCI Communications Corp.* v. *American Telephone and Telegraph Co.*, 44 ATRR 112 (7th Cir., Jan. 20, 1983).

[99] Marshall C. Howard, *Legal Aspects of Marketing* (New York: McGraw-Hill Book Co., 1964), pp. 45–46.

[100] Scherer, *Industrial Market Structure . . .* , op. cit., p. 571.

companies may be able to establish prices that are profitable for them but unprofitable for smaller firms that must pay more for inputs.

Without question, the Robinson–Patman Act is one of the most confusing,
complicated, and questionable pieces of antitrust legislation ever passed by the
U.S. Congress.[101] It has been attacked for discouraging price competition and
promoting price uniformity. There is virtual unanimity among students of the
act that its motivation was a desire to limit competition, not enhance it. In a
Supreme Court decision rendered in 1952, Justice Jackson described the act as
"complicated and vague in itself and even more so in its context. Indeed, the
Court of Appeals seems to have thought it almost beyond understanding."[102]
His observation is no less valid today than it was three decades ago. Because
of the confusion surrounding the act, its significance in antitrust enforcement
has faded. Although it was once the basis for numerous actions by the Federal
Trade Commission, few government-initiated actions are now brought under
it.[103] Nevertheless, the act cannot be dismissed as unimportant. As Gellhorn
points out, its rule influences almost all pricing decisions of every major business in the country, and *private* treble damage actions are often founded on it.[104]

In this chapter we focus primarily on the major section [i.e., Section 2(a)]
of the act and those additional sections that are directly related from a pricing
policy perspective. We return to a discussion of additional aspects of the act
(i.e., those having to do with brokerage fees, functional discounts, and promotional allowances) in Chapters 6 and 7. To understand the pricing implications
of the act, it is, however, necessary to dissect Section 2(a), which states:

> It shall be unlawful for any person engaged in commerce . . . either directly or
> indirectly, to *discriminate in price* between *different purchasers* of *commodities of
> like grade and quality,* where either or any of the purchases involved in such dis-
> crimination are in commerce, where such commodities are *sold* for use, consump-
> tion, or resale within . . . [any area] . . . under the jurisdiction of the United
> States, and where the effect of such discrimination may be to *substantially lessen
> competition* or tend to create a monopoly in any line of commerce, or to injure,
> destroy, or prevent competition with any person who either grants or *knowingly
> receives* the benefit of such discrimination, or with customers of either of them.

We have taken the liberty of italicizing various words and phrases in Section
2(a) because we believe that each demands special explanation. In addition,
the act also specifies that price discrimination may be justified if (1) it is carried out to dispose of perishable or obsolete goods, or under a closeout or
bankruptcy sale; (2) it merely makes due allowance for differences in "the cost
of manufacture, sale, or delivery resulting from the differing methods or quantities" in which the commodity is sold or delivered; or (3) it is affected "in

---

[101] See Corwin D. Edwards, *The Price Discrimination Law* (Washington, D.C.: The Brookings Institution,
1959); and Frederick M. Rowe, *Price Discrimination under the Robinson–Patman Act* (Boston: Little, Brown &
Co., 1962).

[102] *FTC* v. *Ruberoid Co.,* 343 U.S. 470 at 483 (1952).

[103] Gellhorn, op. cit., p. 364.

[104] Ibid., p. 366.

good faith to meet an equally low price of a competitor." We also address each of the latter two justifications. It should be pointed out at the outset, however, that because many of the cases brought under the Robinson–Patman Act have been disposed of by consent order and other informal processes, the legal principles now regarded as applicable have been established in relatively few litigated cases.[105]

Discriminate in Price

The term "discriminate in price" is not defined in the Robinson–Patman Act. In the *Anheuser–Busch* case,[106] the Supreme Court interpreted it to mean *any* price differential, although in an earlier case, the Court looked for "substantial" price differentials.[107] Price differentials, the Court reasoned, harm the position of companies that buy at higher prices, and thus harm competition. When price differentials exist, the seller may, however, avoid liability by showing that the lower price was available to all purchasers, including the purchaser claiming injury.[108] But the Court has required that, in addition to the implied offer, there must also be functional availability as well. For example, in *FTC* v. *Morton Salt Company*,[109] the defendant had offered a 6 percent discount to all purchasers who bought in carload quantities. To obtain the highest possible discount, though, required such massive cumulative purchases of salt over the course of a year that the discounts were, in actuality, only available to a few large companies. The Court ruled that, in light of the lack of functional availability, Morton was guilty of price discrimination.

Different Purchasers

Liability does not occur under the act unless there are at least two *actual* sales or contracts for sale. A sale to one buyer and an offer to another at a different price will not constitute discrimination in price between different purchasers.[110] In addition, the act does not apply to leases where the lease does not envision a sale. A lease agreement containing an option to purchase may, however, be within the purview of the act.

In situations where vertical integration is involved, it is unlikely that the courts will view transfers among divisions as separate "purchasers." But it is possible that transfers that are, in actuality, arms-length bargains struck between *separate* sales subsidiaries within the same corporation will be scrutinized as to their possible discriminatory effect.[111] In these cases, the status of

---

[105] Neale and Goyder, op. cit., p. 215.

[106] *Anheuser–Busch, Inc.* v. *FTC,* 289 F.2d 835 (7th Cir., 1961).

[107] *FTC* v. *Morton Salt Co.,* 334 U.S. 37 (1948).

[108] Rowe, op. cit., p. 97.

[109] 334 U.S. 37 (1948).

[110] *Bruce's Juices, Inc.* v. *American Can Co.,* 330 U.S. 743 (1947).

[111] James Rahl and Ronald Kennedy, *Cases and Materials on Antitrust Law,* Northwestern University School of Law, Multilith, 1981.

the subsidiaries as purchasers will be determined on the basis of an examination of intrafirm procedures, corporate policies, and the amount of control that the parent has over the subsidiaries.

Commodities of Like Grade and Quality . . . Are Sold

Discriminatory pricing is scrutinized under the Robinson–Patman Act only if the actual *sale* of *goods* or commodities is involved; there are no provisions in the act addressing the sale of *services*. Promotional services themselves can be discriminatory when provided differentially to purchasers of commodities. These latter regulations concerning marketing strategy imposed by Section 2(e) of the act will be addressed in Chapter 7.

Where products are of different materials or workmanship levels, they are not ordinarily considered to be of "like grade and quality," but where the differences are small and do not affect the basic use of the goods, then selling at price differentials has been attacked. For example, the Supreme Court ruled in 1966 that the Borden Company had engaged in price discrimination by selling physically homogeneous canned evaporated milk at two prices, one for cans sold under the Borden label and a lower price for cans sold under private labels to retail food chains.[112] The Court believed that "perceived" product differentiation failed to constitute an "actual" difference in grade and quality under the act's interpretation. The impact of this case for marketing practice might have been profound had not an appellate court ruled on remand that no injury to competition resulted if "a price differential between a premium and nonpremium brand reflects no more than a consumer preference for the premium brand," since it merely represents "a rough equivalent of the benefit by way of the seller's national advertising and promotion which the purchaser of the more expensive branded product enjoys."[113] This latter ruling appears to endorse the efficacy of subjective consumer preferences influenced by promotion as a justification for price differentials. However, it should be carefully noted that such a ruling, as Scherer points out, "appears logically inconsistent with the Supreme Court's condemnation of such differentials in the Clorox merger case," discussed earlier in this text.[114]

The difference in consumers' perceptions of brands extends beyond the private label versus national brand area. When Anheuser–Busch lowered the price of its "premium" beer (Budweiser) to compete more intensively with "nonpremium" beers, such as Falstaff, in St. Louis in an attempt to induce more purchases from a retail chain, the court viewed the new price as under-

---

[112] *FTC* v. *Borden Co.,* 383 U.S. 637 (1966).

[113] *Borden Co.* v. *FTC,* 381 F.2d 175 at 181 (1967). This court also noted that Borden's private label milk was available to all buyers; this meant that the price differential between regular and private label brands could not substantially lessen competition. The Supreme Court had emphasized this availability concept in its 1966 decision.

[114] Scherer, *Industrial Market Structure . . . ,* op. cit., p. 575n. See Chapter 4 of this text for a discussion of the Clorox merger case. Scherer also observes, in the same footnote referred to here, that "Robinson–Patman Act interpretations have never been distinguished for their consistency with the other antitrust laws."

cutting the price of the nonpremium brands, even though Budweiser's price was meeting and not beating the nonpremium price.[115] Perceived differences were viewed by the court as evidence of an actual difference in grade and quality, even though the beers were physically identical. Anheuser–Busch's pricing behavior could not, therefore, be justified by the "meeting competition" defense outlined later in this chapter.

Substantially Lessen Competition

The Robinson–Patman Act prohibits discrimination only when the effect may be to lessen competition substantially. The act does not make discriminatory pricing illegal per se. There is, however, considerable controversy about whether the act and related court rulings have been more protective of competition or of competitors. Most scholars, both economic and legal, seem to agree with a position close to the one articulated by Asch:

> it seems fair to observe that the courts have made little inquiry into the competitive implications of price discrimination or nondiscriminatory price differences. In place of inquiry and analysis the courts have substituted an assumption: if differentials in price give some competitors an advantage over others, harm to competition is implied. In other words, a price difference that hurts one or more *competitors* is interpreted as hurting *competition.*[116]

The courts and the FTC have tended to hold to the view that evidence of predatory intent to destroy a *competitor* can help determine whether *competition* itself is being injured. Such an intent might be inferred by sustained below-cost selling. Other factors to consider are the number of firms in the market and the market share of the discriminating seller.[117]

Predatory pricing is, as we have already seen, circumscribed by Section 2 of the Sherman Act. Why, then, is there need for another law that seemingly does the same thing? An explanation is provided by Sullivan:

> [Section 2 of the Sherman Act] . . . forbids such discriminations where used by a firm with monopoly power or by a firm which, by use of these along with other devices, threatens to attain such power. The Robinson–Patman provision amplifies Section 2 of Sherman by making such conduct unlawful because of its threat to competitors even when it is used by a firm that neither possesses monopoly power nor is close enough to possessing it to be caught by the ["attempt to monopolize"] concept [of Section 2].[118]

Despite the frequent focus on *competitors,* the courts have ruled that *competition* and not injury to competitors is a critical factor in determining the legality or illegality of price discrimination.[119] The injury to competition need not

---

[115] *Anheuser–Busch, Inc.* v. *FTC,* op. cit.

[116] Peter Asch, *Economic Theory and the Antitrust Dilemma* (New York: John Wiley & Sons, Inc., 1970), p. 344.

[117] Howard, op. cit., p. 55.

[118] Sullivan, op. cit., p. 684.

[119] For example, see Anheuser–Busch, op. cit.

be actual to be unlawful, but a remote possibility of injury is not sufficient for illegality. Because of the requirement of injury to competition, a time and space dimension must be applied in price discrimination cases. In one case, for example, a sulfur producer had a 10-year contract with a fertilizer manufacturer to supply a fixed quantity of sulfur every year at a specified price or at the price charged to the fertilizer firm's competitors, whichever was lower. In times of high prices, the stipulated price was lower than that charged to other customers. Therefore, the sulfur firm attempted to have the contract declared illegal as unlawful price discrimination. The court ruled that the lower price was legal so long as the other firms were offered the same prices and terms at the time the contract was made.[120]

Injury to any of three levels of competition may bring price discrimination under the prohibition of the Robinson–Patman Act.

Primary Level.

The bulk of case law under the Robinson–Patman Act focuses on the harm that price discrimination may do to competition between powerful and less powerful buyers. There are still important cases, however, in which the contention is that a supplier uses price discrimination as a weapon against his own competitors. Thus, competition between two sellers (primary level) may be injured when one of them gives discriminatory prices to some customers. This was the situation in the *Utah Pie* case.[121] The Utah Pie Company was a local concern that sold its frozen pies in Salt Lake City at low prices due to its low costs. It had 66 percent of the market. Several national concerns (Continental, Pet Milk, and Carnation) competed with Utah Pie in Salt Lake City by cutting their prices below what they charged in other markets. In some cases, these prices were below average total cost (including overhead allowances). The Supreme Court ruled that the evidence in the case was sufficient for a jury to decide that Continental, Pet, and Carnation had engaged in predatory tactics and whether competition had been lessened, even though over the 4-year period of competitive activity Utah's market share had declined only to 45 percent, the Utah market for frozen pies had grown 500 percent, and the company's sales and earnings had expanded. On remand, the court affirmed a judgment in favor of Utah Pie.

Since the *Utah Pie* decision, there has been continuing controversy over the circumstances under which injury to primary level competition can reasonably be found and over the closely related question of what constitutes predatory pricing under both the Robinson–Patman Act and Section 2 of the Sherman Act. Some of the rules suggested by the debate over this issue were outlined in the preceding section on predatory pricing. For example, during the 1970s two

[120] *Texas Gulf Sulphur Co.* v. *J. R. Simplot Co.*, 418 F.2d 793 (9th Cir. 1969).

[121] *Utah Pie Company* v. *Continental Baking Co.*, 386 U.S. 685 (1967). Another important case here is *L. L. Moore* v. *Mead's Fine Bread Company*, 348 U.S. 115 (1954), where Mead cut its wholesale price in Moore's market area but nowhere else, forcing Moore out of business.

appellate court decisions[122] rejected Robinson–Patman primary level injury claims, stressing, among other things, that prices had not been cut below marginal or average variable cost, the test of predation advocated by Areeda and Turner.[123] Nevertheless, the Federal Trade Commission has historically insisted that a full or total cost test be applied, including prorated overhead, and not merely a marginal or average variable cost test.

Secondary Level.

Competition between two customers of a seller may be affected if the seller differentiates between them in price. In effect the seller is aiding one customer and harming the other in their mutual competition, and this is sufficient to cause substantial lessening of competition. The effect on competition between buyers generally arises through the ability of the favored buyer to lower his selling prices and draw customers away from the disfavored buyer. This is not always straightforward, however, as the circumstances in the *Morton Salt* case proved.[124] The commodity involved, salt, constituted a very small percentage of the assortment of goods carried by a retail store. Price competition on salt would not seem to be very influential in determining consumer patronage. Yet, the Supreme Court found that, in this circumstance, Robinson–Patman Act protection could be provided by applying it to each individual article, because food store sales consist of numerous small items. On the other hand, where the product sold under the discriminatory price is only a small component part of a total product being produced by the buyer and is found to play only a minor role in determining the price of the total product, the required effect on competition may be lacking.[125]

The Robinson–Patman Act has also been employed to impede delivered pricing or basing-point schemes. Previously in this chapter, it was shown how such schemes might be an instrument of industry-wide collusion to avoid price competition. However, even if successfully brought, such cases pose an enforcement problem, because there is nothing to prevent individual firms in an industry from continuing tacitly to apply the established formula in their pricing decisions without any further collusion.[126] To combat this problem, the Federal Trade Commission seized upon the fact that, within them, delivered pricing mechanisms have an element of price discrimination. Thus, it could be reasoned that the essence of price discrimination is that customers are treated differently. This condition is present regardless of whether only freight absorption, only phantom freight, or both, exist in a pricing system.

Freight absorption is a situation where a seller charges less than his full

---

[122] *International Air Industries, Inc.* v. *American Excelsior Co.*, 517 F.2d 714 (1975) and *Pacific Engineering & Production Co. of Nevada* v. *Kerr–McGee Corp. et al.*, 551 F.2d 790 (1977), *cert. denied*, 434 U.S. 879 (1977).

[123] Areeda and Turner, op. cit.

[124] *FTC* v. *Morton Salt Co.*, op. cit.

[125] *Minneapolis–Honeywell Regulator Co.* v. *FTC*, 191 F.2d 76 (7th Cir. 1951).

[126] Neale and Goyder, op. cit., p. 245.

cost of transporting merchandise to a buyer in order to remain competitive with other sellers who are located closer to the buyer. (For example, Republic Steel located in Cleveland, Ohio, may "absorb freight" in order to win a customer in Chicago who can purchase its requirements from U.S. Steel located close by in Gary, Indiana.) Phantom freight is charged when the amount charged a customer for freight includes a surplus over the actual freight cost. (In the preceding example, if Cleveland, Ohio, were a basing point from which delivered prices are calculated and if U.S. Steel agreed to the basing-point formula, then U.S. Steel's customers in Chicago would be charged the freight costs from Cleveland, not from Gary. The difference between the freight costs it would actually incur and the freight costs it charges would be *phantom freight.*) If phantom freight is charged to some, those who are charged are treated less favorably than those who are not. But if freight is absorbed for some, those for whom it is *not* absorbed are similarly treated in a worse fashion than those for whom it is.[127] This reasoning served as the foundation for the decisions in the Glucose cases,[128] where it was shown that if geographic pricing of the basing-point variety results in major cost advantages for buyers (e.g., candy manufacturers) near the point, it is not only discriminatory but it is also likely to lessen competition substantially within the meaning of the law.

Since the Glucose cases, all delivered pricing cases have involved issues of collusive price fixing.[129] As Neale and Goyder observe,

> It seems unlikely that the use of the Robinson–Patman Act to reinforce these cases has been of real advantage in enforcement, and for this reason it may well be abandoned. In the end no legal rule has emerged that prevents the individual supplier from quoting delivered prices by reference to basing-points. In the absence of collusion, he may invade the "natural" markets of other suppliers and by "absorbing" freight meet the competition of the going price in these markets.[130]

Here it appears the Robinson–Patman Act has not been able to provide a shield to competitors from bona fide competition.

Tertiary Level.

If a manufacturer discriminates in prices between two wholesalers such that the customers of one wholesaler are favored over those of the other, competition is being injured by the price discrimination. For example, in *Standard Oil Co. v. FTC,*[131] Standard sold gasoline to large wholesalers (jobbers) and to retailers (service stations) directly. The jobbers bought in tank-car loads (8,000

---

[127] Asch, op. cit., p. 337.

[128] *Corn Products Refining Co.* v. *FTC,* 324 U.S. 726 (1945) and *FTC* v. *A. E. Staley Mfg. Co.,* 324 U.S. 746 (1945).

[129] For example, Weyerhaeuser Co., Georgia–Pacific Corp., and Willamette Industries were, in 1981, found guilty of charging "phantom" freight rates as part of a conspiracy to maintain high prices. See Kathryn Christensen, "Three Plywood Companies Lose Appeal of Antitrust Verdict on 'Phantom' Rates," *Wall Street Journal,* Sept. 9, 1981, p. 48.

[130] Neale and Goyder, op. cit., p. 248.

[131] 340 U.S. 231 (1950).

to 12,000 gallons), and the service stations bought in tank-wagon loads (700 to 800 gallons). The jobbers purchased the gasoline at $1^1/2¢$ per gallon less than the stations; hence, the jobbers could sell gas to their retail stations at prices less than the other retail stations who received their gas directly from Standard. Competition was affected at the tertiary or retail level because of Standard's discriminatory pricing.

Cost Justification Defense

If it can be shown that a price difference does or is likely to substantially lessen competition, then this finding constitutes a prima facie case under the Robinson–Patman Act. But the defendant is permitted to show that the price difference was due to differences in cost arising from different quantities sold or different methods of sale or delivery and hence that it was a justifiable difference and not an unlawful discrimination. The burden of proof is on the seller. For example, Morton Salt might have escaped the charge of price discrimination had it been able to show that its various discounts (including the largest cumulative quantity discount) made "only due allowance" for reduced costs of selling to the larger customers.

The principal drawback of the cost justification defense is the difficulty of demonstrating or proving the cost saving. First, the burden of proving it falls on the seller. Second, this burden generally requires a complete cost study;[132] conjectures of experts are usually considered inadequate. Third, it is far from an easy matter to define the applicable "cost." Using the *Morton Salt* case[133] again, it would have been necessary to show not merely that lower prices to certain customers corresponded to lower selling costs, but that the price differentials were *precisely* matched by cost differentials. Such evidence is very difficult to derive. As Asch points out,

> A company may be aware that large-volume customers cost less per unit to serve. But precisely how much less—especially when the company distributes many products or when part of its gain is seen to be "better" planning and timing of deliveries—may be impossible to estimate.[134]

Mere estimates of cost, even supported by expert testimony, will generally not meet with FTC approval. The record shows that few firms have been able, in litigation, to justify price differences on the basis of cost.[135]

As difficult as it is to use the cost justification defense effectively, it would be even more difficult to use if a seller had to provide cost data concerning each individual buyer. The courts have recognized the right of sellers to group buyers into homogeneous categories that have significant cost differences from other categories. The classification must, however, be on the basis of those

[132] See *Automatic Canteen Co.* v. *FTC*, 346 U.S. 61 (1953).

[133] *FTC* v. *Morton Salt Co.,* op. cit.

[134] Asch, op. cit., p. 340.

[135] Howard, op. cit., p. 62.

cost differences and not reflect irrelevant organizational features such as ownership (e.g., chain stores versus independent stores).[136]

Because of their importance in pricing, it is important to understand that quantity discounts *are* permitted under Section 2(a) to the extent that they are justified by cost savings. Such discounts must usually reflect cost savings in deliveries made to one place at one time. This places limitations on the use of cumulative quantity discounts. And the cost justification defense is subject to a qualifying proviso under which the Federal Trade Commission may set quantity limits beyond which even cost-justified quantity discounts may not be granted. This constraint might be imposed if it can be determined that only a few very large buyers can qualify for the largest discount category in a seller's pricing schedule, as was the situation in the *Morton Salt* case.[137] Although the FTC may establish maximum discounts or quantity limits, its only attempt to use this power was unsuccessful because of a basic discrepancy between the FTC's order and the evidence on which it was based.[138]

Good Faith Defense

Section 2(b) of the Robinson–Patman Act allows a firm to charge lower prices to some of its customers than others if it is done "in good faith to meet an equally low price of a competitor." If good faith can be shown, the discrimination is not illegal even if there has been a substantial lessening of competition, but the burden of proving good faith falls on the defendant.

Several requirements must be met before the good faith defense can be employed:

The Price Being Met Must Be Lawful.

It cannot be produced by collusion nor can it be an unjustified discriminatory price offered by a competing seller. For example, the Supreme Court ruled in the *A. E. Staley Co.* case[139] (one of the previously mentioned Glucose cases) that the "good faith" defense could not apply when the prices met were themselves illegal, stemming from an illegal discriminatory system. (In this case, Staley had copied Corn Product's basing-point system so as to maintain pricing parity in the industry.) A seller does not have to prove the price he is meeting is lawful, but in order to be in good faith, as required, he must make some effort to find out if it is.[140]

The Price Must Be Met and Not Undercut.

Price reductions on a "premium" product to the level of "standard" products can be a form of illegal price discrimination. If the public is willing to

---

[136] *U.S.* v. *Borden Co.*, 350 U.S. 460 (1962).

[137] *FTC* v. *Morton Salt Co.*, op. cit.

[138] See *FTC* v. *B. F. Goodrich et al.*, 242 F.2d 31 (1957).

[139] *FTC* v. *A. E. Staley Mfg. Co.*, op. cit.

[140] Howard, op. cit., pp. 60–61.

pay a higher price for the "premium" product, the equal prices may be considered beating and not meeting competition.[141]

The requirement that a seller make an effort to ascertain whether his offered price meets or beats a competitor's lawful offer presents severe problems. In *U.S.* v. *United States Gypsum Co.,*[142] a case referred to earlier in this chapter during the discussion of exchanging price information, competing sellers who engaged in price verification were found to have violated Section 1 of the Sherman Act. The Supreme Court also held that the Robinson–Patman good faith defense did not require and could not justify direct price verification. In other words, the meeting competition defense is available even in the absence of absolute certainty by the seller as to the competitor's price. Nor is there any automatic obligation on the seller to verify reports of his competitors' prices if he has only "vague, generalized doubts" about the reliability of information given to him by his own customer.[143] This observation is buttressed by findings in a 1975 FTC case against A&P where the Supreme Court accepted Borden's discriminatory pricing as meeting competition "in good faith," even though Borden's reduced price was "a shot in the dark" based on limited information revealed by A&P about a competitive bid by another dairy seeking A&P's milk business.[144] In these cases, the Supreme Court has been concerned to avoid having the "good faith" defense used as a justification for collusion. However, this puts sellers in precarious positions. When, through experience in an industry, a seller has reason to doubt a reported competitor's price, the defense of meeting competition is unavailable, and yet direct verification is unlawful. He is caught between a rock and a hard place.

The Competition Being Met Must Be at the Primary Level.

Granting a discriminatory price to some customers to enable them to meet their own competition is not protected. The seller must be in actual competition with the other sellers who are making the lower prices available. Thus, Sun Oil Company could not grant discriminatory price concessions to certain franchised dealers to help them meet lower market prices in a gasoline price war they were facing. It was Sun's dealers' competitors, not its own competitors, who were cutting prices.[145]

The question of whether the good faith defense is applicable to gaining new customers as well as to retaining old customers is basically unsettled. The Federal Trade Commission has argued that a company is only allowed to grant price discriminations "in good faith" to retain old customers. However,

---

[141] See *Anheuser–Busch, Inc.* v. *FTC*, op. cit.

[142] 438 U.S. 422 (1978). Another issue in meeting prices has to do with geography. Falls City Industries, a brewer in Louisville Ky., charged lower prices in Kentucky than it did in Indiana. When sued by Vanco Beverage, one of its distributors in Indiana, the Supreme Court ruled that Falls City was entitled to show that it set its prices in order to meet competition on an area-wide basis and was not limited to defending its prices on a customer-by-customer basis. See *Falls CIty Industries, Inc, v Vanco Beverage, Inc.,*455 U.S. 988 (1982).

[143] Neale and Goyder, op. cit., p. 227.

[144] *Great Atlantic & Pacific Tea Co., Inc.* v. *FTC*, 99 U.S. 925 (1975).

[145] *FTC* v. *Sun Oil Co.,* 83 U.S. 358 (1963). Also, see Howard, op. cit., p. 57.

the 7th Circuit Court overruled this view in holding that the law does not distinguish old and new customers.[146]

Because of the difficulties encountered by companies in trying to apply both the cost justification and good faith defenses and the likelihood that, in certain instances, the act merely protects competitors from competition, it is little wonder that there has been considerable question about the act's ultimate value and equity.

Sales at "Unreasonably Low Prices"

Section 3 of the Robinson–Patman Act also attacks price discrimination, making it illegal to discriminate against competitors of a purchaser, to sell at prices lower in one part of the country, or to sell goods at "unreasonably low prices" for the purpose of destroying competition or eliminating a competitor. Section 3 is a criminal statute outside the jurisdiction of the Federal Trade Commission. It cannot be used as the basis for private treble-damage actions because it is technically not a part of the antitrust laws; as a result, it has largely lain dormant.[147] In one of the rare cases brought under Section 3, National Dairy Products Corporation was charged with having violated Section 3 by selling milk in certain markets at unreasonably low prices, utilizing its virtually nationwide presence in order to finance price wars against small dairies in certain towns.[148] The Court held that Section 3 is constitutional, notwithstanding the vagueness of its provisions. It also noted that the practice of making unjustifiable sales below cost has been a violation of the Sherman Act for years and that the legislative history of Section 3 shows that it was aimed at predatory pricing practices. But it also pointed out that sales at such low prices may be legitimate, such as when used to meet competition, clear out obsolete stocks, and so on. The prices attached to goods in these special circumstances would not cause an inference of predation and would not be unreasonably low.

Price Discrimination by Buyers

One of the main purposes of the Robinson–Patman amendments to the Clayton Act was to curb the power of the big buyer. One manifestation of that purpose is the prohibition of fees to "dummy" brokers, a constraint that will be discussed in Chapter 6. The main manifestation, however, was the inclusion of Section 2(f) of the act. Section 2(f) makes it illegal for a buyer "knowingly to induce or receive a discrimination in price" prohibited by other sections of the act. Because only those price discriminations that are prohibited by other sections can give rise to buyers' liability, Section 2(f) is totally derivative in nature. Where a seller has a defense that justifies a discriminatory price (e.g., one that is cost justified or made in good faith to meet competition), the buyer cannot be condemned for having "induced" the price discrimination.[149] The

---

[146] *Sunshine Biscuits, Inc.* v. *FTC,* 306 F.2d 48 (7th Cir. 1962).

[147] See Howard, op. cit., pp. 50–51.

[148] *U.S.* v. *National Dairy Products Corp.,* 372 U.S. 29 (1963).

plaintiff must prove that the buyer not only received illegal price concessions, but that it had good reason to believe the concessions were illegal.

Perhaps the most important recent case of this kind is one to which reference was made earlier, *Great Atlantic & Pacific Tea Co., Inc.* v. *FTC*.[150] In this case, A&P told its supplier, Borden, that a price offer from Borden's competitor, Bowman, was sufficiently attractive that "you [Borden] people . . . are not even in the ball park." To retain A&P's business, Borden submitted a new offer containing a large discount and informed A&P that it was pricing to meet the competitive bid, although it did not know the specifics of Bowman's offer. Borden implied that its discount was discriminatory and could not be cost justified. In fact, its bid not only met, but undercut, Bowman's offer, a fact that only A&P knew for certain. In its case against A&P, the FTC found that A&P had illegally induced discrimination. But when the case was appealed to the Supreme Court, the Court ruled that A&P had not acted illegally because Borden had had a valid defense to charges of price discrimination (i.e., it had acted in good faith to meet the imprecise competitive threat with which it was confronted). The Court held that A&P could not be held liable for violating Section 2(f) unless Borden's discriminatory prices were illegal. Otherwise, A&P would have no valid defense under other sections of the Robinson–Patman Act.[151]

What this convoluted and tortuous wording means is that the buyer who seeks and receives price concessions is clearly in the position of having "knowingly" induced differential prices, but, in order to defend himself, he must rely for his defense on the proposition that the differential was not an illegal discrimination. Under the Robinson–Patman Act, the only factors that can save the buyer from a violation are the supplier's cost savings or his good faith in meeting competition. Thus, the only way in which a buyer can be judged in violation of the act is if, in the process of the case, the seller is shown to have done something illegal as well. While it is possible to understand the reasoning underlying these kinds of rulings, it is also evident that the *A&P* case, along with those preceding it, is simply another chapter in the strange, strange saga of the act. As Neal and Goyder point out,

> Although Congress in passing the Robinson–Patman Act was exercised about the coercive use of buying power, the main provisions of the Act still strike against the supplier who grants the discrimination rather than against the buyer who benefits from it. This seems a little hard, like punishing a child for giving a toy away to a bully; especially so when there is so much difficulty about establishing the supplier's defenses of "cost-justification" and "meeting competition."[152]

There may, however, be a limit to how far the derivative nature of Section 2(f) will go in protecting discriminatory price-inducing buyers. In the *A&P* case, the Supreme Court said there was no affirmative duty on A&P to dis-

---

[149] See *Automatic Canteen Co.* v. *FTC*, op. cit.

[150] 440 U.S. 69 (1979).

[151] Scherer, *Industrial Market Structure . . .* , op. cit., p. 574.

[152] Neale and Goyder, op. cit., p. 228.

close to Borden that it had beaten and not met Bowman's bid. However, where the buyer actively misrepresents a bid, a lower court has found the buyer liable.[153]

The *A&P* case probably stands for a much broader rule than the derivative nature of Section 2(f). In that case, the policies of the Sherman Act and the Robinson–Patman Act once again came directly into conflict. To require A&P to tell Borden whether it had beaten Bowman's bid would have been to give Borden the means of iteratively determining exactly what Bowman's bid was. This prior knowledge of a competitor's prices has been a consistent concern in cases brought under Section 1 of the Sherman Act and was a central issue in the condemnation of U.S. Gypsum's "price verification" scheme mentioned earlier in this chapter.[154]

The difficulty with enforcing Section 2(f) of the Robinson–Patman Act should not be seen as an opportunity for buyers to induce discriminatory prices, because such behavior might also be condemned by means of Section 5 of the Federal Trade Commission Act on the ground that this use of coercive power is an unfair method of competition. Likewise, it is per se illegal for buyers to coerce favors from suppliers in the form of special promotional allowances and services, as discussed later in Chapter 7. Also, the Federal Trade Commission has won a number of cases using Section 2(f) against wholesalers of replacement parts for cars who, in order to strengthen their bargaining positions, formed themselves into cooperatives in order to obtain a discount not available to other nonaligned independent wholesalers. The actions of the wholesalers were illegal because the wholesalers knew very well that the prices they were paying through their cooperative were substantially lower than prices paid by nonmember wholesalers, that their orders and shipments were handled in exactly the same way they were prior to the formation of the cooperative when each wholesaler purchased autonomously, and that there were no cost savings or "meeting competition" defenses that were applicable to their situation.[155] The main objection that one could raise to such cases is that they basically involved relatively small businessmen (auto parts wholesalers) who operate in direct competition with large chain stores, oil companies, and car dealers. It would seem that the FTC would have larger "fish to fry" than this if it really wanted to concern itself with discriminatory pricing activity on the part of buyers. More recent complaints against larger firms, such as Kroger and Boise Cascade, give some indication that the FTC is starting to challenge the discriminatory activities of major corporations.

CONCLUSION

Virtually no area of marketing practice creates more legal problems for marketing executives than pricing. This is because there is a definite, explicit belief on the part of Congress, the courts, and the antitrust enforcement agencies

[153] *Kroger Co.* v. *FTC,* 438 F.2d 1372 (6th Cir. 1971).
[154] *U.S.* v. *United States Gypsum Co.,* op. cit.
[155] *General Auto Supplies* v. *FTC,* 346 F.2d 311 (7th Cir. 1965).

that prices are mechanisms by which resources become efficiently and effectively allocated throughout the economy. If these mechanisms are somehow artificially constrained, then the probability of misallocation is increased markedly. Such a belief is behind the major efforts in recent history to deregulate a number of industries, such as trucking, airlines, and communication.

The most overt act of "tampering" that a marketing executive can undertake is price fixing. This practice, as widespread as it has been in so many different industries, prevents the price mechanism from working at all. Again and again, the courts and the enforcement agencies have reiterated their outright distaste for price fixing. In fact, they are more quick to apply criminal penalties against price fixers than they are against any other antitrust violation. Price fixing is per se illegal, whether it is engaged in by competitors or among members of a channel of distribution.

But some marketing executives are convinced that too much price competition is destructive, and, therefore, they have occasionally been overly zealous in their attempts to avoid it. This is especially true in industries typified by high fixed costs and overcapacity. There, the desire to stabilize prices is particularly intense, because the temptation to cut prices to "ruinous" levels to obtain incremental sales is almost irresistible. Short of overt agreements to fix prices, executives have used their industry trade associations to institute exchanges of price information or have attempted to develop elaborate pricing formulas so that delivered prices throughout their industries will be similar. In the absence of overt agreements to set prices, none of these activities is illegal per se. Indeed, price exchanges exist in a number of industries, and delivered pricing is still being used in a variety of different forms. But both of these activities are suspect, and if challenged, the courts are certain to take into consideration the intent of the executives (i.e., was the activity really instituted to fix prices?) in the context of the structure of the industry (i.e., does a price exchange or an industry-wide delivered pricing scheme induce rigidities into what might otherwise be a more competitive marketplace?). In addition, the Federal Trade Commission is increasingly inclined to apply Section 5 of the FTC Act to other practices, such as price signaling, which merely *facilitate* price fixing. And it has now become clear that the professional services areas, such as health care and engineering, are subject to the same scrutiny regarding horizontal restraints of trade as the manufacturing and distribution areas.

On the other hand, it seems as though the courts have become increasingly lenient with regard to the issue of parallel pricing in oligopolistic industries. Modern economic theory has taught that such pricing behavior is to be expected, and the courts have basically accepted this thesis as fact. They will, however, look for "plus" factors that encourage or induce parallel pricing, such as the circulation of letters among industry members that discuss "appropriate" pricing behavior.

One area of general confusion, however, is predatory pricing. It is not at all clear where one draws the line between healthy and unhealthy price competition. How can it be determined that the prices set by one firm are predatory? Isn't part of the competitive "game" to knock one's opponent out of the box?

One answer seems to be that if such behavior could permit a firm to achieve monopoly and/or market domination, then the consequences of such behavior are not in the best interests of the society and the economy. But the rules establishing when prices are predatory are far from clear or well established. It appears that the Areeda–Turner test, which defines predatory pricing as those policies that yield returns below average variable or marginal cost, whichever is lower, is presently the most popular standard. But other arguments say that predation involves not only below-cost pricing but all sorts of other activities designed to destroy competitors, and that these additional activities, including among them the intent of the alleged predator, ought to be taken into account as well.

Hand in glove with the confusion surrounding predatory pricing, but increasing the confusion by a factor of ten or more, are the court decisions and enforcement agency activities surrounding the Robinson–Patman Act. Discriminatory prices really seem to be the heart of price competition; it is only rational to charge different prices to different customers if those customers are typified by different demand elasticities, even if the prices cannot be cost justified or are not set to meet competitors' prices. However, if those discriminatory prices result in a substantial lessening of competition on the primary, secondary, or tertiary level of distribution, then they are illegal.

Twenty years ago, Grether made the following telling comment about the Robinson–Patman Act. Every word he said is applicable to the act today.

> Many objective investigators, observers, legal practitioners, and government officials agree that while the act has in some minimal sense helped to equalize competition as intended (i.e., the buying power and advantages of mass buyers have been reduced to some unknown degree), enforcement under it has disclosed so many uncertainties, difficulties, and occasions for arbitrary action, often contrary to the purposes of antitrust enforcement, as to suggest either repeal or basic revision. Political observers are agreed, too, that neither repeal nor fundamental revision are likely in the near future. Hence, any increase in the effectiveness of enforcement must arise out of the policies and procedures of the Federal Trade Commission and the character of the reviews by the courts. The responsibilities placed upon the Commission are so heavy and ambiguous, and so vague in terms of specific determination, that much depends upon the quality and motivation of the enforcement personnel and the political climate in Washington.[156]

If the political climate in Washington and at the FTC at the time the present book was written were to continue into the future, it is likely that, for all intents and purposes, the act would be basically dead and buried as a major antitrust enforcement vehicle. However, different administrations have different agendas, and the act may once again be called into play to further certain social and economic goals. But now, at least, it appears that private lawsuits will be the main means by which some life will be maintained in it. Given all its weaknesses, it is questionable, as Scherer has sarcastically pointed out, wheth-

---

[156] E. T. Grether, *Marketing and Public Policy* (Englewood Cliffs, N.J.: Prentice-Hall, Inc., 1966), p. 59.

er the circle of the act's beneficiaries extends much wider than the attorneys who earn sizable fees interpreting its complex provisions.[157]

Evidence of a more tempered approach to possible Robinson–Patman violations was seen in 1982 when the Federal Trade Commission rejected an antitrust settlement it had negotiated in 1980 with Times Mirror Company over the way the *Los Angeles Times* grants discounts to large retail advertisers.[158] The *Times* offers a cumulative discount in advertising rates based on the number of lines an advertiser buys each year. In 1977, the FTC argued that the rate schedule was not based on cost and alleged that it unfairly discriminated against smaller companies who had to pay more for ads than some of their direct competitors, simply because their advertising volume was not as great. In 1982, the FTC reversed itself, reasoning that the facts of the case indicated that there would be little, if any, economic harm to small advertisers resulting from the *Times'* cumulative discount rate. On the other hand, just as U.S. antitrust authorities seem to be stepping back from an enforcement of the Robinson–Patman Act, the European Commission has given indications that it intends to introduce price-equality and cost-justification principles into European Community law.[159] Robinson–Patman-type violations are increasingly being challenged in Europe, which simply means that pricing "nightmares" will continue to be part of a marketing executive's nocturnal activities for decades to come.

---

[157] Scherer, *Industrial Market Structure . . .* , op. cit., p. 581.

[158] See *In the Matter of Times Mirror Company, Federal Trade Commission docket no. 9103* (July 8, 1982). See, also, Margaret Garrard Warner, "FTC Drops Charges against Times Mirror over Discounts Granted to Big Advertisers," *Wall Street Journal*, July 8, 1982, p. 10.

[159] See "The EC Cracks Down on Price Discrimination," *Business Week*, Dec. 7, 1981, p. 45.

Case 1
American Tobacco Co. et al. *v.* United States

NO. 18. CERTIORARI TO THE CIRCUIT COURT OF APPEALS FOR
THE SIXTH CIRCUIT.*
Argued November 7, 8, 1945.—Decided June 10, 1946.

MR. JUSTICE BURTON delivered the opinion of the Court.

The petitioners are The American Tobacco Company, Liggett & Myers Tobacco Company, R. J. Reynolds Tobacco Company,[1] American Suppliers,
Inc., a subsidiary of American, and certain officials of the respective companies who were convicted by a jury, in the District Court of the United States
for the Eastern District of Kentucky, of violating §§1 and 2 of the Sherman
Anti-Trust Act, pursuant to an information filed July 24, 1940, and modified
October 31, 1940.

Each petitioner was convicted on four counts: (1) conspiracy in restraint of
trade, (2) monopolization, (3) attempt to monopolize, and (4) conspiracy to
monopolize. Each count related to interstate and foreign trade and commerce
in tobacco. No sentence was imposed under the third count as the Court held
that that count was merged in the second. Each petitioner was fined $5,000 on
each of the other counts, making $15,000 for each petitioner and a total of
$255,000. Seven other defendants were found not guilty and a number of the
original defendants were severed from the proceedings pursuant to stipulation.

The Circuit Court of Appeals for the Sixth Circuit, on December 8, 1944,
affirmed each conviction, 147 F. 2d 93. All the grounds urged for review of
those judgments were considered here on petitions for certiorari. On March
26, 1945, this Court granted the petitions but each was "limited to the question whether actual exclusion of competitors is necessary to the crime of monopolization under §2 of the Sherman Act." 324 U. S. 836. On April 19, 1945,
Reynolds, et al., filed a petition for rehearing and enlargement of the scope of
review in their case but it was denied. 324 U. S. 891. This opinion is limited to
the convictions under §2 of the Sherman Act[2] and deals especially with those
for monopolization under the second count of the information.

---

[1] Here referred to as American, Liggett and Reynolds.

[2] "SEC. 2. Every person who shall monopolize, or attempt to monopolize, or combine or conspire with any
other person or persons, to monopolize any part of the trade or commerce among the several States, or with
foreign nations, shall be deemed guilty of a misdemeanor, and, on conviction thereof, shall be punished by fine
not exceeding five thousand dollars, or by imprisonment not exceeding one year, or by both said punishments,
in the discretion of the court." 26 Stat. 209, 15 U.S.C. §2.

The present opinion is not a finding by this Court one way or the other on the many closely contested issues of fact. The present opinion is an application of the law to the facts as they were found by the jury and which the Circuit Court of Appeals held should not be set aside. The trial court's instruction did not call for proof of an "actual exclusion" of competitors on the part of the petitioners. For the purposes of this opinion, we shall assume, therefore, that an actual exclusion of competitors by the petitioners was not claimed or established by the prosecution. Simply stated the issue is: Do the facts called for by the trial court's definition of monopolization amount to a violation of §2 of the Sherman Act?

The position of the petitioners in the cigarette industry from 1931 to 1939 is clear from the following tables:

Percentage of Total U. S. Production of Small Cigarettes—1931–1939.

	1931	1932	1933	1934	1935	1936	1937	1938	1939
American	39.5	36.6	33.0	26.1	24.0	22.5	21.5	22.7	22.9
Liggett	22.7	23.0	28.1	27.4	26.0	24.6	23.6	22.9	21.6
Reynolds	28.4	21.8	22.8	26.0	28.1	29.5	28.1	25.3	23.6
Lorillard	6.5	5.2	4.7	4.1	3.8	4.3	4.7	5.1	5.8
Brown & Williamson	0.2	6.9	5.5	8.3	9.6	9.6	9.9	9.9	10.6
Philip Morris	0.9	1.4	0.8	2.0	3.1	4.1	5.4	5.7	7.1
Stephano	0.1	0.1	0.2	0.5	1.4	1.9	2.5	3.1	3.3
Axton-Fisher	0.7	3.1	4.4	4.4	3.0	2.2	2.4	2.7	2.4
Larus	0.2	1.0	0.2	0.6	0.7	0.8	1.0	1.3	1.3
Combined Percentages of American, Liggett and Reynolds	90.7	81.4	83.9	79.5	78.0	76.7	73.3	71.0	68.0

Volume of Cigarette Production—1931–1939. (Billions of cigarettes.)

	1931	1932	1933	1934	1935	1936	1937	1938	1939
Total U. S. Production	117.4	106.6	114.9	130.0	140.0	158.9	170.0	174.7	180.7
American	46.2	39.0	37.9	33.9	33.5	35.8	36.6	39.0	41.4
Liggett	26.6	24.6	32.2	35.6	36.3	39.1	40.2	39.3	39.0
Reynolds	33.3	23.2	26.2	33.8	39.4	46.9	47.8	43.5	42.6
Lorillard	7.6	5.5	5.4	5.3	5.3	6.8	8.1	8.8	10.5
Brown & Williamson	0.3	7.3	6.3	10.8	13.4	15.2	16.8	17.1	19.1
Philip Morris	1.0	1.5	0.9	2.6	4.4	6.4	9.2	9.7	12.8
Stephano	0.1	0.1	0.2	0.7	2.0	3.0	4.2	5.4	6.0
Axton-Fisher	0.8	3.3	5.0	5.7	4.2	3.5	4.1	4.5	4.3
Larus	0.3	1.0	0.3	0.7	1.0	1.2	1.7	2.2	2.3
Combined volume of American, Liggett and Reynolds	106.1	86.8	96.3	103.3	109.2	121.8	124.6	121.8	123.0

The first table shows that, although American, Liggett and Reynolds gradually dropped in their percentage of the national domestic cigarette production from 90.7% in 1931 to 73.3%, 71% and 68%, respectively, in 1937, 1938 and 1939, they have accounted at all times for more than 68%, and usually for more than 75%, of the national production. The balance of the cigarette production has come from six other companies. No one of those six ever has produced more than the 10.6% once reached by Brown & Williamson in 1939.

The second table shows that, while the percentage of cigarettes produced by American, Liggett and Reynolds in the United States dropped gradually from 90.7% to 68%, their combined volume of production actually increased from 106 billion in 1931 to about 125 billion, 122 billion and 123 billion, respectively, in 1937, 1938, and 1939. The remainder of the production was divided among the other six companies. No one of those six ever has produced more than about 19 billion cigarettes a year, which was the high point reached by Brown & Williamson in 1939.

The further dominance of American, Liggett and Reynolds within their special field of burley blend cigarettes, as compared with the so-called "10 cent cigarettes," is also apparent. In 1939, the 10 cent cigarettes constituted about 14½% of the total domestic cigarette production. Accordingly, the 68% of the total cigarette production enjoyed by American, Liggett and Reynolds amounted to 80% of that production within their special field of cigarettes. The second table shows a like situation. In 1939, the 10 cent cigarettes accounted for 25.6 billion of the cigarettes produced. Deducting this from the 57.7 billion cigarettes produced by others than American, Liggett and Reynolds left only about 32 billion cigarettes of a comparable grade produced in that year by competitors of the "Big Three" as against the 123 billion produced by them. In addition to the combined production by American, Liggett and Reynolds in 1939 of over 68% of all domestic cigarettes, they also produced over 63% of the smoking tobacco and over 44% of the chewing tobacco. They never were important factors in the cigar or snuff fields of the tobacco industry.

The foregoing demonstrates the basis of the claim of American, Liggett and Reynolds to the title of the "Big Three." The marked dominance enjoyed by each of these three, in roughly equal proportions, is emphasized by the fact that the smallest of them at all times showed over twice the production of the largest outsider. Without adverse criticism of it, comparative size on this great scale inevitably increased the power of these three to dominate all phases of their industry. "Size carries with it an opportunity for abuse that is not to be ignored when the opportunity is proved to have been utilized in the past." *United States* v. *Swift & Co.,* 286 U. S. 106, 116. An intent to use this power to maintain a monopoly was found by the jury in these cases.

The record further shows that the net worth of American, Liggett and Reynolds in terms of their total assets, less current liabilities, rose from $277,000,000 in 1912 to over $551,000,000 in 1939. Their net annual earnings, before payment of interest and dividends, rose from about $28,000,000 in 1912 to over $75,000,000 in 1939. The record is full of evidence of the close relationship between their large expenditures for national advertising of cigarettes and resulting volumes of sales. In each of the years 1937, 1938 and 1939, American, Liggett and Reynolds expended a total of over $40,000,000 a year for advertising. Such advertising is not here criticized as a business expense. Such advertising may benefit indirectly the entire industry, including the competitors of the advertisers. Such tremendous advertising, however, is also a widely published warning that these companies possess and know how to use a powerful offensive and defensive weapon against new competition. New competition dare not enter such a field, unless it be well supported by comparable national advertising. Large inventories of leaf tobacco, and large sums required for payment of federal taxes in advance of actual sales, further emphasize the effectiveness of a well financed monopoly in this field against potential competitors if there merely exists an intent to exclude such competitors. Prevention of all potential competition is the natural program for maintaining a monopoly here, rather than any program of actual exclusion. "Prevention" is cheaper and more effective than any amount of "cure."

With this background of a substantial monopoly, amounting to over two-thirds of the entire domestic field of cigarettes, and to over 80% of the field of comparable cigarettes, and with the opposition confined to several small competitors, the jury could have found from the actual operation of the petitioners that there existed a combination or conspiracy among them not only in restraint of trade, but to monopolize a part of the tobacco industry. The trial court described this combination or conspiracy as an "essential element" and "indispensable ingredient" of the offenses charged. It is therefore only in conjunction with such a combination or conspiracy that these cases will constitute a precedent. The conspiracy so established by the verdicts under the second count appears to have been one to fix and control prices and other material conditions relating to the purchase of raw material in the form of leaf tobacco for use in the manufacture of cigarettes. It also appears to have been one to fix and control prices and other material conditions relating to the distribution and sale of the product of such tobacco in the form of cigarettes. The jury found a conspiracy to monopolize to a substantial degree the leaf market and the cigarette market. The jury's verdicts also found a power and intent on the part of the petitioners to exclude competition to a substantial extent in the tobacco industry.

I.

The verdicts show that the jury found that the petitioners conspired to fix prices and to exclude undesired competition against them in the purchase of the domestic type of flue-cured tobacco and of burley tobacco. These are raw materials essential to the production of cigarettes of the grade sold by the petitioners and also, to some extent, of the 10 cent grade of cigarettes which constitutes the only substantial competition to American, Liggett and Reynolds in the cigarette field of the domestic tobacco industry. The tobaccos involved in these cases are the flue-cured, burley and Maryland tobaccos. The flue-cured or bright tobacco is grown in a number of areas called "belts." These are in Virginia, North Carolina, South Carolina, Georgia and Florida. The tobacco takes its name of flue-cured from the "curing" process to which it is subjected and which consists of hanging the tobacco leaves in barns heated by a system of flues. Between 50% and 60% of the total flue-cured product is for export to England. The petitioners purchased a combined total of between 50% and 80% of the domestic flue-cured tobacco. The burley tobacco is produced largely in the burley belt in Kentucky and Tennessee. It is cured without heating by exposing the leaves to the air in barns in which they are hung. The petitioners purchased from 60% to 80% of the annual crop of burley. The Maryland tobacco is grown in the southern part of that State. Some of it is sold in auction markets, the rest is packed in hogsheads and sold in two Baltimore warehouses by the Maryland Tobacco Growers' Association and by commercial merchants. The greater part of the Maryland tobacco was purchased by petitioners. The crops in the more southerly belts mature first and the burley crops are not ready for market until late fall. When the tobacco is ready for market the farmers strip, sort and grade the leaves according to their judgment as to quality, tie them into bundles called "hands" (except in Georgia where the tobacco remains loose), and truck them to tobacco auction markets. In the possession of the farmers the crops are perishable as they require a redrying process. Under the modern system of marketing, the tobacco cannot be stored to await another season. The farmers have no facilities for redrying the tobacco and therefore must sell their crops in the season in which those crops are raised or they will lose them. The petitioners kept large enough tobacco stock on hand to last about three years. The value of these stocks was over $100,000,000 for each company and these stocks assured their independence of the market in any one year. Auction markets for the sale of leaf tobacco have been in operation for many years and were well established long before the dissolution of the tobacco trust in 1911. Such markets are located in 75 towns in the flue-cured region and 42 towns in the burley area. There are four Maryland markets. Since the crop in the Georgia Belt matures first, the markets in that belt open first, usually about August 1. The auctioneers then follow the marketing seasons to the North, reaching the "Old Belt" in North Carolina and Virginia in the latter part of September. The dates for opening the markets in the flue-cured belts are set by the Tobacco Association of the United States of which buyers, including petitioners, warehousemen and others connected with the industry, but not including farmers, are members. Burley sales begin in Lexington, Kentucky, which is the principal market, on the first Monday in December. The other burley markets open the next day. Sales continue, excepting at Christmas time, for the next few months.

The Government introduced evidence showing that, although there was no written or express agreement discovered among American, Liggett and Reynolds, their practices included a clear course of dealing. This evidently convinced the jury of the existence of a combination or conspiracy to fix and control prices and practices as to domestic leaf tobacco, both in restraint of trade as such, and to establish a substantially impregnable defense against any attempted intrusion by potential competitors into these markets.

It appeared that petitioners refused to purchase tobacco on these markets unless the other petitioners were also represented thereon. There were attempts made by others to open new tobacco markets but none of the petitioners would participate in them unless the other petitioners were present. Consequently, such markets were failures due to the absence of buyers. It appeared that the tobacco farmers did not want to sell their tobacco on a market in which the only purchasers were speculators or dealers. The prices paid under such circumstances were likely to be low in order that the purchasers eventually might resell the tobacco to the manufacturing companies. The foreign purchasers likewise would not participate without the presence of the petitioners. In this way the new tobacco markets and their locations were determined by the unanimous consent of the petitioners and, in arriving at their determination, the petitioners consulted with each other as to whether or not a community deserved a market.

The Government presented evidence to support its claim that, before the markets opened, the petitioners placed limitations and restrictions on the prices which their buyers were permitted to pay for tobacco. None of the buyers exceeded these price ceilings. Grades of tobacco were formulated in such a way as to result in the absence of competition between the petitioners. There was manipulation of the price of lower grade tobaccos in order to restrict competition from manufacturers of the lower priced cigarettes. Methods used included the practice of the petitioners of calling their respective buyers in, prior to the opening of the annual markets, and giving them instructions as to the prices to be paid for leaf tobacco in each of the markets. These instructions were in terms of top prices or price ranges. The price ceilings thus established for the buyers were the same for each of them. In case of tie bids the auctioneer awarded the sale customarily to the buyer who bid first. Under this custom the buyers representing the petitioners often made bids on various baskets of tobacco before an opening price could be announced so that they might have their claim to the tobacco recognized at the understood ceiling price in the case of tie bids. Often a buyer would bid ahead by indicating that he wanted a certain basket further along in the line of baskets and, in such cases, the tobacco in question was awarded to such buyer without the mention of any price, it being understood that it was sold at the top price theretofore previously determined upon.

Where one or two of the petitioners secured their percentage of the crop on a certain market or were not interested in the purchase of certain offerings of tobacco, their buyers, nevertheless, would enter the bidding in order to force the other petitioners to bid up to the maximum price. The petitioners were not so much concerned with the prices they paid for the leaf tobacco as that each should pay the same price for the same grade and that none would secure any advantage in purchasing tobacco. They were all to be on the same basis as far as the expenses of their purchasers went. The prices which were set as top prices by petitioners, or by the first of them to purchase on the market, became, with few exceptions, the top prices prevailing on those markets. Competition also was eliminated between petitioners by the purchase of grades of tobacco in which but one of them was interested. To accomplish this, each company formulated the grades which it alone wished to purchase. The other companies recognized the grades so formulated as distinctive grades and did not compete for them. While the differences between the grades so formulated were distinguishable by the highly trained special buyers, they were in reality so minute as to be inconsequential. This element, however, did not mean that a company could bid any price it wished for its especially formulated grades of tobacco. The other companies prevented that by bidding up the tobacco, at least to a point where they did not risk being awarded the sale to themselves. Each company determined in advance what portion of the entire crop it would purchase before the market for that season opened. The petitioners then separately informed their buyers of the percentage of the crop which they wished to purchase and gave instructions that only such a percentage should be purchased on each market. The purchases were spread evenly over the different markets throughout the season. No matter what the size of the crop might be, the petitioners were able to purchase their predetermined percentages thereof within the price limits determined upon by them, thus indicating a stabilized market. The respective petitioners employed supervisors whose functions were to see that the prices were the same on one market as on another. Where, because of difference in appraisals of grades or other similar factors, the bidding was out of line with the predetermined price limits or there was a tendency for prices to vary from those on other markets, the supervisors sought to maintain the same prices and grades on different markets. This was sought to be achieved by instructions to buyers to change the prices bid or the percentages purchased, and such actions proved to be successful in maintaining and equalizing the prices on the different markets.

At a time when the manufacturers of lower priced cigarettes were beginning to manufacture them in quantity, the petitioners commenced to make large purchases of the cheaper tobacco leaves used for the manufacture of such lower priced cigarettes. No explanation was offered as to how or where this tobacco was used by petitioners. The compositions of their respective brands of cigarettes calling for the use of more expensive tobaccos remained unchanged during this period of controversy and up to the end of the trial. The Government claimed that such purchases of cheaper tobacco evidenced a combination and a purpose among the petitioners to deprive the manufacturers of cheaper cigarettes of the tobacco necessary for their manufacture, as well as to raise the price of such tobacco to such a point that cigarettes made therefrom could not be sold at a sufficiently low price to compete with the petitioners' more highly advertised brands.

II.

The verdicts show also that the jury found that the petitioners conspired to fix prices and to exclude undesired competition in the distribution and sale of their principal products. The petitioners sold and distributed their products to jobbers and to selected dealers who bought at list prices, less discounts. Almost all of the million or more dealers who handled the respective petitioners' products throughout the country consisted of such establishments as small storekeepers, gasoline station operators and lunch room proprietors who purchased the cigarettes from jobbers. The jobbers in turn derived their profits from the difference between the wholesale price paid by them and the price charged by them to local dealers. A great advantage therefore accrued to any dealer buying at the discounted or wholesale list prices. Selling to dealers at jobbers' prices was called "direct selling" and the dealers as well as the jobbers getting those prices were referred to as being on the "direct list." The list prices charged and the discount allowed by petitioners have been practically identical since 1923 and absolutely identical since 1928. Since the later date, only seven changes have been made by the three companies and those have been identical in amount. The increases were first announced by Reynolds. American and Liggett thereupon increased their list prices in identical amounts.

The following record of price changes is circumstantial evidence of the existence of a conspiracy and of a power and intent to exclude competition coming from cheaper grade cigarettes. During the two years preceding June, 1931, the petitioners produced 90% of the total cigarette production in the United States. In that month tobacco farmers were receiving the lowest prices for their crops since 1905. The costs to the petitioners for tobacco leaf, therefore, were lower than usual during the past 25 years, and their manufacturing costs had been declining. It was one of the worst years of financial and economic depression in the history of the country. On June 23, 1931, Reynolds, without previous notification or warning to the trade or public, raised the list price of Camel cigarettes, constituting its leading cigarette brand, from $6.40 to $6.85 a thousand. The same day, American increased the list price for Lucky Strike cigarettes, its leading brand, and Liggett the price for Chesterfield cigarettes, its leading brand, to the identical price of $6.85 a thousand. No economic justification for this raise was demonstrated. The president of Reynolds stated that it was "to express our own courage for the future and our own confidence in our industry." The president of American gave as his reason for the increase, "the opportunity of making some money." See 147 F.2d 93, 103. He further claimed that because Reynolds had raised its list price, Reynolds would therefore have additional funds for advertising and American had raised its price in order to have a similar amount for advertising. The officials of Liggett claimed that they thought the increase was a mistake as there did not seem to be any reason for making a price advance but they contended that unless they also raised their list price for Chesterfields, the other companies would have greater resources to spend in advertising and thus would put Chesterfield cigarettes at a competitive disadvantage. This general price increase soon resulted in higher retail prices and in a loss in volume of sales. Yet in 1932, in the midst of the national depression with the sales of the petitioners' cigarettes falling off greatly in number, the petitioners still were making tremendous profit as a result of the price increase. Their net profits in that year amounted to more than $100,000,000. This was one of the three biggest years in their history.

Before 1931, certain smaller companies had manufactured cigarettes retailing at 10 cents a package, which was several cents lower than the retail price for the leading brands of the petitioners. Up to that time, the sales of the 10 cent cigarettes were negligible. However, after the above described increase in list prices of the petitioners in 1931, the 10 cent brands made serious inroads upon the sales of the petitioners. These cheaper brands of cigarettes were sold at a list pice of $4.75 a thousand and from 1931 to 1932 the sales of these cigarettes multiplied 30 times, rising from 0.28% of the total cigarette sales of the country in June, 1931, to 22.78% in November, 1932. In response to this threat of competition from the manufacturers of the 10 cent brands, the petitioners, in January, 1933, cut the list price of their three leading brands from $6.85 to $6 a thousand. In February, they cut again to $5.50 a thousand. The evidence tends to show that this cut was directed at the competition of the 10 cent cigarettes. Reports that previously had been sent in by various officials and representatives to their companies told of the petitioners' brands losing in competition with the 10 cent brands. The petitioners were interested in a sufficiently low retail price for their products so that they would defeat the threat from the lower priced cigarettes and found that, in order to succeed in their objective, it was necessary that there be not more than a 3 cent differential on each package at retail between the cheaper cigarettes and their own brands. The petitioners' cuts in their list prices and the subsequent reductions in the retail prices of their products resulted in a victory over the 10 cent brands. The letters of petitioners' representatives to their companies reported upon the progress of this battle, giving an account of the decline in sales of the 10 cent brands because of the price reductions in the "15-cent brands," and prophesying that certain of the 10 cent brands would "pass out of the picture." Following the first price cut by petitioners, the sales of the 10 cent brands fell off considerably. After the second cut they fell off to a much greater extent. When the sale of the 10 cent brands had dropped from 22.78% of the total cigarette sales in November, 1932, to 6.43% in May, 1933, the petitioners, in January, 1934, raised the list price of their leading brands from $5.50 back up to $6.10 a thousand. During the period that the list price of $5.50 a thousand was in effect, Camels and Lucky Strikes were being sold at a loss by Reynolds and American. Liggett at the same time was forced to curtail all of its normal business activities and cut its advertising to the bone in order to sell at this price. The petitioners, in 1937, again increased the list prices of their above named brands to $6.25 a thousand and in July, 1940, to $6.53 a thousand.

Certain methods used by the petitioners to secure a reduction in the retail prices of their cigarettes were in evidence. Reynolds and Liggett required their retailers to price the 10 cent brands at a differential of not more than 3 cents below Camel and Chesterfield cigarettes. They insisted upon their dealers correcting a greater differential by increasing the retail price of the 10 cent brands to 11 cents with petitioners' brands at 14 cents a package, or by requiring that petitioners' brands be priced at 13 cents with the lower priced cigarettes at 10 cents a package. Salesmen for Liggett were instructed to narrow the differential to 3 cents, it being deemed of no consequence whether the dealer raised the price of the 10 cent brands or reduced the price of Chesterfields. Reynolds referred to a differential of more than 3 cents as "discriminatory" on the ground that the dealer then would make a higher gross profit on the higher priced cigarettes than on the 10 cent brands. After the list price reductions were made and at the height of the price war, the petitioners commenced the distribution of posters advertising their brands at 10 cents a package and made attempts to have dealers meet these prices. Among the efforts used to achieve their objectives, petitioners gave dealers direct list privileges of purchase, together with discounts, poster advertising displays, cash subsidies and free goods. In addition to the use of these inducements, petitioners also used threats and penalties to enforce compliance with their retail price program, removed dealers from the direct lists, cancelled arrangements for window advertising, changed credit terms with a resulting handicap to recalcitrant dealers, discontinued cash allowances for advertising, refused to make deals giving free goods, and made use of price cutters to whom they granted advantageous privileges to drive down retail prices where a parity, or price equalization, was not maintained by dealers between brands of petitioners or where the dealers refused to maintain the 3 cent differential between the 10 cent brands and the leading brands of petitioners' cigarettes. There was evidence that when dealers received an announcement of the price increase from one of the petitioners and attempted to purchase some of the leading brands of cigarettes from the other petitioners at their unchanged prices before announcement of a similar change, the latter refused to fill such orders until their prices were also raised, thus bringing about the same result as if the changes had been precisely simultaneous.

III.

It was on the basis of such evidence that the Circuit Court of Appeals found that the verdicts of the jury were sustained by sufficient evidence on each count. The question squarely presented here by the order of this Court in allowing the writs of certiorari is whether actual exclusion of competitors is necessary to the crime of monopolization in these cases under §2 of the Sherman Act. We agree with the lower courts that such actual exclusion of competitors is not necessary to that crime in these cases and that the instructions given to the jury, and hereinbefore quoted, correctly defined the crime. A correct interpretation of the statute and of the authorities makes it the crime of monopolizing, under §2 of the Sherman Act, for parties, as in these cases, to combine or conspire to acquire or maintain the power to exclude competitors from any part of the trade or commerce among the several states or with foreign nations, provided they also have such a power that they are able, as a group, to exclude actual or potential competition from the field and provided that they have the intent and purpose to exercise that power. See *United States v. Socony-Vacuum Oil Co.,* 310 U.S. 150, 226, n. 59 and authorities cited.

It is not the form of the combination or the particular means used but the result to be achieved that the statute condemns. It is not of importance whether the means used to accomplish the unlawful objective are in themselves lawful or unlawful. Acts done to give effect to the conspiracy may be in themselves wholly innocent acts. Yet, if they are part of the sum of the acts which are relied upon to effectuate the conspiracy which the statute forbids, they come within its prohibition. No formal agreement is necessary to constitute an unlawful conspiracy. Often crimes are a matter of inference deduced from the acts of the person accused and done in pursuance of a criminal purpose. Where the conspiracy is proved, as here, from the evidence of the action taken in concert by the parties to it, it is all the more convincing proof of an intent to exercise the power of exclusion acquired through that conspiracy. The essential combination or conspiracy in violation of the Sherman Act may be found in a course of dealing or other circumstances as well as in an exchange of words. *United States* v. *Schrader's Son,* 252 U.S. 85. Where the circumstances are such as to warrant a jury in finding that the conspirators had a unity of purpose or a common design and understanding, or a meeting of minds in an unlawful arrangement, the conclusion that a conspiracy is established is justified. Neither proof of exertion of the power to exclude nor proof of actual exclusion of existing or potential competitors is essential to sustain a charge of monopolization under the Sherman Act.

In the present cases, the petitioners have been found to have conspired to establish a monopoly and also to have the power and intent to establish and maintain the monopoly. To hold that they do not come within the prohibition of the Sherman Act would destroy the force of that Act. Accordingly, the instructions of the trial court under §2 of the Act are approved and the judgment of the Circuit Court of Appeals is

Affirmed.

Case 2
Great Atlantic & Pacific Tea Co., Inc. *v.*
Federal Trade Commission

CERTIORARI TO THE UNITED STATES COURT OF APPEALS FOR
THE SECOND CIRCUIT

No. 77-654. Argued December 4, 1978—Decided February 22, 1979

MR. JUSTICE STEWART delivered the opinion of the Court.

The question presented in this case is whether the petitioner, the Great Atlantic & Pacific Tea Co. (A&P), violated §2(f) of the Clayton Act, 38 Stat. 730, as amended by the Robinson-Patman Act, 49 Stat. 1526, 15 U. S. C. §13(f),[1] by knowingly inducing or receiving illegal price discriminations from the Borden Co. (Borden).

The alleged violation was reflected in a 1965 agreement between A&P and Borden under which Borden undertook to supply "private label" milk to more than 200 A&P stores in a Chicago area that included portions of Illinois and

---

[1] Title 15 U. S. C. §13(f) provides:

"It shall be unlawful for any person engaged in commerce, in the course of such commerce, knowingly to induce or receive a discrimination in price which is prohibited by this section."

Title 15 U. S. C. §§13(a) and (b) provide in pertinent part:

"(a) . . . It shall be unlawful for any person engaged in commerce, in the course of such commerce, either directly or indirectly, to discriminate in price between different purchasers of commodities of like grade and quality, where either or any of the purchases involved in such discrimination are in commerce, where such commodities are sold for use, consumption, or resale within the United States or any Territory thereof or the District of Columbia or any insular possession or other place under the jurisdiction of the United States, and where the effect of such discrimination may be substantially to lessen competition or tend to create a monopoly in any line of commerce, or to injure, destroy, or prevent competition with any person who either grants or knowingly receives the benefit of such discrimination or with customers of either of them: *Provided,* That nothing herein contained shall prevent differentials which make only due allowance for differences in the cost of manufacture, sale, or delivery resulting from the different methods or quantities in which such commodities are to such purchasers sold or delivered. . . .

"(b) . . . Upon proof being made, at any hearing on a complaint under this section, that there has been discrimination in price or services or facilities furnished, the burden of rebutting the prima-facie case thus made by showing justification shall be upon the person charged with a violation of this section, and unless justification shall be affirmatively shown, the Commission is authorized to issue an order terminating the discrimination: *Provided, however,* That nothing herein contained shall prevent a seller rebutting the prima-facie case thus made by showing that his lower price or the furnishing of services or facilities to any purchaser or purchasers was made in good faith to meet an equally low price of a competitor, or the services or facilities furnished by a competitor."

Indiana. This agreement resulted from an effort by A&P to achieve cost savings by switching from the sale of "brand label" milk (milk sold under the brand name of the supplying dairy) to the sale of "private label" milk (milk sold under the A&P label).

To implement this plan, A&P asked Borden, its longtime supplier, to submit an offer to supply under private label certain of A&P's milk and other dairy product requirements. After prolonged negotiations, Borden offered to grant A&P a discount for switching to private-label milk provided A&P would accept limited delivery service. Borden claimed that this offer would save A&P $410,000 a year compared to what it had been paying for its dairy products. A&P, however, was not satisfied with this offer and solicited offers from other dairies. A competitor of Borden, Bowman Dairy, then submitted an offer which was lower than Borden's.[2]

At this point, A&P's Chicago buyer contacted Borden's chain store sales manager and stated: "I have a bid in my pocket. You [Borden] people are so far out of line it is not even funny. You are not even in the ball park." When the Borden representative asked for more details, he was told nothing except that a $50,000 improvement in Borden's bid "would not be a drop in the bucket."

Borden was thus faced with the problem of deciding whether to rebid. A&P at the time was one of Borden's largest customers in the Chicago area. Moreover, Borden had just invested more than $5 million in a new dairy facility in Illinois. The loss of the A&P account would result in underutilization of this new plant. Under these circumstances, Borden decided to submit a new bid which doubled the estimated annual savings to A&P, from $410,000 to $820,000. In presenting its offer, Borden emphasized to A&P that it needed to keep A&P's business and was making the new offer in order to meet Bowman's bid. A&P then accepted Borden's bid after concluding that it was substantially better than Bowman's.

I.

Based on these facts, the Federal Trade Commission filed a three-count complaint against A&P. Count I charged that A&P had violated §5 of the Federal Trade Commission Act by misleading Borden in the course of negotiations for the private-label contract, in that A&P had failed to inform Borden that its second offer was better than the Bowman bid.[3] Count II, involving the same conduct, charged that A&P had violated §2(f) of the Clayton Act, as amended

[2] The Bowman bid would have produced estimated annual savings of approximately $737,000 for A&P as compared with the first Borden bid, which would have produced estimated annual savings of $410,000.

[3] Section 5(a) of the Federal Trade Commission Act, 38 Stat. 719, as amended, 15 U. S. C. § 45(a), provides in relevant part:

"(1) Unfair methods of competition in or affecting commerce, and unfair or deceptive acts or practices in or affecting commerce, are declared unlawful."

by the Robinson–Patman Act, by knowingly inducing or receiving price discriminations from Borden. Count III charged that Borden and A&P had violated§5 of the Federal Trade Commission Act by combining to stabilize and maintain the retail and wholesale prices of milk and other dairy products.

An Administrative Law Judge found, after extended discovery and a hearing that lasted over 110 days, that A&P had acted unfairly and deceptively in accepting the second offer from Borden and had therefore violated §5 of the Federal Trade Commission Act as charged in Count I. The Administrative Law Judge similarly found that this same conduct had violated §2(f). Finally, he dismissed Count III on the ground that the Commission had not satisfied its burden of proof.

On review, the Commission reversed the Administrative Law Judge's finding as to Count I. Pointing out that the question at issue was what amount of disclosure is required of the buyer during contract negotiations, the Commission held that the imposition of a duty of affirmative disclosure would be "contrary to normal business practice and, we think, contrary to the public interest." Despite this ruling, however, the Commission held as to Count II that the identical conduct on the part of A&P had violated §2(f), finding that Borden had discriminated in price between A&P and its competitors, that the discrimination had been injurious to competition, and that A&P had known or should have known that it was the beneficiary of unlawful price discrimination.[4] The Commission rejected A&P's defenses that the Borden bid had been made to meet competition and was cost justified.[5]

A&P filed a petition for review of the Commission's order in the Court of Appeals for the Second Circuit. The court held that substantial evidence supported the findings of the Commission and that as a matter of law A&P could not successfully assert a meeting-competition defense because it, unlike Borden, had known that Borden's offer was better than Bowman's.[6] Finally, the court held that the Commission had correctly determined that A&P had no cost-justi-

[4] The Commission also found that the interstate commerce requirement of §2(f) was satisfied.

[5] Under §§2(a) and (b) of the Act, a seller who can establish either that a price differential was cost justified or offered in good faith to meet competition has a complete defense to a charge of price discrimination under the Act. *Standard Oil Co.* v. *FTC,* 340 U. S. 231. See n. 1, *supra.*

With respect to the meeting-competition defense, the Commission stated that even though Borden as the seller might have had a meeting-competition defense, A&P as the buyer did not have such a defense because it knew that the bid offered was, in fact, better than the Bowman bid. With respect to the cost-justification defense, the Commission found that Commission counsel had met the initial burden of going forward as required by this Court's decision in *Automatic Canteen Co. of America* v. *FTC,* 346 U. S. 61, and that A&P had not then satisfied its burden of showing that the prices were cost justified, or that it did not know that they were not.

The Commission upheld the Administrative Law Judge's dismissal of Count III of the complaint.

[6] The Court of Appeals, like the Commission, relied on *Kroger Co.* v. *FTC,* 438 F. 2d 1372 (CA6), for the proposition that a buyer can be liable under §2(f) of the Act even if the seller has a meeting-competition defense. The *Kroger* case involved a buyer who had made deliberate misrepresentations to a seller in order to induce price concessions. While the Court of Appeals in this case did not find that A&P had made any affirmative misrepresentations, it viewed the distinction between a "lying buyer" and a buyer who knowingly accepts the lower of two bids as without legal significance. See n. 15, *infra.*

fication defense. 557 F. 2d 971. Because the judgment of the Court of Appeals raises important issues of federal law, we granted certiorari. 435 U.S. 922.

II.

The Robinsin–Patman Act was passed in response to the problem perceived in the increased market power and coercive practices of chainstores and other big buyers that threatened the existence of small independent retailers. Notwithstanding this concern with buyers, however, the emphasis of the Act is in § 2(a), which prohibits price discriminations by sellers. Indeed, the original Patman bill as reported by Committees of both Houses prohibited only seller activity, with no mention of buyer liability.[7] Section 2(f), making buyers liable for inducing or receiving price discriminations by sellers, was the product of a belated floor amendment near the conclusion of the Senate debates.[8]

As finally enacted, §2(f) provides:

> "That it shall be unlawful for any person engaged in commerce, in the course of such commerce, knowingly to induce or receive a discrimination in price *which is prohibited by this section.*" (Emphasis added.)

Liability under §2(f) thus is limited to situations where the price discrimination is one "which is prohibited by this section." While the phrase "this section" refers to the entire §2 of the Act, only subsections (a) and (b) dealing with seller liability involve discriminations in price. Under the plain meaning of §2(f), therefore, a buyer cannot be liable if a prima facie case could not be established against a seller or if the seller has an affirmative defense. In either situation, there is no price discrimination "prohibited by this section."[9] The legislative history of §2(f) fully confirms the conclusion that buyer liability under§2(f) is dependent on seller liability under §2(a).[10]

The derivative nature of liability under §2(f) was recognized by this Court in *Automatic Canteen Co. of America* v. *FTC,* 346 U. S. 61. In that case, the Court stated that even if the Commission has established a prima facie case of price discrimination, a buyer does not violate §2(f) if the lower prices received

---

[7] II. R. 8442, 74th Cong., 1st Sess. (1935); S. 3154, 74th Cong., 1st Sess. (1935).

[8] F. Rowe, Price Discrimination Under the Robinson–Patman Act 423 (1962). Section 2(f) has been described by commentators as an "afterthought." *Id.,* at 421; J. McCord, Commentaries on the Robinson–Patman Act 96 (1969).

[9] Commentators have recognized that a finding of buyer liability under §2(f) is dependent on a finding of seller liability under §2(a). McCord, *supra,* at 96 ("[Section] 2(f) cannot be enforced if a prima facie case could not be established against the seller on the basis of the transaction in question under Section 2(a) or if he could sustain an affirmative defense thereto"); Rowe, *supra,* at 421 ("the legal status of the buyer is derivative from the seller's pricing legality under the Act"); H. Shniderman, Price Discrimination in Perspective 136 (1977) (a buyer can be liable under §2(f) only if the price received "cannot be excused by any defenses provided to the seller").

[10] In presenting the Conference Report to the House, Representative Utterback summarized the meaning of §2(f) by stating: "This paragraph makes the buyer liable for knowingly inducing or receiving any discrimination in price which is unlawful under the first paragraph [§2(a)] of the amendment." 80 Cong. Rec. 9419 (1936).

are either within one of the seller's defenses or not known by the buyer not to be within one of those defenses. The Court stated:

> "Thus, at the least, we can be confident in reading the words in §2(f), 'a discrimination in price which is prohibited by this section,' as a reference to the substantive prohibitions against discrimination by sellers defined elsewhere in the Act. It is therefore apparent that the discriminatory price that buyers are forbidden by §2(f) to induce cannot include price differentials that are not forbidden to sellers in other sections of the Act. . . . For we are not dealing with a 'discrimination in price'; the 'discrimination in price' in §2(f) must be one 'which is prohibited by this section.' Even if any price differential were to be comprehended within the term 'discrimination in price,' §2(f), which speaks of prohibited discriminations, cannot be read as declaring out of bounds price differentials within one or more of the 'defenses' available to sellers, such as that the price differentials reflect cost differences, fluctuating market conditions, or bona fide attempts to meet competition, as those defenses are set out in the provisos of §§2(a) and 2(b)." 346 U. S., at 70–71 (footnotes omitted).

The Court thus explicitly recognized that a buyer cannot be held liable under §2(f) if the lower prices received are justified by reason of one of the seller's affirmative defenses.

III.

The petitioner, relying on this plain meaning of §2(f) and the teaching of the *Automatic Canteen* case, argues that it cannot be liable under §2(f) if Borden had a valid meeting-competition defense. The respondent, on the other hand, argues that the petitioner may be liable even assuming that Borden had such a defense. The meeting-competition defense, the respondent contends, must in these circumstances be judged from the point of view of the buyer. Since A&P knew for a fact that the final Borden bid beat the Bowman bid, it was not entitled to assert the meeting-competition defense even though Borden may have honestly believed that it was simply meeting competition. Recognition of a meeting-competition defense for the buyer in this situation, the respondent argues, would be contrary to the basic purpose of the Robinson–Patman Act to curtail abuses by large buyers.

A.

The short answer to these contentions of the respondent is that Congress did not provide in §2(f) that a buyer can be liable even if the seller has a valid defense. The clear language of §2(f) states that a buyer can be liable only if he receives a price discrimination "prohibited by this section." If a seller has a valid meeting-competition defense, there is simply no prohibited price discrimination.

A similar attempt to amend the Robinson–Patman Act judicially was rejected by this Court in *FTC* v. *Simplicity Pattern Co.,* 360 U. S. 55. There the

Federal Trade Commission had found that a manufacturer of dress patterns had violated §2(e) of the Clayton Act, as amended by the Robinson–Patman Act, by providing its larger customers services and facilities not offered its smaller customers.[11] The manufacturer attempted to defend against this charge by asserting that there had been no injury to competition and that its discriminations in services were cost justified. Since liability under §2(e), unlike §2(a), does not depend upon competitive injury or the absence of a cost-justification defense, the manufacturer's primary argument was that "it would be 'bad law and bad economics' to make discriminations unlawful even where they may be accounted for by cost differentials or where there is no competitive injury." 360 U. S., at 67 (footnote omitted). The Court rejected this argument. Recognizing that "this Court is not in a position to review the economic wisdom of Congress," the Court stated that "[w]e cannot supply what Congress has studiously omitted." *Ibid.* (footnote omitted). The respondent's attempt in the present case to rewrite §2(f) to hold a buyer liable even though there is no discrimination in price "prohibited by this section" must be rejected for the same reason.[12]

B.

In the *Automatic Canteen* case, the Court warned against interpretations of the Robinson–Patman Act which "extend beyond the prohibitions of the Act and, in so doing, help give rise to a price uniformity and rigidity in open conflict with the purposes of other antitrust legislation." 346 U. S., at 63. Imposition of §2(f) liability on the petitioner in this case would lead to just such price uniformity and rigidity.[13]

In a competitive market, uncertainty among sellers will cause them to compete for business by offering buyers lower prices. Because of the evils of collusive action, the Court has held that the exchange of price information by competitors violates the Sherman Act. *United States* v. *Container Corp.,* 393 U. S. 333. Under the view advanced by the respondent, however, a buyer, to avoid liability, must either refuse a seller's bid or at least inform him that his

---

[11] Section 2(e) provides:
"It shall be unlawful for any person to discriminate in favor of one purchaser against another purchaser or purchasers of a commodity bought for resale, with or without processing, by contracting to furnish or furnishing, or by contributing to the furnishing of, any services or facilities connected with the processing, handling, sale, or offering for sale of such commodity so purchased upon terms not accorded to all purchasers on proportionally equal terms." 15 U. S. C. §13(e).

[12] Contrary to the respondent's suggestion, this interpretation of §2(f) is in no way inconsistent with congressional intent. "[T]he buyer whom Congress in the main sought to reach was the one who, knowing full well that there was little likelihood of a defense for the seller, nevertheless proceeded to exert pressure for lower prices." *Automatic Canteen Co. of America* v. *FTC,* 346 U. S., at 79. Here, by contrast, we conclude that a buyer is not liable if the seller *does* have a defense under §2(b).

[13] More than once the Court has stated that the Robinson–Patman Act should be construed consistently with broader policies of the antitrust laws. *United States* v. *United States Gypsum Co.,* 438 U. S. 422; *Automatic Canteen Co. of America* v. *FTC, supra,* at 74.

bid has beaten competition. Such a duty of affirmative disclosure would almost inevitably frustrate competitive bidding and, by reducing uncertainty, lead to price matching and anticompetitive cooperation among sellers.[14]

Ironically, the Commission itself, in dismissing the charge under §5 of the Federal Trade Commission Act in this case, recognized the dangers inherent in a duty of affirmative disclosure:

> "The imposition of a duty of affirmative disclosure, applicable to a buyer whenever a seller states that his offer is intended to meet competition, is contrary to normal business practice and, we think, contrary to the public interest.

> "We fear a scenario where the seller automatically attaches a meeting competition caveat to every bid. The buyer would then state whether such bid meets, beats, or loses to another bid. The seller would then submit a second, a third, and perhaps a fourth bid until finally he is able to ascertain his competitor's bid." 87 F. T. C. 1047, 1050–1051.

The effect of the finding that the same conduct of the petitioner violated §2(f), however, is to impose the same duty of affirmative disclosure which the Commission condemned as anticompetitive, "contrary to the public interest," and "contrary to normal business practice," in dismissing the charge under §5 of the Federal Trade Commission Act. Neither the Commission nor the Court of Appeals offered any explanation for their apparent anomaly.

As in the *Automatic Canteen* case, we decline to adopt a construction of §2(f) that is contrary to its plain meaning and would lead to anticompetitive results. Accordingly, we hold that a buyer who has done no more than accept the lower of two prices competitively offered does not violate §2(f) provided the seller has a meeting-competition defense.[15]

---

[14] A duty of affirmative disclosure might also be difficult to enforce. In cases where a seller offers differing quantities or a different quality product, or offers to serve the buyer in a different manner, it might be difficult for the buyer to determine when disclosure is required.

[15] In *Kroger Co.* v. *FTC,* 438 F. 2d 1372, the Court of Appeals for the Sixth Circuit held that a buyer who induced price concessions by a seller by making deliberate misrepresentations could be liable under §2(f) even if the seller has a meeting-competition defense.

This case does not involve a "lying buyer" situation. The complaint issued by the FTC alleged that "A&P accepted the said offer of Borden with knowledge that Borden had granted a substantially lower price than that offered by the only other competitive bidder and without notifying Borden of this fact." The complaint did not allege that Borden's second bid was induced by any misrepresentation. The Court of Appeals recognized that the *Kroger* case involved a "lying buyer," but stated that there was no meaningful distinction between the situation where "the buyer lies or merely keeps quiet about the nature of the competing bid." 557 F. 2d 971, 983.

Despite this background, the respondent argues that A&P did engage in misrepresentations and therefore can be found liable as a "lying buyer" under the rationale of the *Kroger* case. The misrepresentation relied upon by the respondent is a statement allegedly made by a representative of A&P to Borden after Borden made its second bid which would have resulted in annual savings to A&P of $820,000. The A&P representative allegedly told Borden to "sharpen your pencil a little bit because you are not quite there." But the Commission itself referred to the comment only to note its irrelevance, and neither the Commission nor the Court of Appeals mentioned it in considering the §2(f) charge against A&P. This is quite understandable, since the comment was allegedly made *after* Borden made its second bid and therefore cannot be said to have induced the bid as in the *Kroger* case.

Because A&P was not a "lying buyer," we need not decide whether such a buyer could be liable under §2(f) even if the seller has a meeting-competition defense.

IV.

Because both the Commission and the Court of Appeals proceeded on the assumption that a buyer who accepts the lower of two competitive bids can be liable under §2(f) even if the seller has a meeting-competition defense, there was not a specific finding that Borden did in fact have such a defense. But it quite clearly did.

A.

The test for determining when a seller has a valid meeting-competition defense is whether a seller can "show the existence of facts which would lead a reasonable and prudent person to believe that the granting of a lower price would in fact meet the equally low price of a competitor." *FTC* v. *A. E. Staley Mfg. Co.,* 324 U. S. 746, 759–760. "A good-faith belief, rather than absolute certainty, that a price concession is being offered to meet an equally low price offered by a competitor is sufficient to satisfy the §2(b) defense." *United States* v. *United States Gypsum Co.,* 438 U. S. 422, 453.[16] Since good faith, rather than absolute certainty, is the touchstone of the meeting-competition defense, a seller can assert the defense even if it has unknowingly made a bid that in fact not only met but beat his competition. *Id.,* at 454.

B.

Under the circumstances of this case, Borden did act reasonably and in good faith when it made its second bid. The petitioner, despite its longstanding relationship with Borden, was dissatisfied with Borden's first bid and solicited offers from other dairies. The subsequent events are aptly described in the opinion of the Commission:

> "Thereafter, on August 31, 1965, A&P received an offer from Bowman Dairy that was lower than Borden's August 13 offer. On or about September 1, 1965, Elmer Schmidt, A&P's Chicago unit buyer, telephoned Gordon Tarr, Borden's Chicago chain store sales manager, and stated, 'I have a bid in my pocket. You [Borden] people are so far out of line it is not even funny. You are not even in the ball park.' Although Tarr asked Schmidt for some details, Schmidt said that he could not tell Tarr anything except that a $50,000 improvement in Borden's bid 'would not be a drop in the [bucket].' Contrary to its usual practice, A&P

---

[16] Recognition of the right of a seller to meet a lower competitive price in good faith may be the primary means of reconciling the Robinson–Patman Act with the more general purposes of the antitrust laws of encouraging competition between sellers. As the Court stated in *Standard Oil Co.* v. *FTC,* 340 U. S., at 249:

"We need not now reconcile, in its entirety, the economic theory which underlies the Robinson –Patman Act with that of the Sherman and Clayton Acts. It is enough to say that Congress did not seek by the Robinson–Patman Act either to abolish competition or so radically to curtail it that a seller would have no substantial right of self-defense against a price raid by a competitor."

then offered Borden the opportunity to submit another bid." 87 F. T. C., at 1048 (Footnotes and record citations omitted.)

Thus, Borden was informed by the petitioner that it was in danger of losing its A&P business in the Chicago area unless it came up with a better offer. It was told that its first offer was "not even in the ball park" and that a $50,000 improvement "would not be a drop in the bucket." In light of Borden's established business relationship with the petitioner, Borden could justifiably conclude that A&P's statements were reliable and that it was necessary to make another bid offering substantial concessions to avoid losing its account with the petitioner.

Borden was unable to ascertain the details of the Bowman bid. It requested more information about the bid from the petitioner, but this request was refused. It could not then attempt to verify the existence and terms of the competing offer from Bowman without risking Sherman Act liability. *United States* v. *United States Gypsum Co., supra.* Faced with a substantial loss of business and unable to find out the precise details of the competing bid, Borden made another offer stating that it was doing so in order to meet competition. Under these circumstances, the conclusion is virtually inescapable that in making that offer Borden acted in a reasonable and good-faith effort to meet its competition, and therefore was entitled to a meeting-competition defense.[17]

Since Borden had a meeting-competition defense and thus could not be liable under §2(b), the petitioner who did no more than accept that offer cannot be liable under §2(f).[18]

Accordingly, the judgment is reversed.

It is so ordered.

---

[17] The facts of this case are thus readily distinguishable from *Corn Products Co.* v. *FTC,* 324 U. S. 726, and *FTC* v. *A. E. Staley Mfg. Co.,* 324 U. S. 746, in both of which the Court held that a seller had failed to establish a meeting-competition defense. In the *Corn Products* case, the only evidence to rebut the prima facie case of price discrimination was testimony by witnesses who had no personal knowledge of the transactions in question. Similarly, in the *Staley Mfg. Co.* case, unsupported testimony from informants of uncertain character and reliability was insufficient to establish the defense. In the present case, by contrast, the source of the information was a person whose reliability was not questioned and who had personal knowledge of the competing bid. Moreover, Borden attempted to investigate by asking A&P for more information about the competing bid. Finally, Borden was faced with a credible threat of a termination of purchases by A&P if it did not make a second offer. All of these factors serve to show that Borden did have a valid meeting-competition defense. See *United States* v. *United States Gypsum Co.,* 438 U. S., at 454.

[18] Because we hold that the petitioner is not liable under §2(f), we do not reach the question whether Borden might also have had a cost-justification defense under §2(a).

6

Antitrust Issues and Marketing Channel Strategy

The long-term viability of any individual marketing channel member (e.g., a manufacturer, a wholesaler, or a retailer) depends on, among other things, the ability of the distribution system within which it is embedded to compete effectively with the systems of rival firms.[1] For this reason, various channel members frequently seek to exercise control over the functioning of the channel as a whole so that the resources of the channel are marshalled and directed in such a way as to promote maximum impact at the end-user level. A channel member can achieve complete control over the channel via vertical integration. Where integration is either inefficient, strategically inappropriate, or financially infeasible, a number of alternative means to achieving control exist. Foremost among them is the imposition of vertical restrictions—restraints on the behavior of channel members imposed by agreement among firms or individuals at successive levels of distribution.

There are a large number of marketing policies that suppliers can imple-

---

[1] For a discussion of the management of marketing channel relationships, see Louis W. Stern and Adel I. El-Ansary, *Marketing Channels,* 2nd ed. (Englewood Cliffs, N.J.: Prentice-Hall, Inc., 1982). Some of the information in this chapter is drawn from Chapter 8 in the Stern and El-Ansary text.

ment that are aimed at controlling or incentivizing their distribution systems. And there are numerous antitrust precedents that deal with these policies, because some of them represent blatant restraints of trade. A critical issue that has evolved in antitrust cases over the past 20 years is whether certain of these policies, while severely restricting *intrabrand* competition, are actually promoting, or at least not substantially lessening, *interbrand* competition. Intrabrand competition is defined as competition among wholesalers or retailers of the same brand (e.g., Coca-Cola, Chevrolet, or Apple). Interbrand competition is defined as competition among all the suppliers of different brands of the same generic product (e.g., brands of soft drinks, automobiles, or personal computers). By restricting intrabrand competition via instituting certain stipulations regarding resellers' activities, a supplier can supposedly motivate its wholesalers and retailers to give appropriate attention to the supplier's brand. This "appropriate attention," in turn, generates interbrand competition as the resellers of Brand X attempt to win out over the resellers of Brand Y in the sales and servicing of Product Z.

As appealing as this argument must sound to marketing strategists who would like to implement a variety of distribution policies, the issues are frequently more complex than this. Control over distribution is sought for many reasons, some of which are highly opportunistic and self-serving. Furthermore, not all distribution policies deal with intrabrand competition; several involve restricting interbrand competition directly by foreclosing competitors from resellers' outlets. Therefore, despite the increasingly sophisticated rationale that is being employed to defend vertical restrictions in distribution, there are scores of reasons why marketing executives should remain alert to potential antitrust problems. While control over distribution practices may make abundant sense from a marketing perspective in a variety of different situations, there is no mandate from the Congress, the courts, or the enforcement agencies that indicates that executives are free to exert such control without considerable scrutiny.

In this chapter, we examine the antitrust issues surrounding the use of the following vertical restrictions:

Exclusive dealing
Tying contracts
Territorial and customer restrictions
Resale price maintenance
Reciprocity
Refusals to deal

We also examine the constraints on the granting of functional discounts to different categories of channel members. Finally, we look at the policy of vertical integration. In doing so, we indicate where expansion by both external (e.g., by merger or acquisition) and internal means is circumscribed and explore some of the legal problems associated with operating dual distribution systems in which customers are also competitors.[2]

EXCLUSIVE DEALING

Exclusive dealing is the requirement by a seller or lessor that its customers sell or lease only its products, or at least no products in direct competition with the seller's products. A variant of exclusive dealing, requirement contracts, is subject to the same legal constraints as exclusive dealing arrangements. Under a requirements contract, a buyer agrees to purchase all or a part of his requirements of a product from one seller, usually for a specified period of time. Such arrangements clearly reduce the freedom of choice of the buyer. They also have the possibly undesirable effect of foreclosing a potential customer to alternate sellers, and vice versa, during the period stipulated in the agreement.

The use of exclusive dealing or requirements contracts is not illegal per se. These arrangements are generally viewed under a modified rule of reason, which has meant that they are subject to a measure of the effect of foreclosure on competing sellers.[3] Such marketing policies in distribution channels are mainly circumscribed by Section 3 of the Clayton Act, which stipulates that

> it shall be unlawful for any person . . . to lease or make a sale or contract for sale of goods, wares, merchandise, machinery, supplies or other commodities, whether patented or unpatented, . . . on the condition, agreement, or understanding that the lessee or purchaser thereof shall not use or deal in the goods, . . . of a competitor or competitors of the lessor or seller, where the effect of such lease, sale, or contract for sale or such condition, agreement or understanding may be to substantially lessen competition or tend to create a monopoly in any line of commerce.

However, they may also violate Section 1 of the Sherman Act and Section 5 of the Federal Trade Commission Act. Under the Sherman Act, various types of exclusive contracts may be deemed unlawful restraints of trade when a dominant firm is involved and when the contracts go so far beyond reasonable business needs as to have the necessary effect, or disclose a clear intention, of suppressing competition.[4] Under the FTC Act, the Federal Trade Commission has the power to stop such trade restraints in their incipiency without proof that they amount to an outright violation of Section 3 of the Clayton Act or other provisions of the antitrust laws. In other words, the FTC, using Section 5, has broad powers to declare "unfair" practices that conflict with the basic

---

[2] We have purposely excluded discussion of the various franchise disclosure laws, because we have chosen to focus on antitrust and consumer protection issues in this text. Furthermore, most of these laws vary from state to state, and our emphasis here is almost exclusively on federal law and federal court decisions. For an excellent outline on franchising law, see Franchising Committee, Section of Antitrust Law, "Franchising as a Distribution Channel: Outline of Relevant Law," *Antitrust Law Journal* 49, Issue 2 (1981), pp. 791–803.

[3] Ernest Gellhorn, *Antitrust Law and Economics in a Nutshell* (St. Paul, Minn.: West Publishing Co., 1976), p. 291.

[4] A. D. Neale and D. G. Goyder, *The Antitrust Laws of the U.S.A.*, 3rd ed. (New York: Cambridge University Press, 1980), p. 266.

policies of the Sherman Act and the Clayton Act, even though such practices may not constitute a violation of those laws. We will return to an examination of situations where the Sherman Act and the FTC Act have been applied against exclusive dealing or requirements contracts, but first we will turn our attention to the major cases where such arrangements have been attacked under Section 3 of the Clayton Act, which remains the dominant statute in this marketing policy area.

Major Cases

The first major case involving exclusive dealing to reach the Supreme Court under Section 3 of the Clayton Act was *Standard Fashion Co.* v. *Magrane–Houston Co.*[5] Here, a manufacturer of paper patterns for women's clothing exacted from its customers (mainly department and "notions" stores, which, in aggregate, represented 40 percent of all pattern retailers nationally) a promise not to handle competitors' patterns. The customers agreed to buy substantial quantitites of patterns, maintain a considerable inventory, and deal with Standard Fashion exclusively. The Court held that the arrangement was unlawful, arguing that the Clayton Act was aimed at stopping restraints "in their incipiency" and that foreclosing 40 percent of all outlets could seriously impede the ability of alternative suppliers to compete.

Nearly 30 years later, in the now infamous *Standard Stations* case,[6] the Court reinforced the *Standard Fashion* decision, but in a very roundabout manner. In the western states that it served, Standard Oil of California's total sales amounted to 23 percent of all gasoline sold in 1946. Its sales to its own service stations and to independent service stations amounted to 14 percent, divided about equally between the two distribution networks. The balance of the 23 percent was sold to industrial users. Standard had six major competitors who among them supplied 42 percent of the gasoline sold at retail as against Standard's 14 percent. All the major suppliers used exclusive supply contracts similar to those employed by Standard. Under Standard Oil's contracts, nearly 6,000 independent service stations (16 percent of the service stations in the western states) agreed to purchase all their requirements of one or more products. By far the greatest number of contracts concerned gasoline and other oil products only.

A major issue in the case was whether the Court was going to adopt a standard that was developed in an earlier case involving contracts tying the supply of salt to the use of patented machines.[7] The Court had condemned the tying contracts simply on the basis that the volume of business foreclosed was not insignificant or insubstantial. There was no question that the arrangement in *Standard Stations* met the "quantitative substantiality" test of this earlier

[5] 258 U.S. 346 (1922).

[6] *Standard Oil Company of California, et al.* v. *U.S.*, 337 U.S. 293 (1949).

[7] *International Salt Co.* v. *U.S.*, 332 U.S. 392 (1947).

case where only $500,000 of salt sales had been foreclosed to competitors. The main question was whether tying contracts were inherently more restrictive than requirements contracts or exclusive dealing arrangements, thus justifying a looser test of their effect on competition. The answer, supplied by Mr. Justice Frankfurter, was that the latter contracts and arrangements had some redeeming benefits, of which the following were most prominent:

In the case of the buyer, they may

—assure supply,
—afford protection against increases in price,
—enable long-term planning on the basis of known costs, and
—obviate the expense and risk of storage in the quantity necessary for a commodity having fluctuating demand.

From the seller's point of view, they may

—make possible the substantial reduction of selling expenses,
—give protection against price fluctuations,
—offer the possibility of a predictable market (which is of particular advantage to a newcomer to the field wanting to know what capital expenditures are justified), and
—permit establishing a foothold against the counterattacks of entrenched competitors.[8]

This line of thinking seemingly should have led the Court to apply a rule of reason and consider the economic effects of the arrangements used by Standard Oil. But in a curious twist, the Court fell back on arguments amazingly similar to those in *Standard Fashion* and in the case involving the tying contract for salt. It noted that the market was concentrated, because the largest seven firms (including Standard) controlled 65 percent of the market, and that entry was apparently restricted, because market shares had stabilized after the contractual arrangements were introduced. In this setting, the Court held that foreclosure of a substantial share of the retail market (i.e., Standard's independent service stations represented 7 percent of the market) establishes a sufficient foundation to infer that the arrangement may substantially lessen competition. Furthermore, it argued that Standard's contracts created "a potential clog on competition," and emphasized that exclusive contracts were pervasive in the market, being employed not only by Standard but by Standard's competitors as well.

The Court's decision contains a very powerful (and rather strange) message for all those parties seeking to influence Court decisions on the basis of economic and marketing principles. Mr. Justice Frankfurter noted in his opinion that while Standard's competitive position had not improved during the period covered by the exclusive arrangements, it was impossible to say *what would have happened* to its position in the absence of the contracts. In turn, he argued that the courts were not qualified to make predictions about effects on

---

[8] *Standard Oil Company of California, et al.* v. *U.S.*, 337 U.S. 293 at 306–307 (1949).

competition. In other words, the Court refused to become embroiled in economic and marketing analysis, and therefore decided that it had better hold on to a relatively straightforward quantitative test in terms of the amount of business foreclosed by the restrictive contracts.[9] In the end, then, a presumption was made against such arrangements involving a substantial volume of business because of the "serious difficulties" that would attend any effort to apply the necessary tests of competitive effects. Thus, the Court seemed to argue for a rule of reason approach, while actually applying a per se test modified by the significance of commerce affected.

However, in a case decided in 1961, the Court's economic impact analysis was considerably more intensive, both as to markets likely to be affected and the probable effect of the particular foreclosure, than that given in *Standard Stations*. The decision did not expressly overrule *Standard Stations*, but it significantly modified some of the more restrictive interpretations of the circumstances in which exclusive dealing arrangements would be allowed. For once the Court appeared to be moving from a per se approach toward a rule of reason balancing approach. The case, *Tampa Electric Co. v. Nashville Coal Co. et al.*,[10] involved a contract between Nashville Coal and Tampa Electric, a Florida public utility producing electricity, covering Tampa's expected requirements of coal (i.e., not less than 500,000 tons per year) for a period of 20 years. Before any coal was delivered, Nashville declined to perform the contract on the ground that it was illegal under the antitrust laws. (In actuality, the price of coal had jumped, making the arrangement less profitable for the coal company.) Tampa brought suit, arguing that the contract was both valid and enforceable.

Quantitatively, the commerce over the 20-year period of the contract would amount to $128 million, and on this basis the district court and the court of appeals found a violation. But the Supreme Court, in a suprising move, held flatly that "the dollar volume, by itself, is not the test,"[11] thereby rejecting "quantitative substantiality" as the standard to be used in these situations. To be illegal, the Court explained such arrangements must have a tendency to work a substantial, not merely remote, lessening of competition in the relevant competitive market. Mr. Justice Clark, speaking for the majority, indicated that "substantiality" was to be determined by taking into account the following factors:

—the relative strength of the parties involved,
—the proportionate volume of commerce involved in relation to the total volume of commerce in the relevant market area, and
—the probable immediate and future effects which pre-emption of that share of the market might have on effective competition within it.[12]

[9] Neale and Goyder, op. cit., p. 269. See, also, Peter Asch, *Economic Theory and the Antitrust Dilemma* (New York: John Wiley & Sons, Inc., 1970), p. 352.

[10] 365 U.S. 320 (1961).

[11] Ibid., at 333.

[12] Ibid., at 333.

The district court and the court of appeals had accepted the argument that the contract foreclosed a substantial share of the market, because Tampa's requirements equaled the total volume of coal purchased in the state of Florida before the contract's inception. The Supreme Court, in an interesting piece of economic reasoning, defined the relevant market as the *supply* market in an eight-state area, noting that mines in that coal-producing region were eager to sell more coal in Florida. When the market was defined as the entire multi-state Appalachian coal region, the foreclosure amounted to less than 1 percent of the tonnage produced each year. The Court concluded that given the nature of the market (i.e., the needs of a utility for a stable supply at reasonable prices over a long period of time as well as the level of concentration) the small percentage of foreclosure did not actually or potentially cause a substantial reduction of competition nor tend toward a monopoly.

In their summary of the *Tampa Electric* case, Neale and Goyder point out that

> The Court, finding for Tampa, distinguished earlier cases on a number of grounds. In this case, there was no seller with a dominant position in the market, as in *Standard Fashion*, nor were there myriad outlets with substantial sales volume coupled with an industry-wide practice of relying upon exclusive contracts, as in *Standard Stations*.[13]

The decision in this case indicates that the type of goods or merchandise, the geographic area of effective competition, and the substantiality of the competition foreclosed must all be assessed in determining illegality or legality. It also indicates that exclusive dealing arrangements or requirements contracts that are negotiated by sellers possessing a very small share of the relevant market have a good chance of standing up in court.[14] The critical issue may involve the definition of the relevant market; firms with large shares may still be circumscribed.

The observation about firms with relatively small market shares was supported in *U.S.* v. *J. I. Case Co.*[15] The company's salesmen had apparently pressured Case's dealers to act as exclusive agents for its farm machinery. Such pressure was officially disowned by the company, which blamed it on overzealous sales work. Beyond the absence of an overt exclusive agreement, the district court found that the instances of pressure that had been shown did not damage competition. The decision to dismiss the case was based primarily on the fact that J. I. Case was by no means the largest in its field, that other manufacturers were able to find dealers for their goods, and that the dealers clearly preferred to deal in one manufacturer's line. In such situations, evidence that the arrangement is not an involuntary one, imposed by the seller on the buyer, may save it from illegality.[16]

---

[13] Neale and Goyder, op. cit., p. 273.

[14] F. M. Scherer, *Industrial Market Structure and Economic Performance,* 2nd ed. (Chicago: Rand McNally College Publishing Co., 1980), pp. 585–586.

[15] 101 F. Supp. 856 (1951).

[16] Neale and Goyder, op. cit., p. 273.

Sherman and FTC Act Cases

Exclusive dealing and requirements contracts are also subject to scrutiny under the Sherman Act and FTC Act. Thus, under the Sherman Act, a dominant firm, American Can Company, was found to restrain trade unreasonably when it required food-processing lessees of its can-closing machinery to buy all their supply of cans on 5-year contracts.[17] Under Section 5 of the Federal Trade Commission Act, the Supreme Court decided that Brown Shoe Company, one of the world's largest shoe manufacturers, could be prohibited by the FTC from using exclusive dealerships.[18] In this case, approximately 650 dealers of the Brown Shoe Company, about 1 percent of all shoe retailers in the United States, had agreed to concentrate on purchases of Brown shoes in return for assistance with shop design, group insurance, and other promotional help. The FTC believed that this franchise plan was an example of an "incipient attempt" to reduce competition in the shoe trade, even though the record contained no evidence of the market share affected or of the extent to which competing shoe suppliers were foreclosed. Furthermore, the agreements could be terminated at any time by the dealers. Actual (in Sherman Act cases) or potential (in Clayton Act cases) injury to competition has to be shown before such arrangements can be declared unlawful. But in *FTC* v. *Brown Shoe*, the Supreme Court held that, because the agreements were in conflict with the spirit of the Sherman and the Clayton Acts, the FTC was not required under the FTC Act to prove actual or potential injury to competition. (In other words, all the FTC has to show is high likelihood that there may be an injury.) This finding means that exclusive dealing and requirements contracts are more vulnerable to prosecution under Section 5 of the FTC Act than under provisions of the other antitrust laws.

TYING CONTRACTS

Tying contracts exist when a seller, having a product or service that buyers want (the *tying product*), refuses to sell it unless a second (*tied*) product or service is also purchased, or at least is not purchased from anyone other than the seller of the tying product. Thus, a manufacturer of motion picture projectors (the tying product) might insist that only his film (the tied product) be used with the projectors, or a manufacturer of shoe machinery (the tying product) might insist that lessees of the machinery purchase service contracts (tied service) from him for the proper maintenance of the machinery. A tying agreement in effect forecloses competing sellers from the opportunity of selling the tied commodity or service to the purchaser. Indeed, like exclusive dealing arrangements, the critical issue in the condemnation of tying contracts is the foreclosing of competition from a marketplace. But tying contracts are viewed much more negatively by the courts than exclusive dealing arrangements or re-

[17] *U.S. v. American Can Co., et al.*, 87 F. Supp. 18 (1949).
[18] *Brown Shoe Co., Inc. v. FTC*, 384 U.S. 316 (1966).

quirements contracts. For example, in making the distinction between a requirements contract and a tying contract in the *Standard Stations* case mentioned previously, Justice Frankfurter stated that tying arrangements "serve hardly any purpose beyond the suppression of competition. . . ."[19] The courts have often viewed tie-ins with concern because, as they have reasoned, such arrangements force buyers into giving up the purchase of substitutes for the tied product, and they may destroy the free access of competing suppliers of the tied product to the consuming market. Thus, tying agreements are seen to have the anticompetitive effect of limiting competition in the market for the tied product.

Similar to exclusive dealing, tying is also circumscribed by the Sherman Act, the Clayton Act, and the FTC Act. Given the overwhelmingly negative attitude on the part of the courts toward tying, it is little wonder that use of such arrangements would rarely be approved. Indeed as Sullivan points out, "a black letter statement of the current law" would probably assert three propositions:

1. That a tie violates Section 1 of the Sherman Act whenever the seller possesses any discernible degree of market power in the tying product and the tie effects more than a *de minimus* amount of commerce.
2. That a tie also violates Section 3 of the Clayton Act when it meets that test, so long as there is a "sale or lease" of a commodity or a contract therefore.[20]
3. That any tie violating Section 1 alone or Sections 1 and 3 also violates Section 5 of the FTC Act.[21]

But, as Sullivan also points out, "statements of this kind, useful as they can be at times, are terribly simplistic and for that reason dangerous."[22] In other words, many have argued that tying agreements are, like price fixing, per se illegal on the basis of the propositions listed previously. But, as we shall see, there seems to be a bit more latitude as compared to price fixing.

Major Cases

Numerous cases are important in this area of distribution policy. Here we briefly touch on only a few of the more prominent in order to provide some notion of how the Supreme Court has wrestled with this marketing activity over the years.

Back in the 1930s, IBM leased its patented tabulating equipment on the condition that it be used only with punch cards made and sold by it, even though it had leased its machine to the government on the basis that, with a

---

[19] *Standard Oil Company of California* v. *U.S.*, 337 U.S. 293 (1949) at 305.

[20] Section 3 of the Clayton Act is inapplicable to tying contracts for the sales of land, or when the tying item is the provision of services rather than of "goods, wares, merchandise, machinery, supplies or other commodities . . . ," whereas the Sherman Act applies to every kind of contract.

[21] Lawrence A. Sullivan, *Handbook of the Law of Antitrust* (St. Paul, Minn.: West Publishing Co., 1977), p. 434.

[22] Ibid.

15 percent increase in lease costs, the government could use its own cards. IBM asserted that improperly made cards could injure the machine and damage its goodwill. In a case against IBM, decided in 1936, the Court commented that a less restrictive alternative would be to publish specifications for cards that would not damage the machines and to restrict the machine to use with cards meeting these specifications.[23] In condemning the tying agreement, the Court examined whether IBM had power in the tying product, and alluded to the patent that IBM had on its machine. It also noted that IBM and its competitors marketed their products in the same way (i.e., with tying agreements) and that the amount of commerce in punch cards covered by the restraint was quantitatively substantial (some $3 million per year), adding up to 81 percent of the entire punch card market. In short, the Court went through a search of a number of market facts before making its judgment. However, in the next important case, *International Salt Co.* v. *U.S.*,[24] the Court, as indicated in the preceding section on exclusive dealing, developed a more rigorous legal standard by condemning the tying agreement (salt purchases from International were tied to the purchase of International's patented machines) on the basis of foreclosure of a certain dollar volume. The record of the case showed nothing relevant to monopoly power beyond the fact that annual sales of salt for use in the machines amounted to about $500,000. The decision in *International Salt* was the first time the Court labeled tying a per se offense, arguing that "it is unreasonable, per se, to foreclose competitors from any substantial market," and that the volume of business involved in this case "cannot be said to be insignificant or insubstantial."[25]

In more recent cases, however, the Court has tried to clarify and amend the bright line standard of *International Salt*. For example, in 1953, the Supreme Court said in its *Times–Picayune* decision[26] that tying contracts are illegal per see under Section 3 of the Clayton Act if the seller enjoys a monopolistic position in the market for the tying product *or* if a substantial volume of commerce in the tied product is restrained. Then, in 1958, it said that tying agreements are unreasonable per se under Section 1 of the Sherman Act if the seller has "sufficient economic power" with respect to the tying product to appreciably restrain trade in the tied product.[27] Because Section 3 of the Clayton Act is restricted in its coverage to *commodities*,[28] the 1958 case, which involved tying agreements used by Northern Pacific Railroad Company, was brought under the Sherman Act because it concerned the purchasing or leasing of *land*. The railroad company had, in the late nineteenth century, been granted by Congress approximately 40 million acres of land in the Northwest in return

[23] *International Business Machines Corp.* v. *U.S.*, 298 U.S. 131 (1936).

[24] 332 U.S. 392 (1947).

[25] Ibid. at 396.

[26] *Times–Picayune Publishing Co.* v. *U.S.*, 345 U.S. 594 (1953).

[27] *Northern Pacific Railroad Company* v. *U.S.*, 356 U.S. 1 (1958).

[28] See footnote 20.

for its construction of a railway line from Lake Superior to the Pacific Coast. Over the years, most of this land had been sold or leased out subject to the terms of a "preferential routing" clause, under which the purchaser or lessee was obliged to ship over Northern Pacific's lines all commodities produced or manufactured on the land. Mr. Justice Black, for the majority, pointed out that the tying agreement served little or no legitimate purpose, foreclosed competing suppliers from an open market in the tied product, and prevented buyers from exercising a free choice.

The most recent major case to come before the Supreme Court dealt with the tying of credit to the purchase of prefabricated homes.[29] Fortner Enterprises, the plaintiff, was a corporation formed by an experienced real estate developer for the purpose of developing a tract of homes. U.S. Steel's home division, the defendant, marketed prefabricated homes. To enhance the attractiveness of its offerings to developers, U.S. Steel formed a subsidiary corporation solely for the purpose of extending credit to its customers. Fortner sought financing from U.S. Steel, and credit was extended to cover all of Fortner's development costs as well as the price of purchasing homes from U.S. Steel. However, Fortner became dissatisfied with the agreement, claiming the prefabricated homes were defective, and sued for treble damages under the tying arrangement doctrine of the Sherman Act. After long and protracted litigation, the case was finally laid to rest in 1977. The finding of the Supreme Court may reflect the willingness of the Burger Court to consider a wide range of facts in deciding tying cases. In his summation, Mr. Justice Stevens stated that the trial record contained no evidence that U.S. Steel or its subsidiaries had any market power that gave them a cost advantage over banks or other financial institutions in the credit market; nor was there any element of "uniqueness" in the credit as a tying product comparable to either the landholdings of Northern Pacific or the patent strength of International Salt. As Mr. Justice Stevens concluded, "The ususual credit bargain offered to Fortner proves nothing more than a willingness to provide cheap financing in order to sell expensive homes." In summary, the *Fortner* case indicates that, in the absence of monopoly or economic power in the tying product, such tying arrangements are not illegal. Here the lack of "uniqueness" indicated to the Court that the economic power involved was insignificant.

Patents, Copyrights, and Trademarks

Determining whether the seller has sufficient "economic power" in the tying product market to appreciably restrain competition in the tied product market is critical in tying contract cases. When the tying product is patented, copyrighted, or, in certain circumstances, simply trademarked, the requisite economic power is presumed.

---

[29] *Fortner Enterprises, Inc.* v. *U.S. Steel Corporation,* 97 U.S. 861 (1977).

Patents.

We have already discussed the relationship between patents and antitrust in Chapter 2 and made reference to cases involving tying contracts. When the tying product is patented, there is no doubt that some element of monopoly power exists. Courts have consistently ruled that a patent on a tying product supplies, prima facie, the monopolistic element necessary to condemn the arrangement. The patent issue was significant in both the *IBM* and the *International Salt* cases. In such situations, it is reasoned that the holder of a legal monopoly (a patent) in one market is using that leverage to monopolize another market.

In addition, tying provisions in a patent license constitute patent misuse (as a matter of patent law) and will operate to deny the holder relief for infringement of the patent. For example, in *Morton Salt* v. *Suppiger Co.*,[30] Morton, which manufactured a patented machine that dispensed salt, had licensed canners to use the machine only in connection with purchases of Morton salt. Morton was denied infringement relief against a defendant who manufactured and sold a machine that infringed Morton's patent. It should be noted, however, that the doctrine of patent misuse may have somewhat broader scope than an antitrust violation, because the former does not depend on a showing of anticompetitive effect.[31]

Copyrights.

The major case involving tying agreements and copyrights concerned motion picture distribution, a line of trade that has historically been riddled with anticompetitive practices. In *U.S.* v. *Loew's Inc.*,[32] six major distributors were charged with violating Section 1 of the Sherman Act by making the sale of one or more feature films to television stations conditional on the purchase of other films. The practice had forced buyers to purchase undesirable films to obtain the features they wanted. For example, to get *Treasure of Sierra Madre, Casablanca, Sergeant York, Johnny Belinda,* and *The Man Who Came to Dinner,* WTOP (a Washington television station) also had to purchase such films as *Nancy Drew, Troubleshooter, Tugboat Annie Sails Again, Kid Nightingale, Gorilla Man,* and *Tear Gas Squad.* The test of illegality rested on an assessment of the market power held by the seller. The Court held that "sufficient economic power" lay in the uniqueness of the tying product, because the most desirable films were, of course, copyrighted. In other words, the presence of a copyright on the tying good creates the presumption of the requisite market power. Moreover, since 24 contracts were involved, comprising payments ranging from $60,000 to over $2,500,000, the requirement that a "not insubstantial amount" of interstate commerce be affected was also met.

[30] 314 U.S. 488 (1942).

[31] Gellhorn, op. cit., pp. 278–279n.

[32] 371 U.S. 45 (1962).

Trademarks.

The presumption of a requisite economic power was extended to trademarks by the 9th Circuit Court of Appeals in 1971 in a case involving franchising.[33] Under franchise agreements, an individual (franchisee) or group of individuals is usually permitted to set up an outlet of a national or regional chain in return for a capital investment and a periodic fee to the parent company (the franchisor). In some cases, the parent company also requires the franchise holders to buy various supplies, such as meat, baked goods, and paper cups in the case of restaurants, either from the corporation or an approved supplier. In franchising, the tying product is the franchise itself, and the tied products are the supplies that the franchisee must purchase to operate his business.[34] Companies with such requirements have argued that they are necessary in order to maintain the quality of their services and reputation. However, critics of such agreements assert that franchisors often require franchisees to purchase supplies and raw materials at prices far above those of the competitive market.[35] The potential for a conflict of interest on the part of franchisors is high, especially when the volume of revenue generated by sales of supplies is taken into account, as shown in Table 6-1. For example, in 1982, franchised convenience food stores, like 7-11, purchased over $154 million in products and services from their franchisors, such as Southland Corp., the overwhelming proportion of which were purchases of food.

Under the Lanham Act, as pointed out in Chapter 2, there is a duty on a trademark owner to maintain control over the use of the mark by his licensees. In franchising, the primary tying "product" is the trademark itself (e.g., "McDonald's," "Budget" Rent-a-Car, "Sheraton" Hotels). Therefore, tying agreements that link the trademark to supplies have been sustained by the courts only when franchisors have been able to prove that their trademarks are inseparable from their supplies and that the tied products (the supplies) are, in fact, essential to the maintenance of quality control. For example, in a lawsuit involving Baskin–Robbins, a franchised chain of ice cream stores, certain franchisees contended that Baskin–Robbins ice cream products were unlawfully tied to the sale of the Baskin–Robbins trademark.[36] However, the tie-in claim was disallowed because the franchisees did not establish that the trademark was a separate product from the ice cream; in tying cases, two distinct products must be involved in order for tying to be present.

In its decision, the 9th Circuit Court of Appeals distinguished between two

---

[33] *Siegel* v. *Chicken Delight, Inc.,* 448 F.2d 43 (9th Cir. 1971), *cert. denied,* 405 U.S. 95 (1972).

[34] A survey conducted by Hunt and Nevin indicated that about 70 percent of over 600 fast-food franchisee respondents were required to purchase at least some of their operating supplies from their franchisors and that the supplies so obtained represented 50 percent of the franchisees' total purchases. S. D. Hunt and J. R. Nevin, "Tying Agreements in Franchising," *Journal of Marketing* 39 (July 1975), pp. 24–25.

[35] Almost half the respondents of Hunt and Nevin's survey who purchase supplies from their franchisors believed that they were paying higher prices for the supplies than they would have had to pay in the open market. Ibid. See, also, *The Impact of Franchising on Small Business,* Hearings Before the Subcommittee on Urban and Rural Economic Development (Washington, D.C.: U.S. Government Printing Office, 1970), p. 5.

[36] *Norman E. Krehl, et al.* v. *Baskin–Robbins Ice Cream Company, et al.,* 42 F.2d 115 (8th Cir. 1982).

Table 6-1.

Total Sales of Products and Services by Franchisors to Franchisees: 1982[a]

Kinds of Franchised Business	Total	Merchandise (Nonfood) for Resale	Supplies (such as Paper Goods, etc.)	Food Ingredients	Other
TOTAL ALL FRANCHISING[b]	6,621,178	4,369,333	533,214	1,518,675	199,956
Automotive products and services	1,929,241	1,912,123	6,969	0	10,149
Business aids and services	75,464	18,005	19,815	0	37,644
Construction, home improvement, maintenance and cleaning services	150,592	109,383	12,614	0	28,595
Convenience stores	154,927	25	0	150,602	4,300
Educational products and services	34,193	2,509	10,684	0	21,000
Restaurants (all types)	1,140,587	62,000	346,489	691,956	39,542
Hotels, motels, and campgrounds	65,248	753	56,485	260	7,750
Laundry and drycleaning services	1,236	26	140	0	1,070
Recreation entertainment, and travel	4,498	2,240	1,226	0	1,032
Rental services (auto–truck)	2,662	0	2,662	0	0
Rental services (equipment)	23,747	2,907	505	0	20,335
Retailing (nonfood)	2,269,120	2,214,850	47,016	0	7,254
Retailing (food other than convenience stores)	732,025	14,467	24,416	675,857	17,285
Miscellaneous	37,638	29,445	4,193	0	4,000

Source: U.S. Department of Commerce, Franchising in the Economy 1980–1982 (Washington, D.C.: U.S. Government Printing Office, Jan. 1982), p. 35.

[a] Estimated by respondents.

[b] Does not include automobile and truck dealers, gasoline service stations, and soft drink bottlers for which data were not collected.

kinds of franchising systems: (1) the business format system and (2) the distribution system. It stated that a business format system is usually created merely to conduct business under a common trade name. The franchise outlet itself is generally responsible for the production and preparation of the system's end product; the franchisor merely provides the trademark and, in some cases, supplies used in operating the franchised outlet and producing the system's product (e.g., Budget Rent-a-Car, Sir Speedy Instant Printing). Under a distribution type system, the franchised outlets, according to the court, serve merely as conduits through which the trademarked goods of the franchisor flow to the ultimate consumer. These goods are generally manufactured by the franchisor or by its licensees according to detailed specifications. In this context, instead of identifying a business format, the trademark serves merely as representation of the end product marketed by the system (e.g., Chevrolet automobile dealerships, Texaco gas stations). Consequently, sales of substandard products under the trademark would dissipate goodwill and reduce the value of the trademark. The Court felt that the Baskin–Robbins Ice Cream Company is representative of a distribution-type system.

The decision in the *Baskin–Robbins* case is similar to that in a lawsuit against Carvel (a soft ice cream franchise), where the court concluded that Carvel's ingredient supply restrictions were justified by the need for quality control connected with the problem of ingredient secrecy.[37] In addition, in a lawsuit involving Dunkin' Donuts, the court stated that such tying agreements may be justified not only when the franchisor is attempting to maintain product quality, but also when it is attempting to enter a new market or industry *or* to preserve its market identity.[38]

In a decision involving the Chock Full O'Nuts Corporation, it was held that the franchisor "successfully proved its affirmative defense (to tying charges) of maintaining quality control with regard to its coffee and baked goods."[39] On the other hand, Chock Full O'Nuts was unsuccessful in defending its tying practices with respect to a number of other products (e.g., french fries, soft drink syrups, napkins, and glasses). The latter adverse finding paralleled that in an antitrust case involving Chicken Delight.[40] The parent company's contract requiring Chicken Delight franchisees to purchase paper items, cookers, fryers, and mix preparations from the franchisor was declared to be a tying contract in violation of Section 1 of the Sherman Act. Chicken Delight failed in its attempt to convince the court that its system should be considered a single product. The paper products were viewed as illegally tied to the franchise because they were easily reproducible. The issue of the cookers, fryers, and spice items was less clearcut, and the court left it to a jury to decide whether they were justifiably tied on the basis of quality control of the finished prod-

---

[37] *Susser* v. *Carvel Corp.*, 332 F.2d 505 (2nd Cir. 1964).

[38] *Ungar* v. *Dunkin' Donuts of America, Inc.*, 531 F.2d 1211 (3d. Cir. 1976).

[39] *In re Chock Full O'Nuts Corp. Inc.*, 3 Trade Reg. Rep. 20, 441 (Oct. 1973).

[40] *Siegel* v. *Chicken Delight, Inc.*, op. cit.

uct. The jury eventually determined that quality control could have been effected by means other than a tie-in and thus rejected the franchisor's claims.

Tying agreements were also involved in the *Brown Shoe* case, referred to in the preceding section on exclusive dealing.[41] Under Brown's franchise plan, held to be unfair and illegal by the Federal Trade Commission, independent dealers were given what was admittedly a valuable package of services—architectural plans, merchandising records, the help of a Brown field representative, and an option to participate in inexpensive group insurance—in return for a simple promise of the dealer–franchisee to concentrate on the Brown Shoe line and not to handle "conflicting" lines. Justice Hugo Black, in writing the Supreme Court's decision, stated that the records showed "beyond doubt" that Brown's program required shoe retailers "unless faithless to their contractual obligations with Brown, substantially to limit their trade with Brown's competitors." The conclusion in this case was that franchising poses a restraint to trade if the parent company places unreasonable limitations on the right of the franchisee to make his own business decisions.

Related Policies Subject to Scrutiny

Policies similar to or having the effect of tying agreements have also been challenged. For example, tires, batteries, and accessories have been sold in service stations of major oil companies in two different ways:

1. *Purchase–resale agreements.* Under this plan, the products are purchased from the manufacturer by the oil company and resold to gasoline wholesalers and retailers.
2. *Sales commission plans.* Under these plans, the products are sold directly to gasoline wholesalers and retailers by the manufacturer. The oil company receives a commission on all sales, and in return it assists with promotion.

In three cases ending in 1968, the courts held that the sales commission plan is inherently coercive because of the control that the oil company has over its dealers.[42] Market exclusion of other brands will result, and thus the plans are an unfair practice whether illegal intent is shown or not. In the *Atlantic Refining* case the Supreme Court confirmed this view.[43] The merits of purchase–resale agreements were not ruled upon by the courts.

In addition, the Federal Trade Commission has used Section 5 of the FTC Act to challenge retailers to stop making, carrying out, or enforcing anticompetitive leasing agreements. These agreements or boycotts, which are also similar to tying contracts, have given a retailer the right to be the only retailer of its kind (e.g., drugstore) in a shopping center, the right to reject or accept the opportunity to operate an additional outlet in a shopping center

[41] Ibid.

[42] Donald F. Dixon, "Market Exclusion and Dealer Coercion in Sponsored TBA Sales," *Journal of Marketing* 35 (Jan. 1971), pp. 62–63.

[43] *Atlantic Refining Co.* v. *FTC,* 381 U.S. 357 (1965).

where it already has one ("rights of first refusal"), the right to prohibit or control the entrance of tenants into shopping centers, and the right to restrict the business operations of other tenants in shopping centers.[44] For example, FTC consent orders in 1976 and 1979 prohibited Sears, Roebuck[45] and Federated Department Stores,[46] respectively, from making or forcing any agreement with shopping center developers that

> prohibit entry into centers of particular tenants or classes of tenants (e.g., discount stores) or allows Sears or Federated to approve tenant entry;
>
> grants Sears or Federated the right to approve floor space to others or their use of it;
>
> specifies that tenants shall sell their merchandise at any particular price or within any range of prices, fashions, or quality (when the latter terms connote price);
>
> limits discount advertising, pricing, or selling;
>
> limits the types of merchandise or services that tenants may sell;
>
> prescribes minimum hours of operation;
>
> grants Sears or Federated the right to approve tenant location; or
>
> provides for radius restrictions upon tenants.

These prohibitions apply to all shopping centers, including those developed and built by Sears' wholly owned subsidiary, Homart Development Company.

Another form of tying arrangement is called "full-line forcing." This is where a seller's leverage with regard to a tying product is used to force a buyer to purchase his whole line of goods. This policy is not illegal unless the buyer is prevented from handling competitors' products. In the case of a farm machinery manufacturer, a court held that the practice was within the law, but inferred that full-line forcing that caused the exclusion of competitors from this part of the market might be illegal if a substantial share of business were affected.[47] Block-booking imposed by motion picture distributors and producers on independent theatre owners can also be viewed as full-line forcing. This practice compels theaters to take many pictures they do not want in order to obtain the ones they do. Independent producers have consequently been unable to rent their films to theaters whose programs were thus crowded with the products of the major firms. Such practices have typically been held to be illegal, especially when copyrights are involved relative to the films used as tying mechanisms.[48]

---

[44] "Order against Drug Chain Bans Shopping Center Lease Restrictions," *FTC News Summary* (Oct. 10, 1975), p. 1. See also "Antitrust Action in Shopping Malls," *Business Week* (Dec. 8, 1975), p. 51. In survey results released by the FTC on Mar. 13, 1981, it was pointed out that "larger stores in shopping centers have generally abandoned the practice of exercising excessive power over smaller stores and discounters in lease arrangements." See "Shopping Centers Complying with an FTC Decision on Leasing Practices," *FTC News Summary* (Mar. 20, 1981), p. 2.

[45] "Order Against Sears, Roebuck Bans Anticompetitive Shopping Center Conduct," *FTC News Summary* (Oct. 29, 1976), p. 1.

[46] "FTC Shopping Center Order Would Ban Control by Department Stores," *FTC News Summary* (Jan. 19, 1979), p. 1.

[47] *U.S.* v. *J. I. Case Co.,* 101 F. Supp. 856 (1951).

[48] *U.S.* v. *Paramount Pictures,* 334 U.S. 131 (1948); *U.S.* v. *Loew's Inc.,* 371 U.S. 45 (1962).

Other instances prohibiting the use of full-line forcing have occurred. For example, in 1976, E&J Gallo Winery, the largest seller of wine in the United States, consented to a Federal Trade Commission order prohibiting the company from, among other things, requiring its wholesalers to distribute any Gallo wines in order to obtain other kinds.[49] And, in 1977, Union Carbide Corporation agreed to a consent order prohibiting the company from requiring its dealers to purchase from it their total requirements of six industrial gases (acetylene, argon, helium, hydrogen, nitrogen, and oxygen) and from making the purchase of the six gases a prerequisite for dealers buying other gases or welding products.[50]

The Per Se Issue

In spite of references to the per se illegality of tying contracts in a number of cases, it is still necessary to determine when conditions of economic power exist. In theory, where no leverage exists in a product, there can be no tying arrangement by coercion; the buyer can always go elsewhere to purchase.[51] Thus, plaintiffs must prove more than the existence of a tie. As Sullivan points out, they must also show that the tying product is successfully differentiated and that the commerce affected by the tie is not *de minimus*.[52] The presumption against tying arrangements is not quite as strong as the per se rule against price-fixing conspiracies. As summed up by Scherer,

> Violation will not be found unless there is appreciable monopoly power in the tying good market or unless a substantial volume of sales is foreclosed in the tied good market. For relatively small sellers of unpatented products, these conditions are not likely to be satisfied. Small companies attempting to break into a new market under the protection of tying contracts may also escape censure. And the courts have been willing to consider extenuating circumstances such as the need to exercise control over complementary goods or services to ensure satisfactory operation of the tying product.[53]

Some of these extenuating circumstances, beyond those detailed previously relative to franchising, can be found when two products are made to be used jointly and one will not function properly without the other.[54] In other situations, if a company's goodwill depends on proper operation of equipment, a service contract may be tied to the sale or lease of the machine. Thus, in *U.S. v. Jerrold Electronics*,[55] the Supreme Court approved a tie-in of engineering

---

[49] "Consent Agreement Cites E & J Gallo Winery," *FTC News Summary* (May 21, 1976), p. 1. See, also, "Gallo Winery Consents to FTC Rule Covering Wholesaler Dealings," *Wall Street Journal,* May 20, 1976, p. 15.

[50] "Union Carbide Settles Complaint by FTC on Industrial-Gas Sales; Airco to Fight," *Wall Street Journal,* May 20, 1977, p. 8.

[51] Marshall C. Howard, *Legal Aspects of Marketing* (New York: McGraw-Hill Book Co., 1964), p. 98.

[52] Sullivan, op. cit., p. 439.

[53] Scherer, op. cit., p. 584.

[54] See *ILC Peripherals Leasing Corp. (Memorex)* v. *International Business Machines Corp.,* 458 F. Supp. 423 (N.D. Cal. 1978).

[55] 187 F. Supp. 545 (E.D. Pa. 1960), *aff'd per curiam.* 365 U.S. 567 (1961).

service contracts to the purchase of highly innovative, complex community television antennae systems. There was reason to believe that, in the absence of a compulsory tie-in, customers might attempt to service their own antenna apparatus, a task for which few were qualified. Such efforts could have led to unsatisfactory performance of the equipment and damage to Jerrold's innovative business. But the Court only approved the tie-in during the early, developmental stages of the business. It held that it would cease to be reasonable once the technical requirements of the system were more widely understood and individual failures would no longer materially prejudice the future of the whole industry. In addition, the practicality of alternatives to the tying arrangement appears to be crucial as well. If a firm will suffer injury unless it can protect its product, and there is no feasible alternative, the courts are likely to go along with tying agreements. Nevertheless, even though all these extenuating circumstances have been recognized, the general rule that industry would be wise to follow is that tying agreements are inherently anticompetitive in their impact and, thus, while not strictly per se illegal, are very close to it. As Neale and Coyder put it,

> Provided that the person imposing the tie-in has sufficient economic power with respect to the tying product to restrain free competition in the market for the tied product to some degree, and a not "insubstantial" amount of interstate commerce is affected, tying contracts will almost certainly now be held illegal, under whichever Act the action is brought.[56]

Having said all this, it is highly instructive to note that, in 1982, the Justice Department (under the Reagan Administration) dismissed a tying case filed by it in 1979 (under the Carter Administration) against Mercedes–Benz. The complaint alleged that Mercedes–Benz of North America (MBNA) violated Section 1 of the Sherman Act by conditioning the sales of Mercedes–Benz automobiles on its dealers' purchase of replacement parts from MBNA. In dropping the case, the assistant attorney general in charge of the Antitrust Division, William Baxter, said that "tying arrangements of the sort involved in this case . . . do not harm competition by creating market power. Instead, they merely allow firms to capture, in a particular way, the value of customer preference for the particular brand or trade name."[57] Elimination of the tying provisions would, he said, be "unlikely to yield any economic benefits." Whether or not the courts adopt this theme obviously remains to be seen. Suffice it to say here that the effects of the first two policy areas addressed in this chapter, exclusive dealing and tying agreements, can be traced directly to a potential lessening or *interbrand* competition rather than intrabrand competition. By instituting exclusive dealing policies, a supplier prohibits a reseller from selling directly competing brands. And in using a tying arrangement or contract, competition of other brands with the tied brand is immediately

---

[56] Neale and Goyder, op. cit., p. 276.

[57] See "Justice Department Dismisses Tying Cast against Mercedes–Benz," 42 *ATRR* 587 (Mar. 18, 1982) at 587–588. Also see "Judge to Review Move Ending Antitrust Suit against Mercedes–Benz," *Wall Street Journal*, May 28, 1982, p. 32.

foreclosed. Therefore, it is very difficult to defend either exclusive dealing or tying on the same basis as one might defend territorial and customer restrictions, the next policy areas to be addressed.

TERRITORIAL AND CUSTOMER RESTRICTIONS

In contrast to exclusive dealing arrangements, requirements contracts, and tying agreements, territorial and customer restrictions are often designed to reduce *intra*brand competition—competition among wholesalers or retailers of the same brand. A territorial restriction either prevents or discourages a middleman from selling outside a particular area, while a customer restriction prohibits a middleman from selling to specific customers or classes of customers regardless of their location.

The rationale behind restricting intrabrand competition is that by protecting resellers of its brand from competition among themselves a supplier will improve their effectiveness against resellers of other brands. Specifically, a supplier establishes territorial or customer restrictions in order to provide an incentive for distributors to make necessary investments in plant, equipment, or inventory; to generate important support activities (e.g., point-of-sale promotion, repairs, customer service); and/or to achieve the widest and deepest possible coverage of a geographical area or market segment. Distributors might be unwilling to perform these activities in the absence of such incentives because of the possibility of "free riders." For example, a retailer that provides advertising and showrooms may discover that consumers take advantage of his services and then make their purchases from another retailer—a free rider —who does not provide any services but offers the product at a lower price. Confronted with such consumer behavior, retailers may all decide to lower their service levels, despite their supplier's insistence that such amenities are necessary relative to competition from other suppliers' brands. However, irrespective of intention or strategic rationale, both territorial and customer restrictions are clearly restraints of trade and, therefore, are subject to close scrutiny under the antitrust laws.

Territorial Restrictions

Territorial restrictions range from absolute confinement of reseller sales intended to completely foreclose intrabrand competition to "lesser" territorial allocations designed to inhibit such competition. These lesser allocations include areas of primary responsibility, profit pass-over arrangements, and location clauses.[58]

Absolute confinement involves a promise by a reseller that he will not sell

---

[58] For a complete discussion of these restrictions and the legal issues surrounding their use, see ABA Antitrust Section, *Vertical Restrictions Limiting Intrabrand Competition* (Chicago: American Bar Association, 1977).

outside his assigned territory. Often combined with such a promise is a pledge by the supplier not to sell anyone else in that territory. Such a pledge is known as the granting of an *exclusive* distributorship or franchise. When absolute confinement is combined with an exclusive distributorship, the territory can be considered "airtight."[59] On the other hand, an area of primary responsibility requires the reseller to use his best efforts to maintain effective distribution of the supplier's goods in the territory specifically assigned to him. Failure to meet performance targets may result in termination, but the reseller is free to sell outside his area, and other wholesalers or retailers may sell in his territory.

Profit pass-over arrangements require that a reseller who sells to a customer located outside his assigned territory compensate the reseller in whose territory the customer is located. Such compensation is ostensibly to reimburse the second reseller for his efforts to stimulate demand in his territory and for the cost of providing services upon which the first reseller might have capitalized. Finally, a location clause specifies the physical site of a reseller's place of business. Such clauses are used to "space" resellers in a given territory so that each has a "natural" market to serve comprised of those customers who are closest to the reseller's location. However, the reseller may sell to any customer walking through his door. Furthermore, the customers located closest to him may decide to purchase at more distant locations than his.

The antitrust enforcement agencies' attitude has historically been that effective competition involves *both* intrabrand and interbrand competition. Consequently, any attempts to confine wholesalers' or retailers' selling activities to one area may be viewed by these agencies as either restraints of trade or as unfair methods of competition and therefore may be challenged under the Sherman Act or under Section 5 of the FTC Act. For example, in 1958, the Justice Department brought suit against the White Motor Company, charging, among other things, that its franchises, which limited the area in which its dealers could sell or solicit customers, constituted an agreement to restrain trade. The decision by the lower courts concurred with the Justice Department's argument and held that such exclusive territorial arrangements were illegal per se, regardless of their competitive effects.[60] The Supreme Court refused to accept a per se rule for territorial restrictions and remanded the case for Court retrial.[61] Before a retrial could be held in the lower courts, White accepted a consent decree to drop the exclusive territorial provisions in its franchise agreements.

Less than 5 years after its decision in *White Motors*, the Court responded in a much different fashion when the issue of territorial restrictions came before it again. In *U.S. v. Arnold, Schwinn & Co.*,[62] the defendant used three types of

---

[59] See Robert Pitofsky, "The *Sylvania* Case: Antitrust Analysis of Non-Price Vertical Restrictions," *Columbia Law Review* 78 (Jan. 1978), pp. 3–4.

[60] *White Motor Co.* v. *U.S.*, 194 F. Supp. 562 (1961).

[61] *White Motor Co.* v. *U.S.*, 372 U.S. 253 (1963).

[62] *U.S.* v. *Arnold, Schwinn and Co., et al.*, 388 U.S. 365 (1967).

marketing arrangements: (1) sales to wholesale distributors who resold to franchised retailers; (2) consignment or agency arrangements with distributors who
sold to retailers; and (3) direct shipments to franchised retailers with a commission paid to the distributor who had taken the order. On the wholesale level, territorial restrictions limited distributor sales to exclusive territories.
(Schwinn also restricted the customers to whom distributors and retailers
could sell.) In his opinion for the Court, Justice Fortas distinguished
Schwinn's outright sales to distributors and dealers from its agency and consignment transactions. Arguing that to allow a supplier to control goods after
a sale would violate the "ancient rule against restraints on alienation," he stated that

> once the manufacturer has parted with title and risk, he has parted with do
> minion over the product, and his effort thereafter to restrict territory or persons
> to whom the product may be transferred—whether by explicit agreement or by
> silent combination or understanding with his vendee—is a *per se* violation of
> Section 1 of the Sherman Act.[63]

Thus, the territorial (and the customer) restrictions imposed by Schwinn on its
distributors and dealers were found to be per se violations of the Sherman Act
unless Schwinn was willing to retain title, risk, and dominion over its bicycles,
that is, to sell them on a consignment basis or vertically integrate.[64] It should
be noted, however, that when the actual remedy was imposed by the District
Court, Schwinn was not prohibited from designating areas of prime responsibility for its distributors nor from designating the location of the place of
business in its franchise agreements. Schwinn also retained the right to select
its distributors and franchised dealers and to terminate dealerships for cause
so long as such arrangements did not involve exclusive dealing clauses.[65]

The per se ruling in the *Schwinn* case proved to be immensely unpopular
among businessmen, legal scholars, and even among judges. Therefore, when
the Supreme Court handed down a decision in the *Sylvania*[66] case on June 23,
1977, which overturned the Schwinn decision, there was cause for celebration.
The *Sylvania* decision held that territorial restrictions should be judged by the
"rule of reason" on a case by case basis. Because of the significance of the
Sylvania case to the establishing of distribution policies, it is important to devote some time to understanding what transpired in it.

Prior to 1962, Sylvania, a manufacturer of television sets, sold its sets
through both independent and company-owned distributors to a large number
of independent retailers. RCA dominated the market at the time with 60 to 70
percent of national sales; Zenith and Magnavox were major rivals. Sylvania
had only 1 to 2 percent of the market. In 1962, Sylvania decided to abandon
efforts at "saturation distribution" and chose instead to phase out its whole-

---

[63] Ibid., at 382.

[64] See Betty Bock, *Antitrust Issues in Restricting Sales Territories and Outlets* (New York: The Conference Board, 1967), for a complete discussion of the case.

[65] "*U.S.* v. *Arnold, Schwinn and Co., et al.,*" *Journal of Marketing* 33 (Jan. 1969), p. 107.

[66] *Continental T.V., Inc.* v. *GTE Sylvania Inc.,* 433 U.S. 36 (1977).

salers and sell directly to a small group of franchised retailers. Sylvania retained sole discretion to determine how many retailers would operate in any geographic area and, in fact, at least two retailers were franchised in every metropolitan center of more than 100,000 people. Dealers were free to sell anywhere and to any class of customers, but agreed to operate only from locations approved by Sylvania.

Continental TV was one of Sylvania's most successful retailers in northern California. After a series of disagreements arising from Sylvania's authorizing a new outlet near one of Continental's best locations, Continental opened a new outlet in Sacramento although its earlier request for approval for that location had been denied. Sylvania than terminated Continental's franchise. Continental brought a lawsuit against Sylvania, citing the precedent established in the *Schwinn* decision regarding the per se illegality of territorial restrictions. The Court sided with Sylvania, which argued that the use of its territorial allocation policy permitted its marketing channels to compete more successfully against those established by its large competitors.

In its decision, the Court favored the promotion of *inter*brand competition, even if *intra*brand competition were restricted. It indicated that customer and territorial restrictions encourage interbrand competition by allowing the manufacturer to achieve certain efficiencies in the distribution of his products. Specifically, Mr. Justice Powell, citing Preston,[67] commented that there are a number of ways in which manufacturers can use such restrictions to compete effectively against other manufacturers . . . for example,

> —new manufacturers and manufacturers entering new markets can use the restrictions in order to induce competent and aggressive retailers to make the kind of investment of capital and labor that is often required in the distribution of products unknown to the consumer;

and

> —established manufacturers can use them to induce retailers to engage in promotional activities or to provide service and repair facilities necessary to the efficient marketing of their products.[68]

And, in a footnote, the Court recognized that marketing efficiency is not the only legitimate reason for a manufacturer's desire to exert control over the manner in which its products are sold and serviced, because society increasingly demands the manufacturer directly assume responsibility for the safety and quality of its products.[69]

Thus, the upshot of the Sylvania decision is that territorial restraints will not be found to be per se illegal if they do not have a "pernicious effect on competition without redeeming value." Increased interbrand competition appears to be of sufficient "redeeming value." Of course, such restraints may still

---

[67] Lee E. Preston, "Restrictive Distribution Arrangements: Economic Analysis and Public Policy Standard," *Law and Contemporary Problems* 30 (1965), pp. 506–529.

[68] *Continental TV, Inc.* v. *GTE Sylvania Inc.*, 433 U.S. 36 at 41 (1977).

[69] Ibid., n. 23. See also the discussion of product liability and trademark law in Chapter 2 of this text.

be attacked as unreasonable restraints in violation of Section 1 of the Sherman Act or Section 5 of the Federal Trade Commission Act, but the burden will be on the plaintiff to prove that they are unreasonable. For example, in 1982, the Federal Trade Commission ruled that Beltone Electronics Corporation's requirements that its dealers sell only within assigned geographical territories and deal exclusively in Beltone hearing aids "have not unreasonably restrained competition."[70] The FTC concluded that the complaint should be dismissed because complaint counsel did not show an adverse effect on interbrand competition necessary for a successful challenge to the vertical restraints.

Even in the face of the FTC's *Beltone* decision, it appears that the status of such restraints imposed by successful marketers with substantial market power and/or market shares will remain clouded pending further *court* decisions.[71] Also, lawsuits challenging such restraints will likely be more complex and costly due to the requisite economic evidence that will be required to prove certain restraints unreasonable. The effect of this should be to reduce the amount of private litigation involving such restraints.[72]

On the other hand, territorial restrictions that may appear superficially to have been imposed vertically (i.e., by a supplier), but which are in reality the product of concerted activity of dealers or distributors who are horizontal competitors, are per se illegal, even after *Sylvania*.[73] In other words, when dealers agree among themselves not to interpenetrate each other's markets or to solicit the same customers, or when they induce their supplier to impose upon them such restrictions, the law is clearly violated. Thus, in a case concerning a collective attempt by Los Angeles Chevrolet dealers and GM officials to prevent some dealers from bootlegging cars to unfranchised automobile supermarkets, the Supreme Court ruled that such horizontal agreements constitute "a classic conspiracy" in restraint of trade.[74] In *U.S.* v. *Topco Associates, Inc.*[75] and

[70] *In the matter of Beltone Electronics Corporation,* Federal Trade Commission Docket No. 8928, July 7, 1982.

[71] The FTC brought suit against the exclusive territorial restrictions used by Coca-Cola and Pepsi-Cola, two companies with considerably more economic power in their markets than Sylvania had in the television set market, but before the case could be fully resolved in the courts, Congress passed a law ["Soft Drink Interbrand Competition Act," 15 USC 3501, Public Law 96-308 (S.598), enacted July 9, 1980], creating a special exemption from the antitrust laws for the territorial restrictions used in the soft drink industry to a loser standard than the rule of reason. For a suggested approach in such cases, see E. F. Zelek, Jr., L. W. Stern, and T. W. Dunfee, "A Rule of Reason Model After *Sylvania*," *California Law Review* 68 (1980), pp. 801–836. For an application of the model, see L. W. Stern, E. F. Zelek, Jr., and T. W. Dunfee, "A Rule of Reason Analysis of Territorial Restrictions in the Soft Drink Industry," *Antitrust Bulletin* 27 (Summer 1982). See, also, John F. Cady, "Reasonable Rules and Rules of Reason: Vertical Restrictions on Distributors," *Journal of Marketing* 46 (Summer 1982), pp. 27–37; and Saul Sands and Robert J. Posch, Jr., "A Checklist of Questions for Firms Considering a Vertical Territorial Distribution Plan," *Journal of Marketing* 46 (Summer 1982), pp. 38–43.

[72] Many of these conclusions have been drawn from James G. Hiering and Richard L. Reinish, "Vertical Restraints on Distribution: Continental TV, Inc. v. GTE Sylvania, Inc.," office memorandum of Keck, Cushman, Mahin & Cate, Chicago, Ill., July 1, 1977. See also Robert E. Weigand, "Policing the Market Channel—It May Get Easier," in R. F. Lusch and P. H. Zinszer (eds.), *Contemporary Issues in Marketing Channels* (Norman, Okla.: University of Oklahoma, 1979), pp. 105–111.

[73] See *Continental TV, Inc.* v. *GTE Sylvania, Inc.,* op. cit., at 58, n. 28.

[74] *U.S.* v. *General Motors Corp. et al.,* 384 U.S. 127 (1966).

[75] *U.S.* v. *Topco Associates, Inc.,* 405 U.S. 596 (1972).

U.S. v. *Sealy, Inc.,*[76] competing companies created wholly owned trademark licensors, and the licensors then granted each competitor an exclusive area in which to manufacture and/or distribute the trademarked products. In both cases, the Supreme Court declared the arrangements illegal, concluding that the trademark licenses were merely facades to mask an allocation of markets by pre-existing competitors.

Customer Restrictions

A supplier may wish to impose restrictions on to whom a wholesaler or retailer may resell his goods and services. These arrangements may be very desirable for suppliers in the marketing of some goods, since they can reserve certain large customers to themselves for direct sales and also control the reselling of their goods throughout the channel. Posner has pointed out the economic rationale underlying the use of such restrictions, as follows:

> There may be a class of customers who, because of size, sophistication, or special needs, do not require dealer services. The manufacturer may be in a better position than any dealer to provide these customers with whatever presale services they do require. If so, the manufacturer who allows his dealers to compete with him for such an account is inviting them to take a free ride on his services. He provides the services at a cost that he hopes to recoup in the price charged these customers; the dealers then offer the customers a lower price, which they can do since they do not incur any services expense with respect to these customers. In such a case, forbidding dealers to compete for these accounts is just like limiting competition among dealers in order to prevent some of them from taking a free ride on presale services provided by others.[77]

The exact status of customer restrictions in distribution is somewhat cloudy. In the previously mentioned *White Motor* case,[78] the Supreme Court reversed a summary judgment that had declared per se illegal a franchise agreement reserving national accounts to the manufacturer. In *Schwinn*, the defendant had prohibited its wholesalers and its franchised retailers from selling its products to nonfranchised retailers (e.g., discount stores). Such a restriction was declared, as indicated previously, per se illegal. While the situation in the *Sylvania* case did not directly involve customer restrictions, the Supreme Court found that the intent and the competitive impact of customer restrictions are indistinguishable from territorial restrictions. Thus, following *Sylvania*, restrictions of this type become illegal when it can be shown that their effects tend to reduce competition.

Despite the *Sylvania* ruling, it would be risky to assume that a supplier is completely free to dictate to wholesalers or retailers the classes and kinds of customers to whom they may resell its product or brand. First, no clear guide-

[76] *U.S.* v. *Sealy, Inc.,* 388 U.S. 350 (1967).

[77] Richard A. Posner, *Antitrust Law: An Economic Perspective* (Chicago: University of Chicago Press, 1976), p. 162.

[78] *White Motor Co.* v. *U.S.,* 372 U.S. 253 (1963).

lines exist.[79] Second, there is a different tone between establishing territorial limits and setting customer restrictions. Establishing territorial limits or boundaries basically involves the exercise of reward power on the part of a supplier (e.g., the granting of an intrabrand monopoly within a defined geographical area). On the other hand, setting customer restrictions represents, for the most part, an exercise of coercive power (e.g., prohibitions on selling to specific classes of customers, such as discount stores).[80] They may also be considered horizontal agreements not to compete made between direct-selling suppliers and their resellers. Therefore, despite Posner's interesting rationalization, the uncertainty surrounding the legality of customer restrictions may continue until another precedent-setting Supreme Court decision on the matter is handed down, whenever that may be.

RESALE PRICE MAINTENANCE

Resale price maintenance is the specification by a supplier, typically a manufacturer, of the prices below or above which resellers, typically wholesalers and retailers, may not sell its products. The enactment of such a policy is a matter related to distribution channel strategy, which explains why the topic is addressed in this chapter rather than in Chapter 5.

Resale price maintenance was one of the few channel policy areas where the use of coercive power was sanctioned, in a positive manner, by federal laws. Originally, resale price maintenance (so-called Fair Trade) laws were passed by states (starting with California in 1931) enabling manufacturers to fix resale prices for their goods if they chose to do so. The U.S. Congress passed the Miller–Tydings Act in 1937 and the McGuire Act in 1952 exempting retail price fixing by manufacturers from the federal antitrust laws in states that permitted such vertical pricing arrangements. However, by the end of 1975, the repeal of state Fair Trade laws had proceeded to the point where resale price maintenance was enforceable against contracting parties in only 22 states. And, as a final blow, Congress passed the Consumer Goods Pricing Act[81] late in 1975, repealing the Miller–Tydings and McGuire acts. This meant that the Fair Trade agreements that were previously exempted from the Sherman Act's prohibitions against vertical price restraints became per se unlawful.[82]

---

[79] Emmet J. Bondurant, "Antitrust Considerations in the Selection and Modification of Distribution Systems," *Antitrust Law Journal* 49, Issue 2 (1981), p. 777. The setting of "minimum standards" for dealers, a de facto means of instituting resale price restrictions, is permissible, according to *In the Matter of U.S. Pioneer Electronics Corp.*, Federal Trade Commission docket No. C-2755, Nov. 5, 1982.

[80] For a discussion of the use of various power bases in distribution as well as some of their legal implications, see Louis W. Stern and Adel I. El-Ansary, *Marketing Channels*, 2nd ed. (Englewood Cliffs, N.J.: Prentice-Hall, Inc., 1982).

[81] Public Law No. 94-145, 89 Stat. 801.

[82] The history of resale price maintenance legislation is fascinating. For colorful accounts, see Scherer, op. cit., pp. 590–594 and Joseph C. Palamountain, Jr., *The Politics of Distribution* (Cambridge, Mass.: Harvard University Press, 1955), pp. 235–253. For a complete outline of the legal status of resale price maintenance, see John W. Clark, Oliver F. Green, Jr., and Paul E. Slater, "Resale Price Maintenance: Outline of Relevant Law," *Antitrust Law Journal* 49, Issue 2 (1981), pp. 839–843.

Ostensibly, resale price maintenance (Fair Trade) laws were supposed to facilitate a manufacturer's desire to influence prices at the retail level; however, their initial development was instigated through the collective efforts of coalitions of small, independent retailers who wished to be protected from the direct price competition of mass merchandisers and discounters.[83] In more recent history, though, there have been some logical economic arguments raised explaining the potential significance of resale price maintenance by manufacturers as a mechanism for inducing service competition among resellers.[84] In fact, as Scherer points out, resale price maintenance is, in some respects, "analogous in motivation and effect to vertical territorial restrictions."[85] If there is merit to the contention that impeding intrabrand competition may further interbrand competition (as was postulated previously), then perhaps resale price maintenance ought to be treated in the same manner as customer and territorial restrictions (i.e., as a rule of reason offense). Posner puts the argument neatly when he writes,

> Resale price maintenance is more flexible than exclusive territories as a method of limiting price competition among dealers, and it may be the only feasible method where effective retail distribution requires that dealers be located close to one another; any free-rider or other arguments that are available to justify exclusive territories are equally available to justify resale price maintenance.[86]

He has also argued that the distinction between price and nonprice restriction is "indefensible."

> To forbid a dealer or distributor to sell outside of its territory, when it is the only distributor or dealer of the manufacturer's brand in the territory, has if anything a greater adverse effect on intrabrand competition than fixing the price at which it may resell the product. The territorial restriction affects both price and service competition; the price restriction affects only price competition.[87]

Because Posner has had a profound effect on thinking about these matters, as witnessed by the number of citations to his works in the *Sylvania* decision alone,[88] it is important to review briefly some of the legal history of resale price maintenance just in case the Posnerian perspective were to gain favor among the antitrust enforcement agencies and even among the members of the Supreme Court. If it did gain favor, it would require a conceptual about-face from much of the reasoning previously employed.

Such an about-face is not a remote possibility. During its 1983–84 session, the Supreme Court agreed to review a case in which Spray-Rite Service Corporation, now defunct, sued Monsanto Company after Mosanto had cut off

---

[83] See Palamountain, op. cit., pp. 235–253.

[84] See Posner, op. cit., pp. 147–167. See also Richard A. Posner, "The Next Step in the Antitrust Treatment of Restricted Distribution: Per Se Legality," *University of Chicago Law Review* 48 (Winter 1981), pp. 6–26.

[85] Scherer, op. cit., p. 590.

[86] Posner, "The Next Step . . . ," op. cit., p. 9.

[87] Ibid., p. 9.

[88] *Continental TV, Inc.* v. *GTE Sylvania, Inc.,* op. cit.

Spray-Rite's distributorship of herbicides in northern Illinois in 1968. Monsanto said it severed the relationship because Spray-Rite would not adopt company programs to promote the sale of herbicides. But Spray-Rite said Monsanto acted because the distributor would not join in an effort to fix the prices at which the herbicides were sold. Spray-Rite claimed that Monsanto had previously complained about price cutting. A district court jury awarded Spray-Rite $3.5 million in damages, which was tripled to $10.5 million. In 1982, the 7th Circuit Court of Appeals in *Spray-Rite Service Corp. v. Monsanto Co.* (684 F.2d 1226, 7th Cir. 1982) upheld the verdict. The Justice Department, adopting Posner's perspective, entered the case as a friend-of-the-court on behalf of Monsanto. In its brief, the Justice Department argued that vertical price-fixing should be judged on a rule of reason basis because it does not always reduce competition. In fact, according to the Justice Department's brief, fixing prices in distribution can sometimes stimulate competition and enhance consumer welfare. Indeed, the issue of resale price maintenance became one of the most hotly debated antitrust topics throughout industry, Congress, and the Executive branch of government during the entire Reagan Administration. The Supreme Court's decision, when it is finally delivered, may resolve this debate or it may simply leave it up in the air.

Some Significant Cases

In *Dr. Miles Medical Company* v. *John D. Park and Sons Company*,[89] the classic case on resale price maintenance, the Supreme Court held that it was an undue restraint of trade and hence per se illegal under the Sherman Act for a manufacturer to require his dealers by contract to maintain prescribed retail prices. The decision was based on the argument that a manufacturer parts with control over his goods when he sells them and is not entitled to lay down conditions by express contract that restrict competition in future sales at other levels in the marketing channel. Specifically, the Court saw no difference between fixing prices by contract in this manner and an actual horizontal agreement among the dealers. It stated that Miles, the manufacturer, could have fared no better "with its plan of identical contracts than could the dealers themselves if they had formed a combination and endeavored to establish the same restrictions, and thus to achieve the same result, by agreement with each other."

Even if the perpetrator of the vertical price fixing is the holder of a copyright or a patent or a trademark, the per se prohibition is supposed to apply. In referring to a patent held by General Electric, for example, Chief Justice Taft stated, in 1926, that "where a patentee makes the patented article, and sells it, he can exercise no future control over what the purchaser may wish to do with the article after his purchase. It has passed beyond the scope of the patentee's rights."[90] The argument is that the patent or copyright or trademark

[89] 220 U.S. 373 (1911).
[90] *U.S.* v. *General Electric Company*, 272 U.S. 476 (1926).

holder has basically obtained his reward and exhausted his property rights when he sells his product.[91]

The issue of vertical price fixing has even been raised relative to goods sold on consignment. At one time, General Electric retained title, dominion, and risk to all of its light bulbs sold through retail outlets and also set the final prices at which its bulbs could be resold. In the same case as the one just cited in which Chief Justice Taft made the observation about patented products, it was decided that the consignment arrangement was legitimate and that where the manufacturer both retains title and bears substantial risks of ownership (e.g., acts of God, obsolescence, possible price declines), the antitrust laws do not prevent him from dictating the terms of sale, including retail prices.[92] However, as Gellhorn has insightfully noted, the focus under *GE* was on the *method* of the manufacturer's control over the resale price and not its *effect* on competition or consumer welfare.[93] Therefore, it is not surprising to find that, in 1964, the Court backed away from the *GE* position and refused to apply the *GE* precedent to facts that were at most superficially distinguishable.[94] The upshot of all this is that, although the setting of a consignee's resale prices was once considered lawful where the seller retained title to the consigned goods, the consignment arrangement may now be held to be unlawful per se if employed as a cloak for vertical price fixing.

The blanket prohibition against *all* forms of resale price maintenance was reinforced when the Court held in 1968 that a newspaper publisher violated Section 1 of the Sherman Act when it disciplined a distributor that had ceased to adhere to the *maximum* resale prices set by the publisher.[95] And the Court restated its position in the *Sylvania* decision when it pointed out, in a footnote, that resale price maintenance continues to be per se illegal, despite its findings with respect to customer and territorial restrictions.[96] It is important to note, though, that, in his concurring opinion in *Sylvania*, Mr. Justice White suggested that the Court, in light of its blessing for the use of the rule of reason in the analysis of the legality of vertical restrictions generally, might well wish to reconsider its previous ruling that resale price maintenance should be illegal per se.

Despite the insights generated by the logic of Posner's economic arguments, the settled law is clear and univocal, at least at the present time. As summed up by Sullivan, it states that

> The seller has no interest sufficient to warrant such restraint; neither the seller's general good will as a maker or vendor nor its interest as the holder of a

[91] See *U.S.* v. *Paramount Pictures, Inc.,* 334 U.S. 131 (1948), and *U.S.* v. *Sealy, Inc.,* 338 U.S. 350 (1967).

[92] *U.S.* v. *General Electric Company,* op. cit.

[93] Gellhorn, op. cit., p. 263.

[94] See *Simpson* v. *Union Oil Co.,* 377 U.S. 13 (1964); also, see Sullivan's analysis of the superficial nature of the distinction between *Simpson* and *GE* in Sullivan, op. cit., p. 388.

[95] *Kiefer–Stewart Company,* v. *Joseph E. Seagram & Sons, Inc.,* 340 U.S. 211 (1951), and *Albrecht,* v. *The Herald Co.,* 390 U.S. 145 (1968).

[96] *Continental TV, Inc.,* v. *GTE Sylvania, Inc.,* op. cit. at 51, n. 18. The per se proscription of vertical price fixing was reinforced in *California Liquor Dealers* v. *Midcal Aluminum,* 445 U.S. 97 (1980).

trademark or a patent on the item sold outweighs the public interest in assuring that buyers remain free to resell at prices dictated by their individual responses to the competitive conditions which they face in the resale market.[97]

Because of this conclusion, the antitrust enforcement agencies have a mandate to scrutinize each and every attempt to specify or maintain resale prices. In the not-too-distant past, they have done so quite vigorously. In particular, the FTC has obtained consent order agreements from, among others, garment, high fidelity component, carpet, detergent, cookware, ski equipment, and cosmetics manufacturers relative to their vertical pricing-fixing activities.[98] In a number of situations, the consent orders prohibit the manufacturers from

Fixing or controlling resale prices.

Suggesting or recommending resale prices to customers for a set number of years.

Preticketing products with resale prices.

Policing customers' resale prices.

Communicating with any customer or prospective customer concerning a deviation from any resale price.

Terminating or taking any other action against customers because of their resale prices.

Withholding advertising or other allowances from customers because of their resale prices.

Nevertheless, in keeping with the Reagan Administration's lenient attitude with regard to vertical restrictions, the Federal Trade commission in 1983 refused to appeal a lower court's ruling on a case against Russell Stover Candies, Inc. which had been brought under the Carter Administration.[99] Russell Stover was originially found to have violated antitrust law by coercing retailers into selling candy at "suggested retail prices" with threats to terminate dealers. A federal court in St. Louis reversed the FTC's finding in the fall of 1982, and the FTC then voted 2-2 on whether to appeal. Under FTC rules, a tie vote means that the agency cannot take action. James Miller, the FTC Chairman, voted against seeking Supreme Court review because of his belief

[97] Sullivan, op. cit., p. 377.

[98] "Jonathan Logan Apparel Subject of Consent Order Affecting Sales Practices," *FTC News Summary,* May 18, 1979, p. 1; "FTC Complaint Against Levi Strauss Alleges Price Fixing and Other Anticompetitive Acts," *FTC News Summary* May 14, 1976, p. 1; "Public Comment on Two Orders Banning Price Fixing of Hi-Fi Components Accepted and Invited," *FTC News Summary,* May 7, 1976, p. 3; "Consent Order Banning Resale Price Fixing of Rugs and Carpet Issued," *FTC News Summary,* Aug. 27, 1976, p. 2; "Two Clothing Companies Agree Not to Set Retail Prices, Says FTC," *FTC News Summary,* Aug. 27, 1976, p. 2; "Two Clothing Companies Agree Not to Set Retail Prices, Says FTC," *FTC News Summary,* May 25, 1979, p. 2; "FTC Accepts and Invites Comment on Consent Order Banning Resale Price Fixing by Copco, Inc.," *FTC News Summary,* May 6, 1977, p. 2; "FTC Accepts and Invites Comment on Consent Order Banning Resale Price Fixing by Olin Ski Co., Inc.," *FTC News Summary,* May 10, 1977, p. 2; "The Pricing Police Take a Sterner Line," *Business Week,* June 14, 1976, p. 27; "Germaine Monteil May Not Set Retailers' Prices, Under Final Federal Trade Commission Order," *FTC News Summary,* Nov. 26, 1982, p. 4. During the Carter Administration, the Justice Department became active in the vertical price fixing area. See Robert E. Taylor, "Livack Gets Attention of Business with Novel Antitrust Prosecution," *Wall Street Journal,* Oct. 31, 1980, p. 27; and "Cuisinarts Is Fined on Felony Charges in Antitrust Case," *Wall Street Journal,* Dec. 22, 1980, p. 9.

[99] *Russell Stover Candies, Inc. v. FTC,* 1983-2 Trade cas. ¶ 65,640 (8th Circuit, September 29, 1983). See also Jeanne Saddler, "FTC Decided It Won't Appeal Its Reversal in Russell Stover Prices Case to Top Court," *Wall Street Journal,* December 16, 1983, p. 46 and "Russell Stover Violated Antitrust Laws By Fixing Resale Prices," *FTC News Summary,* July 16, 1982, p. 1.

that the retailers whom Stover was allegedly coercing could have stocked many other brands of boxed chocolates if Stover refused to sell to them. It should be noted, however, that there is nothing inherently illegal about suppliers suggesting or recommending resale prices. What has been held to be illegal is any attempt to enforce them, such as by threatening to terminate dealers who do not comply with them.

RECIPROCITY

Reciprocity is the practice of making decisions at least partly on the basis of whether the vendor is also a customer. In some cases the relationship may be more complex, involving three or more customer–vendors in a circular arrangement. Reciprocity comes down to doing business with your friends.[100] Business reciprocity has come under antitrust scrutiny, especially if there is an inequality of bargaining power in the relationship. This may arise from differences in the relative sizes of the firms.[101] The antitrust laws regulate reciprocity, because sellers influence their customers to buy not only on the basis of marketing competition, but also because the buyer wishes to sell his own products to the seller. Indeed, as Sullivan points out, the social concern about reciprocity is markedly similar to that with respect to tying arrangements.

> The ideal is that each market transaction be made on the competitive merits of that particular transaction. If a firm has power in one market as a buyer and exercises that power to gain an advantage as a seller in a different market, the ideal is frustrated. Part of the second market is foreclosed to competing sellers and a buyer in that market, because of its interests as a seller elsewhere, may be deprived of the freedom to decide from whom it prefers to buy.[102]

There is a set of cases concerned with determining the division between illegal and legal reciprocity. In general, reciprocity is illegal under two circumstances.[103]

1. Coercive reciprocity involving the use of pressure may be illegal as an unfair trade practice.
2. A merger that may cause a reciprocity program to be formed will violate Section 7 of the Clayton Act if the reciprocity may reduce competition.[104]

This latter circumstance can come about when a firm that operates a reciprocity program merges with another firm, and one of the two has a customer that sells to the other. In some cases a corporate policy against reciprocity will shield a merger from Section 7.[105] We will return later in this chapter to the issue of reciprocity stemming from vertical mergers.

Noncoercive reciprocity is legal so long as the policy is not aggressive, is outside of a merger context, and is not supported with elaborate records of

[100] Reed Moyer, "Reciprocity: Retrospect and Prospect," *Journal of Marketing* 34 (Oct. 1970), p. 47.

[101] Howard, op. cit., p. 93.

[102] Sullivan, op. cit., p. 491.

[103] Moyer, op. cit., p. 48.

[104] See *U.S.* v. *General Dynamics Corp.*, 258 F. Supp. 36 (S.D.N.Y. 1966), and *FTC* v. *Consolidated Foods Corp.*, 380 U.S. 592 (1965).

[105] Moyer, op. cit., p. 53. For a discussion of Section 7 of the Clayton Act, see Chapter 4.

purchases and sales from and to other firms. The Federal Trade Commission has held that where reciprocity is prevalent and systematized and where a substantial amount of commerce is involved, there is a violation of Section 5 of the Federal Trade Commission Act.[106] For example, the FTC issued three cease and desist orders under Section 5 against the practice of reciprocity in the 1930s.[107] In *Waugh Equipment,* as an illustration, two traffic managers of the Armour Company bought stock in a small firm manufacturing special draft gears for the railroad industry. They gave preference to routing Armour's huge meat shipments to railroads that purchased gears from their company. As a result, the gear-making firm moved from seventh place (with a 1 percent market share) to first place (with a 35 percent market share) in its industry in only six years. A 1971 case in which a major tire manufacturer and its three subsidiaries were barred from any reciprocity purchases from their suppliers indicated that the Justice Department was willing to pursue such practices under Section 1 of the Sherman Act in addition to their willingness to raise the issue in vertical merger cases.[108] However, it should be noted that it is very difficult to draw a line between "coercive" reciprocity and the situation where two firms do business "voluntarily" with each other because it is to their mutual advantage.

Indicative of the Reagan Administration's relatively relaxed stance toward the potential dangers of vertical restraints, the Justice Department in 1981 dropped a reciprocity case against General Electric Company, which had been filed by a previous administration in 1972.[109] The lawsuit charged GE with making reciprocal purchasing arrangements with customers and suppliers since 1965. The government had originally alleged that these arrangements prevented GE competitors from selling to GE customers and that they limited the number of suppliers that could sell to GE. The rationale used for dropping the case was that "the passage of time had reduced the significance of the case and the value of injunctive relief."[110] Likewise, the FTC has brought very few cases involving reciprocal dealing over the past decade and, in fact, in 1983, actually freed Southland Corp., the Dallas-based owner of the 7-Eleven convenience-store chain, from a 1974 order barring it from reciprocal dealing.

REFUSALS TO DEAL

A seller can select his own distributors or dealers according to his own criteria and judgment. He may also announce in advance the circumstances under which he would refuse to sell to distributors or dealers. These two commercial

[106] "Federal Trade Commission Statement on Reciprocity," *Journal of Marketing* 35 (Apr. 1971), pp. 76–77.

[107] *Waugh Equipment Co.,* 15 FTC 232 (1931); *Mechanical Manufacturing Co.,* 16 FTC 67 (1932); and *California Packing Corp.,* 25 FTC 379 (1937).

[108] *U.S.* v. *General Tire and Rubber Co., Aerojet-General Corp., A. M. Byers Co., and RKO General Inc.,* CCH 73,303 (D.C. N. Ohio, Oct. 1970); BNA ATRR No. 486 (Nov. 3, 1970), A-16. Perhaps the most far-reaching aspect of this consent decree was the requirement that the position of trade relations director of General Tire and that of corporate relations director in a subsidiary had to be abolished and that no employee could be assigned any trade relations function because of the reciprocity practice challenged in this case.

[109] "G.E. Antitrust Suit Filed 9 Years Ago Is Dropped by U.S.," *Wall Street Journal,* Oct. 15, 1981, p. 20.

[110] Ibid.

"freedoms" were recognized in *U.S.* v. *Colgate & Co.*[111] in 1919 and are referred to as the "Colgate Doctrine." The doctrine was formally recognized by Congress in Section 2(a) of the Robinson–Patman Act, which reads "nothing herein contained shall prevent persons engaged in selling goods, wares, or merchandise in commerce from selecting their own customers in *bona fide* transactions and not in restraint of trade."

One of the major legal issues involved in refusals to deal is whether the refusal can be characterized as a combination or conspiracy between firms on the same or different levels of a marketing channel to exclude other firms from that channel. For example, in *Eastern States Retail Lumber Dealers' Association* v. *U.S.,*[112] the association had circulated lists of wholesale lumber dealers who were known to be selling at retail as well. After circulation of the lists, members generally stopped buying from the companies that had been named. Although individual firms have a right to refuse to deal with other firms, concerted boycotts by groups of firms, such as by the lumber retailers, have long been regarded as per se violations of Section 1 of the Sherman Act.[113] In the *Colgate* case, the Court held that so long as refusal to deal is exercised *unilaterally,* that is, by the seller alone, and not by the seller in concert either with other sellers or other buyers, it should not be characterized as conspiratorial.[114] In a now famous statement, the Court observed that

> In the absence of any purpose to create or maintain a monopoly, the act does not restrict the long recognized right of trader or manufacturer engaged in an entirely private business, freely to exercise his own independent discretion as to parties with whom he will deal; and, of course, he may announce in advance the circumstances under which he will refuse to sell.[115]

A major problem with the *Colgate* case was that it dealt with Colgate's right to refuse to deal with a retailer who was not adhering to its resale price maintenance policies. We have already seen that price maintenance was declared per se illegal in 1911 in *Dr. Miles Medical Co.* v. *John D. Park & Sons Co.,*[116] a case that preceded *Colgate* by 8 years. The facts in the *Colgate* case centered on Colgate's action to cease supplying a retailer in the absence of a *specific contract* to maintain prices, but in the presence of a clear policy statement on the part of Colgate indicating that price cutters would be dropped as customers. Because of the tension between the *Colgate* decision and the main body of law generated previous to the *Colgate* decision, the Court has, as Sullivan observes, "repeatedly drawn distinctions which have limited and contained the implication of the original holding."[117] Indeed, after a number of

---

[111] 250 U.S. 300 (1919).

[112] 234 U.S. 600 (1914).

[113] See, also, *Fashion Originators' Guild of America, Inc.* v. *FTC,* 312 U.S. 457 (1941); *Klor's Inc.* v. *Broadway–Hale Stores, Inc.,* 359 U.S. 207 (1959); *U.S.* v. *Parke, Davis & Co.,* 362 U.S. 29 (1960); and *U.S.* v. *General Motors Corporation et al.,* 384 U.S. 127 (1966).

[114] See Sullivan, op. cit., p. 392.

[115] *U.S.* v. *Colgate & Co.,* 250 U.S. 300 (1919) at 307.

[116] 220 U.S. 373 (1911).

[117] Sullivan, op. cit., p. 393.

decisions dealing with the right of refusal to deal, the "right" has been narrowly confined. Suppliers may formally cut off dealers for valid business reasons, such as failure to pay or poor performance in sales or service, but where the suppliers have set up restrictive, regulated, or programmed distribution systems and there are complaints that the dealers who are being cut off have somehow stepped out of line with the edicts of the programmed system, the right to refuse to deal may be a severely constrained defense in treble-damage actions brought against the suppliers by the dealers.

A large number of litigated cases continue to be generated under Sections 1 and 2 of the Sherman Act involving decisions by suppliers or franchisors to modify their distribution systems by terminating an existing dealer, and substituting a new dealer on an exclusive or nonexclusive basis, or as part of a conversion from representation by independent middlemen to a vertically integrated system.[118] While it appears as though the original selection of distributors or dealers for a new product poses no legal problems, it is increasingly clear that the cutting off or termination of existing distributors and dealers does pose such problems, even in the absence of group boycotts or conspiracies. As Neale and Goyder observe,

> once a manufacturer has selected a dealer he will be unable subsequently, without risking a treble-damage action, to drop him merely because he refuses to comply with the manufacturer's policy in any particular respect, unless that policy is one which in all circumstances does not constitute a violation of the antitrust laws.[119]

Thus, when exclusive dealing, customer or territorial restrictions, or other types of vertical restraints have been applied by a supplier within its distribution network and when a dealer is cut off from that network, the dealer may take the supplier to court, charging that the refusal to deal was based on the supplier's desire to maintain an unlawful practice. The orientation toward litigation in these cases has been furthered by particularistic legislation, such as the Automobile Dealers Franchise Act of 1956, which entitles a car dealer to sue any car manufacturer who fails to act in good faith in connection with the termination, cancellation, or nonrenewal of the dealer's franchise. It is open to the manufacturer, however, to produce evidence that the dealer has himself not acted in good faith and that its own action was thereby justified. In nearly all the cases to date, this defense has been successful.[120]

On the other hand, a number of different circuit court decisions have approved the right of a manufacturer to construct his own distribution channel and to alter it over time, depending on his assessment of marketplace conditions.[121] For example, the 9th Circuit stated in *Golden Gate Acceptance Corp.* v. *General Motors Corp.*[122] that "it is not a violation of the Sherman Act for a

---

[118] For a review of such cases, see Bondurant, op. cit., pp. 783–789.

[119] Neale and Goyder, op. cit. p. 282.

[120] Ibid.

[121] See Bondurant, op. cit., for a listing of relevant cases.

[122] 597 F.2d 676 (9th cir. 1979) at 678.

manufacturer to conspire with others to simply switch distributors at one of its exclusive franchises and to cease doing business with a former dealer." And in another case, the 2nd Circuit held that where a manufacturer simply decides on its own to substitute one dealer for another, and cuts off the former dealer, its decision to sell exclusively to a new dealer "does not amount to an antitrust 'conspiracy' with the latter, even though the manufacturer has agreed with the new dealer to transfer patronage to him and to terminate sales to the former dealer."[123] The court in this case went on to note that it is equally permissible for a manufacturer to abandon its "entire distribution system in favor of another system, whether it be to improve distribution, maximize profits or for some other legitimate competitive reason."[124] Irrespective of these findings, however, the scope and the potency of the original *Colgate* doctrine has been severely limited. As one court has said, "The Supreme Court has left a narrow channel through which a manufacturer may pass even though the facts would have to be of such Doric simplicity as to be somewhat rare in this day of complex business enterprise."[125]

FUNCTIONAL DISCOUNTS

Each level in the marketing channel performs certain specific tasks and takes certain risks as labor is divided among the various institutions and agencies responsible for making goods and services available to end users. Historically, when there was little vertical integration and when independent wholesalers sold to numerous, relatively small retail outlets, each level in the channel was rewarded differently (e.g., the wholesaler got a larger price discount from the manufacturer than the retailer). In addition, each level in the channel dealt with a specific class of customer (i.e., the wholesaler sold only to retailers, and retailers only to consumers). Therefore, the discounts given to wholesalers and retailers, called functional discounts because they are payments for unique functions performed,[126] could differ without being an antitrust violation, because wholesalers and retailers normally performed different functions in different markets and thus did not compete against each other. However, in more recent years the distinctions in distribution systems have blurred as wholesalers have formed voluntary chains and as retailers have integrated wholesaling functions; therefore, the antitrust questions are much more difficult.

Functional or trade discounts are not specifically referred to in the Robinson–Patman Act or elsewhere, and yet there are clearly instances where price discrimination is being practiced due to confusing classifications of middlemen. For example, K-Mart, a major discount store chain, performs

---

[123] *Fuchs Sugars & Syrups, Inc.* v. *Amstar Corp.*, 602 F.2d 1025 (2d. Cir. 1979).

[124] Ibid.

[125] *George W. Warner & Co.* v. *Black & Decker Mfg. Co.*, 277 F.2d 787 (2d. Cir. 1960) at 790.

[126] Wholesalers and retailers can receive *both* functional discounts *and* quantity discounts. Functional discounts are granted by functions performed, while quantity discounts are given on the basis of amount purchased.

many of its own wholesaling functions. It receives in large lots from manufacturers, breaks bulk, assorts merchandise, and reships merchandise from its warehouses to its retail stores. However, it is generally classified as a "retailer" and, therefore, is supposedly entitled only to the *functional* discounts given to retailers. (It can, of course, avail itself of whatever *quantity* discounts are offered by its suppliers.) If K-Mart cannot receive a wholesaler's functional discount as well (assuming that such discounts are granted by its suppliers), then it is being discriminated against.

The problem here is obviously one of classification. And if K-Mart were to be given both trade discounts (a wholesaler's and a retailer's), then independent wholesalers who resell to independent retailers would argue that their customers (small retailers) are not able to compete with the major chains, like K-Mart, on an equal footing because the wholesalers would only be entitled to receive the wholesaler discount.

The problem is horribly complex, and no easy solution is in hand. (Some companies have dropped their functional discount structures entirely in order to avoid the problem; they simply offer quantity discounts.) In attempting to cope with this issue, the Federal Trade Commission has been forced to pass upon the methods by which middlemen are classified. When it challenges functional discounts, it relies on the provision of the Robinson–Patman Act that condemns substantial lessening of or injury to competition. However, sellers have been permitted to use the cost savings and good faith defenses detailed in Chapter 5 to defend their discriminatory functional discount structures. Putting it another way, functional discounts are lawful under the Robinson–Patman Act as long as they are offered on the same terms to all competing buyers of the same class or as long as the discounts granted do not exceed cost savings of the seller.

Several cases are worthy of mention regarding these issues. Perhaps the most famous is *Standard Oil Co. (Indiana)* v. *FTC* in which Standard's wholesale (jobber) customers received a tank-car discount, while its direct retailer customers received the lower tank-wagon discount.[127] It was found that some of the retailers supplied by the jobbers bought gasoline cheaper than retailers supplied by Standard direct. The FTC saw a danger to third-line (retail level) competition in this situation, because jobber-supplied retailers were able to underprice Standard-supplied retailers. In another case, Ruberoid, an important manufacturer of asbestos and asphalt roofing materials, was selling to wholesalers, retailers, and "applicators" or roofing contractors at different discount levels.[128] There was a great deal of competition at the retail level among all three of these marketing channel members, and therefore, the FTC said, in effect, that the designation given to any particular firm for price discount purposes was to be disregarded. Ruberoid was ordered to give equal treatment to firms that in fact competed with one another in the resale of the product.

[127] 340 U.S. 231 (1951).

[128] *FTC* v. *Ruberoid Company*, 343 U.S. 470 (1952).

And, in a third important case, Mueller Company sold products for water and gas distribution systems to wholesalers, some of whom inventoried certain items and some did not.[129] Mueller gave the first set of wholesalers an additional 10 percent discount on the inventoried items. The FTC found this action to be a violation of the Robinson–Patman Act because, it reasoned, Mueller had given these wholesalers a business advantage (i.e., having the high-volume items on hand for immediate delivery to customers) by subsidizing them. But the FTC also found that the opportunity to be an inventory-carrying wholesaler was not open to all wholesalers but only open to those selected by Mueller. If the opportunity had been available to all, it is possible that the functional discount might not have been viewed as so anticompetitive.

In general, the FTC has held that classifications of customers must not be arbitrary, that they must conform strictly to the nature of the operations undertaken by different types of customers, and that buyers at the sale level who compete directly with one another, such as independent retailers, mail order houses, and chain stores, must be put in the same class.[130] This conclusion does not, however, make the whole issue of functional discounts any more clear. Indeed, as Neale and Goyder point out, "the treatment of functional discounts under the Robinson–Patman Act remains an area of unanswered questions and obscurities in antitrust."[131] Perhaps some of the murkiness will be removed when a case against Boise Cascade Corporation is decided. In a complaint filed in 1980, the FTC charged Boise Cascade with knowingly receiving illegal discounts from its office-products suppliers.[132] Boise Cascade purchases office supplies from manufacturers and resells them to both retail dealers and large commercial users. In selling to commercial users, Boise competes against retail stationers and other office-products dealers who buy from the same manufacturers. The FTC charged that, on goods purchased for resale to commercial users, Boise's Office Products Division receives discounts that are not available to other retail dealers, giving Boise a competitive advantage.

It appears that there are two legal standards that might be applied by the FTC to this case.[133] One of them arises from a 1955 FTC lawsuit involving the Doubleday Co.[134] In that case, the FTC indicated that discriminatory prices may be legal if justified by special services or functions performed for manufacturers by the company receiving the discount. This might include such things as carrying a complete line of products or keeping a warehouse fully stocked. The other standard stemming from the above-mentioned Mueller decision says that an otherwise illegal price discrimination can be justified only if the discount matches actual cost savings the manufacturer derives from special

---

[129] *Mueller Co.*, 60 FTC 120 (1962).

[130] See Clair Wilcox, *Public Policies toward Business*, 4th ed. (Homewood, Ill.: Richard D. Irwin, Inc., 1971), p. 207.

[131] Neal and Goyder, op. cit., p. 241.

[132] "Boise Cascade Charged with Receiving Illegal Discounts," *FTC News Summary*, May 9, 1980, p. 2.

[133] Ibid.

[134] *Doubleday & Co.*, 52 FTC 169 (1955).

services the buyer performs. In the Mueller case, the FTC expressly overturned its Doubleday ruling.

VERTICAL INTEGRATION

The marketing manager is faced with another set of legal constraints when considering vertical integration. Vertical integration in the channel may come about through forward or backward integration by a producer or a wholesaler and by backward integration by a retailer. Integration may be brought about by the creation of a new business function by existing firms (internal expansion) or by acquisition of the stock or the assets of other firms (mergers).

The two methods of creating integration are fundamentally different in their relationship to the law. Internal expansion is primarily regulated by Section 2 of the Sherman Act, which prohibits monopoly or attempts to monopolize any part of the interstate or foreign commerce of the United States. External expansion is regulated by Section 7 of the Clayton Act and its amendment, the Celler–Kefauver Act, which, as mentioned in Chapter 4 when discussing horizontal and conglomerate mergers, prohibits the purchase of stock or assets of other firms if the effects may be to substantially lessen competition or tend to create a monopoly in any line of commerce in any part of the country. Vertical integration via external expansion has also been regulated under Sections 1 and 2 of the Sherman Act. For example, in the *Columbia Steel* case to which reference was made in Chapter 4, the government charged, under Section 1, that United States Steel, as a dominant supplier of rolled-steel "semis," was illegally restraining trade in acquiring the business of a substantial user of "semis," because the result would be that the user (Consolidated Steel) would in the future take all its requirements of "semis" from U.S. Steel, thereby foreclosing that part of the market for "semis" from competitors.[135] In this case, the merger was permitted to stand because the Supreme Court ruled that the amount of competition foreclosed was too small to involve a significant restraint of trade. However, for reasons detailed in Chapter 4, the Sherman Act is particularly weak in attacking mergers and, therefore, reliance has predominately been placed on Section 7 of the Clayton Act.[136]

In general, there is a strong bias in court cases in favor of internal expansion versus external expansion. In fact, in the *Philadelphia National Bank* case, the Supreme Court explicitly stated that "one premise of an antimerger statute such as Section 7 is that corporate growth by internal expansion is socially preferable to growth by acquisition."[137] On the other hand, the *Merger Guidelines* issued by the Justice Department on June 14, 1982, and reproduced at the end of Chapter 4 are, by omission of detailed discussion of likely trans-

---

[135] *U.S.* v. *Columbia Steel Co.,* 334 U.S. 495 (1948).

[136] Under the wording of Section 7 of the Clayton Act, it is not necessary to prove that the restraint involved has actually restrained competition. It is enough that it "may tend" to substantially lessen competition.

[137] *U.S.* v. *Philadelphia National Bank,* 374 U.S. 321 at 370 (1963).

gressions, permissive with respect to vertical mergers.[138] Justice Department challenges will not likely be forthcoming unless particular, unusual circumstances suggest that the mergers will lead to monopolies or have strong horizontal consequences. The *Merger Guidelines* explicitly specify only three competitive problems from vertical mergers:

1. *Barriers to entry from vertical mergers*: Three conditions are necessary (but not sufficient) for competitively objectionable barriers to entry to exist: (a) the degree of vertical integration between the two markets must be so extensive that entrants to one market (the "primary" market) also would have to enter the other market (the "secondary" market) simultaneously; (b) the requirement of entry at the secondary level must make entry at the primary level significantly more difficult and less likely to occur; and (c) the structure or other characteristics of the primary market must be otherwise so conducive to noncompetitive performance that the increased difficulty of entry is likely to affect its performance.
2. *Facilitating collusion through vertical mergers*: (a) a high level of vertical integration by upstream firms into the associated retail market may facilitate collusion in the upstream market by making it easier to monitor price, and (b) the elimination of a particularly disruptive buyer in a downstream market may facilitate collusion in the upstream market.
3. *Evasion of rate regulation*: non-horizontal mergers may be used by monopoly public utilities subject to rate regulation as a tool for circumventing that regulation.

In any event, integration, whether by merger or internal expansion, may result in the lowering of costs and make possible more effective management of marketing channel relations.[139] It may also be a means of avoiding many of the legal problems previously discussed, because an integrated firm is free to control prices and allocate products to its integrated units without conflict with the laws governing restrictive distribution policies.

Vertical Integration by Merger

The major legal consideration in a vertical merger is the effect the merger will have on competition among firms at the various distributive levels involved in the merger. As Justice Douglas stated in his dissenting opinion in *Columbia Steel*, "Competition is never more irrevocably eliminated than by buying the customer for whose business the industry has been competing."[140] If a merger will tend to foreclose a source of supply to independent firms at the buyer's level or to foreclose a market to other firms at the seller's level, the merger can be questioned. This is because, as Gellhorn points out, the newly acquired

---

[138] "Merger Guidelines, Issued by Justice Department on June 14, 1982, and Attorney General's Statement and FTC's Policy State on Horizontal Mergers," *Bureau of National Affairs*, Special Supplement, Vol. 42, No. 1069 (June 17, 1982), S-9–S-11.

[139] For a discussion of the benefits and costs of vertical integration, see Oliver E. Williamson, *Market and Hierarchies: Analysis and Antitrust Implications* (New York: Free Press, 1975); Frederick R. Warren-Boulton, *Vertical Control of Markets: Business and Labor Practices* (Cambridge, Mass: Ballinger Publishing Co., 1978); and Michael E. Porter, *Competitive Strategy* (New York: Free Press, 1980).

[140] *U.S.* v. *Columbia Steel Co.*, op. cit., at 537.

firm may decide to deal only with the acquiring firm, thereby altering competition in three markets: among the acquiring firm's suppliers, customers, or competitors.[141]

> Suppliers may find that they no longer have a market for their goods, retail outlets may be deprived of supplies, and competitors may find that both supplies and outlets are blocked. The concern, just as in the case of vertical restraints, is that such foreclosures may substantially lessen competition.[142]

Indeed, one might look at the effects of vertical mergers in the same way as one might scrutinize the legality of exclusive dealing under Section 3 of the Clayton Act. In both cases, it is the foreclosure of substantial markets to competitors that makes exclusive arrangements questionable.

In determining whether a merger will reduce competition, the two critical variables initially examined are the definition of the line of commerce and the market involved. In vertical as in horizontal and conglomerate merger cases, the analysis starts by defining relevant markets and then asks what percentage of the unintegrated portions of the upstream and downstream markets are being linked by the merger. A key issue to be resolved is what share of the customer or supply market is being foreclosed. If the relevant market is defined narrowly enough, almost any merger can be questioned. For example, in 1917, du Pont bought 23 percent of the common stock of General Motors and began supplying GM with finishes and fabrics. The amount of business that flowed to du Pont from GM was large; in 1947, total purchases amounted to over $26 million. This represented a substantial portion of the automobile industry's requirements for finishes and fabrics because GM accounted for almost half the industry's annual sales. In a case brought by the Justice Department against du Pont,[143] the Court rejected du Pont's argument that *all industrial* finishes and fabrics belonged in the relevant market. Instead, it confined the market to *automotive* finishes and fabrics. This had the effect of exaggerating the impact of the merger on these sales. For example, the foreclosure of paint sales was only 3.5 percent of total industrial finishes but 24 percent of automotive uses.

The *du Pont–GM* case was tried under Section 7 of the Clayton Act *prior* to the 1950 amendment. The Supreme Court's first opportunity to interpret the amended Section 7 came in *Brown Shoe,*[144] a case for which the horizontal merger aspects were discussed previously in Chapter 4. It should be recalled from the previous discussion that Brown Shoe Company was, at the time of the case, the fourth largest shoe manufacturer in the United States, accounting for about 4 percent of the national output of shoes. Brown Shoe merged with G. R. Kinney Corporation, which both manufactured and retailed shoes. Brown Shoe owned or controlled, through franchises or agreements, approxi-

---

[141] Gellhorn, op. cit., pp. 305–306.

[142] Ibid.

[143] *U.S.* v. *E.I. du Pont de Nemours and Co. et al.,* 353 U.S. 586 (1957).

[144] *Brown Shoe Co., Inc.* v. *U.S.,* 370 U.S. 279 (1962).

mately 1,230 retail outlets. Kinney operated some 400 outlets, but represented the largest family-style shoe-store chain in the United States. The Kinney retail stores sold only 1.2 percent of all national retail shoe sales by dollar volume, but the annual retail sales exceeded $42 million. However, Kinney's manufacturing plants supplied Kinney's retail outlets with only 20 percent of their shoes. This was the crux of the decision against the vertical aspects of the merger. Although the merger involved leading firms in the shoe industry, it would not have produced a company whose size would overwhelm the industry. Nevertheless, the Court noted, "in this industry, no merger between a manufacturer and an independent retailer would involve a larger potential market foreclosure."[145]

In looking at the vertical aspects of the *Brown Shoe* case, the Court started by defining relevant markets and the asking what percentage of the unintegrated portions of the upstream and downstream markets were linked by the merger. It indicated that, unless the percentage foreclosed approached monopoly proportions, the share would not itself be determinative. In *Brown Shoe,* the share was neither a monopoly nor at a minimum (*de minimus*). Therefore, other factors were examined, such as the purpose of the agreement. The Court acknowledged the desire, grounded in legislative history, to save failing companies and to allow small companies to merge in order to enable them to compete better. But it noted that, in the Brown–Kinney merger, large companies were involved. Also, both past history and the testimony of Brown Shoe's president indicated that Brown Shoe would force its shoes into Kinney stores by virtue of ownership; that is, the potential for foreclosure would be exploited. Finally, the Court noted the trend toward concentration in the industry and the possibility that locally controlled units would increasingly come under national control via such means as vertical mergers.

The Court emphasized that it is necessary to look beyond market share statistics into the historical and economic background of affected markets before pronouncing judgment. In other words, it endorsed a rule of reason approach for vertical merger cases brought under Section 7.[146] What the rule of reason approach amounts to is that the parties must argue many elements, attempting to show that anticompetitive effects are or are not unreasonable. Among the relevant elements are market shares, the total quantitative amount of business involved, the trend to concentration in the industry, whether or not the defendant would have entered the market without a merger, the possibility of price or supply squeezes, the barriers to entry into the industry, and the existing level of concentration in the industry. Thus, Ford Motor Company's merger of Autolite was found to be unlawful because (1) the merger foreclosed 10 percent of the spark-plug market to other sellers (i.e., Ford's purchases represented 10 percent of the market of spark plugs); (2) Ford was going to start its own manufacture of spark plugs, but bought Autolite instead; (3) the automotive after-market normally replaced the same type of spark plug put in the

---

[145] Ibid., at 331–332.

[146] The rule of reason was applied in *Reynolds Metals Co.* v. *FTC,* 309 F.2d 223 (1962).

original equipment; therefore, the acquisition of Autolite by Ford would mean that the spark-plug market would become exactly like the concentrated car market; and (4) the barriers to entry for new spark-plug firms would be extremely high after the acquisition.[147]

Many joint ventures also have "vertical" overtones and may be subject to the same kind of scrutiny that vertical mergers receive. For example, in 1980, the Justice Department opposed a proposed joint venture/merger of Showtime, owned by Viacom International, and The Movie Channel, owned by American Express and Warner Communications, with three movie companies —Paramount Pictures, Universal Studios, and Warner Brothers. It was felt that the joint venture/merger might have impaired competition in cable television because it would have foreclosed to competitive pay-television channels the licensing of motion pictures distributed by the movie companies. In 1980, the companies accounted for 50 percent of all pay-TV film rentals. Showtime and The Movie Channel were to be the exclusive outlets for the pay-TV film rentals for a nine-month period.

As indicated earlier in this chapter and in Chapter 4, vertical mergers creating the opportunity for forcing reciprocal buying agreements upon suppliers or buyers are also subject to attack under the Clayton Act.[148] For example, Consolidated Foods, a large processor and distributor of food products, purchased Gentry, Inc., a processor of dehydrated onion and garlic, putting Consolidated in a position to require its suppliers to obtain onion and garlic from Gentry as a condition of doing business with Consolidated. The FTC objected to such uses of reciprocity and filed suit to force Consolidated to divest itself of Gentry.[149] The Court found that the particular practice in this situation (which Consolidated admitted following) was moving in the direction of coercion and "foreclosure" as well as possible "price squeezing," and stated, "the establishment of the power to exert pressure on customers because those customers are also suppliers, when such power was acquired by merger, is in violation of Section 7 of the Clayton Act."[150]

In another case, General Dynamics Corporation, the nation's largest defense contractor in 1962, used its power as a lever to force firms that sold to it to buy their carbon dioxide and other industrial gas requirements from it.[151] General Dynamics had acquired Liquid Carbonic, a carbon dioxide producer, in 1957 with the idea of developing a sales program encouraging its suppliers to buy carbon dioxide from Liquid Carbonic. General Dynamics compiled a list of suppliers that needed carbon dioxide and arranged contacts between Liquid Carbonic executives and these companies. The evidence showed that, in at least two instances, purchases were made from Liquid Carbonic based on

---

[147] *Ford Motor Co.* v. *U.S.*, 405 U.S. 562 (1972).

[148] See, also, Louis W. Stern and John R. Grabner, Jr., *Competition in the Marketplace* (Glenview, Ill.: Scott, Foresman & Co. 1970), p. 96.

[149] *FTC* v. *Consolidated Food Corporation*, 380 U.S. 592 (1965).

[150] Ibid.

[151] *U.S.* v. *General Dynamics Corporation*, 258 F. Supp. 36 (S.D.N.Y. 1966).

General Dynamics' use of reciprocity. Thus, the merger violated Section 1 of the Sherman Act. However, as Scherer points out, proving that reciprocal buying is a probable consequence of mergers has generally been difficult; as a result, few mergers have been struck down on reciprocal purchasing grounds, and the government has experienced several noteworthy defeats.[152]

Vertical Integration by Internal Expansion

This form of integration is limited only by the laws preventing monopoly or attempts to monopolize. As Neale and Goyder observe,

> The law on vertical integration, as on all these monopolization problems, comes back in the end to the intent and purpose of the parties. Where the purpose is to exclude competition or create monopoly power, vertical integration may be vulnerable like any other device; where it is a reasonable step to take on its commercial merits and the remaining competition appears effective, vertical integration as such is unlikely to fall foul of the law.[153]

There are, however, instances of internal expansion creating such problems, although they are relatively rare. For example, one of these was Alcoa's practice of selling ingot aluminum at a relatively high price, while selling fabricated aluminum at a relatively low price, thereby putting its ingot customers who also sold fabricated aluminum in a price squeeze. Its ability to do so was directly related to its vertically integrated operations; the practice was held to be a violation of Section 2 of the Sherman Act.[154] Another example was in the *A&P* case, where the company was found in 1946 to be employing its wholesale produce subsidiary, the Atlantic Commission Company, as a "dummy" brokerage firm to obtain discriminatory advantages over its competitors.[155] A consent decree accepted in 1954 provided that ACCO be dissolved. And a third example is provided in the *Paramount* case, which involved five of the major producers of motion pictures who also operated first-run theaters in the larger cities and chains of smaller theaters throughout the country.[156] The government charged that these concerns had favored their own theaters in supplying films, and had required block booking, minimum admission charges, and protracted intervals between successive showings in leasing films to others, thus making it difficult for independent producers and distributors to compete. The Supreme Court insisted that production and exhibition be divorced, and the five companies were broken into ten, five of them producers and five operating chains of theaters. As a result, markets were opened to independent producers, and films were made readily available to independent exhibitors.

On the whole, a firm is ordinarily free to integrate backward or to set up its own distribution and retailing systems unless this would overconcentrate

---

[152] Scherer, op. cit., p. 559. See also Peter O. Steiner, *Mergers* (Ann Arbor: University of Michigan Press, 1975), pp. 244–248.

[153] Neale and Goyder, op. cit., pp. 147–148. See, also, Wilcox, op. cit., pp. 136–138.

[154] *U.S.* v. *Aluminum Co. of America,* 148 F.2d (2nd Cir. 1945).

[155] *U.S.* v. *N.Y. Great A & P Tea Company,* 67 E. Supp. 626 (1946).

[156] *U.S.* v. *Paramount Pictures,* 334 U.S. 131 (1948).

the market for its product. Also, Section 7 of the Clayton Act specifically permits a firm to set up subsidiary corporations to carry on business or extensions thereof if competition is not substantially lessened.[157] Except for the unusual limitations applicable to business activities resulting in monopoly, an internal expansion is generally not challengeable under the antitrust laws.[158]

Problems Created by Dual Distribution

The term *dual distribution* describes a wide variety of marketing arrangements by which a manufacturer or a wholesaler reaches its final markets by employing two or more different types of channels for the same basic product. However, a dual arrangement that often creates controversy is the one that involves manufacturers marketing their products through competing vertically integrated *and* independently owned outlets on either the wholesale or the retail level.[159] This kind of practice is customary in some lines of trade, such as the automotive passenger tire, paint, and petroleum industries. Dual distribution also takes place when a manufacturer sells similar products under different brand names for distribution through different channels.[160] This latter kind of dual distribution comes about because of market segmentation, or because of sales to distributors under "private" labels.

In all dual distribution situations, conflict among channel members is likely to be relatively high. But serious legal questions arise mainly in two situations: (1) when price "squeezing" is suspected or (2) when horizontal combinations or conspiracies are possible between competitors. The first situation brings about issues comparable to those found when examining the legality of and difficulties associated with the use of functional discounts. The second relates to potential restraints of trade arrived at in concert by vertically integrated firms and their customers. It should be noted at the outset, though, that the Supreme Court has yet to rule squarely on whether dual distribution systems fall within the rule of per se illegality. While dual distribution is not itself a violation of the Sherman Act, any action taken by a supplier engaged in full distribution that affects the prices at which its customers resell its products or inhibits the ability of those customers to compete with the supplier has the potential of being found in violation of Section 1 of the Sherman Act, unless the supplier can convince the court that the decision was motivated solely by legitimate business reasons and not by a desire on the part of the supplier to restrain competition.[161]

[157] *Industrial Buildings Material, Inc.* v. *Interchemical Corp.*, 437 F. 2d 1336 (9th Cir. 1970).

[158] Gellhorn, op. cit., p. 306. Some cases involving subsidiary corporations have been brought under Section 1 of the Sherman Act. For example, in 1983, the Supreme Court agreed to consider whether joint conduct of a subsidiary and its parent corporation can constitute an agreement or conspiracy in restraint of trade. (*Copperweld Corp.* v. *Independence Tube Corp.*, N. 82-1260, U.S. Sup. Ct., *cert granted*, 6/20/83).

[159] E. T. Grether, *Marketing and Public Policy* (Englewood Cliffs, N.J.: Prentice-Hall, Inc., 1966), p. 84. The issue of dual distribution was a "hot topic" during the Carter Administration. The Justice Department was prepared to bring criminal charges against dual distribution arrangements. See "Justice Takes Aim at Dual Distribution," *Business Week*, July 7, 1980, pp. 24–25.

[160] L. E. Preston and A. E. Schramm, Jr., "Dual Distribution and Its Impact on Marketing Organization," *California Management Review* 8 (Winter 1965), p. 61.

[161] Bondurant, op. cit., p. 778.

Price Squeezes.

A seller operating at only one market level in competition with a powerful vertically integrated firm might be subject to a price "squeeze" at his particular level. For example, a manufacturer of fabricated aluminum might be under pressure from price increases by his raw material (ingot) supplier. If the supplier were also a fabricator, it could take its gain from the price increase (which represents higher costs to the customer–competitor) and use all or a portion of the increased returns for marketing activities at the fabricating level. This was exactly the scenario of the Alcoa situation recounted previously.[162] A number of lower court decisions have declared unlawful an integrated supplier's attempt to eliminate a customer as a competitor by undercutting the customer's prices and placing the customer in a price squeeze.[163]

In 1982, the Federal Trade Commission dismissed a 1976 case brought against General Motors regarding a possible price squeeze in the distribution of GM crash parts[164] (e.g., fenders, doors, bumpers, and hoods). General Motors sells its crash parts exclusively to its franchised automobile dealers. Independent body shops purchase the parts from the GM dealers. The GM dealers generally charge the independents, their competitors in the collision repair business, more for the parts than what the dealers initially paid GM. For this reason, and because the dealers are the sole source of these parts, the 1976 complaint said that GM's distribution system disadvantaged and discriminated against those other commercial repairers. In its 1982 decision, the FTC acknowledged that the independent body shops are competitively harmed by GM's distribution system but found that the injury "barely" met the required legal showing of substantial injury to competition. The Commission concluded that the injury was offset by a showing of substantial business justification for the system. It may be a gross understatement to say that independent body shops did not find the FTC's decision very consoling, especially since the FTC also found that a major cause for independent body shop failure rates "is the fact that they pay, on the average, 17.7% more for GM crash parts than their competitors, the dealer–installers."[165]

The same kind of competitive inequality arises from the granting of functional discounts when different functional categories may be represented by buyers who, at least in part of their trade, are in competition with each other. Oil jobbers, for example, sometimes sell at retail, and they may use their functional discount received as jobbers to advantage in competition with retailers.[166] Such pricing raises the possibility of Robinson–Patman Act as well as Sherman Act violations.

---

[162] *U.S.* v. *Aluminum Co. of America*, 148 F. 2d 416 (2nd Cir. 1945).

[163] See for example *Columbia Metal Culvert Co., Inc.* v. *Kaiser Aluminum & Chemical Corp.*, 579 F. 2d 20 (3d Cir. 1978); *Coleman Motor Co.* v. *Chrysler Corp.*, 525 F. 2d 1338 (3d Cir. 1975); *Industrial Building Materials, Inc.* v. *Inter-Chemical Corp.*, 437 F 2d 1336 (9th Cir. 1970).

[164] *In re General Motors Corp.*, Federal Trade Commission docket no. 9077, July 1, 1982. See, also, "FTC Finds General Motors Has Business Justification to Continue Its Crash Parts Distribution System; Overturns Administrative Law Judge's Decision, *FTC News Summary*, July 16, 1982, p. 2.

[165] Ibid.

[166] *Standard Oil Co. of Indiana* v. *FTC*, 340 U.S. 231 (1950).

When a supplier to an independent retailer also competes with the retailer by owning its own outlets, the possibility of a price squeeze exits if the integrated supplier is more aggressive in setting retail prices at his own outlets than it is in setting wholesale prices to the independent. Such a possibility was no doubt behind the passage of a law in Maryland (upheld by the U.S. Supreme Court in 1978) that prohibits oil producers or refiners from directly operating gasoline outlets.[167] The law, which permits oil companies to own retail stations as long as they do not use their own employees or agents to run them, also forbids discrimination among dealers in the supply and price of gasoline. It is analogous to legislation proposed in numerous other states designed to halt the trend of oil companies opening their own cut-rate, gasoline-only stations in competition with dealer-operated stations. The specific impetus for the law was dealer complaints that oil companies gave their own stations preferential treatment when gasoline was in short supply at the time of the 1973 Arab oil boycott.

Horizontal Combinations or Conspiracies.

In dual distribution situations, the distinction between purely vertical restraints and horizontal restraints may be critical in determining the legality of a marketing activity. Section 1 of the Sherman Act is not violated by the purely unilateral action of a supplier; there must be at least one additional party present whom the court may find combined or conspired with the supplier. As Bondurant has documented, the courts have not found it difficult to identify a host of potential conspirators.[168] Indeed, Bondurant has carefully cataloged a number of lower court decisions in this area, showing that when a supplier or a franchisor has integrated forward to the level of some of its customers, the following activities may be challenged and prohibited or circumscribed, depending on the specific situation:

1. Establishing territorial boundaries between the supplier and its customer/competitors;
2. Publishing lists of suggested resale prices;
3. Preventing or impeding price competition on the part of customer/competitors via such actions as raising prices to or withdrawing discounts from them; and
4. Reserving certain national accounts and/or preventing customer/competitors from competing for such accounts.[169]

And in one case, the court of appeals reversed a district court and held that, where a manufacturer has dominant or monopoly power over a given product, it must *preserve* the independent distributor of its products.[170] According to the court of appeals, the public benefits by being able to buy from a distributor who may handle competing products. A dominant manufacturer may replace

---

[167] See Carol H. Falk, "Justices Uphold Bar to Oil Firms' Retail Outlets," *Wall Street Journal,* June 15, 1978, p. 3; "The Oil Majors Retreat from the Gasoline Pump," *Business Week,* Aug. 7, 1978, pp. 50–51.

[168] Bondurant, op. cit., p. 778n.

[169] Ibid., pp. 779–783.

[170] *Industrial Building Materials, Inc.* v. *Interchemical Corp.,* op. cit.

a distributor, but he may not enter into competition with him and destroy him.

In sum, dual distribution is not unlawful per se, and each case must be appraised in terms of its special circumstance. However, as Bondurant warns,

> the existence of direct competition between the supplier and its customers inevitably requires that the supplier's business decisions that affect the ability of its customers to compete be subjected to close antitrust scrutiny to determine the real motivation for the supplier's action.[171]

The question of intent will be crucial. The decision may rest on the issues raised in the *Sylvania* case[172] discussed earlier in this chapter. There, a balancing of the effects of a marketing policy on *intra*brand and *inter*brand competition was mandated by the Supreme Court in situations involving vertical restraints.

CONCLUSION

In setting marketing channel policy, there seem to be a host of ways in which marketing executives can run afoul of the antitrust laws. However, because of the *Sylvania* decision, many of these potential offenses will be analyzed by the courts under a rule of reason approach rather than viewed as per se illegal. And even in those situations where decisions have tended toward a per se approach, there are still opportunities for a firm to show that it does not meet the standards set for illegality. In other words, with the exception of vertical price fixing, there is no policy area in distribution that can be called an outright per se illegal offense. And there are even ways in which the vertical price-fixing prohibition is being circumvented. For example, manufacturers are permitted, under a 1982 ruling by the Federal Trade Commission involving U.S. Pioneer Electronics Corp.,[173] to set "minimum standards" for dealers, a de facto means for instituting resale restrictions and for cutting off supplies to discounters.[174]

This does not mean that marketing executives can now relax about the law. On the contrary, almost every aspect of their vertical relationships is covered, in one form or another, by the antitrust umbrella. Consider, once again, the long list of policies discussed in this chapter:

1. *Exclusive dealing.* The requirement by a seller or lessor that its customer sell or lease only its products or at least no products in direct competition with the seller's products. Such a policy is illegal if the requirement may substantially lessen competition and is circumscribed by all three of the major antitrust acts—Sherman, Clayton and FTC. The dominant statute here is, however, Section 3 of the Clayton Act.

---

[171] Bondurant, op. cit., p. 783.

[172] *Continental T.V., Inc.* v. *GTE Sylvania Inc.*, 433 U.S. 36 (1977).

[173] *In the Matter of U.S. Pioneer Electronics Corp.*, Federal Trade Commission docket No. C-2755, Nov. 5, 1982.

[174] See Claudia Ricci, "Discounters, Alleging Price-Fixing, are Fighting Cuts in their Supplies," *Wall Street Journal*, June 21, 1983, p. 35.

2. *Tying contracts.* The requirement by a seller or lessor that its customers take other products in order to obtain a product that they desire. As with exclusive dealing, such a requirement is illegal when it may substantially lessen competition. The three major antitrust laws may be applied here, too.
3. *Territorial restrictions,* particularly the granting of exclusive territories. The granting by a seller of a geographical monopoly to a buyer relative to the resale of its product or brand. Such a policy is circumscribed by the Sherman Act and the FTC Act. The major emphasis in the analysis of such cases is on the potential effect of *intrabrand* restrictions on *interbrand* competition.
4. *Customer (resale) restrictions.* The requirement by a seller that its customers can resell its products only to specified clientele. (The seller frequently agrees not to compete for those clientele reserved for the customers.) This policy area is treated similarly to territorial restrictions under the antitrust laws.
5. *Resale price maintenance.* The requirement by a seller that a buyer can resell its products only above or below a specified price or at a stipulated price. Price maintenance (fair trade) laws have been nullified by the repeal of the Miller–Tydings and McGuire acts. Price maintenance is per se illegal and is mainly circumscribed by the Sherman Act.
6. *Reciprocity.* The requirement by a buyer that those from whom it purchases must also be buyers of its products. Such a policy, which has frequently been compared to tying arrangements, is prohibited by Section 5 of the FTC Act when a substantial amount of commerce is involved and where reciprocity is prevalent and systematized. It is particularly circumscribed when it is established by coercion.
7. *Refusals to deal.* The right of the seller to choose its own customers or to stop serving a given customer. This threat obviously underlies the commercial enforcement of the above-mentioned policies. Although its use is permitted under Section 2(a) of the Robinson–Patman Act, it is forbidden if it fosters restraint of trade or is employed as to substantially lessen competition.
8. *Functional discounts.* The granting by a seller of price reductions to resellers on the basis of their positions in the marketing channel and the nature and scope of their marketing functions. Although no law directly deals with such discounts, they are circumscribed indirectly by the Robinson–Patman Act and the FTC Act in circumstances where they are allocated unfairly in such a way as to substantially lessen competition.

Vertical integration via internal expansion seems to be positively sanctioned by the antitrust enforcement agencies so long as it does not lead to monopolization in restraint of trade, a horizontal consequence negatively sanctioned by the Sherman Act. On the other hand, vertical integration by merger is more heavily scrutinized and may be illegal if there is significant evidence that the merger will foreclose competition at any level in a marketing channel. In the case of mergers, Section 7 (the Celler–Kefauver Amendment) of the Clayton Act comes into play and can be used if the agencies or private parties believe that there may be a tendency for the merger, once consummated, to substantially lessen competition. Thus, as mentioned in Chapter 4, mergers can be challenged in their incipiency.

The policy of vertically integrating often leads to dual distribution conflicts when sellers become competitors of some of their independently owned resellers. Although there are no additional laws beyond those mentioned earlier that limit the practice of dual distribution, this phenomenon has undergone considerable scrutiny in Congress, and it is not at all unlikely that legislation may be forthcoming to limit its practice, especially if it can be shown that small independent middlemen are being severely hurt by it.

It should be noted once again that this chapter, like all the other chapters in this book, has focused only on federal law. The states have become much more active in the antitrust arena over the past two decades, and thus marketing executives would make a serious mistake if they were to ignore the vast outpouring of legislation regulating distribution practices in each of the states in which the products of their companies are sold. Unfortunately, no comprehensive compendium of state laws regulating distribution is available. Marketing executives must, therefore, rely on state-by-state analyses in order to uncover relevant guidelines.

Case 1

Continental T. V., Inc. et al. *v.* GTE Sylvania, Inc.

Certiorari to the United States Court of Appeals for the Ninth Circuit

No. 76-15. Argued February 28, 1977—Decided June 23, 1977

MR. JUSTICE POWELL delivered the opinion of the Court.

Franchise agreements between manufacturers and retailers frequently include provisions barring the retailers from selling franchised products from locations other than those specified in the agreements. This case presents important questions concerning the appropriate antitrust analysis of these restrictions under §1 of the Sherman Act, 26 Stat. 209, as amended, 15 U. S. C. §1, and the Court's decision in *United States* v. *Arnold, Schwinn & Co.*, 388 U.S. 365 (1967).

Respondent GTE Sylvania Inc. (Sylvania) manufactures and sells television sets through its Home Entertainment Products Division. Prior to 1962, like most other television manufacturers, Sylvania sold its televisions to independent or company-owned distributors who in turn resold to a large and diverse group of retailers. Prompted by a decline in its market share to a relatively insignificant 1% to 2% of national television sales,[1] Sylvania conducted an intensive reassessment of its marketing strategy, and in 1962 adopted the franchise plan challenged here. Sylvania phased out its wholesale distributors and began to sell its televisions directly to a smaller and more select group of franchised retailers. An acknowledged purpose of the change was to decrease the number of competing Sylvania retailers in the hope of attracting the more aggressive and competent retailers thought necessary to the improvement of the company's market position.[2] To this end, Sylvania limited the number of franchises granted for any given area and required each franchisee to sell his Sylvania products only from the location or locations at which he was franchised.[3] A franchise did not constitute an exclusive territory, and Sylvania retained sole discretion to increase the number of retailers in an area in light of the success or failure of existing retailers in developing their market. The revised market-

---

[1] RCA at that time was the dominant firm with as much as 60% to 70% of national television sales in an industry with more than 100 manufacturers.

[2] The number of retailers selling Sylvania products declined significantly as a result of the change, but in 1965 there were at least two franchised Sylvania retailers in each metropolitan center of more than 100,000 population.

[3] Sylvania imposed no restrictions on the right of the franchisee to sell the products of competing manufacturers.

ing strategy appears to have been successful during the period at issue here, for by 1965 Sylvania's share of national television sales had increased to approximately 5%, and the company ranked as the Nation's eighth largest manufacturer of color television sets.

This suit is the result of the rupture of a franchiser–franchisee relationship that had previously prospered under the revised Sylvania plan. Dissatisfied with its sales in the city of San Francisco,[4] Sylvania decided in the spring of 1965 to franchise Young Brothers, an established San Francisco retailer of televisions, as an additional San Francisco retailer. The proposed location of the new franchise was approximately a mile from a retail outlet operated by petitioner Continental T. V., Inc. (Continental), one of the most successful Sylvania franchisees.[5] Continental protested that the location of the new franchise violated Sylvania's marketing policy, but Sylvania persisted in its plans. Continental then canceled a large Sylvania order and placed a large order with Phillips, one of Sylvania's competitors.

During this same period, Continental expressed a desire to open a store in Sacramento, Cal., a desire Sylvania attributed at least in part to Continental's displeasure over the Young Brothers decision. Sylvania believed that the Sacramento market was adequately served by the existing Sylvania retailers and denied the request.[6] In the face of this denial, Continental advised Sylvania in early September 1965, that it was in the process of moving Sylvania merchandise from its San Jose, Cal., warehouse to a new retail location that it had leased in Sacramento. Two weeks later, allegedly for unrelated reasons, Sylvania's credit department reduced Continental's credit line from $300,000 to $50,000.[7] In reponse to the reduction in credit and the generally deteriorating relations with Sylvania, Continental withheld all payments owed to John P. Maguire & Co., Inc. (Maguire), the finance company that handled the credit arrangements between Sylvania and its retailers. Shortly thereafter, Sylvania terminated Continental's franchises, and Maguire filed this diversity action in the United States District Court for the Northern District of California seeking recovery of money owed and of secured merchandise held by Continental.

The antitrust issues before us originated in cross-claims brought by Continental against Sylvania and Maguire. Most important for our purposes was the claim that Sylvania had violated §1 of the Sherman Act by entering into and enforcing franchise agreements that prohibited the sale of Sylvania products other than from specified locations.[8] At the close of evidence in the jury

[4] Sylvania's market share in San Francisco was approximately 2.5%—half its national and northern California average.

[5] There are in fact four corporate petitioners: Continental T. V., Inc., A & G Sales, Sylpac, Inc., and S. A. M. Industries, Inc. All are owned in large part by the same individual, and all conducted business under the trade style of "Continental T. V." We adopt the convention used by the court below of referring to petitioners collectively as "Continental."

[6] Sylvania had achieved exceptional results in Sacramento, where its market share exceeded 15% in 1965.

[7] In its findings of fact made in conjunction with Continental's plea for injunctive relief, the District Court rejected Sylvania's claim that its actions were prompted by independent concerns over Continental's credit. The jury's verdict is ambiguous on this point. In any event, we do not consider it relevant to the issue before us.

[8] Although Sylvania contended in the District Court that its policy was unilaterally enforced, it now concedes that its location restriction involved understandings or agreements with the retailers.

trial of Continental's claims, Sylvania requested the District Court to instruct the jury that its location restriction was illegal only if it unreasonably restrained or suppressed competition. App. 5-6, 9-15. Relying on this Court's decision in *United States* v. *Arnold, Schwinn & Co., supra,* the District Court rejected the proffered instruction in favor of the following one:

> "Therefore, if you find by a preponderance of the evidence that Sylvania entered into a contract, combination or conspiracy with one or more of its dealers pursuant to which Sylvania exercised dominion or control over the products sold to the dealer, after having parted with title and risk to the products, you must find any effort thereafter to restrict outlets or store locations from which its dealers resold the merchandise which they had purchased from Sylvania to be a violation of Section 1 of the Sherman Act, regardless of the reasonableness of the location restrictions." App. 492.

In answers to special interrogatories, the jury found that Sylvania had engaged "in a contract, combination or conspiracy in restraint of trade in violation of the antitrust laws with respect to location restrictions alone," and assessed Continental's damages at $591,505, which was trebled pursuant to 15 U. S. C. §15 to produce an award of $1,774,515. App. 498, 501.[9]

On appeal, the Court of Appeals for the Ninth Circuit, sitting en banc, reversed by a divided vote. 537 F. 2d 980 (1976). The court acknowledged that there is language in *Schwinn* that could be read to support the District Court's instruction but concluded that *Schwinn* was distinguishable on several grounds. Contrasting the nature of the restrictions, their competitive impact, and the market shares of the franchisers in the two cases, the court concluded that Sylvania's location restriction had less potential for competitive harm than the restrictions invalidated in *Schwinn* and thus should be judged under the "rule of reason" rather than the *per se* rule stated in *Schwinn.* The court found support for its position in the policies of the Sherman Act and in the decisions of other federal courts involving nonprice vertical restrictions.[10]

We granted Continental's petition for certiorari to resolve this important question of antitrust law. 429 U. S. 893 (1976).[11]

---

[9] The jury also found that Maguire had not conspired with Sylvania with respect to this violation. Other claims made by Continental were either rejected by the jury or withdrawn by Continental. Most important was the jury's rejection of the allegation that the location restriction was part of a larger scheme to fix prices. A pendent claim that Sylvania and Maguire had willfully and maliciously caused injury to Continental's business in violation of California law also was rejected by the jury, and a pendent breach-of-contract claim was withdrawn by Continental during the course of the proceedings. The parties eventually stipulated to a judgment for Maguire on its claim against Continental.

[10] There were two major dissenting opinions. Judge Kilkenny argued that the present case is indistinguishable from *Schwinn* and that the jury had been correctly instructed. Agreeing with Judge Kilkenny's interpretation of *Schwinn,* Judge Browning stated that he found the interpretation responsive to and justified by the need to protect " 'individual traders from unnecessary restrictions upon their freedom of action.' " 537 F. 2d, at 1021. See n. 21, *infra.*

[11] This Court has never given plenary consideration to the question of the proper antitrust analysis of location restrictions. Before *Schwinn* such restrictions had been sustained in *Boro Hall Corp.* v. *General Motors Corp.,* 124 F. 2d 822 (CA2 1942). Since the decision in *Schwinn,* location restrictions have been sustained by three Courts of Appeals, including the decision below. *Salco Corp.* v. *General Motors Corp.,* 517 F. 2d 567 (CA10 1975); *Kaiser* v. *General Motors Corp.,* 396 F. Supp. 33 (ED Pa. 1975), affirmance order, 530 F. 2d 964 (CA3 1976).

II

A

We turn first to Continental's contention that Sylvania's restriction on retail locations is a *per se* violation of §1 of the Sherman Act as interpreted in *Schwinn*. The restrictions at issue in *Schwinn* were part of a three-tier distribution system comprising, in addition to Arnold, Schwinn & Co. (Schwinn), 22 intermediate distributors and a network of franchised retailers. Each distributor had a defined geographic area in which it had the exclusive right to supply franchised retailers. Sales to the public were made only through franchised retailers, who were authorized to sell Schwinn bicycles only from specified locations. In support of this limitation, Schwinn prohibited both distributors and retailers from selling Schwinn bicycles to nonfranchised retailers. At the retail level, therefore, Schwinn was able to control the number of retailers of its bicycles in any given area according to its view of the needs of that market.

As of 1967 approximately 75% of Schwinn's total sales were made under the "Schwinn Plan." Acting essentially as a manufacturer's representative or sales agent, a distributor participating in this plan forwarded orders from retailers to the factory. Schwinn then shipped the ordered bicycles directly to the retailer, billed the retailer, bore the credit risk, and paid the distributor a commission on the sale. Under the Schwinn Plan, the distributor never had title to or possession of the bicycles. The remainder of the bicycles moved to the retailers through the hands of the distributors. For the most part, the distributors functioned as traditional wholesalers with respect to these sales, stocking an inventory of bicycles owned by them to supply retailers with emergency and "fill-in" requirements. A smaller part of the bicycles that were physically distributed by the distributors were covered by consignment and agency arrangements that had been developed to deal with particular problems of certain distributors. Distributors acquired title only to those bicycles that they purchased as wholesalers; retailers, of course, acquired title to all of the bicycles ordered by them.

In the District Court, the United States charged a continuing conspiracy by Schwinn and other alleged co-conspirators to fix prices, allocate exclusive territories to distributors, and confine Schwinn bicycles to franchised retailers. Relying on *United States* v. *Bausch & Lomb Co.*, 321 U. S. 707 (1944), the Government argued that the nonprice restrictions were *per se* illegal as part of a scheme for fixing the retail prices of Schwinn bicycles. The District Court rejected the price-fixing allegation because of a failure of proof and held that Schwinn's limitation of retail bicycle sales to franchised retailers was permissible under §1. The court found a §1 violation, however, in "a conspiracy to divide certain borderline or overlapping counties in the territories served by four Midwestern cycle distributors." 237 F. Supp. 323, 342 (ND Ill. 1965). The court described the violation as a "division of territory by agreement between the distributors . . . horizontal in nature," and held that Schwinn's participation did not change that basic characteristic. *Ibid.* The District Court limited its injunction to apply only to the territorial restrictions on the resale of bicycles purchased by the distributors in their roles as wholesalers. *Ibid.*

Schwinn came to this Court on appeal by the United States from the District Court's decision. Abandoning its *per se* theories, the Government argued that Schwinn's prohibition against distributors' and retailers' selling Schwinn bicycles to nonfranchised retailers was unreasonable under §1 and that the District Court's injunction against exclusive distributor territories should extend to all such restrictions regardless of the form of the transaction. The Government did not challenge the District Court's decision on price fixing, and Schwinn did not challenge the decision on exclusive distributor territories.

The Court acknowledged the Government's abandonment of its *per se* theories and stated that the resolution of the case would require an examination of "the specifics of the challenged practices and their impact upon the marketplace in order to make a judgment as to whether the restraint is or is not 'reasonable' in the special sense in which §1 of the Sherman Act must be read for purposes of this type of inquiry." 388 U. S., at 374. Despite this description of its task, the Court proceeded to articulate the following "bright line" *per se* rule of illegality for vertical restrictions: "Under the Sherman Act, it is unreasonable without more for a manufacturer to seek to restrict and confine areas or persons with whom an article may be traded after the manufacturer has parted with dominion over it." *Id.*, at 379. But the Court expressly stated that the rule of reason governs when "the manufacturer retains title, dominion, and risk with respect to the product and the position and function of the dealer in question are, in fact, indistinguishable from those of an agent or salesman of the manufacturer." *Id.*, at 380.

Application of these principles to the facts of *Schwinn* produced sharply contrasting results depending upon the role played by the distributor in the distribution system. With respect to that portion of Schwinn's sales for which the distributors acted as ordinary wholesalers, buying and reselling Schwinn bicycles, the Court held that the territorial and customer restrictions challenged by the Government were *per se* illegal. But, with respect to that larger portion of Schwinn's sales in which the distributors functioned under the Schwinn Plan and under the less common consignment and agency arrangements, the Court held that the same restrictions should be judged under the rule of reason. The only retail restriction challenged by the Government prevented franchised retailers from supplying nonfranchised retailers. *Id.*, at 377. The Court apparently perceived no material distinction between the restrictions on distributors and retailers, for it held:

> "The principle is, of course, equally applicable to sales to retailers, and the decree should similarly enjoin the making of any sales to retailers upon any condition, agreement or understanding limiting the retailer's freedom as to where and to whom it will resell the products." *Id.*, at 378.

Applying the rule of reason to the restrictions that were not imposed in conjunction with the sale of bicycles, the Court had little difficulty finding them all reasonable in light of the competitive situation in "the product market as a whole." *Id.*, at 382.

B

In the present case, it is undisputed that title to the television sets passed from Sylvania to Continental. Thus, the *Schwinn per se* rule applies unless Sylvania's restriction on locations falls outside *Schwinn's* prohibition against a manufacturer's attempting to restrict a "retailer's freedom as to where and to whom it will resell the products." *Id.*, at 378. As the Court of Appeals conceded, the language of *Schwinn* is clearly broad enough to apply to the present case. Unlike the Court of Appeals, however, we are unable to find a principled basis for distinguishing *Schwinn* from the case now before us.

Both Schwinn and Sylvania sought to reduce but not to eliminate competition among their respective retailers through the adoption of a franchise system. Although it was not one of the issues addressed by the District Court or presented on appeal by the Government, the Schwinn franchise plan included a location restriction similar to the one challenged here. These restrictions allowed Schwinn and Sylvania to regulate the amount of competition among their retailers by preventing a franchisee from selling franchised products from outlets other than the one covered by the franchise agreement. To exactly the same end, the Schwinn franchise plan included a companion restriction, apparently not found in the Sylvania plan, that prohibited franchised retailers from selling Schwinn products to nonfranchised retailers. In *Schwinn* the Court expressly held that this restriction was impermissible under the broad principle stated there. In intent and competitve impact, the retail-customer restriction in *Schwinn* is indistinguishable from the location restriction in the present case. In both cases the restrictions limited the freedom of the retailer to dispose of the purchased products as he desired. The fact that one restriction was addressed to territory and the other to customers is irrelevant to functional antitrust analysis and, indeed, to the language and broad thrust of the opinion in *Schwinn*.[12] As Mr. Chief Justice Hughes stated in *Appalachian Coals, Inc.* v.

---

[12] The distinctions drawn by the Court of Appeals and endorsed in Mr. Justice White's separate opinion have no basis in *Schwinn*. The intrabrand competitive impact of the restrictions at issue in *Schwinn* ranged from complete elimination to mere reduction; yet, the Court did not even hint at any distinction on this ground. Similarly, there is no suggestion that the *per se* rule was applied because of Schwinn's prominent position in its industry. That position was the same whether the bicycles were sold or consigned, but the Court's analysis was quite different. In light of Mr. Justice White's emphasis on the "superior consumer acceptance" enjoyed by the Schwinn brand name, *post*, at 63, we note that the Court rejected precisely that premise in *Schwinn*. Applying the rule of reason to the restrictions imposed in nonsale transactions, the Court stressed that there was "no showing that [competitive bicycles were] not in all respects reasonably interchangeable as articles of competitive commerce with the Schwinn product" and that it did "not regard Schwinn's claim of product excellence as establishing the contrary." 388 U. S., at 381, and n. 7. Although *Schwinn* did hint at preferential treatment for new entrants and failing firms, the District Court below did not even submit Sylvania's claim that it was failing to the jury. Accordingly, Mr. Justice White's position appears to reflect an extension of *Schwinn* in this regard. Having crossed the "failing firm" line, Mr. Justice White attempts neither to draw a new one nor to explain why one should be drawn at all.

United States, 288 U. S. 344, 360, 377 (1933): "Realities must dominate the judgment. . . . The Anti-Trust Act aims at substance."

III

Sylvania argues that if *Schwinn* cannot be distinguished, it should be reconsidered. Although *Schwinn* is supported by the principle of *stare decisis, Illinois Brick Co.* v. *Illinois,* 431 U. S. 720, 736 (1977), we were convinced that the need for clarification of the law in this area justifies reconsideration. *Schwinn* itself was an abrupt and largely unexplained departure from *White Motor Co.* v. *United States,* 372 U. S. 253 (1963), where only four years earlier the Court had refused to endorse a *per se* rule for vertical restrictions. Since its announcement, *Schwinn* has been the subject of continuing controversy and confusion, both in the scholarly journals and in the federal courts. The great weight of scholarly opinion has been critical of the decision,[13] and a number of the federal courts confronted with analogous vertical restrictions have sought to limit its reach.[14] In our view, the experience of the past 10 years should be brought to bear on this subject of considerable commercial importance.

The traditional framework of analysis under §1 of the Sherman Act is fa-

---

[13] A former Assistant Attorney General in charge of the Antitrust Division has described *Schwinn* as "an exercise in barren formalism" that is "artificial and unresponsive to the competitive needs of the real world." Baker, Vertical Restraints in Times of Change: From *White* to *Schwinn* to Where?, 44 Antitrust L. J. 537 (1975). See, e. g., Handler, The Twentieth Annual Antitrust Review — 1967, 53 Va. L. Rev. 1667 (1967); McLaren, Territorial and Customer Restrictions, Consignments, Suggested Retail Prices and Refusals to Deal, 37 Antitrust L. J. 137 (1968); Pollock, Alternative Distribution Methods After *Schwinn,* 63 Nw. U. L. Rev. 595 (1968); Posner, Antitrust Policy and the Supreme Court: An Analysis of the Restricted Distribution, Horizontal Merger and Potential Competition Decisions, 75 Colum. L. Rev. 282 (1975); Robinson, Recent Antitrust Developments: 1974, 75 Colum. L. Rev. 243 (1975); Note, Vertical Territorial and Customer Restrictions in the Franchising Industry, 10 Colum. J. L. & Soc. Prob. 497 (1974); Note, Territorial and Customer Restrictions: A Trend Toward a Broader Rule of Reason?, 40 Geo. Wash. L. Rev. 123 (1971); Note, Territorial Restrictions and Per Se Rules — A Re-evaluation of the *Schwinn* and *Sealy* Doctrines, 70 Mich. L. Rev. 616 (1972). But see Louis, Vertical Distributional Restraints Under *Schwinn* and *Sylvania*: An Argument for the Continuing Use of a Partial Per Se Approach, 75 Mich. L. Rev. 275 (1976); Zimmerman, Distribution Restrictions After *Sealy* and *Schwinn,* 12 Antitrust Bull. 1181 (1967). For a more inclusive list of articles and comments, see 537 F. 2d, at 988 n. 13.

[14] Indeed, as one commentator has observed, many courts "have struggled to distinguish or limit *Schwinn* in ways that are a tribute to judicial ingenuity." Robinson, *supra,* n. 13, at 272. Thus, the statement in *Schwinn* that post-sale vertical restrictions as to customers or territories are "unreasonable without more," 388 U. S., at 379, has been interpreted to allow an exception to the *per se* rule where the manufacturer proves "more" by showing that the restraints will protect consumers against injury and the manufacturer against product liability claims. See, e. g., *Tripoli Co.* v. *Wella Corp.,* 425 F. 2d 932, 936–938 (CA3 1970) (en banc). Similarly, the statement that Schwinn's enforcement of its restrictions had been " 'firm and resolute,' " 388 U. S., at 372, has been relied upon to distinguish cases lacking that element. See, e. g., *Janel Sales Corp.* v. *Lanvin Parfums, Inc.,* 396 F. 2d 398, 406 (CA2 1968). Other factual distinctions have been drawn to justify upholding territorial restrictions that would seem to fall within the scope of the *Schwinn per se* rule. See, e. g., *Carter-Wallace, Inc.* v. *United States,* 196 Ct. Cl. 35, 44–46, 449 F. 2d 1374, 1379–1380 (1971) (*per se* rule inapplicable when purchaser can avoid restraints by electing to buy product at higher price); *Colorado Pump & Supply Co.* v. *Febco, Inc.,* 472 F. 2d 637 (CA10 1973) (apparent territorial restriction characterized as primary responsibility clause). One Court of Appeals has expressly urged us to consider the need in this area for greater flexibility. *Adolph Coors Co.* v. *FTC,* 497 F. 2d 1178, 1187 (CA10 1974). The decision in *Schwinn* and the developments in the lower courts have been exhaustively surveyed in ABA Antitrust Section, Monograph No. 2, Vertical Restrictions Limiting Intrabrand Competition (1977) (ABA Monograph No. 2).

miliar and does not require extended discussion. Section 1 prohibits "[e]very contract, combination . . . , or conspiracy, in restraint of trade or commerce." Since the early years of this century a judicial gloss on this statutory language has established the "rule of reason" as the prevailing standard of analysis. *Standard Oil Co.* v. *United States*, 221 U. S. 1 (1911). Under this rule, the factfinder weighs all of the circumstances of a case in deciding whether a restrictive practice should be prohibited as imposing an unreasonable restraint on competition.[15] *Per se* rules of illegality are appropriate only when they relate to conduct that is manifestly anticompetitive. As the Court explained in *Northern Pac. R. Co.* v. *United States* , 356 U. S. 1, 5 (1958), "there are certain agreements or practices which because of their pernicious effect on competition and lack of any redeeming virtue are conclusively presumed to unreasonable and therefore illegal without elaborate inquiry as to the precise harm they have caused or the business excuse for their use."[16]

In essence, the issue before us is whether *Schwinn's per se* rule can be justified under the demanding standards of *Northern Pac. R. Co.* The Court's refusal to endorse a *per se* rule in *White Motor Co.* was based on its uncertainty as to whether vertical restrictions satisfied those standards. Addressing this question for the first time, the Court stated:

> "We need to know more than we do about the actual impact of these arrangements on competition to decide whether they have such a 'pernicious effect on competition and lack . . . any redeeming virtue' (*Northern Pac. R. Co.* v. *United States, supra,* p. 5) and therefore should be classified as *per se* violations of the Sherman Act." 372 U. S., at 263.

Only four years later the Court in *Schwinn* announced its sweeping *per se* rule without even a reference to *Northern Pac. R. Co.* and with no explanation of

---

[15] One of the most frequently cited statements of the rule of reason is that of Mr. Justice Brandeis in *Chicago Bd. of Trade* v. *United States,* 246 U. S. 231, 238 (1918):

"The true test of legality is whether the restraint imposed is such as merely regulates and perhaps thereby promotes competition or whether it is such as may suppress or even destroy competition. To determine that question the court must ordinarily consider the facts peculiar to the business to which the restraint is applied; its condition before and after the restraint was imposed; the nature of the restraint and its effect, actual or probable. The history of the restraint, the evil believed to exist, the reason for adopting the particular remedy, the purpose or end sought to be attained, are all relevant facts. This is not because a good intention will save an otherwise objectionable regulation or the reverse; but because knowledge of intent may help the court to interpret facts and to predict consequences."

[16] *Per se* rules thus require the Court to make broad generalizations about the social utility of particular commercial practices. The probability that anticompetitive consequences will result from a practice and the severity of those consequences must be balanced against its procompetitive consequences. Cases that do not fit the generalization may arise, but a *per se* rule reflects the judgment that such cases are not sufficiently common or important to justify the time and expense necessary to identify them. Once established, *per se* rules tend to provide guidance to the business community and to minimize the burdens on litigants and the judicial system of the more complex rule-of-reason trials, see *Northern Pac. R. Co.* v. *United States,* 356 U. S., at 5; *United States* v. *Topco Associates, Inc.,* 405 U. S. 596, 609–610 (1972), but those advantages are not sufficient in themselves to justify the creation of *per se* rules. If it were otherwise, all of antitrust law would be reduced to *per se* rules, thus introducing an unintended and undesirable rigidity in the law.

its sudden change in position.[17] We turn now to consider *Schwinn* in light of *Northern Pac. R. Co.*

The market impact of vertical restrictions[18] is complex because of their potential for simultaneous reduction of intrabrand competition and stimulation of interbrand competition.[19] Significantly, the Court in *Schwinn* did not distinguish among the challenged restrictions on the basis of their individual potential for intrabrand harm or interbrand benefit. Restrictions that completely eliminated intrabrand competition among Schwinn distributors were analyzed no differently from those that merely moderated intrabrand competiton among retailers. The pivotal factor was the passage of title: All restrictions were held to be *per se* illegal where title had passed, and all were evaluated and sustained under the rule of reason where it had not. The location restriction at issue here would be subject to the same pattern of analysis under *Schwinn.*

It appears that this distinction between sale and nonsale transactions resulted from the Court's effort to accommodate the perceived intrabrand harm and interbrand benefit of vertical restrictions. The *per se* rule for sale transactions reflected the view that vertical restrictions are "so obviously destructive" of intrabrand competition[20] that their use would "open the door to exclusivity of outlets and limitation of territory further than prudence permits." 388 U. S.,

---

[17] After *White Motor Co.,* the Courts of Appeals continued to evaluate territorial restrictions according to the rule of reason. *Sandura Co.* v. *FTC,* 339 F. 2d 847 (CA6 1964); *Snap-On Tools Corp.* v. *FTC,* 321 F. 2d 825 (CA7 1963). For an exposition of the history of the antitrust analysis of vertical restrictions before *Schwinn,* see ABA Monograph No. 2, pp. 6–8.

[18] As in *Schwinn,* we are concerned here only with nonprice vertical restrictions. The *per se* illegality of price restrictions has been established firmly for many years and involves significantly different questions of analysis and policy. As MR. JUSTICE WHITE notes, *post,* at 69–70, some commentators have argued that the manufacturer's motivation for imposing vertical price restrictions may be the same as for nonprice restrictions. There are, however, significant differences that could easily justify different treatment. In his concurring opinion in *White Motor Co.* v. *United States,* MR. JUSTICE BRENNAN noted that, unlike nonprice restrictions, "[r]esale price maintenance is not only designed to, but almost invariably does in fact, reduce price competition not only *among* sellers of the affected product, but quite as much *between* that product and competing brands." 372 U. S., at 268. Professor Posner also recognized that "industry-wide resale price maintenance might facilitate cartelizing." Posner, *supra,* n. 13, at 294 (footnote omitted); see R. Posner, Antitrust: Cases, Economic Notes and Other Materials 134 (1974); E. Gellhorn, Antitrust Law and Economics 252 (1976); Note, 10 Colum. J. L. & Soc. Prob., *supra,* n. 13, at 498 n. 12. Furthermore, Congress recently has expressed its approval of a *per se* analysis of vertical price restrictions by repealing those provisions of the Miller-Tydings and McGuire Acts allowing fair-trade pricing at the option of the individual States. Consumer Goods Pricing Act of 1975, 89 Stat. 801, amending 15 U. S. C. §§1, 45(a). No similar expression of congressional intent exists for nonprice restrictions.

[19] Interbrand competition is the competition among the manufacturers of the same generic product — television sets in this case — and is the primary concern of antitrust law. The extreme example of a deficiency of interbrand competition is monopoly, where there is only one manufacturer. In contrast, intrabrand competition is the competition between the distributors — wholesale or retail — of the product of a particular manufacturer.

The degree of intrabrand competition is wholly independent of the level of interbrand competition confronting the manufacturer. Thus, there may be fierce intrabrand competition among the distributors of a product produced by a monopolist and no intrabrand competition among the distributors of a product produced by a firm in a highly competitive industry. But when interbrand competition exists, as it does among television manufacturers, it provides a significant check on the exploitation of intrabrand market power because of the ability of consumers to substitute a different brand of the same product.

[20] The Court did not specifically refer to intrabrand competition, but this meaning is clear from the context.

at 379-380.[21] Conversely, the continued adherence to the traditional rule of reason for nonsale transactions reflected the view that the restrictions have too great a potential for the promotion of interbrand competition to justify complete prohibition.[22] The Court's opinion provides no analytical support for these contrasting positions. Nor is there even an assertion in the opinion that the competitive impact of vertical restrictions is significantly affected by the form of the transaction. Non-sale transactions appear to be excluded from the *per se* rule, not because of a greater danger of intrabrand harm or a greater promise of interbrand benefit, but rather because of the Court's unexplained belief that a complete *per se* prohibition would be too "inflexibl[e]." *Id.*, at 379.

Vertical restrictions reduce intrabrand competition by limiting the number of sellers of a particular product competing for the business of a given group of buyers. Location restrictions have this effect because of practical constraints on the effective marketing area of retail outlets. Although intrabrand competition may be reduced, the ability of retailers to exploit the resulting market may be limited both by the ability of consumers to travel to other franchised locations and, perhaps more importantly, to purchase the competing products of other manufacturers. None of these key variables, however, is affected by the form of the transaction by which a manufacturer conveys his products to the retailers.

Vertical restrictions promote interbrand competition by allowing the manufacturer to achieve certain efficiencies in the distribution of his products. These "redeeming virtues" are implicit in every decision sustaining vertical restric-

---

[21] The Court also stated that to impose vertical restrictions in sale transactions would "violate the ancient rule against restraints on alienation." 388 U. S., at 380. This isolated reference has provoked sharp criticism from virtually all of the commentators on the decision, most of whom have regarded the Court's apparent reliance on the "ancient rule" as both a misreading of legal history and a perversion of antitrust analysis. See, *e. g.,* Handler, *supra,* n. 13, at 1684–1686; Posner, *supra,* n. 13, at 295–295; Robinson, *supra,* n. 13, at 270–271; but see Louis, *supra,* n. 13, at 276 n. 6. We quite agree with MR. JUSTICE STEWART's dissenting comment in *Schwinn* that "the state of the common law 400 or even 100 years ago is irrelevant to the issue before us: the effect of the antitrust laws upon vertical distributional restraints in the American economy today." 388 U. S., at 392.

We are similarly unable to accept Judge Browning's interpretation of *Schwinn.* In his dissent below he argued that the decision reflects the view that the Sherman Act was intended to prohibit restrictions on the autonomy of independent businessmen even though they have no impact on "price, quality, and quantity of goods and services," 537 F. 2d, at 1019. This view is certainly not explicit in *Schwinn,* which purports to be based on an examination of the "impact [of the restrictions] upon the marketplace." 388 U. S., at 374. Competitive economics have social and political as well as economic advantages, see *e. g., Northern Pac. R. Co.* v. *United States,* 356 U. S., at 4, but an antitrust policy divorced from market considerations would lack any objective benchmarks. As Mr. Justice Brandeis reminded us: "Every agreement concerning trade, every regulation of trade, restrains. To bind, to restrain, is of their very essence." *Chicago Bd. of Trade* v. *United States,* 246 U. S., at 238. Although MR. JUSTICE WHITE's opinion endorses Judge Browning's interpretation, *post,* at 66–68, it purports to distinguish *Schwinn* on grounds inconsistent with that interpretation, *post,* at 71.

[22] In that regard, the Court specifically stated that a more complete prohibition "might severely hamper smaller enterprises resorting to reasonable methods of meeting the competition of giants and of merchandising through independent dealers." 388 U. S., at 380. The Court also broadly hinted that it would recognize additional exceptions to the *per se* rule for new entrants in an industry and for failing firms, both of which were mentioned in *White Motor* as candidates for such exceptions. 388 U. S., at 374. The Court might have limited the exceptions to the *per se* rule to these situations, which present the strongest arguments for the sacrifice of intrabrand competition for interbrand competition. Significantly, it chose instead to create the more extensive exception for nonsale transactions which is available to all businesses, regardless of their size, financial health, or market share. This broader exception demonstrates even more clearly the Court's awareness of the "redeeming virtues" of vertical restrictions.

tions under the rule of reason. Economists have identified a number of ways in which manufacturers can use such restrictions to compete more effectively against other manufacturers. See, e. g., Preston, Restrictive Distribution Arrangements: Economic Analysis and Public Policy Standards, 30 Law & Contemp. Prob. 506, 511 (1965).[23] For example, new manufacturers and manufacturers entering new markets can use the restrictions in order to induce competent and aggressive retailers to make the kind of investment of capital and labor that is often required in the distribution of products unknown to the consumer. Established manufacturers can use them to induce retailers to engage in promotional activities or to provide service and repair facilities necessary to the efficient marketing of their products. Service and repair are vital for many products, such as automobiles and major household appliances. The availability and quality of such services affect a manufacturer's goodwill and competitiveness of his product. Because of market imperfections such as the so-called "free rider" effect, these services might not be provided by retailers in a purely competitive situation, despite the fact that each retailer's benefit would be greater if all provided the services than if none did. Posner, supra, n. 13, at 285; cf. P. Samuelson, Economics 506-507 (10th ed. 1976).

Economists also have argued that manufacturers have an economic interest in maintaining as much intrabrand competition as is consistent with the efficient distribution of their products. Bork, The Rule of Reason and the Per Se Concept: Price Fixing and Market Division [II], 75 Yale L. J. 373, 403 (1966); Posner, supra, n. 13, at 283, 287–288.[24] Although the view that the manufacturer's interest necessarily corresponds with that of the public is not universally shared, even the leading critic of vertical restrictions concedes that Schwinn's distinction between sale and nonsale transactions is essentially unrelated to any relevant economic impact. Comanor, Vertical Territorial and Customer Restrictions: White Motor and Its Aftermath, 81 Harv. L. Rev. 1419, 1422 (1968).[25] Indeed, to the extent that the form of the transaction is related to

[23] Marketing efficiency is not the only legitimate reason for a manufacturer's desire to exert control over the manner in which his products are sold and serviced. As a result of statutory and common-law developments, society increasingly demands that manufacturers assume direct responsibility for the safety and quality of their products. For example, at the federal level, apart from more specialized requirements, manufacturers of consumer products have safety responsibilities under the Consumer Product Safety Act, 15 U. S. C. §2051 et seq. (1970 ed., Supp. V), and obligations for warranties under the Consumer Product Warranties Act, 15 U. S. C. §2301 et seq. (1970 ed., Supp. V). Similar obligations are imposed by state law. See, e. g., Cal. Civ. Code Ann. §1790 et seq. (West 1973). The legitimacy of these concerns has been recognized in cases involving vertical restrictions. See, e. g., Tripoli Co. v. Wella Corp., 425 F. 2d 932 (CA3 1970).

[24] "Generally a manufacturer would prefer the lowest retail price possible, once its price to dealers has been set, because a lower retail price means increased sales and higher manufacturer revenues." Note, 88 Harv. L. Rev. 636, 641 (1975). In this context, a manufacturer is likely to view the difference between the price at which it sells to its retailers and their price to the consumer as its "cost of distribution," which it would prefer to minimize. Posner, supra, n. 13, at 283.

[25] Professor Comanor argues that the promotional activities encouraged by vertical restrictions result in product differentiation and, therefore, a decrease in interbrand competition. This argument is flawed by its necessary assumption that a large part of the promotional efforts resulting from vertical restrictions will not convey socially desirable information about product availability, price, quality, and services. Nor is it clear that a per se rule would result in anything more than a shift to less efficient methods of obtaining the same promotional effects.

interbrand benefits, the Court's distinction is inconsistent with its articulated concern for the ability of smaller firms to compete effectively with larger ones. Capital requirements and administrative expenses may prevent smaller firms from using the exception for nonsale transactions. See, *e. g.*, Baker, *supra*, n. 13, at 538; Phillips, *Schwinn* Rules and the "New Economics" of Vertical Relation, 44 Antitrust L. J. 573, 576 (1975); Pollock, *supra*, n. 13, at 610.[26]

We conclude that the distinction drawn in *Schwinn* between sale and nonsale transactions is not sufficient to justify the application of a *per se* rule in one situation and a rule of reason in the other. The question remains whether the *per se* rule stated in *Schwinn* should be expanded to include nonsale transactions or abandoned in favor of a return to the rule of reason. We have found no persuasive support for expanding the *per se* rule. As noted above, the *Schwinn* Court recognized the undesirability of "prohibit[ing] all vertical restrictions of territory and all franchising. . . ." 388 U. S., at 379–380.[27] And even Continental does not urge us to hold that all such restrictions are *per se* illegal.

We revert to the standard articulated in *Northern Pac. R. Co.*, and reiterated in *White Motor*, for determining whether vertical restrictions must be "conclusively presumed to be unreasonable and therefore illegal without elaborate inquiry as to the precise harm they have caused or the business excuse for their use." 356 U. S., at 5. Such restrictions, in varying forms, are widely used in our free market economy. As indicated above, there is substantial scholarly and judicial authority supporting their economic utility. There is relatively little authority to the contrary.[28] Certainly, there has been no showing in this case, either generally or with respect to Sylvania's agreements, that vertical restrictions have or are likely to have a "pernicious effect on competition" or that they "lack . . . any redeeming virtue." *Ibid.*[29] Accordingly, we conclude

---

[26] We also note that *per se* rules in this area may work to the ultimate detriment of the small businessmen who operate as franchisees. To the extent that a *per se* rule prevents a firm from using the franchise system to achieve efficiencies that it perceives as important to its successful operation, the rule creates an incentive for vertical integration into the distribution system, thereby eliminating to that extent the role of independent businessmen. See, *e. g.*, Keck, The *Schwinn* Case, 23 Bus. Law. 669 (1968); Pollock, *supra*, n. 13, at 608–610.

[27] Continental's contention that balancing intrabrand and interbrand competitive effects of vertical restrictions is not a "proper part of the judicial function," Brief for Petitioners 52, is refuted by *Schwinn* itself. *United States* v. *Topco Associates, Inc.*, 405 U. S., at 608, is not to the contrary, for it involved a horizontal restriction among ostensible competitors.

[28] There may be occasional problems in differentiating vertical restrictions from horizontal restrictions originating in agreements among the retailers. There is no doubt that restrictions in the latter category would be illegal *per se*, see, *e. g.*, *United States* v. *General Motors Corp.*, 384 U. S. 127 (1966); *United States* v. *Topco Associates, Inc.*, *supra*, but we do not regard the problems of proof as sufficiently great to justify a *per se* rule.

[29] The location restriction used by Sylvania was neither the least nor the most restrictive provision that it could have used. See ABA Monograph No. 2, pp. 20–25. But we agree with the implicit judgment in *Schwinn* that a *per se* rule based on the nature of the restriction is, in general, undesirable. Although distinctions can be drawn among the frequently used restrictions, we are inclined to view them as differences of degree and form. See Robinson, *supra*, n. 13, at 279–280; Averill, Sealy, Schwinn and Sherman One: An Analysis and Prognosis, 15 N. Y. L. F. 39, 65 (1969). We are unable to perceive significant social gain from channeling transactions into one form or another. Finally, we agree with the Court in *Schwinn* that the advantages of vertical restrictions should not be limited to the categories of new entrants and failing firms. Sylvania was faltering, if not failing, and we think it would be unduly artificial to deny it the use of valuable competitive tools.

that the *per se* rule stated in *Schwinn* must be overruled.[30] In so holding we do not foreclose the possibility that particular applications of vertical restrictions might justify *per se* prohibition under *Northern Pac. R. Co.* But we do make clear that departure from the rule-of-reason standard must be based upon demonstrable economic effect rather than—as in *Schwinn*—upon formalistic line drawing.

In sum, we conclude that the appropriate decision is to return to the rule of reason that governed vertical restrictions prior to *Schwinn*. When anticompetitive effects are shown to result from particular vertical restrictions they can be adequately policed under the rule of reason, the standard traditionally applied for the majority of anticompetitive practices challenged under §1 of the Act. Accordingly, the decision of the Court of Appeals is

Affirmed.

---

[30] The importance of *stare decisis* is, of course, unquestioned, but as Mr. Justice Frankfurter stated in *Helvering* v. *Hallock,* 309 U. S. 106, 119 (1940), "*stare decisis* is a principle of policy and not a mechanical formula of adherence to the latest decision, however recent and questionable, when such adherence involves collision with a prior doctrine more embracing in its scope, intrinsically sounder, and verified by experience."

Case 2

United States Steel Corp. et al. v. Fortner Enterprises, Inc.

Certiorari to the United States Court of Appeals For The Sixth Circuit

No. 75-853. Argued November 1, 1976—Decided February 22, 1977

MR. JUSTICE STEVENS delivered the opinion of the Court.

In exchange for respondent's promise to purchase prefabricated houses to be erected on land near Louisville, Ky., petitioners agreed to finance the cost of acquiring and developing the land. Difficulties arose while the development was in progress, and respondent (Fortner) commenced this treble-damages action, claiming that the transaction was a tying arrangement forbidden by the Sherman Act. Fortner alleged that competition for prefabricated houses (the tied product) was restrained by petitioners' abuse of power over credit (the tying product). A summary judgment in favor of petitioners was reversed by this Court. *Fortner Enterprises* v. *United States Steel Corp.*, 394 U. S. 495 (*Fortner I*). We held that the agreement affected a "not insubstantial" amount of commerce in the tied product and that Fortner was entitled to an opportunity to prove that petitioners possessed "appreciable economic power" in the market for the tying product. The question now presented is whether the record supports the conclusion that petitioners has such power in the credit market.[1]

---

[1] As explained at the outset of the opinion, *Fortner I* involved "a variety of questions concerning the proper standards to be applied by a United States district court in passing on a motion for summary judgment in a civil antitrust action." 394 U. S., at 496. Petitioners do not ask us to re-examine *Fortner I*, which left only the economic-power question open on the issue of whether a *per se* violation could be proved. On the other hand, Fortner has not pursued the suggestion in *Fortner I* that it might be able to prove a §1 violation under the rule-of-reason standard. 394 U. S., at 500. Thus, with respect to §1, only the economic-power issue is before us.

In *Fortner I*, the Court noted that Fortner also alleged a §2 violation, namely, that petitioners "conspired together for the purpose of . . . acquiring a monopoly in the market for prefabricated houses." 394 U. S., at 500. The District Court held that a §2 violation had been proved. Although the Court of Appeals did not reach this issue, a remand is unnecessary. It is clear that neither the District Court's findings of fact nor the record supports the conclusion that §2 was violated. The District Court found only that "the defendants did combine or conspire to *increase sales* of prefabricated house packages by United States Steel Corporation by the making of loans to numerous builders containing the tie-in provision" and that "the sole purpose of the loan programs of the Credit Corporation was specifically and deliberately to *increase the share of the market* of United States Steel Corporation in prefabricated house packages. . . ." App. 1603 (emphasis added). But "increasing sales" and "increasing market share" are normal business goals, not forbidden by §2 without other evidence of an intent to monopolize. The evidence in this case does not bridge the gap between the District Court's findings of intent to increase sales and its legal conclusion of conspiracy to monopolize. Moreover, petitioners did not have a large market share or dominant market position. See n. 3, *infra*. No inference of intent to monopolize can be drawn from the fact that a firm with a small market share has engaged in nonpredatory competitive conduct in the hope of increasing sales. Yet as we conclude, *infra*, at 621–622, that is all the record in this case shows.

The conclusion that a violation of §1 of the Sherman Act[2] had been proved was only reached after two trials. At the first trial following our remand, the District Court directed a verdict in favor of Fortner on the issue of liability, and submitted only the issue of damages to the jury. The jury assessed damages, before trebling, of $93,200. The Court of Appeals reversed the directed verdict and remanded for a new trial on liability. 452 F. 2d 1095 (CA6 1971), cert. denied, 406 U. S. 919. The parties then waived the jury; the trial judge heard additional evidence, and entered extensive findings of fact which were affirmed on appeal. 523 F. 2d 961 (1975). Both courts held that the findings justified the conclusion that petitioners had sufficient economic power in the credit market to make the tying arrangement unlawful.

Before explaining why we disagree with the ultimate conclusion of the courts below, we first describe the tying arrangement and then summarize the findings on the economic-power issue.

I

Only the essential features of the arrangement between the parties need be described. Fortner is a corporation which was activated by an experienced real estate developer for the purpose of buying and improving residential lots. One petitioner, United States Steel Corp., operates a "Home Division" which manufactures and assembles components of prefabricated houses; the second petitioner, the "Credit Corp.," is a wholly owned subsidiary, which provides financing to customers of the Home Division in order to promote sales. Although their common ownership and control make it appropriate to regard the two as a single seller, they sell two separate products—prefabricated houses and credit. The credit extended to Fortner was not merely for the price of the homes. Petitioners agreed to lend Fortner over $2,000,000 in exchange for Fortner's promise to purchase the components of 210 homes for about $689,000. The additional borrowed funds were intended to cover Fortner's cost of acquiring and developing the vacant real estate, and the cost of erecting the houses.

The impact of the agreement on the market for the tied product (prefabricated houses) is not in dispute. On the one hand, there is no claim—nor could there be—that the Home Division had any dominance in the prefabricated housing business. The record indicates that it was only moderately successful, and that its sales represented a small fraction of the industry total.[3] On the other hand, we have already held that the dollar value of the sales to respondent was sufficient to meet the "not insubstantial" test described in earlier cases. See 394 U. S., at 501-502. We therefore confine our attention to the

---

[2] 26 Stat. 209, as amended, 15 U. S. C. §1.

[3] In 1960, for example, the Home Division sold a total of 1,793 houses for $6,747,353. There were at least four larger prefabricated home manufacturers, the largest of which sold $16,804 homes in that year. In the following year the Home Division's sales declined while the sales of each of its four principal competitors remained steady or increased.

source of the tying arrangement—petitioners' "economic power" in the credit market.

II

The evidence supporting the conclusion that the Credit Corp. had appreciable economic power in the credit market relates to four propositions: (1) petitioner Credit Corp. and the Home Division were owned by one of the Nation's largest corporations; (2) petitioners entered into tying arrangements with a significant number of customers in addition to Fortner; (3) the Home Division charged respondent a noncompetitive price for its prefabricated homes; and (4) the financing provided to Fortner was "unique," primarily because it covered 100% of Fortner's acquisition and development costs.

The Credit Corp. was established in 1954 to provide financing for customers of the Home Division. The United States Steel Corp. not only provided the equity capital, but also allowed the Credit Corp. to use its credit in order to borrow money from banks at the prime rate. Thus, although the Credit Corp. itself was not a particularly large company, it was supported by a corporate parent with great financial strength.

The Credit Corp.'s loan policies were primarily intended to help the Home Division sell its products.[4] It extended credit only to customers of the Home Division, and over two-thirds of the Home Division customers obtained such financing. With few exceptions, all the loan agreements containing a tying clause comparable to the one challenged in this case. Petitioner's home sales in 1960 amounted to $6,747,353. Since over $4,600,000 of these sales were tied to financing provided by the Credit Corp.,[5] it is apparent that the tying arrangement was used with a number of customers in addition to Fortner.

The least expensive house package that Fortner purchased from the Home Division cost about $3,150. One witness testified that the Home Division's price was $455 higher than the price of comparable components in a conventional home; another witness, to whom the District Court made no reference in its findings, testified that the Home Division's price was $443 higher than a comparable prefabricated product. Whether the price differential was as great as 15% is not entirely clear, but the record does support the conclusion that the contract required Fortner to pay a noncompetitive price for the Home Division's houses.

The finding that the credit extended to Fortner was unique was based on factors emphasized in the testimony of Fortner's expert witness, Dr. Masten, a

---

[4] After reviewing extensive evidence taken from the files of the Credit Corp., including a memorandum stating that "our only purpose in making the loan . . . is shipping houses," the District Court expressly found "that the Credit Corporation was not so much concerned with the risks involved in loans but whether they would help sell houses." App. 1588–1589.

[5] This figure is not stated in the District Court's findings; it is derived from the finding of total sales and the finding that 68% of the sales in 1960 were made to dealers receiving financial assistance from the Credit Corp. See *id.*, at 1589–1590.

professor with special knowledge of lending practices in the Kentucky area. Dr. Masten testified that mortgage loans equal to 100% of the acquisition and development cost of real estate were not otherwise available in the Kentucky area; that even though Fortner had a deficit of $16,000, its loan was not guaranteed by a shareholder, officer, or other person interested in its business; and that the interest rate of 6% represented a low rate under prevailing economic conditions.[6] Moreover, he explained that the stable price levels at the time made the risk to the lender somewhat higher than would have been the case in a period of rising prices. Dr. Masten concluded that the terms granted to respondent by the Credit Corp. were so unusual that it was almost inconceivable that the funds could have been acquired from any other source. It is a fair summary of his testimony, and of the District Court's findings, to say that the loan was unique because the lender accepted such a high risk and the borrower assumed such a low cost.

The District Court also found that banks and federally insured savings and loan associations generally were prohibited by law from making 100% land acquisition and development loans, and "that other conventional lenders would not have made such loans at the time in question since they were not prudent loans due to the risk involved." App. 1596.

Accordingly, the District Court concluded "that all of the required elements of an illegal tie-in agreement did exist since the tie-in itself was present, a not insubstantial amount of interstate commerce in the tied product was restrained and the Credit Corporation did possess sufficient economic power or leverage to effect such restraint." *Id.,* at 1602.

III

Without the finding that the financing provided to Fortner was "unique," it is clear that the District Court's findings would be insufficient to support the conclusion that the Credit Corp. possessed any significant economic power in the credit market.

Although the Credit Corp. is owned by one of the Nation's largest manufacturing corporations, there is nothing in the record to indicate that this enabled it to borrow funds on terms more favorable than those available to competing lenders, or that it was able to operate more efficiently than other lending institutions. In short, the affiliation between the petitioners does not appear to have given the Credit Corp. any cost advantage over its competitors in the credit market. Instead, the affiliation was significant only because the Credit Corp. provided a source of funds to customers of the Home Division. That fact tells us nothing about the extent of petitioners' economic power in the credit market.

---

[6] The prime rate at the time was 5% or 5½%.

The same may be said about the fact that loans from the Credit Corp. were used to obtain house sales from Fortner and others. In some tying situations a disproportionately large volume of sales of the tied product resulting from only a few strategic sales of the tying product may reflect a form of economic "leverage" that is probative of power in the market for the tying product. If, as some economists have suggested, the purpose of a tie-in is often to facilitate price discrimination, such evidence would imply the existence of power that a free market would not tolerate.[7] But in this case Fortner was only required to purchase houses for the number of lots for which it received financing. The tying product produced no commitment from Fortner to purchase varying quantities of the tied product over an extended period of time. This record, therefore, does not describe the kind of "leverage" found in some of the Court's prior decisions condemning tying arrangements.[8]

The fact that Fortner—and presumably other Home Division customers as well—paid a noncompetitive price for houses also lends insufficient support to the judgment of the lower court. Proof that Fortner paid a higher price for the tied product is consistent with the possibility that the financing was unusually inexpensive[9] and that the price for the entire package was equal to, or below, a competitive price. And this possibility is equally strong even though a number of Home Division customers made a package purchase of homes and financing.[10]

The most significant finding made by the District Court related to the unique character of the credit extended to Fortner. This finding is particularly important because the unique character of the tying product has provided critical support for the finding of illegality in prior cases. Thus, the statutory grant of a patent monopoly in *International Salt Co.* v. *United States,* 332 U.

---

[7] See Bowman, Tying Arrangements and the Leverage Problem, 67 Yale L. J. 19 (1957).

[8] See *e. g., United Shoe Machinery* v. *United States,* 258 U. S. 451; *International Business Machines* v. *United States,* 298 U. S. 131; *International Salt Co.* v. *United States,* 332 U. S. 392. In his article in the 1969 Supreme Court Review 16, Professor Dam suggests that this kind of leverage may also have been present in *Northern Pacific R. Co.* v. *United States,* 356 U. S. 1.

[9] Fortner's expert witness agreed with the statement:
"The amount of the loan as a percentage of the collateral or security is only one element in determining its advantage to a borrower. The other relevant factors include the rate of interest charged, whether the lender discounts the amount loaned or charges service for [sic] other fees and maturity in terms of repayment." App. 1686.

[10] Relying on *Advance Business Systems & Supply Co.* v. *SCM Corp.,* 415 F. 2d 55 (CA4 1969), cert. denied, 397 U. S. 920, Fortner contends that acceptance of the package by a significant number of customers is itself sufficient to prove the seller's economic power. But this approach depends on the absence of other explanations for the willingness of buyers to purchase the package. See 415 F. 2d, at 68. In the *Northern Pacific* case, for instance, the Court explained:
"The very existence of this host of tying arrangements is itself compelling evidence of the defendant's great power, at least where, as here, no other explanation has been offered for the existence of these restraints. The 'preferential routing' clauses conferred no benefit on the purchasers or lessees. While they got the land they wanted by yielding their freedom to deal with competing carriers, the defendant makes no claim that it came any cheaper than if the restrictive clauses had been omitted. In fact any such price reduction in return for rail shipments would have quite plainly constituted an unlawfull rebate to the shipper. So far as the Railroad was concerned its purpose obviously was to fence out competitors, to stifle competition." 356 U. S., at 7–8 (footnote omitted).
As this passage demonstrates, this case differs from *Northern Pacific* because use of the tie-in in this case be explained as a form of price competition in the tied product, whereas that explanation was unavailable to the Northern Pacific Railway.

S. 392; the copyright monopolies in *United States* v. *Paramount Pictures, Inc.,* 334 U. S. 131, and *United States* v. *Loew's Inc.,* 371 U. S. 38; and the extensive land holdings in *Northern Pacific R. Co.* v. *United States,* 356 U. S. 1,[11] represented tying products that the Court regarded as sufficiently unique to give rise to a presumption of economic power.[12]

As the Court plainly stated in its prior opinion in this case, these decisions do not require that the defendant have a monopoly or even a dominant position throughout the market for a tying product. See 394 U. S., at 502–503. They do, however, focus attention on the question whether the seller has the power, within the market for the tying product, to raise prices or to require purchasers to accept burdensome terms that could not be exacted in a completely competitive market.[13] In short, the question is whether the seller has some advantage not shared by his competitors in the market for the tying product.

Without any such advantage differentiating his product from that of his competitors, the seller's product does not have the kind of uniqueness considered relevant in prior tying-clause cases.[14] The Court made this point explicitly when it remanded this case for trial:

> "We do not mean to accept petitioner's apparent argument that market power can be inferred simply because the kind of financing terms offered by a lending company are 'unique and unusual.' We do mean, however, that uniquely and un-

---

[11] The Court in *Northern Pacific* concluded that the railroad "possessed substantial economic power by virtue of its extensive landholdings" and then described those holdings as follows:

"As pointed out before, the defendant was initially granted large acreages by Congress in the several Northwestern States through which its lines now run. This land was strategically located in checkerboard fashion amid private holdings and within economic distance of transportation facilities. Not only the testimony of various witnesses but common sense makes it evident that this particular land was often prized by those who purchased or leased it and was frequently essential to their business activities." *Id.,* at 7.

[12] "Since one of the objectives of the patent laws is to reward uniqueness, the principle of these cases was carried over into antitrust law on the theory that the existence of a valid patent on the tying product, without more, establishes a distinctiveness sufficient to conclude that any tying arrangement involving the patented product would have anticompetitive consequences." *United States* v. *Loew's Inc.,* 371 U. S. 38, 46.

[13] "Accordingly, the proper focus of concern is whether the seller has the power to raise prices, or impose other burdensome terms such as a tie-in, with respect to any appreciable number of buyers within the market." 394 U. S., at 504.

Professor Dam correctly analyzed the burden of proof imposed on Fortner by this language. In his article in the 1969 Supreme Court Review 25–26, he reasoned:

"One important question in interpreting the *Fortner* decision is the meaning of this language. Taken out of context, it might be thought to mean that, just as the 'host of tying arrangements' was 'compelling evidence' of 'great power' in *Northern Pacific,* so the inclusion of tie-in clauses in contracts with 'any appreciable numbers of buyers' establishes market power. But the passage read in context does not warrant this interpretation. For the immediately preceding sentence makes clear that market power in the sense of power over price must still exist. If the price could have been raised but the tie-in was demanded in lieu of the higher price, then—and presumably only then—would the requisite economic power exist. Thus, despite the broad language available for quotation in later cases, the treatment of the law on market power is on close reading not only consonant with the precedents but in some ways less far-reaching than *Northern Pacific* and *Loew's,* which could be read to make actual market power irrelevant." (Footnotes omitted).

[14] One commentator on *Fortner I* noted:

"The Court's uniqueness test is adequate to identify a number of situations in which this type of foreclosure is likely to occur. Whenever there are some buyers who find a seller's product uniquely attractive, and are therefore willing to pay a premium above the price of its nearest substitute, the seller has the opportunity to impose a tie to some other good." Note, The Logic of Foreclosure: Tie-In Doctrine after *Fortner* v. *U. S. Steel,* 79 Yale L. J. 86, 93–94 (1969).

usually advantageous terms can reflect a creditor's unique economic advantages over his competitors." 394 U. S., at 505.

An accompanying footnote explained:

"Uniqueness confers economic power only when other competitors are in some way prevented from offering the distinctive product themselves. Such barriers may be legal, as in the case of patented and copyrighted products, *e.g., International Salt; Loew's,* or physical, as when the product is land, *e.g., Northern Pacific.* It is true that the barriers may also be economic, as when competitors are simply unable to produce the distinctive product profitably, but the uniqueness test in such situations is somewhat confusing since the real source of economic power is not the product itself but rather the seller's cost advantage in producing it." *Id.,* at 505 n. 2.

Quite clearly, if the evidence merely shows that credit terms are unique because the seller is willing to accept a lesser profit—or to incur greater risks—than its competitors, that kind of uniqueness will not give rise to any inference of economic power in the credit market. Yet this is, in substance, all that the record in this case indicates.

The unusual credit bargain offered to Fortner proves nothing more than a willingness to provide cheap financing in order to sell expensive houses.[15] Without any evidence that the Credit Corp. had some cost advantage over its competitors—or could offer a form of financing that was significantly differentiated from that which other lenders could offer if they so elected—the unique character of its financing does not support the conclusion that petitioners had the kind of economic power which Fortner had the burden of proving in order to prevail in this litigation.

The judgment of the Court of Appeals is reversed.

So ordered.

7

Legal Aspects of Promotion Strategy: Advertising

Promotional activities of firms take many and varied forms and frequently are combined with other marketing decisions. For example, decisions to change the price or the quality of a product must be communicated to purchasers by promotional efforts if the desired effect on sales volume is to be obtained. Earlier chapters have described the legal issues relating to price and product-related decisions; this chapter focuses on laws and regulations that relate to advertising decisions. The next chapter examines other types of promotional activities, such as games of chance and promotional allowances.

In trying to understand why advertising regulation is shaped as it is, the marketing executive should realize that the basic goal of such regulation is to enhance the amount and accuracy of information available to purchasers.[1] This goal originally was pursued almost exclusively through legal prohibitions on the making of false representations and the use of other deceptive acts or practices. But as our economy has expanded and produced numerous products of increasing complexity, lawmakers were persuaded that more needed to be

---

[1] Federal Trade Commission, Consumer Information Remedies (Washington, D.C.: U.S. Government Printing Office, June 1979), pp. 14.

done to help consumers make informed purchasing decisions. Accordingly, numerous laws have been enacted that require sellers to disclose detailed product information.

Although the goal of providing purchasers with an adequate supply of accurate information about products is relatively noncontroversial, the wide variety of laws regulating promotional activities present numerous traps for the unwary. Laws have been enacted in the name of consumer protection at all levels of government, federal, state, and local. We do not purport to offer definitive guidance for complying with all these forms of regulation; instead, we focus on laws at the federal level that regulate the communicative aspects of promotional activity. These laws are enforced primarily by the Federal Trade Commission, and the bulk of our analysis is on the enforcement approaches of this government agency and the sanctions it imposes on those who use deceptive or unfair promotional practices. We examine specific advertising and other promotional techniques, such as the use of demonstrations and mock-ups in advertising; the use of endorsements and testimonials; and the use of warranties and prices in advertising. Also, we examine laws that allow one firm to bring legal action against the deceptive advertising of a competititor.

ADVERTISING AND THE FEDERAL TRADE COMMISSION

Deceptive Acts or Practices

The Federal Trade Commission (FTC) is a major force in the regulation of promotional practices. The FTC's mandate from Congress is a relatively simple one: to prevent "unfair or deceptive acts or practices" and "unfair methods of competition." The FTC's enforcement activities have added considerable depth and complexity to the meaning of the terms "unfair" and "deceptive." FTC enforcement activities have meaning not only for the enforcement of federal law but also for the enforcement of many state statutes, which use the same terminology in regulating promotional activities. Many of those statutes instruct courts and state enforcement agencies to be guided by FTC decisions. Thus, it is important to examine in some detail the general principles that the FTC has developed to determine when a practice is "deceptive." (The FTC's authority over "unfair" acts and practices will be discussed in later sections.)

The Meaning of Deception.

The Federal Trade Commission Act contains a general prohibition of "acts or practices" that are "deceptive," and a more detailed definition of "false advertising" as it pertains to foods, drugs, devices and cosmetics.

> The term "false advertisement" means an advertisement, other than labeling, which is misleading in a material respect; and in determining whether any adver-

tisement is misleading, there shall be taken into account (among other things) not only representations made or suggested by statement, word, design, device, sound, or any combination thereof, but also the extent to which the advertisement fails to reveal facts material in the light of such representations or material with respect to consequences which may result from the use of the commodity to which the advertisement relates under the conditions prescribed in said advertisement, or under such conditions as are customary or usual.[2]

This definition makes clear that (1) false representations are illegal; (2) representations can be made either expressly or by implication and suggestion (through "designs, devices and sounds"); and (3) failing to disclose material facts can be illegal. While the definition of "false advertising" applies only to foods, drugs, devices, and cosmetics, the principles embodied in the definition are frequently used by the FTC in determining whether any advertising or promotion is "deceptive." As both the formal definition and FTC decisions recognize, seller communications can harm consumers if they make representations that are false or if they do not disclose important facts. These two categories of deception—false representations and material omissions—comprise the main doctrinal interpretations of the FTC's authority to take remedial action against "deceptive acts or practices."[3]

The essence of the FTC's approach to the determination of whether a particular advertisement is deceptive can be captured in a few simple but potent rules:

1. A false representation or omission is actionable if it has the "tendency or capacity" to deceive a significant number of consumers; proof that any consumers actually were deceived is not required.[4]
2. A false representation or omission must relate to facts that are material or important to consumers in their purchasing decisions; insignificant false representations or omissions are not actionable.[5]
3. An ad can make representations by implication as well as expressly, and the question of what representations have been made to consumers is to be re-

---

[2] 15 U.S.C. §55(a)(1).

[3] See, Beales, Craswell, and Salop, *The Efficient Regulation of Consumer Information*, 24 J. Law & Econ. 491 (1981).

[4] *FTC* v. *Colgate–Palmolive Co.*, 380 U.S. 374 (1965). In 1983, a majority of the FTC Commissioners promulgated a formal statement regarding the FTC's enforcement policy against deceptive acts or practices. The majority reduced the underlying principles of deception to three: "First, there must be a representation, omission or practice that is likely to mislead the consumer. . . . Second, we examine the practice from the perspective of the consumer acting reasonably in the circumstances. . . . Third, the representation, omission, or practice must be a 'material' one." Letter to Committee on Energy and Commerce of the House of Representatives, dated October 14, 1983, from FTC Chairman James C. Miller III, reprinted in 45 BNA, ATRR (Oct. 27, 1983), p. 689. Two Commissioners dissented from the promulgation of the policy statement. One Commissioner charged that it was "an ill-conceived and frankly radical attempt to change the law of deception and create new and restrictive legal standards which would constrain the Commission's traditional and important law enforcement activities" (Statement of Commissioner Patricia P. Bailey, id., at 695). Another Commissioner charged that the statement was "internally inconsistent, confusing, and slipshod in use of legal precedent" and would "loosen the reins on dishonesty and unscrupulous behavior." (Statement of Commissioner Michael Pertschuk, id., at 697-98). Whether the new policy statement on deception represents a major change that will lead to different outcomes in any significant number of cases remains unclear.

[5] The materiality standard is a part of the definition of "false advertisement" applying to food, drugs, devices, and cosmetics. See text at note 2, supra. See also *FTC* v. *Simeon Management Corp.*, 532 F.2d 708, 716 (9th Cir. 1976).

solved by the Commission using its expertise; no proof, whether anecdotal or empirical, is required in order for the FTC to find that particular representations were made to consumers.[6]

4. Literal truth is not a defense to a false representation case if the representation, viewed as a whole, conveys a false impression.

5. The knowledge of the advertiser as to the falsity of a representation and the intent of the advertiser to deceive consumers are irrelevant to a finding that a deceptive practice has occurred.[7]

6. A false representation or material omission is actionable even if less than a majority of the recipients of a representation perceive it in a light that is false; the "ignorant and the credulous" are entitled to protection as long as their absolute numbers are "not insignificant."[8]

7. The falsity of a representation is subject to objective proof, but the materiality of a false representation or of an omission is a matter for the FTC's expertise.[9]

The net effect of the interaction of these rules is to leave the FTC with considerable discretion in determining whether a deceptive act or practice has occurred. It is possible for the FTC to condemn a representation or omission with little or no actual evidence that any great proportion of consumers either interpreted a promotion falsely or relied upon a representation in a way which produced actual harm. As one commentator has observed,

---

[6] The FTC frequently does use surveys to determine the meaning of advertising, but it is not required to do so by law. For example, in *Zenith Radio Corp.* v. *FTC,* 143 F.2d 29 (7th Cir. 1944), an advertisement of the number of tubes in a radio was found deceptive since some of the "tubes" were "rectifier tubes," which do not detect, amplify, or receive radio signals. In upholding the FTC's finding that the purchasing public believed that the greater the number of tubes in a radio the better it was at receiving signals, the court stated, "The Commission was not required to sample public opinion to determine what the petitioner was representing to the public. The Commission had a right to look at the advertisement in question, consider the relevant evidence in the record that would aid it in interpreting the advertisements, and then to decide for itself whether the practices engaged in by the petitioner were unfair or deceptive, as charged in the complaint." However, the FTC will consider evidence of consumer understanding of advertising if submitted by a respondent.

[7] See *Doherty, Clifford, Steers and Sheenfield, Inc.* v. *FTC,* 392 F.2d 921 (6th Cir. 1968).

[8] See *Charles of the Ritz Distributors Corp.* v. *FTC,* 143 F.2d 676 (2d Cir. 1944) (upholding FTC's determination that use of the trademark "rejuvenescence" in connection with a cosmetic might deceive "the vast multitude which includes the ignorant, the unthinking and the credulous" into believing that the product would "actually cause . . . youth to be restored"). The FTC has given some indication that advertisers may not be responsible for interpretations of advertising by those with extremely low levels of intelligence. In *Heinz W. Kirchner,* 63 F.T.C. 1282 (1963), *aff'd,* 337 F.2d 751 (9th cir. 1964), a representation that a swimming aide to be worn under a bathing suit was "thin and invisible" was held to be not deceptive. The Commission stated,

"Swim-ezy" is not invisible or impalpable or dimensionless, and to anyone who so understood the representation, it would be false. It is not likely, however, that many prospective purchasers would take the representation thus in its literal sense. True . . . the Commission's responsibility is to prevent deception of the gullible and credulous, as well as the cautious and knowledgeable . . . [T]his principal loses its validity, however, if it is applied uncritically or pushed to an absurd extreme. An advertiser cannot be charged with liability with respect of every conceivable misconception, however outlandish, to which his representations might be subject among the foolish or feeble-minded. . . . A representation does not become "false and deceptive" merely because it will be unreasonably misunderstood by an insignificant and unrepresentative segment of the class of persons to whom the representation is addressed.

When empirical evidence of consumer understanding of a particular advertisement has been presented to the FTC, the FTC has held advertising deceptive when as little as 14 percent of the recipients of a communication interpreted it falsely. For example, in *Benrus Watch Co.,* 352 F.2d 313 (8th cir. 1965), where 14 percent of the purchasers believed that a preticketed price was the product's usual retail price, the representations of savings based on a comparison to that price were found to be deceptive. And in *Firestone Tire & Rubber Co.* v. *FTC.,* 81 F.T.C. 1032, (1972), *aff'd,* 481 F.2d 246 (6th cir. 1973), *cert. denied,* 414 U.S. 1112 (1974), when only 15.3 percent of purchasers interpreted an ad falsely, the FTC nevertheless found the ad deceptive.

[9] Ira Millstein, *The Federal Trade Commission and False Advertising,* 64 Colum. L. Rev. 439, 478–483 (1964).

> [The] law of deception has now developed to the point of virtually eliminating any line between advertisements which are deceptive and advertisements which simply fail to inform. Indeed, it is not too broad a statement to say that present legal doctrine could make every advertisement in the country potentially deceptive.[10]

In 1982, the FTC went so far as to hold that it is deceptive to fail to disclose major product defects. Thus, it has charged that automobile manufacturers deceptively failed to disclose facts indicating transmission failure, premature engine wear, faulty fuel injection pumps, and propensity of fenders to rust prematurely.[11] Whether the failure to disclose information is deceptive may depend upon other representations made in the ad. For example, where a seller made efficacy claims for an over-the-counter analgesic, the FTC held that it was deceptive to fail to disclose the fact that the claim was not supported by "two or more well-controlled clinical studies."[12]

The relatively open-ended concept of deception and the relative freedom of the FTC to find a particular practice or advertising claim to be deceptive have led to demands for a more precise definition of deception.[13] Others have countered that protection against unwise use of FTC power lies in the sound use of discretion and the appointment of high-quality commissioners.[14] While the merits of this debate may never be resolved, it does appear that the FTC is moving in the direction of developing principles and standards for the selection of cases to prosecute. These standards and principles initially were developed by the FTC in 1975 and are receiving renewed emphasis. This "Policy Protocol" (see Appendix A) for dealing with product claims that are alleged to be either deceptive (or unsubstantiated) directs the FTC staff to develop information about several factors that should be considered in the decision of whether to take action against allegedly deceptive claims:

1. The staff is directed to examine advertising so as to be aware of all information provided by the advertisement, both true and allegedly false; implied representations are to be evaluated for their reasonableness.
2. The materiality of all representations, and particularly the allegedly false rep-

[10] Beales, Craswell & Salop, *op. cit.*, pp. 491, 495.

[11] See 44 BNA, ATRR (Jan. 27, 1983), p. 196 and *In re American Honda Motor Co.*, CCH Trade Reg. Rep. ¶21, 846 (1982).

[12] *American Home Products v. FTC*, 695 F.2d 681. (3d Cir. 1982). This doctrine, known as the "substantial question" doctrine was abandoned in 1983 in the cases of *Bristol–Myers Co.*, ___ F.T.C. ___ (1983), and *Sterling Drug, Inc.*, ___ F.T.C. ___ (1983). Under these decisions, drug efficacy claims must be supported by two well controlled clinical studies only if the advertiser represents (either expressly or by implication) that an efficacy claim has been "proven" or "established." These decisions are described in 45 BNA, ATRR (July 14, 1983), pp. 40–41.

[13] The Chairman of the Federal Trade Commission, Mr. James C. Miller, III, has urged Congress to limit the commission's authority to prosecute alleged deceptive practices by, among other things, allowing prosecution of only those deceptions that affect "reasonable consumers." False representations to "vulnerable groups" (i.e., children, elderly) would be actionable only if "the perpetrator knew or should have known that the actual practice was deceptive." See testimony before Senate Commerce Committee, as reported in 42 BNA, ATRR (Mar. 25, 1982), pp. 628–29. The FTC, by a 3-2 vote, recently announced a new verbal formulation of "deception," which includes the requirement that misrepresentations or omissions will be found deceptive only if they mislead "the typical or ordinary consumer acting reasonably in the circumstances, to the consumer's detriment." 45 BNA ATTR (Oct. 27, 1983) p. 689. Considerable controversy exists as to the potential impact of this redefinition of deception.

[14] Testimony of FTC Commissioner Patricia Bailey before House and Senate Commerce Committees, as reported in 42 BNA, ATRR (May 6, 1982), pp. 964, 970.

resentations, is to be assessed, together with the extent of possible harm if
the claims are found to be false. In particular, inquiry is directed to the total
information environment in which consumer decision making takes place and
to the cost to the consumer of either verifying the truth of the claim or
risking the consequences of a false claim (including the cost of validating or
disproving the claim through experience).[15]

3. In addition, the FTC staff is directed to consider several law enforcement issues, including questions such as whether other agencies might best resolve
   the matter, whether inaction would signal firms and encourage them to engage in deception, and whether there is a significant risk of erroneous agency
   action, as well as whether adjudication or rule-making would be the most
   appropriate response to the deception problem.

In short, these guides, if adhered to, would substantially limit the possibility of unwise prosecution of insignificant deceptions by the FTC and would focus action on those deceptions that are genuinely significant (i.e., those that
do affect a large number of consumers who make purchases and suffer losses
because of their reliance on false representations). They would also lessen the
possibility that a firm would be prosecuted for trivial violations of the deception standards.

Implied Representations.

The question of whether an act or practice is "deceptive" under the Federal
Trade Commission Act, or is "false" or "misleading" under other statutes or
common law rules, depends on a determination of what "representations"
have been made. Originally, most courts and the FTC focused strictly on the
literal words used by a seller to determine what had been represented.[16] Gradually, it was recognized that, under some circumstances, "silence speaks louder
than words," and that a speaker can literally "say" one thing while conveying
a different impression. "Implied" representations thus became actionable. For
example, an ad that quotes a survey by saying "no cigarette has less tar than
ours" might be considered deceptive even if the representation literally is true,
if the same survey found that numerous other brands of cigarettes had equally
low levels of tar.[17] The deception could consist of making two implied representations, both of which are false: (1) "our brand is *lowest* in tar," and (2)
"no other brand is as low as we are in tar." While these implications may not

---

[15] The commission has been severely criticized for prosecuting false advertising claims for inexpensive
products where the validity of the claim can be readily assessed by consumers after purchasing and using the
product. One such case involved the product Dry-Ban Spray Deodorant, whose advertising was alleged to
falsely represent that it was completely dry upon application to the underarm. The case was eventually
dismissed, but not after considerable expenditure of time and a decision by the commission itself. One
commissioner, Mayo Thompson, criticized the staff for bringing the case by noting that consumers easily could
verify the truth of the dryness claim by observing how the product actually appeared on application: "A 'Dry
Ban' customer standing in front of his TV set with a dripping armpit is not likely, one supposes, to go out and
buy a second can of the stuff if . . . it is a *literally* dry (non-liquid) anti-perspirant that he wants." *Bristol–Myers
Co.*, 85 F.T.C. 688, 752 (1975).

[16] Kramer, *Marconian Problems, Gutenbergian Remedies: Evaluating the Multiple-Sensory Experience Ad on
the Double-Spaced, Type-Written Page*, 30 Fed. Comm. L.J. 35 (1977).

[17] *P. Lorillard Co.* v. *FTC*, 186 F.2d 52 (4th Cir. 1950).

be strictly logical, a large proportion of an audience probably would jump to the illogical conclusions. The FTC has found these and similar implied representations to have been made in numerous cases.

The Defense of Puffing.

The foregoing material suggests that advertisers must carefully evaluate their advertising in order to make sure that all the express and implied representations that might be communicated to readers or viewers of the ad are true and that any possible false implications are eliminated or properly qualified. But in view of the virtually limitless possibilities for the FTC to find implied representations, this review process can never yield absolute assurance that an ad will safely pass the FTC's tests of deceptiveness. This lack of certainty may encourage advertisers to use forms of advertising that convey no factual representations or at least none that can be condemned as false. This approach to advertising might fit within the FTC's deception safe harbor known as *puffing*.

Puffing has been defined as the use of advertising that praises an item with "subjective opinions, superlatives, or exaggerations, vaguely and generally, stating no specific facts."[18] Modern advertising is filled with the use of puffery. Examples include such statements as "Coca Cola is the real thing," "Our gasoline puts a tiger in your tank," and "Our weight reduction plan is easy."

The use of opinions and indefinite superlatives in advertising has been viewed as acceptable by law enforcement agencies, including the FTC and courts, on several different rationales. First, courts have presumed that purchasers do not rely upon a positive expression of opinion by the seller as to the seller's own product and qualities.[19] This rationale carries overtones of *caveat emptor*, and forces buyers to be somewhat cautious about general statements made by a seller. Second, the FTC, in applying its "capacity to deceive" test, recognizes that certain general statements of praise are not likely to be relied upon by reasonable consumers and, therefore, should not be actionable since they have no tendency or capacity to deceive. Third, some forms of general praise are permissible simply because there is no objective way to establish that the statements are false. With the recent expansion of first amendment protection to truthful commercial speech, this ground may find support in first amendment doctrine that "there is no such thing as a false opinion or idea."[20] If the puff takes the form of a pure statement of opinion and if the law prohibits only false *factual* statements, it may be impossible for a plaintiff (whether governmental or private) to carry its burden of proving that a false representation was made.

---

[18] Ivan Preston, *The Great American Blow-Up: Puffery in Advertising and Selling* (Madison, Wisc.: University of Wisconsin Press, 1975), p. 17.

[19] Restatement (Second) Torts (St. Paul, Minn.: American Law Institute Publishers, 1977), §542, Comment e.

[20] Schauer, *Language, Truth, and the First Amendment: An Essay in Memory of Harry Canter*, 64 Va. L. Rev. 263 (1978).

A seller's privilege to puff has come under increasing criticism by behavioral scientists and others who point out that puffery has the capacity to lead consumers to make false factual implications, even if that process is not strictly logical.[21] They also have demonstrated that consumer attitudes, beliefs, and intentions can be influenced by the use of puffery. Legal scholars have also voiced objections to any broad privilege to deceive through the puffing doctrine. For example, Prosser has noted, "the 'puffing' rule amounts to a seller's privilege to lie his head off, so long as he says nothing specific . . . ."[22]

While the doctrinal basis for tolerating exaggerations, superlatives, and unsupported opinions in selling has been firmly established, it is also clear that the scope of permissible puffing has been reduced in recent years. This reduction has occurred through the increasing willingness of enforcement agencies (particularly the FTC) and courts to recognize that false factual representations can arise by implication from some forms of puffing.

The judicial deference given to Federal Trade Commission findings of fact has given the FTC considerable leeway to find that false factual implications result from some forms of puffery and that such implied representations have a tendency or capacity to deceive a substantial number of consumers. For example, the FTC found that use of the term "Rejuvenescence" (which might be characterized as an exaggerated statement of praise) implied that the product "would actually cause youth to be restored."[23] Since the product (a cosmetic) did not have that ability, a general statement of praise, carrying an implied factual statement, was found to be deceptive because the implied fact was false.

Thus, because the dividing line between permissible puffery and impermissible deception is vague and because false implications of fact can be easily found, there is an increasing risk of liability for using puffery in selling. As one commentator has noted, "A claim that would have been regarded as subjective opinion and legitimate puffery years ago might now be viewed in a different light. Consumerism has forced a new orientation which affects when a puffery defense will be regarded as appropriate."[24] And as behavioral scientists become more adept at measuring the deceptive impact of advertising, it becomes more likely that the puffery defense will be further narrowed and will not encompass any advertising that causes consumers to have false perceptions as to specific factual matters.[25] Thus, if it could be shown that a phrase such as "get the best—get Sealtest" caused consumers to believe that objective standards exist by which the product was actually determined to be the best

[21] Richard Oliver, "An Interpretation of the Attitudinal and Behavioral Effects of Puffery," Journal of Consumer Affairs 13, no. 1 (1979) p. 8. Terrence Shimp, "Social-Psychological (Mis) Representations in Television Advertising," *Journal of Consumer Affairs* 13, no. 1 (1979), p. 28.

[22] William Prosser, 4th ed. *Handbook of the Law of Torts* (St. Paul, Minn.: West Publishing Co., 1971), p. 723.

[23] *Charles of the Ritz Distributors Corp.*, 143 F.2d 676 (2d Cir. 1944).

[24] Comment, 6 Pepperdine L. Rev. 439, 457–58 (1979).

[25] J. Edward Russo, Barbara Metcalf, and Debra Stephens, "Identifying Misleading Advertising," *Journal of Consumer Research* 8, no. 2 (Sept. 1981), p. 119.

in relation to all other products, and when that implication can be shown to be false, an enhanced risk of liability or susceptibility to governmental prosecution exists.[26]

Unfair Acts or Practices

In addition to its authority to prevent deception, the FTC has authority to prevent "unfair acts or practices." The FTC began to use this authority when it proposed a rule that would require a health warning in connection with cigarette marketing.[27] In finding that it was unfair to fail to disclose the health risks connected with cigarette smoking, the FTC identified three factors that it considered in determining whether a practice was unfair: (1) injury to consumers; (2) public policy; and (3) the immoral, unethical, oppressive, or unscrupulous nature of the practice. In 1972, these three criteria seemingly were given approval by the Supreme Court.[28]

In 1975, the FTC embarked upon an ambitious rule-making program using these criteria. But significant concern was expressed about the FTC's activities under this vague prong of its jurisdiction, and in 1980, Congress responded by removing some of the FTC's unfairness authority, that is, the authority to promulgate rules using this criteria if the rules affected "commercial advertising."[29] Congress seemed to be concerned that the first amendment rights of advertisers might be chilled if "unfairness" was used to restrict advertising, but Congress did not prohibit the FTC from taking action against individual instances of unfair advertising by entering cease and desist orders or by seeking civil penalties for violations of prior FTC unfairness precedents.

During the Congressional inquiry into the FTC's use of its unfairness authority, the FTC promulgated a policy statement that clarified its approach to questions of unfairness. The FTC informed Congress that it would abandon any future use of the "unethical, immoral, oppressive or unscrupulous" criterion and instead would place primary emphasis on the "consumer injury" criterion; the "public policy" criterion would be used only secondarily as a check on the correctness of its determination of consumer injury.[30] The FTC also elaborated upon the consumer injury criterion by announcing that consumer injury would be found only if the injury was (1) substantial, (2) not outweighed by competing benefits to consumers or to competition in general, and (3) not avoidable by reasonable actions of consumers. This approach es-

---

[26] Oliver, op. cit., note 21.

[27] Federal Trade Commission Cigarette Advertising Rule, 29 Fed. Reg. 8324, 8355 (1964).

[28] *FTC* v. *Sperry & Hutchinson Co.,* 405 U.S. 233 (1972). The narrow holding of the court in Sperry & Hutchinson simply was that the FTC could consider factors other than those reflected in the letter or spirit of antitrust laws to find that practices were unfair. But the Court quoted with approval the FTC's criteria announced in the cigarette advertising rule.

[29] Federal Trade Commission Improvements Act of 1980. See Holmes, *FTC Regulation of Unfair or Deceptive Advertising: Current Status of the Law* 30 DePaul L. Rev. 555 (1981).

[30] The FTC's Letters to Senators Ford and Danforth are reprinted in *Clearinghouse Review* (Oct. 1981), Appendix E, p. 457.

sentially committed the FTC to the use of cost–benefit analyses in deciding whether to prohibit acts or practices as unfair.

Whether legislative curtailment of the FTC's unfairness jurisdiction will be of great significance to advertisers is questionable. Many commentators have asserted that the FTC can reach almost all the practices it has previously condemned as unfair by expansively using its deception jurisdiction.[31] If, for example, an ad that fails to disclose material information can be considered deceptive (and considerable judicial and scholarly authority supports this proposition),[32] then many unfairness cases could be similarly resolved under deception theories. Since many FTC unfairness cases and rules are based on a failure to disclose information,[33] the FTC could prohibit the same conduct without having to use unfairness as a ground for its actions.

Commentators have been able to identify only two types of cases where the existence of the FTC's unfairness authority may be critical to its ability to restrict advertising. In one area, the FTC has held that the portrayal in advertising of dangerous activities, particularly those involving children, is unfair. For example, an advertisement for bicycles that portrayed children cycling through intersections without stopping was attacked on unfairness grounds.[34] Similarly, a portrayal of the gathering and eating of wild plants was condemned because it might have encouraged people to consume poisonous plants.[35] And the depiction of children cooking food on a stove also was found to be unfair, as was the distribution of free samples of razor blades inside newspapers delivered to homes.[36] These advertisements and practices would be difficult to attack on deception grounds.

The other series of FTC cases based on unfairness that would be jeopardized if the FTC's unfairness jurisdiction were curtailed involves high-pressure personal selling. For example, the use of high-pressure sales tactics aimed at elderly persons and designed to induce them to buy thousands of dollars of dance lessons has been held to be unfair.[37] Since these practices have no representational component, it also would be difficult to attack them on deception grounds.

Advertising Substantiation.

One FTC unfairness doctrine, the "reasonable basis" doctrine, probably would survive any elimination of the FTC's unfairness jurisdiction over advertising, because the same conduct can, in most cases, be attacked under the FTC's deception jurisdiction. Under this doctrine, it is "unfair" to make an af-

---

[31] Beales, Craswell, and Salop, op. cit. note 3.

[32] Ibid.

[33] Robert Gage, *The Discriminating Use of Information Disclosure Rules by the Federal Trade Commission* 26 U.C.L.A. L. Rev. 1037 (1979).

[34] *AMF, Inc.*, 95 F.T.C. 310 (1980).

[35] *General Foods Corp.*, 86 F.T.C. 831 (1975).

[36] *Uncle Ben's, Inc.*, 89 F.T.C. 131 (1977); *Phillip Morris, Inc.*, 82 F.T.C. 16 (1973).

[37] *Arthur Murray Studio, Inc.* v. *F.T.C.*, 458 F.2d 622 (5th Cir. 1972).

firmative product claim without having a reasonable basis to believe that the claim is true. This standard was defined by the FTC in the *Pfizer* case in which Pfizer had made advertising claims that its sunburn medication "Unburn" would "anesthetize nerves" and "relieve pain fast."[38] These claims were challenged on the ground that, at the time they were made, Pfizer had not amassed sufficient evidence as to the validity of the claims. Although the case was eventually dismissed, the FTC unequivocally announced its view that making claims about a product without a reasonable basis to support those claims was an unfair practice.

The FTC uses the reasonable basis rule to require advertisers to furnish the FTC with all evidence that supports any advertising claims questioned by the FTC. [At one time, FTC made this evidence available to the public in the expectation that consumer protection groups would examine the data submitted and would reveal to the public that specific advertising claims were supported weakly or not at all by the data; however, much of this evidence was too voluminous and complex to be easily analyzed by the staff or by consumer groups, and, for this and other reasons, public disclosure of material submitted to the FTC no longer occurs as a matter of routine.] If the FTC feels that the advertising claims are not justified in light of the material submitted, it may commence a formal prosecution.

The FTC has done little to clarify its reasonable basis requirement other than to suggest that as the risk of consumer harm increases if a claim is false, the degree of required substantiation will be higher. In other words, if consumers encounter health or safety risks when claims are false, a reasonable basis for the health or safety claims may consist of nothing less than the highest possible form of substantiation, that is, well-controlled, double-blind scientific experiments.[39] Where the risk of harm from a false claim is minimal, however, the FTC has suggested that a reasonable basis might exist for the claim if clinical experience or general knowledge supports the claim.[40]

One reason why the FTC seldom needs to use its unfairness jurisdiction to impose a substantiation requirement on advertisers is that advertisers often expressly or impliedly represent that claims about a product have been "proven," or that a specific type of testing or verification procedure supports the claims. These representations often are specific and testable as to their truth or falsity, and if found to be false, they can be prohibited under the FTC's authority over deceptive acts or practices. An example of such a representation might be, "In a recent scientific study using a random sample of automobile mechanics, 75% recommended use of our product as the best at preventing excessive engine wear." This sort of representation allows the FTC to explore the truth of the representation directly to determine whether the sample was "random" and the methodology "scientific." If the representation

---

[38] *Pfizer, Inc.,* 81 F.T.C. 23 (1972).

[39] *American Home Products, Inc.,* 98 F.T.C. 136 (1981), aff'd in part, 695 F.2d 681 (3rd Cir. 1983).

[40] *National Dynamics Corp.,* 82 F.T.C. 488 (1973).

is false (i.e., if the level of substantiation claimed by the advertiser did not exist), the practice can be prohibited under the FTC's less controversial deception jurisdiction.

By expansively interpreting advertising and finding that the advertising makes implied representations, the FTC frequently can find representations as to the degree of substantiation; the nature of the support for a claim can be implied by the overall setting of the advertisement. For example, if the ad uses people dressed in laboratory gowns and depicts the use of scientific apparatus, the advertiser may be implying that well-controlled, double-blind, scientific tests leave virtually no doubt about the truth of the product claim being made in the ad. Again, if it turns out that the advertiser conducted only a few trials of the product in the basement, the implied representation of scientific support for the claim is false and is actionable on deception theories; concepts of unfairness simply are unnecessary to deal adequately with the deception being practiced.

The FTC is becoming increasingly specific in its findings as to the degree of substantiation implied in ads making drug effectiveness claims. In a case involving American Home Products Corporation, American Home had advertised that its product, Arthritis Pain Formula Anacin, was superior to other products in its pain relief effectiveness and in its freedom from side effects. The FTC found that the advertising implied that the claims had been "proven" or "established" by evidence considered adequate in the relevant medical and scientific community. The FTC then found that the scientific and medical world would accept a drug effectiveness claim as "established" only if it was supported by at least two adequate and well controlled clinical investigations conducted by independent experts using double-blind studies with placebo controls. Since American Home Products did not possess such studies, the FTC found that the implied claim was false and deceptive.[41]

Federal Trade Commission Remedies

Once the FTC has determined that a firm has engaged in an act or practice that violates the FTC Act, the FTC is empowered to enter an appropriate remedial order against the firm. The simplest form of order is one that merely prohibits the firm from engaging in the particular act or practice that was determined to be deceptive. Thus, if a firm has been found to have made a false performance claim as to a particular product, the FTC will order the firm to cease and desist from making the same performance claim in the future. This order can subject the firm to civil penalties if the order is violated.

But the FTC can do more than enter simple cease and desist orders against deceptive or unfair advertising. It is useful to examine some of the more powerful forms of orders that the FTC can enter; these are: (1) affirmative disclosure orders; (2) corrective advertising orders; and (3) multiple product orders.

---

[41] *American Home Products Corp.*, supra note 39. This part of the FTC's order was affirmed by the Court of Appeals. *American Home Products Corp.* v. *FTC,* 695 F.2d 681 (3d Cir. 1982).

Affirmative Disclosure Orders.

Frequently, the FTC finds that a communication is deceptive because it fails to contain information that relates to a partially true, but deceptively incomplete, representation. In this situation, the FTC's cease and desist orders prohibit the firm from making the true representation without also making the additional disclosure. For example, Geritol (an iron-deficiency anemia remedy) had been advertised by the J.B. Williams Company in a way that suggested its effectiveness as a remedy for any illness characterized by a feeling of tiredness. The FTC found that the advertising was deceptive because it failed to indicate that some tiredness symptoms result from causes for which the Geritol product is totally ineffective. Accordingly, the FTC required all advertising that emphasized the tiredness theme to also disclose that the product "will be of no benefit" for the "great majority of persons" who suffer from tiredness.[42]

The FTC makes extensive use of affirmative disclosure orders. An evaluation of the use of such orders found that they had been used in 220 cases between 1970 and 1977.[43] The evaluation also found that disclosure orders were effective in helping consumers form accurate perceptions about health and safety risks, product values, and product characteristics. Therefore, it can be expected that the FTC will continue to rely heavily on orders of this type.

Corrective Advertising.

Since disclosures must be made by sellers only when future advertising contains the particular claims that were found to be deceptive, the affirmative disclosure order is of little consequence to a firm unless the order relates to a critical product feature. Thus, Geritol can still be advertised as a cure for iron deficiency anemia as long as no claims are made as to its ability to cure all tiredness symptoms. During the early 1970s, concern was expressed that the usual FTC sanction of a cease and desist order was so painless that potential false advertisers would not be sufficiently deterred. Accordingly, it was argued that a sanction known as *corrective advertising* would be a useful new tool in the effort to deter false advertising.

The concept of corrective advertising is that if the FTC found that an advertisement was deceptive, the advertiser would be required to state, in future advertising, that the specific claims made in past advertising were false.[44] Because of the severe damage that such corrections supposedly would inflict on the reputation of the firm, it was believed that advertisers would become more careful about what representations were made in advertising, and, accordingly, the amount of false advertising would diminish.

On several occasions the FTC has indicated that it is empowered to issue corrective advertising orders;[45] it frequently has settled pending cases by

---

[42] *J. B. Williams Company* v. *FTC,* 381 F.2d 884 (6th Cir. 1967).

[43] William Wilkie, *Affirmative Disclosure: A Survey and Evaluation of FTC Orders Issued From 1970–1977* (Washington, D.C.: Federal Trade Commission, June 1980).

[44] Pitofsky, *Beyond Nader: Consumer Protection and Regulation of Advertising,* 90 Harv. L. Rev. 661 (1977).

[45] *Firestone Tire & Rubber Co.,* 81 F.T.C. 1032 (1972), *aff'd,* 481 F.2d 246 (6th Cir. 1973), *cert. denied,* 414 U.S. 1112 (1974); *ITT Continental Baking Co.,* 82 F.T.C. 1183 (1973).

obtaining agreements that past advertising would be corrected in future advertising.[46] But the FTC has ordered corrective advertising in only a few cases
where the responding firm objected or failed to agree to such an order, and
only one of these cases has been reviewed by the courts. That case involved
advertising by the Warner–Lambert Company of its product Listerine.[47]

In the Listerine case, the FTC charged that Listerine had been extensively
promoted as a product that would prevent colds and sore throats or would
lessen their severity. Since these representations were found to be false, the
FTC ordered Warner–Lambert to cease and desist from making these representations. But in addition, the FTC ordered that in any future advertising of
Listerine (and regardless of whether such advertising made any representations
about the efficacy of Listerine in preventing colds or ameliorating cold symptoms), Warner–Lambert must include the statement that "contrary to prior
advertising, Listerine will not help prevent colds or sore throats or lessen their
severity."[48] The FTC ordered that this statement must appear in the next $10
million worth of advertising of Listerine. The FTC's order was upheld by
Court of Appeals for the District of Columbia in all major respects; however,
the Court held that the future advertising did not have to contain the phrase
"contrary to prior advertising," since its use was not necessary to attract the
public's attention to the corrective information and therefore could serve only
to "humiliate" Warner–Lambert (a purpose that the FTC cannot pursue in the
absence of evidence of egregious and deliberate deception).[49]

The FTC's standard for determining when a corrective advertising remedy
is appropriate was approved by the Court of Appeals; it is as follows:

> [I]f a deceptive advertisement has played a substantial role in creating or rein-
> forcing in the public's mind a false and material belief which lives on after the
> false advertising ceases, there is clear and continuing injury to competition and
> to the consuming public as consumers continue to make purchasing decisions
> based on the false belief. Since this injury cannot be averted by merely requiring
> respondent to cease disseminating the advertisement, we may appropriately order
> respondent to take affirmative action designed to terminate the otherwise con-
> tinuing ill effects of the advertisement.[50]

Several factors that were present in the Listerine case suggest that the corrective advertising remedy may be appropriately used in relatively few cases.
In the first place, the claims about Listerine's ability to prevent colds and less-
en the severity of cold symptoms were not substantiated by any studies that
were well controlled; the FTC findings that the claims were false were found
by the Court of Appeals to be "supported by substantial evidence on the

---

[46] *Ocean Spray Cranberries, Inc.,* 80 F.T.C. 989 (1972).

[47] *Warner–Lambert Co.* v. *FTC,* 562 F.2d 749 (D.C. Cir. 1977).

[48] Ibid.

[49] Ibid., at 763.

[50] Ibid., at 762.

record viewed as a whole."[51] Second, the claims had been made for such a long period of time (since 1921) that the FTC reasonably could infer that the claims were important to and believed by many consumers. Third, survey evidence was presented to the FTC that false belief levels were high (on the order of 65%) and did not decline even when no promotion of the product occurred. Thus, the Court of Appeals found little difficulty in approving a corrective advertising remedy on the basis of facts developed before the FTC.

But the question remains as to whether another Court of Appeals would approve a corrective advertising remedy when less compelling evidence existed as to advertising's falsity and its causal connection to false consumer beliefs, and as to the durability and materiality of those false beliefs. The Court of Appeals for the District of Columbia suggested that it would have little difficulty in upholding a corrective advertising remedy even if little or no factual evidence were presented to the FTC on these issues. Although the Court held corrective advertising was appropriate only when an ad created false beliefs that continued to have an impact on purchase decisions, the Court would allow the FTC to enter a corrective advertising order with little, if any, direct proof of these facts:

> It strikes us that if the answer to both questions [about false beliefs and their continuing impact on purchases] is not yes, companies everywhere may be wasting their massive advertising budgets. Indeed, it is more than a little peculiar to hear petitioner assert that its commercials really have no effect on consumer beliefs. For these reasons it might be appropriate in some cases to presume the existence of the two factual predicates for corrective advertising.[52]

Although this statement has no value as precedent in future cases since the facts before the court showed an impact on consumer beliefs (legally, the statement is *dicta*), it leaves open the possibility that such orders might be upheld simply on the basis of an FTC finding that a claim is clearly false. And if corrective advertising has the negative impact on a firm that it is predicted to have, the making of false claims clearly presents firms with substantial risks.

In addition to taking steps to ensure that no false claims are made, firms might resist corrective advertising orders by presenting evidence that any consumer misperceptions will die out fairly rapidly over time after any false advertising ceases. This might be easy to demonstrate in the event that a false claim relates to a feature of a frequently purchased product. Consumers, through their own experience, will be able to ascertain any falsity in a product claim and will not be influenced by the claim in the future.[53] Although some sanction will be appropriate for the making of the false claim, corrective advertising will not be the appropriate remedy. Similarly, evidence that claims other than the false claim were of greater importance to consumers in their decision-making process would negate the materiality requirement for corrective advertising. And, finally, evidence that consumers held pre-existing false be-

---

[51] Ibid., at 753.

[52] Ibid., at 762.

[53] Nelson, *Information and Consumer Behavior*, 78 J. Pol. Econ. 311 (1970).

liefs that were not affected in any way by advertising also might make corrective advertising inappropriate.[54]

Other aspects of the corrective advertising remedy also seem open to question and possible attack in contested proceedings. For example, empirical evidence may demonstrate that corrective advertising involves "overkill," in the sense that the remedy does more than correct consumer misperceptions and actually harms a business in ways having nothing to do with the making of a false claim. Such evidence would allow a challenge to the FTC'c authority on the ground that it is "punitive," or that it is unnecessary to the achievement of the government's only legitimate interest, the prevention of deception.[55] It may even be possible to demonstrate that the placing of correct information on labels is all that is necessary to prevent misinformed purchasing if an appropriately designed label would attract the attention of consumers and eliminate misperceptions.[56]

The requirement that the correction be included in a specific dollar amount of future advertising also seems questionable. For example, if a firm could demonstrate that false belief levels had been reduced to levels that existed before the false claim was made, it would seem that further correction would serve no legitimate governmental interest and would be punitive and therefore beyond the FTC's authority.[57] Such a reduction in false belief levels could occur in a variety of ways, including the passage of time, comprehension of the corrective advertising message, or widespread publicity or dissemination of other important information. Since the FTC must respond to requests to modify orders, the failure to terminate a corrective advertising order when presented with information that the order has no further corrective purpose to achieve probably would be challengeable as an abuse of FTC discretion.[58]

Finally, corrective advertising orders raise difficult issues under the first amendment. The Supreme Court has extended protection to commercial speech and seemingly has held that truthful commercial speech cannot be sanctioned in the absence of a compelling governmental interest and the unavailability of less restrictive alternatives. Since the concept of corrective advertising requires the inclusion of a corrective message regardless of the deceptiveness of the current advertising, there is room for argument that the corrective message is an unconstitutional burden on fully protected truthful speech. The Court in the Listerine case was not required to reach this argument, as it upheld the Commission finding that any advertisement for Listerine would automatically build upon the prior false claims and would im-

---

[54] The research methodology described by Russo et al., supra note 25, should be useful for documenting pre-existing false beliefs.

[55] Note, *Warner–Lambert Co.* v. *FTC: Corrective Advertising Gives Listerine a Taste of Its Own Medicine*, 73 Nw. U.L. Rev. 957, 976 (1979).

[56] Ibid., at 978.

[57] Ibid., at 973–74.

[58] The Federal Trade Commission Improvement Act of 1980 clarifies the obligation of the commission to respond to requests for modification of prior cease and assist orders.

plicitly continue the deception. Such a finding was reasonable in the context of a 50-year history of false cold prevention claims; whether more short-lived campaigns are so memorable that any subsequent campaign will automatically trigger recall of a deceptive message seems highly problematical.[59] No case has yet resolved the question of whether the FTC must possess information to support a finding that consumer recall of a prior false claim would be triggered by any type of future advertising.

It is equally unclear whether the FTC possesses sufficient authority to simply order a respondent to correct a prior deception even if the respondent has no plans to engage in any promotion in the future. The only instances in which the FTC has ordered a respondent to actually correct prior advertising have occurred in cases brought to impose civil penalties on an advertiser; the defendant in those cases agreed to correct prior claims as part of a settlement of the civil penalty action.[60]

Multiple Product Orders.

If the FTC finds that a firm made a false performance claim as to a particular product, the FTC will order the firm to refrain from making false claims in the future about that product. For firms who sell a multitude of products and a variety of product lines, such orders impose very little constraint on future advertising activities and present little risk of inadvertent future violations. To deal with firms that have a history of repetitive violations of the law or that engage in deliberately false advertising, the FTC frequently imposes orders that apply to all future advertising of all products sold by the firm, not just the product that was falsely advertised.

The validity of a multiple product order is well established. The Supreme Court has upheld the authority of the FTC to issue such orders, noting that "those caught violating the Act must expect some fencing in."[61] The appropriateness of such orders is largely left to the discretion of the FTC, and courts will overturn the FTC's judgment only when discretion has been abused. When an advertising campaign involves false claims that were known to be false by the advertiser, the Commission's multiproduct orders have usually been upheld. For example, Sears, Roebuck and Company disseminated print and electronic advertisements claiming that its Lady Kenmore dishwashers completely eliminated the need for prescraping and prerinsing of dishes. These claims were untrue, and Sears was held to have had knowledge of the untruth of the claim (even the owners manual indicated that some presoaking and light scouring were required).[62] The FTC entered an order prohibiting Sears from misrepresenting any test and from making any performance claims with-

---

[59] Note, *Warner–Lambert Co.* v. *FTC,* supra note 47.

[60] See BNA, ATRR, no. 851 (Feb. 16, 1978), p. A-8 (settlement of FTC action against STP Corporation in which STP agreed to pay $500,000 in civil penalties and to spend $200,000 for advertising in major publications having a circulation of 78 million readers).

[61] *FTC* v. *National Lead Co.,* 352 U.S. 419 (1957).

[62] *Sears, Roebuck and Co.,* 95 F.T.C. 406 (1980).

out first possessing a reasonable basis in support of the claims. This order applied to all of Sears' major home appliances. The FTC's order was upheld by the Ninth Circuit Court of Appeals because of the specific circumstances involved in this advertising campaign.[63] The court stated,

> This advertising campaign cost $8 million, ran for four years and appeared in magazines, newspapers and on television throughout the country. The Commission found, and Sears does not dispute, that the campaign's central claim was false. Sears had no reasonable basis for making a claim, and the test which Sears purportedly relied on showed, if anything, that the claim was false. . . . Under the circumstances, Sear's advertising campaign demonstrates "blatant and utter disregard" for the law.[64]

The court also found that a multiproduct order was justified because of the high cost and infrequent purchase by individual consumers. Merely preventing Sears from making false and unsubstantiated claims as to dishwashers would not sufficiently deter Sears from making similar by deceptive claims as to other appliances in future advertising campaigns and would leave the FTC with the job of instituting separate proceedings to secure new orders for each unlawfully advertised product. Under the circumstances, a multiproduct order is warranted.[65]

Other FTC Remedial Powers.

As the preceding discussion has revealed, the ordinary cease and desist order and the ordinary affirmative disclosure order are not particularly harsh sanctions for violating the FTC Act. Firms that escape an FTC challenge to advertising with such a mild sanctions have had a "free bite at the apple." Only if they violate the order by future conduct will more serious consequences result.

The perceived ineffectiveness of the cease and desist order and the affirmative disclosure order led consumer leaders to press for congressional enhancement of FTC remedial authority. Congress responded in 1975 by giving the FTC authority to impose civil penalties for violations of its previous determinations of illegality, even if the penalties are imposed on firms that were not a party to the previous determination. The FTC must establish that any violation of its previous determinations of illegality was done knowingly by the offending firm. Congress also allowed the FTC to petition a court for an order requiring a firm to provide redress to consumers who suffer injury as a result of the firm's violation of the act; in this situation, the FTC must show that the violation was one that a reasonable person would know was dishonest or fraudulent. The enhancement of the FTC's remedial authority by the addition of these provisions drastically diminishes the possibility for firms to obtain a "free bite at the apple" in the future.

---

[63] *Sears, Roebuck and Co.*, 676 F.2d 385 (9th Cir. 1982).

[64] Ibid.

[65] Ibid.

Federal Trade Commission Rule Making

The FTC elucidates the meaning of "unfair" and "deceptive" in ways other than through its entry of cease and desist orders. The most important mechanism for this purpose is the FTC's promulgation of rules that have the force of law and that define with greater specificity the acts and practices that will be considered unfair or deceptive. Congress gave the FTC authority to promulgate Trade Regulation Rules, which define the specific acts and practices that the FTC considers unfair or deceptive.[66] This rule-making authority was coupled with the possibility of enhanced sanctions for engaging in activity that is prohibited by the rule. This enhancement takes two forms: (1) violators of the commands of a rule will be subject to civil penalties,[67] and (2) courts can order consumer redress for economic injury caused by the violation.[68]

In 1980, the Congress sought to limit the FTC's authority to make rules in two respects: first, Congress required the FTC to submit its proposed rules to Congress which could prevent the rules from taking effect by a majority vote of both chambers.[69] The FTC submitted a rule which would require used automobile dealers to disclose defects in the used cars they sold; both houses voted to "veto" the rule,[70] but the Supreme Court held that this method of restricting the authority of the FTC was unconstitutional.[71] Another rule regulating funeral homes was submitted to Congress and became effective when Congress failed to act.[72]

A second limitation on the FTC's rule-making authority is that unfairness cannot be used as a basis for promulgating a rule that restricts advertising. Congress was concerned that the vagueness in the unfairness concept, when coupled with the concern for first amendment protection of commercial speech, might allow the FTC to go too far in restricting the dissemination of information through the broadcast media. This limitation was discussed previously.

The FTC has considered a large number of subjects in its rule-making pro-

---

[66] Federal Trade Commission Act., 15 U.S.C. §57a.

[67] Federal Trade Commission Act, 15 U.S.C. §45(m)(1)(A) (The FTC may seek to recover civil penalties for up to $10,000 for each violation of a rule; the FTC must establish that the rule was violated "with actual knowledge or knowledge fairly implied on the basis of objective circumstances that such act is unfair or deceptive and is prohibited by such rule.")

[68] Federal Trade Commission Act, 15 U.S.C. §57b. If the FTC establishes before a court that a rule has been violated, the court can "grant such relief as the court finds necessary to redress injury to consumers . . . resulting from the rule violation . . . [s]uch relief may include, but shall not be limited to recission or reformation of contracts, the refund of money or return of property, the payment of damages, and public notification respecting the rule violation. . . ."

[69] Federal Trade Commission Improvement Act of 1980, Public Law No. 96-252, §21, 94 Stat. 374 (1980) [as codified at 15 U.S.C. §57a-1 (supp. IV 1980)].

[70] H. Con. Res. 256, 97th Cong., 2d Sess., 128 Cong. Rec. H2856 (May 26, 1982).

[71] *United States Senate v. FTC,* 103 S.Ct. 3556 (1983), *aff'g sub nom., Consumers Union, Inc. v. FTC,* 691 F.2d 575 (D.C. Cir. 1982). The Rule is being reconsidered by the FTC and has not become effective. 45 BNA ATTR (Dec. 15, 1983), pp. 970-71.

[72] Federal Trade Commission, Trade Regulation Rule: Funeral Industry Practices, 16 C.F.R. part 453 (1983). Legal challenges to the validity of the Rule were rejected by the Court of Appeals in *Harry & Bryant Co.* v. *FTC,* 46 BNA ATTR (4th Cir., Jan. 19, 1984), p. 119. This Rule became effective in two stages on January 1, and April 30, 1984. Id.

ceedings. Among others, the FTC had considered or adopted rules dealing with

The terms used in standard-form consumer credit contracts.[73]

Warranty performance in the mobile home industry.[74]

Disclosures and contract provisions in the vocational school industry.[75]

Advertising of ophthalmic goods and services.[76]

Advertising and labeling of protein supplements.[77]

Disclosures in franchising and business opportunity ventures.[78]

Disclosure of R-values in residential thermal insulations.[79]

Sale of hearing aids.[80]

Another rule that would have regulated food advertising was abandoned in 1982.[81]

REGULATION OF SPECIFIC PROMOTIONAL PRACTICES

The preceding discussion has examined how courts and the FTC have applied general laws prohibiting deception and unfairness. This section discusses some specific advertising practices that have been the subject of fairly detailed rules and regulations. The subjects considered include the following:

1. The use of demonstrations or mock-ups in advertising.
2. Using endorsements and testimonials in advertising.
3. The use of prices in promotion.
4. Using warranties in advertising.
5. Advertising of credit.

---

[73] Federal Trade Commission, Proposed Trade Regulation Rule: Credit Practices, 40 Fed. Reg. 16347, April 11, 1975. Portions of the proposed rule have been approved, and certain harsh terms in consumer credit contracts would be banned. See 45 BNA, ATRR (July 21, 1983), pp. 86–87.

[74] Federal Trade Commission, Proposed Trade Regulation Rule: Mobile Homes Sales and Services, 40 Fed. Reg. 23334, May 29, 1975. The final staff report on the rule is contained at 45 Fed. Reg. 53839, Aug. 13, 1980.

[75] Federal Trade Commission, Trade Regulation Rule: Proprietary Vocational and Home Study Schools, 16 C.F.R. part 438 (1982). This rule was set aside by a judicial decision, *Katharine Gibbs School, Inc.* v. *FTC*, 612 F.2d 658 (2d Cir. 1979) and is presently under review at the Federal Trade Commission.

[76] Federal Trade Commission, Trade Regulation Rule, Advertising of Ophthalmic Goods and Services, 16 C.F.R. Part 456 (1982). This rule was also set aside by the court in *American Optometric Association* v. *FTC*, 626 F.2d 896 (D.C. Cir. 1980), and is presently under review at the Federal Trade Commission. A second investigation is under way (known as "eyeglasses II") concerning various state-imposed restrictions on the practice of optometry. See BNA, ATRR, no. 992, Dec. 4, 1980, p. H-1.

[77] Federal Trade Commission, Proposed Trade Regulation Rule: Advertising and Labeling of Protein Supplements, 40 Fed. Reg. 41144, Sept. 5, 1975.

[78] Federal Trade Commission, Trade Regulation Rule: Disclosure Requirements and Prohibitions Concerning Franchising and Business Opportunity Ventures, 16 C.F.R. Part 436 (1982). This rule became effective on July 21, 1979, and requires that franchisors give prospective franchisees information about the past experience and profitability of a franchisor, plus numerous other items of information.

[79] Federal Trade Commission, Trade Regulation Rule: Labeling and Advertising of Home Insulation, 16 C.F.R. Part 460 (1982).

[80] Federal Trade Commission, Proposed Trade Regulation Rule: 40 Fed. Reg. 59746 (Dec. 30, 1975). The Food and Drug Administration has a parallel rule requiring labeling of hearing aids. See 21 C.F.R. § 801.420 (1982).

[81] Federal Trade Commission, Proposed Trade Regulation Rule: Food Advertising, 43 Fed. Reg. 11834 (1978). The Federal Trade Commission, in 1982, announced that it would not proceed with this rule-making proposal. See *FTC News Summary*, Dec. 23, 1982, p. 1.

Deceptive Demonstrations or Mock-ups

The FTC successfully challenged an advertising campaign of Colgate–Palmolive Company designed to demonstrate the superiority of a shaving cream in softening beards by showing that the cream, when applied to sandpaper, allowed the sand to be smoothly and effortlessly shaved off the paper.[82] The advertisement was challenged on the ground that sandpaper was not actually used in the filmed demonstration; rather, sand had been sprinkled on the surface of a piece of plexiglas. This technique was used because the grains in ordinary sandpaper could not be photographed and transmitted over television in a way that would allow the viewer to be convinced that the paper being shaved was sandpaper rather than ordinary paper. Both the FTC and the Supreme Court rejected these photographic difficulties as an excuse for this mild form of deception, holding that if the advertiser chose to represent that the consumer was actually seeing a demonstration, the demonstration must be real and not a mock-up. While both the FTC and the Court were sensitive to the possibility that acutal photographs themselves could be misleading in certain contexts (e.g., the color blue might be transmitted as whiter than the color white, which would transmit as gray, thereby allowing the cleaning power of detergents to be misrepresented), the use of mock-ups without disclosures of the fact that a mock-up is being used is now firmly established as a deceptive practice.

Other difficulties in visually conveying information accurately have come under scrutiny by the FTC. For example, Campbell Soup Company wanted to convey the impression that its vegetable soup contained a large quantity of solids; in order to photograph the soup in a bowl and portray the solid contents (which would not be visible as they sank beneath the surface), clear glass marbles were placed in the soupbowl before the soup was added to the bowl. The FTC found that this practice (which was not disclosed to the viewer) tended to convey the impression that the entire contents of the bowl consisted of solids that came with the soup; since this impression was false, the practice was condemned as violative of the FTC Act.[83]

While the shaving cream and soup cases are fairly obvious examples of deceptive practices, other photographic problems and techniques to circumvent them raise more difficult issues. For example, the heat generated by lighting used in commercial photography will cause frozen products to melt, making the photographic depiction of such products difficult. Can advertisers substitute mashed potatoes for ice cream or clear plastic cubes for ice cubes? The answer will depend upon the purpose of the substitution and the product characteristics portrayed. For example, if an advertisement that depicts the joys of consuming ice cream used mashed potatoes as a substitute for ice cream, no apparent deception of consumers exists. But if the advertisement de-

---

[82] *FTC* v. *Colgate–Palmolive Co.*, 380 U.S. 374 (1965).

[83] *Campbell Soup*, 77 F.T.C. 664 (1970).

picts the texture of the ice cream, the use of a mock-up or substitute probably would run afoul of the *Colgate* case. In short, if an advertisement portrays a photographable characteristic of the product or the result of its use, then the real thing must be used unless the viewer is told that a substitute is being used.

Endorsements and Testimonials

The Federal Trade Commission has given close scrutiny to the use of endorsements and testimonials. The FTC is concerned that such techniques carry an enhanced risk of deceiving purchasers because of the importance that purchasers attach to advertisements that employ the technique. In 1980, it issued a guide as to which practices it would consider deceptive.[84]

What Is an Endorsement?

The FTC's guide applies to an advertising message that "consumers are likely to believe reflects the opinions, beliefs, findings, or experience of a party other than the sponsoring advertiser."[85] The line between an endorsement and an ordinary commendation of the product by the sponsor (which is not covered by the guide) is not always clear. If a well-known personality is used in an advertisement for a product whose qualities are related to the personality's field of expertise, an endorsement is likely to exist. For example, if the ad shows a well-recognized professional golfer hitting the golf balls being advertised, an endorsement by the golfer of the golf balls is clearly implied. Similarly, if a professional automobile racer appears in an ad for tires and comments on the quality of the tires, an endorsement exists. But if unfamiliar persons are used in dramatizations and announcements, no endorsement will be implied; consumers are likely to recognize that such persons are merely communicating the sponsor's views of the product and not the views of other persons about the product.

Celebrity Endorsements.

The use of well-known public figures in advertising is subject to several limitations. Any endorsement must reflect the honest opinion, belief, or experience of the endorser. Furthermore, the endorser may not make claims about the product that the advertiser could not substantiate under general FTC substantiation requirements as noted in the previous discussion of the "reasonable basis" requirement. If the celebrity represents that the product is used by the celebrity, that fact must be true, and the advertiser must have "good reason to believe" that the endorser continues to be a "bona fide user" each time the advertisement is run. Both the advertiser and the endorser can incur liability for violating the bona fide use requirement. For example, singer Pat Boone was

---

[84] Federal Trade Commission, Guides Concerning Use of Endorsements and Testimonials in Advertising, 16 C.F.R. Part 255 (1982). (hereinafter, "F.T.C. Guide")

[85] *Ibid.*, part 255.0(b).

required to contribute to a fund for making refunds to purchasers of an acne remedy who relied upon Boone's false representation that he and his family used the acne remedy.[86]

The advertiser has an affirmative duty to check at "reasonable intervals" on the continued accuracy of the endorsement. For example, if the endorsement reflects the celebrity's preference for the product over competing products, any change in the product being promoted or any change in the products of competitors may make the celebrity's preference obsolete.[87]

Consumer Endorsements.

The use of advertising that depicts actual users of a product and communicates their views will be interpreted by the FTC as representing both that the users are "actual consumers" and that the experiences portrayed are typical. Accordingly, if actors are used instead of "actual consumers," that fact must be disclosed.[88] The experiences portrayed must be substantiated by information showing that the experiences are representative of a "significant proportion" of the experiences of actual users of the product. A disclosure that "not all consumers will get this result" is insufficient to negate the implication that the experiences portrayed are typical; only a clear and conspicuous disclosure of what the generally expected performance would be in the depicted circumstances will suffice to negate the false impression that the portrayal represents the generally expected results.[89] Thus, if the advertisement portrays an owner of the advertised television set who states that the set has needed repair only once during a 2-year period of ownership, the ad will be considered deceptive if the advertiser does not have substantiation that a significant proportion of all users have the same experience. Consumer descriptions of the efficacy of drugs or devices are subjected to the additional requirements that (1) "adequate scientific substantiation" exists for the claim, and (2) the claims are consistent with determinations of the Food and Drug Administration as to the safety and efficacy of the drug.[90]

The appropriateness of these requirements for the use of consumer endorsements and testimonials has been questioned on behavioral grounds. Researchers suggest that consumers do not place any great weight on advertisements portraying "man in the street" evaluations or "hidden camera" portrayals; according to some, the portrayals are devices to attract attention or affect memory in order to induce consumer trial of the product.[91] If the FTC follows its more general protocol for evaluating deceptive advertising, few actions should be brought under these guides for consumer endorsements of low-cost, fre-

---

[86] *Cooga Mooga, Inc.*, 92 F.T.C. 310 (1978).

[87] F.T.C. Guide Part 255.1(b)&(c).

[88] F.T.C. Guide Part 255.2(b).

[89] F.T.C. Guide Part 255.2.

[90] F.T.C. Guide Part 255.2(c).

[91] Nelson, "Advertising as Information," *Journal of Political Economy* 82, Jones, *Celebrity Endorsements: A Case for Alarm and Concern for the Future.* 15 New England L. Rev. 521 (1979–80).

quently purchased products where repeat purchasing is important to the advertiser and where consumers are fully able to evaluate the product claims through actual use of the product.

Expert Endorsements.

Advertising appeals that communicate the results of tests, surveys, experiences, and studies are subjected to even greater scrutiny. These communications frequently relate to product features and benefits that are important to purchasers and lend an additional measure of credibility to the claims made about the product. Accordingly, the FTC guides impose additional requirements on advertisements that use "experts." An *expert endorser* is defined as "an individual, group or institution possessing, as a result of experience, study or training, knowledge of a particular subject, which knowledge is superior to that generally acquired by ordinary individuals.[92]

The first requirement for expert endorsements is that the product qualities being endorsed must be within the area of the endorser's expertise. Former astronaut Gordon Cooper ran afoul of this requirement by endorsing an automobile fuel economy device. Cooper's expertise as an astronaut did not extend to automotive engineering, but the viewing public might infer that Cooper's endorsement was scientifically based. Accordingly, the FTC found that the endorsement was deceptive.[93]

The second requirement for expert endorsements is that they be based on product qualities or features that are relevant and available to purchasers. This requirement would be violated if a hospital's endorsement of a drug were communicated to the public, but the endorsement was based on packaging used only in sales to hospitals.

Finally, the expert endorsement must be based on an actual use of the expertise represented or implied, and the conclusions of the expert must be accurately portrayed. Problems that arise in this area usually result from implied representations that flow from the manner in which the endorsement is portrayed. For example, if a product is advertised as being approved by a "scientific institute," the ad would imply that the institute actually evaluated the product and approved it, using evaluative procedures that were scientific and valid. If those representations are false, the ad will be held deceptive. And if an ad communicates the fact that a product is used by others in their business (e.g., a cleaning product is represented as being used by a cleaning business), the ad may imply that the business has expertise to evaluate alternative products, and that other products were evaluated in side-by-side comparisons and were found inadequate by these cleaning experts. If those implications are false, the ad is deceptive.[94]

---

[92] F.T.C. Guide Part 255.0(d).

[93] *Leroy Gordon Cooper, Jr.,* 94 F.T.C. 674 (1979).

[94] F.T.C. Guide Part 255.3, Example 4.

Using a Seal of Approval of a Third Party.

The practice of using a seal of approval of another entity in connection with promotional activities is a form of an endorsement. The use of seals of approval carries certain risks for advertisers because consumers may infer that the seal implies some form of actual testing and evaluation. For example, the use of a seal of approval may imply that the owner of the seal would not allow its use unless products had passed some objective test of quality. If that implication is false, the use of the seal is deceptive. The FTC obtained a consent order against the National Association of Scuba Diving Schools, which allowed its seal of approval (featuring the words "integrity" "safety," and "instruction,") to be used on scuba diving equipment, even though the equipment had not been tested or evaluated by the association. The seals were affixed to price tags and decals that were shipped to over 200 retailers, who were permitted to attach the decals to any products sold by the retailer. The association also advertised in magazines and on store displays that products could earn its seal of approval; consumers were urged to look for the seal before purchasing.[95]

Disclosing Connections.

In addition to these requirements for endorsements, the FTC requires that unexpected and potentially biasing *connections* between the advertiser and the endorser must be disclosed. Ordinary payments for the services of the expert do not have to be disclosed, but the FTC held that Astronaut Gordon Cooper's endorsement of a fuel economy device should have revealed that Cooper had been promised a share of the future sales of the product.[96] Usual and customary payments to celebrity endorsers do not have to be disclosed, because the public reasonably should expect that celebrities get paid for allowing their names to be associated with a product. However, if a celebrity owns an interest in the firm promoting the product, and if the public is not aware of this connection, the failure to disclose the connection is deceptive. Because singer Pat Boone was not generally known to be the president of the company that was marketing the acne remedy he endorsed, the failure to disclose this connection was improper.[97]

The question of whether payments for consumer endorsements must be disclosed will depend upon the nature of the portrayal of the endorsement, the form of the "payment," and the conditions under which the endorsement was obtained. For example, if a consumer is paid to state that a certain product is preferred over other products, and if the ad portrays the consumer as randomly selected and unbiased, the payment should be disclosed.[98] And if consumers are told in advance that they will be exposed to a new product, that their re-

---

[95] *National Association of Scuba Diving Schools,* 3 CCH Trade Reg. Rep. ¶ 21,921 (May 18, 1982).

[96] *Leroy Gordon Cooper, Jr.,* op. cit.

[97] *Cooga Mooga, Inc.,* 92 F.T.C. 310, 321 (1978).

[98] F.T.C. Guide, part 255.5.

actions will be filmed and used on television, and that if the film is used they will be compensated, then any ad that portrays "spontaneous consumer reaction to our new product" will be deceptive unless it reveals these circumstances. In other words, consumers, under those circumstances, might be expected to make favorable statements about the product regardless of their true beliefs; they value the opportunity to have their images displayed publically and suspect that, if they say the "right thing" about the product, their chances of public exposure will be enhanced. Any portrayal of their "unbiased reaction" is a deception.[99]

Promotions Based on Price

Promotions that feature price have come in for a great deal of regulation, apparently on the theory that purchasers place primary emphasis on price and are likely to be affected by even the slightest degree of inaccuracy regarding a pricing claim. Thus, in addition to general laws regarding deception, extensive regulation exists to make sure that any cents-off promotion on labeling is an accurate representation of a true price reduction.[100] Regulations go even beyond a requirement for honesty regarding savings or price reductions, however; many laws require that prices be calculated in a prescribed fashion or displayed in a particular format.[101]

Price Surveys.

One example of the FTC's concern for accuracy regarding the use of prices involved advertising by Kroger Company.[102] Kroger had employed shoppers to ascertain the prices of 100 to 150 items that were sold in Kroger stores and in the stores of Kroger's competitors; Kroger then published the results of the price comparisons. The ads indicated that, for the items compared (which represented about 2% of the items stocked in a typical retail store), Kroger's prices were equal to or lower than the prices charged by Kroger's competitors; the ad also proclaimed that Kroger was the "price leader." The FTC found that the ads implicitly represented that the surveys were statistically valid and projectible to all items sold by Kroger; this representation was false, thereby making the ads deceptive. While Kroger was permitted to make truthful claims about savings on particular items, it was not allowed to create the inference that similar savings could be obtained on all items throughout the store.

Cents-Off Labeling.

The promotional practice of using cents-off labeling has been regulated by the Federal Trade Commission pursuant to the Fair Packaging and Labeling

[99] Ibid., Example 3.

[100] Federal Trade Commission, Regulations under Section 5(C) of the Fair Packaging and Labeling Act, 16 C.F.R. Part 502 (1982).

[101] See, e.g., Mass. Ann. Stat. ch. 6, § 115A (Mitchie/Law Corp. 1980).

[102] *Kroger Co.*, 98 F.T.C. 639 (1981).

Act.[103] The FTC's rules apply to the use of any labeling of consumer commodities that states or represents by implication that the product is being offered for sale at a price lower than the ordinary and customary retail price. To control deceptive use of the cents-off representation, the FTC prohibits use of that term unless five different conditions are satisfied:

1. The product must have previously been sold at an ordinary or customary price in the recent past.
2. The price reduction must be genuine and equal to or greater than the cents-off representation.
3. The regular price, so designated, must be clearly and conspicuously displayed on shelf signs or on the package.
4. The frequency of a cents-off promotion for any particular size of commodity cannot exceed 3 months within a 12-month period and at least 30 days must elapse between promotions, which, in total, cannot be in effect more than 6 months within any 12-month period.
5. Sales may not exceed 50% of the total volume during a 12-month period.[104]

Packagers and labelers must do some policing of retailers to make sure that the represented savings are actually fully passed on to consumers. The FTC prohibits the furnishing of promotional material where the packager or labeler knows or has reason to know that the retailer will not pass on the savings.[105]

Introductory Offers.

The use of the term "introductory offer" on packaging and labeling, which states or implies that a new commodity is being offered at a price lower than the anticipated ordinary and customary retail sales price, is also regulated by the FTC rules under the Fair Packaging and Labeling Act.[106] For example; the product must in fact be new or changed in a functionally significant and substantial respect or newly introduced into the trade area for the first time. The introductory offer period cannot exceed 6 months in duration. The packager or labeler must intend to offer the commodity at an ordinary and customary price for a reasonably substantial period of time following the duration of the introductory offer promotion. If a specific representation of the savings that will result from a purchase during the introductory period is contained on the label, the packager or labeler must intend to charge a price that will equal the savings represented on the label.

Economy Size Labeling.

The use of promotional labeling that characterizes or suggests that the purchaser will save by purchasing the package size labeled with a term such as "economy size," "economy pack," "budget pack," "bargain size," "value

---

[103] Federal Trade Commission, Regulations under Section 5(C) of the Fair Packaging and Labeling Act, 16 C.F.R. part 502 (1982).

[104] Ibid., at §502.100.

[105] Ibid., §502.100 (c).

[106] Ibid., §502.101.

size," or words of similar import will be deceptive unless (1) the same brand is available in a package of at least one other size, (2) no other such package uses a similar savings representation, and (3) the savings to the purchaser is at least 5 percent as measured by the actual prices of all other packages of the same brand simultaneously offered for sale.[107]

Price Reductions.

The FTC similarly has been concerned about the accuracy of claims that prices have been reduced or lowered. While genuine reductions in price can be advertised without fear of legal action, some care must be exercised in choosing the appropriate comparison price. For example, if a discount chain already has an established price that is below the manufacturer's suggested retail price (where the manufacturer can legally suggest such a price), the discount chain cannot suggest a recent price reduction by comparing its price to the suggested retail price; the appropriate comparison is to the most recently charged price by the discount chain.[108] Critics of these FTC rules have argued that as long as the advertised price is accurate, consumers are not harmed by misleading suggestions of price reductions, because consumers can learn the prices of competitors and judge for themselves as to whether the advertised price is lower than the competition. Nevertheless, the FTC seems to feel that consumers are affected by false claims of price reductions and has declared them to be deceptive. However, the enforcement activity against misleading price reductions seemingly is on the decline.[109]

Bait Advertising and Unavailability of Advertised Products.

Courts and legislatures have been concerned with one particular form of price deception known as *bait advertising*. This practice involves the advertising of an unusually low price coupled with practices at the point of sale to discourage purchase of the advertised item and to encourage purchase of a higher priced (and more profitable) alternative. Frequently, such practices include heavy disparagement of the advertised product ("sure, madam, we will sell it to you but, frankly, it won't last a week") or simply indicating that the supply of the advertised item has been exhausted ("we had no idea this many people would respond to our promotion"). Such practices have been condemned generally.[110] Regulations are addressed to industries that are thought to engage in the practice excessively; the latter category includes supermarkets and has led to an FTC rule on the "unavailability of advertised specials."[111] The rule technically applies only to retail food stores and requires simply that goods be available at the advertised price during the period of the

---

[107] Ibid., §502.102.

[108] Federal Trade Commission, Guides against Deceptive Pricing, 16 C.F.R. Part 233 (1982).

[109] Robert Pitofsky, "Advertising Regulation and the Consumer Movement," in *Issues in Advertising: The Economics of Persuasion,* David Tureck, (ed.) (Washington, D.C.: American Enterprise Institute for Public Policy Research, 1978), pp. 38–42.

[110] Federal Trade Commission, Guides Against Bait Advertising, 16 C.F.R. Part 238 (1982).

[111] Federal Trade Commission, Trade Regulation Rule: Retail Food Store Advertising and Marketing Practices, 16 C.F.R. Part 424 (1982).

advertising. Certain defenses are available in the event that the items actually are not available. For example, if the sale items were ordered in sufficient quantities to meet reasonably anticipated demand but were not available because of shipping difficulties or excessive demand, then the rule is not violated. However, a raincheck must be given that will allow the item (or a similar item of equal or better quality) to be purchased at the same price in the near future; failure to routinely make a raincheck available will result in a violation of the rule. Obviously, the question of what level of demand is "reasonably anticipated" can present difficult questions for courts and enforcement agencies, but prior history of consumer response to similar reductions on comparable items would serve as a rough guide, and failure to have on hand at least that amount would present a serious risk of violating the rule (or similar state laws).

A related problem was addressed by the FTC when it challenged the practice of Sears, Roebuck and Company of giving greater levels of compensation to salespersons for sales of nonadvertised items. Sears had followed the practice in connection with sales of sewing machines. The FTC found Sears in violation of the FTC Act because the practice had a subtle effect on sales efforts and tended to encourage salespersons to "move" a customer to a higher-priced item on which the salesperson's commission would be higher.[112]

Validity of Restrictions on Price Advertising.

Despite the obvious competitive benefits that flow from widespread consumer knowledge of prices, many states have prohibited the advertising of prices for a wide range of goods and services ranging from eyeglasses and prescription drugs through legal, medical, and dental services. Rationales for such prohibitions on price advertising range widely. Prohibitions on drug price advertising were justified as diminishing overuse of drugs and as preserving the professional pharmacist's ability to provide additional services to prescription drug users. Prohibitions on advertising of legal services were justified in part on the ground that the product (lawyer services) could not be adequately standardized, and, thus, consumers might be misled by price advertising of certain types of services and could not accurately compare prices across different providers.

Laws based on these rationales for restricting price advertising by pharmacists and other professionals have been declared unconstitional by the Supreme Court.[113] The Court has held that state restrictions on price advertising violate the first amendment, which protects the freedom of speech of advertisers. Thus, Virginia's ban on the advertising of prescription drug prices by pharmacists has been declared unconstitutional, as has Arizona's ban on the advertising of certain routine legal services such as divorce, will preparation, bankruptcy representation, and changes of name.[114] These cases have not com-

---

[112] *Sears, Roebuck and Co.*, 89 F.T.C. 229 (1977).

[113] *Virginia State Board of Pharmacy* v. *Virginia Citizens Consumer Council Inc.*, 425 U.S. 748 (1976).

[114] *Bates* v. *State Bar of Arizona*, 433 U.S. 350 (1977).

pletely invalidated all restrictions of price advertising, however, as the Court has suggested that states can take action to regulate or prohibit advertising that is deceptive. But for such state regulations to be constitutional, the state must be able to show that no less restrictive means are available to eliminate the deception than the means chosen by the state.[115] Absolute prohibitions of price advertising have little likelihood of meeting this burden. Truthful statements as to price and availability of a product or service rarely are misleading, and even if there is some incomplete or deceptive aspect to the advertising, the less restrictive manner of regulation would simply involve additional disclosure to eliminate the deception. Furthermore, as the Court suggested in the lawyer advertising case, if there is a legitimate concern that, for example, price advertising of divorce services will be misleading because different lawyers will include different components in their "divorce" package, the state can regulate in a less restrictive manner by defining the basic essentials of the service and by requiring lawyers who advertise the service to provide that minimum level of service.[116]

Now that restrictions on the advertising of prices have been removed by the Supreme Court, states have been moving to require retailers to affirmatively disclose prices or price-related information to consumers in ways that make comparative price shopping less costly. For example, some states have required pharmacists to prominently display a listing of the prices charged by the pharmacy for the top sellers among the drugs sold by the pharmacy.[117] Some states require gasoline retailers to prominently display the price of gasoline so that it is visible to passing motorists.[118] And federal regulations require that the price of credit (the actual "finance charge" and the corresponding "annual percentage rate") must be included in advertising that contains other representations about the cost or availability of credit.[119]

Unit Pricing.

One form of price regulation related to promotional activity requires sellers of goods normally sold by, or with an indication of, weight or other standard unit of measurement to compute and prominently display the price of the item per such unit of measurement.[120] The purpose of such regulations is to allow consumers to compare the per unit costs of similar goods that are packaged in dissimilar-sized containers. For example, a shopper may be seeking to purchase a packaged food item and may find several different brands on the shelf, all bearing different prices, and all packaged in differently sized containers. For the shopper who desires to purchase the lowest priced product, formida-

---

[115] *Central Hudson Gas & Electric Corp.* v. *Public Service Commission,* 447 U.S. 557 (1980).

[116] *Bates* v. *State Bar of Arizona,* 433 U.S. 350, 373, n. 28 (1977).

[117] N.Y. Educ. Law, § 6826 (Consol. 1979).

[118] Cal. Bus. & Prof. Code § 13531 (West, 1982 Supp.)

[119] Truth in Lending Act, 15 U.S.C. §§ 1661–1665 (1980); Federal Reserve Board, Regulation Z, 12 C.F.R. §§ 226.16 and 226.24 (1982).

[120] Mass. Ann. Laws, ch. 6, § 115(A) (Mitchie/Law Co-op 1980).

ble computations are necessary to make the determination of which is the lowest priced product. The regulations assist these consumers by requiring the seller to perform the calculations and post the results. Although several empirical studies have cast doubt on the extent to which shoppers actually use these unit-price disclosures, it appears that, if the proper format is employed in disclosing the results of the computations, shoppers will use the information.[121]

Scanning and Price Marking.

A recent technological development has led to legal requirements that prices actually be marked on each product. The use of a universal product identification code (UPC), coupled with use of a machine capable of reading the code and associating the code with the seller's price for the product, has encouraged retailers to not mark prices on products. By the elimination of the labor cost associated with marking prices on goods in grocery stores, consumers supposedly are benefited. But because of consumer concerns about the accuracy of the prices charged during the check-out process (a concern shared by the FTC[122]), and because of consumer desires to have the price of each product physically marked on the product, some states and cities have enacted laws that require retailers to mark each product with its price.

Promotions of Warranties

Decisions about the nature and extent of warranties to offer in connection with products often are accompanied by promotional activities. These activities are constrained by both the general prohibition of deception and by requirements under the Magnuson–Moss Warranty Act for making the terms of warranties available to purchasers before sale. The disclosure, labeling, and presale availability requirements of the act were described in Chapter 3.

The FTC industry guide on deceptive advertising of guarantees sets forth several principles for use in determining whether advertising of guarantees is deceptive.[123] These guides suggest the following:

1. The use of words such as "lifetime guarantee" will be construed as referring to the remaining natural life of the purchaser or original user unless a different term is clearly and conspicuously indicated. For example, if a carburetor was advertised as being "guaranteed for life," but actually was guaranteed only for the life of the car in which it was installed, the ad would be considered deceptive. Any ambiguity about durational representations should be avoided.
2. Statements about the duration of a guarantee will be construed as implying that the product will normally be expected to last for that duration. For ex-

---

[121] J. Edward Russo, Gene Kreiser, and Sally Miyashita, "An Effective Display of Unit Price Information," *Journal of Marketing* 39, (Apr. 1975), p. 11.

[122] *Great A & P Co., Inc.*, 85 F.T.C. 601 (1975)(A & P agreed to reduce the number of price discrepancies in its check-out process to "an acceptable level").

[123] Federal Trade Commission, Guides against Deceptive Advertising of Guarantees, 16 C.F.R. Part 239 (1982).

ample, the statement "guaranteed for 36 months" as applied to batteries should not be used if the battery is known to have a life expectancy of only 18 months.

3. If guarantees are adjusted on a pro rata basis (e.g., using the proportion of the warranty term that has not expired when a defect occurs), this must be disclosed clearly in the advertising. Furthermore, if the price used in making the adjustment is a price other than the price paid by the purchaser, this fact should be clearly and conspicuously disclosed. For example, if tires are sold with a 12-month guarantee at a price of $24.00 but are adjusted using a list price of $48.00, it must be disclosed that a higher list price will be used to make adjustments.

4. Using terms such as "satisfaction or your money back" or "10 day free trial" or similar representations is construed as representing that the full purchase price will be refunded at the option of the purchaser. Any limitations inconsistent with this construction must be disclosed clearly and conspicuously.

Credit Advertising

Consumers have a keen interest in whether the purchase of a product or service can be facilitated by obtaining credit from the seller. The advertising of credit terms clearly imparts useful information to consumers, but management must avoid any representations that, because of the incompleteness of the information disclosed, might mislead consumers as to the amount or availability of credit.

The Federal Truth in Lending Act regulates the use of credit information in advertising.[124] It clearly prohibits the use of false, misleading, or "bait" advertising; ads cannot mention a specific size of down-payment requirement, a specific periodic repayment amount, or any other specific credit terms, unless the creditor "usually and customarily arranges" or will arrange the advertised terms. In addition, the act requires that any rate of interest or finance charge must be expressed as an "annual percentage rate" and must be computed according to the requirements of the act. No other rate can be used in any advertisement; however, the "simple annual rate" or the "periodic rate that is applied to an unpaid balance" may be stated in conjunction with, but not more conspicuously than, the annual percentage rate. If the advertisement mentions any of five specific terms (the amount of the down payment, the amount of any installment payment, the dollar amount of finance charges, the number of installment payments, or the period of repayment), then the advertisement must also disclose the rate of the finance charge expressed as an annual percentage rate, the down payment, and the repayment terms.[125] The disclosures must be made "clearly and conspicuously."

The question of when the terms used in an advertisement will require full disclosure of all terms is not free from doubt, although the use of specific terms seems to compel full disclosure. For example, a statement such as "no down payment" or "no trade-in required" will not trigger the disclosure re-

---

[124] Truth in Lending Act, 15 U.S.C. §§ 1661–1665 a (Supp V, 1982).

[125] 15 U.S.C. § 1664(c) and § 1663(2) and Federal Reserve Board, Regulation Z, 12 C.F.R. §§ 226.16 & 226.24(c) (1983).

quirement, but the phrase "only 5% down" or "as low as $100 down" does compel full disclosure.[126] Similarly, statements such as "you can pay weekly," "monthly payment terms can be arranged," or "take years to repay," do not require full disclosure, whereas statements such as "30-year mortgage," "repayment in as many as 36 monthly installments," or "48-month payments terms," will require full disclosure.[127] Catalog and multiple-page advertisements that mention credit can comply with the disclosure requirements by giving information in a table or schedule that has sufficient detail to permit the down payment, the terms of repayment, and the annual percentage rate to be determined. The location of the table must be clearly referred to whenever credit is mentioned in the catalog or multiple-page advertisement.

Advertising that promotes the use of credit cards also must fully disclose all aspects of a credit transaction under certain circumstances. Thus, if an ad mentions the circumstances under which a finance charge would be imposed ("charge it—you won't be billed until February"), the ad also must clearly and conspicuously disclose the periodic rate expressed as an annual percentage rate and the numerous other charges or fees that might be imposed under credit card plans.

These rules, which implement the Truth and Lending Simplification and Reform Act of 1980, seem difficult to comply with, yet they have reduced greatly the compliance difficulties under prior law of properly including credit information in advertising. In view of these considerable uncertainties, it can only be suggested that the detailed regulations of the Federal Reserve Board and the official interpretations of its staff should be consulted whenever a decision is made to refer to the availability of credit in advertising. The only other safe alternative is to always include in the advertising the annual percentage rate and the full terms of a credit offering. The basic goal of these disclosure requirements is to permit readers of advertising to learn most of the important aspects of a credit transaction, such as the down payment and annual percentage rate, without being misled. Although the annual percentage rate may not be the most important piece of information for consumers in making a credit decision,[128] federal law is now committed to requiring that the annual percentage rate be included in most advertising that mentions any specific aspect of the seller's credit offering.

COMPETITOR ACTIONS AGAINST DECEPTIVE ADVERTISING

Previous sections of this chapter have explored the complexities of the terms "deceptive" and "unfair" in the Federal Trade Commission Act and the enforcement of the act by the Federal Trade Commission. But the FTC is not

[126] Federal Reserve Board, Official Staff Commentary on Reg. Z, § 226.24(c).

[127] Ibid.

[128] National Commission on Consumer Finance, *Consumer Credit in the United States* (Washington, D.C.: U.S. Government Printing Office, 1972).

the only institution that can initiate a proceeding to scrutinize the accuracy and truthfulness of advertising. Numerous laws against false and misleading advertising exist at the state level, and these laws frequently authorize both governmental officials and injured consumers to bring litigation to challenge deceptive advertising practices. But of even greater importance to most firms is the authority given to firms to challenge the false and deceptive advertising of their competitors. This section will explore the circumstances under which the law will permit private enforcement of the policy against false advertising.

The ability of firms to sue one another over misleading advertising has assumed greater importance because of the increasing use of comparative advertising, which has been encouraged by the elimination of both legal and other less formal barriers to comparisons of competing products in advertising. For example, print advertising of cigarettes (which cannot be advertised on television) frequently informs readers of the relative tar and nicotine content of competing cigarettes. Similarly, comparisons are made of product features such as the tread-wear characteristics of automobile tires, the relative fuel economy measures for competing automobiles, the charges for car rentals, and so on. The potential for inflicting harm is very high if the comparisons are false or deceptive.

Economic theory suggests that such comparative advertising provides valuable information to consumers and effectively reduces the cost of consumer search for information, thereby making markets more competitive.[129] And although some contrary evidence exists, research into consumer responses to comparative advertising suggests that consumers pay greater attention to the claims made in the advertising and place greater reliance on the claims of product superiority. Because of the impact of comparative information, the benefits of making false or misleading comparisons are thought to be likely to induce more questionable claims. However, this inducement may be more than offset by the greater probability that litigation over truthfulness will result because of the interest of the firm whose products are falsely portrayed in a less favorable light. Although the law has not always allowed businesses to sue a competitor on the ground that the competitor's advertising (whether comparative or not) is false or deceptive,[130] both the common law and statutes have increasingly allowed an injured competitor to bring suit to challenge false comparative advertising.

Although numerous doctrinal niceties may determine whether suit must be brought in state or federal court,[131] it is now clear that the victim of a false or misleading comparative advertisement or promotion may obtain injunctive relief against a competitor. The question of whether damages can be recovered is much less certain, because it is difficult to establish with any great precision the amount of injury that has been caused by false advertising.

---

[129] Posner, *The Federal Trade Commission*, 37 U. Chi. L. Rev. 47 (1969).

[130] Jordan and Rubin, *An Economic Analysis of the Law of False Advertising*, 8 J. Legal Studies 527 (1979).

[131] Suits may be brought in federal court only if the parties are of different state citizenships or if the action is authorized to be brought pursuant to a federal statute. The Lanham Act is such a federal statute.

Comparative Advertising and the Lanham Act

The most frequently used basis for attacking deceptive comparative advertisements is section 43(a) of the Lanham Act.[132] That statute provides a remedy for persons "likely to be damaged" by "false descriptions or representations" regarding products or services. Comparative advertising campaigns can give rise to legal liability for inaccurate comparisons if the plaintiff shows that (1) the defendant made false statements of fact about its own product; (2) the false statements are material (i.e., they pertain to important aspects of a purchasing decision and have the capacity to deceive many consumers); and (3) the defendant caused the advertised goods or services to enter interstate commerce. (This latter requirement is a peculiar by-product of the language of the statute and its applicability to interstate commerce.)[133] Thus, it is possible for a defendant to make false statements about the plaintiff's product without those statements being actionable under the Lanham Act. However, such false statements may be actionable under state laws of unfair competition or under tort theories of disparagement or libel, as shown later.

The Lanham Act has given rise to numerous lawsuits involving comparative advertising. Much of the litigation is centered on the question of whether the statements of the defendant in promoting its product amounted to "false descriptions or representations." As discussed earlier, the question of exactly what is represented by any particular ad is a different problem for courts to resolve. Although the reaction of the consuming public to an advertisement is clearly the most relevant measure of falsity, courts do not always insist upon proof of consumer reaction through surveys or studies. Instead, courts frequently examine the literal language used in an advertisement, and if the language seems to be clear and unambiguous and is, in addition, clearly false, courts will enjoin the advertising. For example, where a perfume manufacturer claimed that its copy of Chanel perfume was "equal to the original," that claim was found to be false without the need to resort to consumer studies.[134] Similarly, where a claim was made that Triumph was the "national taste test winner" over Merit cigarettes, and where that claim was false, the court entered an injunction without receiving any evidence of the consumer perception of the ad.[135] However, where Anacin pain reliever was advertised as superior to Tylenol for relief of pain associated with inflammation, and where it was alleged that consumers would falsely interpret that claim as a claim of general pain relief superiority, the court accepted and relied upon consumer surveys, which demonstrated that consumers perceived the claim of superiority as a

---

[132] Trade Mark Act of 1946, 15 U.S.C. §1125 (a).

[133] Actions against those who make false representation are authorized only if the person who is making the false representation "shall cause such goods or services to enter into commerce." This requirement seemingly compels the court to find that the defendant made false representations about its own goods.

[134] *Smith* v. *Chanel, Inc.*, 402 F.2d 562 (9th Cir. 1968).

[135] *Philip Morris, Inc.* v. *Loew's Theatres, Inc.*, 511 F. Supp. 855 (S.D.N.Y. 1980). See also, *American Brands* v. *R. J. Reynolds Tobacco Co.*, 413 F. Supp. 1352 (S.D.N.Y. 1976) (Reynolds Tobacco advertised their low-tar cigarette NOW as having "the lowest" tar; but Carlton cigarettes were equally low in tar and the advertisement falsely implied that NOW was the lowest).

generalized superiority claim not restricted to pain associated with inflammation.[136] Since the general superiority claim was false, the court used the
Lanham Act to enjoin the somewhat ambiguous (or at least easily misunderstood) claim made by Anacin.

Even where a claim might be somewhat ambiguous and consumer surveys
would be useful in determining what was represented, courts have excused a
plaintiff from presenting such evidence when the defendant clearly *intended* to
convey a false message. For example, in *McNeil Lab. Inc.* v. *American Home
Products Corporation,*[137] the court relied upon internal memoranda of the defendant as showing an intent to convey a false message; this intent was held to be
effective without a need for proof of actual consumer understanding. The
court noted, "advertisements successfully project the messages they are intended to project, especially when they are professionally designed."[138]

The use of surveys and other measures of consumer attitudes and beliefs in
Lanham Act cases raises additional problems relating to the validity and reliability of the studies. These methodological issues have not been dealt with in
any great detail by the courts. Perhaps this failure can be justified because
courts, in most Lanham Act cases, are usually awarding only an injunction
against the advertising message of the defendant, and are not awarding damages to the plaintiff. Under the circumstances, precision and exactitude in the
design and implementation of a consumer survey may be unnecessary, because
courts, when granting an injunction, are simply preventing the making of
false, or probably false, claims. As long as some reliable evidence indicates
that false claims are being made, and as long as truthful messages are not restrained, little harm is done in granting injunctive relief against a false claim
that has the tendency or capacity to affect consumer beliefs or attitudes. However, when a plaintiff requests monetary relief, courts are more demanding as
to proof that a false representation was made and actually caused harm. One
court has explained its reluctance to award damages, while being relatively receptive to awarding injunctions, by stating that

> No measure of the competition for the mind of the consumer has yet been de-
> vised other than market share, and no evidence has been or probably ever will be
> submitted that would establish [that] a particular market shift was a direct result
> of a false advertisement so that damages could be determined.[139]

The percentage of the audience that must perceive the false message in order for relief to be given under the Lanham Act has never been precisely stated by the courts. The courts frequently enunciate broad rules, such as the rule
that a "substantial segment" of the audience should be deceived, but the precise percentage that would meet this substantiality requirement is never specified. However, the facts of particular cases suggest that at least 20 percent of

[136] *American Home Products Corp.* v. *Johnson & Johnson,* 577 F.2d 160 (2d Cir. 1978).

[137] *McNeilab, Inc.* v. *American Home Products Corp.,* 501 F. Supp. 517 (S.D.N.Y. 1980).

[138] Id.

[139] *Phillip Morris, Inc.* v. *Loew's Theatres, Inc.,* op. cit.

the viewing audience should perceive and remember a deceptive message. In the Anacin–Tylenol dispute, the district court awarded an injunction upon a showing that 20 percent of all those surveyed remembered a claim that Anacin was generally superior to Tylenol. That court rejected as insignificant a showing that 7 percent of the audience recalled a message of Anacin's superiority to Tylenol regarding the propensity of the products to upset the stomach.[140] Injunctions have been issued where 37 percent of the audience received the false message that "Triumph tastes better than Merit,"[141] and where 23 percent of the audience understood an advertisement as claiming falsely that Maximum Strength Anacin was stronger than Extra Strength Tylenol.[142]

Where comparative advertising claims are ambiguous, some courts have refused to interpret advertising claims and have required some empirical evidence of actual consumer misunderstanding. For example, when R. J. Reynolds advertised that NOW cigarettes were the lowest in tar of all cigarettes, the court found that this claim was ambiguous as to whether NOW was the absolute lowest or whether it shared that characteristic with other low tar cigarettes.[143] Since the plaintiff could not produce evidence of consumer reaction to the advertisements, the complaint was dismissed.[144]

Comparative Advertising and Consumer Preference Tests

One frequently used comparative advertising technique involves tests that measure consumer preferences between compared products. One advertising campaign involved Bristol–Myers' shampoo, Body-On-Tap. The advertisement stated, "In shampoo tests with over 900 women . . . , Body-On-Tap got higher ratings than Prell for body. Higher than Flex for conditioning. Higher than Sassoon for strong, healthy looking hair." This claim was based upon a "blind monadic test" in which participants are asked to test only one product and then to rate it on a qualitative scale with respect to numerous attributes. A six-step scale was used, involving the categories "outstanding," "excellent," "very good," "good," "fair," or "poor." Bristol–Myers combined the outstanding and excellent categories for the attribute "strong, healthy looking hair," and found that 36 percent of the women who tested Body-On-Tap found it outstanding or excellent, whereas only 24 percent of the separate group of women who tested Sassoon gave it such ratings.

Sassoon asked for and received a preliminary injunction against the advertising campaign.[145] The court was presented with evidence from a separate consumer perception study, which showed that 95 percent of the viewers of the advertisement inferred that the 900 women involved in the advertising

[140] *American Home Products Corp.* v. *Johnson & Johnson*, 436 F. Supp. 785 (S.D.N.Y. 1977).

[141] *Phillip Morris, Inc.* v. *Loew's Theatres, Inc.*, op. cit.

[142] *McNeilab, Inc.*, v. *American Home Products Corp.*, op. cit.

[143] *American Brands, Inc.* v. *R. J. Reynolds Tobacco Co.*, 413 F. Supp. 1352 (S.D.N.Y. 1976).

[144] Ibid.

[145] *Vidal Sassoon, Inc.* v. *Bristol–Myers Co.*, 661 F.2d 272 (2d Cir. 1981).

claim had tested at least two or more brands of shampoo. The Court of Appeals affirmed the granting of a preliminary injunction by noting that "whether or not the statements made in the advertisements are literally true, section 43(a) of the Lanham Act encompasses more than blatant falsehoods. It embraces 'innuendo, indirect intimations, and ambiguous suggestions' evidenced by the consuming public's misapprehension of the hard facts underlying the advertisement."[146]

The court also examined the Bristol–Myers study and found that, if the remaining categories of rating were used ("very good," "good," "fair," or "poor"), there was only a "statistically insignificant difference of 1% between the ratings of the two shampoos regarding 'strong, healthy looking hair."[147] Holding that the misrepresentations concerning the test results were actionable under the Lanham Act, the court stated,

> While we recognize section 43(a) encompasses only misrepresentations with respect to the "inherent quality or characteristic" of defendant's product, . . . the intent and total effect of the advertisements were to lead consumers into believing that Body-On-Tap was competitively superior, surely a representation regarding its "inherent quality."[148]

The court added,

> Where many of the qualities of a product . . . are not susceptible to objective measurement, it is difficult to see how the manufacturer can advertise its product's "quality" more effectively than through the dissemination of the results of a consumer preference study. In such instances, the medium of consumer tests truly becomes the message of inherent superiority. . . . Where depictions of consumer test results or methodology are so significantly misleading that the reasonably intelligent consumer will be deceived about the product's inherent quality or characteristics, an action under section 43(a) may lie.[149]

State Law Regarding Comparative Advertising

If a plaintiff in a comparative advertising situation is unable to establish that the false representations were made about the defendant's goods or services, the plaintiff will not be able to bring a lawsuit under the Lanham Act.[150] Although a false statement about the plaintiff's goods in a comparative advertising context could be construed as a false statement about the defendant's goods, courts have reluctantly followed the literal requirement in the statute that the false representation pertain to the defendant's goods. Thus, the inability to use the Lanham Act was upheld in *Bernard Foods* v. *Dietene,* where the defendant's product comparisons emphasized the inferiority of the plaintiff's product (mentioning deficiencies in flavor, texture, nutrition, and cost of the

---

[146] Id. at 277.

[147] Id.

[148] Id., at 278.

[149] Id.

[150] *Bernard Food Industries* v. *Dietene Co.,* 415 F.2d 1279 (7th Cir. 1969) *cert. denied,* 397 U.S. 912 (1970).

plaintiff's custard mix), even when accompanied by the statement that the defendant's product was superior to the plaintiff's product "in all major respects."[151] Several courts have questioned, but adhered to, the requirement that the false statement pertain to the defendant's goods. For example, in *Skil Corp.* v. *Rockwell International Corp.*, the court, in referring to the *Bernard Food* decision, stated,

> With due respect to the Court, it does not seem logical to distinguish between a false statement about the plaintiff's product and a false statement about the defendant's product in a case where a particular statement is contained in comparison advertising by the defendant. . . .[152]

In the *Skil* case, the defendant Rockwell's advertising featured comparative product tests on the performance of electric drills and jigsaws manufactured by Rockwell, Skil, and two other companies. Since Rockwell's advertisement included test reports on its own product, the court found little difficulty in finding that false representations were allegedly made about the defendant's own products and were therefore actionable under the Lanham Act.

Where the Lanham Act is not applicable (because the false comparative advertisement does not make false statements about the defendant's own product), the plaintiff may be forced to bring suit under state statutory or common law. Two potential theories of recovery are available: defamation and disparagement. The defamation action protects a plaintiff's public reputation (i.e., the respect, goodwill, confidence, or esteem in which plaintiff is held by the public). The disparagement action, however, protects the plaintiff's interest in making sales of its product free of false representations about its product emanating from the defendant.

The defamation action, where available, may make recovery by a plaintiff easier than in a disparagement action. However, few comparative advertisements attack the plaintiff's business character. One case did prove defamatory; in *Cosgove Studio and Camera Shop, Inc.* v. *Paine*,[153] the plaintiff had placed a newspaper advertisement offering a free roll of film for each roll developed by the plaintiff. The following day the defendant placed an advertisement in the same newspaper implying that those who offer free film were dishonest. The ads stated: "Use common sense . . . you get nothing for nothing! We will not inflate our prices to give you a new roll free, print blurred negatives to inflate the price of your snapshots, hurry-up the developing of your valuable snapshots and ruin them, or use inferior chemicals and paper on your valuable snapshots."[154] Even though plaintiff was not named in the advertisement, the court found the advertisement clearly referred to the plaintiff and was defamatory and therefore actionable. Accordingly, the plaintiff did not have to prove that the defendant knew the statements were false or intended to cause harm

[151] Ibid.

[152] *Skil Corp.* v. *Rockwell International Corp.*, 375 F. Supp. 777, 782 (N.D. Ill. 1974).

[153] 408 Pa. 314 (1962).

[154] Ibid.

to the plaintiff.[155] These requirements must be proved in a disparagement action. In addition, in a disparagement action, the plaintiff must prove special damages, unlike the plaintiff in a defamation action.[156]

The disparagement tort and the Lanham Action are complementary. If a defendant makes false statements about its own product in comparison to plaintiff's product, an action will lie under the Lanham Act. However, if defendant makes false statements about plaintiff's product, an action can be brought under the disparagement theory. Unlike the Lanham Act action, the disparagement action must be brought in state court rather than in federal court.

One other point of difference exists between a disparagement action and a Lanham Act action. The disparagement action is a tort remedy that seeks monetary relief for damages. Under the Lanham Act, either an injunction or monetary damages can be recovered. Because of the difficulty of proving a causal connection between a false representation and a loss of business, plaintiffs have difficulty prevailing in disparagement actions. Whether such plaintiffs are entitled to injunctive relief is not entirely clear. In some states, it is clear that under a theory of unfair competition a plaintiff may obtain an injunction.[157] Furthermore, 16 states have adopted the Uniform Deceptive Trade Practices Act, which allows a plaintiff to obtain an injunction without proving loss of profits or intent to deceive or actual consumer confusion or misunderstanding.[158] The act grants a cause of action for false statements in a wide variety of contexts, including (1) "disparag[ing] the goods, services, or business of another by false or misleading representation[s] of fact"; (2) making false representations that goods or services (a) "have sponsorship, approval, characteristics, ingredients, uses, benefits, or qualities," or (b) "are of a particular standard, quality, or grade," or (c) "are of a particular style or model"; and (3) making false representations that a business "has a sponsorship, approval, status, affiliation or connection." All these activities, "and any other conduct which similarly creates a likelihood of confusion or misunderstanding" are actionable under this act. Thus, under almost any theory and in almost any state, a comparative advertising campaign that is based on false factual information can be the basis of an appropriate injunctive action.

One formerly controversial issue in comparative advertising campaigns has been settled: it is perfectly legal to refer to a compared product by name or

---

[155] In defamation actions that do not involve commercial speech, the Supreme Court has required the plaintiff to establish that the defendant knew the statements were false or negligently failed to ascertain whether the statements were true. See *Gertz v. Robert Welch, Inc.*, 418 U.S. 323 (1974). Whether these requirements will be extended to actions involving defamatory commercial speech is not known at the present time.

[156] In cases not involving defamatory commercial speech, the Supreme Court has indicated that a plaintiff must prove some damage resulting from the false communication; state laws that allowed juries to presume damages resulting from defamatory speech were held unconstitutional. *Gertz v. Robert Welch, Inc.*, op. cit.

[157] *Royer v. Stoody Co.*, 192 F. Supp. 949 (W.D. Okla. 1961), *aff'd*, 374 F.2d 672 (10th Cir. 1967).

[158] National Conference of Commissioners on Uniform State Laws, *Uniform Deceptive Trade Practices Act*, reprinted in 7A Uniform Laws Annotated (St. Paul, Minn.: West Pub. Co., 1978), pp. 35, 65.

trademark. For example, in *Smith* v. *Chanel, Inc.*,[159] the defendant claimed that its perfumes duplicated plaintiff's Chanel No. 5. The Court of Appeals reversed the District Court's award of an injunction that was based solely on the use of the plaintiff's trademark and held that "such advertising may not be enjoined under either the Lanham Act, . . . or the common law of unfair competition, as long as it does not contain misrepresentations or create a reasonable likelihood that purchasers will be confused as to the source, identity, or sponsorship of the advertiser's product."[160] Thus, truthful comparisons using trademarks or trade names are perfectly permissible and serve to advance the consumer interest in learning important characteristics of competing products. However, when falsity is used, those comparisons harm consumers and are actionable under a variety of theories.

CONCLUSION

Advertising is an obviously important component of marketing strategy for many firms. It serves the vital function of communicating information about the firm and its products to potential customers. This information is valuable to potential customers as it reduces search costs and provides other signals about the firm and the attributes of products. The importance of advertising and other communicative promotion to the functioning of our economic system is reflected not only in the tremendous amounts of money spent annually to produce and disseminate advertising, but also in recent decisions of the Supreme Court that protect advertisers against arbitrary governmental actions restricting the right of firms to communicate with the buying public.

But the value of seller-sponsored communications is dependent on the truthfulness and nondeceptiveness of the product messages. The legal restrictions of advertising are designed to minimize the extent of false and misleading representations. This relatively noncontroversial goal is pursued through laws that allow the Federal Trade Commission to prohibit unfair and deceptive advertising and that allow customers and competitors who are injured by false advertising to seek relief through the courts. These laws and legal doctrines present serious risks to firms because of the relative ease with which courts and the FTC can find that an advertisement contains representations that are false, deceptively incomplete, or lacking adequate proof of their truthfulness. Although the law tolerates a fair degree of seller puffing or exaggeration of the value of its products, the privilege to puff is not open ended, and the courts as well as the FTC have considerable latitude to determine that puffing many cause consumers to have false beliefs about a product attribute. Unless the ad makes absolutely no implications whatsoever about any factor that is material

---

[159] *Smith* v. *Chanel, Inc.*, 402 F.2d 562 (9th Cir. 1968).
[160] Ibid., at 563.

to a consumer's purchase decision, there is some risk that the FTC or a court could find the ad deceptive. Such ads, which might feature music, catchy slogans, and happy crowds, might not always be effective as promotion tools when consumers demand more factual advertising. In those circumstances, firms must balance the need to be persuasive against the risk of being found to have overstepped the bounds of truthful advertising.

The FTC's requirement that advertising claims be supported by a "reasonable basis" creates risks that a true claim about a product will nevertheless be condemned because the firm failed to have the required "reasonable basis." This requirement itself is somewhat vague and imprecise, thereby creating additional risks because of uncertainty about the precise legal standard. The FTC seems to be pursuing a policy of demanding higher standards of support for claims that, if false, present health, safety, or large monetary risks to consumers.

The obligation to have support for a product claim can be imposed by the advertiser as well as by the FTC unfairness rule. If an ad represents that a claim is supported by a test, report, or survey, that representation must be true. For example, if an ad makes a representation about the product and then states that the representation "has been *established* by a leading independent laboratory," this claim must be truthful. Claims that the superior efficacy of an over-the-counter drug have been "proven" or "established" must be backed by two well-controlled clinical studies.

The use of certain types of advertising appeals presents a greater risk of violating the law simply because they are subject to extremely detailed and precise requirements. For example, the FTC has established detailed rules for determining the deceptiveness of advertisements that use endorsements and testimonials. Similarly, claims in advertising or on labeling that relate to price reductions or savings discounts have been the subject of detailed FTC rules for determining whether the claims are misleading or deceptive. Ads for certain products are subject to requirements for including specified information in the ad (cigarette advertising must contain a health warning; automobile advertising must disclose the EPA mileage rating if mileage claims are made; and credit advertising must disclose all major credit terms, such as the annual percentage rate, if certain "triggering" information is present in the ad). The compliance problems created by these rules are largely ones of being aware that the advertising is subject to a detailed rule and of making sure that the rule is followed.

Finally, the FTC's unfairness doctrines require that advertising not suggest or encourage activity that might be dangerous. For example, ads using children must not depict the children in activities such as cooking on stoves, using knives, recklessly using toys, picking and eating wild fruit, and the like.

Despite the long-standing position of the law that false and deceptive advertising is harmful to consumers and rightfully can be punished, it is becoming increasingly clear that no simple rules exist to determine when advertising is sufficiently deceptive to be legally condemned. In mass advertising cases, difficult policy questions exist as to what the law should do about ads that are deceptive to some portion of the audience but not deceptive to the remainder. The Supreme Court has not grappled with the many complexities that arise because of its recent extension of first amendment protection to commercial speech. Only as cases resolve these difficult issues will the law against deceptive advertising become less confusing than it now is.

Federal Trade Commission
Policy Planning Protocol
Deceptive and Unsubstantiated Claims

These questions are not cumulative. The answer to less than all of them may indicate the need for action. Moreover, answers to certain of these questions will frequently not be available at all, or may not be available except at considerable cost and delay. Answers to these questions therefore should not be required where obtaining the answers would be unduly burdensome or speculative, or where the answers to other of the questions indicate that the action proposed is a particularly good one, or, of course, where the answers could be obtained only by compulsory process and the action which the Commission is being asked to take is to authorize such process.

A. *Consumer Interpretations of the Claim*

1. List the main interpretations that consumers may place on the claim recommended for challenge, including those that might render the claim true/substantiated as well as those that might render the claim false/unsubstantiated.
2. Indicate which of these interpretations would be alleged to be implications of the claim for purposes of substantiation or litigation. For each interpretation so indicated, state the reasons, if any, for believing that the claim so interpreted would be false/unsubstantiated.

B. *Scale of the Deception or Lack of Substantiation*

3. What is known about the relative proportions of consumers adhering to each of the interpretations listed above in response to Question 1?
4. What was the approximate advertising budget for the claim during the past year or during any other period of time that would reflect the number of consumers actually exposed to the claim? Is there more direct information on the number of consumers exposed to the claim?

C. *Materiality*

5. If consumers do interpret the claim in the ways that would be alleged to be implications, what reasons are there for supposing that these interpretations would influence purchase decisions?
6. During the past year, approximately how many consumers purchased the product* about which the claim was made?
7. Approximately what price did they pay?
8. Estimate, if possible, the proportion of consumers who would have purchased the product only at some price lower than they did pay, if at all,

*Throughout, "product" refers to the particular brand advertised.

412

were they informed that the interpretations identified in response to Question 2 were false.

9. Estimate, if possible, what the advertised product would be worth to the consumers identified by Question 8 if they knew that the product did not have the positive (or unique) attributes suggested by the claim. If the claim can cause consumers to disregard some negative attribute, such as a risk to health and safety, to their possible physical or economic injury, so specify. If so, estimate, if possible, the annual number of such injuries attributable to the claim.

D. *Adequacy of Corrective Market Forces*

10. If the product to which the claim relates is a low ticket item, can consumers ordinarily determine prior to purchase whether the claim, as interpreted, is true or invest a small amount in purchase and then by experience with the product determine whether or not the claim is true? Does the claim relate to a credence quality, that is, a quality of the product that consumers ordinarily cannot evaluate during normal use of the product without acquiring costly information from some source other than their own evaluative faculties?

11. Is the product to which the claim relates one that a consumer would typically purchase frequently? Have product sales increased or decreased substantially since the claim was made?

12. Are there sources of information about the subject matter of the claim in addition to the claim itself? If so, are they likely to be recalled by consumers when they purchase or use the product? Are they likely to be used by consumers who are not aggressive, effective shoppers? If not, why not?

E. *Effect on the Flow of Truthful Information*

13. Will the standard of truth/substantiation that would be applied to the claim under the recommendation to initiate proceedings make it extremely difficult as a practical matter to make the type of claim? Is this result reasonable?

14. What are the consequences to consumers of an erroneous determination by the Commission that the claim is false/unsubstantiated? What are the consequences to consumers of an erroneous determination by the Commission that the claim is true/substantiated?

F. *Deterrence*

15. Is there a possibility of getting significant relief with broad product or claim coverage? What relief is possible? Why would it be significant?

16. Do the facts of the matter recommended present an opportunity to elaborate a rule of law that would be applicable to claims or advertisers other than those that would be directly challenged by the recommended action? If so, describe this rule of law as you would wish the advertising community to understand it. If this rule of law would be a significant precedent, explain why.

17. Does the claim violate a Guide or is it inconsistent with relevant principles embodied in a Guide?

18. Is the fact of a violation so evident to other industry members that, if we do not act, our credibility and deterrence might be adversely affected?

19. Is there any aspect of the advertisement—*e.g.*, the nature of the advertiser, the product, the theme, the volume of the advertising, the memo-

rableness of the ad, the blatancy of the violation — which indicates that an enforcement action would have substantial impact on the advertising community?

20. What, if anything, do we know about the role advertising plays (as against other promotional techniques and other sources of information) in the decision to purchase the product?

21. What is the aggregate dollar volume spent on advertising by the advertiser to be joined in the recommended action?

22. What is the aggregate volume of sales of the advertised product and of products of the same type?

G. *Law Enforcement Efficiency*

23. Has another agency taken action or does another agency have expertise with respect to the claim or its subject matter? Are there reasons why the Commission should defer? What is the position of this other agency? If coordination is planned, what form would it take?

24. How difficult would it be to litigate a case challenging the claim? Would the theory of the proceeding recommended place the Commission in a position of resolving issues that are better left to other modes of resolution, for instance, debate among scientists? If so, explain? Is there a substantial possibility of whole or partial summary judgment?

25. Can the problem seen in the ad be handled by way of a rule? Are the violations widespread? Should they be handled by way of a rule?

H. *Additional Considerations*

26. What is the ratio of the advertiser's advertising expense to sales revenues? How, if at all, is this ratio relevant to the public interest in proceeding as recommended?

27. Does the claim specially affect a vulnerable group?

28. Does the advertising use deception or unfairness to offend important values or to exploit legitimate concerns of a substantial segment of the population, whether or not there is direct injury to person or pocketbook, *e.g.,* minority hiring or environmental protection?

29. Are there additional considerations not elicited by previous questions that would affect the public interest in proceeding?

Case 1
Warner–Lambert Company, *v.* Federal Trade Commission,

United States Court of Appeals
District of Columbia Circuit, 1977

562 F.2d 749

J. SKELLY WRIGHT, Circuit Judge:

The Warner–Lambert Company petitions for review of an order of the Federal Trade Commission requiring it to cease and desist from advertising that its product, Listerine Antiseptic mouthwash, prevents, cures, or alleviates the common cold. The FTC order further requires Warner–Lambert to disclose in future Listerine advertisements that: "Contrary to prior advertising, Listerine will not help prevent colds or sore throats or lessen their severity."[1] We affirm but modify the order to delete from the required disclosure the phrase "Contrary to prior advertising."

I. BACKGROUND

The order under review represents the culmination of a proceeding begun in 1972, when the FTC issued a complaint charging petitioner with violation of Section 5(a)(1) of the Federal Trade Commission Act[2] by misrepresenting the efficacy of Listerine against the common cold.

Listerine has been on the market since 1879. Its formula has never changed. Ever since its introduction it has been represented as being beneficial in certain respects for colds, cold symptoms, and sore throats. Direct advertising to the consumer, including the cold claims as well as others, began in 1921.

Following the 1972 complaint, hearings were held before an administrative law judge (ALJ). The hearings consumed over four months and produced an

---

[1] This requirement terminates when petitioner has expended on Listerine advertising a sum equal to the average annual Listerine advertising budget for the period of April 1962 to March 1972, approximately ten million dollars.

[2] 15 U.S.C. §45(a)(1) (1970). At the time the complaint issued, §5(a)(1) stated that "[u]nfair methods of competition in commerce, and unfair or deceptive acts or practices in commerce, are declared unlawful." This was amended in 1975 to substitute "in or affecting commerce" for the phrase "in commerce." *See* 15 U.S.C. §45(a)(1) (Supp. V 1975).

evidentiary record consisting of approximately 4,000 pages of documentary exhibits and the testimony of 46 witnesses. In 1974 the ALJ issued an initial decision sustaining the allegations of the complaint. Petitioner appealed this decision to the Commission. On December 9, 1975 the Commission issued its decision essentially affirming the ALJ's findings. It concluded that petitioner had made the challenged representations that Listerine will ameliorate, prevent, and cure colds and sore throats, and that these representations were false. Therefore the Commission ordered petitioner to:

> (1) cease and desist from representing that Listerine will cure colds or sore throats, prevent colds or sore throats, or that users of Listerine will have fewer colds than non-users;[3]
> (2) cease and desist from representing that Listerine is a treatment for, or will lessen the severity of, colds or sore throats; that it will have any significant beneficial effect on the symptoms of sore throats or any beneficial effect on symptoms of colds; or that the ability of Listerine to kill germs is of medical significance in the treatment of colds or sore throats or their symptoms;
> (3) cease and desist from disseminating any advertisement for Listerine unless it is clearly and conspicuously disclosed in each such advertisement, in the exact language below, that: "Contrary to prior advertising, Listerine will not help prevent colds or sore throats or lessen their severity." This requirement extends only to the next ten million dollars of Listerine advertising.

Petitioner seeks review of this order. The American Advertising Federation and the Association of National Advertisers have filed briefs as *amici curiae.*

II. SUBSTANTIAL EVIDENCE

The first issue on appeal is whether the Commission's conclusion that Listerine is not beneficial for colds or sore throats is supported by the evidence. The Commission's findings must be sustained if they are supported by substantial evidence on the record viewed as a whole. We conclude that they are.

Both the ALJ and the Commission carefully analyzed the evidence. They gave full consideration to the studies submitted by petitioner. The ultimate conclusion that Listerine is not an effective cold remedy was based on six specific findings of fact.

First, the Commission found that the ingredients of Listerine are not present in sufficient quantities to have any therapeutic effect. This was the testimony of two leading pharmacologists called by Commission counsel. The Commission was justified in concluding that the testimony of Listerine's experts was not sufficiently persuasive to counter this testimony.

Second, the Commission found that in the process of gargling it is impossible for Listerine to reach the critical areas of the body in medically significant concentration. The liquid is confined to the mouth chamber. Such vapors as might reach the nasal passage would not be in therapeutic concentration. Peti-

---

[3] Petitioner does not contest this part of the order on appeal.

tioner did not offer any evidence that vapors reached the affected areas in significant concentration.

Third, the Commission found that even if significant quantities of the active ingredients of Listerine were to reach the critical sites where cold viruses enter and infect the body, they could not interfere with the activities of the virus because they could not penetrate the tissue cells.

Fourth, the Commission discounted the results of a clinical study conducted by petitioner on which petitioner heavily relies. Petitioner contends that in a four-year study schoolchildren who gargled with Listerine had fewer colds and cold symptoms than those who did not gargle with Listerine. The Commission found that the design and execution of the "St. Barnabas study" made its results unreliable. For the first two years of the four-year test no placebo was given to the control group. For the last two years the placebo was inadequate: the control group was given colored water which did not resemble Listerine in smell or taste. There was also evidence that the physician who examined the test subjects was not blinded from knowing which children were using Listerine and which were not, that his evaluation of the cold symptoms of each child each day may have been imprecise, and that he necessarily relied on the non-blinded child's subjective reporting. Both the ALJ and the Commission analyzed the St. Barnabas study and the expert testimony about it in depth and were justified in concluding that its results are unreliable.[4]

Fifth, the Commission found that the ability of Listerine to kill germs by millions on contact is of no medical significance in the treatment of colds or sore throats. Expert testimony showed that bacteria in the oral cavity, the "germs" which Listerine purports to kill, do not cause colds and play no role in cold symptoms. Colds are caused by viruses. Further, "while Listerine kills millions of bacteria in the mouth, it also leaves millions. It is impossible to sterilize any area of the mouth, let alone the entire mouth."

Sixth, the Commission found that Listerine has no significant beneficial effect on the symptoms of sore throat. The Commission recognized that gargling with Listerine could provide temporary relief from a sore throat by removing accumulated debris irritating the throat. But this type of relief can also be obtained by gargling with salt water or even warm water.[5] The Commission found that this is not the significant relief promised by petitioner's advertisements. It was reasonable to conclude that "such temporary relief does not 'lessen the severity' of a sore throat any more than expectorating or blowing one's nose 'lessens the severity' of a cold."

---

[4] People who are given medication for an ailment frequently feel better because they think they should, even though the product has no therapeutic value. This is known as the placebo effect. In order to eliminate the bias of the placebo effect in a clinical study, it is common practice to "blind" the participants, i.e., dispense to the control group a placebo which simulates in taste, smell, and appearance the product being tested. Similarly, to neutralize any subconscious bias of the examiner, it is important to blind him, i.e., prevent him from knowing which subjects received the medication and which did not. A study in which both the subjects and the examiner are blinded is referred to as "double-blind." See JA 914–916.

[5] Petitioner argued that the lower the surface tension of a gargle the greater its ability to remove the irritating debris, and there was evidence that Listerine has a lower surface tension than salt water. However, there was no evidence that this lower surface tension translates into meaningfully greater relief.

In its attack on the Commission's findings, petitioner relies heavily on a recent study of over-the-counter cold remedies by the Food and Drug Administration[6] which petitioner alleges found Listerine "likely to be effective." Its argument is two-pronged: first, that the fact that the Commission's findings differ from the FDA's proves that the Commission's findings are wrong; and second, that it was error for the Commission to refuse to reopen its proceedings when the FDA study was released. We conclude that both of these arguments are without merit for the simple reason that the FDA study does not, to any significant degree, contradict the Commission's findings.

The FDA study is the product of an expert panel appointed in 1972 to study all over-the-counter cold, cough, allergy, bronchodilator, and anti-asthmatic drug products—some 180 ingredients used in as many as 50,000 products. The panel's draft report was issued in February 1976, two months after the FTC issued its order against Listerine. The FTC refused to reopen its proceedings to consider the draft report. In September 1976 the expert panel's report was published, but it has not yet been adopted by the Commissioner of the FDA.[7]

The only evidence pertinent to the effectiveness of Listerine that the FDA panel considered was the St. Barnabas study, and it appears that reference to it was included in the report only as an afterthought.[8] More importantly, the reference which does appear does not endorse or adopt the St. Barnabas study; the FDA report merely describes it and recounts the results.[9] The panel's own conclusions are reflected in the operative language for each ingredient of Listerine:

> There are no well-controlled studies documenting the effectiveness of [eucalyptol/eucalyptus oil, menthol, thymol] as an [antitussive, expectorant, nasal decongestant].

*   *   *   *   *   *

> For use as a mouthwash: Data to demonstrate effectiveness will be required. . . .[10]

Each ingredient of Listerine was placed in Category III, defined as "the available data are insufficient to classify such condition under either [Category I,

---

[6] Petitioner's motion requesting that the court take judicial notice of the FDA study is hereby granted.

[7] 41 Fed.Reg. 38312 (Sept. 9, 1976). The Commissioner stated: "The Commissioner has not yet fully evaluated the report, but has concluded that it should first be issued as a formal proposal to obtain full public comment before any decision is made on the recommendations of the Panel."

[8] The draft report published in February 1976 did not refer to mouthwashes or the St. Barnabas study. After it was issued the panel received a letter, apparently from petitioner, "concerning the fact that no references were made in the report on a submission concerning the use of volatile aromatics in mouthwashes for the symptomatic relief of the common cold." Minutes of the panel's meeting of March 2 and 3, 1976, JA 3045. The panel then voted to add to the sections of the report dealing with menthol, eucalyptol, and thymol (three of Listerine's active ingredients) a paragraph describing the St. Barnabas study. JA 3046.

[9] The effect of rinsing twice daily with an aqueous mixture of volatile substances on the incidence of colds and the severity of the symptoms associated with colds was evaluated in a long-term double-blind, placebo-controlled, subjective study in school children. The results of the study revealed milder nasal symptoms and cough symptoms in individuals using the medicated mouthwash as compared to the placebo. Although the medicated mouthwash contained [eucalyptol, menthol, thymol], the results did not demonstrate the contribution of this component to the overall alleviation of symptoms . . . .

[10] To the extent that the report describes the St. Barnabas study as "double-blind, placebo-controlled," it appears to be in error.

generally recognized as safe and effective] or [Category II, not generally recognized as safe and effective] and for which further testing is therefore required." Petitioner's assertion that this is equivalent to finding the product "likely to be effective" is not supported by the facts.[11]

In sum, the FDA study does not reflect any new data not considered by the FTC. Since the FDA did not consider the extensive record compiled in the FTC proceedings, its conclusion that there is insufficient data about the ingredients of Listerine to justify classifying it as effective or ineffective is not necessarily inconsistent with the FTC's conclusion that Listerine's advertising claims are deceptive. The FTC did not err in refusing to reopen its proceedings to consider the draft FDA study, and the FDA findings do not establish that the FTC's conclusions are wrong.

III. THE COMMISSION'S POWER

Petitioner contends that even if its advertising claims in the past were false, the portion of the Commission's order requiring "corrective advertising" exceeds the Commission's statutory power. The argument is based upon a literal reading of Section 5 of the Federal Trade Commission Act, which authorizes the Commission to issue "cease and desist" orders against violators and does not expressly mention any other remedies.[12] The Commission's position, on the other hand, is that the affirmative disclosure that Listerine will not prevent colds or lessen their severity is absolutely necessary to give effect to the prospective cease and desist order; a hundred years of false cold claims have built up a large reservoir or erroneous consumer belief which would persist, unless corrected, long after petitioner ceased making the claims.

The need for the corrective advertising remedy and its appropriateness in this case are important issues which we will explore *infra*. But the threshold question is whether the Commission has the authority to issue such an order.[13] We hold that it does.

[11] The only place in the FDA report where the phrase "likely to be effective" appears is in the introduction to the report, where the panel outlines its duties. In an apparent reference to Category III, the panel lists as one task:
    Advising the Food and Drug Administration regarding those ingredients which in their judgment are likely to be safe and effective, but for which more data are needed.
41 Fed.Reg. at 38319. Petitioner concludes from this that every ingredient which the panel placed in Category III—including those in Listerine–was found "likely to be effective." This extrapolation is unwarranted. Every other reference to Category III in the report says simply "the available data are insufficient." *See, e.g., id.* at 38312, 38329, 38343, 38359, 38405. Similarly, the notation that data are insufficient is made for each ingredient of Listerine, see note 21, *supra,* while the phrase "likely to be effective" is never used in connection with any of them. We conclude that the panel put in Category III ingredients which were not proven effective or ineffective, in accordance with the mandate of 21 C.F.R.§330.10(a)(5)(iii), and that the phrase "likely to be effective" in the introduction was an aberration.

[12] Section 5(b) provides in pertinent part:
    If upon such hearing the Commission shall be of the opinion that the method of competition or the act or practice in question is prohibited by [this Act], it shall . . . issue . . an order requiring such person, partnership, or corporation to cease and desist from using such method of competition or such act or practice.
15 U.S.C. §45(b) (1970).

[13] For reasons set forth below, we have decided to modify the Commission's order by deleting the phrase "Contrary to prior advertising." All of our discussion of the Commission's power refers to the order as modified.

Petitioner's narrow reading of Section 5 was at one time shared by the Supreme Court. In *FTC* v. *Eastman Kodak Co.* the Court held that the Commission's authority did not exceed that expressly conferred by statute. The Commission has not, the Court said, "been delegated the authority of a court of equity."[14]

But the modern view is very different. In 1963 the Court ruled that the Civil Aeronautics Board has authority to order divestiture in addition to ordering cessation of unfair methods of competition by air carriers.[15] The CAB statute, like Section 5, spoke only of the authority to issue cease and desist orders, but the Court said, "We do not read the Act so restrictively. . . . [W]here the problem lies within the purview of the Board, . . . Congress must have intended to give it authority that was ample to deal with the evil at hand." The Court continued, "Authority to mold administrative decrees is indeed like the authority of courts to frame injunctive decrees. . . . [The] power to order divestiture need not be explicitly included in the powers of an administrative agency to be part of its arsenal of authority. . . ."

Later, in *FTC* v. *Dean Foods Co.*, the Court applied *Pan American* to the Federal Trade Commission.[16] In upholding the Commission's power to seek a preliminary injunction against a proposed merger, the Court held that it was not necessary to find express statutory authority for the power. Rather, the Court concluded, "It would stultify congressional purpose to say that the Commission did not have the . . . power. . . . Such ancillary powers have always been treated as essential to the effective discharge of the Commission's responsibilities."

Thus it is clear that the Commission has the power to shape remedies which go beyond the simple cease and desist order. Our next inquiry must be whether a corrective advertising order is for any reason outside the range of permissible remedies. Petitioner and *amici curiae* argue that it is because (1) legislative history precludes it, (2) it impinges on the First Amendment, and (3) it has never been approved by any court.

A. Legislative History

Petitioner relies on the legislative history of the 1914 Federal Trade Commission Act and the Wheeler–Lea amendments to it in 1938[17] for the proposition that corrective advertising was not contemplated. In 1914 and in 1938 Congress chose not to authorize such remedies as criminal penalties, treble

---

[14] 274 U.S. 619, 623, 47 S.Ct. 688, 689, 71 L.Ed. 1238 (1927) (setting aside order requiring Kodak to divest itself of three laboratories as part of unfair competition remedy).

[15] *Pan American World Airways, Inc.* v. *United States,* 371 U.S. 296, 83 S.Ct. 476, 9 L.Ed.2d 325 (1963).

[16] 384 U.S. 597, 86 S.Ct. 1738, 16 L.Ed.2d 802 (1966). The Court also noted that *Eastman Kodak* had been "repudiated" in *Pan American Id.* at 606 n.4, 86 S.Ct. 1738.

[17] It is true that one Court of Appeals has relied on this history in concluding that the Commission does not have power to order restitution of ill-gotten monies to the injured consumers. *Heater* v. *FTC,* 503 F.2d 321 (9th Cir. 1974). But restitution is not corrective advertising. Ordering refunds to *past* consumers is very different from ordering affirmative disclosure to correct misconceptions which *future* consumers may hold. Moreover, the *Heater* court itself recognized this distinction and expressly distinguished corrective advertising, which it said the Commission is authorized to order, from restitution. 503 F.2d at 323 n.7 and 325 n.13.

damages, or civil penalties, but that fact does not dispose of the question of corrective advertising.

Petitioner's reliance on the legislative history of the 1975 amendments to the Act[18] is also misplaced. The amendments added a new Section 19 to the Act authorizing the Commission to bring suits in federal District Courts to redress injury to consumers resulting from a deceptive practice. The section authorizes the court to grant such relief as it "finds necessary to redress injury to consumers or other persons, partnerships, and corporations resulting from the rule violation or the unfair or deceptive act or practice," including, but not limited to,

> rescission or reformation of contracts, the refund of money or return of property, the payment of damages, and public notification respecting the rule violation or the unfair or deceptive act or practice. . . .[19]

Petitioner and *amici* contend that this congressional grant *to a court* of power to order public notification of a violation establishes that the Commission by itself does not have that power.

We note first that "public notification" is not synonymous with corrective advertising; public notification is a much broader term and may take any one of many forms.[20] Second, the "public notification" contemplated by the amendment is directed at *past* consumers of the product ("to redress injury"), whereas the type of corrective advertising currently before us is directed at *future* consumers. Third, petitioner's construction of the section runs directly contrary to the congressional intent as expressed in a later subsection: "Nothing in this section shall be construed to affect any authority of the Commission under any other provision of law." Moreover, this intent is amplified by the conference committee's report:

> The section . . is not intended to modify or limit any existing power the Commission may have to itself issue orders designed to remedying [*sic*] violations of the law. That issue is now before the courts. It is not the intent of the Conferees to influence the outcome in any way.

We conclude that this legislative history cannot be said to remove corrective advertising from the class of permissible remedies.

B. The First Amendment

Petitioner and *amici* further contend that corrective advertising is not a permissible remedy because it trenches on the First Amendment. Petitioner is correct that this triggers a special responsibility on the Commission to order

---

[18] The Magnuson–Moss Warranty — Federal Trade Commission Improvement Act. 88 Stat. 2183 (1975).

[19] 15 U.S.C. §57b(b) (Supp. V 1975).

[20] For example, it might encompass requiring the defendant to run special advertisements reporting the FTC finding, advertisements advising consumers of the availability of a refund, or the posting of notices in the defendant's place of business.

corrective advertising only if the restriction inherent in its order is no greater than necessary to serve the interest involved. But this goes to the appropriateness of the order in this case, an issue we reach in Part IV of this opinion. *Amici curiae* go further, arguing that, since the Supreme Court has recently extended First Amendment protection to commercial advertising,[21] mandatory corrective advertising is unconstitutional.

A careful reading of *Virginia State Board of Pharmacy* v. *Virginia Citizens Consumer Council* compels rejection of this argument. For the Supreme Court expressly noted that the First Amendment presents "no obstacle" to government regulation of false or misleading advertising. The First Amendment, the Court said,

> as we construe it today, does not prohibit the State from insuring that the stream of commercial information flow[s] cleanly as well as freely.

In a footnote the Court went on to delineate several differences between commercial speech and other forms which may suggest "that a different degree of protection is necessary. . . ." For example, the Court said, they may

> make it appropriate to require that a commercial message appear in such a form, or include such additional information, warnings, and disclaimers, as are necessary to prevent its being deceptive.

The Supreme Court clearly foresaw the very question before us, and its statement is dispositive of *amici's* contention.

C. Precedents

According to petitioner, "The first reference to corrective advertising in Commission decisions occurred in 1970, nearly fifty years and untold numbers of false advertising cases after passage of the Act." In petitioner's view, the late emergence of this "newly discovered" remedy is itself evidence that it is beyond the Commission's authority. This argument fails on two counts. First the fact that an agency has not asserted a power over a period of years is not proof that the agency lacks such power. Second, and more importantly, we are not convinced that the corrective advertising remedy is really such an innovation. The label may be newly coined, but the concept is well established. It is simply that under certain circumstances an advertiser may be required to make affirmative disclosure of unfavorable facts.

One such circumstance is when an advertisement that did not contain the disclosure would be misleading. For example, the Commission has ordered the sellers of treatments for baldness to disclose that the vast majority of cases of thinning hair and baldness are attributable to heredity, age, and endocrine balance (so-called "male pattern baldness") and that their treatment would have

---

[21] *Virginia State Board of Pharmacy* v. *Virginia Citizens Consumer Council, Inc.,* 425 U.S. 748, 96 S.Ct. 1817, 48 L.Ed.2d 346 (1976); *Bigelow* v. *Virginia,* 421 U.S. 809, 95 S.Ct. 2222, 44 L.Ed.2d 600 (1975).

no effect whatever on this type of baldness.[22] It has ordered the promoters of a device for stopping bedwetting to disclose that the device would not be of value in cases caused by organic defects or diseases.[23] And it has ordered the makers of Geritol, an iron supplement, to disclose that Geritol will relieve symptoms of tiredness only in persons who suffer from iron deficiency anemia, and that the vast majority of people who experience such symptoms do not have such a deficiency.[24]

Each of these orders was approved on appeal over objections that it exceeded the Commission's statutory authority.[25] The decisions reflect a recognition that, as the Supreme Court has stated,

> If the Commission is to attain the objectives Congress envisioned, it cannot be required to confine its road block to the narrow lane the transgressor has traveled; it must be allowed effectively to close all roads to the prohibited goal, so that its order may not be by-passed with impunity.

Affirmative disclosure has also been required when an advertisement, although not misleading if taken alone, becomes misleading considered in light of past advertisements. For example, for 60 years Royal Baking Powder Company had stressed in its advertising that its product was superior because it was made with cream of tartar, not phosphate. But, faced with rising costs of cream of tartar, the time came when it changed its ingredients and became a phosphate baking powder. It carefully removed from all labels and advertisements any reference to cream of tartar and corrected the list of ingredients. But the new labels used the familiar arrangement of lettering, coloration, and design, so that they looked exactly like the old ones. A new advertising campaign stressed the new low cost of the product and dropped all reference to cream of tartar. But the advertisements were also silent on the subject of phosphate and did not disclose the change in the product.

The Commission held, and the Second Circuit agreed, that the new advertisements were deceptive, since they did not advise consumers that their reasons for buying the powder in the past no longer applied. The court held that

[22] *Ward Laboratories Inc.* v. *FTC,* 276 F.2d 952 (2d Cir.), *cert. denied,* 364 U.S. 827, 81 S.Ct. 65, 5 L.Ed.2d 55 (1960); *Keele Hair & Scalp Specialists, Inc.* v. *FTC,* 275 F.2d 18 (5th Cir. 1960).

[23] *Feil* v. *FTC,* 285 F.2d 879 (9th Cir. 1960).

[24] *J. B. Williams Co.* v. *FTC,* 381 F.2d 884 (6th Cir. 1967). *Compare Alberty* v. *FTC,* 86 U.S. App.D.C. 238, 182 F.2d 36, *cert. denied,* 340 U.S. 818, 71 S.Ct. 49, 95 L.Ed. 601 (1950), discussed in note 25 *infra.*

[25] In *Alberty* v. *FTC, supra* note 24, this court set aside an order similar to the one upheld in *J. B. Williams Co.* v. *FTC, supra* note 24. The precise holding of *Alberty* is disputed. Several courts have stated that it held only that the Commission must make an express finding that failure to make disclosure is misleading before it can require such disclosure. *Feil* v. *FTC, supra* note 23; *Ward Laboratories, Inc.* v. *FTC, supra* note 22; *Keele Hair & Scalp Specialists, Inc.* v. *FTC, supra* note 22. To the extent that Alberty may have held that the Commission lacked power to order corrective advertising, it has never been followed. The characterization of the required disclosure as "additional interesting, and perhaps useful, information" may or may not have been accurate in *Alberty,* but it grossly understates the case at hand. The disclosure that Listerine does not relieve colds is essential information to correct a widely held, mistaken belief which was cultivated by petitioner's past advertising.

FTC v. *Simeon Management Corp.,* 532 F.2d 708 (9th Cir. 1976), is readily distinguishable on this ground. There an order requiring affirmative disclosure was set aside because there was no evidence that consumers seeing the advertisements formed an incorrect belief or were misled. In short, there was nothing to correct. That is not this case.

it was proper to require the company to take affirmative steps to advise the public.[26] To continue to sell the new powder

> on the strength of the reputation attained through 60 years of its manufacture and sale and wide advertising of its superior powder, under an impression induced by its advertisements that the product purchased was the same in kind and as superior as that which had been so long manufactured by it, was unfair alike to the public and to the competitors in the baking powder business.[27]

In another case[28] the Waltham Watch Company of Massachusetts had become renowned for the manufacture of fine clocks since 1849. Soon after it stopped manufacturing clocks in the 1950's, it transferred its trademarks, good will, and the trade name "Waltham" to a successor corporation, which began importing clocks from Europe for resale in the United States. The imported clocks were advertised as "product of Waltham Watch Company since 1850," "a famous 150-year-old company."

The Commission found that the advertisements caused consumers to believe they were buying the same fine Massachusetts clocks of which they had heard for many years. To correct this impression the Commission ordered the company to disclose in all advertisements and on the product that the clock was not made by the old Waltham company and that it was imported. The Seventh Circuit affirmed, relying on "the well-established general principle that the Commission may require affirmative disclosure for the purpose of preventing future deception."[29]

It appears to us that the orders in *Royal* and *Waltham* were the same kind of remedy the Commission has ordered here. Like Royal and Waltham, Listerine has built up over a period of many years a widespread reputation. When it was ascertained that that reputation no longer applied to the product, it was necessary to take action to correct it.[30] Here, as in *Royal* and *Waltham,* it is the accumulated impact of *past* advertising that necessitates disclosure in

---

[26] The order required Royal to cease using any label which simulated the old familiar label, to incorporate the word "phosphate" as part of the name of the product on all labels and in all advertisements, to cease from representing that the old product had been reduced in price, and to cease from representing that the new product was the baking powder sold by Royal for many years.

[27] *Royal Baking Powder Co.* v. *FTC,* 281 F. 744, 753 (2d Cir. 1922).

[28] *Waltham Watch Co.* v. *FTC,* 318 F.2d 28 (7th Cir.), *cert. denied,* 375 U.S. 944, 84 S.Ct. 349, 11 L.Ed.2d 274 (1963). *See also Waltham Precision Instrument Co.* v. *FTC,* 327 F.2d 427 (7th Cir.), *cert. denied,* 377 U.S. 992, 84 S.Ct. 1918, 12 L.Ed.2d 1045 (1964).

[29] 318 F.2d at 32. *Accord, Ward Laboratories, Inc.* v. *FTC, supra* note 22. The dissent incorrectly states that the Royal and Waltham ads and labels were false on their face (just as selling moonshine in Haig & Haig bottles would be) and that the courts simply ordered the misrepresentations removed. To the contrary, the Royal and Waltham ads and labels were strictly truthful, but they *became* misleading when considered in light of past advertisements. *See* 281 F. at 748–749 and 318 F.2d at 30–31.

[30] In *Royal* and *Waltham* the advertising claims that had given rise to the products' reputations were concededly true when made, but because the products themselves had changed that reputation was no longer deserved. Consumers would have been deceived, in the future, if they had continued to make purchases in reliance upon this reputation. Here, of course, the Commission has determined that Listerine's cold claims were *never* true, and that its reputation as a cold remedy was thus never deserved. What has changed in this case is not the product itself, but the extent of our knowledge of the evidence underlying the advertising claims. But the result here is the same as in the earlier cases—like Royal baking powder or Waltham watches, Listerine continues to enjoy a reputation it does not deserve, and consumers would therefore be deceived if they were to make purchases in reliance upon that reputation.

future advertising.[31] To allow consumers to continue to buy the product on the strength of the impression built up by prior advertising—an impression which is now known to be false—would be unfair and deceptive.[32]

IV. THE REMEDY

Having established that the Commission does have the power to order corrective advertising in appropriate cases, it remains to consider whether use of the remedy against Listerine is warranted and equitable. We have concluded that part 3 of the order should be modified to delete the phrase "Contrary to prior advertising."[33] With that modification, we approve the order.

Our role in reviewing the remedy is limited. The Supreme Court has set forth the standard:

[31] We thus find unpersuasive petitioner's contention that the corrective advertising ordered here is unprecedented in that it seeks "to eliminate perceived future effects of past violations that are wholly unrelated to future conduct . . . ." Petitioner's br. at 26. We agree with the Commission that the "common thread" linking earlier corrective advertising cases extends to the present case as well. *See* JA 894.

The distinctions petitioner seeks to draw between the present case and earlier corrective advertising cases are essentially semantic. It argues that, unlike *Royal, Waltham,* and similar cases, here the Commission made no specific finding that even truthful future Listerine ads would themselves be deceptive without a corrective statement. Petitioner's br. at 38. Similarly, while petitioner appears to concede that continued *sales* of a product under false pretenses may constitute violation of the FTC Act justifying imposition of corrective advertising, it argues that the Commission offered no evidence to support a finding of such a violation here. Petitioner's br. at 26. It seems clear to us that these various different "theories" are in fact simply different ways of describing the same thing. The nature of the violation, and the nature of the remedy required, are no different whether one says that future truthful *ads* will be "deceptive" when viewed against the backdrop of earlier advertising, or that future *sales* to customers who have been misled by earlier advertising will constitute the deceptive practice, or, as the Commission said here, that "there is clear and continuing injury to competition and to the consuming public as consumers continue to make purchasing decisions based on the false belief [that arose from prior deceptive advertisements]." JA 894. The Commission's authority to impose corrective advertising obviously should not turn upon the particular verbal formula chosen in a particular case.

[32] There is also precedent in other contexts for Commission action to dissipate future effects of a company's past wrongful conduct. In *American Cyanamid Co.* v. *FTC,* 363 F.2d 757 (6th Cir. 1966), *after remand,* 401 F.2d 574 (6th Cir. 1968), *cert. denied,* 394 U.S. 920, 89 S.Ct. 1195, 22 L.Ed.2d 453 (1969), the court approved an order requiring the petitioner to grant patent licenses where he had obtained the patent by illegal conduct. The court said his retention of the fruits of his unlawful conduct would itself be an unfair practice and the Commission had the power to prevent it.

In *Lorain Journal Co.* v. *United States,* 342 U.S. 143, 72 S.Ct. 181, 96 L.Ed. 162 (1951), the Supreme Court affirmed a judgment that a newspaper publisher, in an effort to destroy a competing radio station, had unlawfully refused to accept advertising from anyone who advertised on the radio station. The Court approved a District Court order requiring the newspaper to publish each week for 25 weeks a conspicuous notice apprising the public of the terms of the judgment. The order was necessary to prevent the newspaper from continuing to reap the benefits of its wrongful conduct.

While we do not know and do not decide whether our petitioner made its false cold claims in good faith or bad, we do observe that for an advertiser who knowingly advertises falsely a simple cease and desist order provides no real deterrent. He has nothing to lose but attorneys' fees. He gets to use the deceptive advertisements until he is caught—more precisely, until Commission proceedings, which usually drag on for years, are completed against him. By the time the order has become final, the particular campaign has probably been squeezed dry, if not already discarded. In the meantime the seller has increased his market share and reaped handsome profits. The order to cease making the false claims takes none of this away from him. In short, "[a]cease and desist order which commands the respondent only to 'go, and sin no more' simply allows every violator a free bite at the apple." Note, *"Corrective Advertising" Orders of the Federal Trade Commission,* 85 Harv.L.Rev. 477, 482–483 (1971). *See also* Pitofsky, *Beyond Nader: Consumer Protection and the Regulation of Advertising,* 90 Harv.L.Rev. 661, 693–694 (1977); Note, *Corrective Advertising and the FTC: No, Virginia, Wonder Bread Doesn't Build Strong Bodies Twelve Ways,* 70 Mich.L.Rev. 374 (1971).

[33] The Federal Trade Commission Act gives the reviewing court the power to "enter a decree affirming, modifying, or setting aside the order of the Commission . . . ." 15 U.S.C. §45(c) (1970).

The Commission is the expert body to determine what remedy is necessary to eliminate the unfair or deceptive trade practices which have been disclosed. It has wide latitude for judgment and the courts will not interfere except where the remedy selected has no reasonable relation to the unlawful practices found to exist.[34]

The Commission has adopted the following standard for the imposition of corrective advertising:

[I]f a deceptive advertisement has played a substantial role in creating or reinforcing in the public's mind a false and material belief which lives on after the false advertising ceases, there is clear and continuing injury to competition and to the consuming public as consumers continue to make purchasing decisions based on the false belief. Since this injury cannot be averted by merely requiring respondent to cease disseminating the advertisement, we may appropriately order respondent to take affirmative action designed to terminate the otherwise continuing ill effects of the advertisement.

We think this standard is entirely reasonable. It dictates two factual inquiries: (1) did Listerine's advertisements play a substantial role in creating or reinforcing in the public's mind a false belief about the product? and (2) would this belief linger on after the false advertising ceases? It strikes us that if the answer to both questions is not yes, companies everywhere may be wasting their massive advertising budgets. Indeed, it is more than a little peculiar to hear petitioner assert that its commercials really have no effect on consumer belief.

For these reasons it might be appropriate in some cases to presume the existence of the two factual predicates for corrective advertising. But we need not decide that question, or rely on presumptions here, because the Commission adduced survey evidence to support both propositions. We find that the "Product Q" survey data and the expert testimony interpreting them[35] constitute substantial evidence in support of the need for corrective advertising in this case.

We turn next to the specific disclosure required: "Contrary to prior advertising, Listerine will not help prevent colds or sore throats or lessen their severity." Petitioner is ordered to include this statement in every future advertisement for Listerine for a defined period. In printed advertisements it

---

[34] *Jacob Siegel Co.* v. *FTC,* 327 U.S. 608, 612–613, 66 S.Ct. 758, 760, 90 L.Ed. 888 (1946).

[35] The Commission used the results of a series of market surveys known as "Product Q" reports on the "Mouthwash Market." The surveys were conducted by petitioner for its own purposes from 1963 to 1971. According to petitioner's own advertising agency, "Product Q is ideally suited to provide guidance in such vital areas as . . . [h]ow successful are the current advertising campaigns of different brands on awareness, recall, attitudes and sales?" JA 2785–2786. The surveys showed that about 70% of the consumers questioned recalled "effective for colds and sore throats" as a main theme of Listerine advertising. During the summer, when no cold claims had been broadcast for about six months, the percentge fell to only 64%; *i.e.,* the recall of cold claims after six months of silence was very substantial. The surveys also showed that about 60% of consumers questioned believed Listerine was "one of the best" mouthwashes for the quality "effective against colds and sore throats." JA 568–580.

The Commission also relied on the testimony of two experts in the field of consumer marketing surveys. Dr. Bass testified that cold efficacy belief levels would continue at about 60% for two years after colds advertising ceased and would remain high after five years. JA 1591–1592, 1617. Dr. Rossi testified that cold efficacy beliefs would decline at no greater a rate than 5% per year. JA 1522, 1556–1559.

must be displayed in type size at least as large as that in which the principal portion of the text of the advertisement appears and it must be separated from the text so that it can be readily noticed. In television commercials the disclosure must be presented simultaneously in both audio and visual portions. During the audio portion of the disclosure in television and radio advertisements, no other sounds, including music, may occur.

These specifications are well calculated to assure that the disclosure will reach the public. It will necessarily attract the notice of readers, viewers, and listeners, and be plainly conveyed. Given these safeguards, we believe the preamble "Contrary to prior advertising" is not necessary. It can serve only two purposes: either to attract attention that a correction follows or to humiliate the advertiser. The Commission claims only the first purpose for it, and this we think is obviated by the other terms of the order. The second purpose, if it were intended, might be called for in an egregious case of deliberate deception, but this is not one. While we do not decide whether petitioner proffered its cold claims in good faith or bad, the record compiled could support a finding of good faith.[36] On these facts, the confessional preamble to the disclosure is not warranted.

Finally, petitioner challenges the duration of the disclosure requirement. By its terms it continues until respondent has expended on Listerine advertising a sum equal to the average annual Listerine advertising budget for the period April 1962 to March 1972. That is approximately ten million dollars. Thus if petitioner continues to advertise normally the corrective advertising will be required for about one year. We cannot say that is an unreasonably long time in which to correct a hundred years of cold claims. But, to petitioner's distress, the requirement will not expire by mere passage of time. If petitioner cuts back its Listerine advertising, or ceases it altogether, it can only postpone the duty to disclose.[37] The Commission concluded that correction was required and that a duration of a fixed period of time might not accomplish that task, since petitioner could evade the order by choosing not to advertise at all. The formula settled upon by the Commission is reasonably related to the violation it found.

Accordingly, the order, as modified, is *Affirmed.*

[36] Petitioner strenuously urges its good faith and offers in support thereof its reliance on the St. Barnabas study which allegedly supported Listerine's claims, and on previous "acquittals" by the Commission. The Commission reviewed Listerine's cold claims in 1932, 1940, 1951, 1958, and 1962, and took no action against them. JA 2738–2740.

While good faith may be relevant to the fairness of a confessional preamble, it is irrelevant to the need for corrective advertising in general. Innocence of motive is not a defense if an advertisement is prejudicial to the public interest. As the Supreme Court stated in *FTC* v. *Algoma Lumber Co.,* 291 U.S. 67, 81, 54 S.Ct. 315, 321, 78 L.Ed. 655 (1934):

Indeed there is a kind of fraud . . . in clinging to a benefit which is the product of misrepresentation, however innocently made. . . . That is the respondents' plight today, no matter what their motives may have been when they began. They must extricate themselves from it by purging their business methods of a capacity to deceive.

(Citations omitted.)

[37] The ALJ had set the duration of the requirement at two years, but conceded that "[o]ne variable that will have an effect upon what is accomplished is the amount of Listerine advertising respondent may see fit to engage in." JA 585. The Commission's formula takes that variable into account.

SUPPLEMENTAL OPINION ON PETITION
FOR REHEARING

In its petition for rehearing petitioner has urged this court to reconsider its earlier decision affirming, with some modifications, the order of the Federal Trade Commission requiring Warner–Lambert Company to cease and desist from deceptively advertising its product Listerine as a cure for colds or sore throat and affirmatively to correct in its future advertisements the impression created by its prior deceptive advertising. The primary argument raised in the petition for rehearing is that the Commission is barred by the First Amendment from imposing a corrective advertising order in this case. Having considered this claim carefully, it is our conclusion that it must be rejected. Because of the importance of the issues raised, however, we think it desirable to set forth in some detail our reasons for so concluding.

I

In *Virginia State Board of Pharmacy* v. *Virginia Citizens Consumer Council, Inc.,* the Supreme Court rejected prior precedents holding that commercial speech is "wholly outside the protection of the First Amendment." In reaching this conclusion the Court emphasized the interest of consumers in the free flow of truthful information necessary for formulation of intelligent opinions and proper resource allocation. Consistent with this concern, the Court was careful to distinguish truthful commercial speech from that which is false, misleading, or deceptive: "Untruthful speech, commercial or otherwise, has never been protected for its own sake. . . . Obviously, much commercial speech is not provably false, or even wholly false, but only deceptive or misleading. We foresee no obstacle to a State's dealing effectively with this problem." Furthermore, the Court went on to suggest that, because of the "commonsense differences" between commercial speech and other varieties, even commercial speech subject to First Amendment protections may nonetheless enjoy a "different degree of protection" than that normally accorded under the First Amendment.

Applying these principles to the case at bar, there can be no question of the legitimacy of the FTC's role in regulating and preventing false and deceptive advertising. In this case it has been found that Warner–Lambert has, over a long period of time, worked a substantial deception upon the public; it has advertised Listerine as a cure for colds, and consumers have purchased its product with that in mind. That the Commission has authority to prohibit Warner –Lambert from continuing to make such false and deceptive claims in its advertisements is not disputed, for it is only truthful claims which are protected under the First Amendment.[38] Here, however, the FTC has determined on

---

[38] Cease and desist orders aimed at false or deceptive speech may, in theory, have a chilling effect on truthful speech, and be subject to First Amendment scrutiny on that account. In practice, however, this should rarely if ever be necessary. *See* Part II *infra.*

substantial evidence that the deception of the public occasioned by Warner–Lambert's past advertisements will not be halted by merely requiring Warner–Lambert to cease making such claims in the future. To be sure, current and future advertising of Listerine, when viewed in isolation, may not contain any statements which are themselves false or deceptive. But reality counsels that such advertisements cannot be viewed in isolation; they must be seen against the background of over 50 years in which Listerine has been proclaimed—and purchased—as a remedy for colds. When viewed from this perspective, advertising which fails to rebut the prior claims as to Listerine's efficacy inevitably builds upon those claims; continued advertising continues the deception, albeit implicitly rather than explicitly.[39] It will induce people to continue to buy Listerine thinking it will cure colds. Thus the Commission found on substantial evidence that the corrective order was necessary to "dissipate the effects of respondent's deceptive representations."

Under this reasoning the First Amendment presents no direct obstacle. The Commission is not regulating truthful speech protected by the First Amendment, but is merely requiring certain statements which, if not present in current and future advertisements, would render those advertisements themselves part of a continuing deception of the public. As the Supreme Court recognized in *Virginia State Board,* in some cases it may be "appropriate to require that a commercial message appear in such a form, or include such additional information, warnings, and disclaimers, as are necessary to prevent its being deceptive." We must conclude—as did the Commission—that this is such a case.

II

Admittedly, corrective advertising orders such as that imposed here may give rise to concern as to their chilling effect on protected truthful speech. The potential advertiser must consider not only the possibility that he will be forced, at some future date, to abandon his advertising campaign, but also that he may be required to include specific disclaimers in future advertisements. But this danger seems more theoretical than real. As the Supreme Court pointed out in *Virginia State Board,* not only is the truth of commercial speech "more easily verifiable by its disseminator" than other forms of speech, but "[s]ince advertising is the *sine qua non* of commercial profits, there is little likelihood of its being chilled by proper regulation and forgone entirely."

Moreover, whatever incremental chill is caused by a corrective advertising order beyond that which would result from a cease and desist order may well be necessary if the interest of consumers in truthful information is to be served at all. Otherwise, advertisers remain free to misrepresent their products to the public through false and deceptive claims, knowing full well that even if the FTC chooses to prosecute they will be required only to cease an advertising

[39] In this connection it is worth noting that Warner–Lambert currently advertises Listerine's ability to kill germs that cause bad breath. While we have no reason to doubt the truth of this claim, the emphasis on Listerine's germ-killing ability does seem to tie in closely with prior false advertising as to its capacity to alleviate health problems.

campaign which by that point will, in all likelihood, have served its purpose by deceiving the public and already been replaced.

III

A more serious First Amendment problem which may be raised by corrective advertising orders involves the burden thereby imposed upon the constitutional right recognized in *Virginia State Board* to advertise truthfully: the party subject to a corrective advertising order may be precluded from exercising his right to advertise unless he also includes specified statements undermining his prior deceptive claims. On the facts of this case, no burden is imposed upon truthful, protected advertising since, as the Commission makes clear, Listerine's current advertising, if not accompanied by a corrective message, would itself continue to mislead the public. Even if, in the circumstances of this case, the current and future advertising of Listerine is considered constitutionally protected speech, however, we think the corrective advertising order in this case remains appropriate.

The Supreme Court, in invalidating the state ban on advertising of prescription drug prices in *Virginia State Board,* considered the scope of the restriction on First Amendment rights, the governmental purposes and public interests affected by the ban, and the availability of alternative means to accomplish the legitimate governmental objectives. As we have indicated, it is not at all clear, even after *Virginia State Board,* that commercial speech protected by the First Amendment is, apart from "commonsense differences," entitled to the same degree of protection as other forms. Indeed, the opposite conclusion seems the more appropriate one. But in any event, it does seem clear that the corrective advertising order in this case is the least restrictive means of achieving a substantial and important governmental objective and that, on balance, it must be upheld. The governmental interest here, of course, is in protecting citizens against deception—with its attendant waste and misallocation by consumers to the benefit of the wrongdoers—by ensuring that advertising conveys truthful information to the public. As we noted earlier, it is this very interest which was invoked by the *Virginia State Board* Court as support for its conclusion that commercial speech is protected by the First Amendment.

And the facts of this case make it eminently clear that this interest will not be substantially served by the less restrictive remedy—a cease and desist order. Whatever one may conclude as to the effect of Warner–Lambert's long history of deception on the protected status of its current advertising, we see no basis—and none has been offered—for questioning the Commission's conclusion that, absent a corrective remedy, consumers will continue to purchase Listerine as a cure of colds. Indeed, at least one advocate of corrective advertising has urged that such orders not be confined to obvious cases such as *Warner–Lambert* where the proof presented to the Commission of the success of a deceptive campaign is so striking. Noting the long history of a deceptive claim uniquely asserted for Listerine, the absence of consumer confusion as to which mouthwash was effective against colds, and the persuasive evidence that this claim was believed by consumers after the false advertising had ceased, Professor Pitofsky has argued that "[c]omparable proof of deception-perception-memory influence would be virtually impossible in most advertising cases. . . . If the Commission is to do an effective job in regulating deceptive advertising, corrective advertising must apply to more than the one-in-a-million type of ad campaign present in *Warner–Lambert.*" See Pitofsky, *supra,* 90 Harv.L.Rev. at 698.

Finally, the corrective advertising order in this case, by tying the quantity of correction required to the investment in deception, is tailored to serve the legitimate governmental interest in correcting public misimpressions as to the value of Listerine—and no more.[40] Taking all these factors into account, we think it beyond doubt that the FTC order is a valid one.

Petition for rehearing denied.

---

[40] As the Commission itself noted, it may well be impossible to "determine in advance with computer-like precision the minimum amount of corrective advertising which will dispel the otherwise continuing beliefs at issue." Even so, considering the 50 years of deceptive Listerine advertising, continuing inflation with attendant increased advertising costs leaves no doubt that the Commission is requiring a significantly smaller quantity of corrective advertising than prior deceptive advertising. As a result, any imprecision in the order's scope would seem likely to inure to Warner–Lambert's benefit.

Case 2
American Home Products Corp. *v.* Johnson & Johnson

United States Court of Appeals
Second Circuit, 1978

577 F.2d 160

Before LUMBARD and OAKES, Circuit Judges, and WYZANSKI, District
Judge.*

OAKES, Circuit Judge:

Comparative advertising in which the competing product is explicitly
named is a relatively new weapon in the Madison Avenue arsenal.[1] These
cross-appeals by two of the leading manufacturers of analgesics—pain relief
tablets—raise questions regarding the permissible boundaries of this novel approach to consumer persuasion. The parties appeal from an order of the United States District Court for the Southern District of New York, Charles E.
Stewart, *Judge,* enjoining the use in television and printed advertising of certain product superiority claims of "Anacin" over "Tylenol." *American Home
Products Corp.* v. *Johnson & Johnson,* 436 F.Supp. 785 (S.D.N.Y.1977). The
order was issued in an action for a declaratory judgment initiated by appellant
American Home Products Corp. (AHP), the manufacturer of Anacin, against
McNeil Laboratories, Inc., the manufacturer of Tylenol, and its parent corporation, Johnson & Johnson (collectively McNeil), seeking a ruling that the advertising is not false. McNeil counterclaimed, alleging, *inter alia,* that the
advertisments were false and misleading under Section 43(a) of the Lanham
Act, 15 U.S.C. §1125(a). The district court found that the advertising violated
Section 43(a), and accordingly the judgment enjoined AHP from representing
that Anacin provides superior analgesia to Tylenol "in the context of a representation as to any anti-inflammatory property of Anacin. . . ."

AHP argues on appeal that (1) even on the basis of the district court's findings, there is no ground for relief under Section 43(a); (2) the findings are
clearly erroneous in concluding that (a) the Anacin advertising claims greater

---

* Of the District of Massachusetts, sitting by designation.

[1] Note. *The Law of Comparative Advertising: How Much Worse is "Better" Than "Great,"* 76 Colum.L.Rev.
80, 80 (1976).

·pain relief (Claims One and Two); (b) the disputed claim of superiority in reducing pain from inflammatory conditions (Claim Two) is false; and (c) the anti-inflammatory claim for the conditions listed in the advertising (Claim Three) is unsubstantiated; and (3) the terms of the injunction are too indefinite to comply with Fed.R.Civ.P. 65(d).[2] McNeil appeals from the district court's refusal to enjoin those portions of the Anacin advertising which, McNeil asserts, present misleading claims of Anacin's faster onset of analgesia and harmlessness to the stomach. Since we are of the view that Judge Stewart's order is based upon sound legal principles, that his findings are not clearly erroneous, and that the injunction as framed is proper in scope and specificity, we affirm.

I. THE FACTS

AHP's product, Anacin, is a compound of aspirin (ASA), its analgesic component, and caffeine. McNeil's product, Tylenol, affords analgesia through the ingredient acetaminophen (APAP). Anacin advertises more heavily than the other leading aspirin brands. It took over the Number One pain reliever spot from another aspirin-based product, Bayer Aspirin, a few years ago. Since the summer of 1976, however, Tylenol has replaced Anacin as the largest selling over-the-counter (OTC) internal analgesic product. Anacin remains the largest selling aspirin-based analgesic.

The lawsuit arose out of two Anacin advertisements initiated shortly after Tylenol became market leader. The first is a thirty-second television commercial initially aired by CBS in late November, 1976, and by NBC in early December, 1976. It commences with the phrase: "Your body knows the difference between these pain relievers . . . and Adult Strength Anacin," and asserts its superiority to Datril, Tylenol and Extra-Strength Tylenol.[3] The second advertisement was introduced in national magazines in late January, 1977. It carries a similar theme, stating that "Anacin can reduce inflammation that comes with most pain," "Tylenol cannot."[4]

---

[2] AHP also makes a First Amendment claim which was not raised below. Accordingly, we will not consider it on appeal.

[3] The "story board" of the television commercial is printed in Judge Stewart's opinion below, 436 F.Supp. 785, 788 (S.D.N.Y.1977). The script for the commercial reads as follows:
SPOKESMAN: Your body knows the difference between these pain relievers [showing other products] and Adult Strength Anacin. For pain other than headache Anacin reduces the inflammation that often comes with pain. These do not. (SFX: MUTED KETTLE DRUM.) Specifically, inflammation of tooth extraction [,] muscle strain (SFX BUILDS)[,] backache (SFX BUILDS)[,] or if your doctor diagnoses tendonitis[,] neuritis. (SFX FADES.) Anacin reduces that inflammation (SFX OUT) as Anacin relieves pain fast. These do not. Take Adult Strength Anacin.

[4] The print advertisement is reproduced in Judge Stewart's opinion, 436 F.Supp. at 789. It reads in substantial part as follows:

Anacin can reduce inflammation that comes with most pain. Tylenol cannot.
With any of these pains, your body knows the difference between the pain reliever in Adult-Strength Anacin and other pain relievers like Tylenol. Anacin can reduce the inflammation that often comes with these pains.
Tylenol cannot. Even Extra-Strength Tylenol cannot. And Anacin relieves pain fast as it reduces inflammation.
Get fast relief. Take Adult-Strength Anacin. Millions take Anacin with no stomach upset. Anacin.
"These pains" referred to in the text are depicted as located on the human body by spots and include sinusitis, tooth extraction, neuritis, tendonitis, muscular backache, muscle strain, and sprains.

The controversy began when McNeil protested the television commercial to the networks and the magazine advertisement to the print media on the ground that they were deceptive and misleading.[5] McNeil also complained to the National Advertising Division of the Better Business Bureau. These protests were, for the most part, unsuccessful. CBS, NBC and the print media, continued to carry the two advertisements without alteration.[6] As a result of the protests, AHP filed a declaratory judgment action under 28 U.S.C. §2201 and sought to enjoin McNeil from interfering with the dissemination of the commercial and the printed advertisement. McNeil counterclaimed under Section 43(a) of the Lanham Act, 15 U.S.C. §1125(a),[7] urging that the following claims contained in AHP's advertisements were false: (A) that Anacin is a superior analgesic to Tylenol, (B) that Anacin is an efficacious anti-inflammatory drug for the conditions listed in the advertisements,[8] (C) that Anacin provides faster relief than Tylenol, and (D) that Anacin does not harm the stomach. It sought declaratory relief and an injunction prohibiting AHP from continuing to make false claims which disparaged Tylenol.

After denying McNeil's motion for a preliminary injunction, Judge Stewart held an expedited trial on the merits. Principally on the basis of consumer reaction surveys, he concluded that the advertisements made the following representations: (1) the television commercial represented that "Anacin is a superior analgesic generally, and not only with reference to particular conditions such as those enumerated in the ad [see note 3 supra] or to Anacin's alleged ability to reduce inflammation," (Claim One); (2) the print advertisement claimed that "Anacin is a superior analgesic for certain kinds of pain because Anacin can reduce inflammation," (Claim Two); and (3) both advertisements represented that Anacin reduces inflammation associated with the conditions specified in the advertisements. (Claim Three).[9] The district court then concluded that the preponderance of the evidence indicated that Claims One and Two—that Anacin is a superior analgesic in general to Tylenol and a superior analgesic for conditions which have an inflammatory component— were false. The court further held that it could not be determined on the basis of the evidence presented whether OTC dosages of Anacin reduce inflammation to a clinically significant extent in the conditions specified by the adver-

[5] At least two of the television networks have their own guidelines for comparative advertisements. *See* Note, *The Law of Comparative Advertising, supra,* note 1, 76 Colum.L.Rev. at 81 n. 7.

[6] Before ABC would broadcast the commercials it required AHP to change certain language used in the CBS and NBC commercials. "Anacin relieves both pain and its inflammation fast. These do nothing for inflammation" was substituted for "Anacin reduces that inflammation as Anacin relieves pain fast. These do not."

[7] Section 43(a) provides in pertinent part:
Any person who shall . . . use in connection with goods . . . any false description or representation, including words or other symbols tending falsely to describe or represent the same, and shall cause such goods . . . to enter into commerce, . . . shall be liable to a civil action . . . by any person who believes that he is or is likely to be damaged by the use of any such false description or representation. 15 U.S.C. §1125(a).

[8] *See* notes 3–4 *supra.*

[9] The judge also held that the advertising does not represent that Anacin provides faster analgesic action or that Anacin is harmless to the stomach, again on the basis of consumer reaction. *Amercian Home Prods. Corp.* v. *Johnson & Johnson,* 436 F.Supp. 785, 796 (S.D.N.Y.1977). *See* Part III *infra.* Accordingly, no findings on the truth or falsity of these alleged representations were made.

tisements. Thus, Judge Stewart could not reach a definitive conclusion on the truth or falsity of the third claim. Nevertheless, he determined that because the three claims are "integral and inseparable," "the advertisements as a whole make false representations for Anacin and falsely disparages [sic] Tylenol in violation of the Lanham Act." Accordingly, he held that McNeil was entitled to an injunction against AHP, given the "substantial evidence that consumers have been and will continue to be deceived as to the relative efficacy of the two products and that this deception is injuring, and will continue to injure, Tylenol's reputation among consumers." The injunction prohibits AHP from publishing or inducing television, radio or print media to publish

> any advertisement or promotional material which contains, in the context of a representation as to any anti-inflammatory property of Anacin or aspirin sold by AHP, any representation that at over-the-counter levels Anacin or aspirin provides superior analgesia to acetaminophen including Tylenol either (1) generally, or (2) for conditions which are associated with inflammation or have inflammatory components, or (3) because Anacin or aspirin reduces inflammation. . . .

II. THE PRINCIPAL APPEAL

A. *Whether Relief May be Afforded under Section 43(a) on the Basis of the District Court's Findings.*

AHP's first contention is based on the following premises. The advertisements contain no express claim for greater analgesia; they merely assert Anacin's superiority to Tylenol in reducing inflammation, a claim which the district court found not to be false. AHP further assumes that the anti-inflammatory claim was held to be true and is in fact unambiguous. The argument is that a truthful and unambiguous product claim cannot be barred under Section 43(a) even though consumers mistakenly perceive a different and incorrect meaning. Thus, appellants urge, the court erred in finding a violation of Section 43(a) by not relying on express claims of superior pain relief, but by interpreting consumer reaction tests—one of which, incidentally, was introduced by AHP and the other of which was not objected to by AHP—as indicating that consumers derive a message of greater pain relief from the explicit "truthful" claim.

Whatever abstract validity AHP's argument may have, an issue we need not decide, it is clear that in this case the language of the advertisements is not unambiguous. The "truthfulness" of the claims, therefore, cannot be established until the ambiguity is resolved. Moreover, Judge Stewart expressly refused to characterize the anti-inflammatory claims as truthful.[10] But even

---

[10] The flaw in appellant's logic is its conclusion of truthfulness from the district court's candid recognition that it could not determine whether the anti-inflammatory claim was true or false. Judge Stewart did not find this claim truthful:

> Accordingly, we find that there is no reliable evidence showing that ASA reduces inflammation to a clinically significant extent in the conditions listed in the advertisements at OTC dosages. On the other hand, we think that McNeil has not proved by a preponderance of the evidence that this claim is, or tends to be, false. 436 F.Supp. at 801.

assuming the literal truthfulness of the anti-inflammatory claims, appellant's position is no stronger because of the ambiguity of the total message which, as the district court found, conveys additional claims (Claims One and Two).[11]

That Section 43(a) of the Lanham Act encompasses more than literal falsehoods cannot be questioned. Were it otherwise, clever use of innuendo, indirect intimations, and ambiguous suggestions could shield the advertisement from scrutiny precisely when protection against such sophisticated deception is most needed. It is equally well established that the truth or falsity of the advertisement usually should be tested by the reactions of the public. Judge Lasker astutely articulated these legal principles in *American Brands, Inc.* v. *R. J. Reynolds Co., supra*, 413 F.Supp. at 1356–57 (emphasis added), a false advertising case involving ambiguous claims:

> Deceptive advertising or merchandising statements may be judged in various ways. If a statement is actually false, relief can be granted on the court's own findings without reference to the reaction of the buyer or consumer of the product. . . .

The subject matter here is different. We are dealing not with statements which are literally or grammatically untrue . . . . Rather, we are asked to determine whether a statement acknowledged to be *literally true and grammatically correct nevertheless has a tendency to mislead, confuse or deceive*. As to such a proposition "the public's reaction to [the] advertisement will be the starting point in any discussion of the likelihood of deception. . . . If an advertisement is designed to impress . . . customers, . . . the reaction of [that] group [s] [*sic*] will be determinative." 1 Callmann: Unfair Competition, Trademarks & Monopolies at 19.2(a)(1) (3rd ed. 1967). A court may, of course, construe and parse the language of the advertisement. It may have personal reactions as to the defensibility or indefensibility of the deliberately manipulated words. It may conclude that the language is far from candid and would never pass muster under tests otherwise applied—for example, the Securities Acts' injunction that "thou shalt disclose"; but

> the court's reaction is at best not determinative and at worst irrelevant. *The question in such cases is—what does the person to whom the advertisement is addressed find to be the message?*

---

[11] Appellants apparently solely refer to the claims of superior anti-inflammatory effect as the "truthful and unambiguous product claim." We have already pointed out, note 10 *supra*, the fallacy of interpreting the district court's finding of unsubstantiation as a finding of truthfulness. Additionally, appellants err in their failure to recognize that the advertisement must be viewed in its entirety. As stated by Judge Kaufman in *FTC* v. *Sterling Drug, Inc.*, 317 F.2d 669, 674 (2d Cir. 1963):

> It is therefore necessary . . . to consider the advertisement in its entirety and not to engage in disputatious dissection. The entire mosaic should be viewed rather than each tile separately. "[T]he buying public does not ordinarily carefully study or weigh each word in an advertisement. The ultimate impression upon the mind of the reader arises from the sum total of not only what is said but also of all that is reasonably implied." *Aronberg* v. *Federal Trade Commission*, 132 F.2d 165, 167 (7th Cir. 1942).

By paraphrasing the language of the advertisments simply to state that Anacin reduces inflammation while Tylenol cannot, they over-look the obvious ambiguous nature of the advertisements. See note 12 & accompanying text *infra*.

Applying these principles to the facts of this case, we are convinced that the district court's use of consumer response data was proper. We believe that the claims of both the television commercial and the print advertisement are ambiguous. This obscurity is produced by several references to "pain" and body sensation accompanying the assertions that Anacin reduces inflammation.[12] A reader of or listener to these advertisements could reasonably infer that Anacin is superior to Tylenol in reducing pain generally (Claim One) and in reducing certain kinds of pain (Claim Two). Given this rather obvious ambiguity, Judge Stewart was warranted in examining, and may have been compelled to examine, consumer data to determine first the messages conveyed[13] in order to determine ultimately the truth or falsity of the messages.

It was also proper to construe Section 43(a) to prohibit the representations, assuming for the moment the correctness of Judge Stewart's findings on consumer reaction, see Part II, B, 1, *infra*, and on falsity. See Part II, B, 2, *infra*. Contrary to appellant's contentions, Judge Stewart did not use Section 43(a) to prohibit truthful representations mistakenly construed by consumers. See notes 10–11 *supra*. We have here deliberate ambiguity and unsubstantiated anti-inflammatory claims determined by the district court to be understood by the public as proclaiming superior analgesic results.[14] Given the audience reaction to the advertisements, as found by the district court, the statute's proscription of "words or other symbols tending falsely to describe or represent [the goods] " was violated.

[12] The television commercial initially states that "[y]our body knows the difference between these pain relievers . . . and Adult Strength Anacin," thereby suggesting that the individual is going to *feel* the difference in pain reduction from use of Anacin. The reference to superior analgesic properties without mention of inflammation is quite apparent. The commercial then goes on to say that "[f]or pain other than headache Anacin reduces the inflammation that often comes with pain," while the competition does not. This statement is ambiguous because it does not state that "for *conditions* other than headache, Anacin reduces inflammation." It says "for *pain* other than headache," implying that by reducing the inflammation that often comes with pain, the pain is itself reduced. Again, after listing specific ostensibly inflammatory conditions, the television commercial states that "Anacin reduces that inflammation as Anacin relieves pain . . . fast," while the competition does not. Meanwhile, pulsating spots of inflammation of a male body are eliminated as Anacin works by "reliev[ing] pain." Quite clearly the television commercial is purposely ambiguous. Quite clearly a claim for superior analgesic effect is intended.

The printed advertisement is similar. The lead statement that "Anacin can reduce the inflammation that comes with most pain, Tylenol cannot" implies superior reduction of pain. The smaller print states that "[w]ith any of these pains [rather than any of these conditions], your body knows the difference between the pain reliever in Adult-Strength Anacin and other pain relievers like Tylenol." In other words, your body can tell the difference between pain relievers, again strongly suggesting that Adult Strength Anacin provides greater pain relief than Tylenol. After comparing Anacin with Tylenol, the advertisement continues: "And Anacin relieves pain fast as it reduces inflammation," implying that Anacin is superior as a *pain* reliever. At the very least, there is sufficient ambiguity in the advertising in question to justify the district court's examination of consumer data.

[13] AHP concedes that consumer data may be used to determine whether a particular representation has been made, that is, to resolve ambiguity. Brief for Appellant at 22–23. Appellant simply disagrees on whether the advertising statement is unambiguous and truthful.

[14] AHP relies upon *Alfred Dunhill, Ltd.* v. *Interstate Cigar Co.*, 499 F.2d 232 (2d Cir. 1974), in which we refused to extend Section 43(a) to preclude sales of damaged goods bearing the Dunhill brand name, notwithstanding the possibility that consumers would receive the false impression that the goods sold were Dunhill's usual high-quality product. *Dunhill*, however, involved a failure affirmatively to disclose material facts which would have been necessary to prevent purchaser deception. There was no false representation in the sense contemplated by the Lanham Act. The goods sold were Dunhill goods. Here, however, by innuendo if not by direct statement, Anacin is represented as being a superior general analgesic. Appellant's misplaced reliance on the *Dunhill* case, analogizing the truthfulness of the Dunhill name to the "truthfulness" of the anti-inflammatory claims, is caused by its incorrect characterization of the anti-inflammatory claims as truthful.

B. Whether the Findings Are Supported by the Evidence.

1. *The findings that the advertising makes claims of greater pain relief generally and for specific conditions.*

AHP argues that even if Judge Stewart was correct in evaluating consumer perceptions, he arrived at the conclusion that the advertisements claim greater pain relief (Claims One and Two) by misinterpreting the consumer reaction data and erroneously affording no weight to the testimony of market research experts concerning the messages conveyed by the advertising. Initially, we note that the district court did take into account the expert testimony offered by both sides on the meaning of the advertisements. Recognizing that in some circumstances such testimony should be given substantial weight, Judge Stewart refrained from doing so here largely because it was neither reliable nor helpful to an understanding of the test data which it purported to interpret. The testimony, however, was used to corroborate the surveys.

The test data itself has some inherent weaknesses.[15] However, it was in the district court's province as trier of fact to weigh the evidence, and in particular the opinion research. Additionally, the district court's findings, based not only on its analysis of the surveys but also on the corroborating testimony of the market research experts, are entitled to the usual clearly erroneous standard of review under Fed.R.Civ.P. 52(a). And our review of the record reveals that the findings on consumer interpretation of the advertising are not erroneous.

The analysis of its test data by ASI Market Research, Inc. (ASI) which was made for and at the request of AHP and was heavily relied on by Judge Stewart, completely supports his finding that the television commercial made a superiority claim which was not limited to pain associated with inflammation. It states that the commercial

> produced a reasonable level of "competitive superiority" type of recall. It is fairly clear from the qualitative group discussions that the side by side comparison to other named brands was being translated into a general "better than" rather than a specific "better for inflammation."

It also reveals: "[H]eavy symptom-relief response was occurring, predominantly in the area of relief of 'pain.' Relief of headaches was secondary, somewhat more visible for 'Muscle' [another commerical] than for [this commercial]." Translated from survey jargon, the ASI survey concludes that the "Your Body

---

[15] Questions of reliability are raised because the two television commercial tests upon which the district court relied focused, to a considerable extent, on audience recall rather than on immediate impressions. Delayed recall measures consumer interest and advertising persuasiveness as well as message content. The Gallup and Robinson, Inc. (G&R) test was conducted approximately 24 hours after the commercial was aired by the use of telephone interviews with persons who claimed to have watched the program accompanying the commercial. The ASI Market Research, Inc. (ASI) testing was performed at special screenings for a specially selected audience. The viewers were questioned about their reactions both during and one hour after the screening. Some of the people tested by both surveys either had bad memories or paid little attention to the television commercial, resulting in inaccurate descriptions, not only of the claims made but even of the products discussed. But such inaccuracies, we suppose, are to be expected in advertising research.

Knows" television commercial produced a recollection in the selected audience of 250 members that Anacin is a superior pain reliever generally, even though the advertisement may have been phrased in terms of comparing inflammation relief.[16]

AHP's advertising executives may, indeed, have intended to communicate that Anacin is better for relieving pain. They noted that 74% of the specifically selected audience thought of the commercial in terms of pain relief, while none thought of inflammation as such unless attention was directed specifically to inflammation. Nevertheless, they pointed out that because the references to inflammation triggered pain association, it was not necessary that inflammation relief be recalled.[17] What the ASI test shows, then, is the powerful "subliminal" influence of modern advertisements. The survey reveals that the word "inflammation" triggers pain association, and pain association is what both advertisements are all about. The district court properly relied on these conclusions in finding that the commercial claimed general analgesic superiority.[18]

Judge Stewart placed less reliance on the Gallup & Robinson, Inc. (G&R) statistical analysis of the television commercial, largely because the breakdown of responses did not differentiate anti-inflammation messages from general pain relief messages. Instead, he reviewed the G&R verbatim interviews himself and found that they "revealed that the symptom relief reported was general pain relief with relatively few references to the specific conditions listed in the ad or to the reduction of inflammation." AHP objects to the use of this data, asserting principally its unreliability. The district court, however, was well aware of this survey's limitations, as indicated by the detailed discussion of the test's inadequacies. Judge Stewart therefore gave little weight to the conclusions he drew from the responses because he was "not confident that the G&R technique really tested what message the consumer took from the language used as opposed to the broader issue of what mental processes view-

---

[16] AHP contends that because there was insufficient evidence on the methods of coding the consumer responses, the district court could not have interpreted the data meaningfully. More particularly, appellant argues that some of the percentage figures espoused by the court are inaccurate in that non-exclusive categories were treated as exclusive, thereby increasing erroneously the percentage of people who mentioned pain relief generally. McNeil argues that the interpretation of the ASI figures was accurate in all respects. We find it unnecessary, however, to delve into the murky area of statistics evaluation. Both the AHP marketing executives' evaluation of the commercial, *see* note 17 & accompanying text *infra*, and the ASI analysis of its own data conclude that the principal message received by consumers was general analgesic superiority.

[17] The internal memorandum states:
   "Body" was somewhat stronger [than another Anacin commercial] on *pain* mention (74% of those playing back pain vs. 57% for [the other commercial]) as a percentage of total symptom relief.
   In the "Body" commercial, inflammation, per se, was not played back in copy point recall and had to be probed for in the focus group session. It may well be that *recall and/or complete understanding of inflammation is not essential* since 74% of those recalling symptom relief in "Body" mentioned "pain" and 20% mentioned "headache pain" despite the phrase "For pain other than headache" preceding the list of inflammatory symptoms within that commercial. In other words, *inflammation is a word that triggers pain association.*
(Emphasis added.) The subliminal influence is present even though—incredibly enough—the survey showed 46% of the people tested found something in the commercial "hard to believe,"

[18] Moreover, the direct testimony of the AHP expert on consumer reaction data, aptly named Dr. Payne, supports Judge Stewart's finding that a high percentage of viewers reported a message of competitive superiority.

ers went through when they noticed an Anacin ad appear on the screen." In our view, appellant's complaint is groundless.

Appellant attacks the district court's conclusion on the message derived from the print advertisement—"that Anacin was better for relieving pain for some conditions because it reduces inflammation," *id.* at 795—on two grounds. First, AHP argues that Judge Stewart simply misinterpreted the G&R verbatim responses. Appellant contends that while 50% may have reported the message that Anacin reduces inflammation, only about 10% stated that Anacin provides superior analgesia. Moreover, the argument continues, the district court's conclusion that 75% reported superiority in relieving pain for some conditions cannot logically be drawn from the district court's findings that 50% reported the message of reduced inflammation and that 25% reported the message of Anacin's analgesic superiority for certain listed conditions. We think that Judge Stewart's conclusion is fully supported by the responses. The percentage computations may not be precise, but the majority of those who recalled any message reported, either explicitly or by implication, Anacin's superiority as a pain reliever.

Second, AHP urges that since the television commercial and printed advertisement say the same thing, the district court's holding that the printed advertisement made a qualified claim of superior pain relief must be wrong. We refuse to engage in this sort of speculation, given Judge Stewart's careful scrutiny of the consumer surveys. Moreover, the differences in language and in medium of expression likely account for the slightly diverse consumer responses.

We conclude, therefore, that the judge correctly held, principally on the basis of consumer reaction tests, that both advertisements claim greater pain relief. On the assumption that this claim is false, *see* Part II, B, 2, *infra,* as the district court held, it was perfectly proper for the trial court to enjoin future advertisements containing superior analgesic claims.

2. The findings of falsity and inconclusiveness.

Appellant apparently does not attack the district court's finding that Claim One (Anacin is a superior pain reliever in general to Tylenol) is false. It does dispute findings on Claims Two and Three. It first argues: "Even assuming that AHP's advertising claims greater pain relief for inflammatory conditions [Claim Two, we believe], the advertising is truthful. . . ." Second, appellant asserts: "The District Court found that . . . the anti-inflammatory claim for the conditions listed in AHP's advertising [Claim Three] is not false. However, the District Court erred in failing to find expressly that Anacin does reduce inflammation for the listed conditions."

We conclude that Judge Stewart's determination that ASA and APAP are equipotent as pain relievers for inflammatory conditions is not clearly erroneous. It was based on his careful consideration of medical studies, medical literature and expert testimony. The studies, which we have also examined, reveal that with one exception—in the case of rheumatoid arthritis[19]—there is little to indicate that in OTC dosages ASA is more effective in reducing pain from inflammatory conditions[20] than APAP.[21]

The district court recognized that the medical experts' testimony as well as the scientifically unsupported opinions of certain members of the medical community were more conflicting. Judge Stewart was unwilling to give much weight to AHP's experts, who hypothesized that Anacin reduces pain associated with inflammation better than Tylenol, because much of this evidence admittedly consisted of mere speculation. In sum, Judge Stewart found most of the studies on the comparative analgesic effectiveness of ASA and APAP more reliable and convincing. Given the conflicting testimony of each party's experts and the sound scientific basis underlying the studies, we cannot say that Judge Stewart erred in his evaluation and weighing of the evidence.

We also conclude that on the basis of the evidence introduced at trial, the judge was justified in holding that he could not determine whether Anacin, at OTC dosages, reduces inflammation in the conditions listed in the advertisements.[22] We think it unnecessary to detail the conflicting evidence presented on

[19] Two of many studies on rheumatoid arthritis found ASA superior to APAP in pain reduction. With regard to the 1974 test, which found ASA slightly more effective than APAP in reducing pain from rheumatoid arthritis, it repeatedly points out the lack of statistical significance of the subjects' responses. The district court was entitled to rely on this caveat, see 436 F.Supp. at 802, in discounting the weight to be given to the study. Moreover, it appears from our review of the study that ASA and APAP were never directly compared in the same trial group, another factor undermining the test's reliability.

Judge Stewart found the second study, nearly 20 years old, to be methodologically unsound in comparison to the numerous other scientific reports introduced. Additionally, the study does not seem very helpful in resolving the issues below because it measured pain relief by noting differences in grip strength and joint stiffness. We have difficulty, therefore, understanding whether and when its conclusions are directed to pain relief (relevant to Claim Two) or to inflammation relief (relevant to Claim Three).

[20] The conditions specifically examined include postpartum pain, postoperative pain, tonsillectomy and oral surgery.

[21] AHP heavily relies on one statement from a report of the Advisory Review Panel on OTC Internal Analgesic and Antirheumatic Products [hereinafter IAP Report], appointed by the Food and Drug Administration, which states:

The Panel concludes that acetaminophen is effective in relieving the pain of headache, and that it is a general analgesic of proven efficacy as shown by clinical testing. Thus, acetaminophen is considered to be equivalent to aspirin in its analgesic effects, although the lack of anti-inflammatory action *might* make it less useful in conditions having an inflammatory component.

42 Fed.Reg.No.131, Book 2, at 35413 (1977) (emphasis added). We do not disagree with Judge Stewart's characterization of the inference to be drawn from the last clause in this statement as "reputable . . . speculations."

[22] As far as we can tell, even if we were to disagree with the district court's conclusion, the outcome of this case would not be altered because he district court's holding that the advertisements carry the messages that Anacin provides greater pain relief in general and in the specified conditions associated with inflammation would still stand. Appellant seems to concede as much in its Reply Brief at 33 n. 1. Judge Stewart found that even though it could not be determined whether or not OTC dosages of Anacin could or did reduce inflammation for the specified conditions, to the extent that the advertisements claim superior *analgesia* for the specified inflammatory conditions, they are false. He further determined that the claim that Anacin reduces inflammation and Tylenol does not is so integrally connected to the two false analgesic representations—obviously because an inflammation claims trigger pain claims, see notes 16–18 & accompanying text *supra*—that the false claims cannot be avoided even though they may stem from one of undeterminable truth. Declaring the anti-inflammation claims to be truthful would affect neither the existence nor the falsity of the two analgesic claims which consumers report from the ambiguous commercials. Accordingly, enjoining any advertisement "which contains, in the context of a representation as to any anti-inflammatory property of ANACIN," the representation that Anacin is a superior analgesic generally or a superior analgesic for conditions which are associated with inflammation or have inflammatory components, would in all probability be proper. See Part II, A, *supra*.

each of the conditions. For determining the validity of the district court's holding of lack of substantiation, it is sufficient to note that for each condition mentioned in the advertisements there was credible evidence suggesting that Anacin does not reduce inflammation.[23]

There was testimony that aspirin is not used to control *inflammation* following tooth extraction because of its well-documented propensity to increase post-operative hemorrhaging. With respect to neuritis, perhaps an out-moded term, there was evidence that all but two neuropathies are noninflammatory in nature, and that the only two which are inherently inflammatory—leprosy and shingles—are not treated by aspirin. The evidence regarding sinusitis revealed that while aspirin can make the patient more comfortable by reducing fever and relieving headache and muscle ache, it has no effect whatsoever on the underlying sinus infection. There was evidence that aspirin is not used for reduction of inflammation from sprains and strains; indeed it can be counterproductive by prolonging and increasing hemorrhaging at the site of the injury. There was basic disagreement on whether tendonitis, to be distinguished from tenosynovitis, is a degenerative or an inherently inflammatory disease. Thus, it could not be determined whether aspirin at OTC dosages provides any therapeutic effect on tendonitis other than pain relief. Backaches have so many different causes, so many of which are not inherently inflammatory in origin, that the advertising simply cannot be accepted as true.

Moreover, Judge Stewart painstakingly considered the evidence most favorable to appellant's position—studies on aspirin's effectiveness in reducing inflammation from rheumatoid arthritis. However, he concluded that these studies did not sufficiently resolve the question whether at OTC levels Anacin reduces inflammation in the specified conditions,[24] particularly in light of the conflicting medical literature and expert testimony on the subject.

Our discussion of the evidence relied on by the district court is an overall review of the thousands of pages of transcripts and documentary evidence. Nevertheless, we are confident that Judge Stewart's findings, based on his thorough review of the evidence, are not "clearly erroneous."

C. Whether the Injunction is Sufficiently Specific.

AHP argues that the injunctive order, does not comply with Fed.R.Civ.P. 65(d) which requires specificity in terms and description in reasonable detail of the acts sought to be restrained. In particular, appellant asserts that the injunction as framed effectively bars AHP from discussing Anacin's anti-inflammatory benefits in a comparative advertisement because such claims may also

---

[23] At larger than OTC levels, it is less disputed that ASA may reduce inflammation accompanying some of the stated conditions. But the anti-inflammatory claims are based, as they must be, solely on OTC dosages. Otherwise, the advertising would invite the consumer to guess the appropriate levels of intake, a dangerous and potentially fatal practice.

The IAP Report emphasizes the inefficiency and danger of self-medication where anti-inflammatory therapy is desired. *See e.g.,* 42 Fed.Reg.No.131, Book 2, at 35381–82; 35459; 35355.

Judge Stewart expressed similar concerns.

[24] The district court opinion, 436 F.Supp. at 799–800, indicates very careful consideration given to the studies.

contain an implicit representation of superior analgesia. Apparently, AHP objects to the fact that the injunction is not limited to express claims for superior analgesia. We think the district court did a commendable job of drafting an order which specifies, as clearly as possible under the circumstances, the acts to be enjoined. Representations as to any anti-inflammatory properties of Anacin are enjoined only to the extent that they contain or imply three clearly described claims of analgesic superiority at OTC levels. In our view, Rule 65(d) is satisfied. More explicit language, if this is possible, will not diminish AHP's asserted difficulty in determining whether proposed advertising conveys a message of superior pain relief. We note, moreover, that the district court has retained jurisdiction to enable the parties "to apply to this court at any time for such other orders and directions as may be necessary or appropriate for the modification, construction or carrying out of [the] judgment." *American Home Products Corp.* v. *Johnson & Johnson, supra,* 436 F.Supp. 785. If AHP encounters difficulties under the decree, it can apply to the court for guidance at such time.

III. THE CROSS-APPEAL

The district court rejected McNeil's contentions that the printed advertisement contains claims of Anacin's faster onset of analgesia and harmlessness to the stomach. *See* note 9 *supra.* We have some difficulty with this conclusion because the advertisement suggests to us that Anacin produces analgesia faster than Tylenol and that Anacin is gentle to the stomach. But we agree with Judge Lasker's statement in *American Brands, Inc.* v. *R. J. Reynolds Tobacco Co., supra,* 413 F.Supp. at 1357, that "the court's reaction [to language of an advertisement] is at best not determinative and at worst irrelevant."[25] A court should turn to consumers' reactions to determine whether the advertising in question makes false representations, as Judge Stewart did. While the evidence could have supported a contrary result, we cannot hold that his findings of insufficient evidence to sustain either of McNeil's claims are clearly erroneous. The consumer surveys did not sufficiently buttress the contention that the literally true statement of the print advertisement, "[m]illions take Anacin with no stomach upset," produces the message that Anacin causes no harm to the stomach. Only three out of the forty-three women questioned in the G&R survey reported such a claim. This surely was a proper basis for the district court's finding that this number is too small to support, by a preponderance of the evidence, the existence of the representation.

The surveys were contradictory on whether the commercials convey a claim of faster relief. The G&R print advertisement test showed 49% reporting "fast

[25] In short, we do not have the same expertise as the Federal Trade Commission when it interprets the language of an advertisement to determine whether an advertisement is an unfair or deceptive practice in violation of 15 U.S.C. §§45 and 52. Accordingly, we, as judges, must rely more heavily on the reactions of consumers, as found by the finder of fact.

acting." Judge Stewart's review of the verbatims revealed that most of the 49%, about one-third of the test audience, reported a "faster" claim. The ASI data, however, indicated that only 1% of the television viewers reported this message. Judge Stewart rejected the G&R results because he considered the ASI data more reliable, it "so strongly undercut" the G&R data, and the expert testimony supporting the McNeil position simply did not take the ASI study sufficiently into account. 436 F.Supp. at 794–95. We are persuaded by the district court's clearly articulated reasoning that its weighing of the evidence was reasonable.

The judgment is affirmed.

8

Legal Aspects of Sales Promotion and Personal Selling Practices

Chapter 7 focused extensively on advertising strategy and examined the circumstances under which advertising communications might be false, deceptive, or unfair. This chapter focuses on other elements of the promotion mix, such as sales promotion and personal selling. The legality of these latter elements is based more on the way in which the activity is executed than on the truth or falsity of representations. Specifically, the chapter explores legal issues raised by (1) the use of contests, games of chance, and sweepstakes; (2) personal selling techniques; (3) mail-order selling; (4) referral sales; and (5) promotional and brokerage allowances. It should be noted at the outset, though, that while false and deceptive representations to consumers in connection with the promotion practices discussed in this chapter are illegal, we do not focus on issues of deception here. The principles of deception set forth in Chapter 7 are, however, directly applicable to the practices discussed here if those practices have the capacity to deceive consumers.

SWEEPSTAKES AND CONTESTS

Sweepstakes, contests, and games of chance are sales promotion techniques whose use is very much in vogue. These games (as we will refer to them) promise substantial prizes for winners. Entry blanks and game pieces are made available at specified retail outlets. The hope and expectation of the user of this promotional technique is that consumers will visit retail outlets to obtain the pieces and, while there, make retail purchases. If appropriately structured and implemented, these contests and games rarely will be held to be violative of law. However, because of their close resemblance to gambling and lotteries (which are either prohibited or heavily regulated), there is some legal risk associated with using them.

The first task of the firm seeking to use games as a sales promotion device is to avoid having the game classified as a lottery. In most states, gambling is declared to be illegal, and lotteries are considered to be a form of gambling. The Federal Trade Commission considers all lotteries to be unfair or deceptive (unless permitted under state law), and the Federal Communications Act prohibits broadcasters from transmitting information about lotteries.

A game is an illegal lottery if a prize is offered, if winning a prize depends upon chance and not skill, and if the participant is required to give up something of value in order to participate in the game. (This latter requirement is referred to in the law as the giving of "consideration.") Since most games will meet the first two criteria, they can escape condemnation as lotteries only if they fail to meet the third criterion.[1]

The question of when a game of chance will be held to be an illegal lottery because of the presence of "consideration" is not an easy one to resolve. Although most states will not find "consideration" in the mere requirement that the consumer visit a retail outlet in order to obtain game pieces, some older state statutes still contain prohibitions that would find "consideration" in any burden that the game rules impose on the consumer. Generally, however, as long as consumers are not *required* to make a purchase of goods or services in order to obtain a game piece or entry card, the contest will not be condemned as a lottery. In most states, either by court decision or by express statutory amendment, requirements that consumers complete application blanks and send winning game cards by mail are not held to be "consideration." In a state such as Wisconsin, which defines consideration as "anything which is a commercial or financial advantage to the promoter or a disadvantage to any participant,"[2] *any* significant burden on the consumer, unless specifically exempted by the statute, could be found to be "consideration," thereby making the promotional game illegal.

Whether promotional games can require winners to provide interviews and photographs and whether promoters can use photographs in further publicity efforts without violating older state lottery rules is not totally free from doubt. Conceivably, these additional consumer burdens could be attacked as deceptive unless they are conspicuously disclosed when game pieces are distributed. Alternatively, the use of consumer likenesses and names might be held to be "consideration," thereby making the game an illegal lottery.

---

[1] Volner, *The Games Consumers Play: "Give Away" and the Law—A Conflict of Policies*, 25 Fed. Comm. B. J., 121 (1972); Harvey Zuckman and Martin Gaynes, *Communications Law*, 2d ed. (St. Paul, Minn.: West Publishing Co., 1983), p. 418.

[2] Wisconsin Statutes Annotated, §945.01(2)(b)(1)(1981).

Also questionable are any limitations on the number of pieces that any person can obtain on each visit to an outlet. While some form of reasonable limitation is necessary to prevent abuse of the game, strictly enforced "one piece per visit" limitations on the number of pieces distributed to each requesting person might suggest that a purchase actually was necessary, especially if the limit is not applied to those who also make a purchase. Any action that suggests that a purchase is actually required might lead a court to find "consideration."

The Federal Trade Commission has enacted a rule regulating games of chance in the food retailing and gasoline industries.[3] Many states and local governments have enacted laws that are modeled after this FTC rule, and the FTC uses the principles of the rule in determining whether games of chance in other industries are unfair or deceptive. The FTC rule requires that game promoters make certain disclosures and follow prescribed rules to ensure the fairness of the game. Disclosures must be made of (1) the exact number of prizes to be awarded and the odds of winning; (2) the geographic area and total number of outlets participating in the contest; (3) the duration or termination date of the contest; and (4) if a game extends beyond 30 days, disclosure on a weekly basis of unredeemed prizes valued at $25 or more and the revised odds of winning such prizes. The FTC has held that these disclosure requirements do not apply to advertising of games on radio and television, because the length of the disclosures would make most advertising uneconomical.

In addition to these disclosure requirements, the FTC rule requires that (1) all game pieces must be dispersed to retail outlets on a totally random basis rather than being disproportionately disbursed at the beginning of the game; (2) successive games must be separated by a period of time equal to the length of the previous game or 30 days, whichever is less; and (3) a game may not be terminated prior to the distribution of all game pieces, nor can additional game pieces be added during the course of the game.[4]

PERSONAL SELLING AND COERCION

The Federal Trade Commission and virtually all other state lawmaking agencies have been concerned about various aspects of personal selling techniques. For example, virtually all states have rules that regulate personal selling that takes place in the home of the prospective purchaser;[5] and, in 1974, the FTC added its own rule regarding door-to-door selling practices.[6] In addition, even where personal selling takes place on the business premises, courts and agencies have enacted special rules that protect the recipient of the selling message against undue coercion and excessive sales pressure.

[3] Federal Trade Commission, Trade Regulation Rule; Games of Chance in the Food Retailing and Gasoline Industries, 16 C.F.R. Part 419 (1982).

[4] Id.

[5] Sher, *The "Cooling-off" Period in Door-To-Door Sales*, 15 U.C.L.A. Rev. 717 (1968).

[6] Federal Trade Commission, Trade Regulation Rule: Cooling-Off Period for Door-to-Door Sales, 16 C.F.R. Part 429 (1982).

Selling in the Purchaser's Home

Promotional efforts that take place in the purchaser's home are suspect; the purchaser may sign a proposed contract in order to get the salesperson to leave the home rather than because of the desirability of the purchase. While many sales made in the home confer benefits on the purchaser (usually in the form of reduced search costs) and are not tainted with fraud or undue pressure, regulatory authorities have decided that, because of the greater propensities for exploitation and short-circuiting of the consumer's normal search and decision-making process, sales made in the home are presumptively coercive and purchasers should be allowed some form of relief. For example, the FTC rule allows the purchaser to cancel any home solicitation sale for a period of three days following the sale (or three days following the furnishing of a required notice to the buyer of the right to cancel the sale, whichever is longer). The purchaser must be furnished with a form for indicating the desire to cancel the sale; cancellation is accomplished simply by sending the notice to the seller. The purchaser is relieved of any obligation to affirmatively establish that the sale was the result of coercion or undue influence.[7] Most states have rules that are similar to the FTC requirements.

One other aspect of door-to-door selling is monitored and regulated by the FTC. Many salespersons have gained access to a home of a prospective purchaser by misrepresenting the nature or purpose for the call at the purchaser's home. Some common examples of such misrepresentations include representations that the salesperson is "taking a survey" or that the prospective purchaser has "won a gift." The FTC has sanctioned encyclopedia sellers for misrepresenting the nature or purpose of the call at the home; the FTC required salespersons to accurately announce the true purpose of the call (to sell encyclopedias) and to furnish the purchaser with a business card indicating that the person is a sales representative.[8] The selling purpose of the home visit must be made clear at the initial contact.

Coercive selling practices are not necessarily confined to the home. In one case, a dance studio employed a variety of selling techniques to induce customers to sign expensive and long-term dance instruction contracts. Sales pitches using teams of salespersons and lasting several hours were coupled with persuasive methods that prevented the customers from leaving. The pitches emphasized the loneliness of customers and worked the customers into emotional frenzies, which led them to sign the contracts. These coercive techniques were banned by the FTC.[9] And as a result of widespread publicity and complaints about such sales tactics, many states enacted legislation that heavi-

---

[7] Ibid.

[8] *Encyclopedia Britannica, Inc.*, 87 F.T.C. 421 (1976), *aff'd*, 605 F.2d 964 (7th Cir. 1979), *cert. denied*, 445 U.S. 934 (1980); *Grolier, Inc.*, 3 CCH Trade Reg. Rep. ¶21,919 (March 16, 1982), *aff'd*, 699 F.2d 983 (9th Cir. 1983), *cent. denied*, 52 U.S. Law Week (Oct., 1983), p. 3285.

[9] *Arthur Murray Studio, Inc.* v. *F.T.C.*, 458 F.2d 622 (5th Cir. 1972).

ly regulates dance studios and places limits on the dollar value of contracts that can be obtained from a customer.[10]

Little question exists as to the constitutionality of legislation that regulates personal selling. The legal profession's ban on personal solicitation of potential clients was challenged on the ground that it infringed the first amendment commercial speech rights of attorneys. The Supreme Court held that the ban on personal solicitation was constitutional and indicated that states could prohibit attorney-initiated selling of legal services because of the high probability that potential clients would be improperly influenced to retain the soliciting attorney.[11] Since a state's complete prohibition of soliciting is a more severe restriction on commercial speech rights than the FTC's rule (which allows in-home soliciting but also allows contracts to be canceled during the three day cooling-off period), the Supreme Court probably would uphold most forms of regulation of personal selling modeled on the FTC's rule.[12]

Special Restrictions on Personal Selling

Some forms of personal solicitation or promotion are regulated more extensively than others and require higher standards of honesty and fair dealing than most typical buyer–seller relationships. Businesses that are legally classified as fiduciaries have an obligation to disclose all material information before obtaining the consent of a bargaining adversary to engage in a transaction. For example, doctors, lawyers, accountants, and other professionals must exercise a high degree of honesty in advising their clients or patients as to actions that should be undertaken.[13] A seller of insurance, if considered to be an agent of the potential buyer, must disclose all known information and obtain the best insurance policy for the buyer at the least possible known cost.[14] Similarly, those who give investment advice may be required to recommend only those purchases of investment securities that are "suitable" for the particular

---

[10] Ill. Rev. Stat. Ch. 29 §50 (1981).

[11] *Ohralik* v. *Ohio State Bar Ass'n.*, 436 U.S. 447 (1978).

[12] Subsequent Supreme Court cases, such as *Central Hudson Gas & Electric Corp.* v. *Public Service Commission*, 447 U.S. 557 (1980), have imposed a "least restrictive means test" on state regulations restricting commercial speech. Under this test, if the objectives supporting a complete ban on a particular type of advertising could be achieved by alternative means that place fewer restrictions on commercial speech, a complete ban would be unconstitutional. Since a cooling-off period seemingly is less restrictive than a complete ban and allows a state to achieve its objectives of eliminating coercion and undue sales pressure, a complete ban should not be upheld as constitutional.

[13] For example, doctors and hospitals are prohibited from providing treatment to patients without obtaining "the informed consent" of the patient. Unless all risks and possible complications of a proposed medical procedure are explained to a patient, any consent to proceed with the treatment will be without the patient's informed consent and may give rise to physician and hospital liability. Waltz and Scheuneman, *Informed Consent to Therapy*, 64 Nw. U.L. Rev. 628 (1969); Note, *Informed Consent Liability*, 26 Drake L. Rev. 696 (1976–77).

[14] See *Browder* v. *Hanley Dawson Cadillac Co.*, 379 N.E.2d 1209 (Ill. App. 1978). (Automobile sellers, if found to be insurance agents of automobile purchasers, are obligated to disclose the availability of comparable lower cost credit insurance and must disclose all material facts within the agent's knowledge that may in any way affect the transaction, including the agent's possible receipt of a rebate for insurance premiums remitted to an insurance company.)

financial circumstances of the potential purchaser. Thus, investment advisors have been held liable to their customers for recommending the purchase of risky and speculative securities when the client's financial position and age dictated an investment policy of low risk and guaranteed return.[15]

Whether a person will be considered a fiduciary and held to a higher obligation of disclosure of all information material to the purchasing decision will depend on the licensing requirements, if any, for engaging in the particular type of business or profession, and on the law's assessment of the understanding between the alleged fiduciary and the customer. These parties are, within limits, free to agree to the nature of their relationship and the extent to which information disclosure is required. While there is a clear trend in decisions to require bargaining adversaries to disclose more and more information, and while it is possible that this evolution will continue to the point where no meaningful distinction can be made between bargaining adversaries and fiduciaries, nevertheless the law nominally maintains such a distinction.[16] As long as a relationship can be characterized as involving nothing more than a buyer-seller relationship, it seems unlikely that the fiduciary disclosure concept will be imposed on that relationship. Accordingly, in the absence of a statute or rule, and in the absence of deception, a used automobile dealer, for example, will not be required to disclose all that the dealer knows about the automobiles on the used car lot.

MAIL-ORDER SELLING

Selling products by mail is a large and growing business, with annual sales exceeding $80 billion. But mail-order selling also generates an excessive number of complaints from consumers (over 100,000 per year). Not surprisingly, numerous laws have been enacted to deal with these consumer complaints. Both the United States Postal Service and the Federal Trade Commission enforce laws in the area.

Unordered Merchandise

To combat the practice of mailing unordered merchandise to consumers and then sending bills and dunning notices to coerce payment for the goods, Congress enacted a law making it an unfair trade practice under the Federal Trade Commission Act to mail such merchandise (defined as merchandise mailed without the prior express request of the recipient).[17] The statute provides exceptions for the mailing of free samples that are clearly and conspicuously marked as such, and for merchandise mailed by charitable organizations

---

[15] *Clark* v. *John Lamula Investors, Inc.,* 583 F.2d 594 (2d Cir. 1978).

[16] Restatement (Second) Torts (St. Paul, Minn.: American Law Institute Publishers, 1977), §551.

[17] 39 U.S.C. §3009.

soliciting contributions. All mailings of unordered merchandise must bear a clear and conspicuous statement that the recipient may treat the merchandise as a gift and can retain, use, discard, or dispose of the merchandise in any manner without any obligation to the sender. Most states have similar laws. Accordingly, firms contemplating sending of samples of merchandise through the mail should be aware that they can take no action to induce the consumer to pay for the merchandise sent.

Negative Option Mail-Order Plans

The Federal Trade Commission also regulates mail-order selling through two different rules. One rule governs "negative option" plans under which a seller proposes to send merchandise to (and will expect payment from) a consumer unless notice of a rejection is sent by the consumer within a stated time period.[18] This method of selling is used extensively by book and record clubs. The FTC issued its rule in 1973 after receiving numerous complaints regarding the operation of these plans. The complaints included the failure to allow sufficient time to return a rejection notice, the failure to deliver merchandise promised as part of an introductory offer, and the delivery of unacceptable substitute merchandise.

The FTC rule requires sellers who use a negative option plan to disclose all material terms of the plan, including any buyer's obligation to purchase a minimum quantity of merchandise, or to pay postage and handling. The rule also requires that buyers be given a minimum period of 10 days within which to reject a proposed shipment of merchandise. Sellers are required to announce the impending shipment and to furnish a rejection form for use by the purchaser. Sellers must credit the purchaser's account and pay postage for the return of any selections mailed after a consumer has appropriately sent a rejection. Shipments made after a proper rejection are treated as unordered merchandise under the postal statutes. The rule requires sellers to ship any bonus or introductory merchandise within four weeks after an order has been received.

Prompt Shipping Requirements

A second FTC rule is designed to encourage mail-order businesses to promptly ship merchandise that has been ordered.[19] The rule prohibits a seller from soliciting orders unless a reasonable basis exists to believe that shipments will occur within the time stated in the solicitation or, if no time is stated, within 30 days. If the seller is unable to ship within the proper time, the seller must give the buyer an option to either cancel the order and receive a refund of any

---

[18] Federal Trade Commission Trade Regulation Rule: Use of Negative Option Plans by Sellers in Commerce, 16 C.F.R. Part 425 (1982).

[19] Federal Trade Commission, Trade Regulation Rule: Mail Order Merchandise, 16 C.F.R. Part 435 (1982).

amounts paid or to accept a further delay in shipment. Buyers have the continuing right to cancel delayed orders unless a specific time is agreed upon as to the additional period within which the delayed shipment will occur. Sellers must furnish adequate forms and documents for buyers to exercise their options. The FTC obtained a $50,000 civil penalty against a firm that was charged with violating the FTC's rule by misrepresenting the speed with which orders would be filled, paying refunds in the form of credit slips rather than cash, and unfairly retaining customer payments.[20] In addition to the civil penalty, the mail-order merchandiser agreed to notify 500,000 customers of their eligibility for cash refunds or replacement merchandise.

Other laws regulate incidental aspects of mail-order businesses. The postal statutes declare certain matter unmailable because of what is contained on the envelope or package in which the merchandise is mailed.[21] Similarly, sexually oriented advertisements cannot be mailed to persons who have informed the Postal Service that they do not desire to receive such material.[22]

REFERRAL SALES

Many states specifically prohibit sellers from using a sales technique known as a *chain referral*. The technique is used to induce a consumer to enter into a purchase agreement by promising the consumer that the purchase price will be reduced if the consumer refers other potential consumers to the seller.[23] Not all forms of this technique are illegal. For example, if the seller promises to reduce the price simply upon the buyer's furnishing of names of persons to contact, the actual giving of a price reduction is permissible. The technique becomes illegal, however, when the seller conditions the price reduction upon the seller's ability to actually make additional sales to the potential customers referred to the seller by the consumer.[24] Under these circumstances, legislatures apparently believe that consumers are likely to get a false impression about the ease with which price reductions can be obtained. Courts also have found that such schemes are illegal lotteries.

BROKERAGE AND PROMOTIONAL ALLOWANCES

So far in our discussion of the legal issues surrounding promotional strategy, the focus has been on regulations that protect consumers from deceptive or unfair advertising and questionable sales practices. But antitrust legislation ex-

---

[20] *FTC* v. *Star Crest Products of California, Inc.,* FTC News Summary, Mar. 28, 1982.

[21] 18 U.S.C. §§1463, 1718.

[22] 18 U.S.C. §§1735–37; and 39 U.S.C. §§3010, 3011.

[23] David Epstein and Steve Nichols, *Consumer Protection,* 2d ed. (St. Paul, Minn: West Publishing Co., 1976), pp. 38–39. The Uniform Consumer Credit Code, which has been adopted in 20 states, allows a consumer to keep, without having to pay for, any goods sold with this technique. UCCC §3.309 (1974).

[24] See, e.g., Illinois Revised Statutes, Chapter 121 1/2, §262A (1981).

ists in this area that has as its goal the protection of competition. The constraints on promotional activities relating to antitrust are spelled out in specific sections of the Robinson–Patman Act. The first set of constraints deals with the granting of brokerage allowances, and the second deals with allowances given by sellers to buyers for advertising, display, and other similar activities.

Brokerage Allowances

Instead of employing its own sales force, a manufacturer may decide to hire brokers or agents, paying them a commission or an allowance for searching out and finding customers for the manufacturer's products. In a similar fashion, a buyer, such as a retail chain, may hire independent agents to search out and find sources of supply. Thus, as described by Howard,

> "Brokerage" is the pecuniary reward received by the broker from the buyer or seller for the rendering of such services. In the case of a food broker, who acts as the seller's agent, the commission or fee is generally treated by the seller in his accounts as a selling expense. If the buyer were to be permitted to perform the brokerage function himself, he would deduct an amount from the seller's price to compensate for the performance of that function. This is a brokerage discount.[25]

The Robinson–Patman Act was passed in the 1930s at the behest of independent middlemen who believed that large retail chains were receiving major discriminatory concessions from suppliers. In fact, one frustration of these middlemen (including independent food brokers as well as wholesalers and retailers) was the practice of the chains in establishing "dummy" brokers in order to exact lower prices from suppliers.

> These "dummy" brokers would normally not perform any brokerage function but would receive payments from the seller for a fictitious service. Payments received by the "dummy" broker would subsequently be passed on to the buyer. The large buyers, such as A&P, argued that the price concessions were justified because of services rendered by the buyer in contracting directly with sellers.[26]

Thus, as part of the Robinson–Patman Act, Congress incorporated Section 2(c), which makes it unlawful for a buyer of goods (or any agent or representative of the buyer) to receive from or to be paid by the supplier any brokerage or other commission "except for services rendered in connection with the sale or purchase of goods." The sweeping language that is incorporated into this section covers payments by a seller or by the seller's broker to a buyer, to a purchasing agent or broker owned by or affiliated with a buyer, or to an independent purchasing agent or broker selected by and representing the buyer.[27] Thus, only third-party independent brokers can receive a commission for rendering services related to the sale of merchandise. In effect, then, Section 2(c) is a piece of particularistic legislation that protects the existence of brokers.

[25] Marshall C. Howard, *Legal Aspects of Marketing* (New York: McGraw-Hill Book Co., 1964), p. 66.

[26] Joe L. Welch, *Marketing Law* (Tulsa, Okla.: PPC Books, 1980), p. 79.

[27] Lawrence A. Sullivan, *Handbook of the Law of Antitrust* (St. Paul, Minn.: West Publishing Co., 1977), p. 698.

In court cases dealing with this issue, a per se rule has evolved. That is, the plaintiff is not required to prove that a payment has injured competition, and the defendant is not permitted to justify the payment by showing savings in costs. Despite the phrase in the section that outlaws such payments "except for services rendered," the defendant cannot escape conviction by showing that services have been performed, although there are some indications that his latter stance may be weakening, as shown later. In general, the law has been rigidly applied, not only where brokerage has been received by mass distributors, like A&P, but also where it has been collected by independent intermediaries[28] or cooperative buying groups and passed on to their customers.

To enforce Section 2(c), the FTC must make fine-line distinctions between brokerage allowances and functional discounts. The latter are legal, as was pointed out in Chapter 5, although they, too, are circumscribed. Thus, if an organization performs all the functions of an independent merchant wholesaler (i.e., it purchases goods on its own account, makes direct payment to the seller for goods invoiced to it, and performs other wholesaling services such as warehousing and granting credit), it will not violate Section 2(a) when it receives a discount for "services rendered."[29] If the organization performs none of these functions, a payment for a middleman's services is likely to be called a brokerage allowance[30] and could be prosecuted under Section 2(c).

The courts are, however, beginning to give some indication that, in certain circumstances, the "services rendered" section may be interpreted to cover situations where the buyer has relieved the seller (or vice versa) of functions that he would otherwise perform himself or that represent cost savings to him even when independent brokers are involved in the transaction. For example, in *FTC* v. *Henry Broch and Company,*[31] Broch, an independent food broker, reduced its brokerage fee to Canada Foods Ltd. from 5 to 3 percent in order to obtain a large order from J. M. Smucker Company. While the Supreme Court noted that there was no evidence that Smucker had rendered any services to Canada Foods or to Broch or that anything in Smucker's method of dealing justified Smucker's getting a price concession through a reduced brokerage charge, it added, in a very poignant and significant statement, that "we would have quite a different case if there were such evidence. . . ." In other words, as Howard has observed, "it might well be that it could be shown that there were true cost savings attributable to the buyer and that the resulting discriminatory price would be legal. If this were so, . . . then the cost-justification provision of Section 2(a) would become operative."[32] The *Broch* case, among

---

[28] See *Great Atlantic & Pacific Tea Co.* v. *FTC*, 106 F.2d 667 (3d cir. 1939), *cert. denied* 308 U.S. 625 (1940); *Biddle Purchasing Company* v. *FTC*, 96 F.2d 687 (2d cir. 1938), *cert. denied* 305 U.S. 634 (1938); *Independent Grocers Alliance Distributing Co.* v. *FTC*, 203 F.2d 941 (7th cir. 1953); *Modern Marketing Service, Inc.* v. *FTC*, 149 F.2d 970 (7th cir. 1945); *Webb–Crawford Co.* v. *FTC*, 109 F.2d 268 (5th cir. 1940); and *Southgate Brokerage Co.* v. *FTC*, 150 F.2d 607 (5th cir. 1945).

[29] See *Central Retailer-Owned Grocers, Inc.* v. *FTC*, 319 F.2d 410 (7th Cir. 1963).

[30] F. M. Scherer, *Industrial Market Structure and Economic Performance*, 2nd ed. (Chicago: Rand McNally College Publishing Co., 1980), p. 574.

[31] *FTC* v. *Henry Broch and Company*, 363 U.S. 166 (1960).

[32] Howard, op. cit., pp. 68–69. See, also, Sullivan, op. cit., p. 698.

others since then, may be giving a larger and more literal meaning to the "for services rendered" exception.

Promotional Allowances

Sections 2(d) and 2(e) of the Robinson–Patman Act prohibit a seller from granting advertising allowances, offering other types of promotional assistance, or providing services, display facilities, or equipment to any buyer unless similar allowances and assistance are made available to all purchasers. Section 2(d) applies to *payments* by a seller to a buyer for the performance of promotional services; Section 2(e) applies to the actual *provision* of such services (e.g., display racks or signs). Because buyers differ in terms of size of physical establishment and volume of sales, allowances obviously cannot be made available to all customers on the same absolute basis. Therefore, the law stipulates that the allowances be made available to buyers on "proportionately equal terms."

The prohibitions of these sections of the Robinson–Patman Act are absolute and are not dependent on injury to competition. Cost justification of the discrimination is not a defense. In other words, if it can be shown that discriminatory allowances exist and that the firms being discriminated against are in competition with each other, the violation is deemed to be illegal on a per se basis. However, for firms to be "in competition," they must be in sufficient geographical proximity to compete for the same customer groups. If, for example, retailers are involved, only those retailers in a limited market territory need be included when granting allowances. On the other hand, the market might be construed as national if mail-order companies are involved. In the latter situation, a manufacturer (or wholesaler) would have to grant allowances or services to all mail-order companies if he were to grant them to one. In addition, a time dimension is important in defining the domain of the allowance. For example, if advertising allowances are granted one month, they do not have to be granted to another buyer five months later. Otherwise, the initial allowance would determine all future allowances.[33]

Certain stipulations have been made regarding adherence to Sections 2(d) and 2(e).[34] Among them are the following:

1. Allowances may be made only for services actually rendered, and they must not be substantially in excess of the cost of these services to the buyer or their value to the seller.
2. The seller must design a promotional program in such a way that all competing buyers can realistically implement it.
3. The seller should take action designed to inform all competing customers of the existence and essential features of the promotional program in ample time for them to take full advantage of it.
4. If a program is not functionally available to (i.e., suitable for and usable by) some of the seller's competing customers, the seller must make certain that suitable alternatives are offered to such customers.
5. The seller should provide its customers with sufficient information to permit a clear understanding of the exact terms of the offer, including all alterna-

[33] Howard, op. cit., p. 71. See *Atlantic Trading Corp.* v. *FTC,* 258 F.2d 375 (2d cir. 1958).

[34] Federal Trade Commission, *Guides for Advertising Allowances and Other Merchandising Payments and Services,* 16 C.F.R. part 240 (1983).

tives, and the conditions upon which payment will be made or services furnished.

When promotional allowances or merchandising services are provided, the FTC has stipulated that they should be furnished in accordance with a written plan that meets the listed requirements.[35] And, in the case of sellers who market their products directly to retailers as well as sell through wholesalers, it has been mandated that any promotional allowance offered to the retailers must also be offered, on a proportionately equal basis, to the wholesalers. The wholesalers would then be expected to pass along the allowance to their retail customers who are in competition with the direct-buying retailers.[36]

Promotional allowances and services must be made available to all competing customers on proportionately equal terms. No single way to proportionalize is prescribed by law; any method that treats competing customers on proportionately equal terms may be used. Generally, this can be done by basing payments made or services furnished on the dollar volume or on the quantity of goods purchased during a specified period. Furthermore, unlike brokerage allowances, a company that grants a discriminatory promotional allowance may argue that the allowance was given in "good faith" to meet the promotional program of a competitor.[37]

CONCLUSION

In addition to the general obligation to avoid false and deceptive advertising, marketing executives must comply with laws that extensively regulate other promotional practices. Some practices have generated such a large number of consumer complaints that the practices have been singled out for special legal treatment and detailed regulation.

The use of games of chance, contests, or sweepstakes in connection with a sales campaign is subject to detailed regulation because of the similarity of games of chance to illegal gambling. However, if participation in a game is not conditioned on a purchase of a seller's product and does not require a consumer to do more than request the necessary entry forms, the game probably will be legal. But because gambling prohibitions are enacted at the state level, it is necessary to be aware of and comply with all laws in states where the game is played or promoted. In addition, the Federal Trade Commission has enacted a rule on games of chance in the food retailing and gasoline industries, and compliance with this rule requires extensive disclosures about the game and adherence to rules concerning the basic fairness of the game.

Personal selling is constrained by laws at all levels of government, especially if the selling takes place in the home of a consumer. In these sales, consumers must be furnished with a notice that they can cancel the sale within

[35] Ibid., § 240.6.

[36] *FTC* v. *Fred Meyer Company, Inc.,* 390 U.S. 341 (1968).

[37] *FTC* v. *Simplicity Pattern Co.,* 360 U.S. 55 (1959), and *Exquisite Form Brassiere, Inc.* v. *FTC,* 301 F.2d 499 (D.C. cir. 1961).

three days by simply sending the seller a notification of cancellation. In addition, general laws against the use of deceptive practices exist to prevent seller misrepresentations as to the purpose of a call at a consumer's home; consumers cannot be falsely told that the sales agent is calling to award a prize or to take a survey. Other forms of coercive and high-pressure selling techniques are legally prohibited either by general laws or by regulations of specific industries in which such practices are thought to be widespread (e.g., dance instruction). Some businesses, such as insurance and financial advising, must comply with special requirements for honesty and fair dealing with their customers.

Mail-order selling is heavily regulated. Sellers must comply with detailed rules about promptness of filling orders and making refunds if shipment cannot be made in the time promised. Negative-option sales plans, such as those used by book and record clubs, must comply with detailed rules that seek to ensure that the buyer is given ample time to reject a proposed shipment and a convenient method of communicating the rejection. The sending of unordered merchandise and the attempt to collect the value of the merchandise is prohibited; consumers are allowed to treat the merchandise as a gift and can ignore the collection efforts.

In addition to the preceding rules, which directly seek to protect buyers (particularly individuals purchasing goods and services for personal consumption), the antitrust laws, and specifically the Robinson–Patman Act, constrain the granting of incentives that encourage middlemen to provide promotional support in behalf of suppliers. For example, commissions cannot be granted to retailers for the performance of brokerage services. They may only be given to independent brokers who serve as agents for sellers. Otherwise, the granting of such commissions is per se illegal. Buyers and their agents cannot receive compensation from suppliers except for services actually rendered in connection with the sale or purchase of goods. In addition, promotional allowances that are offered to competing middlemen in return for advertising, display, and special marketing efforts can be made available only on proportionately equal terms. If these allowances are not made available on such a basis, they are also *per se* illegal.

Clearly, the promotional strategies of marketing executives are subject to considerable scrutiny. In fact, the legal aspects relating to the elements of the promotion mix (advertising, sales promotion, and personal selling) are nearly as comprehensive as those relating to pricing. The reason for this is relatively straightforward: pricing and promotion practices are often highly visible and/or produce very strong and immediate reactions on the part of consumers and competitors alike. Therefore, the likelihood of some form of regulation is high, and the potential for either public or private enforcement is relatively great. But the promotion area has generally more "gray areas" than pricing in the sense that public policy is not clearly defined, especially with regard to advertising. Therefore, the outcome of lawsuits in this area of marketing is more uncertain.

Case 1
Encyclopaedia Britannica, Inc. *v.* Federal Trade Commission

United States Court of Appeals
Seventh Circuit, 1979

605 F.2d 964

FAIRCHILD, Chief Judge.

This is a petition to review an order of the Federal Trade Commission holding that certain practices of petitioners, Encyclopaedia Britannica, Inc. and its subsidiary, Britannica Home Library Services, Inc. (hereinafter referred to jointly as Britannica) violated §5 of the Federal Trade Commission Act, 15 U.S.C. §45(a)(1),[1] and ordering Britannica to cease and desist from certain practices. Some of the cease and desist provisions of the orders were so framed as to forbid certain customary sales and promotional activity unless specified notices were given. These notice provisions are the subject of this review.

I. THE AGENCY PROCEEDING

Encyclopaedia Britannica, Inc. is a New York Corporation with its principal place of business in Chicago. As is widely known, Britannica publishes, sells, and distributes encyclopedias, textbooks, general reference works, and other educational and literary products throughout the world. The primary sales method is direct selling at the homes of customers.

The complaint which initiated the proceeding before the Commission was issued December 11, 1972. It charged deceptive practices in recruitment of sales representatives, in sales presentations to members of the public, in obtaining leads to persons who will allow Britannica sales representatives into their homes, in seeking subscriptions to book promotions, and in collection procedures. On December 16, 1974, after trial hearings, ALJ Barnes entered very extensive findings, conclusions, and a remedial order. In respects not material on this review, the ALJ found deceptive and unfair practices in recruiting advertisements, in certain sales devices, a mail order program, and the use

---

[1] At the time this proceeding was instituted, 15 U.S.C. §45(a)(1) provided: "Unfair methods of competition in commerce, and unfair or deceptive acts or practices in commerce, are declared unlawful." This section has since been amended in ways not relevant to this appeal.

of types of collection letters. On this review, Britannica has narrowed its challenges to remedial provisions relating to deception on initial contact of salesmen with consumers, and to deception in certain advertised offerings.

A. The ALJ summarized his detailed findings concerning "Initial Contact With Consumers," in part as follows:

> "The primary means by which EB [Britannica] sells its products and services is through the door-to-door solicitation of consumers. . . . EB's salesmen utilize numerous devices which disguise the purpose of the salesman's initial contact with prospects—devices which essentially are ruses for gaining admission into prospects' homes 'not in the role of a salesman'. . . . These devices are approved by EB's management, are made available to its salesmen, and the salesmen are trained by EB to effectively use such devices.—
>
> "One ploy used to gain entrance into prospects' homes is the Advertising Research Analysis questionnaire. This form questionnaire is designed to enable the salesman to disguise his role as a salesman and appear as a surveyor engaged in advertising research. EB fortifies the deception created by the questionnaire with a form letter from its Director of Advertising—for use with those prospects who may question the survey role. These questionnaires are thrown away by salesmen without being analyzed for any purpose whatsoever.—
>
> "Thus, the record is clear that EB's sales representatives misrepresented and failed to disclose the purpose of the initial contact with prospects. These practices were authorized and condoned by EB. . . ."

The portions of the ALJ's order challenged by Britannica and remedying the practices above described require Britannica to cease and desist from:

> "D. Visiting the home or place of business of any persons for the purpose of soliciting the sale, rental or lease of any publications, merchandise or service, unless at the time admission is sought into the home or place of business of such person, a card 3 inches by 5 inches in dimension, with all words in 10-point bold-face type, with the following information, and none other, in the indicated order, is presented to such person:
>
> (1) the name of the corporation;
> (2) the name of the salesperson;
> (3) the term 'Encyclopedia Sales Representative' [or other applicable product];
> (4) the terminology: 'The purpose of this representative's call is to solicit the sale of encyclopedias' [or other applicable product]; and
> (5) the statement: This card should be kept as part of your permanent records of this transaction.

[Paragraph 5 was deleted from the order by the Commission.]

> "E. Failing to give the card, required by Paragraph II D, above, to each such person, to direct each such person to read the information contained on such card, and to provide each such person with an adequate opportunity to read the card before engaging any such person in any sales solicitation."

In discussing the remedial order, the ALJ said he had "taken into consideration . . . (1) the numerous violations of law by respondents which this record establishes, consisting of conduct which has been declared unlawful by the Commission over the years, (2) the fact that this order must be designed to

protect the general consuming public which includes the ignorant, the unthinking and the credulous . . . , (3) respondents' past record of unlawful conduct as determined in previous Commission proceedings, [1952 and 1961
orders concerning representations with respect to allegedly 'special' prices and
the like] and (4) the fact that '. . . once the Government has successfully borne
the considerable burden of establishing a violation of law, all doubts as to the
remedy are to be resolved in its favor'. . . ."

With respect to the Initial Contact deception, the ALJ wrote as follows:

> "The Order contains provisions which prohibit respondent from misrepresent-
> ing the purpose of contacting persons in their homes or places of business, and
> require respondent to clearly inform prospects in telephone talks and at the door
> that the purpose of the visit is to solicit the sale of respondent's products or
> services. This will correct respondent's misrepresentations and deceptions as
> shown by the record. As one of EB's former corporate officials testified, the abil-
> ity to gain admittance into the home is essential to respondent's business opera-
> tions (Balsano, Tr. 1542). Thus, elimination of misrepresentations and deceptions
> in gaining admittance into homes is crucial to this Order as well. There is no
> conceivable business or other justification for misrepresenting the purpose of a
> salesman's visit. A homeowner is entitled to know the purpose behind any visit
> by a salesman. The time has arrived to put an end to deceptions of this type.
> "For these reasons, the Order entered herewith requires EB's salesmen to pres-
> ent the prospect with a card which clearly discloses the purpose of the visit. Re-
> spondent strenuously objects to such an Order provision (RPF III-7; RM, p. 43;
> RRM, p. 17); however, no satisfactory alternatives are suggested. The use of a
> disclosure card should prove effective to eliminate misrepresentations and decep-
> tions in obtaining appointments with homeowners, or in gaining admittance into
> homes. If this provision proves unduly onerous, relief from this provision can be
> requested at a later date.
> "The Order also requires respondent's salesmen to give the prospect an oppor-
> tunity to read the card at the door before any sales presentation can commence.
> This seems ample disclosure of the purpose of the salesman's visit. Thus, com-
> plaint counsel's proposal for different size cards depending upon the method of
> initial contact with a prospect seems superfluous and is rejected."

The requirement of the Card-at-the-Door was debated in the briefs of counsel on appeal to the Commission. Britannica pointed to testimony that the required presentation of the card would have a devastating effect upon a
rational interchange between salesman and prospect. Britannica proposed as
less drastic alternatives (1) the requirement of oral disclosure and of training
of sales personnel to make such disclosures, and (2) the requirement that the
sales representative present an ordinary business card, disclosing his title as
"Sales Representative."

Commission counsel argued several aspects of the greater effectiveness of
the prescribed card, as compared with an ordinary business card, in giving
persons clear notice of the caller's sales purpose and an opportunity to protect
themselves from unwanted harassment.

The opinion of the Commission dealt specifically with Britannica's concern
over the Card-at-the-Door requirement. Adverting in detail to evidence that
Britannica's sales representatives have been trained to conceal the sales purpose of seeking admission to a home, the Commission concluded that "[t]he

company-described disguise techniques necessitate inclusion of an order provision requiring clear and conspicuous disclosure of the fact that the representative is a salesman and of the true purpose of gaining entry into the home."

The Commission concluded that the prescribed advice to the customer to keep the card did "not appear to be necessary in order to provide a clear and conspicuous disclosure of the nature and purpose of the call" and omitted that prescription.

B. The ALJ summarized his detailed findings concerning "Lead-Getting Activities," in part, as follows:

> "EB's magazine and direct-mail advertisements as well as contest entry cards, used to obtain the names of persons who will be contacted by EB's salespersons for the purpose of persuading such persons to purchase EB's products, do not disclose the fact that persons who respond will be contacted by EB's salespersons. —
>
> ". . . Respondent also points out that EB's salesmen usually telephone prospects prior to visiting them personally. These fact differences do not change the basic deception inherent in EB's methods. EB's magazine advertisements affirmatively mislead the public into believing that all materials and information will come by mail—direct from the publisher. . . . Some of the contest entry cards indicate EB is giving away prizes in celebration of its 200th anniversary, that there is no obligation in filling out a card. —
>
> "The *sole* purpose of these activities is to obtain leads to prospects. The only way to protect the public, to correct the misrepresentations in respondent's lead-getting activities, is to inform the public of the true motives behind respondent's offers of free information and prizes—that respondent has a profit motive and will seek to sell its products to those who respond to its devices. These are material facts the public should know. Disclosure that a salesman may call to make a sales presentation of respondent's products and services will correct respondent's misrepresentations and make these material facts available to the public."

The portions of the ALJ's order challenged by Britannica and remedying the practices above described require Britannica to cease and desist from:

> "A. Disseminating or causing to be disseminated any advertisement or promotional material which solicits participation in any contest, drawing or sweepstakes, or solicits any response to any offer of merchandise, service or information unless any such solicitation clearly and conspicuously discloses the following statement in 10-point bold-face type:
> *NOTICE TO CONSUMER*—PERSONS WHO REPLY AS REQUESTED MAY BE CONTACTED BY A SALESPERSON FOR THE PURPOSE OF SELLING [insert name of applicable product].
> "B. Providing any return card, coupon or other device which is used to respond to any advertisement or promotional material covered by Paragraph II A above, unless the following statement clearly and conspicuously appears in 10-point bold-face type in immediate proximity to the space provided for a signature or other identification of the responding party:
> *NOTICE TO CONSUMER*—PERSONS WHO RETURN THIS [insert name of applicable device] MAY BE CONTACTED BY A SALESPERSON FOR THE PURPOSE OF SELLING [insert name of applicable product]."

In discussing these portions of the remedial order, the ALJ wrote as follows:

"EB is prohibited by the Order from disseminating any promotional material or providing any contest entry card which does not clearly disclose that any person responding to such materials may be contacted by a salesperson. This provision does not require that a salesperson call, but merely informs the public of respondent's intent in disseminating such materials and the risks or obligations which may be involved. This is information the public should have, and it does not unduly interfere with any of respondent's business operations."

On appeal to the Commission, Britannica argued that the disclosure is unnecessary and in any event is not the least drastic alternative. Britannica took issue with the choice of words, and suggested that at most there might be a requirement that Britannica disclose in clear print that the responding individual may be contacted to see if he would desire further information on the particular product.

In response, Commission counsel emphasized the support in the record for the fact that a substantial number of consumers do not want visits from encyclopedia salespersons, and that by failing to disclose that those who respond are subject to an unannounced visit by a salesperson, Britannica obtains a greater number of responses.

The opinion of the Commission treated specifically the portion of the order requiring these disclosures in advertising or promotional material which solicits participation in contests and the like, or solicits a response to an offer of merchandise, service, or information. It said:

"The Commission has determined that these order provisions are needed to inform the consumer that the card or coupon response will trigger the delivery of material and information by a sales representative whose call is for the purpose of selling. Such knowledge cannot be gleaned by the consumer who reads the ads or who enters the contest. The ads mislead the consumer in that the wording portrays all information as coming by mail and direct from the publisher. A number of contest entry cards portray the give-away merely as a celebration of the company's bicentennial and suggest that a consumer who fills in the card will not be imposed upon. We reject respondent's contention that disclosure is unnecessary and that the language of the disclosure is 'negative.' "

The Commission's order was issued March 9, 1976.

Britannica does not challenge the sufficiency of the evidence to support the findings of violation, nor does it challenge the propriety of a remedial order. Rather, Britannica focuses its attack on the provisions requiring specified disclosures on initial contact with prospective customers and in certain types of lead-getting material. Britannica argues that these remedial provisions should be set aside because: (1) the disclosures ordered by the Commission are not the least restrictive alternative for curing deception; (2) the Commission failed to state reasons for its choice of remedy in violation of the Administrative Procedure Act, 5 U.S.C. §557(c); (3) the Commission's order unconstitutionally infringes on Britannica's First Amendment right to advertise and solicit sales; (4) the Commission abused its discretion in its method of enforcement; and (5) Britannica did not have an opportunity to rebut information it believes the Commission considered in selecting the remedy. We will now consider each of these contentions, respectively.

II. WHETHER THE COMMISSION EXCEEDED ITS STATUTORY AUTHORITY IN REQUIRING THE AFFIRMATIVE DISCLOSURES IN THIS CASE

Once a violation of the Act has been found, our role in reviewing the remedy is a narrow one. As the Supreme Court has stated:

> The Commission is the expert body to determine what remedy is necessary to eliminate the unfair or deceptive trade practices which have been disclosed. It has wide latitude for judgment and the courts will not interfere except where the remedy selected has no reasonable relation to the unlawful practices found to exist.

Jacob Siegel Co. v. *FTC*, 327 U.S. 608, 612–13, 66 S.Ct. 758, 760, 90 L.Ed. 888 (1946). *See also, e.g., Gilbertville Trucking Co.* v. *U.S.*, 371 U.S. 115, 130, 83 S.Ct. 217, 9 L.Ed.2d 177 (1962); *L. G. Balfour Co.* v. *FTC*, 442 F.2d 1, 23 (7th Cir.1971).[2] If an FTC order bears no reasonable relationship to the unlawful conduct, however, courts may narrow the scope of the order accordingly. *E. g., Chrysler Corp.* v. *FTC*, 182 U.S.App.D.C. 359, 366, 561 F.2d 357, 364 (1977); *ITT Continental Baking Co.* v. *FTC*, 532 F.2d 207, 220–21 (9th Cir.1976). Similarly, courts may modify FTC orders if a less onerous remedy would have the same effect in furthering the governmental interest of preventing deception as the remedy chosen, *FTC* v. *Royal Milling Co.*, 288 U.S. 212, 53 S.Ct. 335, 77 L.Ed. 706 (1933). *Cf., Beneficial Corp.* v. *FTC*, 542 F.2d 611 (3d Cir.1976), *cert. denied* 430 U.S. 983, 97 S.Ct. 1679, 52 L.Ed.2d 377 (1977). However, the Commission in framing its remedy is "not limited to prohibiting the precise misrepresentations that had occurred in the past." *National Com'n. on Egg Nutrition* v. *FTC*, 570 F.2d 157, 163–64. As the Supreme Court has stated:

> We think it reasonable for the Commission to frame its order broadly enough to prevent respondents from engaging in similarly illegal practices in future advertisements. As we said in *Federal Trade Comm'n* v. *Ruberoid Co.*, 343 U.S. 470, 473, 72 S.Ct. 800, 96 L.Ed. 1081: '[T]he Commission is not limited to prohibiting the illegal practice in the precise form in which it is found to have existed in the past.' Having been caught violating the Act, respondents 'must expect some fencing in.' *Federal Trade Comm'n* v. *National Lead Co.*, 352 U.S. 419, 431, 77 S.Ct. 502, 1 L.Ed.2d 438.

FTC v. *Colgate–Palmolive Co.*, 380 U.S. 374, 395, 85 S.Ct. 1035, 1048, 13 L.Ed.2d 904 (1965). *Cf. National Society of Professional Engineers* v. *United States*, 435 U.S. 679, 698, 98 S.Ct. 1355, 55 L.Ed.2d 637 (1978).

We have no hesitancy in concluding that the requirement of the disclosures on initial contact and in the so-called promotional materials were reasonably related to the deceptive practices found. We do not think Britannica seriously contends that required disclosure in some form is an improper remedy, and the choice the Commission made as to form and content of the disclosures

---

[2] It is well established that the Commission is authorized to require affirmative action as a remedy in addition to a cease and desist order. *E.g., Warner Lambert Co.* v. *FTC*, 183 U.S. App.D.C. 230, 237, 562 F.2d 749, 756 (1977); *Waltham Watch Co.* v. *FTC*, 318 F.2d 28 (7th Cir.), *cert. denied* 375 U.S. 944, 84 S.Ct. 349, 11 L.Ed.2d 274 (1963).

could not be deemed an abuse of discretion. These choices were well within the range.

III. WHETHER THE COMMISSION ADEQUATELY ARTICULATED THE REASONS FOR ITS CHOICE OF PRESCRIBED FORMS OF DISCLOSURE

Britannica contends that the remedial provisions under attack must be set aside because the Commission failed to state reasons for its discretionary choice of forms of disclosure. Britannica points to the requirement of 5 U.S.C. §557(c) (Administrative Procedure Act), that "All decisions . . . shall include a statement of . . . findings and conclusions, and the reasons or basis therefor, on all the material issues of . . . discretion presented on the record. . . . " *See also, Burlington Truck Lines* v. *U. S.*, 371 U.S. 156, 83 S.Ct. 239, 9 L.Ed.2d 207 (1942), faulting the ICC for failure to make findings and an analysis to justify its choice between two different available and apparently adequate remedies.

We have set out or summarized the findings, conclusions, and comments of the ALJ and Commission concerning the deceptive practices at which these remedies are directed. There is emphasis on the studied character of the deceptions. We think these clearly set forth adequate reasons for requiring affirmative disclosure of the sales purposes involved rather than a simple command to cease the deception. Britannica suggested to the ALJ and the Commission less onerous forms of disclosure, *i.e.*, oral rather than written (except for an ordinary business card) in the initial contact and less blunt reference to the sales purpose of the contact to be expected by a person answering a promotional ad.

It is true that the ALJ and Commission made no express comparison between the suggested less onerous forms of disclosure and the form adopted. With respect to the initial contact, the ALJ wrote that the card as ordered "should prove effective" and "no satisfactory alternatives are suggested." The Commission asserted the need for "clear and conspicuous disclosure" and indicated its consideration of that standard in deciding to omit the portion of the card suggesting that the recipient keep it. We think there is the clearest implication from these remarks in the context of the record that the alternatives had been considered and been found not to be adequately effective.

With respect to the required disclosure in lead-getting activities, the ALJ wrote "this is information the public should have, and it does not unduly interfere with any of respondent's business operations." The Commission asserted that the provisions "are needed," and rejected Britannica's contention that the language is "negative." Again it seems clear to us that the suggested alternative had been considered and found not to be adequately effective.

Burlington is readily distinguishable. There the available remedies were quite different, and the Court found every indication that the remedy not chosen would have been effective. In the present case, the matters at issue are only the form of the disclosure to be required, and it seems clear, though not expressly stated, that the Commission considered the less onerous forms suggested and decided they would not be adequately effective. We do not consider that the Administrative Procedure Act, nor *Burlington* requires us to set aside the challenged provisions because the Commission did not expressly make the comparison.

IV. WHETHER THE ORDER OF THE COMMISSION INFRINGES ON BRITANNICA'S CONSTITUTIONAL RIGHT TO ADVERTISE AND SOLICIT SALES

The proposition that commercial speech enjoys some degree of First Amendment protection can no longer be seriously questioned. *See, e.g., Bates* v. *State Bar of Arizona,* 433 U.S. 350, 97 S.Ct. 2691, 53 L.Ed.2d 810 (1977); *Virginia Pharmacy Board* v. *Virginia Consumer Council,* 425 U.S. 748, 96 S.Ct. 1817, 48 L.Ed.2d 346 (1976); *National Com'n on Egg Nutrition, supra.* It is also beyond question, however, that deceptive advertising is subject to regulation. As the Supreme Court stated in *Bates* v. *State Bar of Arizona, supra,* 433 U.S. at 383, 97 S.Ct. at 2708:

> Advertising that is false, deceptive, or misleading of course is subject to restraint. See *Virginia Pharmacy Board* v. *Virginia Consumer Council,* 425 U.S. at 771–772, and n. 24, 96 S.Ct., at 1830–1831. Since the advertiser knows his product and has a commercial interest in its dissemination, we have little worry that regulation to assure truthfulness will discourage protected speech. *Id.,* at n. 24, 96 S.Ct., at 1830. And any concern that strict requirements for truthfulness will undesirably inhibit spontaneity seems inapplicable because commercial speech generally is calculated. Indeed, the public and private benefits from commercial speech derive from confidence in its accuracy and reliability. Thus, the leeway for untruthful or misleading expression that has been allowed in other contexts has little force in the commercial arena.

While Britannica does not dispute the general proposition that deceptive advertising can be regulated, it does argue that the affirmative disclosures required by the Commission in this case go beyond the constitutionally permissible.

A remedy for deceptive advertising which is broader than is necessary to prevent future deception or correct past deception is impermissible under the First Amendment. *E.g., National Com'n. on Egg Nutrition, supra,* 570 F.2d at 164; *Beneficial Corp.* v. *FTC, supra,* 542 F.2d at 619. In *National Com'n. on Egg Nutrition, supra,* the FTC ordered a trade association to cease and desist from disseminating advertisements containing statements to the effect that there is no scientific evidence that eating eggs increases the risk of heart disease. The FTC also ordered the trade association to include in any future advertisements or public statements it made regarding the relationship between eating eggs and heart disease the affirmative statement that many medical experts believe eating eggs may increase the risk of heart disease. This court modified this aspect of the order as overbroad under the First Amendment:

The First Amendment does not permit a remedy broader than that which is necessary to prevent deception. . . . The . . . [additional statement] in its present form would require NCEN [the trade association] to argue the other side of the controversy, thus interfering unnecessarily with the effective presentation of the pro-egg position. The desired preventive effect can be achieved by requiring the disclosure that there is a controversy among the experts and NCEN is presenting its side of that controversy. The additional statement in the form now ordered by the FTC should be required only when NCEN chooses to make a representation as to the state of the available evidence or information concerning the controversy. As thus modified, the challenged condition would not unnecessarily curtail NCEN's right to present its position. 570 F.2d at 164.

Similarly, in *U.S.* v. *National Soc. of Professional Engineers,* 181 U.S.App.D.C. 41, 555 F.2d 978 (1977), *aff'd* 435 U.S. 679, 98 S.Ct. 1355, 55 L.Ed.2d 637 (1978), the court held that an engineering society violated §1 of the Sherman Act by adopting and enforcing a rule against competitive fee bidding. The Court of Appeals, however, also held (in a ruling not reviewed by the Supreme Court) that a requirement that the Society state affirmatively that it does not consider competitive bidding to be unethical was contrary to the First Amendment:

In view of the foregoing, we affirm the district court's decree, except in one respect in which we think the decree is overbroad: It not only enjoins the Society from adopting any policy statement which describes price competition as 'unethical,' but also orders the Society to state affirmatively that it does not consider competitive bidding to be unethical. To force an association of individuals to express as its own opinion judicially dictated ideas is to encroach on that sphere of free thought and expression protected by the First Amendment. 555 F.2d at 984.

Finally, in *Beneficial Corp.* v. *FTC, supra,* the Third Circuit modified a Commission order which required excision of a short copyrighted and heavily promoted phrase from its advertising material when revision of the context within which the phrase was used could eliminate deception.

In the present case, however, the Commission order does not require Britannica to argue a side of a controversy to which it is opposed as in *Egg Nutrition* or *National Soc. of Professional Engineers,* nor does it require Britannica to delete a copyrighted phrase as in *Beneficial Corp.* Rather, the order of the Commission directs truthful disclosure of Britannica's purposes. Both the public and consumers have a strong interest "that the stream of commercial information flow cleanly as well as freely." *Virginia State Board, supra,* 425 U.S. at 772, 96 S.Ct. at 1831. "Indeed, the public and private benefits from commercial speech derive from confidence in its accuracy and reliability." *Bates, supra,* 433 U.S. at 383, 97 S.Ct. at 2708. Moreover, in light of the Commission's finding that clear and conspicuous disclosure is required to prevent future deception by Britannica, we are not persuaded that a remedy ordered by the Commission is not the least restrictive alternative which will adequately further the legitimate governmental interest of the prevention of deception.

V. THE COMMISSION'S METHOD OF ENFORCEMENT
AGAINST BRITANNICA

The Commission has wide discretion in selecting its methods of remedying deceptive and unfair practices. *E.g., NLRB* v. *Bell Aerospace Co.,* 416 U.S. 267, 290–95, 94 S.Ct. 1757, 40 L.Ed.2d 134 (1974); *FTC* v. *Universal-Rundle Corp.,* 387 U.S. 244, 251–52, 87 S.Ct. 1622, 18 L.Ed.2d 749 (1967); *Moog Industries* v. *FTC,* 355 U.S. 411, 413, 78 S.Ct. 377, 2 L.Ed.2d 370 (1958); *SEC* v. *Chenery Corp.,* 332 U.S. 194, 202–03, 67 S.Ct. 1575 91 L.Ed. 1995 (1947). This discretion extends to the decision whether to proceed by rulemaking or adjudication. *E.g., Bell Aerospace Co., supra,* 416 U.S. at 294, 94 S.Ct. 1757; *SEC* v. *Chenery Corp., supra,* 332 U.S. at 203, 67 S.Ct. 1575.

Despite the Commission's discretionary power to proceed by adjudication, Britannica argues that the Commission has no power to enter radically different orders against direct competitors.[3]

The Commission has the power to act against one firm practicing an industry-wide illegal practice. *E.g., FTC* v. *Universal-Rundle Corp., supra,* 387 U.S. at 251, 87 S.Ct. 1622; *L. G. Balfour Co.* v. *FTC,* 442 F.2d 1, 24 (1971); *Rabiner & Jontow, Inc.* v. *FTC,* 386 F.2d 667, 669 (2d Cir. 1967); *Johnson Products Co.* v. *FTC,* 549 F.2d 35, 41 (7th Cir. 1977). The Commission must be accorded wide latitude in its enforcement strategy for "the Commission alone is empowered to develop that enforcement policy best calculated to achieve the ends contemplated by Congress and to allocate its available funds and personnel in such a way as to execute its policy efficiently and economically." *Moog Industries, Inc.* v. *FTC,* 355 U.S. 411, 413, 78 S.Ct. 377, 379, 2 L.Ed.2d 370 (1958).

Nevertheless, the discretion of the Commission is not unlimited and may be "overturned . . . [for] a patent abuse of discretion." *Moog Industries, supra,* at 414, 78 S.Ct. at 380; *Johnson Products Co., supra,* 549 F.2d at 41. If the Commission elects to litigate against similarly situated competitors, for example, it cannot place one competitor at a competitive disadvantage by arbitrarily treating one violator differently from another, *Garrett* v. *F.T.C.,* 168 U.S.App.D.C. 266, 270, 513 F.2d 1056, 1060 (1975). As this court has stated:

> [T]he Commission's orders are to serve a remedial and not a punitive function, . . . and the Commission may not issue orders which would arbitrarily destroy one of many violators in the market. . . . It is the responsibility of the Commission to perform a 'reasonable evaluation' of the competitive situation to ascertain whether a particular order would be contrary to the purpose of the laws sought to be enforced.

L. G. Balfour Co., supra, 442 F.2d at 24 (citations omitted).

---

[3] Britannica also contends that the Commission violated 5 U.S.C. §555(e) of the Administrative Procedure Act by denying its petition for rule making without analysis or reasons. Whatever the merit of this argument, however, it has no bearing on the validity of the Commission's order after an adjudicative proceeding in this case. Rule making proceedings and adjudicative proceedings are not necessarily mutually exclusive. See *Lehigh Portland Cement Co.* v. *FTC,* 291 F.Supp. 628 (E.D.Va. 1968), *aff'd* 416 F.2d 971 (4th Cir. 1969).

The facts of this case, however, do not support Britannica's claim of discriminatory treatment. It is true, as Britannica points out, that an earlier order against a minor competitor required only oral disclosure. *P. F. Collier & Son Corp.* v. *FTC,* 427 F.2d 261, 265–66, footnote 6 (6th Cir. 1970), *cert. denied* 400 U.S. 926, 91 S.Ct. 188, 27 L.Ed.2d 186 (1970). Use of a less exacting remedy in a case litigated almost a decade prior to the present controversy does not, however, establish discriminatory enforcement. To establish such a claim, a competitor would have to show not only that competitors were treated differently, but that no rational reason exists to support the differential treatment. Differences in remedy may be attributable to any number of reasons including a realization that earlier remedies were ineffective. A prior insufficient order does not necessitate the insufficiency of all later orders. *P. F. Collier, supra,* 427 F.2d at 276.

Recent action by the Commission further demonstrates that Britannica has not been put at a competitive disadvantage as a result of discriminatory enforcement. In a proceeding against Grolier, a principal competitor of Britannica, the Commission imposed a remedy virtually identical to the disputed provisions in this case after a finding that Grolier has been engaging in the same practices as Britannica. *In the Matter of Grolier, Inc.,* FTC Docket No. 8879. The record, therefore, does not support a claim of discriminatory enforcement by the Commission.

The order under review will be affirmed and enforced.

Case 2
Federal Trade Commission *v.* Henry Broch & Co.

363 U.S. 166 (1960)

MR. JUSTICE DOUGLAS delivered the opinion of the Court.

Section 2(c) of the Clayton Act, as amended by the Robinson-Patman Act,[1] makes it unlawful for "any person" to made an allowance in lieu of "brokerage" to the "other party to such transaction." The question is whether that prohibition is applicable to the following transactions by respondent.

Respondent is a broker or sales representative for a number of principals who sell food products. One of the principals is Canada Foods Ltd., a processor of apple concentrate and other products. Respondent agreed to act for the Canada Foods for a 5% commission. Other brokers working for the same principal were promised a 4% commission. Respondent's commission was higher because it stocked merchandise in advance of sales. Canada Foods established a price for its 1954 pack of apple concentrate at $1.30 per gallon in 50-gallon drums and authorized its brokers to negotiate sales at that price.

The J. M. Smucker Co., a buyer, negotiated with another broker, Phipps, also working for Canada Foods, for apple concentrate. Smucker wanted a lower price than $1.30 but Canada Foods would not agree. Smucker finally offered $1.25 for a 500-gallon purchase. That was turned down by Canada Foods, acting through Phipps. Canada Foods took the position that the only way the price could be lowered would be through reduction in brokerage. About the same time respondent was negotiating with Smucker, Canada Foods told respondent what it had told Phipps, that the price to the buyer could be reduced only if the brokerage were cut; and it added that it would make the sale at $1.25—the buyer's bid—if respondent would agree to reduce its brokerage from 5% to 3%. Respondent agreed and the sale was consummated at that price and for that brokerage. The reduced price of $1.25 was

[1] Section 2(c) makes it unlawful for "*any person* . . . to pay or grant . . . anything of value as a commission, brokerage, or other compensation, or *any allowance or discount in lieu thereof,* except for services rendered in connection with the sale or purchase of goods . . . either to the other party to such transaction or to an . . . intermediary therein. . . ." (Emphasis supplied.) 49 Stat. 1527.

thereafter granted Smucker on subsequent sales. But on sales to all other customers, whether through respondent or other brokers, the price continued to be $1.30 and in each instance respondent received the full 5% commission. Only on sales through respondent to Smucker were the selling price and the brokerage reduced.

The customary brokerage fee of 5% to respondent would have been $2,036.84. The actual brokerage of 3% received by respondent was $1,222.11. The reduction of brokerage was $814.73 which is 50% of the total price reduction of $1,629.47 granted by Canada Foods to Smucker.

The Commission charged respondent with violating §2(c) of the Act, and after a hearing and the making of findings entered a cease-and-desist order against respondent. The Court of Appeals, while not questioning the findings of fact of the Commission, reversed. 261 F.2d 725. The case is here on writ of certiorari, 360 U.S. 908.

The Robinson–Patman Act was enacted in 1936 to curb and prohibit all devices by which large buyers gained discriminatory preferences over smaller ones by virtue of their greater purchasing power. A lengthy investigation revealed that large chain buyers were obtaining competitive advantages in several ways other than direct price concessions[2] and were thus avoiding the impact of the Clayton Act.[3] One of the favorite means of obtaining an indirect price concession was by setting up "dummy" brokers who were employed by the buyer and who, in many cases, rendered no services. The large buyers demanded that the seller pay "brokerage" to these fictitious brokers who then turned it over to their employer. This practice was one of the chief targets of §2(c) of the Act.[4] But it was not the only means by which the brokerage function was abused[5] and Congress in its wisdom phrased §2(c) broadly, not only to cover the other methods then in existence but all other means by which brokerage could be used to effect price discrimination.[6]

The particular evil at which §2(c) is aimed can be as easily perpetrated by a seller's broker as by the seller himself. The seller and his broker can of course agree on any brokerage fee that they wish. Yet when they agree upon one,

[2] See Final Report on the Chain-Store Investigation, S. Doc. No. 4, 74th Cong., 1st Sess. (1935).

[3] Section 2 of the Clayton Act as originally enacted in 1914 (38 Stat. 730) applied only to price discriminations the effect of which was to "substantially lessen competition or tend to create a monopoly." This section was modified and retained in §2(a) as amended by the Robinson–Patman Act. See note 7, infra.

[4] See S. Rep. No. 1502, 74th Cong., 2d Sess., p. 7; H. R. Rep. No. 2287, 74th Cong., 2d Sess., pp. 14–15; Federal Trade Comm'n v. Simplicity Pattern Co., 360 U. S. 55, 69.

[5] In the Final Report on the Chain-Store Investigation, note 2, supra, Congress had before it examples not only of large buyers demanding the payment of brokerage to their agents but also instances where buyers demanded discounts, allowances, or outright price reductions based on the theory that fewer brokerage services were needed in sales to these particular buyers, or that no brokerage services were necessary at all. Id., at 25, 63. These transactions were described in the report as the giving of "allowances in lieu of brokerage" (id., at 62) or "discount[s] in lieu of brokerage." Id., at 27.

[6] The Report of the House Judiciary Committee described the brokerage provision as dealing "with the abuse of the brokerage function for purposes of oppressive discrimination." H. R. Rep. No. 2287, 74th Cong., 2d Sess., p. 14. And although not mentioned in the Committee Reports, the debates on the bill show clearly that §2(c) was intended to proscribe other practices such as the "bribing" of a seller's broker by the buyer. See 80 Cong. Rec. 7759–7760, 8111–8112.

only to reduce it when necessary to meet the demands of a favored buyer, they use the reduction in brokerage to undermine the policy of §2(c). The seller's broker is clearly "any person" as the words are used in §2(c)—as clearly such as a buyer's broker.

It is urged that the seller is free to pass on to the buyer in the form of a price reduction any differential between his ordinary brokerage expense and the brokerage commission which he pays on a particular sale because §2(a)[7] of the Act permits price differentials based on savings in selling costs resulting from differing methods of distribution. From this premise it is reasoned that a seller's broker should not be held to have violated §2(c) for having done that which is permitted under §2(a). We need not decide the validity of that premise, because the fact that a transaction may not violate one section of the Act does not answer the question whether another section has been violated. Section 2(c), with which we are here concerned, is independent of §2(a) and was enacted by Congress because §2(a) was not considered adequate to deal with abuses of the brokerage function.

Before the Act was passed the large buyers, who maintained their own elaborate purchasing departments and therefore did not need the services of a seller's broker because they bought their merchandise directly from the seller, demanded and received allowances reflecting these savings in the cost of distribution. In many cases they required that "brokerage" be paid to their own purchasing agents. After the Act was passed they discarded the façade of "brokerage" and merely received a price reduction equivalent to the seller's ordinary brokerage expenses in sales to other customers. When haled before the Commission, they protested that the transaction was not covered by §2(c) but, since it was a price reduction, was governed by §2(a). They also argued that because no brokerage services were needed or used in sales to them, they were entitled to a price differential reflecting this cost saving. Congress had anticipated such a contention by the "in lieu thereof" provision. Accordingly, the Commission and the courts early rejected the contention that such a price reduction was lawful because the buyer's purchasing organization had saved the seller the amount of his ordinary brokerage expense.

In *Great Atlantic & Pacific Tea Co.* v. *Federal Trade Comm'n,* 106 F.2d 667 (C. A. 3d Cir. 1939), a buyer sought to evade §2(c) by accepting price reductions equivalent to the seller's normal brokerage payments. The court upheld the Commission's view that the price reduction was an allowance in lieu of brokerage under §2(c) and was prohibited even though, in fact, the seller had "saved" his brokerage expense by dealing directly with the select buyer. The

---

[7] Section 2(a), 15 U. S. C. §13(a), provides, in relevant part: "It shall be unlawful for any person engaged in commerce . . . to discriminate in price between different purchasers of commodities of like grade and quality . . . where the effect of such discrimination may be substantially to lessen competition or tend to create a monopoly . . . or prevent competition with any person who either grants or knowingly receives the benefit of such discrimination, or with customers of either of them: *Provided,* That nothing . . . shall prevent differentials which make only due allowance for differences in the cost of manufacture, sale, or delivery resulting from the differing methods or quantities in which such commodities are . . . sold or delivered."

buyer also sought to justify its price reduction on the ground that it had rendered valuable services to the seller. The court rejected this argument also. Although that court's interpretation of the "services rendered" exception in §2(c) has been criticized,[8] its conclusion that the price reduction was an allowance in lieu of brokerage within the meaning of §2(c) has been followed[9] and accepted.[10]

We are asked to distinguish these precedents on the ground that there is no claim by the present buyer that the price reduction, concededly based in part on a saving to the seller of part of his regular brokerage cost on the particular sale, was justified by the elimination of services normally performed by the seller or his broker. There is no evidence that the buyer rendered any services to the seller or to the respondent nor that anything in its method of dealing justified its getting a discriminatory price by means of a reduced brokerage charge. We would have quite a different case if there were such evidence and we need not explore the applicability of §2(c) to such circumstances. One thing is clear—the absence of such evidence and the absence of a claim that the rendition of services or savings in distribution costs justified the allowance does not support the view that §2(c) has not been violated.

The fact that the buyer was not aware that its favored price was based in part on a discriminatory reduction in respondent's brokerage commission is immaterial. The Act is aimed at price discrimination, not conspiracy. The buyer's intent might be relevant were he charged with receiving an allowance in violation of §2(c). But certainly it has no bearing on whether the respondent has violated the law. The powerful buyer who demands a price concession is concerned only with getting it. He does not care whether it comes from the seller, the seller's broker, or both.

Congress enacted the Robinson–Patman Act to prevent sellers and sellers' brokers from yielding to the economic pressures of a large buying organization by granting unfair preferences in connection with the sale of goods. The form in which the buyer pressure is exerted is immaterial and proof of its existence is not required. It is rare that the motive in yielding to a buyer's demands is not the "necessity" for making the sale. An "independent" broker is not likely to be independent of the buyer's coercive bargaining power. He, like the seller, is constrained to favor the buyers with the most purchasing power. If respondent merely paid over part of his commission to the buyer, he clearly would

---

[8] See Report of the Attorney General's National Committee to Study the Antitrust Laws (1955) 192, 193; Oppenheim, Federal Antitrust Legislation: Guideposts to a Revised National Antitrust Policy, 50 Mich. L. Rev. 1139, 1207, n. 178; Rowe, Price Discrimination, Competition, and Confusion: Another Look at Robinson–Patman, 60 Yale L. J. 929, 957–958.

[9] *Southgate Brokerage Co.* v. *Federal Trade Comm'n, supra,* note 11. See also cases cited, note 10, *supra.*

[10] In speaking of these interpretations of §2(c), a leading authority said;
"Here too the Commission and the court have applied the Congressional intent with precision. If Congress envisaged the evil as the transmission of brokerage commissions to the buyer, then to permit the buyer to get the same thing under 2(a) in another form and name would deprive 2(c) of all substance." Oppenheim, Administration of the Brokerage Provision of the Robinson–Patman Act, 8 Geo. Wash. L. Rev. 511, 535.

have violated the Act. We see no distinction of substance between the two transactions. In each case the seller and his broker make a concession to the buyer as a consequence of his economic power. In both cases the result is that the buyer has received a discriminatory price. In both cases the seller's broker reduces his usual brokerage fee to get a particular contract. There is no difference in economic effect between the seller's broker splitting his brokerage commission with the buyer and his yelding part of the brokerage to the seller to be passed on to the buyer in the form of a lower price.

We conclude that the statute clearly applies to payments or allowances by a seller's broker to the buyer, whether made directly to the buyer, or indirectly, through the seller. The allowances proscribed by §2(c) are those made by "any person" which, as we have said, clearly encompasses a seller's broker. The respondent was a necessary party to the price reduction granted the buyer. His yielding of part of his brokerage to be passed on to the buyer was a *sine qua non* of the price reduction. This is not to say that every reduction in price, coupled with a reduction in brokerage, automatically compels the conclusion that an allowance "in lieu" of brokerage has been granted. As the Commission itself has made clear, whether such a reduction is tantamount to a discriminatory payment of brokerage depends on the circumstances of each case. *Main Fish Co., Inc.,* 53 F. T. C. 88. Nor does this "fuse" provisions of §2(a), which permits the defense of cost justification, with those of §2(c) which does not; it but realistically interprets the prohibitions of §2(c) as including an independent broker's allowance of a reduced brokerage to obtain a particular order.

It is suggested that reversal of this case would establish an irrevocable floor under commission rates. We think that view has no foundation in fact or in law. Both before and after the sales to Smucker, respondent continued to charge the usual 5% on sales to other buyers. There is nothing in the Act, nor is there anything in this case, to require him to continue to charge 5% on sales to all customers. A price reduction based upon alleged savings in brokerage expenses is an "allowance in lieu of brokerage" when given only to favored customers. Had respondent, for example, agreed to accept a 3% commission on all sales to all buyers there plainly would be no room for finding that the price reductions were violations of §2(c). Neither the legislative history nor the purposes of the Act would require such an absurd result, and neither the Commission nor the courts have ever suggested it. Here, however, the reduction in brokerage was made to obtain this particular order and this order only and therefore was clearly discriminatory.

The applicability of §2(c) to sellers' brokers under circumstances not distinguishable in principle from the present case is supported by a 20-year old administrative interpretation. Beginning in 1940, four years after the Act was passed, the Commission restrained the practice of brokers who, whether buying and selling on their own account or acting on behalf of the seller, sold goods to purchasers who bought through them direct at a reduced price reflecting the savings made by the elimination of the services of a local broker. This practice was held to a violation of §2(c), not §2(a).[11]

If we held that §2(c) is not applicable here, we would disregard the history which we have delineated, overturn a settled administrative practice, and approve a construction that is hostile to the statutory scheme—one that would leave a large loophole in the Act. Any doubts as to the wisdom of the economic theory embodied in the statute are questions for Congress to resolve.

Reversed.

---

[11] See *Albert W. Sisk & Son,* 31 F. T. C. 1543 (1940); *C. F. Unruh Brokerage Co.,* 31 F. T. C. 1557 (1940); *C. G. Reaburn & Co.,* 31 F. T. C. 1565 (1940); *William Silver & Co.,* 31 F. T. C. 1589 (1940); *H. M. Ruff & Son,* 31 F. T. C. 1573 (1940); *Thomas Roberts & Co.,* 31 F. T. C. 1551 (1940); *American Brokerage Co.,* 31 F. T. C. 1581 (1940); *W. E. Robinson & Co.,* 32 F. T. C. 370 (1941); *Custom House Packing Corp.,* 43 F. T. C. 164 (1946).

We need not view this administrative practice as laying down an absolute rule that §2(c) is violated by the passing on of savings in broker's commissions to direct buyers, for here, as we have emphasized, the "savings" in brokerage were passed on to a single buyer who was not shown in any way to have deserved favored treatment.

Antitrust Issues
and Achieving Market
Dominance

Marketing strategy is usually formulated with an eye toward obtaining high returns on an organization's investments. Executives often believe that the route to this goal is to achieve effective impact (generally translated into high market shares) within the segments that their organizations have targeted for attack. To accomplish this impact, the organization must somehow significantly differentiate its product and services from those of competitors, efficiently employing the resources of the organization and sagaciously manipulating marketing mix elements. Some of the actions taken by executives are strictly market oriented. That is, the focus of their efforts is to win customers by dint of the attractiveness of their organizations' offerings. Other actions are competition oriented. That is, the strategies adopted are calculated to impede the progress of competitors by predatory or exclusionary means, such as foreclosing distribution channels to them. In most cases, there is a mixture of market-centered and competitor-centered strategies found in the "battle" plans of most organizations. Whatever the combination, the end result desired is the garnering of market power so that prices may be set significantly in excess of costs, leading to abundant profits for the firm. Indeed, the articulation of a marketing strategy is, in theory, an organization's attempt to spell out, explicitly, its contemplated route to the obtaining of a monopoly. In other words, if everything the organization laid down in its plan were to work out perfectly, then the organization should, theoretically at least, attract all the customers in the market, discourage all existing and potential competitors from staying in or entering the market, and thereby lead to the organization's total dominance of the market. Marketing, then, involves the pursuit of monopoly or, at the least, market dominance.

Clearly, very few organizations ever come close to achieving dominance. But when they do achieve it or approach it, then there may be questions raised by the antitrust enforcement agencies and competitors about how they accomplished the feat. Indeed, the greater the market occupancy of an organization, the more likely that its complex of marketing strategies and practices is going to raise genuine public issues. And frequently these issues involve questions related to the behavior the organization enacted in its march to the top. In other words, questions associated with market-oriented versus competition-oriented strategies become germane in uncovering the intentions of the executives responsible for directing the organization's ultimately successful moves in the marketplace.

This chapter deals with the antitrust issues surrounding truly successful organizations—those that have been so effective that they have achieved dominance in the specific market or submarkets that they targeted. In examining these issues, we have adopted an historical treatment, because the court cases in this area of the law have evolved in a patterned way. Given the importance of precedent here, it is meaningful to trace this evolution. Furthermore, history is important because, while there have been significant changes in court interpretations over time, there is no guarantee that the thinking and philosophy of the courts, and particularly of the Supreme Court, will not once again be strongly influenced by the decisions made and reasoning used in the early monopolization cases.

THE MEANING OF MONOPOLIZATION

The firm that actually succeeds too well may be the subject of an antitrust suit brought under Section 2 of the Sherman Act. Section 2 states that

> Every person who shall monopolize, or attempt to monopolize, or combine or conspire with any other person or persons to monopolize any part of the trade or commerce among the several states, or with foreign nations, shall be deemed guilty of a felony. . . .

A key question, of course, is, "What does monopolization mean?" While Section 2 has strong structural overtones, suggesting that *monopoly* is somehow to be prohibited, the word "monopolize" is action oriented and addresses conduct rather than outcomes. A firm has "monopolized" if it has deliberately adopted a course of market conduct through which it has obtained or maintained the power to control price or exclude competition.[1] However, any firm with at least *some* control over the terms and conditions at which it supplies its products or services to its customers possesses a degree of *monopoly power*, as the latter term is used by economists. Certainly, this is not what the framers of the Sherman Act had in mind when they constructed Section 2. The legal definition of monopoly seems to encompass only those firms that could be called "dominant" in a particular market, that is, firms possessing a *very high* degree of monopoly power.[2] In other words, *monopolization* is an active process aimed at securing *monopoly* or market dominance.

Monopoly is the outcome of monopolizing a *market*. Therefore, Section 2 cases, similar to the Clayton Act, Section 7 merger cases discussed in Chapter 4, generally begin by addressing the issue of just what is the *relevant market* for the product or service being offered by the defendant firm. Generically, as Shepherd and Wilcox have put it,

> A market is a grouping of buyers and sellers, communicating quickly and exchanging goods which are substitutable. . . . Substitutability in demands is the basic criterion (but substitutability in supply may also be a factor). Substitutability is measured by the cross-elasticity of demand among goods which may be inside or outside the market. . . .
>
> To define a market, one needs to know (a) the nature of the product and its alternatives, (b) the consumers' subjective images of the product, and (c) geographic limits on interchanging the products.[3]

As indicated in the discussion of the relevant market concept in Chapter 4, achieving consensus on the boundaries of a market is no simple matter. Slight alterations in the definition can have major consequences for the outcomes of antitrust cases, as Table 9-1 implies.

Once a definition of the relevant market is established, Section 2 cases usually proceed by comparing the sales of the defendant with those of other sellers who compete with the defendant. Then this market share is used as a rough index of the defendant's market power, along with other factors such as the likelihood of entry. If market share is very high, primary attention in these cases is turned to the defendant firm's behavior or to how it achieved the share (and concomitant market power) attributed to it.

MAJOR PRECEDENT-SETTING CASES

There have been a large number of Section 2 cases. Some are seminal; others simply serve to reinforce the theme established by the case or cases immediately preceding or succeeding them. Here we focus on the decisions that most commentators would agree make up the basic core of Section 2 cases, leaving aside those that are either peripheral or redundant.

[1] Lawrence A. Sullivan, *Handbook of the Law of Antitrust* (St. Paul, Minn.: West Publishing Co., 1977), p. 29.

[2] Peter Asch, *Economic Theory and the Antitrust Dilemma* (New York: John Wiley & Sons, 1970), p. 236.

[3] William G. Shepherd and Clair Wilcox, *Public Policies toward Business,* 6th ed. (Homewood, Ill.: Richard D. Irwin, Inc., 1979), p. 121.

Table 9-1.

Differing Definitions of the Relevant Market in Selected Antitrust Cases

| Case (year decided) | Relevant Market and the Resulting Share According to the | | | Action Taken |
	1. Defense (percent)	2. Agency or Other Plaintiff (percent)	3. Court in Final Action (percent)	
Alcoa (1945)	All ingot and scrap (33)	Ingot sold (90)	Ingot sold (90)	Alcoa convicted
Times–Picayune (1953)	All local advertising (33)	Advertising in morning newspapers (100)	All newspaper advertising	Acquitted
du Pont "Cellophane" (1956)	Flexible packaging (18)	Cellophane (75–100)	Flexible packaging materials (18)	Acquitted
du Pont–General Motors (1957)	Automotive finishes and fabrics (1 to 3)	GM purchases of these items (60 to 100)	GM purchases (60–100)	Convicted
Bethelehem–Youngstown merger (1958)	Structural metals and plastics (1 to 3)	Regional steel markets (25 plus)	Regional steel markets (25 plus)	Merger enjoined
Brown Shoe (1962)	All shoes (5)	Various types of shoes, in various cities (up to 50)	Specific markets (up to 50)	Merger enjoined
Philadelphia National Bank (1963)	National banking (trivial)	Philadelphia banking (36)	Philadelphia banking (36)	Merger enjoined
Rome Cable (1964)	All conductor wire (3)	Bare aluminum conductor (33)	Bare aluminum conductor and others (33)	Merger enjoined
Continental Can and Hazel–Atlas (1964)	Glass and metal containers are separate markets	Containers (25)	Containers (25)	Merger enjoined
Pabst–Blatz (1966)	National beer market (5)	Wisconsin beer market (24)	Wisconsin beer market (24)	Merger enjoined
Von's Grocery (1966)	Los Angeles retail grocery (7.5)	Los Angeles retail grocery (7.5)	Los Angeles retail grocery (7.5)	Merger enjoined
Grinnell (1966)	All protective services ("low")	Accredited central station protective services (87)	Accredited central station protective services (87)	Conviction
Telx v. IBM (1975)	All computer equipment (30)	Computer equipment "plug-compatible" with IBM equipment (80+)	All computer equipment (30)	IBM acquitted

Source: William G. Shepherd and Clair Wilcox, *Public Policies toward Business*, 6th ed. (Homewood, Ill.: Richard D. Irwin, Inc., 1979), p. 123.

Standard Oil (1911)

While a few cases preceded it, dealing mainly with railroad combinations,[4] *U.S.* v. *Standard Oil Co. of New Jersey* was the first blockbuster case of its kind in U.S. history.[5] It challenged the Standard Oil Trust headed by John D. Rockefeller. The trust had managed to maintain a 90 percent share of the kerosene and lubricating oil markets throughout most of the pre-automobile and pre-electricity eras of the 1880s and 1890s. It accomplished this feat by acquiring more than 120 of its former rivals, securing discriminatory rail freight rates and rebates, foreclosing crude oil supplies to competitors by buying up pipelines, and conducting business espionage. And, if this were not enough, it allegedly waged predatory price wars to drive rivals out of business or to soften them up for a takeover.[6] In fact, the mere listing of its predatory practices filled some 57 pages of the trial record.

The Supreme Court, while clearly impressed with Standard Oil's size and market dominance, indicated that the crime of monopolization involves not merely the acquisition of a monopoly position but, more importantly, the intent to acquire the position and exclude rivals from the industry. The market share achieved by Standard Oil was significant only when viewed in light of the exploitative or predatory practices in which it had engaged. Indeed, the Court took pains to explain that Section 2 was an adjunct to Section 1, which condemned *unreasonable* restraints of trade. However, Section 1 dealt with combinations and conspiracies; therefore, Section 2 was drafted, according to the Court's interpretation, to deal with a *single* firm seeking monopoly power. The Court pointed out that the law was not established by Congress to prohibit "normal methods of industrial development," but rather blatant acts disclosing a monopolistic intent. If the acts unduly restrained competition, going beyond "normal" business practice, then intent could be inferred. The upshot of the *Standard Oil* decision was that, for firms having monopoly power (in the legal sense of the term, i.e., a dominant firm within an industry), restraints of trade that would be illegal under Section 1 must necessarily constitute illegal monopolizing under Section 2.

Almost immediately after the Court issued its decision in *Standard Oil*, it handed down a virtually identical decision against the Tobacco Trust.[7] The Tobacco Trust controlled 95 percent of cigarrette sales. It had achieved this market position via a host of predatory practices: excluding rivals from sources of supply, buying plants to shut them down, using selective predatory pricing, and selling "fighting brands" at a loss to destroy competitors. Similar to *Standard Oil*, it was not American Tobacco's actual domination of the to-

---

[4] See *Northern Securities Co.* v. *U.S.*, 193 U.S. 197 (1904) and *U.S.* v. *Union Pacific Railroad Co.*, 222 U.S. 61 (1912).

[5] 221 U.S. 1 (1911).

[6] See Chapter 5 of this text for a discussion of predatory pricing, re Standard Oil.

[7] *U.S.* v. *American Tobacco Co.*, 221 U.S. 106 (1911).

bacco market, but the means by which domination was achieved, that was decisive in its downfall.

The *Standard Oil* and *American Tobacco* decisions were followed by a small but important set of cases in which the government successfully challenged a number of trusts. The du Pont group of explosives manufacturers was split into three parts.[8] Eastman Kodak was found to have monopolized the manufacture and sale of photographic apparatus and supplies.[9] And the glucose, thread, and farm machinery monopolies were also successfully prosecuted, as well as a group of railroads dominating the anthracite coal industry.[10]

United States Steel (1920)

U.S. v. *United States Steel Corporation*[11] must be viewed as a relatively bizarre case, irrespective of one's leanings on antitrust matters. While U.S. Steel never achieved the power in its markets comparable to the power achieved by the oil and tobacco trusts in theirs, the company was, at the time of the suit, an industrial colossus. Formed in 1901, it was a combination of 12 concerns, themselves resulting from earlier combinations of 180 separate companies with over 300 plants. When the trial began, it controlled one-half of the supply of steel in the nation. Judge Gary, the head of the corporation, was famous for hosting dinners at which prices were discussed among competitors and during which the infamous Pittsburgh-plus delivered pricing system was concocted. Yet U.S. Steel was exonerated. The reasons why are spelled out next.

First, it is important to note that, unlike Standard Oil and American Tobacco, U.S. Steel was not accused of trying to drive rivals from the industry through predatory pricing and other practices. On the contrary, in the words of the Court, its behavior was exemplary:

> It resorted to none of the brutalities or tyrannies that the cases illustrate of other combinations. It did not secure freight rebates; it did not increase its profits by reducing the wages of its employees . . . , by lowering the quality of its products, nor by creating an artificial scarcity of them; . . . it did not undersell its competitors in some localities by reducing prices there below those maintained elsewhere . . . ; there was no evidence that it attempted to crush its competitors or drive them from the market.[12]

Second, the firm had not really achieved monopoly power. The Judge Gary dinners only served to prove its lack of monopoly; had it had a truly monopolistic position it would not have had to meet with competitors to try and fix prices. It could have fixed prices on its own. Indeed, the Court reasoned that the corporation had intended to monopolize the industry, but that it had not succeeded in doing so. Following on this line of reasoning, Mr. Justice Mc-

---

[8] *U.S.* v. *E.I. du Pont de Nemours & Co.*, 188 Fed. 127 (1911).

[9] *U.S.* v. *Eastman Kodak Co.*, 226 Fed. 62 (1915).

[10] *U.S.* v. *Corn Products Refining Co.*, 234 Fed. 964 (1916); *U.S.* v. *American Thread Co.*, settled by consent decree in 1913; *U.S.* v. *Reading Co.*, 253 U.S. 26 (1920); *U.S.* v. *Lehigh Valley Railroad Co.*, 254 U.S. 255 (1920).

[11] 251 U.S. 417 (1920).

[12] Ibid.

Kenna took the position that, because market power had not been shown to exist (the corporation did not have control over the industry), the case was an attack on the sheer size of U.S. Steel. He concluded, "the law does not make mere size an offense or the existence of unexerted power an offense. It . . . requires overt acts. . . . It does not compel competition nor require all that is possible."[13]

Third, U.S. Steel's market share was declining. And, fourth, the government, in presenting its case against the corporation, clearly made a horrendous blunder. As Asch points out, "United States Steel's monopoly position was assumed as an obvious fact in the government's argument. When this 'fact' was rejected by the Court, the government's position was undermined, for it had not sought to emphasize the *attempt* to monopolize. . . ."[14] Thus, with all the dinners and collusive behavior, U.S. Steel was let off. Apparently, it would not have been considered to have successfully monopolized its industry unless its dominance had approached that of a pure monopolist.

Despite these important nuances, the *U.S. Steel* decision is very significant from a marketing perspective, because it was the first major decision to show that a large firm acting in a supposedly exemplary fashion from a market conduct viewpoint would be permitted to continue its previously successful marketing activities. The case was preceded or succeeded almost immediately by three cases involving industrial giants that reached the same basic conclusion. Thus, in 1918, United Shoe Machinery Corporation successfully defended itself against a monopolization charge stemming from its acquisition of over 50 shoe machinery producers holding complementary patents.[15] The Court accepted the corporation's argument that the combination was formed to achieve economies of vertical integration and to remove the serious danger of costly patent litigation among the various firms that it eventually acquired. In 1916, in a case against American Can Company, a district court observed that American "had done nothing of which any competitor or any consumer of cans complains, or anything which strikes a disinterested outsider as unfair or unethical," adding that it was "frankly reluctant to destroy so finely adjusted an industrial machine."[16] And finally, in 1927, the Supreme Court in a case against International Harvester Company directly followed the lead of the *U.S. Steel* decision when it stated that the law "does not make the mere size of a corporation, however impressive, or the existence of unexerted power on its part, an offense, when unaccompanied by unlawful conduct in the exercise of its power."[17] As related in Chapter 5, the price leadership that International Harvester exercised within its industry was rejected as offering evidence of monopoly.

---

[13] Ibid., at 451.

[14] Asch, op. cit., p. 242.

[15] *U.S.* v. *United Shoe Machinery Co. of New Jersey,* 247 U.S. 32 (1918).

[16] *U.S.* v. *American Can Company,* 230 Fed. 859 (1916) at 861 and 903.

[17] *U.S.* v. *International Harvester Company,* 274 U.S. 693 (1927) at 708.

Alcoa (1945)

The *Alcoa* decision would no doubt be viewed antagonistically by any marketing executive in any major U.S. corporation.[18] In one fell swoop, it brushed aside the logic behind *Standard Oil, American Tobacco,* and *U.S. Steel* and established new ground rules for judging monopolization cases.

The decision was written by Learned Hand, a Circuit Court judge, because a quorum of the Supreme Court could not be obtained. Four Supreme Court justices had been associated with earlier litigation involving Alcoa, and therefore a three-member panel of Circuit Court judges was empowered by Congress, as a court of last resort, to hear the case. The opinion of the court focused on two central issues: (1) whether Alcoa possessed a monopoly and (2) whether it had exhibited the intent essential to find monopolization.[19] As mentioned earlier, the initial question generally asked in getting at the first issue involves defining the relevant market and then calculating the defendant's share of that market. Indeed, the relevant market definition was critical in this case.

Alcoa was (and still is) a major, vertically integrated producer of aluminum. That is, not only does it produce ingots, but it also fabricates aluminum from the ingots it makes. It sells both ingots and fabricated aluminum on the open market in competition with other producers. In the lawsuit, concern was focused primarily on Alcoa's share of ingot production. In calculating Alcoa's share, debate centered on whether or not to include secondary or scrap aluminum in the denominator and whether or not to include Alcoa's total ingot production, including that which it kept for its own fabrication process, in the numerator. Depending on what was included or excluded, the final results varied markedly. For example,

- If the market were defined to include secondary (scrap) as well as primary ingot, and if Alcoa's relevant production were defined to exclude ingot that it produced *and* fabricated—that is, did not supply to the open market—the company's share of the market was about 33 percent.
- If the market were defined to include secondary and primary aluminum, but Alcoa's total production (including ingot not placed on the market) were taken as its relevant output, the company's share was about 64 percent.
- If the market were defined to include primary but to exclude secondary aluminum, and Alcoa's total production were taken, the market share would be about 90 percent. (The remaining 10 percent was accounted for by foreign imports.)[20]

Judge Hand favored the third definition because he reasoned that Alcoa's decisions with regard to ingot production would be directly influenced by the amount of scrap available, and since the corporation was one of the major generators of scrap, it could forecast demand for primary ingot relatively accu-

---

[18] *U.S.* v. *Aluminum Company of America,* 148 F.2d 416 (1945).

[19] See F. M. Scherer, *Industrial Market Structure and Economic Performance,* 2nd ed. (Chicago: Rand McNally College Publishing Company, 1980), p. 531.

[20] See Asch, op. cit., p. 243.

rately. Indeed, it could manipulate the market for both by taking into account in its output decisions the effect of scrap reclamation on future prices.

Once the relevant market was decided and the market share determined, Judge Hand then announced that a 90 percent share was clearly a monopoly, a 64 percent share might be, and a 33 percent share clearly was not. This comment has supplied a rule of thumb for all Section 2 cases since then, even though the rationale for the demarcations was never made clear.

Judge Hand next said that because it was a monopoly, the company had violated the law. He justified this pronouncement on the logic that Alcoa was engaged in illegal price fixing. Because it was the only seller, it must, of necessity, be the fixer of prices for the industry. As he stated, "[Alcoa] must sell at some price and the only price at which it could sell is a price which it itself fixed. Thereafter the power and its exercise must needs coalesce." In other words, price fixing was found to be inherent in monopoly. If a firm is all alone in a market, it must be fixing prices, thereby exercising its monopoly power.

He also addressed the critical issue of intent, observing that, given a company of Alcoa's dominance, it is not necessary to show brutal, ruthless, or otherwise unpalatable behavior to bring it within the prohibitions of the Sherman Act. As long as the company worked to achieve and retain its monopoly position, it violated the law. In supporting this line of reasoning, he pointed to Alcoa's building up of ore reserves and electric power sources and production capacity in advance of demand, saying,

> It was not inevitable that it should always anticipate increases in the demand for ingot and be prepared to supply them. Nothing compelled it to keep doubling and redoubling its capacity before others entered the field. It insists that it never excluded competitors; but we can think of no more effective exclusion than progressively to embrace each new opportunity as it opened and to face every newcomer with new capacity already geared into a great organization, having the advantage of experience, trade connections and the elite of personnel.[21]

With regard to the likelihood of being a "good" monopolist, Judge Hand indicated that it might be possible to find a corporation that "does not seek but cannot avoid" the control of a market, is a "passive beneficiary" of monopoly power, or has had monopoly power "thrust upon" it. This statement of permissible monopoly is a considerable distance from the definition of "good" monopolizing used in the *Standard Oil* case: achievement of a dominant position via "normal methods of industrial development."

Anyone at all familiar with the workings of the commercial marketplace has to be shaken by Judge Hand's pronouncements. Neale and Goyder, two British observers of the U.S. antitrust scene, put the situation very politely when they state, "An extreme interpretation of [Judge Hand's] view would impute illegal intent to a firm with monopoly power even on account of its very efficiency, if exclusionary effects were shown to result."[22] And a hard-liner on antitrust issues who is generally in favor of strong and vigorous antitrust en-

---

[21] *U.S.* v. *Aluminum Company of America*, op. cit., at 431.

[22] A. D. Neale and D. G. Goyder, *The Antitrust Laws of the U.S.A.*, 3rd ed. (New York: Cambridge University Press, 1980), p. 110.

forcement across the board, Lawrence Sullivan, is a bit less charitable when he writes, "To require that a firm, to avoid violation, must fail to expand in response to opportunities for profitable growth is to insist upon rather perverse market conduct."[23] There were instances of questionable intent on the part of Alcoa, such as its price squeezing tactics referred to in Chapter 6 and some exclusive dealing contracts with electric power companies, which excluded potential competitors, but the court made it clear that, while it enjoined the repetition of such practices in the future, it was holding Alcoa guilty of monopolization "regardless of such practices." Apparently, a major motivation behind Judge Hand's decision was a noneconomic one, because in his opinion he wrote that it was one of the purposes of the antitrust laws "to perpetuate and preserve for its own sake and in spite of possible cost, an organization of industry into small units which can effectively compete with each other."[24]

Under Judge Hand's presumptive illegality test, the government need only prove a defendant's monopoly position, and then the burden would shift to the defendant to show that it had not abused its position or that the monopoly was unavoidable.[25] Such a defense would be very difficult to accomplish. Three years later, in *U.S.* v. *Griffith Amusement Co.*, Justice Douglas picked up the main theme generated by Judge Hand when, in a repudiation of the *U.S. Steel* doctrine, he observed that "monopoly power, whether lawfully or unlawfully acquired, may itself constitute an evil and stand condemned under Section 2 even though it remains unexercised."[26]

United Shoe Machinery (1953)

The second *United Shoe Machinery* case represented an even more extreme extension of the *Alcoa* decision.[27] The facts presented to the court in 1953 were in most essentials unchanged from those considered 35 years earlier when the company was cleared of the charge of monopolization. United Shoe was found to supply somewhere between 75 and 85 percent of the machines used in the boot and shoe industry, although there was no tariff on imported machines and almost every industrial process could be carried out on machines made by other companies. United Shoe refused to sell its machines; it only leased them for long terms (10 years). Also, if a customer turned a machine back early, a fee was charged that was smaller if the customer took another machine from United Shoe as opposed to taking one from a competitor. The company also had a pricing structure that accepted lower profit margins on machines subject to competition. Finally, machine repair service was provided at no separate charge.

The case was tried before Judge Charles Wyzanski in federal district court

---

[23] Sullivan, op. cit., p. 96.

[24] *U.S.* v. *Aluminum Company of America*, op. cit., at 427.

[25] Gellhorn, op. cit., p. 148.

[26] *U.S.* v. *Griffith Amusement Co.*, 334 U.S. 100 (1948) at 107.

[27] *U.S.* v. *United Shoe Machinery Corp.*, 110 F. Supp. 295 (1953), affirmed per curiam, 347 U.S. 521 (1954).

in Massachusetts, and Wyzanski's decision was affirmed by the Supreme Court. Wyzanski recognized that the above-mentioned practices were in one sense "normal methods of industrial development"; yet, as he stated in his main conclusion,

> they are not practices which can be properly described as the inevitable consequences of ability, natural forces, or law. . . . They are contracts, arrangements and policies which, instead of encouraging competition based on pure merit, further the dominance of a particular firm. In this sense they are unnatural barriers: they unnecessarily exclude actual and potential competition: they restrict a free market. While the law allows many enterprises to use such practices, the Sherman Act is now construed by superior courts to forbid the continuance of effective market control based in part upon such practices.[28]

Falling back on Judge Hand's decision in *Alcoa,* Judge Wyzanski argued that monopoly is lawful only if it is "thrust upon" the monopolist. A company's monopoly power is unlawful if that power is the result of barriers erected by its own business methods (even though not predatory, immoral, or restraining trade in violation of Section 1 of the Sherman Act). The firm can, supposedly, still escape if it shows that the barriers are exclusively the result of superior skill, superior products, natural advantages, technological or economic efficiency, scientific research, low margins of profit maintained permanently and without discrimination, legal licenses, or the like.

In a manner similar to Judge Hand's, Judge Wyzanski also disposed of the question of intent in this case:

> Defendant intended to engage in the leasing practices and pricing policies which maintained its market power. That is all the intent the law requires when both the complaint and the judgment rest on a charge of "monopolizing," not merely "attempting to monopolize." Defendant having willed the means, has willed the end.[29]

In other words, efforts to maintain a very large market share are the crux of the violations found in both *United Shoe* and *Alcoa.*[30] Furthermore, if intentions to monopolize can be shown via uncovering specific behaviors, then it supposedly follows that the effect (monopoly) was intended. The results, coupled with evidence of seemingly "normal methods of industrial development," could serve to prove a violation.

Du Pont (1956)

More than anything, the *du Pont Cellophane* case was a debate over the means and methodology for establishing relevant product markets.[31] Du Pont produced almost 75 percent of the cellophane in the United States. Therefore, on the basis of the *Alcoa* and *United Shoe* decisions, du Pont should have been

[28] Ibid., at 346.

[29] Ibid.

[30] For an excellent analysis, see Cárl Kaysen, *United States* v. *United Shoe Machinery Corp.* (Cambridge, Mass.: Harvard University Press, 1956).

[31] *U.S.* v. *E. I. du Pont de Nemours and Co.,* 351 U.S. 377 (1956).

declared a monopolist and, without much more additional effort, been found guilty of monopolization. Du Pont countered that cellophane was not a distinct product, because it competed with other flexible packaging materials such as aluminum foil, wax paper, saran wrap, polyethlene, and the like. With these goods in the relevant product market, du Pont's market share declined to less than 20 percent, well below the monopoly threshold established by Judge Hand in *Alcoa.*

In its decision, the Supreme Court observed that what was needed "is an appraisal of the cross-elasticity of demand in the trade. . . ." The essence of the majority opinion was that the extent of cross-elasticity of demand (defined as the percentage change in the quantity demanded of one product divided by the percentage change in the price of another) for cellophane and other wrapping materials was crucial. The relevant market was, according to the Court, in those products that had "reasonable interchangeability" with cellophane for the purposes for which they were produced, considering "price, use and technical qualitites."

The Court never did pursue actual cross-elasticity measures. In fact, there is a real question as to whether such measures, as formally defined, would even be meaningful, given their total preoccupation with price changes (as opposed to changes in other levels of the marketing mix) and their static nature. Rather, the Court relied on a much more subjective feel for the relevant market based on its own perception of "reasonable interchangeability." It pointed out that cellophane, despite distinctive property combinations that gave it market advantages, "has to meet competition from other materials in every one of its uses. . . ." The government did not challenge statistics showing that cellophane provided less than 7 percent of bakery products wrappings, 25 percent for candy, 32 percent for snacks, 35 percent for meats and poultry, 47 percent for fresh produce, and 34 percent for frozen foods. These data indicated that cellophane shared its markets with other materials and were interpreted by the Court as evidence of competitiveness among wrappings. The sometimes significant price differences between cellophane and other materials were explained away by the Court on the basis that packaging materials represent a very small proportion of the total cost of packaged goods, and, therefore, the actual price of the packaging material would have minor importance to customers.

While this latter assumption is highly questionable, along with a number of others relating to price differences between cellophane and its competitors,[32] there can be no doubt that the *du Pont Cellophane* case should represent, for marketing executives at least, an oasis in a very uncomfortable desert. In fact, there was broad agreement that the Court had been influenced by du Pont's brilliant record of research, development, and innovation, and therefore was willing to look hard for an excuse to applaud rather than chastise the company. One wonders why, if this conjecture is true, United Shoe Machinery wasn't accorded the same courtesy. One answer might be that United Shoe's share of its relevant market might have led the Court to infer that United

---

[32] See George W. Stocking and Willard F. Mueller, "The Cellophane Case and the New Competition," *American Economic Review* 45 (March 1955), pp. 29–63.

Shoe's intent in using, say, leasing as a marketing strategy to maintain its market position was anticompetitive. The Court doesn't get to the question of intent until after it has decided on relevant market and market share issues. If du Pont's market share had been higher, then the Court might have applied the same reasoning used in *Alcoa* and *United Shoe*, and thereby might have condemned du Pont by further finding evidence of attempts on the company's part to maintain its market share. Another answer might be that the spectacular nature of du Pont's innovations gave an added luster to the company that United Shoe did not have. Also, there was no relevant market issue in the *United Shoe* case that the Court might have used to United Shoe's advantage. The company had a very large share of an easy-to-define market.

Grinnell (1966)

The *Grinnell* case[33] represents a very significant turning point in Section 2 cases, because it laid the foundation for a new way of thinking about "intent" which was carried forward into the contemporary cases discussed later. Indeed, it was the beginning of a break from the strictly structural diagnosis of monopoly and monopolization used in *Alcoa, United Shoe*, and, to a large extent, *du Pont Cellophane.*

Grinnell had acquired three companies in the insurance-accredited central station property protection (burglary and fire) business and then had engaged in a number of allegedly predatory and exclusionary tactics. The Court defined the relevant market as "accredited, central station property protection services" rather than as the wide variety of different services (e.g., guard dogs, night watchmen, single alarm systems, etc.) that could be used to provide protection against robbery and fires. Under this narrow definition, Grinnell was calculated to have a market share of 87 percent. Therefore, if one were to follow the *Alcoa* and *United Shoe* reasoning, the only question remaining would be whether Grinnell did *anything* to attempt to achieve or maintain its market share. It would be virtually impossible not to find a violation.

Even though it did condemn Grinnell, the Court did so for different reasons than those found in *Alcoa* and *United Shoe*. In the latter cases, the fact that both Alcoa and United Shoe had grown and developed as a consequence of their superior marketing abilities was used against them. In the *Grinnell* case, the Court stated that it is necessary to prove "willful acquisition or maintenance" of monopoly power as distinguished from "growth or development as a consequence of a superior product, business acumen, or historic accident."[34] In other words, in challenging a corporation under Section 2, the Justice Department or private parties would have to show that the practices used to acquire or maintain a large market share were "bad." Unlike *Alcoa* in particular, normal business methods would probably not be viewed negatively. A return to a concept of intent similar to that used in *Standard Oil* was signaled by the *Grinnell* decision.

[33] *U.S.* v. *Grinnell Corp.*, 384 U.S. 563 (1966).
[34] Ibid., at 570–71.

CONTEMPORARY CASES

There have been a number of major monopoly and monopolization cases since
the time of the *Grinnell* case that have never made it to the Supreme Court
but that are significant in that they provide some insights into the changing
tenor of the times. A number of these cases have been brought by the Federal
Trade Commission under Section 5 of the Federal Trade Commission Act,
which regulates unfair methods of competition. While all have been settled or
disposed of in one way or another, only two have required significant changes
on the part of the defendant; in the other six the defendants have either been
lightly admonished for misdeeds or been dismissed without penalty. This
record is far different from the days of *Alcoa, Griffith, United Shoe,* and
Grinnell. However, it should be reemphasized that *none* of the cases discussed
next were heard by the Supreme Court. Given its present composition,
though, it is unlikely that the end results would have been significantly different from the results actually achieved. But that is pure conjecture, and the
Court would still have had to deal with the precedents discussed previously.

IBM (1975, 1978, 1979, 1982)

During the period 1965–1978, International Business Machines Corporation
attracted approximately 20 private domestic treble-damage antitrust suits
charging it with monopoly and monopolization and one massive public suit
brought by the U.S. Justice Department. The four most notorious private suits
involved Telex,[35] Memorex,[36] Transamerica,[37] and California Computer Products.[38] All were similar, and therefore we will only describe the gist of one of
them here. The public suit requires special and separate attention.

Telex v. IBM.

In 1972, Telex sued IBM, claiming that IBM used predatory pricing to stop
its entry into the market for disk and tape drives that were "plug compatible"
with IBM equipment. IBM has long been the dominant producer of central
processing units and is also a large supplier of peripheral equipment. IBM reacted to competition from Telex by making substantial price cuts on various
peripheral pieces and by offering discounts to customers who leased equipment for a period of one or two years. It also countered competition for memory units by integrating the main memory component, previously separate,
into the central processing unit.

The district court agreed with Telex and accepted Telex's definition of the
relevant market as being "peripheral equipment plug-compatible to the central

---

[35] *Telex Corporation* v. *International Business Machines Corp.,* 510 F.2d 894 (10th Cir. 1975).

[36] *ILC Peripherals Leasing Corp. (Memorex)* v. *International Business Machines Corp.,* 458 F. Supp. 423
(N.D. Cal. 1978).

[37] *Transamerica Computer Co.* v. *International Business Machines Corp.,* 481 F. Supp. 965 (N.D. Cal. 1979).

[38] *California Computer Products* v. *International Business Machines Corp.,* 613 F.2d 727 (9th Cir. 1979).

processing units manufactured by IBM." Under this definition, IBM's share of the market was between 80 and 90 percent on many kinds of equipment, thus meeting the standard for monopoly established in the earlier cases. But the 10th Circuit Court of Appeals held that peripheral equipment compatible with *all* systems, including IBM's, should be the relevant market, and this ruling meant that IBM's share was much lower than the district court had found. Even more important than the relevant market definition, however, was the fact that the Circuit Court ruled that IBM's actions had not been abusive. In other words, the court relied on the concept of intent developed in the *Grinnell* case and argued that IBM was entitled to adopt "normal business practices" to defend its market share against competitors. As discussed in Chapter 5, it was shown that IBM's price cuts were not predatory, because the reductions resulted in prices that still yielded IBM reasonable profits. IBM's response to competition was held to be "conduct well within the boundaries of permitted competition." The 9th Circuit Court of Appeals in the *California Computer Products* case echoed the sentiment of the 10th Circuit in the *Telex* case when it said,

> IBM's price cuts were a part of the very competitive process the Sherman Act was designed to promote. To accept Cal. Comp.'s position would be to hold that IBM could not compete if competition would result in injury to its competitors, an ill-advised reversal of the Supreme Court's pronouncement that the Sherman Act is meant to protect the competitive process, not competitors.[39]

U.S. v. IBM.

The Justice Department filed a complaint on January 17, 1969, in the Southern District Court of New York charging that IBM held a monopoly, that a pattern of price discrimination prevented effective competition by smaller specialized producers, and that the introduction of the major 360 line of computers in 1965 was done in a way that eliminated competition.[40] The tone of the charge was remarkably similar to that used in the *United Shoe Machinery* case. The Justice Department did not allege that IBM was engaged in gross violations of the law. Rather, the government claimed that by the subtle timing of its products, its pricing, and its designs, IBM had "smothered" existing and potential competition. The Justice Department believed that, even though an individual business practice might not be illegal in itself, the pattern of IBM's conduct illustrated an intent to monopolize and, therefore, should be attacked under the Sherman Act.[41] The government's original charges against IBM focused on sizable "general-purpose" computers and peripheral products sold to companies for business use. The charges of monopolization did not include personal or minicomputers nor did they include enormous computers used almost solely for scientific research.

[39] Ibid.

[40] *U.S.* v. *International Business Machines Corp.*, S.D. New York, complaint filed Jan. 17, 1969.

[41] See William M. Carley, "Dismissal of IBM Antitrust Case Assailed by Ex-Justice Aide Who Supervised Suit," *Wall Street Journal*, Feb. 5, 1982, p. 10.

In January 1982, thirteen years after the complaint was filed, the Justice Department, following the recommendation of Assistant Attorney General William Baxter, dropped its suit. In making the recommendation, Baxter suggested that the case was founded on a "no-fault monopolization" theory similar to that espoused in *Alcoa* and *United Shoe* by which the government need not prove illegal acts in order to condemn the market position of a company.[42] The Reagan Administration's position was that, in order to find monopolization, it is necessary to show evidence of "serious business improprieties that are intended to interfere with competitors, other than by improving the situations of one's consumers.[43] If such evidence cannot be presented, then "a company that is large and has a large market share is free and should be free to go on competing aggressively, keeping its prices down and capturing an even larger market share if it can."[44] In making the announcement regarding the dropping of the lawsuit, Baxter indicated that past enforcement efforts had been too strict on dominant firms that had achieved and held their positions through efficiency, rather than through predatorily pricing products below long-run costs or other illegal acts. And finally he added that, even if the government were to have won the case against IBM, there was no available relief or remedy that would make any sense. Breaking up IBM "would be totally disproportionate to the nature and scope of the violations that we might be able to prove."[45]

AT&T (1982)

Motivated by a long-standing desire to separate Western Electric from AT&T,[46] the Justice Department brought suit against AT&T for the third time.[47] In a complaint filed on November 20, 1975, in the District of Columbia, the Justice Department charged AT&T with monopolization under Section 2 of the Sherman Act.[48] Slightly over six years later, on the same day that the Justice Department dropped its suit against IBM, it announced a settlement of the AT&T case. Thus, in one afternoon, two of the most monumental cases in antitrust history were brought to a close. The accomplishment, irrespective of what one's feelings about the specifics of the cases and their settlements might be, was nothing short of stupendous.

The critical incentive behind AT&T's willingness to settle the case was supposedly the company's desire to free itself from a 1956 federal consent decree[49]

---

[42] See Robert E. Taylor, "Antitrust Enforcement Will Be More Selective, Two Big Cases Indicate," *Wall Street Journal*, Jan. 11, 1982, p. 6.

[43] Ibid.

[44] Ibid.

[45] Ibid.

[46] See *U.S.* v. *Western Electric, Inc., et al.*, CCH 1956 Trade Cases, Para. 68, 246.

[47] See discussion of AT&T situation in Shepherd and Wilcox, op. cit., pp. 151–153.

[48] *U.S.* v. *American Telephone & Telegraph Co. et al.*, District of Columbia, complaint filed Nov. 20, 1975.

[49] *U.S.* v. *Western Electric, Inc.*, op. cit.

that prohibited it from competing in unregulated businesses. The Justice Department's case against AT&T was based on its belief that AT&T used its local telephone monopoly to subsidize its other businesses and, thus, to harm competitors. Therefore, when AT&T agreed to divest itself of its 22 local telephone operating companies as part of the settlement, the concerns of the Justice Department were alleviated.[50] AT&T's decision may also have been prompted by the fact that, if the district court had ruled against it and if the decision were upheld on appeal, the company would have had to face the prospect of divestiture by the court as well as of scores of private damage lawsuits seeking to follow along behind the government's victory. The settlement leaves other parties with the task of proving that AT&T violated the law in impeding their competitive efforts.[51] Apart from the issue of motivation, there can be no doubt that the AT&T settlement is one of the most significant antitrust developments since the Supreme Court ordered the dissolution of the Standard Oil Trust and the Tobacco Trust. Furthermore, the conclusion of the *AT&T* matter indicates to some antitrust observers that when the government presents a strong case in a well-managed trial it can dissolve a monopoly within a reasonable period, something that it has not been able to accomplish very often even though it has achieved favorable decisions in a number of cases.[52]

Berkey–Kodak (1979)

In 1972, Kodak simultaneously introduced the so-called 110-size or "pocket" Instamatic camera and film to fit it. It alerted its film-processing laboratories in advance of the introduction so that they could make necessary adjustments prior to the launch. Berkey, a film-processor, wholesaler, and retailer of photographic equipment, and, up until 1978, a camera manufacturer, alleged that Kodak's competitors were at an unfair disadvantage because of Kodak's ability to capitalize on its innovation, given its dominant position in the camera and film markets already.[53]

The Second Circuit Court of Appeals held that Kodak was entitled to enjoy the lead-time over other camera manufacturers arising from its invention of the pocket camera.[54] It also held that a vertically integrated business (cameras, film, and film processing) does not offend against Section 2 of the Sherman Act simply because one department benefits from its association with

---

[50] See James A. White, "In Antitrust Accord, AT&T Bets on Future by Writing Off Past," *Wall Street Journal*, Jan. 11, 1982, p. 1; "IBM Antitrust Lawsuit Dropped by U.S.; AT&T Settlement Begins 6-Year Revamping," *Wall Street Journal*, Jan. 11, 1982, p. 3; and Stephen Wermiel, "AT&T Settlement Upheld by High Court, Clearing Way for Divesting of Local Units," *Wall Street Journal*, Mar. 1, 1983, p. 2.

[51] General Dynamics has picked up the challenge. See "General Dynamics Sues AT&T, Alleges Antitrust Breach in Telecommunications," *Wall Street Journal*, Dec. 30, 1982, p. 22.

[52] Taylor, op. cit., p. 1.

[53] Berkey is a major customer of Kodak as well. Up to the time of the trial, the companies had enjoyed a long and positive relationship.

[54] *Berkey Photo, Inc.* v. *Eastman Kodak Co.*, 603 F.2d 263 (2d Cir. 1979), *cert. denied*, 444 U.S. 1093 (1980).

another that has monopoly power. Kodak's ability to introduce the new film format at the same time as the new camera was "solely a benefit of integration and not, without more, a use of Kodak's power in the film market to gain a competitive advantage in cameras." In the decision, Judge Irving Kaufman, chief judge of the 2nd Circuit, wrote,

> It is the possibility of success in the marketplace, attributable to superior performance, that provides the incentives on which the proper functioning of our competitive economy rests. If a firm that has engaged in the risks and expense of research and development were required to share with its rivals the benefits of those endeavors, this incentive would very likely be vitiated.[55]

Not only had Berkey sought treble damages, but it had also insisted that Kodak modify its method of new product introduction by notifying its competitors prior to introduction about the features and details associated with its new products. The court clearly held that both of these requests were unwarranted.

Kodak was, however, found guilty of violating the antitrust laws by conspiring with General Telephone & Electronics Corp.'s Sylvania division and with General Electric Company in the introduction of certain flash devices. Berkey also claimed that Kodak had overbilled it for film and photographic paper. The latter charge was still unresolved when Kodak agreed to settle the remaining issues in the case in 1981 for $6.75 million.[56]

Kellogg (1982)

In 1972, the Federal Trade Commission charged the major breakfast cereal producers—Kellogg, General Mills, General Foods, and Quaker Oats—with a shared monopoly.[57] In other words, the charge of monopolization was levied not against a single dominant firm, but against four (later three; Quaker Oats was dropped from the suit) companies who together controlled 90 (or 81) percent of ready-to-eat cereal sales. In its complaint, the FTC staff stated that the companies had acted as though they were one loose monopoly, setting prices for products among themselves, saturating the market with scores of their products to the exclusion of competition, engaging in self-space allocation conspiracies, and refusing to sell private labels to large retail supermarket chains. However, on September 1, 1981, Administrative Law Judge Alvin Berman ruled that the FTC's lawyers had failed to prove the price fixing and monopolization charges, and approximately 4½ months later, the Federal Trade Commission dismissed the case, adopting Judge Berman's findings.[58]

The FTC staff's case rested on a broad interpretation of the Federal Trade Commission Act's Section 5, which prohibits unfair methods of competition.

---

[55] Ibid.

[56] "Kodak to Pay Berkey Photo $6,750,000, Settling Eight-Year Civil Antitrust Suit," *Wall Street Journal,* Sept. 24, 1981, p. 14.

[57] *In the matter of Kellogg Co. et al.,* docket no. 8934, complaint filed January 24, 1972.

[58] *In the matter of Kellogg Co. et al.* initial decision, docket no. 8883, Sept. 1, 1981; *In the matter of Kellogg Co. et al.,* order denying appeal and vacating initial decision, docket no. 8883, Jan. 15, 1982.

In his decision, Judge Berman said that the staff had failed to prove that Kellogg always announced price changes first and that the cereal companies had not operated independently of one another. He saw no attempt on the part of the companies to curtail competition by their introduction of new products; rather, he said it appeared to be a straightforward response to "consumers' desire for variety in breakfast." Introduction of new brands was a legitimate means of competition. The staff also failed to show that the companies charged higher prices than those the competition would permit or that they realized "monopoly profits." The judge could find no evidence of any tacit agreement among the companies not to compete for shelf space in retail stores because of an alleged acquiescence to a shelf space allocation plan developed by Kellogg. Finally, he rejected the FTC counsel's assertion that the companies wasted money on excessive advertising.

> I start with the basic assumption that advertising is a viable and legitimate method of competition. And complaint counsel have failed to demonstrate that the large volume of advertising in the . . . industry does not have a competitive basis or that it reflects the existence of supra-competitive profits.[59]

General Foods (1982)

In a complaint issued on July 14, 1976, the FTC charged General Foods Corporation with violations of Section 5 of the FTC Act and Section 2(a) of the Robinson–Patman Act. It asserted that General Foods had used unfair methods of competition and attempted to monopolize the coffee market through its Maxwell House Division. Specifically, the FTC alleged that the company had responded to the eastward expansion of Procter & Gamble's Folger brand by

- predatory pricing, that is, sustained pricing below costs;
- using a "fighting brand," which is a brand aimed at a specific competitor to disrupt its marketing efforts;
- attempting to impose restrictions on where competing firms could sell; and
- using extensive consumer and trade promotions in both new and previously established marketing areas to deter the entry of new brands.[60]

Between 1971 and 1976, General Foods had achieved a market share of 45 percent of noninstant coffee in the East and more than 50 percent in some of the larger cities in the region.

On January 25, 1982, Administrative Law Judge Lewis Parker ruled that General Foods' actions in the eastern region were "legitimately defensive."[61] He noted that as a result of a one-third decline in coffee consumption between

[59] "FTC Judge Dismisses Charges that Cereal Companies Avoided Competition, Under a Shared Monopoly," *FTC News Summary*, vol. 50–81, Sept. 18, 1981, p. 1. See also *In the matter of Kellogg Co. et al.*, initial decision, op. cit.

[60] See *In the matter of General Foods Corp.*, initial decision, docket no. 9085, Jan. 25, 1982, and "Unfair Competition Charges against General Foods Dismissed; Judge Finds Maxwell House Actions 'Legitimately Defensive,' *FTC News Summary*, Feb. 5, 1982, p. 2. See also "General Foods Cleared by FTC Aide over Coffee Markets," *Wall Street Journal*, Feb. 4, 1982, p. 12.

[61] *In the matter of General Foods Corp.*, op. cit. For a comparable decision in an industrial goods setting, see *In the matter of E. I. du Pont de Nemours & Company*, initial decision, docket no. 9108, Sept. 4, 1979.

1968 and 1978, coffee companies were only able to maintain sales or to grow by taking market share away from competitors as opposed to expanding the market. This caused manufacturers to intensify their marketing and promotional activity. It was during this period that Maxwell House's major competitor, Folger, entered the East. According to Judge Parker, the aggressive pricing and sales activities by the Maxwell House Division in the early to mid-1970s stemmed from a justifiable business goal; the division was trying to prevent Procter & Gamble from entering the market in the Northeast.[62]

Borden (1976), Xerox (1975), and Exxon (1981)

Three additional monopolization cases warrant mention, although it is likely none of them will find a large place in legal history. In the first of these, Borden, maker of ReaLemon, was charged with monopolizing the reconstituted lemon juice market through exclusionary tactics, such as assorted predatory pricing and promotional tactics.[63] The case, which was decided by an administrative law judge in 1976, was unique in two respects. First, in defining the relevant market, the law judge accepted the FTC staff's suggestion to omit the juice from lemons as being directly competitive with reconstituted lemon juice. Second, upon finding Borden guilty (Borden had, in fact, severely harrassed its tiny principal competitor, Golden Crown), the Commission as a whole denied the major remedy suggested by the staff—trademark licensing—deeming it unnecessary to curb Borden's monopoly power. (Borden had over 80 percent of the reconstituted lemon juice market.) The commission instead enjoined Borden from selling juice "below its cost or at unreasonably low prices" with the effect of eliminating competition. And, in 1983, a majority of the five-member commission, representing the economic philosophy of the Reagan Administration, went one step farther by voting to abandon its original order in favor of a negotiated agreement that would only bar Borden from setting ReaLemon prices below the level of certain variable costs under a formula that excludes some of the costs associated with developing and marketing the product.[64] The formula is closely in line with the Areeda–Turner test for predatory pricing mentioned in Chapter 5.

In the second case, Xerox was charged by the FTC with monopolizing the market for plain paper copiers and the entire market for office copiers.[65] By leasing rather than selling its machines, Xerox was able to develop a finely tuned system of price discrimination, based on numbers of runs, number of copies per run, special large user discounts, and still other complicated conditions.[66] The case paralleled, in many respects, *United Shoe Machinery*. The

---

[62] *In the matter of General Foods Corp.*, op. cit.

[63] *In the matter of Borden, Inc.*, initial decision, docket no. 8978, Aug. 19, 1976.

[64] "FTC Settles 'ReaLemon' Pricing Case with Borden," *FTC News Notes*, Vol. 39–83, June 17, 1983, p. 1 and Margaret Garrand Warner, "FTC to Relax Pricing Order against Borden," *Wall Street Journal*, Mar. 2, 1983, p. 46.

[65] *In the matter of Xerox Corp.*, decision and order, 86 FTC 364 (1975).

[66] See Shepherd and Wilcox, op. cit., p. 150.

FTC complaint was settled through a consent decree making Xerox's extensive portfolio of copying machine patents available for licensing at a royalty rate not exceeding 1.5 percent. Although some of the discriminatory pricing was dropped, it was rapidly replaced by even more complex plans. Xerox's market share has, however, declined significantly since 1975, and in light of the decline, the FTC in 1983 modified its original 1975 order to allow Xerox more marketing latitude.

Finally, in 1973, the Federal Trade Commission filed a complaint against Exxon and seven other large oil companies.[67] The complaint alleged that the companies had "maintained and reinforced a non-competitive market structure in the refining of crude oil" in the eastern and Gulf Coast states of the United States, in violation of Section 5 of the FTC Act. In actuality, the basic theory was one of "shared monopoly," similar to the cereal case discussed previously. The FTC's demands for discovery of a vast amount of documentation and the defendants' active opposition to its requests meant that, eight years later, the trial had still not begun. With the administrative law judge's decision in the cereal case a negative one and with the prospect of being bogged down in a situation that could very easily go nowhere, the FTC, in keeping with the overall philosophical trend established by the Reagan administration, dropped the entire proceeding in 1981.

PROBLEMS WITH MONOPOLIZATION CASES

Even if a dyed-in-the-wool monopolist could be found that had achieved its position through all sorts of predatory practices, there would still be enormous problems involved in proving monopolization or in remedying the situation, once proved. First, big monopolization cases are generally so complex and difficult that they are impractical tools to use in restructuring huge companies. And when they have been used for restructuring purposes, the results have not been very impressive. As Scherer points out,

> the *direct* impact of Sherman Act Section 2 in lessening market concentration has been modest. Between 1890 and 1970, the courts have ordered structural reorganization in only 32 Section 2 cases—all but 7 of them before 1950. A few of the orders have been drastic. . . . But most have been mild . . .[68]

The only major exception in recent history has been the *AT&T* settlement. But it should be remembered that AT&T was a regulated monopoly, which made the Solomon-like decision to split off the 22 operating companies somewhat easier to accomplish. It was relatively clear that the operating companies had somehow to remain regulated, although the final organization of the rest of the company and the relationship of the operating companies to the original parent may not be settled for many years to come.[69] The situation in monopo-

---

[67] *In the matter of Exxon Corp. et al.,* docket no 8934, complaint filed July 18, 1973.

[68] Scherer, op. cit., p. 540.

[69] Margaret Garrard Warner, "Reagan Plans to Back Bill to Supplement Proposed Antitrust Accord with AT&T," *Wall Street Journal,* Feb. 16, 1982, p. 4.

lization cases is likely to be closer to the dilemma expressed in Baxter's statement relative to IBM: "Even if the government won this case, there is no relief I could recommend in good conscience."[70] Furthermore, the times often militate against restructuring. As Federal Trade Commissioner Patricia Bailey stated early in 1982 when explaining why it was pointless to hear the staff's appeal on the cereal case, "it is unlikely that the FTC could restructure any industry without a clear Congressional mandate to do so. . . . The evidence is clear that Congress is opposed to restructuring at this time."[71]

Second, the costs of litigating a monopoly case are simply staggering. It cost the Federal Trade Commission nearly $6 million to prosecute the cereal case, for example. The amount spent by corporations generally is not made public, but there is little doubt that, for a major case, it would dwarf the $6 million figure. As Easterbrook has observed,

> The larger the stakes, the more the parties will invest in litigating. In a $5 billion case, it is worth investing as much as $50 million to obtain a 1 percent increase in the chance of prevailing. And when the defendants invest more in litigating, the government must do so too.[72]

Third, it is in the defendant's best interest to throw up as many intellectual roadblocks as possible and to create maximum confusion so that eventually the judge and/or the jury wears out and some kind of a settlement is reached prior to an actual decision. The defendant will generally challenge the definition of the market, generate information about the cost of production under current and future conditions, contend that the challenged practices contribute to efficiency rather than exclusion, and on and on. Again, as Easterbrook has so appropriately observed, "The cases become so sprawling that they overwhelm the critical sense of judges and juries, who can scarcely comprehend what the fuss is about."[73]

Fourth, given the length of time it takes to try a monopolization case (e.g., 13 years for IBM, 10 years for Kellogg, and neither of these were brought to a final resting place in the courts), it is no wonder that the results, whatever they are, are likely to be obsolete. Technological change, new competition (both foreign and domestic), shifting taste patterns, and so on, all tend to make the marketplace highly dynamic. With the pace of change being what it is, it is highly likely that only those individuals who thrive on risk would wish to predict the state of any market 10 to 13 years out into the future. This does not mean that monopolistic transgressions should go unpunished; it simply means that there is bound to be significant confusion about the appropriate punishment once a monopolization case gets to the end of its long and tortuous road.

Finally, the treble-damage possibility motivates private litigation in this

---

[70] Taylor, op. cit., p. 6. See, also, the discussion in Easterbrook, op. cit.

[71] "FTC Dismisses Charges That Cereal Companies Avoided Competition, Under a Shared Monopoly," op. cit.

[72] Frank H. Easterbrook, "Breaking Up Is Hard to Do," *AEI Journal on Government and Society*, Nov./Dec. 1981, p. 31.

[73] Ibid.

area. Indeed, this is an age of litigation, and it is frequently difficult to see the rationale behind certain suits. Sometimes, antitrust suits seem motivated by peevish reactions to failures in the marketplace. It has become commonplace to sue "dominant" firms for monopolization.[74] Lawsuits have, to a certain extent, become a competitive weapon—another element of the marketing mix, as it were. "If you can't beat 'em, sue 'em," might be a legitimate motto for some business enterprises. Indeed, as Neale and Goyder point out when discussing the *Berkey–Kodak* and *Telex–IBM* decisions,

> These cases may be seen as a realistic and healthy reaction by the courts against the possibility that if companies with market power like Kodak and IBM were too readily seen as fair game for treble-damage actions, they might see themselves as forced to provide a "feather-bed" environment for competitors in their industries; and this would be anti-competitive rather than in the spirit of antitrust.[75]

POTENTIAL PROBLEMS: THE EUROPEAN SITUATION

Just when the antitrust monopolization issue seems to be reaching an equilibrium in this country, problems appear to be arising in Europe over many of the same concerns with which our courts have seemingly already begun to come to grips. In December 1980, the executive committee of the European Community (Common Market) started an investigation of whether IBM had abused its market position in Western Europe.[76] Specifically, the executive committee charged that IBM dominated the European computer market and alleged that IBM abused its dominant position in a number of ways, including combining the computer's main memory with the central processing unit so that competitors were precluded from selling certain of their own memory devices. In addition, the committee charged that when IBM first announced a new product, it did not disclose technical details on "interfaces" (the points at which various parts of computer systems plug together); instead, IBM provided those details only when it first shipped a new product to customers, which was sometimes as long as 18 months following announcement of the product. Such actions, the commission alleged, in effect "froze" most of the European computer market during the period between announcement and shipment.[77] One remedy that has been proposed by the Europeans would compel IBM to disclose certain technical data even before the first shipment of a new product.[78] Clearly, the whole proceeding smacks of *Telex, California Computer Products,* and *Berkey–Kodak* all wrapped together. The feeling of *deja vu* is ominous. And, in fact, to make the situation even more like history repeating itself, two

---

[74] See Shepherd and Wilcox, op. cit., p. 152.

[75] Neale and Goyder, op. cit., p. 121.

[76] See "IBM's Antitrust Troubles Are Not Finished Yet," *Business Week,* Jan. 25, 1982, p. 24; Debbie C. Tennison, "IBM Antitrust Suit in Common Market Could Have Widespread Ramifications," *Wall Street Journal,* Mar. 1, 1982, p. 5; and William M. Carley, "Critics See Impropriety in European Lobbying by Antitrust Chief," *Wall Street Journal,* Mar. 31, 1982. p. 1.

[77] See Carley, "Critics See Impropriety. . . ," op. cit.

[78] Ibid.

competitors that both make computer equipment compatible with IBM, Amdahl Corporation and Memorex Corporation, have entered the European case as complainants against IBM. However, it should be noted that the European Community's antitrust law focuses much more on the abuse of power than on corporate intent relative to attaining or maintaining large market shares. Therefore, the result in Europe could be different from the result in the United States, depending on the evidence provided as to IBM's conduct abroad.

Another indication of possible problems for U.S. firms operating in Europe was the announcement by the West German Cartel Office that it would ban the 1981 acquisition of Rothmans Tobacco (Holdings) Ltd. by Philip Morris, Inc., as it applies to the West German cigarette market.[79] The Rothmans German subsidiary, Martin Brinkmann AG, had a 16.8 percent share of the German cigarette market in 1982, and Philip Morris' German subsidiary had a 14.4 percent share. West Germany is Europe's largest cigarette consuming market. In announcing the ban, the Cartel Office was, for the first time, attempting to block the effects of an international merger in West Germany. It was also the first time that the Cartel Office issued a ruling against two foreign companies. Even though the Cartel Office's decision was not legally binding and is being appealed in the West German courts, it represents another, very obvious instance of European questioning with respect to dominant firms. While the issue involved is a merger rather than strictly monopolization, which has been the subject of this chapter, there is a serious overlap that should prompt concern among marketing executives.

CONCLUSION

A major evolution has taken place in the way in which the achievements of successful firms are judged under the antitrust laws. In the very beginning of antitrust enforcement of Section 2 of the Sherman Act, the decisions of the Supreme Court focused almost exclusively on the conduct of the defendants. The Court refused to condemn "normal methods of industrial development," but instead looked for evidence of truly predatory and exclusionary behavior that impelled a firm (like Standard Oil of New Jersey or American Tobacco) to a dominant position in its industry. The Court insisted, though, that mere size was no offense; even though a firm might be enormous, this fact alone did not mean that it was necessarily in violation of the Sherman Act. During this "conduct" era, the Court condemned only flagrant abuses of "monopoly power." If it was not convinced that the defendant in question had actually achieved the requisite amount of monopoly power, it was prone to overlook and/or excuse what sometimes appeared to be flagrant abuses, as the 1920 *U.S. Steel* decision indicates.

---

[79] John M. Geddes and Janet Guyon, "Germany Bars Philip Morris Acquisition Plan," *Wall Street Journal,* Mar. 5, 1982, p. 5.

All Section 2 cases tend to follow a similar process: first, a relevant market is defined; second, the market share of the defendant firm is calculated; and third, if the market share is very high, then the means by which the firm achieved or maintained the market share are scrutinized. Starting with the *Alcoa* decision in 1945, emphasis shifted from conduct to structural factors or conditions. During the "structural" era, the major focus was on the definition of the relevant market and the calculation of market share. If a defendant's market share was found to be very high (e.g., above 70 percent), then the courts were satisfied that a violation of Section 2 had taken place if the firm had used *any* means, normal or abnormal, to achieve or maintain it. In other words, if it could be shown that the firm had taken steps to achieve or maintain its "monopoly" position (even if these steps were ones that any marketing executive would have been expected to take under similar circumstances), then the firm (e.g., *Alcoa, United Shoe Machinery Corp.*) was deemed to have engaged in monopolization in violation of Section 2.

The *Grinnell* case in 1966 ushered in the modern era of Section 2 decisions, one that most marketing executives find more palatable than the "structural" era. Since 1966, the courts have combined *both* structure and conduct analyses in a much more comprehensive fashion. While the three-step process outlined previously is still basically the same as it has always been, the finding of a large market share is a prerequisite only for searching for *questionable* conduct that may have led to the acquisition or maintenance of the market share. In other words, growth or development as a consequence of "superior product, business acumen, or historic accident" is not to be condemned. Rather, plaintiffs must prove "skillful acquisition or maintenance" of monopoly power on the part of defendants. This means that plaintiffs must show that the conduct of defendants is outside the realm of "normal methods of industrial development." The major focus has, once again, shifted to "abnormal" intent.

The contemporary belief on the part of the antitrust enforcement agencies seems to be that some of the precedents established in such monopolization cases as *Alcoa* and *United Shoe* have wrongly prevented large companies from competing vigorously and from providing consumers with the full benefits of greater efficiency that large companies can often achieve. The "modern" view is that past antitrust enforcement was too "tough" on dominant companies that achieved and maintained their positions through efficiency rather than through predatorily pricing products below long-run costs or other illegal acts. There is, however, no guarantee that the contemporary perspective will continue or that the Supreme Court will not fall back on the precedents existing prior to the *Grinnell* case. This is why an historical treatment has been adopted in this chapter. The marketing executive must be forewarned of the kinds of challenges to successful marketing strategy that have been made in the past and the criteria under which those successes were judged.

Monopolization cases are a nightmare for all parties involved. They are extremely cumbersome, costly, and, frequently, inconclusive. Their inconclusiveness stems from the fact that, even if violations are found, functional remedies are extremely difficult to construct. Perhaps the only truly successful monopolization case in the past half-century was the one involving *AT&T,* but, even there, a settlement, rather than a court decision, was arrived at, which has taken years and years to sort out. And *AT&T* involved a regulated company, making the suggested remedy more easy to suggest than remedies for nonregulated companies. Nevertheless, monopolization cases often serve very useful purposes, because they restrain dominant firms from future destructive acts toward their competitors and/or they encourage such firms to voluntarily adopt more open postures with respect to the sharing of critical information with smaller firms, such as data about product planning and introduction.

Just as the question of how to deal with monopoly and monopolization issues seems to be reaching some kind of an equilibrium in the United States, these same issues are being rekindled in Western Europe. The European Community, operating under a different set of antitrust laws from those in the United States, is concerned about abuses of monopoly power and has begun to challenge the conduct of some major multinational corporations. It would be naive to think that the European officials would not avail themselves of the lessons the United States has learned through the enforcement of the Sherman Act or that they would not study major U.S. cases in order to gain deeper insights into the competitive process. Where they will end up, though, is not at all certain. In fact, it is entirely possible that they will adopt a harder "line" than that found in the contemporary monopolization decisions outlined in this chapter. If this is likely to be the situation, then dominant firms may find their marketing practices increasingly challenged by the European Community.

Case 1
United States *v.* Aluminum Co. of America

Court of Appeals of the United States, Second Circuit, 1945. 14S F.2d 416.

Before L. HAND, SWAN, and AUGUSTUS N. HAND, CIRCUIT JUDGES.

L. HAND, Circuit Judge. This appeal comes to us by virtue of a certificate of the Supreme Court, under the amendment of 1944 to §29 of 15 U.S.C.A. The action was brought under §4 of that title, praying the district court to adjudge that the defendant, Aluminum Company of America, was monopolizing interstate and foreign commerce, particularly in the manufacture and sale of "virgin" aluminum ingot, and that it be dissolved; and further to adjudge that that company and the defendant, Aluminum Limited, had entered into a conspiracy in restraint of such commerce. It also asked incidental relief. The plaintiff filed its complaint on April 23, 1937, naming sixty-three defendants. . . . At the date of judgment there were fifty-one defendants who had been served and against whom the action was pending. We may divide these, as the district judge did, into four classes: Aluminum Company of America, with its wholly owned subsidiaries, directors, officers and shareholders. (For convenience we shall speak of these defendants collectively as "Alcoa," that being the name by which the company has become almost universally known.) Next, Aluminum Limited, with its directors, officers and shareholders. (For the same reason we shall speak of this group as "Limited.") Third: the defendant, Aluminum Manufacturers, Inc., which may be treated as a subsidiary of "Alcoa." Fourth: the defendant Aluminum Goods Manufacturing Company, which is independent of "Alcoa," as will appear. The action came to trial on June 1, 1938, and proceeded without much interruption until August 14, 1940, when the case was closed after more than 40,000 pages of testimony had been taken. The judge took time to consider the evidence, and delivered an oral opinion which occupied him from September 30, to October 9, 1941. Again he took time to prepare findings of fact and conclusions of law which he filed on July 14, 1942; and he entered final judgment dismissing the complaint on July 23rd, of that year. The petition for an appeal, and assignments of error, were filed on September 14, 1942, and the petition was allowed on the next day. On June 12, 1944, the Supreme Court, declaring that a quorum of six justices qualified to hear the case was wanting, referred the appeal to this court under §29 of Title 15, already mentioned. The district judge's opinion, reported in D.C., 44 F.Supp. 97, discussed the evidence with the utmost particularity; it

501

took up every phase and every issue with the arguments of both parties, and provided a reasoned basis for the subsequent findings of fact and conclusions of law. For the purposes of this appeal we need not repeat the greater part of the facts; so far as it is necessary, we do so, leaving acquaintance with the remainder to the opinion itself. Although the plaintiff challenged nearly all of the 407 findings of fact, with negligible exceptions these challenges were directed, not to misstatements of the evidence, but to the judge's inferences—alleged to be "clearly erroneous." . . .

I. ALCOA's MONOPOLY OF "VIRGIN" INGOT

"Alcoa" is a corporation, organized under the laws of Pennsylvania on September 18, 1888; its original name, "Pittsburgh Reduction Company," was changed to its present one on January 1, 1907. It has always been engaged in the production and sale of "ingot" aluminum, and since 1895 also in the fabrication of the metal into many finished and semi-finished articles. It has proliferated into a great number of subsidiaries, created at various times between the years 1900 and 1929, as the business expanded. Aluminum is a chemical element; it is never found in a free state, being always in chemical combination with oxygen. One form of this combination is known as alumina; and for practical purposes the most available material from which alumina can be extracted is an ore, called, "bauxite." Aluminum was isolated as a metal more than a century ago, but not until about 1886 did it become commercially practicable to eliminate the oxygen, so that it could be exploited industrially. One, Hall, discovered a process by which this could be done in that year, and got a patent on April 2, 1889, which he assigned to "Alcoa," which thus secured a legal monopoly of the manufacture of the pure aluminum until on April 2, 1906, when this patent expired. Meanwhile Bradley had invented a process by which the smelting could be carried on without the use of external heat, as had theretofore been thought necessary; and for this improvement he too got a patent on February 2, 1892. Bradley's improvement resulted in great economy in manufacture, so that, although after April 2, 1906, anyone could manufacture aluminum by the Hall process, for practical purposes no one could compete with Bradley or with his licensees until February 2, 1909, when Bradley's patent also expired. On October 31, 1903, "Alcoa" and the assignee of the Bradley patent entered into a contract by which "Alcoa" was granted an exclusive license under that patent, in exchange for "Aloca's" promise to sell to the assignee a stated amount of aluminum at a discount of ten per cent below "Alcoa's" published list price, and always to sell at a discount of five per cent greater than that which "Alcoa" gave to any other jobber. Thus until February 2, 1909, "Alcoa" had either a monopoly of the manufacture of "virgin" aluminum ingot, or the monopoly of a process which eliminated all competition.

The extraction of aluminum from alumina requires a very large amount of electrical energy, which is ordinarily, though not always, most cheaply

obtained from water power. Beginning at least as early as 1895, "Alcoa" secured such power from several companies by contracts, containing in at least
three instances, covenants binding the power companies not to sell or let power to anyone else for the manufacture of aluminum. "Alcoa"—either itself or
by a subsidiary—also entered into four successive "cartels" with foreign manufacturers of aluminum by which, in exchange for certain limitations upon its
import into foreign countries, it secured covenants from the foreign producers,
either not to import into the United States at all or to do so under restrictions, which in some cases involved the fixing of prices. These "cartels" and
restrictive covenants and certain other practices were the subject of a suit filed
by the United States against "Alcoa" on May 16, 1912, in which a decree was
entered by consent on June 7, 1912, declaring several of these covenants unlawful and enjoining their performance; and also declaring invalid other restrictive covenants obtained before 1903 relating to the sale of alumina.
("Alcoa" failed at this time to inform the United States of several restrictive
covenants in water-power contracts: its justification—which the judge accepted—being that they had been forgotten.) "Alcoa" did not begin to manufacture alumina on its own behalf until the expiration of a dominant patent in
1903. In that year it built a very large alumina plant at East St. Louis, where
all of its alumina was made until 1939, when it opened another plant in Mobile, Alabama.

None of the foregoing facts are in dispute, and the most important question
in the case is whether the monopoly in "Alcoa's" production of "virgin" ingot, secured by the two patents until 1909, and in part perpetuated between
1909 and 1912 by the unlawful practices, forbidden by the decree of 1912,
continued for the ensuing twenty-eight years; and whether, if it did, it was unlawful under §2 of the Sherman Act, 15 U.S.C.A. §2. It is undisputed that
throughout this period "Alcoa" continued to be the single producer of "virgin" ingot in the United States; and the plaintiff argues that this without more
was enough to make it an unlawful monopoly. It also takes an alternative position: that in any event during this period "Alcoa" consistently pursued unlawful exclusionary practices, which made its dominant position certainly
unlawful, even though it would not have been, had it been retained only by
"natural growth." Finally, it asserts that many of these practices were of
themselves unlawful, as contracts in restraint of trade under §1 of the Act, 15
U.S.C.A. §1. "Alcoa's" position is that the fact that it alone continued to
make "virgin" ingot in this country did not, and does not, give it a monopoly
of the market; that it was always subject to the competition of imported "virgin" ingot, and of what is called "secondary" ingot; and that even if it had
not been, its monopoly would not have been retained by unlawful means, but
would have been the result of a growth which the Act does not forbid, even
when it results in a monopoly. We shall first consider the amount and character of this competition; next, how far it established a monopoly; and finally, if
it did, whether that monopoly was unlawful under §2 of the Act.

From 1902 onward until 1928 "Alcoa" was making ingot in Canada

through a wholly owned subsidiary; so much of this as it imported into the
United States it is proper to include with what it produced here. In the year
1912 the sum of these two items represented nearly ninety-one per cent of the
total amount of "virgin" ingot available for sale in this country. This percentage varied year by year up to and including 1938: in 1913 it was about seventy-two per cent; in 1921 about sixty-eight per cent; in 1922 about seventy-two;
with these exceptions it was always over eighty per cent of the total and for
the last five years 1934–1938 inclusive it averaged over ninety per cent. The effect of such a proportion of the production upon the market we reserve for the
time being, for it will be necessary first to consider the nature and uses of
"secondary" ingot, the name by which the industry knows ingot made from
aluminum scrap. This is of two sorts, though for our purposes it is not important to distinguish between them. One of these is the clippings and trimmings
of "sheet" aluminum, when patterns are cut out of it, as a suit is cut from a
bolt of cloth. The chemical composition of these is obviously the same as that
of the "sheet" from which they come; and, although they are likely to accu-
mulate dust or other dirt in the factory, this may be removed by well known
processes. If a record of the original composition of the "sheet" has been preserved, this scrap may be remelted into new ingot, and used again for the
same purpose. It is true that some of the witnesses—Arthur V. Davis, the
chairman of the board of "Alcoa" among them—testified that at each
remelting aluminum takes up some new oxygen which progressively deterio-
rates its quality for those uses in which purity is important; but other
witnesses thought that it had become commercially feasible to remove this im-
purity, and the judge made no finding on the subject. Since the plaintiff has
the burden of proof, we shall assume that there is no such deterioration. Nevertheless, there is an appreciable "sales resistance" even to this kind of scrap,
and for some uses (airplanes and cables among them), fabricators absolutely
insist upon "virgin": just why is not altogether clear. The other source of
scrap is aluminum which has once been fabricated and the article, after being
used, is discarded and sent to the junk heap, as for example, cooking utensils,
like kettles and pans, and the pistons or crank cases of motorcars. These are
made with a substantial alloy and to restore the metal to its original purity
costs more than its worth. However, if the alloy is known both in quality and
amount, scrap, when remelted, can be used again for the same purpose as before. In spite of this, as in the case of slippings and trimmings, the industry
will ordinarily not accept ingot so salvaged upon the same terms as "virgin."
There are some seventeen companies which scavenge scrap of all sorts, clean
it, remelt it, test it for its composition, make it into ingots and sell it regularly
to the trade. There is in all these salvage operations some inevitable waste of
actual material; not only does a certain amount of aluminum escape altogether, but in the salvage process itself some is skimmed off as scum and thrown
away. The judge found that the return of fabricated products to the market as
"secondary" varied from five to twenty-five years, depending upon the article;
but he did not, and no doubt could not, find how many times the cycle could
be repeated before the metal was finally used up.

There are various ways of computing "Alcoa's" control of the aluminum market—as distinct from its production—depending upon what one regards as competing in that market. The judge figured its share—during the years 1929–1938, inclusive—as only about thirty-three percent; to do so he included "secondary," and excluded that part of "Alcoa's" own production which it fabricated and did not therefore sell as ingot. If, on the other hand, "Alcoa's" total production, fabricated and sold, be included, and balanced against the sum of imported "virgin" and "secondary," its share of the market was in the neighborhood of sixty-four per cent for that period. The percentage we have already mentioned—over ninety—results only if we both include all "Alcoa's" production and exclude "secondary". That percentage is enough to constitute a monopoly; it is doubtful whether sixty or sixty-four percent would be enough; and certainly thirty-three per cent is not. Hence it is necessary to settle what he shall treat as competing in the ingot market. That part of its production which "Alcoa" itself fabricates, does not of course ever reach the market as ingot; and we recognize that it is only when a restriction of production either inevitably affects prices, or is intended to do so, that it violates §1 of the Act. Apex Hosiery Co. v. Leader, 310 U.S. 469, 501, 60 S.Ct. 982,84 L.Ed. 1311, 128 A.L.R. 1044. However, even though we were to assume that a monopoly is unlawful under §2 only in case it controls prices, the ingot fabricated by "Alcoa," necessarily had a direct effect upon the ingot market. All ingot—with trifling exceptions—is used to fabricate intermediate, or end, products; and therefore all intermediate, or end, products which "Alcoa" fabricates and sells, pro tanto reduce the demand for ingot itself. The situation is the same, though reversed, as in Standard Oil Co. v. United States, 221 U.S. 1, 77, 31 S.Ct. 502, 523, 55 L.Ed. 619, 34 L.R.A.,N.S., 834, Ann.Cas.1912D, 734, where the court answered the defendants' argument that they had no control over the crude oil by saying that "as substantial power over the crude product was the inevitable result of the absolute control which existed over the refined product, the monopolization of the one carried with it the power to control the other." We cannot therefore agree that the computation of the percentage of "Alcoa's" control over the ingot market should not include the whole of its ingot production.

As to "secondary," as we have said, for certain purposes the industry will not accept it at all; but for those for which it will, the difference in price is ordinarily not very great; the judge found that it was between one and two cents a pound, hardly enough margin on which to base a monopoly. Indeed, there are times when all differential disappears, and "secondary" will actually sell at a higher price: i.e. when there is a supply available which contains just the alloy that a fabricator needs for the article which he proposes to make. Taking the industry as a whole, we can say nothing more definite than that, although "secondary" does not compete at all in some uses, (whether because of "sales resistance" only, or because of actual metallurgical inferiority), for most purposes it competes upon a substantial equality with "virgin." On these facts the judge found that "every pound of secondary or scrap aluminum which is sold in commerce displaces a pound of virgin aluminum which otherwise would, or might have been, sold." We agree: so far as "secondary" supplies the demand of such fabricators as will accept it, it increases the amount of "virgin" which must seek sale elsewhere; and it therefore results that the supply of that part of the demand which will accept only "virgin" becomes greater in proportion as "secondary" drives away "virgin" from the demand which will accept "secondary." (This is indeed the same argument which we used a moment ago to include in the supply that part of "virgin" which "Alcoa" fabricates; it is not apparent to us why the judge did not think it applicable to that item as well.) At any given moment therefore "secondary" competes with "virgin" in the ingot market; further, it can, and probably does, set a limit or "ceiling" beyond which the price of "virgin" cannot go, for the cost of its production will in the end depend upon the expense of scavenging and reconditioning. It might seem for this reason that in estimating "Alcoa's" control over the ingot market, we ought to include the supply of "secondary," as the judge did. Indeed, it may be thought a paradox to say that anyone has the monopoly of a market in which at all times he must meet a competition that limits his price. We shall show that it is not.

In the case of a monopoly of any commodity which does not disappear in use and which can be salvaged, the supply seeking sale at any moment will be made up of two components: (1) the part which the putative monopolist can immediately produce and sell; and (2) the part which has been, or can be, reclaimed out of what he has produced and sold in the past. By hypothesis he presently controls the first of these components; the second he has controlled in the past; although he no longer does. During the period when he did control the second, if he was aware of his interest, he was guided, not alone by its effect at that time upon the market, but by his knowledge that some part of it was likely to be reclaimed and seek the future market. That consideration will to some extent always affect his production until he decides to abandon the business, or for some other reason ceases to be concerned with the future market. Thus, in the case at bar "Alcoa" always knew that the future supply of ingot would be made up in part of what it produced at the time, and, if it was as farsighted as it proclaims itself, that consideration must have had its share in determining how much to produce. How accurately it could forecast the effect of present production upon the future market is another matter. Experience, no doubt, would help; but it makes no difference that it had to guess; it is enough that it had an inducement to make the best guess it could, and that it would regulate that part of the future supply, so far as it should turn out to have guessed right. The competition of "secondary" must therefore be disregarded, as soon as we consider the position of "Alcoa" over a period of years; it was as much within "Alcoa's" control as was the production of the "virgin" from which it had been derived. This can be well illustrated by the case of a lawful monopoly: e.g. a patent or a copyright. The monopolist cannot prevent those to whom he sells from reselling at whatever prices they please. United States v. General Electric Co., 272 U.S. 476, 484, 47 S.Ct. 192, 71 L.Ed. 362. Nor can he prevent their reconditioning articles worn by use, unless they in fact make a new article. Wilson v. Simpson, 9 How. 109, 123, 13 L.Ed. 66. At any moment his control over the market will therefore be limited by that part of what he has formerly sold, which the price he now charges may bring upon the market, as second hand or reclaimed articles. Yet no one would think of saying that for this reason the patent or the copyright did not confer a monopoly. Again, consider the situation of the owner of the only supply of some raw material like iron ore. Scrap iron is a constant factor in the iron market; it is scavenged, remelted into pig, and sold in competition with newly smelted pig; an owner of the sole supply of ore must always face that competition and it will serve to put a "ceiling" upon his price, so far as there is enough of it. Nevertheless, no one would say that, even during the period while the pig which he has sold in the past can so return to the market, he does not have a natural monopoly. Finally, if "Alcoa" is right, precisely the same reasoning ought to lead us to include that part of clippings and trimmings which a fabricator himself saves and remelts—"process scrap"—for that too pro tanto reduces the market for "virgin." It can make no difference whether the original buyer reclaims, or a professional scavenger. Yet "Alcoa" itself does not assert that such "process scrap" competes; indeed it was at pains to prove that this scrap was not included in its computation of "secondary."

We conclude therefore that "Alcoa's" control over the ingot market must be reckoned at over ninety per cent; that being the proportion which its production bears to imported "virgin" ingot. If the fraction which it did not supply were the produce of domestic manufacture there could be no doubt that this percentage gave it a monopoly—lawful or unlawful, as the case might be. The producer of so large a proportion of the supply has complete control within certain limits. It is true, if by raising the price he reduces the amount which can be marketed—as always, or almost always, happens—he may invite the expansion of the small producers who will try to fill the place left open; nevertheless, not only is there an inevitable lag in this, but the large producer is in a strong position to check such competition; and, indeed, if he has retained his old plant and personnel, he can inevitably do so. There are indeed limits to his power; substitutes are available for almost all commodities, and to raise the price enough is to evoke them. United States v. Corn Products Refining Co., D.C., 234 F. 964, 976; United States v. Associated Press, D.C. 52 F.Supp. 362, 371; Fashion Originators Guild v. Federal Trade Commission, 2 Cir., 114 F.2d 80, 85. Moreover, it is difficult and expensive to keep idle any part of a plant or of personnel; and any drastic contraction of the market will offer increasing temptation to the small producers to expand. But these limitations also exist when a single producer occupies the whole market: even then, his hold will depend upon his moderation in exerting his immediate power.

The case at bar is however different, because, for aught that appears there may well have been a particularly unlimited supply of imports as the price of ingot rose. Assuming that there was no agreement between "Alcoa" and foreign producers not to import, they sold what could bear the handicap of the tariff and the cost of transportation. For the period of eighteen years—1920–

1937—they sold at times a little above "Alcoa's" prices, at times a little under; but there was substantially no gross difference between what they received and what they would have received, had they sold uniformly at "Alcoa's" prices. While the record is silent, we may therefore assume—the plaintiff having the burden—that, had "Alcoa" raised its prices, more ingot would have been imported. Thus there is a distinction between domestic and foreign competition: the first is limited in quantity, and can increase only by an increase in plant and personnel; the second is of producers who, we must assume, produce much more than they import, and whom a rise in price will presumably induce immediately to divert to the American market what they have been selling elsewhere. It is entirely consistent with the evidence that it was the threat of greater foreign imports which kept "Alcoa's" prices where they were, and prevented it from exploiting its advantage as sole domestic producer; indeed, it is hard to resist the conclusion that potential imports did put a "ceiling" upon those prices. Nevertheless, within the limits afforded by the tariff and the cost of transportation, "Alcoa" was free to raise its prices, as it chose, since it was free from domestic competition, save as it drew other metals into the market as substitutes. Was this a monopoly within the meaning of §2? The judge found that, over the whole half century of its existence, "Alcoa's" profits upon capital invested, after payment of income taxes, had been only about ten per cent, and, although the plaintiff puts this figure a little higher, the difference is negligible. The plaintiff does indeed challenge the propriety of computing profits upon a capital base which included past earnings that have been allowed to remain in the business; but as to that it is plainly wrong. An argument is indeed often made in the case of a public utility, that the "rate-base" should not include earnings re-invested which were greater than a fair profit upon the actual investment outstanding at the time. That argument depends, however, upon the premise that at common law— even in the absence of any commission or other authority empowered to enforce a "reasonable" rate—it is the duty of a public utility to charge no more than such a rate, and that any excess is unlawfully collected. Perhaps one might use the same argument in the case of a monopolist; but it would be a condition that one should show what part of the past earnings were extortionate, for not all that even a monopolist may earn is caput lupinum. The plaintiff made no such attempt, and its distinction between capital, "contributed by customers" and capital, "contributed by shareholders," has no basis in law. "Alcoa's" earnings belonged to its shareholders, they were free to withdraw them and spend them, or to leave them in the business. If they chose to leave them, it was no different from contributing new capital out of their pockets. This assumed, it would be hard to say that "Alcoa" had made exorbitant profits on ingot, if it is proper to allocate the profit upon the whole business proportionately among all of its products—ingot, and fabrications from ingot. A profit of ten per cent in such an industry, dependent, in part at any rate, upon continued tariff protection, and subject to the vicissitudes of new demands, to the obsolescence of plant and process—which can never be accurately gauged in advance—to the chance that substitutes may at any moment be discovered which will reduce the demand, and to the other hazards which attend all industry; a profit of ten per cent, so conditioned, could hardly be considered extortionate.

There are however, two answers to any such excuse; and the first is that the profit on ingot was not necessarily the same as the profit of the business as a whole, and that we have no means of allocating its proper share to ingot. It is true that the mill cost appears; but obviously it would be unfair to "Alcoa" to take, as the measure of its profit on ingot, the difference between selling price and mill cost; and yet we have nothing else. It may be retorted that it was for the plaintiff to prove what was the profit upon ingot in accordance with the general burden of proof. We think not. Having proved that "Alcoa" had a monopoly of the domestic ingot market, the plaintiff had gone far enough; if it was an excuse, that "Alcoa" had not abused its power, it lay upon "Alcoa" to prove that it had not. But the whole issue is irrelevant anyway, for it is no excuse for "monopolizing" a market that the monopoly has not been used to extract from the consumer more than a "fair" profit. The Act has wider purposes. Indeed, even though we disregarded all but economic considerations, it would by no means follow that such concentration of producing power is to be desired, when it has not been used extortionately. Many people believe that possession of unchallenged economic power deadens initiative, discourages thrift and depresses energy; that immunity from competition is a narcotic, and rivalry is a stimulant, to industrial progress; that the spur of constant stress is necessary to counteract an inevitable disposition to let well enough alone. Such people believe that competitors, versed in the craft as no consumer can be, will be quick to detect opportunities for saving and new shifts in production, and be eager to profit by them. In any event the mere fact that a producer, having command of the domestic market, has not been able to make more than a "fair" profit, is no evidence that a "fair" profit could not have been made at lower prices. United States v. Corn Products Refining Co., supra, 1014, 1015 (234 F. 964). True, it might have been thought adequate to condemn only those monopolies which could not show that they had exercised the highest possible ingenuity, had adopted every possible economy, had anticipated every conceivable improvement, stimulated every possible demand. No doubt, that would be one way of dealing with the matter, although it would imply constant scrutiny and constant supervision, such as courts are unable to provide. Be that as it may, that was not the way that Congress chose; it did not condone "good trusts" and condemn "bad" ones; it forbade all. Moreover, in so doing it was not necessarily actuated by economic motives alone. It is possible, because of its indirect social or moral effect, to prefer a system of small producers, each dependent for his success upon his own skill and character, to one in which the great mass of those engaged must accept the direction of a few. These considerations, which we have suggested only as possible purposes of the Act, we think the decisions prove to have been in fact its purposes.

It is settled, at least as to §1, that there are some contracts restricting competition which are unlawful, no matter how beneficent they may be; no industrial exigency will justify them; they are absolutely forbidden. Chief Justice Taft said as much of contracts dividing a territory among producers, in the often quoted passage of his opinion in the Circuit Court of Appeals in United States v. Addystone Pipe & Steel Co., 6 Cir., 85 F. 271, 291, 46 L.R.A. 122. The Supreme Court unconditionally condemned all contracts fixing prices in United States v. Trenton Potteries Co., 273 U.S. 392, 397, 398, 47 S.Ct. 377, 71 L.Ed. 700, 50 A.L.R. 989: and whatever doubts may have arisen as to that decision from Appalachian Coals Inc. v. United States, 288 U.S. 344, 53 S.Ct. 471, 77 L.Ed. 825, they were laid by the United States v. Socony-Vacuum Co., 310 U.S. 150, 220–224, 60 S.Ct. 811, 84 L.Ed. 1129. It will now scarcely be denied that the same notion originally extended to all contracts—"reasonable," or "unreasonable"—which restrict competition. United States v. Trans-Missouri Freight Association, 166 U.S. 290, 327, 328, 17 S.Ct. 540, 41 L.Ed. 1007; United States v. Joint Traffic Association, 171 U.S. 505, 575–577, 19 S.Ct. 25, 43 L.Ed. 259. The decisions in Standard Oil Co. v. United States, 221 U.S. 1, 31 S.Ct. 502, 55 L.Ed. 619, 34 L.R.A.,N.S., 834, Ann.Cas.1912D, 734, and American Tobacco Co. v. United States, 221 U.S. 106, 31 S.Ct. 632, 55 L.Ed. 663, certainly did change this, and since then it has been accepted law that not all contracts which in fact put an end to existing competition are unlawful. Starting, however, with the authoritative premise that all contracts fixing prices are unconditionally prohibited, the only possible difference between them and a monopoly is that while a monopoly necessarily involves an equal, or even greater, power to fix prices, its mere existence might be thought not to constitute an exercise of that power. That distinction is nevertheless purely formal; it would be valid only so long as the monopoly remained wholly inert; it would disappear as soon as the monopoly began to operate; for, when it did—that is, as soon as it began to sell at all—it must sell at some price and the only price at which it could sell is a price which it itself fixed. Thereafter the power and its exercise must needs coalesce. Indeed it would be absurd to condemn such contracts unconditionally, and not to extend the condemnation to monopolies; for the contracts are only steps toward that entire control which monopoly confers: they are really partial monopolies.

But we are not left to deductive reasoning. Although in many settings it may be proper to weigh the extent and effect of restrictions in a contract against its industrial or commercial advantages, this is never to be done when the contract is made with intent to set up a monopoly. As much was plainly implied in Swift & Co. v. United States, 196 U.S. 375, 396, 25 S.Ct. 276, 49 L.Ed. 518, where the court spoke of monopoly as being the "result" which the law seeks to prevent; and, although the language on pages 60 and 61 of Standard Oil Co. v. United States, 221 U.S. 1, 31 S.Ct. 502, 55 L.Ed. 619, 34 L.R.A.,N.S., 834, Ann.Cas.1912D, 734, is not altogether clear, it seems to presuppose as a premise that a monopoly is always an "unreasonable restraint of trade." Again, the opinion in Sugar Institute v. United States, 297 U.S. 553,

598, 56 S.Ct. 629, 642, 80 L.Ed. 859, borrowing from Appalachian Coals Inc. v. United States, supra, 288 U.S 344, 374, 53 S.Ct. 471, 77 L.Ed. 825, said: "Accordingly we have held that a co-operative enterprise otherwise free from objection, which carries with it no monopolistic menace" need not always be condemned. These were indeed only thrown out as steps in the argument; but Fashion Originators Guild v. Federal Trade Commission, 312 U.S. 457, 61 S.Ct. 703, 85 L.Ed. 949, was a ruling. . . . Perhaps, it has been idle to labor the point at length; there can be no doubt that the vice of restrictive contracts and of monopoly is really one, it is the denial to commerce of the supposed protection of competition. To repeat, if the earlier stages are proscribed, when they are parts of a plan, the mere projecting of which condemns them unconditionally, the realization of the plan itself must be proscribed.

We have been speaking only of the economic reasons which forbid monopoly; but as we have already implied, there are others, based upon the belief that great industrial consolidations are inherently undesirable, regardless of their economic results. In the debates in Congress Senator Sherman himself in the passage quoted in the margin showed that among the purposes of Congress in 1890 was a desire to put an end to great aggregations of capital because of the helplessness of the individual before them.[1] Another aspect of the same notion may be found in the language of Mr. Justice Peckham in United States v. Trans-Missouri Freight Association, supra, at page 323 (166 U.S. 290, 17 S.Ct. 540, 41 L.Ed. 1007). That Congress is still of the same mind appears in the Surplus Property Act of 1944, 50 U.S.C.A. Appendix §1611 et seq., and the Small Business Mobilization Act, 50 U.S.C.A.Appendix §1101 et seq. Not only does §2(d) of the first declare it to be one aim of that statute to "preserve the competitive position of small business concerns," but §18 is given over to directions designed to "preserve and strengthen" their position. In United States v. Hutcheson, 312 U.S. 219, 61 S.Ct. 463, 85 L.Ed. 788, a later statute in pari materia was considered to throw a cross light upon the Antitrust Acts, illuminating enough even to override an earlier ruling of the court. Throughout the history of these statutes it has been constantly assumed that one of their purposes was to perpetuate and preserve, for its own sake and in spite of possible cost, an organization of industry in small units which can effectively compete with each other. We hold that "Alcoa's" monopoly of ingot was of the kind covered by §2.

It does not follow because "Alcoa" had such a monopoly, that it "monopolized" the ingot market: it may not have achieved monopoly; monopoly may

---

[1] "If the concerted powers of this combination are intrusted to a single man, it is a kingly prerogative, inconsistent with our form of government, and should be subject to the strong resistance of the State and national authorities . . .." 21 Cong. Record, 2457.

"The popular mind is agitated with problems that may disturb social order, and among them all none is more threatening than the inequality of condition, of wealth, and opportunity that has grown within a single generation out of the concentration of capital into vast combinations to control production and trade and to break down competition. These combinations already defy or control powerful transportation corporations and reach State authorities. They reach out their Briarean arms to every part of our country. They are imported from abroad. Congress alone can deal with them, and if we are unwilling or unable there will soon be a trust for every production and a master to fix the price for every necessity of life . . ." 21 Cong. Record, 2460. See also 21 Cong. Record 2508. [By the court.]

have been thrust upon it. If it had been a combination of existing smelters which united the whole industry and controlled the production of all aluminum ingot, it would certainly have "monopolized" the market. In several decisions the Supreme Court has decreed the dissolution of such combinations, although they had engaged in no unlawful trade practices. Perhaps we should not count among these Northern Securities Co. v. United States, 193 U.S. 197, 327, 24 S.Ct. 436, 48 L.Ed. 679, because it was decided under the old dispensation which ended with Standard Oil Co. v. United States, supra, (221 U.S. 1, 31 S.Ct. 502, 55 L.Ed. 619, 34 L.R.A.,N.S., 834, Ann.Cas.1912D, 734); but the following cases were later. United States v. Union Pacific R. Co., 226 U.S. 61, 88. 33 S.Ct. 53, 57 L.Ed. 124; International Harvester v. Missouri, 234 U.S. 199, 209, 34 S.Ct. 859, 58 L.Ed. 1276, 52 L.R.A.,N.S., 525; United States v. Reading Co., 253 U.S. 26, 57–59, 40 S.Ct. 425, 64 L.Ed. 760; United States v. Southern Pacific Co., 259 U.S. 214, 230, 231, 42 S.Ct. 496, 66 L.Ed. 907. We may start therefore with the premise that to have combined ninety per cent of the producers of ingot would have been to "monopolize" the ingot market; and, so far as concerns the public interest, it can make no difference whether an existing competition is put an end to, or whether prospective competition is prevented. The Clayton Act itself speaks in that alternative: "to injure, destroy, or prevent competition." §13(a) 15 U.S.C.A. Nevertheless, it is unquestionably true that from the very outset the courts have at least kept in reserve the possibility that the origin of a monopoly may be critical in determining its legality; and for this they had warrant in some of the congressional debates which accompanied the passage of the Act. In Re Greene, C.C.Ohio, 52 F. 104, 116, 117; United States v. Trans-Missouri Freight Association, 8 Cir., 58 F. 58, 82, 24 L.R.A. 73. This notion has usually been expressed by saying that size does not determine guilt; that there must be some "exclusion" of competitors; that the growth must be something else than "natural" or "normal"; that there must be a "wrongful intent," or some other specific intent; or that some "unduly" coercive means must be used. At times there has been emphasis upon the use of the active verb, "monopolize," as the judge noted in the case at bar. United States v. Standard Oil Co., C.C.Mo., 173 F. 177, 196; United States v. Whiting, D.C., 212 F. 466, 478; Patterson v. United States, 6 Cir., 222 F. 599, 619; National Biscuit Co. v. Federal Trade Commission, 2 Cir., 299 F. 733, 738. What engendered these compunctions is reasonably plain; persons may unwittingly find themselves in possession of a monopoly, automatically so to say: that is, without having intended either to put an end to existing competition, or to prevent competition from arising when none had existed; they may become monopolists by force of accident. Since the Act makes "monopolizing" a crime, as well as a civil wrong, it would be not only unfair, but presumably contrary to the intent of Congress, to include such instances. A market may, for example, be so limited that it is impossible to produce at all and meet the cost of production except by a plant large enough to supply the whole demand. Or there may be changes in taste or in cost which drive out all but one purveyor. A single producer may be the survivor out of a group of active competitors, merely by virtue of his superior skill, foresight and industry. In such cases a strong argument can be made that, although, the result may expose the public to the evils of monopoly, the Act does not mean to condemn the resultant of these very forces which it is its prime object to foster: finis opus coronat. The successful competitor, having been urged to compete, must not be turned upon when he wins. The most extreme expression of this view is in United States v. United States Steel Corporation, 251 U.S. 417, 40 S.Ct. 293, 64 L.Ed. 343, 8 A.L.R. 1121, and which Sanford, J., in part repeated in United States v. International Harvester Corporation, 274 U.S. 693, 708, 47 S.Ct. 748, 71 L.Ed. 1302. It so chances that in both instances the corporation had less than two-thirds of the production in its hands, and the language quoted was not necessary to the decision; so that even if it had not later been modified, it has not the authority of an actual decision. But, whatever authority it does have was modified by the gloss of Cardozo, J., in United States v. Swift & Co., 286 U.S. 106, p. 116, 52 S.Ct. 460, 463, 76 L.Ed. 999, when he said, "Mere size . . . is not an offense against the Sherman Act unless magnified to the point at which it amounts to a monopoly . . . but size carries with it an opportunity for abuse that is not to be ignored when the opportunity is proved to have been utilized in the past." "Alcoa's" size was "magnified" to make it a "monopoly"; indeed, it has never been anything else; and its size, not only offered it an "opportunity for abuse," but it "utilized" its size for "abuse," as can easily be shown.

It would completely misconstrue "Alcoa's" position in 1940 to hold that it was the passive beneficiary of a monopoly, following upon an involuntary elimination of competitors by automatically operative economic forces. Already in 1909, when its last lawful monopoly ended, it sought to strengthen its position by unlawful practices, and these concededly continued until 1912. In that year it had two plants in New York, at which it produced less than 42 million pounds of ingot; in 1934 it had five plants (the original two, enlarged; one in Tennessee; one in North Carolina; one in Washington), and its production had risen to about 327 million pounds, an increase of almost eight-fold. Meanwhile not a pound of ingot had been produced by anyone else in the United States. This increase and this continued and undisturbed control did not fall undesigned into "Alcoa's" lap; obviously it could not have done so. It could only have resulted, as it did result, from a persistent determination to maintain the control, with which it found itself vested in 1912. There were at least one or two abortive attempts to enter the industry, but "Alcoa" effectively anticipated and forestalled all competition, and succeeded in holding the field alone. True, it stimulated demand and opened new uses for the metal, but not without making sure that it could supply what it had evoked. There is nc dispute as to this: "Alcoa" avows it as evidence of the skill, energy and initiative with which it has always conducted its business; as a reason why, having won its way by fair means, it should be commended, and not dismembered. We need charge it with no moral derelictions after 1912; we may assume that all it claims for itself is true. The only question is whether it falls within the exception established in favor of those who do not seek, but cannot avoid, the control of a market. It seems to us that that question scarcely survives its statement. It was not inevitable that it should always anticipate increases in the demand for ingot and be prepared to supply them. Nothing compelled it to keep doubling and redoubling its capacity before others entered the field. It insists that it never excluded competitors; but we can think of no more effective exclusion than progressively to embrace each new opportunity as it opened, and to face every newcomer with new capacity already geared into a great organization, having the advantage of experience, trade connections and the elite of personnel. Only in case we interpret "exclusion" as limited to manoeuvres not honestly industrial, but actuated solely by a desire to prevent competition, can such a course, indefatigably pursued, be deemed not "exclusionary." So to limit it would in our judgment emasculate the Act; would permit just such consolidations as it was designed to prevent.

"Alcoa" answers that it positively assisted competitors, instead of discouraging them. That may be true as to fabricators of ingot; but what of that? They were its market for ingot, and it is charged only with a monopoly of ingot. We can find no instance of its helping prospective ingot manufacturers. We do not forget the Southern Aluminum Company in whose origin it did have some part; though that was over before the end of 1914 and was in any event scarcely late enough to count. We are speaking not of its purchase of the remains of the plant in 1915; we are not suggesting—as the plaintiff argues—that that was a move to keep the plant out of the ingot market; we are speaking of the original venture. . . .

We disregard any question of "intent." Relatively early in the history of the Act—1905—Holmes, J., in Swift & Co. v. United States, supra, (196 U.S. 375, 396, 25 S.Ct. 276, 49 L.Ed. 518), explained this aspect of the Act in a passage often quoted. Although the primary evil was monopoly, the Act also covered preliminary steps, which, if continued, would lead to it. These may do no harm of themselves; but if they are initial moves in a plan or scheme which, carried out, will result in monopoly, they are dangerous and the law will nip them in the bud. For this reason conduct falling short of monopoly, is not illegal unless it is part of a plan to monopolize, or to gain such other control of a market as is equally forbidden. To make it so, the plaintiff must prove what in the criminal law is known as a "specific intent"; an intent which goes beyond the mere intent to do the act. By far the greatest part of the fabulous record piled up in the case at bar, was concerned with proving such an intent. The plaintiff was seeking to show that many transactions, neutral on their face, were not in fact necessary to the development of "Alcoa's" business, and had no motive except to exclude others and perpetuate its hold upon the ingot market. Upon that effort success depended in case the plaintiff failed to satisfy the court that it was unnecessary under §2 to convict "Alcoa" of practices unlawful of themselves. The plaintiff has so satisfied us, and the issue of intent ceases to have any importance; no intent is relevant except that which is relevant to any liability, criminal or civil: i.e. an intent to bring about the forbidden act. Note 59 of United States v. Socony-Vacuum Oil Co., supra, 310 U.S. 150 on page 226, 60 S.Ct. 811, on page 845, 84 L.Ed. 1129, on which "Alcoa" appears so much to rely, is in no sense to the contrary. Douglas, J., was answering the defendants' argument that, assuming that a combination had attempted to fix prices, it had never had the power to do so, for there was too much competing oil. His answer was that the plan was unlawful, even if the parties did not have the power to fix prices, provided that they intended to do so; and it was to drive home this that he contrasted the case then before the court with monopoly, where power was a necessary element. In so doing he said: "An intent and a power . . . are then necessary," which he at once followed by quoting the passage we have just mentioned from Swift & Co. v. United States, supra, 196 U.S. 375, 25 S.Ct. 276, 49 L.Ed. 518. In order to fall within §2, the monopolist must have both the power to monopolize, and the intent to monopolize. To read the passage as demanding any "specific," intent, makes nonsense of it, for no monopolist monopolizes unconscious of what he is doing. So here, "Alcoa" meant to keep, and did keep, that complete and exclusive hold upon the ingot market with which it started. That was to "monopolize" that market, however innocently it otherwise proceeded. So far as the judgment held that it was not within §2, it must be reversed.[Case remanded to the district court.]*

---

* Only the first part of the opinion dealing with the question of whether Alcoa monopolized the market in "virgin" aluminum ingot in violation of Section 2 of the Sherman Act is reprinted here, because it is the part directly pertinent to the subject matter of this chapter.

Case 2

United States *v.* Grinnell Corp. et al.

Appeal From The United States District Court For The District of Rhode Island.

No. 73. Argued March 28–29, 1966.—Decided June 13, 1966.

MR. JUSTICE DOUGLAS delivered the opinion of the Court.

This case presents an important question under §2 of the Sherman Act,[1] which makes it an offense for any person to "monopolize . . . any part of the trade or commerce among the several States." This is a civil suit brought by the United States against Grinnell Corporation (Grinnell), American District Telegraph Co. (ADT), Holmes Electric Protective Co. (Holmes) and Automatic Fire Alarm Co. of Delaware (AFA). The District Court held for the Government and entered a decree. All parties appeal,[2] the United States because it deems the relief inadequate and the defendants both on the merits and on the relief and on the ground that the District Court denied them a fair trial. We noted probable jurisdiction. 381 U. S. 910.

Grinnell manufactures plumbing supplies and fire sprinkler systems. It also owns 76% of the stock of ADT, 89% of the stock of AFA, and 100% of the stock of Holmes.[3] ADT provides both burglary and fire protection services; Holmes provides burglary services alone; AFA supplies only fire protection service. Each offers a central station service under which hazard-detecting devices installed on the protected premises automatically transmit an electric signal to a central station.[4] The central station is manned 24 hours a day. Upon receipt of a signal, the central station, where appropriate, dispatches guards to

---

[1] 26 Stat. 209, as amended, 15 U. S. C. §2 (1964 ed.).

[2] Expediting Act §2, 32 Stat. 823, as amended, 15 U. S. C. §29 (1964 ed.); *United States* v. *Loew's, Inc.,* 371 U. S. 38.

[3] These are the record figures. Since the time of the trial, Grinnell's holdings have increased. Counsel for Grinnell has advised this Court that Grinnell now holds 80% of ADT's stock and 90% of the stock of AFA.

[4] Among the various central station services offered are the following:

    (1) *automatic burglar alarms;*

    (2) *automatic fire alarms;*

    (3) *sprinkler supervisory service* (any malfunctions in the fire sprinkler system—*e.g.,* changes in water pressure, dangerously low water temperatures, etc.—are reported to the central station); and

    (4) *watch signal service* (night watchmen, by operating a key-triggered device on the protected premises, indicate to the central station that they are making their rounds and that all is well; the failure of a watchman to make his electrical report alerts the central station that something may be amiss).

the protected premises and notifies the police or fire department direct. There are other forms of protective services. But the record shows that subscribers to accredited central station service (*i.e.,* that approved by the insurance underwriters) receive reductions in their insurance premiums that are substantially greater than the reduction received by the users of other kinds of protection service. In 1961 accredited companies in the central station service business grossed $65,000,000. ADT, Holmes, and AFA are the three largest companies in the business in terms of revenue: ADT (with 121 central stations in 115 cities) has 73% of the business; Holmes (with 12 central stations in three large cities) has 12.5%; AFA (with three central stations in three large cities) has 2%. Thus the three companies that Grinnell controls have over 87% of the business.

Over the years ADT purchased the stock or assets of 27 companies engaged in the business of providing burglar or fire alarm services. Holmes acquired the stock or assets of three burglar alarm companies in New York City using a central station. Of these 30, the officials of seven agreed not to engage in the protective service business in the area for periods ranging from five years to permanently. After Grinnell acquired control of the other defendants, the latter continued in their attempts to acquire central station companies— offers being made to at least eight companies between the years 1955 and 1961, including four of the five largest nondefendant companies in the business. When the present suit was filed, each of those defendants had outstanding an offer to purchase one of the four largest nondefendant companies.

In 1906, prior to the affiliation of ADT and Holmes, they made a written agreement whereby ADT transferred to Holmes its burglar alarm business in a major part of the Middle Atlantic States and agreed to refrain forever from engaging in that business in that area, while Holmes transferred to ADT its watch signal business and agreed to limit its activities to burglar alarm service and night watch service for financial institutions. While this agreement was modified several times and terminated in 1947, in 1961 Holmes still restricted its business to burglar alarm service and operated only in those areas which had been allocated to it under the 1906 agreement. Similarly, ADT continued to refrain from supplying burglar alarm service in those areas earlier allocated to Holmes.

In 1907 Grinnell entered into a series of agreements with the other defendant companies and with Automatic Fire Protection Co. to the following effect:

AFA received the exclusive right to provide central station sprinkler supervisory and waterflow alarm and automatic fire alarm service in New York City, Boston and Philadelphia, and agreed not to provide burglar alarm service in those cities or central station service elsewhere in the United States.

Automatic Fire Protection Co. obtained the exclusive right to provide central station sprinkler supervisory and waterflow alarm service everywhere else in the United States except for the three cities in which AFA received that exclusive right, and agreed not to engage in burglar alarm service.

ADT received the exclusive right to render burglar alarm and nightwatch service throughout the United States. (Under ADT's 1906 agreement with Holmes, however, it could not provide burglar alarm services in the areas for which it had given Holmes the exclusive right to do so.) It agreed not to furnish sprinkler supervisory and waterflow alarm service anywhere in the country and not to furnish automatic fire alarm service in New York City, Boston or Philadelphia (the three cities allocated to AFA). ADT agreed to connect to its central stations and systems installed by AFA and Automatic.

Grinnell agreed to furnish and install all sprinkler supervisory and waterflow alarm actuating devices used in systems that AFA and Automatic would install, and otherwise not to engage in the central station protection business.

AFA and Automatic received 25% of the revenue produced by the sprinkler supervisory waterflow alarm service which they provided in their respective territories; ADT and Grinnell received 50% and 25%, respectively, of the revenue which resulted from such service. The agreements were to continue until February 1954.

The agreements remained substantially unchanged until 1949 when ADT purchased all of Automatic Fire Protection Co.'s rights under it for $13,500,000. After these 1907 agreements expired in 1954, AFA continued to honor the prior division of territories; and ADT and AFA entered into a new contract providing for the continued sharing of revenues on substantially the same basis as before.[5] In 1954 Grinnell and ADT renewed an agreement with a Rhode Island company which received the exclusive right to render central station service within Rhode Island at prices no lower than those of ADT and which agreed to use certain equipment supplied by Grinnell and ADT and to share its revenues with those companies. ADT had an informal agreement with a competing central station company in Washington, D. C., "that we would not solicit each other's accounts."

ADT over the years reduced its minimum basic rates to meet competition and renewed contracts at substantially increased rates in cities where it had a monopoly of accredited central station service. ADT threatened retaliation against firms that contemplated inaugurating central station service. And the record indicates that, in contemplating opening a new central station, ADT officials frequently stressed that such action would deter their competitors from opening a new station in that area.

The District Court found that the defendant companies had committed *per se* violations of §1 of the Sherman Act as well as §2 and entered a decree. 236 F.Supp.244.

---

[5] In 1959, ADT complained that AFA's share of the revenues was excessive. AFA replied, in a letter to the president of Grinnell (which by that time controlled both ADT and AFA), that its share was just compensation for its continued observance of the service and territorial restrictions: "[*T*]*he geographic restrictions placed upon us plus the requirement that we confine our activities to sprinkler and fire alarm services exclusively,* since 1907 and presumably into the future, has definitely retarded our expansion in the past to the benefit of ADT growth. . . . [AFA's] contribution must also include the many things that helped make ADT big." (Emphasis added.)

I.

The offense of monopoly under §2 of the Sherman Act has two elements: (1) the possession of monopoly power in the relevant market and (2) the willful acquisition or maintenance of that power as distinguished from growth or development as a consequence of a superior product, business acumen, or historic accident. We shall see that this second ingredient presents no major problem here, as what was done in building the empire was done plainly and explicitly for a single purpose. In *United States* v. *du Pont & Co.,* 351 U. S. 377, 391, we defined monopoly power as "the power to control prices or exclude competition." The existence of such power ordinarily may be inferred from the predominant share of the market. In *American Tobacco Co.* v. *United States,* 328 U. S. 781, 797, we said that "over two-thirds of the entire domestic field of cigarettes, and . . . over 80% of the field of comparable cigarettes" constituted "a substantial monopoly." In *United States* v. *Aluminum Co. of America,* 148 F. 2d 416, 429, 90% of the market constituted monopoly power. In the present case, 87% of the accredited central station service business leaves no doubt that the congeries of these defendants have monopoly power— power which, as our discussion of the record indicates, they did not hesitate to wield—if that business is the relevant market. The only remaining question therefore is, what is the relevant market?

In case of a product it may be of such a character that substitute products must also be considered, as customers may turn to them if there is a slight increase in the price of the main product. That is the teaching of the *du Pont* case (*supra,* at 395, 404), *viz.,* that commodities reasonably interchangeable make up that "part" of trade or commerce which §2 protects against monopoly power.

The District Court treated the entire accredited central station service business as a single market and we think it was justified in so doing. Defendants argue that the different central station services offered are so diverse that they cannot under *du Pont* be lumped together to make up the relevant market. For example, burglar alarm services are not interchangeable with fire alarm services. They further urge that *du Pont* requires that protective services other than those of the central station variety be included in the market definition.

But there is here a single use, *i.e.,* the protection of property, through a central station that receives signals. It is that service, accredited, that is unique and that competes with all the other forms of property protection. We see no barrier to combining in a single market a number of different products or services where that combination reflects commercial realities. To repeat, there is here a single basic service—the protection of property through use of a central service station—that must be compared with all other forms of property protection.

In §2 cases under the Sherman Act, as in §7 cases under the Clayton Act (*Brown Shoe Co.* v. *United States,* 370 U. S. 294, 325) there may be submarkets that are separate economic entities. We do not pursue that question here. First, we deal with services, not with products; and second, we conclude that the accredited central station is a type of service that makes up a relevant market and that domination or control of it makes out a monopoly of a "part" of trade or commerce within the meaning of §2 of the Sherman Act. The defendants have not made out a case for fragmentizing the types of services into lesser units.

Burglar alarm service is in a sense different from fire alarm service; from waterflow alarms; and so on. But it would be unrealistic on this record to break down the market into the various kinds of central station protective services that are available. Central station companies recognize that to compete effectively, they must offer all or nearly all types of service.[6] The different forms of accredited central station service are provided from a single office and customers utilize different services in combination. We held in *United States* v. *Philadelphia Nat. Bank,* 374 U. S. 321, 356, that "the cluster" of services denoted by the term "commercial banking" is "a distinct line of commerce." There is, in our view, a comparable cluster of services here. That bank case arose under §7 of the Clayton Act where the question was whether the effect of a merger "in any line of commerce" may be "substantially to lessen competition." We see no reason to differentiate between "line" of commerce in the context of the Clayton Act and "part" of commerce for purposes of the Sherman Act. See *United States* v. *First Nat. Bank & Trust Co.,* 376 U. S. 665, 667–668. In the §7 national bank case just mentioned, *services,* not *products* in the mercantile sense, were involved. In our view the lumping together of various kinds of *services* makes for the appropriate market here as it did in the §7 case.

There are, to be sure, substitutes for the accredited central station service. But none of them appears to operate on the same level as the central station service so as to meet the interchangeability test of the *du Pont* case. Nonautomatic and automatic local alarm systems appear on this record to have marked differences, not the low degree of differentiation required of substitute services as well as substitute articles.

Watchman service is far more costly and less reliable. Systems that set off an audible alarm at the site of a fire or burglary are cheaper but often less reliable. They may be inoperable without anyone's knowing it. Moreover, there is a risk that the local ringing of an alarm will not attract the needed attention and help. Proprietary systems that a customer purchases and operates are available; but they can be used only by a very large business or by government and are not realistic alternatives for most concerns. There are also protective services connected directly to a municipal police or fire department.

---

[6] Thus, of the 38 nondefendant firms operating a central service station protective service in the United States in 1961, 24 offered all of the following services: automatic fire alarm; waterflow alarm and sprinkler supervision; watchman's reporting and manual fire alarm; and burglar alarm. Of the other firms, 11 provided no watchman's reporting and manual fire alarm service; six provided no automatic fire alarm service; and two offered no sprinkler supervisory and waterflow alarm service. Moreover, of the 14 firms not providing the full panoply of services, 10 lacked only *one* of the above-described services. Appellant ADT's assertion that "very few accredited central stations furnish the full variety of services" is flatly contradicted by the record.

But most cities with an accredited central station do not permit direct, connected service for private businesses. These alternate services and devices differ, we are told, in utility, efficiency, reliability, responsiveness, and continuity, and the record sustains that position. And, as noted, insurance companies generally allow a greater reduction in premiums for accredited central station service than for other types of protection.

Defendants earnestly urge that despite these differences, they face competition from these other modes of protection. They seem to us seriously to overstate the degree of competition, but we recognize that (as the District Court found) they "do not have unfettered power to control the price of their services . . . due to the fringe competition of other alarm or watchmen services." 236 F. Supp., at 254. What defendants overlook is that the high degree of differentiation between central station protection and the other forms means that for many customers, only central station protection will do. Though some customers may be willing to accept higher insurance rates in favor of cheaper forms of protection, others will not be willing or able to risk serious interruption to their businesses, even though covered by insurance, and will thus be unwilling to consider anything but central station protection.

The accredited, as distinguished from nonaccredited service, is a relevant part of commerce. Virtually the only central station companies in the status of the nonaccredited are those that have not yet been able to meet the standards of the rating bureau. The accredited ones are indeed those that have achieved, in the eyes of underwriters, superiorities that other central stations do not have. The accredited central station is located in a building of approved design, provided with an emergency lighting system and two alternate main power sources, manned constantly by at least a required minimum of operators, provided with a direct line to fire headquarters and, where possible, a direct line to a police station; and equipped with all the devices, circuits and equipment meeting the requirements of the underwriters. These standards are important as insurance carriers often require accredited central station service as a condition to writing insurance. There is indeed evidence that customers consider the unaccredited service as inferior.

We also agree with the District Court that the geographic market for the accredited central station service is national. The activities of an individual station are in a sense local as it serves, ordinarily, only that area which is within a radius of 25 miles. But the record amply supports the conclusion that the business of providing such a service is operated on a national level. There is national planning. The agreements we have discussed covered activities in many States. The inspection, certification and rate-making is largely by national insurers. The appellant ADT has a national schedule of prices, rates, and terms, though the rates may be varied to meet local conditions. It deals with multistate businesses on the basis of nationwide contracts. The manufacturing business of ADT is interstate. The fact that Holmes is more nearly local than the others does not save it, for it is part and parcel of the combine presided over and controlled by Grinnell.

As the District Court found, the relevant market for determining whether the defendants have monopoly power is not the several local areas which the individual stations serve, but the broader national market that reflects the reality of the way in which they built and conduct their business.

We have said enough about the great hold that the defendants have on this market. The percentage is so high as to justify the finding of monopoly. And, as the facts already related indicate, this monopoly was achieved in large part by unlawful and exclusionary practices. The restrictive agreements that preempted for each company a segment of the market where it was free of competition of the others were one device. Pricing practices that contained competitors were another. The acquisitions by Grinnell of ADT, AFA, and Holmes were still another. Grinnell long faced a problem of competing with ADT. That was one reason it acquired AFA and Holmes. Prior to settlement of its dispute and controversy with ADT, Grinnell prepared to go into the central station service business. By acquiring ADT in 1953, Grinnell eliminated that alternative. Its control of the three other defendants eliminated any possibility of an outbreak of competition that might have occurred when the 1907 agreements terminated. By those acquisitions it perfected the monopoly power to exclude competitors and fix prices.[7]

The judgment below is affirmed except as to the decree. We remand for further hearings on the nature of the relief consistent with the views expressed herein.

It is so ordered.

---

[7] Since the record clearly shows that this monopoly power was consciously acquired, we have no reason to reach the further position of the District Court that once monopoly power is shown to exist, the burden is on the defendants to show that their dominance is due to skill, acumen, and the like.

10

Conjectures about the Future of Antitrust and Consumer Protection Law Enforcement

Throughout this text attempts to editorialize have been purposively suppressed. While some opinions and conjectures are evident in every chapter, particularly in the conclusion sections, a strenuous effort has been made to provide factual material in a way that could be digested by marketing executives and students without having to unravel the facts from the personal biases of the authors. Nor have we interjected the opinions of others. For example, we have avoided the debates of legal theories that always rage in law review articles.[1] We have no intention of breaking with our tradition here, but we do believe that it would be useful to conjecture briefly about the future of law enforcement in antitrust and consumer protection so that executives, in particular, might have some reasonably informed predictions about the likely legal environment they will be facing. They can then place these predictions within their calculus as they map marketing strategy.

In this chapter, we first look at controversies surrounding the appropriate goals of antitrust and consumer protection enforcement. This discussion then

[1] Exceptions are those issues where controversy is the rule rather than the exception, such as predatory pricing and advertising substantiation.

leads to an examination of contemporary criticisms of traditional perspectives regarding enforcement. Next, we explore some general issues in enforcement that will continue to concern business for years to come. Finally, we make a brief statement about the likely future of enforcement.

THE GOALS OF ANTITRUST
AND CONSUMER PROTECTION

Antitrust

The antitrust laws of the United States were designed to encourage competition. But competition is really not an end, but a means to an end. There is considerable controversy over just what the end result of "competition" (as furthered by the antitrust laws) ought to be. In fact, there is even controversy over what it really means to have "a little" or "a lot" of competition.

According to Asch, the antitrust rationale basically rests on a number of familiar propositions:

> that producers and sellers put forth their best efforts when threatened by effective rivals; that the economic desires of society are fulfilled when no individuals or groups within the market place possess the power to exploit; in short, that competition as a market force compels the best possible economic results.[2]

From this rationale, it is clear that public policies toward competition are not motivated solely—perhaps not even primarily—by economic objectives. Some individuals hold, for example, that the Sherman Act and the Clayton Act were rooted in the congressional belief that excess corporate power must be restrained to assure fair competition, prevent exploitation of the consumer, and protect democratic institutions.[3] For example, Justice William O. Douglas in the *Columbia Steel* case four decades ago stated this position clearly by saying that

> Industrial power should be decentralized so that the fortunes of the people will not be dependent on the whim or caprice, the political prejudices, the emotional stability of a few self-appointed men. The fact that they are not vicious men but respectable men is irrelevant.[4]

Carried to its farthest extreme, the sociopolitical goal underlying these sentiments has been taken to mean that Congress, by passing the antitrust laws, desired to "promote competition through the protection of viable, small, locally owned businesses,"[5] even though this might involve some impairment of overall economic efficiency.

To others, the goals of antitrust are tied directly to the goals of economic performance. Historically, economists have generally accepted six goals as

---

[2] Peter Asch, *Economic Theory and the Antitrust Dilemma* (New York: John Wiley & Sons, Inc., 1970), p. 2.

[3] Willard F. Mueller, "The Anti-Antitrust Movement," keynote address for a Conference on Industrial Organization and Public Policy, Middlebury College, Middlebury, Vermont, Apr. 16, 1981, p. 1.

[4] *U.S.* v. *Columbia Steel Co.,* 344 U.S. 495 (1948).

[5] *Brown Shoe Co.* v. *U.S.,* 370 U.S. 294 (1962).

suitable criteria for establishing desirable economic performance: (1) allocative efficiency; (2) technical efficiency; (3) relatively low selling costs; (4) product performance and technological progress; (5) equitable income distribution; and (6) full employment.[6] Over time, however, more stress has been placed on the "efficiency" goals—allocative and technical. Simply put, allocative efficiency is "making what consumers want" and technical or productive efficiency is "making these goods with the fewest scarce resources."[7] Accomplishment of other goals via antitrust is inappropriate, according to these arguments. Thus, "the sole goal of antitrust is economic efficiency" was a statement made in 1982 by William Baxter, assistant attorney general in charge of the Antitrust Division of the Justice Department.[8] Under this philosophy, the common central purpose of the antitrust laws is to maximize wealth by producing what consumers want at the lowest cost.[9] Others, adopting a similar perspective, argue that the only important question regarding the enforcement of the antitrust laws is the question as to which institutions and practices are necessary to keep the U.S. economy productive, especially relative to foreign competition.[10]

Clearly, there is a significant gap between the more sociopolitical perspectives and the strictly economic efficiency perspectives. In reality, such constructs as allocative and technical efficiency were probably unknown to the drafters of the Sherman Act; indeed, many of the economic theories and analyses underlying these constructs did not exist in 1890.[11] Therefore, while the efficiency goals may be very important now, it is difficult, if not impossible, to link these goals to the original intent of Congress.

Consumer Protection

There appear to be three main goals of consumer protection legislation: (1) restricting the communication of false information; (2) requiring the disclosure of information about products; and (3) preventing the marketing of products that are unsafe or fail to meet government safety standards. Like antitrust, there is controversy surrounding these goals, but the controversy is not over the goals themselves, but rather on just how stringently and adamantly the goals should be pursued. For example, very few individuals of any political persuasion oppose at least some form of government activity against the dissemination of false information or the sale of unsafe products. However, many would argue that government should only deal with the most extreme cases of deception, and that the marketplace will take care of the rest. In other words, if someone is deceived, then he or she simply won't purchase the product

---

[6] See Louis W. Stern and John R. Grabner, Jr., *Competition in the Marketplace* (Glenview, Ill.: Scott, Foresman & Co., 1970), pp. 48–68.

[7] Ward S. Bowman, Jr., *Patent and Antitrust Law* (Chicago: University of Chicago Press, 1973).

[8] Robert E. Taylor, "A Talk with Antitrust Chief William Baxter," *Wall Street Journal,* Mar. 4, 1982, p. 22.

[9] Bowman, op. cit., p. 1.

[10] See Lester C. Thurow, *The Zero-Sum Society* (New York: Basic Books, 1980).

[11] See Hans B. Thorelli, *The Federal Antitrust Policy* (Stockholm: Stockholms Hogskola, 1954).

again and eventually the deception will be expunged) The argument is a bit more tricky with regard to safety issues, but many persons would favor a more laissez-faire and less restrictive regulatory policy.

The critical point here is to understand why consumer protection laws are really needed in the first place. With regard to communication of information, a major reason seems to relate to economics and, in fact, ties in with the underlying rationale for antitrust—encouraging competition. If consumers are well informed and armed with honest data, they will make choices that will end up maximizing their welfare, thereby promoting allocative efficiency. With regard to product safety, the primary goal is one of preventing serious injuries inflicted on those who cannot properly analyze the potential harm of a product. While there may well be an economic rationale underlying the need for product safety regulation, the basic purpose underlying this concern is humanitarian as opposed to purely economic. The controversy over goals raises questions about how much protection is enough, and this controversy, along with the efficiency versus "way-of-life" debate in antitrust, is reflected in the differing perspectives discussed next. The weight of current opinion, however, seems to favor the emphasis of efficiency criteria and relaxed enforcement.

CONTEMPORARY VERSUS TRADITIONAL PERSPECTIVES

It is important to elaborate on contemporary antitrust and consumer protection perspectives, because these perspectives may provide a means of forecasting the future direction of policy and enforcement. Almost all the discussion in the preceding chapters revolves around what has been and what exists at present, particularly with respect to the state of the law and legal precedent. But the future will undoubtedly be strongly influenced by the new economic thinking that is embodied in the contemporary perspective. Exactly where this thinking will take antitrust and consumer protection is not clear, but the direction is rather obvious.

Antitrust

Basically, the contemporary antitrust perspective is rooted in the "Chicago School" of economics, which was spawned at the University of Chicago by Milton Friedman, George Stigler, and their colleagues. The Chicago School theory stresses the notion that antitrust policy should focus on the prices consumers have to pay. The heart of the theory is the belief, now based on empirical evidence, that prices are not necessarily dependent upon the number of competitors in any given market. While Chicago School economists and their disciples condemn price fixing and collusion among competitors (because of the adverse effects of such actions on the processes of allocative efficiency), they argue that it is wrong to conclude from a study of the structure of an industry (e.g., the degree of economic concentration) that a small number of companies automatically means less competition and higher prices. In fact, they believe that prices would not necessarily be lower if an industry were fragmented, because of the economies of scale that are available to firms in relatively concentrated industries. While a correlation exists between concentration and profit margins, evidence has been generated indicating that the margins widen not because prices increase but because *costs decrease* due to the efficiencies of concentration.[12] Examples of declining prices in the wake of high economic concentration can be found in such stable industries as major home appliances (e.g., refrigerators, stoves) and in such high-technology industries as computers.[13]

Chicago School economists have long contended that antitrust law overprotects inefficient small businesses and impedes business growth and business arrangements that increase efficiency.[14] One corollary of their theory is that the limits to absolute size should be determined by the marketplace. For example, conglomerate firms, such as ITT, General Dynamics, Litton Industries, and du Pont, become too large only when their size results in diseconomies of scale that erode their profits. At this point, a conglomerate will usually divest itself of some of its subsidiaries; it does not need government prodding to do so. Therefore, according to the Chicago School, most conglomerate mergers should be permissible. The same belief is true for vertical mergers. When a customer acquires a supplier, or vice versa, the result is frequently procompetitive because, as a result of the merger, the two parties will achieve lower costs. Only horizontal mergers are seen as *potentially* anticompetitive. But even here, such mergers can lead to greater efficiencies, which translate into lower prices for the consumer. Therefore, horizontal mergers would not be prohibited under the "new thinking" on a per se basis.[15]

Thurow, an economist at M.I.T., would go one step further. He advocates abolishing the antitrust laws altogether.[16] He bases his suggestion on five main beliefs:

1. The antitrust laws only serve to hinder U.S. competitors who must live by a code that their foreign competitors can ignore.
2. The general rise in income tends to greatly increase the relevant market in which firms compete. Most goods people buy today are not psychological necessities but luxuries that could be substituted by other goods.
3. The huge conglomerate enterprise enhances competition because monopoly

---

[12] Sam Peltzman, "The Gains and Losses from Industrial Concentration," *Journal of Law and Economics* 20 (Oct. 1977), pp. 229–263. For a critique of University of Chicago economist Peltzman's study, see F. M. Scherer, "The Causes and Consequences of Rising Industrial Concentration," *Journal of Law and Economics* 22 (Apr. 1979), pp. 191–208. See, also, the discussion in F. M. Scherer, *Industrial Market Structure and Economic Performance*, 2nd ed. (Chicago: Rand McNally College Publishing Co., 1980), pp. 288–292.

[13] "Antitrust Grows Unpopular," *Business Week*, Jan. 12, 1981, p. 90.

[14] See Richard A. Posner, *Antitrust Law: An Economic Perspective* (Chicago: University of Chicago Press, 1976); and William M. Landes and Richard A. Posner, "Market Power in Antitrust Cases," *Harvard Law Review* 94 (Mar. 1981), pp. 937–996.

[15] See Edward Meadows, "Bold Departures in Antitrust," *Fortune*, Oct. 5, 1981, p. 180.

[16] Thurow, op. cit., pp. 147–148. Also see Lester C. Thurow, "Let's Abolish the Antitrust Laws," *New York Times*, Oct. 19, 1980, and "Abolish the Antitrust Laws," *Duns Review*, Feb. 1981, pp. 72–74.

rents are inherently limited in an economy full of large conglomerate firms willing to invade one another's domains.

4. It is not obvious that anything of economic value is accomplished even if an antitrust case is won by the government.

5. The antitrust laws are preoccupied with price competition. Price is clearly only one of the many competitive weapons . . . and in many areas not the most useful or used weapon.[17]

The bottom line for Thurow is productivity, and he feels strongly that the antitrust laws and their enforcement have not focused on this critical dimension of our economy. He believes that resources would be better spent on research and development and new plant and equipment, instead of on lawyers and economists who prepare the prosecution and defenses of alleged antitrust violations.

On the other hand, the more traditional industrial organization economists, as represented by the works of Joe S. Bain[18] and F. M. Scherer,[19] focus on the significance of market power. Rather than assuming that large firms will be more competitive, especially in concentrated industries, the traditional perspective argues that these firms will use their power to exact a toll from the market in the form of higher prices and higher profits. One major mechanism such firms employ in building insularity from competition is to erect barriers to the entry of new competitors into their markets. The more that these firms are able to exact "monopoly profits," the lower will be the allocative efficiency in the economy. The traditional theory, upon which many of the antitrust cases reported in this book are based, postulates a stream of causation running from market structure (economic concentration) to market conduct (predatory and exclusionary behavior) to market performance (allocative and technical efficiency, among other indexes). Therefore, if it is possible to regulate the structure of industries, then it would be possible to influence their performance, from a social welfare perspective.

In general, a larger and larger group of economists have begun to adopt the viewpoint that antitrust policies enacted prior to 1980 did more harm than good. These policies, it is argued, prevented companies from making horizontal mergers with smaller, faltering companies. In addition, the antitrust policies of the past allegedly resulted in strong competitors sheltering weak inefficient ones because of the concern over antitrust enforcement if the former grew too large. The policies also supposedly resulted in attention being focused unnecessarily on vertical restrictions in distribution, because such restrictions may have little negative effect on interbrand competition and, in fact, may enhance it. For instance, according to this argument, a lawsuit by the Justice Department started under the Carter Administration against Cuisinart, the home food processor, for fixing retail prices was unnecessary, because imitators of the Cuisinart were already undercutting Cuisinart's high

---

[17] Thurow, *The Zero-Sum Society*, op. cit., pp. 147–148.

[18] Joe S. Bain, *Industrial Organization*, 2nd ed. (New York: John Wiley & Sons, Inc., 1968).

[19] F. M. Scherer, *Industrial Market Structure*, op. cit.

rigid prices prior to the complaint being filed. In other words, Cuisinart's retail pricing policy encouraged entry into the market.[20]

The sentiments expressed above were reflected in the policies and perspectives adopted by the Reagan Administration, particularly as articulated in the period 1981–1984 by Attorney General William French Smith, Assistant Attorney General William Baxter, and Federal Trade Commission Chairman James C. Miller, III. During this time, Smith stated that he would request prison sentences for price fixers but would seek to eliminate antitrust restraints that he believed hampered competition. He adopted the Chicago School's theory with regard to concentration, saying, "We must recognize that bigness in business doesn't necessarily mean badness. Efficient firms shouldn't be hobbled under the guise of antitrust enforcement."[21] Baxter was even more outspoken; he said

> I have a fairly deep-seated conviction that companies always [or] almost invariably act to maximize what they perceive to be their best profit opportunity, [and] that generally results in favorable outcomes that shouldn't be interfered with.[22]

Furthermore, he argued that "the intellectual underpinnings of the case against vertical and conglomerate mergers have been thoroughly discredited,"[23] and he concentrated the efforts of his division almost exclusively on activities that increased the risk of collusive behavior.[24] The *Merger Guidelines* issued by his division underscored his intentions, as discussed in Chapter 4. Baxter also argued, following the Chicago School, that courts had too often declared vertical restrictions illegal. "A vertical problem is either a horizontal problem in disguise or no problem at all."[25] He tended to ignore supplier-generated policies such as tying agreements, exclusive dealing arrangements, territorial and customer restrictions, and resale price maintenance. Such practices were challenged by his division only if they had horizontal effects, such as encouraging competitors to fix prices and restrain production.[26]

To a significant extent, Miller's outlook was identical to that of Smith and Baxter. However, he was also sharply critical of the past activities of the Federal Trade Commission, believing that its role had been too expansive. He even questioned the whole notion of independent agencies, arguing that such agencies are not sufficiently responsive to Congress and to the president.[27] He

---

[20] See John A. Jenkins, "Trustbusters Busted?" *TWA Ambassador* (Mar. 1982), p. 16.

[21] "Attorney General to Seek Prison Terms for Price-Fixers, Fewer Antitrust Curbs," *Wall Street Journal,* June 25, 1981, p. 6.

[22] Robert E. Taylor and Stan Crock, "Reagan Team Believes Antitrust Legislation Hurts Big Business," *Wall Street Journal,* July 8, 1981, p. 1.

[23] Meadows, op. cit., p. 182. As evidence of Baxter's orientation, recall the du Pont–Conoco merger, which was approved shortly after the Reagan Administration took office.

[24] Ibid.

[25] Ibid.

[26] Taylor and Crock, op. cit., p. 17. See also "The Antitrust Revolution," *Fortune,* July 11, 1983, pp. 29–32, and Robert E. Taylor, "Critics of Justice Agency's Antitrust Chief Assail his Unit's Effectiveness and Morale," *Wall Street Journal,* May 16, 1983, p. 25.

[27] "FTC Chief Miller Questions Agency Role in Consumer Protection, Antitrust Areas," *Wall Street Journal,* Oct. 27, 1981, p. 6.

brought about a reduction in the agency's budget and severely restricted some of its programs, including eliminating a number of its regional offices. From an enforcement perspective, Miller held that the FTC had historically placed too little emphasis on challenging horizontal restraints, such as price fixing. A devotee of Adam Smith, Miller was convinced that "People of the same trade seldom meet together, even for merriment and diversion, but the conversation ends in a conspiracy against the public, or in some contrivance to raise prices."[28] He also took a strong stand against exempting any group (e.g., doctors and dentists) or industry from the enforcement of the antitrust laws. He stated publicly that the FTC could not "effectively accomplish its mission if . . . a significant sector of our economy is . . . immunized, sanctified, and set aside as a privileged class."[29]

Consumer Protection

A philosophic debate similar to the one involving antitrust has surrounded consumer protection, pitting a new "school" against more traditional perspectives. This debate can be most easily examined by focusing on one specific issue that has been the subject of a great deal of the controversy, the attack on false, misleading, or deceptive seller representations, particularly those contained in advertising. The traditional premise was that the costs sustained by consumers because of false information are greater than the costs sustained by sellers in eliminating the false information. Therefore, from a cost–benefit viewpoint, regulation was clearly warranted. The traditional premise further held that, because false information causes consumers to make erroneous purchases, the ensuing misallocation of resources is too high a price for society, as well as specific individuals, to pay.

The contemporary perspective, similar in tone to the Chicago School, questions these premises. The argument here is that sellers have very little incentive to make false claims about products when consumers can easily detect any falsity by examination of the product before purchase or by purchasing the product and evaluating its performance. Only if sellers have no interest in repeat sales of the product is there a significant risk of false advertising, and, in that case, consumers supposedly are skeptical of false advertising claims and do not rely on them.[30] Under this theory, the interest of sellers in repeat sales and the interest of competitors in avoiding losses of sales because of consumer misperceptions will combine to clear the market of false representations.[31] Excessive government prosecution of questionable factual representa-

---

[28] Adam Smith, *The Wealth of Nations*, Cannan Edition (New York: The Modern Library, 1937), p. 128, as quoted in "Prepared Statement of James C. Miller III before the Committee on Commerce, Science and Transportation of the United States Senate," July 24, 1981, p. 3.

[29] " 'Unfair and Deceptive Practices' Standards Need Definition," FTC's Miller Tells Senate Committee," *FTC News Summary* 23–82 (Mar. 26, 1982), p. 1. See also "The FTC's Miller Puts His Faith in the Free Market," *Business Week*, June 27, 1983, pp. 66–70.

[30] Phillip Nelson, "Advertising as Information," *Journal of Political Economy* 82 (July 1974), pp. 729–754.

[31] Richard A. Posner, *Regulation of Advertising by the Federal Trade Commission* (Washington, D.C.: American Enterprise Institute for Public Policy Research, 1973).

tions about products is, according to this perspective, likely to lead to increased use of noninformation types of advertising, thereby depriving consumers of a relatively costless source of data about products.[32]

On the other hand, the contemporary perspective also recognizes the difficulty of predicting what would happen if false advertising laws were abolished or repealed, because it is not known whether the low level of false advertising that presently occurs in the United States is due to the deterrent effect of existing law.[33] Furthermore, government enforcement of laws against false advertising supposedly confers benefits on those sellers who advertise truthfully. Consumers should also give greater credence to advertising in general if they know that government will act against false advertising.[34]

Again, parallel to antitrust, the contemporary perspective was reflected in the consumer protection policies and enforcement efforts of the Reagan Administration. At the FTC, Chairman Miller appointed as heads of important FTC bureaus persons who were extremely critical of many of the FTC's consumer protection activities, which had been based on the traditional perspective. For example, Timothy J. Muris, the director of the FTC's Bureau of Consumer Protection from 1981 to 1983, made the following comment about the activism of the FTC during the 1970s:

> Under a variety of specific initiatives during the past decade, the agency has tried to reshape vital parts of the American economy and to promote the theoretical views, policy preferences, and social order of the incumbent commissioners and staff. In general, the FTC has failed to base its efforts on sound economic analysis. . . . Fundamental inconsistencies regarding economic analysis surface frequently in FTC programs. For example, some FTC actions deregulate an industry on the theory that market forces best protect consumers, while others regulate an industry on the theory that market forces harm consumers.[35]

Muris extended his criticism to the FTC's failure to consider the costs of rule making. He also questioned the FTC's regulation of deceptive advertising on two grounds: (1) its failure to insist on "proof of actual harm to consumers";[36] and (2) its tendency to find "advertisements deceptive that would fool only a small number of gullible people yet did convey meaningful information to others."[37] In addition, he criticized the merits of the FTC's program that requires advertisers to have substantiation for their claims on the ground that substantiation of truthful claims often imposes a needless cost that is passed on to consumers.[38] Basically, both Miller and Muris believed that consumers are, for

[32] Donald F. Turner, "Commentary," in David G. Tuerck, ed., *Issues in Advertising: The Economics of Persuasion* (Washington, D.C.: American Enterprise Institute for Public Policy Research, 1978), p. 52.

[33] Ibid., p. 50.

[34] Roland M. McKean, "Commentary," in Tuerck, ed., op. cit., pp. 65–66.

[35] Kenneth W. Clarkson and Timothy J. Muris, *The Federal Trade Commission: Letting Competition Serve Consumers,* Law and Economic Center, University of Miami, Working Paper No. 81-2, pp. 23–24.

[36] Ibid., p. 25.

[37] Ibid.

[38] Ibid., p. 26.

the most part, capable of fending for themselves. Their beliefs were very much in line with the contemporary perspective, and, as a result, many of the consumer protection programs instituted by the FTC prior to 1980 received relatively little attention and/or enforcement during the Reagan Administration.

GENERAL ISSUES IN THE ENFORCEMENT OF ANTITRUST AND CONSUMER PROTECTION LAWS

Regardless of the validity of pre-1980 antitrust and consumer protection laws and their enforcement, constraints are built into the U.S. system of justice that make legal change very difficult. First, in the antitrust area, over 95 percent of the civil cases filed in federal courts each year are private (i.e., company versus company). Even if the government assumes a lower profile with respect to its own enforcement efforts, much case law will be generated by suits that do not involve the government. A respected antitrust lawyer, commenting on a number of lower court cases, has observed that

> Although it is difficult to predict which private actions will eventually make substantive contributions to the body of antitrust law, it is clear that the economic impact of private antitrust litigation is increasing.[39]

Second, in the consumer protection area, private product liability lawsuits are the only means by which individuals can obtain redress for injuries caused by unsafe products. In the deception area, while the FTC has been the principal enforcer of deception laws and while private enforcement of deception standards has been sporadic and minimal, there is a distinct possibility that this could change. Enforcement of *state* antideception laws by the attorneys general of the individual states and by private parties is likely to increase. All states have laws that are similar or identical to the Federal Trade Commission law that prohibits unfair and deceptive acts or practices, and these laws can be enforced by private parties and by state governments. A dramatic increase in the number of reported cases decided under state consumer protection acts has been documented.[40] Thus, a decline in consumer protection activity at the federal level may not mean a great deal from the perspective of marketing executives who are concerned with such matters. In fact, it may compound the problem, because rather than simply concentrating attention on a monolithic enforcer (the FTC), they must now watch 50 different enforcement agencies, in addition to facing the possibility of consumer lawsuits. And an increase in another form of private litigation in the consumer protection area also is possible. This litigation involves suits in federal courts initiated by competitors who have been injured by false or deceptive advertising claims, especially those claims that emanate from comparative advertising campaigns.[41]

[39] Richard W. Pogue, "Recent Antitrust Developments," Jones, Day, Reavis & Rogue, Cleveland, Ohio, 1982, p. 7-1.

[40] Paul Bloom and Stephen Greyser, *Exploring the Future of Consumerism* (Cambridge, Mass.: Marketing Science Institute, Report 81-102, July 1981), p. 24.

[41] See Chapter 7 for examples of challenged comparative advertising campaigns.

Third, as a general observation, it is obvious that our society has become increasingly litigious. The continuous growth in the number of lawyers, coupled with judicial decisions that allow attorneys to advertise, is clearly going to result in more lawsuits. In an intensely competitive climate, lawyers seeking business have already begun to place advertisements informing consumers about allegedly defective and dangerous products and offering their services if problems arise in using these products. A federal judge has been quoted as saying, "We have long had the litigating habit, but in recent years the habit has become an addiction."[42] John Opel, president and chief executive officer of IBM (a corporation that has faced its full share of lawsuits), observed that

> Instead of dealing with problems informally and using the law only when necessary, we too often and too quickly turn to the courts to resolve an issue. Litigation has become a knee-jerk reaction to conflict rather than a last resort to work things out.[43]

He has made the following suggestions for stemming the tide of litigation:

- curb meritless lawsuits (people or organizations who press a nuisance lawsuit and lose would have to pay not only court costs, but also the defending side's legal fees);
- eliminate contingency fees or at least limit the amount of money that an attorney can make from a single case;
- use mediation and arbitration to settle disputes;
- accelerate the legal process;
- limit product liability suits and give greater weight to contributory negligence or consumer recklessness;
- restrict treble-damages in antitrust suits to hard core illegalities, such as price-fixing conspiracies (only actual damages should be awarded in grey-zone cases);
- increase federal judgeships; and
- end abuses in discovery (limit the right of either party in a lawsuit to search through the other's files for possible evidence).[44]

Regardless of the merit of these proposals, it is obvious that the problems underlying them are large and pose serious impediments for policy makers seeking to change the direction of law enforcement.

Fourth, aggravating the above-mentioned factors (i.e., the preponderance of *private* lawsuits and the increasing amount of litigation generally) is the fact that, once a lawsuit begins, the length of time absorbed by the suit, both in terms of man-hours of effort and in terms of calendar time, can be immense. As pointed out in Chapter 9, the IBM case brought by the Justice Department in 1969 took 13 years to bring to a settlement and the cereal case took 10 years before being concluded by the Federal Trade Commission. And if a case

---

[42] Quoted in John R. Opel, "Our Litigious Society," *Outlook* (a publication of Booz, Allen & Hamilton, Inc.), Fall/Winter 1980, p. 1.

[43] Ibid. Opel reports that the United States has 15 times as many lawyers per capita as does Japan, which may in part explain the disparity in the amount of litigation in the two societies.

[44] Ibid., pp. 8–10.

were to move up through the appeals system, it may not ever be heard by the Supreme Court, where major precedents are established, because the Court hears only about 160, or 3 percent, of the 5,100 cases filed each term. These figures include *all* subject areas, not just antitrust and consumer protection. While in 1982 the justices issued more opinions (141) and listened to arguments in more cases (184) than at any time in the preceding several decades, the probabilities are still very low that any given case will be heard by them.[45] Furthermore, even if one successfully petitions the Supreme Court, the time delay until a final decision is made is very long. For example, a petition filed in July 1982 and voted on in late fall 1982 would not have been argued until October 1983 and would not have been decided until the spring of 1984.

Finally, as we have emphasized frequently throughout this text, precedent is changed very slowly; so slowly, in fact, that if the Supreme Court believes that the application of a previous decision to a current case is inappropriate, the Court will make every effort to distinguish the two cases rather than overrule the existing precedent. If this is impossible, the Court will likely reinterpret only as much of the prior decision as will make the desired outcome consistent. Only in rare and extreme cases will this process (called *stare decisis*) be upset and precedent specifically overruled. The beliefs of the enforcement agencies may, therefore, have little effect, in the short-run at least, on precedent. The agencies can, however, determine which cases to bring and, probably more important, which commercial practices to ignore. Their activity or inactivity can clearly change the regulatory climate facing industry. They can also attempt to influence the outcomes of cases by stepping into suits on the side of defendants, particularly by filing friend-of-the-court (*amicus curiae*) briefs. This latter strategy was successfully employed in a case decided in 1983 by the Supreme Court involving the use of the good faith defense in the Robinson–Patman Act.[46] The Justice Department and the Federal Trade Commission also played an active role in Marathon Oil's securing a preliminary injunction enjoining Mobil Corp. from acquiring more than 50 percent of Marathon's common stock in 1981.[47] In fact, the filing of *amicus curiae* briefs became a major thrust of the Justice Department in its effort to infuse the contemporary perspective into court decisions during the Reagan Administration.

---

[45] Stephen Wermiel, "High Court Term Focuses Attention on Big Workload, Antitrust Rulings," *Wall Street Journal*, July 6, 1982, p. 21.

[46] Falls City Industries, a brewer in Louisville, Ky., invoked the "meeting competition in good faith" defense when it was sued under the Robinson–Patman Act by Vanco Beverage, one of its distributors in Indiana. Falls City charged lower prices in Kentucky than it did in Indiana, a price structure it defended as a necessary competitive response to market conditions in the two states. The Supreme Court ruled that Falls City was entitled to show that it set its prices in order to meet competition on an *areawide* basis and was not limited to defending its prices on a customer-by-customer basis. The Justice Department and the Federal Trade Commission supported Fall City's Supreme Court appeal. The Justice Department has long been hostile to the Robinson–Patman Act. It urged the Court to interpret the "good faith" defense as broadly as possible as a way of making the statute more flexible. See *Falls City Industries Inc., v. Vanco Beverage Inc.*, 455 U.S. 988 (1982).

[47] *Marathon Oil Co.* v. *Mobil Corp.*, 530 F. Supp. 315, *aff'd*, 669 F.2d 378 (6th Cir. 1981).

THE FUTURE OF ANTITRUST AND CONSUMER PROTECTION

While we believe that marketing executives would do well to abide by the warnings implied above with respect to private enforcement, state laws, and litigation in general, there can be no doubt that the decade of the 1980s was one of reassessment regarding antitrust and consumer protection enforcement efforts. The threatening environment provided by the Antitrust Division and the FTC during the decades of the 1960s and 1970s disappeared. The disappearance was primarily based on the contemporary perspectives discussed previously. These perspectives were adopted, almost completely, by the Reagan Administration. Perhaps the major impetus for the abrupt change was not only the political mood of the country, which became more conservative, but also the existence of a severe recession combined with new forms of foreign competition that U.S. industry had not faced previously. Attention shifted to eliminating inflation and unemployment and to increasing the competitiveness of American firms. Such issues as deceptive advertising, vertical restrictions in distribution, discriminatory pricing, and even mergers among competitors do not attract much attention when the economy is sour and when people are unemployed.

The lack of genuine public interest in antitrust and consumer protection issues provided a vacuum into which the philosophies of the "new right" moved quickly. For example, the FTC, under Miller and Muris, announced its intent to pursue only those deception cases where the public benefit of prosecution was clear and where there was substantial consumer injury. As discussed in Chapter 7, the FTC's 1981 policy protocol for investigation and prosecution of deceptive advertising cases suggested that very few such cases would meet the FTC's standards for prosecution. The potential for the FTC becoming a "paper tiger" was high, certainly with respect to borderline conduct.

On the other hand, such a prognosis may be moot, because technological developments may lessen the need for government intervention. The emergence of cable television, satellite transmission of communications, and videodisks, along with other innovations, will undoubtedly provide consumers with an increased ability to exercise informed purchasing choices. Special programs and mechanisms geared to enhance product knowledge and buying skills will be available. To the extent that purchasers have available and rely on hard data (e.g., gas mileage comparisons, R-ratings, etc.), which can be easily provided via these mechanisms, the significance of deception will be reduced. False, incomplete, and inaccurate promotional activities will lose their power to influence consumers, making legal constraints on deception (and, thus, the need for vigorous enforcement) superfluous. Of course, it is entirely possible that none of these positive results will transpire from the increase in information brought about by technological innovations. In that event, one might well ask whether regulatory intervention is warranted at all if consumers demonstrate their lack of interest in obtaining accurate and complete information by ignoring information made available to them.

The technological revolution aside, it is our belief that during more prosperous times when resources are more plentiful, there is likely to be considerable attention to antitrust and consumer protection issues. Despite the contemporary perspective, it is not academia or government that will really determine the pace of enforcement, but industry itself. Unfair competitive practices, predation, and deception hurt industry directly, and it is highly likely that, as multinational competition continues to intensify, marketing executives will want to reevaluate the "rules of the game" and assure themselves that there is a referee readily available to make certain that the game is played fairly. In fact, they may even prefer a police squad to a referee. Contrary to what most laymen think, executives want to have the rules clearly defined, and, for the most part, they are generally willing to abide by them out of self-interest. Indeed, from industry's perspective, it is possible that deregulation, especially as it is applied to antitrust and consumer protection issues, may go too far. If it does, there will be a reaction to bring it back to a more comfortable level.

For the immediately foreseeable future, however, what marketing executives can expect are vacillating enforcement efforts and changing political and economic philosophies as the country evaluates the performance of the "new right" and as administrations come and go. Precedent, therefore, will become even more important, because it will lend a sense of stability and continuity to the "rules of the game." It is for this reason that this text is written as it is, giving heavy emphasis to precedent. To a large extent, this approach provides information on some of the more enduring rules and guidelines for marketing behavior.

Index

Subject Index

A&P (Great Atlantic & Pacific Tea Co.), 273, 275, 276, 291–299, 342
Abandonment of trademarks, 56
Absolute confinement of reseller sales, 319–320
Actual damages, 12–13
Administrative agency rules, 4
Adulteration, of food products, 103
Advertised specials, unavailability of, 396
Advertising, 369–444
  affirmative disclosure orders and, 381
  bait, 396–397
  cases, 415–444
  cease and desist orders and, 380
  comparative, 57–58, 402–409
    consumer preference tests, 405–406
    Lanham Act, 403–409
    state law regarding, 406–409
  corrective, 381–385
  of credit terms, 400–401
  deceptive, 370–377
    competitor actions against, 401–409
    defense of puffing, 375–377
    implied representations, 374–375
    meaning of deception, 370–374
    remedies available to the FTC, 380–386
  demonstrations or mock-ups in, 389–390
  endorsements and testimonials in, 390–394
  false, 370–371
  multiple product orders and, 385–386
  of price reductions, 396
  price, restrictions on, 397–398
  pricing claims in, 394–399
  rule-making authority of the FTC and, 387–388
  substantiation for, 378–380
  unfair, 377
  warranties created by, 79
Advisory opinions
  of the Antitrust Division, 6
  Federal Trade Commission, 8
Affirmative disclosure orders, 381
Agriculture, U.S. Department of (USDA), 103, 104
Alcoa (Aluminum Company of America), 342, 344, 482–484, 501–515
Allowances
  brokerage, 453–455, 457
  promotional, 455–457
American Brands, 181
American Can Company, 38, 307, 481
American Home Products Corp., 380, 432–444
American Suppliers, Inc., 280–290
American Tobacco Company, The, 280–290
Anheuser-Busch, 266–267
Anti-Monopoly, Inc., 65–75
Antitrust Division of the Department of Justice, 5, 158
  advisory opinions of, 6
  civil actions and, 6
  criminal cases and, 5–6
  discretion of, 9
Antitrust Improvements Act (1976), 157–158
Antitrust laws
  Antitrust Division and, 6–7
  contemporary versus traditional perspectives on, 526–530
  cross-licensing agreements or patent pools and, 36–37

Federal Trade Commission and, 7
future of, 535–536
general issues in the enforcement of, 532–534
goals of, 524–525
marketing channel strategy and, 300–348
  customer restrictions, 324–325
  exclusive dealing, 302–307
  functional discounts, 334–337, 334–337
  reciprocity, 330–331
  refusals to deal, 331–334
  resale price maintenance, 325–330
  territorial restrictions, 319–324
  tying contracts, 307–319
  vertical integration, 337–346
mergers and, 154–160
patents and, 29, 31, 32, 35–38
pricing strategy and, 237–279
  discriminatory pricing, 263–276
  exchanging price information, 245–250
  parallel pricing, 250–257
  predatory pricing, 257–263
  price fixing, 238–245
Antitrust policy, 10
Areas of primary responsibility, 320
Areeda-Turner test, 261, 262, 278, 494
Artistic works, see Copyright
Assignment of trademarks, 57
Association of Stop-N-Shop Supermarkets, 242
AT&T, 490–491
Atlantic Commission Company, 342
Autolite Sparkplug Company, 15, 340–341
Automobile Dealers Franchise Act, 333

Bait advertising, 396–397
Barriers to entry, from vertical mergers, 338
Base-point pricing systems, 255–256
Baskin-Robbins, 312, 314
Beltone Electronics Corporation, 323
Bendix Corporation, 173–174
Berkey Photo, Inc., 491–492
Bethlehem Steel Corporation, 162
Bid-rigging agreements, 241
"Big Foot" trademark, 51
Boise Cascade Corporation, 336
Borden Company, 266, 273, 275, 276, 291–299, 494–495
Bowman Corp., 275
Brand names, 43
Bristol-Myers Co., 405–406
Broch, Henry, and Company, 454–455, 469–474
Brokerage allowances, 453–455, 457
Brown Shoe Co., 307
Brown Shoe Company, 162, 307, 315, 339–340
Burger King, 47

Campbell Soup Company, 389
Carnation, 268
Carvel, 314
Catalog sales, warranties and, 88
Cease and desist orders, Federal Trade Commission, 8, 14, 380
Celebrity endorsements, 390–391
Celler-Kefauver Amendment (or Act) (1950), 3, 154, 157, 159, 162–163, 347
  mergers and, 337
Cement Manufacturers' Protective Association, 247

Cents-off labeling, 394–395
Certification mark, 44
Chain referral sales, 452
Chanel No. 5, 57
Chicago Board of Trade, 243–244
Chicken Delight, 314–315
Child Protection Act of 1966, 107
Child Protection and Toy Safety Act of 1969, 107
Chock Full O'Nuts Corporation, 314
Civil actions, Antitrust Division and, 6
Civil investigative demands (CIDs), 6
Civil penalties, 11
   Federal Trade Commission actions for, 8–9
Civil remedies, 10
   See also Damages; Injunctions
Class actions, 13
Clayton Act, 3
   exclusive dealing and, 302, 303
   mergers and, 154, 157, 160
   monopolization and, 477
   patents and, 35
   reciprocity and, 330
   Robinson-Patman amendments to, see Robinson-
      Patman Act
   tying contracts and, 308, 309
   vertical integration and, 337, 342
   vertical mergers and, 341
Clorox Company, 168, 229–235, 266
Coercion, personal selling and, 447–450
Colgate & Co., 332
Colgate Doctrine, 332, 334
Colgate-Palmolive Company, 389
Collective marks, 44
Collusion
   FTC on factors facilitating, 209
   in parallel pricing, 253–254
   vertical mergers and, 200–201
Combinations, horizontal, 345–346
Commercial speech, 4
Common law
   product quality and, 77, 90
   warranties and, 82
Common Market (European Community), 497
Comparative advertising, 57–58, 402–409
   consumer preference tests and, 405–406
   Lanham Act and, 403–409
   state law regarding, 406–409
Compco Corp., 62–64
Complaints, Federal Trade Commission, 7
Compulsory licensing
   of copyrights, 41–42
   of patents, 38
Concentration ratios
   government merger guidelines on, 176–178, 190–193,
      197
Confidential information, protection of, 20–26
Conglomerate market power, 167
Conglomerate mergers, 152, 167–72
   concentration ratios and, 178–179
   deep-pocket, 168–169
   diversification via, 180–181
   Justice Department guidelines on, 178–179
   potential entrant, 169–172
Conscious parallelism, doctrine of, 252, 253, 255
Consent orders (Federal Trade Commission), 8
Consequential damages, for warranty breach, 79
Consolidated Foods, 341

Consolidated Steel, 337
Conspiracies, horizontal, 345–346
Constitution, U.S., 2–4
Consumer endorsements, 391–392
Consumer Expectations and Risk-Utility test, 96
Consumer Goods Pricing Act, 325
Consumer preference tests, comparative advertising and,
   405–406
Consumer Product Safety Act, 3, 106, 108–109
Consumer Product Safety Commission (CPSC), 77, 94,
   106–110
Consumer protection policy, 10
Consumer protection laws
   future of, 535–536
   general issues in the enforcement of, 532–534
   goals of, 524–525
   traditional versus contemporary perspectives on, 530–
      532
Consumer redress, Federal Trade Commission and, 9
Contests, 445–447
Continental, 268
Continental Can Corporation, 161, 165
Continental TV, 332, 349–361
Contracts, employee, for protection of secrets, 23–24
Controlling circumstance exception to laws on exchanging
   price information, 247, 249
Copies of unpatented products, 25–26
Copyright, 20, 38–42
   compulsory licensing of, 41–42
   duration of, 41
   formalities of obtaining and protecting a, 40
   licensing of, 41–42
   loss of rights in, 14
   rights of the owner of a, 42
   subject matter protected by, 39–40
   tying contracts and, 311
Copyright Act of 1909, 39
Copyright Act of 1976, 3, 38–39
Copyright Office, 40
Copyright Royalty Tribunal, 41
Corrective advertising, 381–385
Cosmetics, regulation of, 104–106
Cost justification defense to discriminatory pricing, 271–
   272
Cost of litigation, 15
Credit advertising, 400–401
Criminal cases, Antitrust Division and, 5–6
Criminal sanctions, 11
Cross-licensing, 36–37
Cuisinarts, Incorporated, 58, 528–529
Customer restrictions, 324–325, 347

Damages
   actual, 12–13
   for copyright infringement, 42
   multiple, 11–12
   punitive, 12
   for trademark infringement, 49–50
   for warranty breaches, 79
Day-Brite Lighting, Inc., 62–64
Dealers
   exclusive, 346
   refusals to deal, 331–334
Deceptive acts or practices, 370–377
Deceptive advertising, see Advertising
Deceptive trademarks, 55
Deep-pocket mergers, 168–169

Defects, product, 92–96
Delivered prices, 255–257
Demonstrations, in advertising, 389–390
Design defects, 94–96
Designs, patents on, 27
Deviation from the Norm test, 94
Devices, 104
Disclaimer of implied warranties, 83–85
Disclosure requirements, of Magnuson-Moss Warranty
    Act, 87–89
Discounts, functional (trade), 334–337
Discretion of enforcement agencies, 9–10
Discriminatory pricing, 263–276
    actual sale of goods or commodities required in, 266–
        267
    by buyers, 274–276
    cost justification defense to, 271–272
    definition of "discriminate in price," 265
    different purchasers required in, 265–266
    good faith defense to, 272–274
    substantial lessening of competition required for, 267–
        271
    "unreasonably low prices" and, 274
Discriminatory royalty obligations, 34
Distribution
    dual, 343–346
    licensing of patents and, 34–36
Distributors
    exclusive, 320–324
    refusals to deal, 331–334
Divestiture, 15
Door-to-door sales, 448–449
    warranties and, 88
Doubleday Co., 336, 337
Drugs
    copying of, 26
    regulation of, 104–106
du Pont, E.I., de Nemours and Company, 15, 22, 243,
    339, 480, 485–487
Dual distribution, 343–346
Dunkin' Donuts, 314

Eastman Kodak, 480, 491–492
Economy size labeling, 395–396
Efficiencies defense, 174, 179, 202
El Paso Natural Gas Co., 170
Employee agreements, protection of trade secrets by, 23–
    24
Encyclopaedia Britannica, Inc., 458–468
Endorsements
    celebrity, 390–391
    connections between advertiser and endorser, 393
    consumer, 391–392
    definition of, 390
    expert, 392
Enforcement policy, 9
Ethyl Corp., 243
European Community (Common Market), 497
Exclusive dealing, 302–307, 346
Exclusive distributorship (or franchise), 320–324
Expert endorsements, 392
Express warranties, 77–80
Exxon Corporation, 48–49

Failing firm defense, 172–173, 179, 202–203, 210–212
Fair Packaging and Labeling Act (FPLA), 111–112, 394–
    395
Fair Trade laws, 325, 326

Fair use exception in copyright law, 42
False advertising, 370–371
False representations, 371
Falstaff Brewing Corp., 170–171
Faltering firm defense, 179
Family names as trademarks, 53
Federal Hazardous Substances Act, 107
Federal Power Commission, 170
Federal Reserve Board, 401
Federal Trade Commission (FTC), 7–9, 55, 529–532
    advertising and, see Advertising
    advisory opinions of, 8
    cease and desist orders of, 7, 14
    complaints issued by, 7
    consent orders of, 8
    consumer redress and, 9
    deep-pocket mergers and, 168–169
    disclosure requirements of Magnusson-Moss Warranty
        Act and, 87–89
    discretion of, 9
    discriminatory pricing and, 269, 271–276
    efficiencies defense to mergers challenged by, 174, 202
    exclusive dealing and, 302–303, 307
    faltering firm defense to mergers challenged by, 179
    function of, 7
    functional discounts and, 335–337
    games as a sales promotion device and, 446–447
    industry guides of, 8
    injunctions, 9
    jurisdiction of, 7
    mail-order selling and, 450–452
    merger guidelines of, 174–175, 179, 204–213
        See also Horizontal mergers — Federal Trade
        Commission statement on
    mergers and, 152, 154–157
    personal selling techniques and, 447–450
    policy planning protocol for deceptive and
        unsubstantiated claims, 412–414
    presale availability rule and, 89
    price fixing and, 277
    price signaling and, 243
    price squeezes and, 334
    reciprocity and, 330–331
    resale price maintenance and, 329–330
    rules issued by, 8
    vertical mergers and, 341
Federal Trade Commission Act, 3, 7, 9
    advertising and, see Advertising
    mailing of unordered merchandise and, 450–451
    parallel pricing and, 256–257
    reciprocity and, 331
    territorial restrictions and, 320, 323
    tying contracts and, 308
Federal Truth in Lending Act, 400
Fiduciaries, personal selling by, 449–450
First National Supermarkets Inc., 242
Fisher Foods Inc., 242
Fitness for a particular purpose, implied warranties of,
    80–82
FMC Corporation (FMC), 117–128
Food, Drug, and Cosmetic Act, 3, 105–106, 115–116
Food and Drug Administration (FDA), 31, 103–106
Food identity standards, 103–104
Food products, regulation of, 103–104
Ford Motor Company, 12, 15, 129–150, 340–341
Foreign words as trademarks, 54–55
Fortner Enterprises, 310, 362–368

Fram Corporation, 173–174
Franchises
  exclusive, 320–324
  trademarks and, 312, 314
Freedom of speech, 4
Freight absorption, 269–270
Functional discounts, 334–337, 347

Gallo, E. & J., Winery, 317
Games of chance, as sales promotion technique, 445–447
General Dynamics Corporation, 165, 341
General Electric Company (GE), 34, 327, 331
General Foods, 168–169
General Foods Corporation, 168–169, 493–494
General Mills Fun Group, Inc., 65–75
General Motors Corporation, 15, 339, 344
  Toyota and, 180
General Talking Pictures Corp. (GTP), 35
Generic drugs, 104–105
Generic names
  Anti-Monopoly case, 65–75
  preventing trademark from becoming, 56–57
Gentry, Inc., 341
Geographic markets
  in FTC merger guidelines, 213
  government merger guidelines and, 176, 187–189
  horizontal mergers and, 159–160, 162
Geographic names as trademarks, 53
Georgia-Pacific Corp., 245
Geritol, 381
Good faith defense to discriminatory pricing, 272–274
Goodyear Corp., 51
Great Atlantic & Pacific Tea Co., see A&P
Grinnell Corporation, 516–522
GTE-Sylvania, 321–324, 328, 349–361

Habitability, warranty of, 82
Hanover Bank, 166
Hazardous substances, 107
Hazel-Atlas, 165
Heileman Brewery, 177, 178
Herfindahl-Hirschman Index (HHI), 167, 176–177, 182,
  190–192
Horizontal combinations or conspiracies, 345–346
Horizontal mergers, 152, 159–167
  factors relevant in testing, 159–168
  Federal Trade Commission statement on, 204–213
    background, 204
    collusion, factors facilitating, 209
    efficiency considerations, 209–210
    Failing Company defense and related arguments,
      210–212
    market definition, 212–213
    market power/duration factors, 206–207
    market share considerations, 204–205
  geographic markets and, 159–160, 162
  Justice Department guidelines on, 190–196
  product markets and, 159–160

**IBM (International Business Machines Corp.), 308–309,
  488–490, 497–498**
Ideas submitted by outsiders, 24–25
Implied representations, 374–375
Implied warranties, 77–78, 80–85
  disclaimer of, 83–85
  of merchantability and fitness for a particular purpose,
    80–83
Incidental damages, for warranty breach, 79
Industry guides, 8

Infringement
  of copyright, 42
  of trademarks, 48–51, 54, 56
Injuctions, 14
  Federal Trade Commission, 9
Injuries, liability for, see Product liability
Innocent infringement defense, in trademark cases, 54
Innovations
  submitted by outsiders, 24–25 See also Patents
Instructions, inadequate, 93–94
International Business Machines Corp., see IBM
International Harvester Company, 481
Intrabrand competition, restrictions on, 319
  See also Customer restrictions; Territorial restrictions
Inventions, see Patents

Johnnie Walker trademark, 47, 52
Johnson & Johnson, 432–444
Judicial decisions, 4–5
Justice Department
  Antitrust Division of, 5, 158
    advisory opinions of, 6
    civil actions and, 6
    criminal cases and, 5–6
    discretion of, 9
  efficiencies defense to mergers challenged by, 174, 202
  merger guidelines of, 174–179, 183–203, 337–338
    defenses, 202–203
    horizontal effect from non-horizontal mergers, 196–202
    horizontal mergers, 190–196
    market definition and measurement, 184–190
    purpose and underlying policy assumptions, 183–184

K-Mart, 334–335
Kellogg Company, 492–493
Kennecott Copper Corporation, 173
Kerr-McGee, 262
Kinney, G.R., Corporation, 162, 214–228, 339–340
Kroger Company, 394

Labeling, 110–112
  cents-off, 394–395
  economy size, 395–396
  introductory offers represented on, 395
  Magnuson-Moss Warranty Act requirements, 86–88
Lanham Act, 45, 50, 312
  comparative advertising and, 403–409
Laws, nature and hierarchy of, 2–5
Legal system, overview of, 2–5
Legislation, 4
Liability
  for breach of warranty, 78–79
  in price fixing, 245
  product, see Product liability
License, loss of, 13
Licensing
  compulsory
    of copyrights, 41–42
    of patents, 38
  of copyrights, 41–42
  of patents, 32–38
    antitrust limits of, 33–36
    challenging patents and obtaining remedies, 37–38
    cross-licensing and patent pools, 36–37
    distribution strategy, 34–36
    pricing strategy, 34
    refusals to license, 33–34
    royalties, 33, 34
  of trademarks, 57

Liggett & Myers Tobacco Company, 280–290
"Likelihood of confusion" test, 48–49
Limit pricing, 167
Liquid Carbonic, 341
Listerine, 382
Literary and artistic works, see Copyright
Location clauses, 320
Loss of bargain, 79
Lotteries, as sales promotion technique, 446–447
LTV Corporation, 173
Lykes Steel, 173

McGuire Act, 325
McKesson & Robbins, 239
Magnuson-Moss Warranty Act (MMWA), 3, 84–89, 399
  availability of text of warranty under, 88–89
  catalog and mail-order sales under, 88
  disclosure requirements of, 87–89
  door-to-door sales under, 88
  full warranty requirements under, 86–87
  litigation regarding warranties and, 89
  presale availability requirements of, 84, 89
Mail-order sales, 450–452, 457
  warranties and, 88
Maine, Unfair Sales Act of, 263
Manufacturers Trust Co., 166
Manufacturing process defects, 92–93
Maple Flooring Manufacturers' Association, 246–247
Marathon Oil Company, 534
Marine Bancorporation, 171
Market, definition of, in Justice Department guidelines, 184
Market concentration, government merger guidelines on, 176–178, 190–193, 197
Market extension mergers, 152
Marketing channel strategies, 300–348
  cases, 349–368
  copyrights, 311
  customer restrictions, 324–325
  exclusive dealing, 302–307
  functional discounts, 334–337
  reciprocity, 330–331
  refusals to deal, 331–334
  resale price maintenance, 325–330
  territorial restrictions, 319–324
  typing contracts, 307–319
    major cases, 308–310
    patents, 311
    per se issue, 317–319
    related policies, 315–317
    trademarks, 312, 314–315
  vertical integration and, 337–346
Market shares
  in Federal Trade Commission policy statement, 204
  in Justice Department merger guidelines, 189–190
Marks, see Trademarks
Mercedes-Benz of North America (MBNA), 318
Merchantability, implied warranty of, 81–83
Mergers
  cases, 214–235
  conglomerate, 152, 167–172
    concentration ratios and, 178–179
    deep-pocket, 168–169
    diversification via, 180–181
    Justice Department guidelines on, 178–179
    potential entrant, 169–172
  deep-pocket, 168–169
  definitions of, 152

efficiencies defense, 174, 179, 202
failing firm defense, 172–173, 179, 202–203, 210–212
Federal Trade Commission and, 152, 154–157
  policy statement of, 174–175, 179, 204–213
  government response to, 154–159
  horizontal, see Horizontal mergers
  Justice Department guidelines on, 174–179, 183–203, 337–338
    defenses, 202–203
    horizontal effect from non-horizontal mergers, 196–202
    horizontal mergers, 190–196
    market definition and measurement, 184–190
    purpose and underlying policy assumptions, 183–184
  market extension, 152
  non-horizontal, horizontal effect from, 196–202
  number and assets of, 152–154
  potential entrant, 169–172
  product extension, 152
  toehold defense, 173–174
  vertical, 152, 178
    barriers to entry from, 338
    collusion and, 200–201
    marketing channels and, 337–341
Miller-Tydings Act, 325
Minimum markup laws, 268
Mock-ups, in advertising, 389–390
Monopolization, 476–522
  cases, 501–502
  contemporary cases, 488–495
    AT&T (1982), 490–491
    Berkey-Kodak (1979), 491–492
    Borden (1976), 494–495
    Exxon (1981), 494–495
    General Foods (1982), 493–494
    IBM (1975, 1978, 1979, 1982), 488–490
    Xerox (1975), 494–495
  European situation and, 497–498
  major precedent-setting cases, 477, 479–487
    Alcoa (1945), 482–484
    Du Pont (1956), 485–487
    Grinnell (1966), 487
    United States Steel (1920), 480–481
    Standard Oil (1911), 479–480
  meaning of, 476–477
  patents and, 29, 31
  problems with cases involving, 495–497
  See also Antitrust laws
Monopoly game, 65–75
Monsanto Company, 326–327
Montgomery Ward & Co., 89
Morton Salt Company, 311
Mueller Company, 336, 337
Multiple damages, 11–12
Multiple products orders, 385–386

Nalco Chemical Corp., 243
Naragansett Brewing Co., 170–171
Nashville Coal Co., 305
National Association of Scuba Diving Schools, 393
National Dairy Products Corporation, 274
Negative option mail-order plans, 451
Negligence rule, product liability and, 90–91
New York Stock Exchange, 244
Nolo contendere, plea of, 5
Non-horizontal mergers, 178
  horizontal effect from, 196–202
Northern Pacific Railroad Company, 309–310

Ofrex Group Ltd., 181
Oligopolistic industries, parallel pricing in, 250
Olin Mathieson, 170
Omissions, material, 371–372
Outsiders, use of ideas submitted by, 24–25

Pacific Engineering & Production Co., 262
Pacific Northwest Pipeline Corporation, 170
Packaging, 110–112
   introductory offers represented on, 395
Parallel pricing, 250–257
   collusion required in, 253–254
   conscious parallelism doctrine and, 252, 253, 255
   delivered prices and, 255–257
   price leadership and, 255
   significant cases in, 251–253
Parens patriae suits, 13
Patent and Trademark Office, U.S., 29–30, 52
Patent pools, 36–37
Patents, 19–20
   acquisition by purchase or exclusive license, 31
   antitrust laws and, 29, 31, 32, 35–36
   challenging, 37–38
   criteria for patentability, 29
   definition of, 26
   domain of, 27–28
   duration of, 26–27
   infringement of, 32
   licensing of, 32–37
      antitrust limits of, 33–36
      challenging patents and obtaining remedies,
         37–38
      cross-licensing and patent pools, 36–37
      distribution strategy, 34–36
      pricing strategy, 34
      refusals to license, 33–34
      royalties, 33, 34
   loss of rights in, 14
   nonuse of patented invention, 31
   process of applying for and obtaining, 29–30
   rationale for, 28
   scope of patent rights, 31–33
   tying contracts and, 311
Patient package inserts, 106
Peabody Coal, 173
Penalties for violations of the law, 10–15
Penn-Salt, 170
Per se doctrine, price fixing and, 238–239, 242–245
Personal injury, liability for, *see* Product liability
Personal selling, 447–450, 456
   case, 458–459
Pet Milk, 268
Pfizer, 379
Phantom freight, 270
Pinto automobile case, 129–150
Potential entrant mergers, 169–172
PPG industries, Inc., 243
Predatory pricing, 257–263, 277–278
   Areeda-Turner test of, 494
   classic cases of, 258–259
   controversy over, 259–263
   sales-below-cost laws and, 263
Presale availability requirements, of Magnuson-Moss
   Warranty Act, 84, 89
Price advertising, validity of restrictions on, 397–398
Price differentials, 265
   See also Discriminatory pricing
Price discrimination, *see* Discriminatory pricing

Price fixing, 238–245, 277
   dominant cases in, 239–241
   frequency of, 241–242
   liability in, 245
   patent licensing and, 34, 37
   per se doctrine and, 238–239, 242–245
   price signaling as, 243
Price information, exchange of, 245–250, 277
   controlling circumstance exception and, 247, 249
   rules of thumb on, 249–250
   significant cases in, 246–249
Price leadership, 255
Price reductions, claims of, 396
Prices (pricing)
   cases, 280–299
   delivered, 255–257
   discriminatory, *see* Discriminatory pricing,
   licensing of patents and, 34
   marketing, scanning and, 399
   parallel, 250–257
      collusion required in, 253–254
      conscious parallelism doctrine and, 252, 253, 255
      delivered prices and, 255–257
      price leadership and, 255
      significant cases in, 251–253
   predatory, 257–263, 277–278
      Areeda-Turner test of, 494
      classic cases of, 258–259
      controversy over, 259–263
      sales-below-cost laws and, 263
   promotions based on, 394
   resale price maintenance, 325–330
   unit, 111–112, 398–399
Price signaling, 243
Price squeezes, 343–345
Price surveys, 394
Price verification system, 249
Price wars, 236–237
Pricing, *see* Prices
Private lawsuits, 18
Proctor & Gamble Co., 24, 168, 229–235
Product defects, 92–96
Product extension mergers, 152
Product liability, 85, 89–110
   defenses to actions, 97–98
   design defects and, 94–96
   negligence rule and, 90–91
   res ipsa loquitur doctrine and, 91
   strict liability in tort doctrine and, 92
   tort law and, 90–94
   warranties and, 79
Product markets
   government merger guidelines and, 175, 185–186, 212
   horizontal mergers and, 159–160
Product quality, 76–114
   cases concerning, 117–152
   common law and, 90
   regulatory agencies and, 90
Product safety, 76–77
   Consumer Product Safety Commission and, 106–110
   See also Product liability
Product substitutability, in Justice Department merger
   guidelines, 185–186
Product substitution, in Justice Department merger
   guidelines, 186–187
Profit pass-over arrangements, 320
Promotional allowances, 455–457
   case, 469–474

Promotions
    price as basis of, 394–399
    of warranties, 399–400
Prompt shipping requirements, 451–452
Puffing, 80, 375–377
Punitive damages, 12

Quality, *see* Product quality

Rate regulation, non-horizontal mergers used to evade, 201–202
Reader's Digest Corporation, 11
Reciprocity, 330–331, 347
Reconditioned products, trademark used for, 58–59
Referral sales, 452
Refund orders, Federal Trade Commission, 9
Refusals to deal, 331–334, 347
Refusals to license, 33–34
Regulation(s)
    of drugs, devices, and cosmetics, 104–106 of food
        products, 103–104
    packaging and labeling, 110–112
Regulatory agencies
    product quality and, 90
    See also Regulation; *and specific agencies*
Relevant markets, horizontal mergers and, 160–161
Remedies for violations of the law, 10–15
Repackaged products, trademark and trade names used
    for, 59
Repair services, trademark used by, 58
Replacement parts, trademark or trade names used for, 58
Reprocessed products, trademark and trade names used
    for, 59
Requirement contracts, 302–307
Resale price maintenance, 325–330, 347
Res ipsa loquitur, doctrine of, 91
Restatement (second) of Torts test, 94–95
Risk-utility test, 95–96
R.J. Reynolds Tobacco Company, 280–290, 405
Robinson-Patman Act, 237, 238, 453
    brokerage allowances and, 453
    discriminatory pricing and, 263–276
    functional discounts and, 335, 336
    parallel pricing and, 256
    predatory pricing and, 278
    price squeezes and, 344
    promotional allowances and, 455–457
    refusals to deal and, 332
Robot-Coupe International Corporation, 57–58
Rockwell International Corp., 407–409
Rohm & Haas, 36
Royalties, patent licensing, 33, 34
Ruberoid, 335
Rules, 9
Russell Stover Candies, Inc., 329–330

Safety, product, 76–77, 106–110
    See also Product liability
Safety standards, 108–109
Sales
    mail-order, 450–452, 457
    personal, 447–450
    referral, 452
Sales-below-cost laws, 263
Salespersons
    warranties created by, 79
    See also Personal selling
Sales promotion, sweepstakes and contests used for, 445–447
Sanctions for violation of law, 10–15

Schlitz Brewery, 177, 178
Schwinn & Co., 320–321
Seals of approval of third parties, 393
Sears, Roebuck and Company, 14, 25, 385–386, 397
Secrets, *see* Trade secrets
Service mark, 44
Sherman Act, 3, 237
    dual distribution and, 343, 345
    exclusive dealing and, 302–303, 307
    mergers and, 154–157, 160
    monopolization and, 476–477
    parallel pricing and, 250, 251, 256
    patents and, 32, 34, 35
    predatory pricing and, 257
    price fixing and, 238, 239, 241
    reciprocity and, 331
    refusals to deal and, 332–334
    resale price maintenance and, 325, 327, 328
    territorial restrictions and, 320, 321, 323
    tying contracts and, 308, 309
    vertical integration and, 337, 342
Shipping requirements, prompt, 451–452
Shopping Bag Stores in Los Angeles, 165
Singer Corp., 37
Smucker, J. M., Company, 454, 469–474
Southland Corp., 331
Speech, freedom of, 4
Spray-Rite Service Corporation, 326–327
Standard Oil Company of Indiana, 270–271, 335
Standard Oil of California, 303
Standard Oil Trust, 258–259, 261, 479–480
State and local laws
    disclaimer of implied warranty under, 84
    on trade names, 55
Stiffel Company, 25
Strict liability in tort doctrine, 92
Stroh Brewery, 177
Sun Oil Company, 273
Supreme Court, U.S., 10
    See also individual cases in the law Case Index
Sweepstakes, 445–447

Tampa Electric Co., 305–306
Telex Corporation, 488–489
Territorial restrictions, 319–324, 347
Testimonials, 390
    See also Endorsements
Texxon trademark, 49
Tobacco Trust, 479–480
Toehold defense, 173–174
Toyota, General Motors and, 180
Toys, 107
Trade discounts, 334–337
Trademark Act of 1946 (Lanham Act), 3
Trademarks, 20, 43–59
    abandonment of, 56
    actual use of, as registration requirement, 46–47
    comparative advertising using, 57–58
    copyright protection not applicable to, 40
    deceptive, 55
    defined, 43
    extension of, to different products, 47–48
    family names as, 53
    foreign words as, 54–55
    general principles of law of, 44–46
    as generic names, 56–57
    geographic names as, 53
    guides for choosing, 52–55

Trademarks *(Continued)*
  infringement of, 48–51, 54, 56
  laudatory descriptions of quality as, 53–54
  legal considerations in choosing, 50–52
  licensing or assigning, 57
  loss of rights in, 14
  permissible uses of another's, 57–59
  protection against loss of rights, 56–57
  reconditioned products' use of, 58–59
  registration of, 45–46
  relief available for infringement of, 49–50
  repackaging and reprocessing and use of, 59
  repair services' use of, 58
  replacement parts' use of, 58
  secondary meaning of, 52–53
  specific prohibitions against registration of, 51–52
  state restrictions on, 55
  strong versus weak, 52–55
  trade names distinguished from, 43–44
  tying contracts and, 312, 314–315
  types of, 44
Trade names, 43–44
  licensing or assigning, 57
  permissible uses of another's, 57–59
  protection of, 52
  repackaging and reprocessing and use of, 59
  state restrictions on, 55
Trade Regulation Rules, 8, 387
Trade secrets, 19–26
  defined, 21
  employee agreements for protection of, 23–24
  factors considered in protection of, 21–22
  protection of, 20–26
Truth and Lending Simplification and Reform Act, 401
Tying contracts, 35–36, 307–319, 347
  copyrights and, 311
  major cases, 308–310
  patents and, 311
  per se issue and, 317–319
  policies similar to or having the effect of, 315–317
  trademarks and, 312, 314–315

Unfair acts or practices, 377–380
Unfair competition, trademark law and, 45
Uniform Commercial Code (UCC)
  disclaimer of implied warranties under, 83–84
  implied warranties of merchantability and fitness for a
    particular purpose under, 80–82
  remedies for warranty breach under, 85–86
  warranties under, 78–80
Uniform Deceptive Trade Practices Act, 408
Union Carbide Corporation, 317
Unit pricing, 111–112, 398–399

United Electric Coal Company, 165
United Shoe Machinery Corporation, 481, 484–485
U.S. Pioneer Electronics Corp., 346
United States Steel Corp., 310, 337, 362–368, 480–481
Universal product identification code (UPC), 399
Unordered merchandise, mailing of, 450–451
Unpatented products, privilege to copy, 25–26
Unreasonable seller test, 95
Unsafe products, *see* Product safety
Urea formaldehyde insulation, 107–108
Utah Pie Company, 268

"V-8" trademark, 47–48
Vertical integration
  dual distribution and, 343–346
  by internal expansion, 337, 341–342
  marketing channels and, 337–341
  by merger, 337–341
Vertical mergers, 152, 178
  barriers to entry from, 338
  collusion and, 200–201
  marketing channels and, 337–341
Vertical restrictions, *see* Marketing channel strategies
Vidal Sassoon, Inc., 405–406
Volkswagen name and mark, 58
Von's Grocery Co., 165

Warner-Lambert Company, 382, 415–431
Warnings or instructions, inadequate, 93–94
Warranties, 77–92
  creation of, 79
  damages for breaches of, 79
  express, 77–80
  full or limited, 86–87
  of habitability, 82
  implied, 77–78, 80–85
  limiting remedies for breach of, 85–86
  Magnuson-Moss Warranty Act and, 84–87
  presale availability of terms of, 83, 89
  promotions of, 399–400
  under Uniform Commercial Code (UCC), 78–80
Western Electric Co., 35
West German Cartel Office, 498
Westinghouse, 34
Weyerhaeuser Co., 245
Wheeler-Lea Act, 3
White Consolidated Industries, Inc., 173
White Motor Company, 173, 320, 324
Willamette Industries, Inc., 245
Williams, J.B., Company, 381

Xerox Corporation, 494–495

Youngstown Sheet & Tube Co., 162

Author Index

Altrogger, Phyllis, 11n.
Areeda, Phillip, 204n., 205n., 209n., 210n., 258n., 259n.,
    261, 262, 269
Asch, Peter, 267, 271, 305n., 477n., 481, 482n., 524

Bailey, Patricia P., 371n., 373n., 496
Bain, Joe S., 31n., 35n., 528
Bassett, 48n.
Baxter, William, 318, 490, 496, 525, 529
Beales, 371n., 373n., 378n.

Benbow, Terence H., 247n., 249n.
Berman, Alvin, 492
Black, Hugo, 310, 315
Bloom, Paul, 532n.
Bock, Betty, 158, 159n., 321n.
Bok, 205n.
Bondurant, Emmet J., 325n., 333n., 345
Boone, Pat, 390–391, 393
Bowman, Ward S., Jr., 28n., 29, 33n., 525n.
Brodley, Joseph F., 261n.

Brown, Stephen A., 247n.
Burditt, George M., 247n.
Burger, Warren, 158, 159, 254

Cady, John F., 323n.
Carley, William M., 263n., 489n., 497n.
Christensen, Kathryn, 245n., 270n.
Clark, John W., 325n.
Clark, Justice, 253, 305–306
Clarkson, Kenneth W., 531n.
Coffingberger, 84n.
Collier, 103n.
Cook, C. Lee, Jr., 32n., 34n.
Cooper, Gordon, 392
Craswell, 371n., 373n., 378n.
Crock, Stan, 529n.

Demsetz, 207n.
Dobbs, 24n.
Douglas, William O., 338, 484, 524
Drinkhall, 24n.
Dunfee, Thomas W., 160n., 169n., 323n.

Easterbrook, Frank H., 496
Edwards, Corwin D., 264n.
Egan, Susan S., 247n.
El-Ansary, Adel I., 300n., 325n.
Elzinga, Kenneth G., 162n.
Enis, Ben M., 49n.
Epstein, David G., 13n.
Erickson, Myron L., 169n.

Falk, Carol H., 345n.
Fisher, 205n., 209n., 210n.
Flannery, Thomas A., 110n.
Flax, Steven, 245n.
Fortas, Abe, 321
Frankfurter, Justice, 304–305, 308
Friedman, Lawrence M., 4n.
Friedman, Milton, 526

Gage, Robert, 377n.
Gary, Judge, 480
Geddes, John M., 498n.
Gellhorn, Ernest, 29n., 33n., 34n., 157n., 164–165, 167n., 250, 260, 264n., 302n., 311n., 328, 338, 342n., 484n.
Gibson, Frank F., 169n.
Goyder, D. G., 5n., 163n., 164n., 168n., 245n., 247n., 248n., 253, 254n., 255, 256n., 257, 265n., 269n., 270, 275, 302n., 305n., 306, 318, 333, 336, 341–342, 483, 497
Grabner, John R., Jr., 341n., 525n.
Green, Oliver F., Jr., 325n.
Grether, E. T., 154n., 278, 343n.
Greyser, Stephen, 532n.
Guyon, Janet, 498n.

Hand, Learned, 482–486
Harlan, 165
Harper, Donald V., 241n.
Hay, George A., 260–261
Hiering, James G., 323n.
Hogarty, Thomas F., 162n., 162n.
Holmes, 377n.
Holmes, Oliver Wendell, Jr., 4n.
Howard, Marshall C., 263n., 267n., 271n., 317n., 453, 454, 455n.
Hunt, S. D., 312n.
Hurwitz, James D., 262n.

Jackson, Justice, 264
Jacobs, Sanford L., 32n.
Jenkins, John A., 529n.
Jordan, 402n.
Joskow, Paul L., 263n.

Kamien, Morton I., 28, 38n.
Kaufman, Irving, 492
Kaysen, Carl, 485n.
Kennedy, Ronald, 265n.
Kitch, Edmund, 24n.
Klevorick, Alvin K., 263n.
Klitzke, 21n.
Koten, John, 180n.
Kotler, Philip, 2n.
Kramer, 374n.
Kreiser, Gene, 399n.

Lande, 205n., 209n., 210n.
Landes, William M., 206n., 527n.
Lauter, 96n.
Levy, Sidney J., 49n., 55n.

McCord, J., 294n.
McGee, John S., 259n.
McGovern, 99n.
McKean, Roland M., 531n.
McKenna, Justice, 480–481
McManis, C., 39n., 40n.
Mann, H. Michael, 244n.
Meadows, Edward, 178n., 178n., 527n., 529n.
Merrill, 103n.
Metcalf, Barbara, 376n.
Miller, James C., III, 210n., 211n., 371n., 373n., 529–532, 535
Millspaugh, 84n.
Millstein, Ira, 372n.
Miyashita, Sally, 399n.
Moyer, Reed, 330n.
Mueller, Willard F., 486n., 524n.
Muris, Timothy J., 210n., 531–532, 535
Murphy, John R., 32n., 32n., 34n.

Narver, John C., 167n., 169n.
Neale, Aran D., 5n., 163n., 164n., 168n., 245n., 247n., 248n., 253, 254n., 255, 256n., 257, 265n., 269n., 270, 275, 302n., 305n., 306, 318, 333, 336, 341–342, 483, 497
Nelson, Phillip, 383n., 391n., 530n.
Nevin, J. R., 312n.
Nichols, William H., 252n.
Nickles, Steve H., 17n.

Oliver, Richard, 376n., 377n.
Opel, John, 533
Osborne, 56n.

Palamountain, Joseph C., Jr., 325n., 326n.
Panitch, Ronald, 23n.
Parker, Lewis, 493–494
Pattishall, 47n.
Pautler, 205n.
Peltzman, Sam, 527n.
Pertschuk, Michael, 371n.
Pitofsky, Robert, 205n., 320n., 381n., 396n.
Pogue, Richard W., 532n.
Pooley, James, 21n.
Porter, Michael E., 338n.
Posch, Robert J., Jr., 323n.
Posner, Richard A., 161, 172, 174, 167n., 174n., 206n., 255n., 260n., 324–326, 328, 402n., 527n., 530n.

Powell, Justice, 322
Preston, Ivan, 375n.
Preston, Lee E., 322, 343n.
Priest, 92n.
Prosser, William L., 4n., 376n.

Rahl, James, 265n.
Reagan, Ronald, 490, 494, 529
Reinish, Richard L., 323n.
Reitz, Curtis R., 84n.
Rockefeller, John D., 258
Roering, Kenneth J., 49n.
Rook, Dennis W., 49n., 55n.
Ross, Irwin, 245n.
Rowe, Frederick M., 264n., 265n., 294n.
Rubin, 402n.
Rupert, 33n., 34n.
Russo, J. Edward, 376n., 399n.

Salop, 371n., 373n., 378n.
Samuels, 86n.
Sands, Saul, 323n.
Schauer, 375n.
Scherer, F. M., 7n., 28n., 32, 37, 38n., 154n., 162n., 164,
     166, 171n., 207n., 238n., 244, 245n., 250n., 254n.,
     259n., 260n., 262, 263n., 266, 278–279, 306n., 317,
     325n., 326, 341, 454n., 482n., 495, 527n., 528
Scheuneman, 449n.
Schramm, A. E., Jr., 343n.
Schwartz, Nancy L., 28, 38n.
Sheperd, William G., 27n., 30, 30n., 173, 477, 490n.,
     497n.
Sher, 446n.
Shimp, Terrence, 376n.
Shniderman, H., 294n.
Sidel, Arthur, 23n.
Silbertson, Z. A., 28n., 38n.
Slater, Paul E., 325n.
Smith, Adam, 530
Smith, Richard A., 241n.
Smith, William French, 529
Steiner, Peter O., 341n.
Stephens, Debra, 376n.

Stern, Louis W., 160n., 169n., 300n., 323n., 325n., 341n.,
     525n.
Stevens, Justice, 310
Stewart, Potter, 165
Stigler, George, 207n., 526
Stocking, George W., 486n.
Sturdivant, Frederick D., 168n.
Sullivan, Lawrence A., 5n., 160, 240, 248, 249, 252n.,
     253, 254n., 257, 258n., 267, 308, 317, 328–329,
     330, 453n., 454n., 477n., 484

Taft, William H., 327, 328
Taylor, C. A., 28n., 38n.
Taylor, Robert E., 167n., 177n., 178n., 329n., 490n.,
     491n., 496n., 525n., 529n.
Tennison, Debbie C., 497n.
Thompson, Mayo, 374n.
Thorelli, Hans B., 525n.
Thurow, Lester C., 525n., 527–528
Turner, Donald F., 204n., 205n., 209n., 210n., 258n.,
     259n., 261, 262, 269, 531n.

Volner, 446n.

Waltz, 449n.
Warner, Margaret G., 243n., 494n., 495n.
Warren, Earl, 158, 159, 239
Warren-Boulton, Frederick R., 338n.
Ways, Max, 161
Weigand, Robert E., 323n.
Welch, Joe L., 161n., 453n.
Wermiel, Stephen, 13n., 491n., 534n.
White, Byron, 328
White, Chief Justice, 258
White, James A., 491n.
Wilcox, Clair, 27, 30, 27n., 37n., 173, 249, 256n., 336n.,
     477, 490n., 495n., 497n.
Wilkie, William, 381n.
Williamson, 210n.
Williamson, Oliver E., 259n., 262, 338n.
Wyzanski, Charles, 484–485

Yamey, B. S., 261n.
Yao, Margaret, 242n.

Zelek, E. F., 323n.

Case Index

A & M Produce Co. v. FMC Corp. **(1982), 117–128**
Addystone Pipe & Steel; U.S. v. (1899), 510
Advance Business Systems & Supply Co. v. *SCM Corp.*
     (1969), 366n.
Alaria v. *Vanier* (1958), 122n.
Albrecht v. *The Herald Co.* (1968), 328
Algoma Lumber Co.; F.T.C. v. (1934), 427n.
Aluminum Co. of America; U.S. v. (1945), 342, 344, 478,
     482–488, 490, 499, 501–515, 519
Aluminum Co. of America; U.S. v. (1964), 161–162, 164,
     208n.
American Brands, Inc. v. *R. J. Reynolds Co.* (1976), 403n.,
     405, 436, 443
American Brokerage Co. (1940) (FTC ruling), 473–474
American Can Co.; U.S. v. (1916), 481
American Can Co., et al.; U.S. v. (1949), 307
American Column and Lumber Co. v. *U.S.* (1921), 246
American Cyanamic Co. v. *F.T.C.* (1966), 425n.
American Home Products, Inc. (1983) (FTC ruling), 379
American Home Products Corp. v. *F.T.C.* (1966), 425n.

American Home Products Corp. v. *Johnson & Johnson*
     (1978), 404–405, 432–444
American Honda Motor Co.; in re (1982), 373n.
American Industrial Fastener Corp. v. *Flushing Enterprises,*
     Inc. (1973), 35n.
American Linseed Oil Co.; U.S. v. (1923), 246
American Optometric Assoc. v. *F.T.C.* (1980), 388n.
American Telephone & Telegraph Co. et al.; U.S. v. (1975),
     490–491, 495, 500
American Thread Co.; U.S. v. (1913), 480
American Tobacco Co.; U.S. v. (1911), 258–259, 479–480,
     482
American Tobacco Co.; U.S. v. (1946), 252–254, 280–290,
     510, 519
American-Marietta Co. v. *Krigsman* (1960), 58
AMF, Inc. (1980) (FTC ruling), 378
Anheuser-Busch, Inc. v. *F.T.C.* (1961), 265, 267, 273n.
Anti-Monopoly, Inc. v *General Mills Fun Group, Inc.*
     (1982), 65–75
Anti-Monopoly I, 65–75

Anti-Monopoly II, 65–75
Apex Hosiery Co. v. *leader,* 505
Appalachian Coals, Inc. v. *U.S.* (1933), 354–355, 511
Aqua Slide 'N' Dive Corp. v. *Consumer Product Safety Council* (1978), 109
Arizona v. *Maricopa County Medical Society* (1982), 242
Arnold, Schwinn & Co.; U.S. v. (1967), 320–322, 324, 349, 351–361
Aronberg v. *F.T.C.* (1942), 436n.
Aronson v. *Quick Point Pencil Co.* (1979), 22n.
Arthur Murray Studio, Inc. v. *F.T.C.* (1972), 378, 448
ASG Industries v. *Consumer Product Safety Commission* (1979), 109n.
Associated Press; U.S. v. 507
Atlantic Refining Co. v. *F.T.C.* (1965), 315
Atlas Powder Co. v. *Ewing* (1952), 104
Aurora Products Canada, Ltd. v. *Tyco Industries, Inc.* (1982), 22n.
Automatic Canteen Co. of America v. *F.T.C.* (1953), 271n., 274n., 293n., 294–297

Bada Co. v. Montgomery Ward & Co., 66
Balfour, L.G., Co. v. *F.T.C.* (1971), 463, 467
Barker v. *Lull Engineering Co.* (1977), 4n., 397, 398, 465
Bates v. *State Bar of Arizona* (1977), 96, 136–138
Bausch & Lomb Co.; U.S. v. (1944), 352
Beef/Eater Restaurants, Inc. v. *James Burrough, Ltd.* (1968), 52
Bell, Robert K., Enterprises, Inc. v. *Consumer Product Safety Commission* (1980), 109n.
Bell Aerospace Co.; NLRB v. (1974), 467
Belton Electronics Corp.; in the matter of (1982), 323
Bendix Corp. v. *F.T.C.* (1970), 174n.
Beneficial Corp. v. *F.T.C.* (1977), 463, 465, 466
Berkey Photo, Inc. v. *Eastman Kodak Co.* (1980), 491–492, 497
Bernard Foods v. *Dietene* (1970), 406–407
Bethelehem Steel Corp.; U.S. v. (1958), 162, 166–167, 218n., 219n., 227n., 478
B. F. Goodrich, et al.; U.S. v. (1957), 272n.
Biddle Purchasing Co. v. *F.T.C.* (1938), 454n.
Big O Tire Dealers, Inc. v. *Goodyear Tire & Rubber Co.* (1976), 51
Bigeow v. *State of Virginia* (1975), 422
Blue Bell, Inc.; U.S. v. (1975), 211n.
Blue Shield of Virginia v. *McCready* (1982), 245n.
Borden Co.; U.S. v. (1962), 272
Borden Co.; F.T.C. v. (1966), 266
Borden Co. v. *F.T.C.* (1967), 266
Borden, Inc.; in the matter of (1976), 494
Boro Hall Corp. v. *General Motors Corp.* (1942), 351n.
Bottone; U.S. v. (1966), 24n.
Bristol-Meyers Co. v. *F.T.C.* (1983), 373
Broch, Henry, & Co.; F.T.C. v. (1960), 454, 469–474
Browder v. *Hanley Dawson Cadillac Co.* (1978), 449n.
Brown Shoe Co., Inc. v. *U.S.* (1962), 160n., 161, 163–166, 214–228, 233, 235, 315, 339, 340, 478, 519–520, 524
Brown Shoe Co., Inc. v. *F.T.C.* (1966), 307
Brown Shoe Co., Inc.; F.T.C. v., 307
Bruce's Juices, Inc. v. *American Can Co.* (1947), 265
Burger King of Florida, Inc. v. *Hoots* (1968), 47
Burlington Truck Lines v. *U.S.* (1942), 464–465

California Computer Products v. International Business Machines Corp. (1979), 259, 488, 489
California Liquor Dealers v. *Midcal Aluminum* (1980), 328n.
Campbell Soup (1970) (FTC ruling), 389

Capsonic Group, Inc. v. *Plas-Met Corp.* (1977), 23n.
Case, J.I., Co.; U.S. v. (1951), 306, 316
Cement Institute; F.T.C. v. (1948), 256
Cement Manufacturers' Protective Assoc. v. *U.S.* (1925), 247, 249
Central Hudson Gas & Electric Corp. v. *Public Service Commission* (1980), 4n., 398, 449n.
Central Retailer-Owner Grocers, Inc. v. *F.T.C.* (1963), 454n.
Champion Spark Plug Co. v. *Sanders* (1949), 58–59
Charles of the Ritz Distributors Corp. v. *F.T.C.* (1944), 372n.
Chemetron Corp. v. *McLouth Steel Corp.* (1974), 127n.
Chicago Board of Trade v. *U.S.* (1918), 243–244, 356n., 358n.
Chock Full O'Nuts Corp., Inc. ; in re (1973), 314
Chrysler Corp. v. *F.T.C.* (1977), 463
Cintrone v. *Hertz Truck Leasing & Rental Service* (1965), 82n.
Citizens & Southern National Bank; U.S. v. (1975), 166n.
Citizens Publishing Co. v. *U.S.* (1964), 172–173
Citizens Publishing Co. v. *U.S.* (1969), 211n.
Clairol, Inc. v. *Boston Discount Center of Berkeley, Inc.* (1979), 59n.
Clark v. *John Lamula Investors, Inc.* (1978), 450
Coffer v. *Standard Brands, Inc.* (1976), 81n.
Coleman Motor Co. v. *Chrysler Corp.* (1975), 344n.
Colgate & Co.; U.S. v. (1919), 332–334
Colgate-Palmolive Co.; F.T.C. v. (1965), 371, 389, 390, 463
Columbia Metal Culvert Co., Inc. v. *Kaiser Aluminum & Chemical Corp.* (1978), 344n.
Columbia Steel Co.; U.S. v. (1948), 155, 219n., 337, 338, 524
Compare Alberty v. *F.T.C.* (1950), 423
Compco Corp. v. *Day-Brite Lighting, Inc.* (1964), 62–64
Consolidated Foods Corp.; F.T.C. v. (1965), 330n., 341
Consumers Union, Inc. v. *F.T.C.* (1982), 387
Container Corp. of America; U.S. v. (1969), 248, 250, 296
Continental Can Co.; U.S. v. (1964), 161, 164–165, 478
Continental T.V., Inc. et al. v. *GTE-Sylvania, Inc.* (1977), 35n., 321–324, 326, 328, 346, 349–361
Copperweld Corp. v. *Independence Tube Corp.* (1983), 342n.
Corn Products Refining Co.; U.S. v. (1916), 480, 507, 509
Corn Products Refining Co. v. *F.T.C.* (1945), 270, 299n.
Cosgove Studio and Camera Shop, Inc. v. *Paine* (1962), 407
C-O Two Fire Equipment Co. v. *U.S.* (1952), 252–254
Craig v. *The American District Telegraph Co.* (1977), 82n.
Cuisinarts, Inc. v. *Robot-Coupe International Corp.* (1981), 57–58
Custom House Packing Corp. (1946) (FTC ruling), 473–474

Davis v. Hearst , 141
Dawes v. *Superior Court,* 145–146
Dawn Donut Co. v. *Hart's Food Stores. Inc.* (1959), 45
Dawson Chemical Co. v. *Rohm & Haas Co.* (1980), 36n.
Dean Foods Co.; F.T.C. v., 420
DeGraff v. *Myers Foods, Inc.* (1958), 81n.
Doherty, Clifford, Steers and Sbeenfield, Inc. v. *F.T.C.* (1968), 372n.
Donnelly v. *Southern Pacific Co.* (1941), 142
Drayton v. *Jiffe Chemical Corp.* (1975), 93
Dr. Miles Medical Co. v. *John D. Park and Sons Co.* (1911), 327, 332
Dunhill, Alfred, Ltd. v. *Interstate Cigar Co.* (1974), 437n.
du Pont, E.I., de Nemours & Co.; U.S. v. (1911), 480
du Pont, E.I., de Nemours & Co.; U.S. v. (1956), 478, 485–487

du Pont, E.I., de Nemours & Co.; *U.S.* v. (1957), 339, 478
du Pont, E.I., de Nemours & Co.; *U.S.* v. (1961), 15, 219, 519
du Pont, E.I., de Nemours & Co. et al. v. *Christopher (1970)*, 22n.
du Pont, E.I., de Nemours & Co. v. *Yoshida International, Inc.* (1975), 71, 72

Eastern States Retail Lumber Dealers' Association v. U.S. (1914), 250, 332
Eastman Kodak Co.; *U.S.* v. (1915), 480
Eastman Kodak Co.; *F.T.C.* v. (1927), 420
Egan v. *Mutual of Omaha Insurance Co.*, 144–145
E.I. du Pont de Nemours & Co., see *du Pont, E.I., de Nemours & Co.*
El Paso Natural Gas Co.; *U.S.* v. (1964), 169–170
Encyclopaedia Britannica, Inc. (1979) (FTC ruling), 448
Encyclopaedia Britannica, Inc. v. *F.T.C.* (1979), 358–468
Evans v. *General Motors Corp.* (1966), 96n.
Exquisite Form Brassiere, Inc. v. *F.T.C.* (1961), 456
Exxon Corp.; *in the matter of* (1973), 494–495
Exxon Corp. v. *Texas Motor Exchange of Houston, Inc.* (1980), 48

Fall City Industries, Inc. v. Vanco Beverage, Inc. (1982), 534n.
Falstaff Brewing Corp.; *U.S.* v. (1973), 170–171
Fashion Originators' Guild of America, Inc. v. *F.T.C.*, 332n., 507, 511
Feil v. *F.T.C.* (1960), 423
Finance Corp. v. *Murphree* (1980), 120n.
Firestone Tire & Rubber Co. (1974) (FTC ruling), 381
Firestone Tire & Rubber Co. v. *F.T.C.* (1973), 372n.
First National Bank & Trust Co.; *U.S.* v., 520
Foglio, 138
Ford Motor Co. v. *U.S.* (1972), 15n., 341
Fortner Enterprises, Inc. v. *United States Steel Corp.* (1977), 310, 362
Friedman v. *Rogers* (1979), 55
Fuchs Sugars & Syrups, Inc. v. *Amstar Corp.* (1979), 334
Futurecraft Corp. v. *Clary Corp.* (1962), 22n.

Galanis v. Proctor & Gamble Corp. (1957), 24n.
Garrett v. *F.C.C.* (1975), 467
Garza v. *Spudnik Equipment Co.* (1982), 93
Gaston v. *Hunter* (1978), 94n.
General Auto Supplies v. *F.T.C.* (1965), 276
General Dynamics Corp.; *U.S.* v. (1966), 330n., 341
General Dynamics Corp.; *U.S.* v. (1974), 165–166, 171, 173, 208n., 211n.
General Electric Co.; *U.S.* v. (1926), 34n., 327, 328, 506
General Foods Corp. (1975) (FTC ruling), 378
General Foods Corp. v. *F.T.C.* (1967), 168–169
General Foods Corp.; *in the matter of*, (1982), 493–494
General Motors Corp. et al; *U.S.* v. (1966), 323, 332n., 360n.
General Talking Pictures Corp. v. *Western Electric Co.* (1938), 35
General Tire and Rubber Co.; *U.S.* v. (1970), 331
Generix Drug Corp.; *U.S.* v. (1983), 105
Gertz v. *Robert Welch, Inc.* (1974), 408n.
Gilbertville Trucking Co. v. *U.S.* (1962), 463
Goddard v. *General Motors Corp. (1979)*, 86n.
Golden Gate Acceptance Corp. v. *General Motors Corp.*, 333–334
Goldfarb v. *Virginia State Bar Assoc.* (1975), 244n.
Goldstein v. *California* (1973), 39
Gottschalk v. *Benson* (1972), 27n.
Graham v. *Scissor-Tail, Inc.*, 123–124

Great Atlantic & Pacific Tea Co. v. *F.T.C.* (1939), 471
Great Atlantic & Pacific Tea Co. v. *F.T.C.* (1940), 454n.
Great Atlantic & Pacific Tea Co.; *U.S.* v. (1946), 342
Great Atlantic & Pacific Tea Co. v. *F.T.C.* (1975), 273
Great Atlantic & Pacific Tea Co. v. *F.T.C.* (1979), 275–276, 291–299
Greater Buffalo Press, Inc.; *U.S.* v. (1971), 211n.
Great Lakes Chemical Corp.; *F.T.C.* v. (1982), 211n.
Green; *in re*, 512
Greenman v. *Yuba Power Products, Inc.* (1963), 94
Griffith Amusement Co.; *U.S.* v., 484, 488
Grimshaw v. *Ford Motor Co.* (1981), 12n., 96n., 129–150
Grinnel Corp. et al.; *U.S.* v. (1966), 478, 487–489, 499, 516–522
Grolier, Inc. (1983) (FTC ruling), 448
Grolier, Inc.; *in the matter of*, 468
GTE-Sylvania, Inc. v. *Consumer Product Safety Commission* (1980) 110n.
Guide v. *Desperak* (1956), 30n.

Hagenbuch v. Snap-On Tools Corp. (1972), 80
Handrigan v. *Apex Warwick, Inc.* (1971), 81n.
Harley-Davidson Motor Co., 222
Harris v. *Belton* (1968), 81n.
Hartford-Empire Co. v. *U.S.* (1945), 31n., 37n.
Heatbath Corp. v. *Ikfovits* (1969), 21n.
Heater v. *F.T.C.* (1974), 420n.
Holiday Inns, Inc. v. *Holiday Out in America* (1973), 52n.
Huck Mfg. Co.; *U.S.* v. (1965), 34n.
Huff v. *White Motor Co.* (1977), 96
Hutcheson; *U.S.* v., 511

Ideal Toy Corp. v. Plawner Toy Mfg. Co. (1982), 26n.
ILC Peripherals Leasing Corp. v. *International Business Machines Corp.* (1978), 259, 262, 311, 317, 488
ILG Industries, Inc. v. *Scott* (1971), 21n.
Illinois Brick Co. v. *State of Illinois* (1977), 245, 355
Incollingo v. *Ewing* (1971), 93
Independent Grocers Alliance Distributing Co. v. *F.T.C.* (1953), 454n.
Industrial Buildings Materials, Inc. v. *Interchemical Corp.* (1970), 342, 344, 345
Intemco, Inc. v. *Randustrial Corp.* (1976), 80
Internationl Air Industries, Inc. v. *American Excelsior Co.* (1975), 269
International Business Machines Corp. v. *U.S.*, 366n.
International Business Machines Corp.; *U.S.* v. (1969), 489–490
International Harvester Co. v. *Missouri*, 512
International Harvester Co.; *U.S.* v. (1927), 255, 481, 513
International Salt Co. v. *U.S.* (1947), 36, 222, 303, 309, 311, 366–368
International Shoe Co. v. *F.T.C.*, 222
Interstate Circuit, Inc., et al. v. *U.S.* (1939), 251–254
Inwood Laboratories, Inc. v. *Ives Laboratories, Inc.* (1982), 26
ITT Continental Baking Co. (1973) (FTC ruling), 381
ITT Continental Baking Co. v. *F.T.C.*, (1976), 463

Jeffreys v. Hickman (1971), 82n.
Jerrold Electronics; *U.S.* v. (1961), 36, 227n., 317–318
Johnson & Johnson v. *Carter-Wallace, Inc.* (1980), 50n.
Johnson Products Co. v. *F.T.C.* (1977), 467
John Walker & Sons, Ltd. v. *Modern Shoe Co.* (1954), 52
John Walker & Sons, Ltd. v. *Tampa Cigar Co.* (1955), 52

Kaiser v. General Motors Corp. (1975), 351n.
Kaiser Aluminum & Chemical Corp. v. *Consumer Product Safety Commission* (1979), 110n.

Kaiser Aluminum & Chemical Corp. v. *F.T.C.* (1981), 208n.
Katharine Gibbs School, Inc. v. *F.T.C.* (1979), 388n.
Keele Hair & Scalp Specialists, Inc. v. *F.T.C.* (1960), 423
Kellogg Co. v. *National Biscuit Co.* (1938), 64
Kellogg Co. et al, in the matter of (1972), 492–493
Kennecot Copper Corp. v. *F.T.C.* (1971), 173n.
Kewanee Oil Co. v. *Bicron Corp.* (1974), 22n.
Kiefer-Stewart Co. v. *Joseph E. Seagram & Sons, Inc.* (1951), 328
King-Seely Thermos Co. v. *Aladdin Industries, Inc.* (1963), 71, 72
Kirchner, Heinz W. (1964) (FTC ruling), 372n.
Klor's Inc. v. *Broadway-Hale Stores, Inc.* (1959), 332n.
Krehl, Norman E. v. *Baskin-Robbins Ice Cream Co. et al.* (1982), 57n., 312
Kroger Co. (1981) (FTC ruling), 394
Kroger Co. v. *F.T.C.* (1971), 276, 293, 297n.

Lehigh Portland Cement Co. v. *F.T.C.* **(1969), 467n.**
Lehigh Valley Railroad Co.; *U.S.* v. (1920), 480
Leroy Gordon Cooper, Jr. (1979) (FTC ruling), 392
Lever Brothers.; *U.S.* v. (1963), 211n.
Li v. *Yellow Cab Co.*, 141, 142
Line Material Co.; *U.S.* v. (1949), 34n.
Loew's Inc.; *U.S.* v. (1962), 311n., 316, 367, 368
Lorain Journal Co. v. *U.S.* (1951), 425n.
Lorillard, P., Co. v. *F.T.C.* (1950), 374
Louisiana Pacific Corp.; *U.S.* v. (1983), 7n.

Main Fish Co., Inc. **473**
Manufacturers Hanover Trust Co.; *U.S.* v. (1965), 166n.
Maple Flooring Manufacturers' Assoc. v. *U.S.* (1925), 246, 247
Marathon Oil Co. v. *Mobile Corp.* (1981), 158n., 534
Marine Bancorporation; *U.S.* v. (1974), 166n., 171
Maze v. *Bush Brothers & Co.* (1971), 81n.
MCI Communications Corp. v. *American Telephone and Telegraph Co.* (1983), 263n.
McKesson & Robbins, Inc.; *U.S.* v. (1956), 239n.
McNeil Lab. Inc. v. *American Home Products Corp.* (1980), 404, 405
Meyer, Fred, Co., Inc.; *F.T.C.* v. (1968), 456
Micallef v. *Miehle Co.* (1976), 94
Minneapolis-Honeywell Regulator Co. v. *F.T.C.* (1951), 269
Modern Marketing Service, Inc. v. *F.T.C.* (1945), 454n.
Montgomery Ward & Co. v. *F.T.C.* (1982), 89
Montgomery Ward & Co. v. *N.Y. Dept. of Motor Vehicles* (1982), 13n.
Moog Industries v. *F.T.C.* (1958), 467
Moore v. *Mead's Fine Bread Co.* (1954), 261n., 268n.
Morton Salt Co. v. *Suppiger Co.* (1945), 311
Morton Salt Co.; *F.T.C.* v. (1948), 265, 269, 271, 272

National Biscuit Co. **v. F.T.C., 512**
National Commission on Egg Nutrition v. *F.T.C.*, 463, 465
National Dairy Products Corp.; *U.S.* v. (1963), 274
National Dynamics Corp. (1973) (FTC ruling), 379
National Lead Co.; *F.T.C.* v. (1957), 385, 463
National Malleable & Steel Castings Co.; *U.S.* v. (1958), 255
National Society of Professional Engineers v. *U.S.* (1978), 244n., 463, 466
Nordstron v. *White Metal Rolling & Stamping Corp.* (1969), 92n.
Northern Pacific Railroad Co. v. *U.S.* (1958), 309–310, 356–357, 358n., 360, 366n., 367, 368
Northern Securities Co. v. *U.S.* (1904), 479n., 512
Nutrilab, Inc. v. *Schweiker* (1982), 105n.

Ocean Spray Cranberries, Inc. **(1972) (FTC ruling), 382**
Ohralik v. *Ohio State Bar Assoc.* (1978), 449
One Hazardous Product; *U.S.* v. (1980), 110n.
Otter Tail Power Co. v. *U.S.* (1973), 32n.
Overland Bond & Investment Corp. v. *Howard* (1972), 81n.

P.F. Collier & Son Corp. **v. F.T.C. (1970), 468**
Pabst Brewing Co.; *U.S.* v. (1966), 162
Pacific Engineering and Production Co. of Nevada v. *Kerr-McGee Corp.* (1977), 262, 269
Pan American World Airways, Inc. v. *U.S.* (1963), 420
Paramount Pictures; *U.S.* v. (1948), 316, 328n., 342, 367
Parke, Davis & Co.; *U.S.* v. (1960), 332n.
Penn-Olin Chemical Co.; *U.S.* v. (1964), 170n., 233
People v. *Watson* (1956), 122n.
Peterson v. *Hubschman Construction Co.* (1979), 82n.
Pfizer, Inc. (1972) (FTC ruling), 379
Philadelphia National Bank; *U.S.* v. (1963), 161–162, 164, 166–167, 233, 337, 478, 520
Phillip Morris, Inc. (1973) (FTC ruling), 378
Phillip Morris, Inc. v. *Loew's Theaters* (1980), 403–405
Phillips Petroleum Co.; *U.S.* v. (1973), 211n.
Piedot v. *Zenith Radio Corp.* (1941), 21n.
Pillsbury Co. (1979), 208n., 211n.
Pillsbury Mills, Inc., 233
Pratt v. *Winnebago Inc.* (1979), 87n.
Procter & Gamble Co.; *F.T.C.* v., 168–169, 229–235

Rabiner & Jontow, Inc. **v. F.T.C. (1967), 467**
Reaburn, C. G., & Co. (1940) (FTC ruling), 473–474
Readers Digest v. *F.T.C.* (1981), 11n.
Reading Co.; *U.S.* v. (1920), 480, 512
Redarowicz v. *Ohlendorf* (1982), 82n.
Reed Roller Bit Co.; *U.S.* v. (1967), 211n.
Reichhold Chemicals, Inc. (1978), 211n.
Resort Car Rental Systems, Inc. v. *F.T.C.* (1975), 55n.
Reynolds Metals Co. v. *F.T.C.* (1962), 340n.
Riley v. *Ford Motor Co.* (1971), 85n., 86n.
Roach v. *Kononen* (1974), 95n.
Robinson, W.E., & Co. (1941) (FTC ruling), 473–474
Rome Cable (1964), 478
Royal Baking Powder Co. v. *F.T.C.* (1922), 424–425
Royal Milling Co.; *F.T.C.* v. (1933), 463
Royer v. *Stoody Co.* (1967), 408
Ruberoid Co.; *F.T.C.* v. (1952), 264, 335, 463
Ruff, H.M., & Son (1940) (FTC ruling), 473–474
Ruggeri v. *Minnesota Mining & Mfg. Co.* (1978), 93

Salco Corp. **v. General Motors Corp. (1975), 351n.**
Sambo's Restaurants, Inc. v. *City of Ann Arbor* (1981), 55n.
Sandura Co. v. *F.T.C.* 357n.
Sarkes Tarzian, Inc. v. *Audio Devices, Inc.* (1958), 22n.
Schrader's Son; *U.S.* v., 290
Schroeder, 146
SCM Corp. v. *Langis Foods, Ltd.* (1976), 47n.
Sealy, Inc.; *U.S.* v. (1967), 324, 328n.
Searle, G.D., & Co. v. *Superior Court* (1975), 145n.
Sears, Roebuck & Co. (1977) (FTC ruling), 397
Sears, Roebuck & Co. (1980) (FTC ruling), 385
Sears, Roebuck & Co. (1982) (FTC ruling), 386
Sears, Roebuck & Co. v. *Stiffel Co.* (1964), 25, 62–64
Sears, Roebuck & Co. v. *F.T.C.* (1982), 14n.
SEC v. *Chenery Corp.* (1947), 467
Selchow & Righter Co. v. *Western Printing & Lithographing Co.*, 69
Seley v. *G.D. Searle, Inc.* (1981), 106n.
Self v. *General Motors Corp.*, 140
Siegel, Jacob, Co. v. *F.T.C.* (1946), 426, 463

Siegel v. *Chicken Delight, Inc.* (1972), 57*n.*, 312, 314
Simeon Management Corp.; *F.T.C.* v. (1976), 371*n.*, 423*n.*
Simplicity Pattern Co.; *F.T.C.* v. (1959), 295–296, 456, 470*n.*
Simpson v. *Union Oil Co.* (1964), 328*n.*
Singer Mfg. Co. v. *U.S.* (1963), 37*n.*
Sisk, Albert W., & Son (1940) (FTC ruling), 473–474
Skelton v. *General Motors Corp.* (1981), 84*n.*
Skil Corp. v. *Rockwell International Corp.* (1974), 407
Smith v. *Chanel, Inc.* (1968), 403, 409
Snap-On Tools Corp. v. *F.T.C.* (1963), 357*n.*
Socony-Vacuum Oil Co.; *U.S.* v. (1940), 240–242, 290, 510, 515
Southern Pacific Co.; *U.S.* v., 512
Southgate Brokerage Co. v. *F.T.C.* (1945), 454*n.*, 472
Southland Mower Co. v. *Consumer Product Safety Commission* (1980), 109
Special Equipment Co. v. *Coe* (1945), 31
Sperry & Hutchinson Co.; *F.T.C.* v. (1972), 377
Spray-Rite Service Corp. v. *Monsanto Co.* (1982), 327
Staley, A. E., Mfg. Co.; *F.T.C.* v. (1945), 270, 272, 298, 299
Standard Fashion Co. v. *Magrane-Houston Co.* (1922), 303, 304, 306
Standard Oil Co.; *U.S.* v., 512
Standard Oil Co. of California, et al. v. *U.S.* (1949), 218, 222, 225, 303–306, 308
Standard Oil Co. of Indiana v. *F.T.C.* (1950), 270, 293*n.*, 298*n.*, 335, 344
Standard Oil Co. of New Jersey v. *U.S.* (1911), 258–259, 356, 479–480, 482, 483, 487, 505, 510, 512
Stanley Works v. *F.T.C.* (1973), 208*n.*
Star Crest Products of California; *F.T.C.* v. (1982), 452
State Fair of Texas v. *Consumer Product Safety Commission* (1979), 109*n.*
Sterling Drug, Inc. v. *F.T.C.* (1963), 436*n.*
Sterling Drug, Inc. v. *F.T.C.* (1983), 373
Sugar Institute v. *U.S.*, 510–511
Sun Oil Co.; *F.T.C.* v. (1963), 273
Sunshine Biscuits, Inc. v. *F.T.C.* (1962), 273
Susser v. *Carvel Corp.* (1964), 314
Swift & Co. v. *U.S.*, 510, 514, 515
Swift & Co.; *U.S.* v. 282, 513

Tampa Electric Co. **v.** *Nashville Coal Co. et al.* **(1961), 221–222, 305–306**
Taylor v. *Superior Court*, 141
Telex Corp. v. *International Business Machines Corp.* (1975), 259, 260, 311, 478, 488–489, 497
Tennessee Valley Ham Co., Inc. v. *Bergland* (1980), 104
Theater Enterprises, Inc. v. *Paramount Film Distributing Corp. et al* (1954), 252–254
Thomas Roberts & Co. (1940) (FTC ruling), 473–474
Times-Picayune Publishing Co. v. *U.S.* (1953), 309, 478
Toole v. *Richardson-Merrell, Inc.*, 143, 146
Topco Associates, Inc.; *U.S.* v. (1972), 323–324, 356*n.*, 360*n.*
Transamerica Computer Co. v. *International Business Machines Corp.* (1979), 311, 488
Trans-Missouri Freight Assoc.; *U.S.* v., 510, 512
Trenton Potteries Co.; *U.S.* v. (1927), 239–240, 246, 510
Triangle Conduit and Cable Co. et al. v. *F.T.C.* (1948), 256*n.*
Tripoli Co. v. *Wella Corp.* (1970), 359*n.*
Turner v. *General Motors Corp.* (1979), 95*n.*

Uloth **v.** *City Tank Corp.* **(1978), 93***n.*
Uncle Ben's, Inc. (1977) (FTC ruling), 378
Ungar v. *Dunkin' Donuts of America, Inc.* (1976), 314
Union Carbide Corp. v. *Ever-Ready, Inc.* (1976), 46
Union Pacific Railroad Co.; *U.S.* v. (1912), 479*n.*
United Shoe Machinery v. *U.S.*, 366*n.*
United Shoe Machinery Corp.; *U.S.* v. (1954), 38*n.*, 484–490, 495, 499
United Shoe Machinery Co. of New Jersey; *U.S.* v. (1918), 481
United States Gypsum Co.; *U.S.* v. (1948), 33*n.*
United States Gypsum Co.; *U.S.* v. (1978), 249, 254, 273, 276, 296*n.*, 298, 299
U.S. Pioneer Electronics Corp.; *in the matter of* (1982), 346
United States Senate v. *F.T.C.* (1983), 387
United States Steel Corp.; *U.S.* v. (1920), 480–483, 498, 513
United States Steel Corp. v. *Fortner Enterprises, Inc.* (1977), 362–368
Universal City Studio v. *Sony Corp.* (1982), 42
Universal-Rundle Corp.; *F.T.C.* v. (1967), 467
Univis Lens Co.; *U.S.* v. (1942), 35*n.*
Unruh, C. F., Brokerage Co. (1940) (FTC ruling), 473–474
Utah Pie Co. v. *Continental Baking Co.* (1967), 268

Vandermark **v.** *Ford Motor Co.* **(1964), 84***n.*
Vendo Co. v. *Stoner* (1974), 23*n.*
Vidal Sassoon, Inc. v. *Bristol-Myers Co.* (1981), 405
Virginia State Board of Pharmacy v. *Virginia Citizens Consumer Council, Inc.* (1976), 2*n.*, 397, 422, 428–430, 465–466
Vizzini v. *Ford Motor Co.* (1977), 97*n.*
Volkswagen v. *Church* (1969), 58
Volkswagenwerk Aktiengesellschaft v. *Karadizian* (1971), 58*n.*
Von's Grocery Co.; *U.S.* v. (1966), 165, 478

Wall Products Co. **v.** *National Gypsum Co.* **(1971), 255***n.*
Waltham Precision Instrument Co. v. *F.T.C.* (1964), 424–425
Waltham Watch Co. v. *F.T.C.* (1963), 424–425, 463*n.*
Ward Laboratories, Inc. v. *F.T.C.* (1960), 423, 424*n.*
Warner, George W., & Co. v. *Black & Decker Mfg. Co.* (1960), 334
Warner-Lambert Co. v. *F.T.C.* (1977), 382, 384*n.*, 385*n.*, 415–431, 463*n.*
Weaver v. *American Oil Co.*, 125
Webb-Crawford Co. v. *F.T.C.* (1940), 454*n.*
Webster v. *Blue Chip Tea Room, Inc.* (1964), 81*n.*
Western Electric, Inc.; *U.S.* v. (1956), 490*n.*
White Motor Co. v. *U.S.* (1961), 320
White Motor Co. v. *U.S.* (1963), 320, 324, 355, 356, 358*n.*, 360
Whiting, U.S. v., 512
William Silver & Co. (1940) (FTC ruling), 473–474
Williams, J.B., Co. v. *F.T.C.* (1967), 381, 423
Wilson v. *Simpson*, 507
Winston Research Corp. v. *Minnesota Mining and Mfg. Co.* (1965), 21*n.*

Xerox Corp.; *in the matter of* **(1975), 494–495**

Zenith Radio Corp. **v.** *F.T.C.* **(1944), 372***n.*
Zirpola v. *Adam Hat Stores, Inc.* (1939), 81*n.*